"This book is a celebration of mindfulness as a fully scientific, well-adapted system for an active life in the West. Every intervention presented here is a living proof that Mindfulness has become a prominent antidote to our Western malaise: a hyperactive, distracted and scattered mind that knows no satisfaction. As part of this burnout society, in which we are constantly everywhere and nowhere, this book, driven by both academic passion and deep compassion, signifies a landmark in our understanding of human suffering and its cure."
Shai Tubali, author of *Indestructible You: Building a Self that cannot be Broken*

"Cleary written, enjoyable and mind-expanding, this book is a must-read! The chapters go well beyond providing a theoretical understanding, updating and organizing the expansive variety of mindfulness-based work with page-turning case examples and wide-ranging transformative activities that we could all begin using immediately."
Francis Kaklauskas PsyD CGP FAGPA, lead editor of *Brilliant Sanity: Buddhist Approaches to Psychotherapy*

"Encyclopaedic in its range, this book performs a vitally important role. It collates and succinctly describes every significant mindfulness therapy and program, and so provides an essential resource for anyone who practices or studies mindfulness, and anyone who would like to benefit from it."
Steve Taylor Ph.D., author of *The Leap*, and *Spiritual Science*.

Handbook of Mindfulness-Based Programmes

Handbook of Mindfulness-Based Programmes: Mindfulness Interventions from Education to Health and Therapy offers the first comprehensive guide to all prominent, evidence-based mindfulness programmes available in the West.

The rapid growth of mindfulness in the Western world has given rise to an unprecedented wave of creative mindfulness programmes, offering tailor-made mindfulness practices for school teachers, students, parents, nurses, yoga teachers, athletes, pregnant women, therapists, care-takers, coaches, organisational leaders and lawyers. This book offers an in-depth engagement with these different programmes, emphasising not only the theory and research but also the practice. Exercises and activities are provided to enable the reader to first understand the programme and then experience its unique approach and benefits.

Handbook of Mindfulness-Based Programmes will enrich your knowledge and experience of mindfulness practice, whether you are a practitioner, researcher or simply interested in the application of mindfulness.

Itai Ivtzan is a positive psychologist, an associate professor at Naropa University, and an honorary senior research associate at University College London. He has spent much time studying, writing books and teaching classes in the field of meditation.

Handbook of Mindfulness-Based Programmes

Mindfulness Interventions from Education to Health and Therapy

Edited by Itai Ivtzan

LONDON AND NEW YORK

First published 2020
by Routledge
2 Park Square, Milton Park, Abingdon, Oxon OX14 4RN

and by Routledge
52 Vanderbilt Avenue, New York, NY 10017

Routledge is an imprint of the Taylor & Francis Group, an informa business

© 2020 selection and editorial matter, Itai Ivtzan; individual chapters, the contributors

The right of Itai Ivtzan to be identified as the author of the editorial material, and of the authors for their individual chapters, has been asserted in accordance with sections 77 and 78 of the Copyright, Designs and Patents Act 1988.

All rights reserved. No part of this book may be reprinted or reproduced or utilised in any form or by any electronic, mechanical, or other means, now known or hereafter invented, including photocopying and recording, or in any information storage or retrieval system, without permission in writing from the publishers.

Trademark notice: Product or corporate names may be trademarks or registered trademarks, and are used only for identification and explanation without intent to infringe.

British Library Cataloguing-in-Publication Data
A catalogue record for this book is available from the British Library

Library of Congress Cataloging-in-Publication Data
A catalog record has been requested for this book

ISBN: 978-1-138-24093-3 (hbk)
ISBN: 978-1-138-24094-0 (pbk)
ISBN: 978-1-315-26543-8 (ebk)

Typeset in Times New Roman
by Apex CoVantage, LLC

This one is dedicated to my students. We all grow together.

I would like to offer a special thanks to the following individuals; their editing work was invaluable for this book: Alexandra Fouracres, Tarli Young, Abigail Boughton-Thomas, Cassandra Michael, Duncan Reid, Gemma Bullivant, Melissa Edwards, and Tanya Heasley.

Contents

1 Handbook of Mindfulness-Based Programmes: an introduction 1
ITAI IVTZAN

SECTION I
Mindfulness programs in therapy 5

2 Acceptance and Commitment Therapy 7
JENNIFER E. KRAFFT, GRAYSON M. BUTCHER, MICHAEL E. LEVIN, AND MICHAEL P. TWOHIG

3 Cultivating wise mind in dialectical behavior therapy through mindfulness 18
DAWN M. SALGADO, ANDREW W. WHITE, DAPHNA PETERSON, AND LINDA A. DIMEFF

4 Mindfulness-Based Stress Reduction: theory, practice and evidence base 29
DIANE REIBEL AND DONALD MCCOWN

5 Mindfulness-Based Positive Behavior Support 42
NIRBHAY N. SINGH, GIULIO E. LANCIONI, JEFFREY CHAN, CARRIE L. MCPHERSON, AND MONICA M. JACKMAN

6 Mindfulness-Based Mind Fitness Training (MMFT): mindfulness training for high-stress and trauma-sensitive contexts 53
KELSEY L. LARSEN AND ELIZABETH A. STANLEY

7 Mindfulness-Based Emotional Balance: history of development, curriculum, and research 64
MARGARET CULLEN, GONZALO BRITO-PONS, AND ROBERT W. ROESER

SECTION II
Mindfulness programs in families 77

8 Mindfulness-Based Childbirth and Parenting: preparing a new generation for birthing and beyond 79
NANCY BARDACKE AND LARISSA G. DUNCAN

9 Coping with the stress of parenting: the mindful parenting program 92
LISA-MARIE EMERSON AND SUSAN BÖGELS

10 Mindfulness-Based Relationship enhancement for couples 105
NATHAN BOHY AND JAMES W. CARSON

11 Mindful Mamas: mindfulness-based yoga for depressed women entering motherhood 112
LAUREL M. HICKS, BARBARA BROOKENS-HARVEY, AND MARIA MUZIK

12 A ceremony of losses: mindfulness for elders and caregivers 123
LUCIA MCBEE AND ANTONELLA BURANELLO

SECTION III
Mindfulness programs in health-care 141

13 Promoting healing through mindful medical practice 143
PATRICIA LYNN DOBKIN

14 Mindfulness-Based Cancer Recovery: an adaptation of MBSR for people with cancer and their caregivers 160
LINDA E. CARLSON, ERIN ZELINSKI, KIRSTI TOIVONEN, AND MICHELLE FLYNN

15 Mindful Sport Performance Enhancement (MSPE) 173
KEITH A. KAUFMAN, CAROL R. GLASS, AND TIMOTHY R. PINEAU

16 Mindfulness-Based Eating Awareness Training (MB-EAT) 191
JEAN L. KRISTELLER

17 Mindfulness-Based Therapy for Insomnia 204
JASON C. ONG AND RACHEL MANBER

SECTION IV
Mindfulness programs in education   217

18 Cultivating Awareness and Resilience in Education: The CARE for
    teachers program   219
    PATRICIA A. JENNINGS, ANTHONY A. DEMAURO, AND POLINA MISCHENKO

19 "Wellness Works in Schools": The practice and research of a
    mindfulness program in urban middle schools   231
    CHERYL T. DESMOND, WYNNE KINDER, LAURIE B. HANICH, AND OBIORAM
    C-B CHUKWU

20 Mindfulness for adolescents: A review of the learning to BREATHE program   241
    JENNIFER L. FRANK, KIMBERLY M. KOHLER, LAMIYA KHAN, AND PATRICIA
    C. BRODERICK

21 Audio-guided Mindful-Based Social Emotional Learning (MBSEL)
    training in school classrooms: The inner explorer program   251
    JUTTA TOBIAS MORTLOCK

SECTION V
Mindfulness programs in children and adolescents   265

22 Still Quiet Place: Sharing mindfulness with children and adolescents   267
    AMY SALTZMAN

23 Mindfulness-Based Cognitive Therapy for Children   282
    JENNIFER LEE AND RANDYE J. SEMPLE

SECTION VI
Mindfulness programs at work   295

24 Mindful leadership   297
    JUTTA TOBIAS MORTLOCK AND JENNIFER ROBINSON

25 Mindfulness practice and the law: Jurisight and the skillful means to
    greet the legal profession   313
    SCOTT ROGERS AND SARAH STUART

SECTION VII
Mindfulness programs in addiction — 325

26 Mindfulness-Oriented Recovery Enhancement: a review of its theoretical underpinnings, clinical application, and biobehavioral mechanisms — 327
ERIC L. GARLAND, ANNE K. BAKER, MICHAEL R. RIQUINO, AND SARAH E. PRIDDY

27 Mindfulness-Based Relapse Prevention for addictive behaviors — 341
VANESSA SOMOHANO, TAYLOR SHANK, AND SARAH BOWEN

SECTION VIII
Mindfulness programs in compassion — 355

28 Mindful Self-Compassion (MSC) — 357
CHRISTOPHER GERMER AND KRISTIN NEFF

29 Mindfulness-Based Compassionate Living (MBCL): a deepening programme for those with basic mindfulness skills — 368
ERIK VAN DEN BRINK AND FRITS KOSTER

SECTION IX
Mindfulness programs in psychological flourishing — 383

30 Mindfulness-Based Strengths Practice (MBSP) — 385
ROGER BRETHERTON AND RYAN M. NIEMIEC

31 Mindfulness Based Flourishing Program (positive mindfulness program) — 403
TARLI YOUNG AND ITAI IVTZAN

Index — 415

Chapter 1

Handbook of Mindfulness-Based Programmes
An introduction

Itai Ivtzan

When we think about mindfulness we frequently picture a monk, wearing orange robes, sitting rigidly for hours, days, maybe even weeks, with his hands resting on his thighs and without moving his body. Although we can indeed practice mindfulness in this way, it is only one option amongst an infinite list of possibilities. This is because mindfulness is not about what we do, or which posture we adopt; it is about our way of being. We practice mindfulness every time our mind (our attention) is one with the activity we are performing. Yes, it is as simple as that. When your mind and activity are one, you are present in the moment; your mind does not wander, and you are free of judgement, criticism, avoidance, and many other cognitive processes that take place in our normal state of consciousness.

But what is that normal state of consciousness? It is usually characterised by contemplation of things other than the activity in which you are engaged. For example, when you speak to your friend while thinking about an email from your boss; when you read the email from your boss while thinking about tonight's date; when you sit with your date while thinking about a task you need to do for work; when you complete this task while thinking of your lunch; when you eat your lunch while thinking of your friend. This is a vicious circle in which we are constantly anywhere but in the present moment. This creates a duality between what we do and where we are (mentally). Such duality distances us from our experiences of life, from ourselves, and from our loved ones. If we are not present as things happen, as we feel and eat and talk and make love and write, we are not in touch with the heart of the experience, the essence of the moment. This is exactly what mindfulness therefore offers: a unity of mind and action, a presence. When these come together our experiences are transformed. We know from scientific research that being mindful changes our experiences, making them more meaningful and enjoyable while enabling us to become more efficient and engaged with life.

Mindfulness research has been conducted with many different groups and the results have consistently demonstrated the important impact mindfulness can have on very different experiences. For example, we now know that practicing mindfulness when we eat makes the food taste better and makes us more aware of the point at which we have had enough and need to stop eating. Practicing mindfulness when we have sex makes the experience more sensual, enjoyable, and connected. And one final example, which I find wonderful because of its mundanity, mindfulness has been found to have an extraordinary impact on the experience of washing the dishes! In such as study, participants are randomly assigned to either "traditional" or "mindful" groups. The first group of participants washes the dishes in a traditional way. This involves washing the dishes while thinking about different things (as most of us do when we wash the dishes). This is the duality I referred to earlier: the activity (washing the dishes) and the attention (wandering into thoughts and images that have nothing to do with the activity at that moment) are disconnected, cleaving the here-and-now experience into two elements that fight for control over one's consciousness. The second group of participants, however, washes the same number of dishes mindfully for the same length of time. What does it mean to wash the dishes mindfully? If mindfulness is all about unity of activity and attention, then all I would need to do is devote my full attention to the activity. For example, I would notice the temperature of the water, feel the texture of the plates and cutlery, notice the feel of the liquid soap as it touches my hand, become aware of how the soap smells; these are all examples of presence. My mind is not wandering off into irrelevant thoughts and instead is fully aware of and embracing the experience and activity of the moment. The results of such studies indicate that participants in the "mindful" washing group exhibited a significant increase in positive emotions and a corresponding decrease in negative emotions. Such benefits were not found in the "traditional" washing group. The same pattern of results can be seen in numerous other mindfulness studies: whatever the circumstances, whatever the activity, integrating a mindful way of being into our lives offers a meaningful transformation.

The discussion above lays the foundations for this book. We now realise that we can implement mindfulness in any population, at any age, for any challenge, and in any circumstances – to support both individuals and groups. A nurse could be seeking mindfulness to help her deal with patients, a teacher might need it to reduce burnout, students may find it helps them to concentrate, employees could improve the quality of their relationships with colleagues, the elderly could find it helps them accept the losses experienced with aging, athletes could concentrate better and improve their performance, and therapists could deepen their feelings of empathy with a client. However, each of these populations is different in many ways, which needs to be taken into account in the delivery of mindfulness so that a personalised and relevant experience is provided for each practitioner.

This realisation has initiated an abundance of mindfulness programmes in the West, each comprising different practices that utilise a variety of exercises and creative approaches and are constructed in a way that feels "right" for each specific practitioner or group of practitioners. For this book I have chosen to select well-established programmes, with a clear rationale, which have demonstrated creativity and wisdom in their application of mindfulness. These programmes have also been scientifically studied and have been shown to provide the practitioner with a positive transformation.

The book is divided into sections, each covering a different theme or population. In each section there is a list of chapters describing different mindfulness programmes. The first section is *Mindfulness programmes in therapy*, which takes the reader through different therapeutic approaches that integrate mindfulness to deepen psychological healing. The second section is entitled *Mindfulness Programmes in Families* and offers a variety of programmes to support parenting, childbirth, relationships, and growing old. The next section, *Mindfulness programmes in health-care*, shows how mindfulness programmes can be integrated into medical practice while also supporting people who are recovering from cancer, eating disorders, and insomnia. As part of the *mindfulness programmes in education* this book offers a variety of mindfulness practices for both teachers and students. The next section, *Mindfulness programmes in children and adolescents*, focuses specifically on child-oriented mindfulness programmes while the following section, *Mindfulnessprogrammes at work*, focuses on leadership and law. The next section, *Mindfulness programmes in addiction* then describes two mindfulness-based approaches that can help with addiction and substance abuse. *Mindfulness programmes in compassion*, on the other hand, is a section in which the emphasis is on the relationship between mindfulness and compassion, offering programmes that deepen both self-compassion and compassion to others. The final section, *Mindfulness programmes in psychological flourishing*, describes two mindfulness programmes that focus on flourishing through strengths, hope, meaning, and other concepts derived from positive psychology. Thus, this is an indisputably diverse group of sections and mindfulness programmes, providing the reader with a full spectrum of knowledge and experience of mindfulness applications.

When I see the long and varied list of mindfulness programmes in this book I feel both excited and proud. Excited because of the incredible potential these programmes offer to improve people's lives, thereby making the world a slightly better place. Proud because in the West we have taken an Eastern-based practice and translated it into a practice that is relevant to the Western world in a 21st century marked by turmoil. I hope you enjoy this wonderful development in the history of mindfulness practice.

Section I

Mindfulness programs in therapy

Chapter 2

Acceptance and Commitment Therapy

Jennifer E. Krafft, Grayson M. Butcher, Michael E. Levin, and Michael P. Twohig

Introduction

Acceptance and Commitment Therapy (ACT; Hayes, Strosahl, & Wilson, 1999) is a transdiagnostic psychotherapy shown to be effective for a variety of problem areas, including but not limited to mood and anxiety disorders (Bluett, Homan, Morrison, Levin, & Twohig, 2014; Twohig & Levin, in press). ACT is considered a contextual cognitive behavioural approach to psychotherapy that has developed out of both traditional behaviour analysis and contemporary interest in mindfulness and acceptance processes. The defining aspect of contextual psychotherapies is an emphasis on targeting "the context and function of psychological events" rather than their content, often through the use of mindfulness and acceptance techniques (Hayes, Villatte, Levin, & Hildebrandt, 2011, pp. 157–158). The goal of this chapter is to introduce ACT as a therapeutic approach. Furthermore, because ACT is a product of a reticulated approach to scientific development, the critical elements underlying ACT need to be introduced: its underlying philosophical assumptions and behaviour analytic account of cognition.

Getting to the roots

ACT is guided by a pragmatic philosophy of science called *functional contextualism* (Hayes et al., 1999). The core assumption of functional contextualism is its truth criterion, known as *effective action*, which refers to the goal of predicting and influencing behavioural events with precision, scope and depth. This means that a psychotherapy based in functional contextualism needs to align with other fields of knowledge (e.g., psychology must adhere to principles in biology), use concepts that apply across many areas (e.g., reinforcement has broad applicability), and have specificity in explaining how these concepts apply to an event (e.g., there are specific parameters to reinforcement). The other core assumption of functional contextualism is the focus on the *whole event*, which situates all therapeutic and scholarly analyses in the larger environmental context. Events are not looked at in isolation as that would exclude important functional elements.

The foundation for ACT

The role of mindfulness in ACT is rooted in Relational Frame Theory (RFT), a behavioural account of human language and cognition (Hayes, Barnes-Holmes, & Roche, 2001). The core assertion of RFT is that humans have the unique ability to learn to relate events, regardless of their formal properties. A simple example is the relation between objects and the nouns that label them, such as when humans learn that the spoken word "dog" is the *same as* an actual dog, and the written word "d-o-g" is the same as an actual dog. As a result of learning these two relations, a language-able human knows the written word is the same as the spoken word even with no direct training regarding their equivalence. It is derived automatically. This is expansive. It has been shown that this occurs with many other types of frames such as comparatives (more than, bigger than, worth more). Thus, given the ability to relate things, one can respond to just about anything without needing to have previously interacted with it. The automaticity and expansiveness of this thinking process fits well with how many mindfulness approaches conceptualize cognition; one good example is the restless and frantic "monkey mind."

Not only is language expansive and automatic, it also can transform experiences that are "thought about." More technically, the function of a stimulus can be transformed due to what it is verbally related to. For example, if a child is taught that dogs are dangerous, the child will likely show an emotional response to many dogs, the spoken word dog, and the written word dog. A child might even avoid going to new places if told dogs might be there. One clinically important feature of this is that therapists can either target the relational frames themselves (the actual information), or the context that informs what function should be transferred (and therefore the impact of the relations on behaviour). ACT uses acceptance and mindfulness techniques to alter the context that informs the function to be transferred (for instance, noticing a thought as just a thought versus relating to the thought as absolutely true information that must be acted on).

The psychological flexibility model

The basic research underlying ACT highlights a primary source of psychological suffering, the tendency for behaviour to be overly guided by internal experiences (thoughts, feelings, urges), or attempts to avoid these experiences, at the expense of more effective or meaningful action. This process is referred to as psychological inflexibility, and it is the core pathological process targeted in ACT. ACT conceptualizes psychopathology and psychological health as two sides of the same coin, characterized by a set of generally effective psychological flexibility processes and a corresponding set of generally ineffective psychological inflexibility processes.

There are six functionally defined processes, which directly address promoting psychological flexibility. The six interrelated processes are acceptance, defusion, contact with the present moment, self as context, values, and committed action (see Figure 2.1). Each process is described briefly here and in greater detail in the "ACT in Practice" section. In ACT, mindfulness is defined as the combination of four of the component processes of psychological flexibility, namely, acceptance, defusion, present moment awareness, and self as context. The other two process of change, values and behavioural commitments, are seen as the active and overt sides of psychological flexibility.

Acceptance: Acceptance describes the action of actively and willingly interacting with ongoing inner experiences without attempting to regulate their occurrence. Like all aspects of psychological flexibility, acceptance is a means to another end. By actively and willingly accepting inner experiences, even those considered unwelcome or uncomfortable, acceptance increases contact with the breadth of experiences and fosters contexts in which one may act more flexibly and in tune with values. By shifting the focus away from regulating

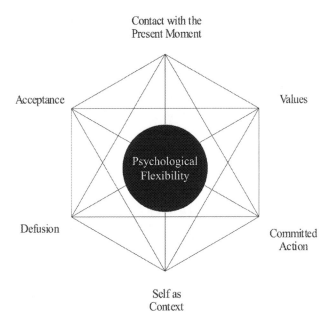

Figure 2.1 The six psychological flexibility processes.
Source: Copyright Steven C. Hayes. Used by permission.

unwelcome inner experiences, acceptance can be seen as the opposite strategy of *experiential avoidance*: a pattern of attempting to reduce or avoid contact with unwanted inner experiences, which narrows one's repertoire of effective action and overall functioning (Hayes, Wilson, Gifford, Follette, & Strosahl, 1996).

Defusion: Cognitive defusion describes the process of relating to thoughts in a non-literal way. In other words, cognitive defusion is the ability to respond to thoughts as simply thoughts, urges as urges, and sensations as sensations. This view contrasts with another common way that people relate to inner experiences: in terms of how truthful, logical, or rational they are.

Present moment awareness: Present moment awareness, or contact with the present moment, involves shifting and maintaining attention on what is occurring here and now. Present moment awareness encompasses flexible attention to both external and internal environmental stimuli and bears a strong similarity to the "attending" or "awareness" aspect of popular definitions of mindfulness (e.g., Kabat-Zinn, 1994; Bishop et al., 2004; or Langer, 2000).

Self as context: Sometimes called a *transcendent sense of self*, self as context refers to contact with oneself as an ongoing observer, aware of yet distinct from, one's experience. Self as context is contrasted with the more typical, pathological self as content, wherein an individual overly identifies with the literal content that is used to describe them (such as through their "self stories"). When individuals encounter a sense of self as context, they report identifying with an observing frame of mind that is itself boundless. Self as context means contacting a sense of being the container, rather than what is contained. For example, you are the sky and your thoughts and feelings are passing clouds.

Values: Values refer to what is deeply and personally meaningful to an individual in terms of how they act in the world. More technically, values are verbally constructed consequences for patterns of activity that enhance the reinforcing qualities of engaging in that activity. Values connect specific behaviours to their meaning in each moment. Values are different from goals in that they are abstractions from meaningful patterns of activities, instead of those activities themselves. For example, a father might have the goal of coaching his child's sports team, which is connected to the value of being a good parent. Because values are abstractions, it is helpful to clarify them and explicate how they connect with daily life. Values function as a positive aspect of language which helps augment one's focus on meaningful, vital patterns of action (Wilson & Dufrene, 2009).

Committed action: ACT is ultimately a behavioural approach, which is to say that each ACT process is a means to change how individuals function in the world. Committed action describes the class of actions in which a person intentionally engages to move towards values-consistent goals. As such, some clarity in regard to values is necessary to engage in committed action.

Operationalizing mindfulness processes

Whereas mindfulness has variously been described as an outcome, process, technique, or method, ACT views mindfulness as the set of four interrelated psychological processes – acceptance, defusion, present moment awareness, and self as context – which foster effective, flexible, and values-driven action (Fletcher & Hayes, 2005). These processes are regarded as interrelated. One unique aspect of the conceptualization of mindfulness in ACT is that it is based on basic verbal processes identified in RFT research. This lower-level research helps define mindfulness in ACT as "defused, accepting, open contact with the present moment and the private events it contains as a conscious human being experientially distinct from the content being noticed" (Fletcher & Hayes, 2005).

Empirical support

ACT is a transdiagnostic approach and has been applied to, and shown to be effective with, an impressive breadth of issues, not all of which fit neatly within clinical diagnoses (A-Tjak et al., 2015). Within the clinical realm, ACT has been shown to be effective for depressive disorders (Twohig & Levin, in press), anxiety and OCD spectrum disorders (Bluett et al., 2014), and substance use disorders (Lee, An, Levin, & Twohig, 2015), among other problem areas. Readers interested in further information on the efficacy and effectiveness of ACT are encouraged to investigate the meta-analyses published on this topic such as A-Tjak et al. 2015 and Öst 2014.

ACT in practice

Introduction

ACT is not defined by a specific set of techniques. Instead, at a fundamental level implementing ACT involves targeting theoretically specified processes of change in order to foster psychological flexibility and increase quality of life (Westrup, 2014). This means that if a clinician brings ACT exercises into the therapy room in a way that is not consistent with enhancing psychological flexibility (for example, teaching a client to "name their mind" as a strategy to control worry; Hayes et al., 1999), they are no longer implementing ACT. Conversely, if a therapist introduces a new metaphor or exercise that helps a client to recognize thoughts as thoughts, this is defusion work, whether or not the exercise is described in any ACT books or protocols.

The process-based nature of ACT allows clinicians freedom and creativity in discovering how they can foster psychological flexibility in each of their clients. In turn, it requires a solid understanding of the principles and processes that define ACT as well as focused, mindful attention on what is happening in the therapy room (Luoma, Hayes, & Walser, 2007).

During a therapy session, therapists delivering ACT attend to the function of clients' behaviour in each moment and identify and target psychological inflexibility as it shows up, in order to encourage contact with new ways of behaving. ACT also tends to involve extensive use of role-plays and metaphors to provide opportunities for experiential learning.

The number of sessions involved in a course of ACT can vary widely depending on the problem area and progress observed over time. That said, clinical trials of ACT commonly involve eight to twelve sessions (Bluett et al., 2014; Öst, 2014). ACT can be implemented in group or individual therapy formats and have been successfully implemented in brief interventions such as workshops (Hayes, Pistorello, & Levin, 2012).

A relatively typical course of ACT will be described. However, as mentioned previously, ACT is a therapy that entails immense flexibility. Depending on a client's starting point and progress, an ACT therapist may address each of the six psychological flexibility processes in a single session or devote most of the course of therapy to a specific process. In addition, while the ACT processes are introduced individually, the six processes of psychological flexibility are interrelated at their core. For example, when introducing values, new areas of fusion or avoidance may be encountered and it may be useful to shift to targeting mindful acceptance. Each of the six processes supports one another and working on one often brings up another.

One aspect of ACT that is distinct from many therapeutic orientations, although common in mindfulness, is that the processes that are targeted in ACT are considered to be equally applicable to clients and clinicians (Luoma et al., 2007). As such, it is important for clinicians to develop self-awareness with respect to ACT processes. For instance, a clinician who finds herself avoiding in-session exposure because she is worried about causing distress can recognize this as a type of experiential avoidance, open up, and consider how to proceed in a way that is consistent with the value of helping her client grow. It can also be highly beneficial for the therapist to model psychological flexibility. For instance, the therapist who caught herself avoiding exposure could model awareness and willingness by sharing what she noticed with her client. This stance can also help therapists to increase empathy and develop a collaborative, egalitarian relationship.

Session overview

Dropping emotional control and preparing for acceptance

It is common for ACT to begin with one or more sessions devoted to identifying the current system of responses to unwanted internal experiences, and how well it works. Typically, a class of experientially avoidant behaviours that serve the purpose of attempting to control these experiences can be identified, including internal attempts to suppress or alter unwanted thoughts and feelings as well as avoidance of situations expected to trigger those thoughts and feelings. For example, a client bothered by panic attacks may avoid not only places or activities that occasion panic, but also engage in cognitive avoidance or distraction. This can help clients recognize the range of behaviours that can serve as attempts to control and avoid unpleasant internal experiences. Mindfulness is widely considered to include an attitude of acceptance towards internal experience (Bishop et al., 2004), and this step lays the groundwork for acceptance by building recognition of when and how non-acceptance occurs.

After identifying a set of experientially avoidant behaviours, these strategies are discussed further to determine if they have worked to decrease suffering in the short term, or in the long term, and what these strategies cost. This discussion is designed to engender a sense of "creative hopelessness," a growing awareness that the current approach is not working to regulate the internal events in order to begin developing the willingness to do something genuinely different with those internal events. It is important to keep the focus on actual experience as the ultimate judge of what works to control the internal events. The therapist's job is not to convince or persuade the client to give up a control agenda, but to help guide the client in exploring his/her own experience.

Early sessions may introduce further discussion of the ineffectiveness of attempts at control, and the paradox that striving for control of internal experience may not only make control more unachievable, but also lessen quality of life. This paradox can be highlighted by drawing contrasts between the internal and external world. For instance, a clinician may use the following technique:

> "I'm going to ask you to do a few simple things, and observe how well you can do them. I want you to try your very hardest to do them. The first thing is . . . don't move your arms. Keep working hard at that, do your very best, make sure your arms are not moving." [*Allow some time to notice how this works.*]
>
> "The next thing is . . . don't think of a pink elephant. No matter what, make sure you aren't thinking about a big, pink elephant". [*Again, allow some time to notice how this works.*]

This exercise is concluded by asking how the two attempts compared. In general, it is easy to not move, while the thought of a pink elephant comes automatically. There are several metaphors that are also commonly introduced to develop a new perspective on the struggle for control, such as falling into quicksand: the more someone struggles, the more they sink.

Acceptance

As clients begin to recognize that rigid emotional control is unworkable and costly, it is common to shift into introducing acceptance as an alternative. As mentioned previously, acceptance is an active embrace of internal experiences in each moment, with a stance of openness, curiosity, and awareness – the opposite of experiential avoidance. This intentional, open attitude towards experience is considered an essential component of mindfulness (Bishop et al., 2004). Sometimes the term "willingness" is used in ACT because it better represents the sense of acceptance as an active, warm stance. Acceptance is not the same as wanting or liking an experience, and this can be an important point of clarification. For example, it makes perfect sense that experiencing intrusive memories of a life-threatening car accident would not be pleasant or desirable. However, letting those memories return without struggling with them may enable the freedom to engage in new patterns of behaviour. As with the other ACT processes, becoming more accepting is not an end in itself, but a way to draw closer to values. As such, exposure to painful thoughts and feelings, both in session and out of session, is framed in the context of valued action. For example, an individual who struggles with binge eating and values their health might be asked if they could notice and make space for their painful emotions and urges to binge if it helped them get closer to their value of health.

There are numerous metaphors and exercises that can help in developing greater acceptance. In a commonly used exercise, clients write a difficult internal experience on a card and are presented different ways of interacting with the card. First, the clinician holds the card up and asks the client to push back against it. The client feels how much work it is to fight against the card. Next, the card is crumpled up as small as possible. Other ways of avoiding or distancing self from the difficult internal experience can also be acted out. Finally, the client is asked to try letting the card sit on their open hands, and holding it gently, like a butterfly. At each step, space is left to notice what it is like to interact with one's experience in this way. These types of experiential exercises can help to develop a sense of what acceptance might involve. As another example, mindfulness meditation exercises may be used to help guide clients in actively noticing the experiences of difficult emotions, thoughts, and sensations purely for what they are and without trying to fight them.

Cognitive defusion

Cognitive fusion refers to the human tendency to "buy into" cognitions, taking them literally and allowing them power over behaviour. Although the ability to talk about things and have them treated as reality is essential for communication with others, there are other times when taking language literally is less helpful. For example, when a client has the thought, *I'm not smart enough for college*, and takes this thought literally, they are more likely to quit studying or quit school entirely. Whether a thought is "positive" or "negative," buying into thoughts can restrict behaviour in unworkable ways. For example, from the thoughts "I'm a kind person" and "Kind people don't get angry," it may be derived that it is necessary to avoid expressing anger or frustration even when this pattern of behaviour damages the ability to have meaningful relationships. Defusion involves changing how one relates to thoughts by perceiving them as what they truly are, in order to alter their impact on behaviour. Bringing mindful awareness to thoughts helps to increase recognition of thoughts as thoughts, supporting defusion. This ability to shift perspective on one's internal experience is also referred to as "decentering" or "distancing," and is a target of other mindfulness-based interventions such as Mindfulness-Based Cognitive Therapy (Segal, Williams, & Teasdale, 2002).

One classic defusion exercise, often referred to as "Milk, Milk, Milk" (Hayes et al., 1999), involves quickly repeating a word or phrase. Eventually the word tends to lose its meaning and be perceived as a series of sounds. This exercise is often started using neutral words or phrases like "milk," but later incorporating words or phrases that are more personally relevant, such as "failure." Another simple defusion exercise involves labeling the process of thinking. For example, after having the thought, *I'm broken*, stating, "I'm having the thought that I'm broken," and even, "I'm noticing I'm having the thought that I'm broken," can help to engender distance from thoughts. Labelling thoughts in this manner can help foster a new, less literal perspective on thoughts and develop a context in which thoughts do not necessarily determine behaviour.

These cognitive defusion exercises provide examples of how ACT uses a number of non-meditative experiential exercises to target processes often emphasized in mindful meditation such as decentering/defusing from thoughts. This may arguably enhance clinician flexibility in how cognitive fusion is targeted, increasing the ability to adapt to clients who struggle with "eyes closed" mindfulness exercises and providing greater variation in mindfulness training to support applying skills to relevant life situations.

Present moment awareness

Many ACT manuals suggest starting sessions with a brief mindfulness exercise (e.g., Westrup, 2014), to help become attuned to what shows up during the time working together. Attending to ongoing experience in a present, moment-by-moment fashion supports acceptance and defusion because it allows opportunities for recognizing thoughts and feelings as transient internal experiences. In addition, developing present moment awareness helps to increase contact with the direct contingencies of experience. For example, by staying present during social situations, individuals with social anxiety can notice how people respond to them rather than being caught up in worries that they will be judged negatively. ACT makes use of structured mindfulness exercises such as mindful eating and mindful breathing to teach present moment awareness. Many exercises also target present moment awareness along with other ACT processes. For instance, the "Leaves on a stream" exercise (Luoma et al., 2007), which involves noticing thoughts and visualizing setting them on a leaf and letting the leaf drift down a stream, over and over, supports both present moment awareness and cognitive defusion. ACT also makes use of informal mindfulness during regular activities, and there is a particular emphasis on "getting present" during sessions.

Self as context

Developing a sense of self as context can also be an important part of ACT. This sense of self as an ongoing observer of experience is cultivated through open awareness in the present moment, and lies in stark contrast to a conceptual, verbally defined sense of self. It is common to be defined through self-narrative: for example, "I am a good mother," "I am someone who quits when things get hard," "I am an activist." While there is nothing problematic about having these types of narratives about the self, they can contribute to the narrowing of behaviour when held tightly. For example, if being a "good mother" is essential to a woman's sense of self, she might avoid talking with her child about difficult topics such as substance use or self-harm because it could involve learning information that might contradict the "good mother" narrative. In contrast, the observing self provides a context for difficult thoughts and feelings to occur without defining one's experience. Self as context is often introduced using metaphors such as "the chessboard" (Hayes et al., 1999). In exploring the metaphor, thoughts and feelings that are struggled with are treated like pieces on the board. No matter how much the pieces fight and battle, the board remains the same, and it can be moved in any direction while holding all the pieces. Mindfulness practices such as meditation can also bring clients in touch with a sense of the self as a context that contains, but is broader than, internal experiences.

Values

Values are flexible in the sense that there are generally many different behaviours that can be linked to a specific value, and the awareness that these behaviours are tied to a value makes engaging in them more reinforcing. Values are not goals to be attained, but qualities of action that can be contacted in each moment. For instance, a health goal might be completing a 5k run, while the value of health could be contacted in every moment of training and nourishing one's body along the way. A life connected with values is vital, engaged, and meaningful. All work in ACT is designed to enable movement towards values. As such, every session tends to involve touching on values at least briefly. However, it may make sense to devote several sessions to the topic of values, particularly if values are unclear or values are driven by fear or compliance. There are many exercises and tools available that can help to clarify values. One popular one is the tombstone exercise (Hayes et al., 1999), which involves thinking to the future and considering how one would want to be remembered after dying in order to identify one's most essential values. Mindfulness and acceptance, as described in the four processes above, support the ability to pursue values even when difficult thoughts and feelings show up.

Committed action

ACT is fundamentally a behaviour therapy, and the goal of a course of ACT is to develop expanding patterns of behaviour that are consistent with values. As such, all the other processes are important to the extent that they enable engagement in value-driven, committed action. In therapy, this often takes the form of behavioural commitments linked to goals and values with the support of the other ACT processes. This process is similar to traditional behaviour therapy – for example, behavioural commitments may involve exposure to social interaction for a person with social anxiety, scheduled smoking for a smoking cessation program, or commitments to engage in meaningful actions towards a partner in couples therapy. However, behavioural change is always linked back to values, which can entail a shift in framing when introducing traditional behavioural methods such as exposure or behavioural activation that are typically framed as a way to regulate emotions (Hayes et al., 2012). When difficulty is encountered in following through on a commitment, this often indicates work is needed in another ACT process. For example, the client who approaches a new social situation may become fused with thoughts such as *no one here likes me*, leading them to experience distress that they are unwilling to make room for, and leave the situation. Committed action is woven throughout treatment, but it is particularly emphasized in later sessions, after the development of mindfulness skills such as greater awareness, willingness, and defusion, with one to two sessions (or more) focused on committed action as needed.

Termination in ACT is not based on symptom reduction, but on the development of psychological flexibility. The most important evidence of progress is seeing the client's behaviour expanding in ways that allow living a more meaningful, engaged life. If a client struggling with depression is continuing to experience self-critical thoughts, but finds that he can hold those thoughts in mindful awareness, make room for them, and still engage in meaningful activities, then treatment has been successful from an ACT perspective. Doing what works to support clients in living a life that they value is what defines ACT above all else. As such, ACT makes extensive use of mindfulness skills and techniques, but they are always employed towards the purpose of enabling clients to behave differently, in a manner more consistent with their values.

Online resources

To learn more about ACT, related mindfulness-based and contextual cognitive behavioural therapies, or the basic research underlying this work, you can visit the Association for Contextual Behavioral Science (ACBS) at https://contextualscience.org. ACBS is an international professional community that is the intellectual "home" for ACT among other contextual behavioural therapies. The website offers a vast array of resources for professionals who join ACBS including access to ACT treatment protocols, videos, audio files, measures, publications, and training opportunities.

References

A-Tjak, J. G. L., Davis, M. L., Morina, N., Powers, M. B., Smits, J. A. J., & Emmelkamp, P. M. G. (2015). A meta-analysis of the efficacy of acceptance and commitment therapy for clinically relevant mental and physical health problems. *Psychotherapy and Psychosomatics, 84*, 30–36.

Bishop, S. R., Lau, M., Shapiro, S., Carlson, L., Anderson, N. D., Carmody, J., . . . Devins, G. (2004). Mindfulness: A proposed operational definition. *Clinical Psychology: Science and Practice, 11*, 230–241.

Bluett, E. J., Homan, K. J., Morrison, K. L., Levin, M. E., & Twohig, M. P. (2014). Acceptance and Commitment Therapy for anxiety and OCD spectrum disorders: An empirical review. *Journal of Anxiety Disorders, 28*, 612–624.

Fletcher, L., & Hayes, S. C. (2005). Relational frame theory, acceptance and commitment therapy, and a functional analytic definition of mindfulness. *Journal of Rational-Emotive and Cognitive-Behavior Therapy, 23*, 315–336.

Hayes, S. C., Barnes-Holmes, D., & Roche, B. (Eds.). (2001). *Relational Frame Theory: A Post-Skinnerian account of human language and cognition.* New York, NY: Plenum Press.

Hayes, S. C., Luoma, J. B., Bond, F. W., Masuda, A., & Lillis, J. (2006). Acceptance and Commitment Therapy: Model, processes and outcomes. *Behaviour Research and Therapy, 44*, 1–25.

Hayes, S. C., Pistorello, J., & Levin, M. E. (2012). Acceptance and Commitment Therapy as a unified model of behavior change. *The Counseling Psychologist, 40*, 976–1002.

Hayes, S. C., Strosahl, K. D., & Wilson, K. G. (1999). *Acceptance and commitment therapy: An experiential approach to behavior change.* New York, NY: Guilford Press.

Hayes, S. C., Villatte, M., Levin, M., & Hildebrandt, M. (2011). Open, aware, and active: Contextual approaches as an emerging trend in the behavioral and cognitive therapies. *Annual Review of Clinical Psychology, 7*, 141–168.

Hayes, S. C., Wilson, K. G., Gifford, E. V., Follette, V. M., & Strosahl, K. (1996). Experiential avoidance and behavioral disorders: A functional dimensional approach to diagnosis and treatment. *Journal of Consulting and Clinical Psychology, 64*, 1152–1168.

Kabat-Zinn, J. (1994). *Wherever you go, there you are.* New York, NY: Hyperion.

Langer, E. J. (2000). Mindful learning. *Current Directions in Psychological Science, 9*, 220–223.

Lee, E. B., An, W., Levin, M. E., & Twohig, M. P. (2015). An initial meta-analysis of Acceptance and Commitment Therapy for treating substance use disorders. *Drug and Alcohol Dependence, 155*, 1–7.

Luoma, J. B., Hayes, S. C., & Walser, R. D. (2007). *Learning ACT: An acceptance & commitment therapy skills-training manual for therapists.* Oakland, CA: New Harbinger.

Öst, L. G. (2014). The efficacy of acceptance and commitment therapy: An updated systematic review and meta-analysis. *Behaviour Research and Therapy, 61*, 105–121.

Segal, Z. V., Williams, J. M. G., & Teasdale, J. D. (2002). *Mindfulness-based cognitive therapy for depression: A new approach to preventing relapse*. New York, NY: Guilford Press.

Twohig, M. P., & Levin, M. E. (in press). Acceptance and commitment therapy as a treatment for anxiety and depression: A review. *Psychiatric Clinics*.

Westrup, D. (2014). *Advanced Acceptance and Commitment Therapy: The experienced practitioner's guide to optimizing delivery*. Oakland, CA: New Harbinger.

Wilson, K. G., & Dufrene, T. (2009). *Mindfulness for two: An acceptance and commitment therapy approach to mindfulness in psychotherapy*. Oakland, CA: New Harbinger.

Chapter 3

Cultivating wise mind in dialectical behavior therapy through mindfulness

Dawn M. Salgado, Andrew W. White, Daphna Peterson, and Linda A. Dimeff

> It is the mark of a wise mind to be able to entertain a thought without accepting it.
> – Aristotle

Program overview

Dr. Marsha Linehan originally developed dialectical behavior therapy (DBT) in the 1980s for the treatment of chronically suicidal individuals with borderline personality disorder (Linehan, 1993a). Predicated on a biosocial approach, as well as dialectical philosophy, behaviorism, and Eastern and Western contemplative practices, DBT extended from traditional cognitive behavioral therapy (CBT) with its incorporation of both change- and acceptance-based strategies used within individual psychotherapy, group skills training, and telephone coaching and consultation.

A key principle in DBT is the client's cultivation of one's inner wisdom and intuition, known in DBT as "Wise Mind". Considered a core DBT skill, Wise Mind is the synthesis of reactant, mood-dependent behavior that is purely under the control of one's emotions ("Emotion Mind") and a more logical, analytical, task-focused behavior ("Reasonable Mind"). Linehan's (1993a) core belief is that Wise Mind, and an individual's innate capacity for profound wisdom, exists within an individual no matter their history or current functioning. DBT consists of four distinct skill modules (i.e., Mindfulness, Distress Tolerance, Emotion Regulation, and Interpersonal Effectiveness) with mindfulness consistently presented to clients in the first two weeks of each module. In summary, the cultivation of "Wise Mind" through acceptance-based strategies such as mindfulness allows for not only the active integration of Reasonable Mind and Emotion Mind but also the active integration with other skills to allow clients to pursue a life worth living.

Theoretical background and research

While working with female clients engaging in chronically suicidal behavior, including non-suicidal self-injurious (NSSI) behavior, Linehan (1993a) began recognizing the limitations of traditional CBT. Specifically, she found that the change-centered focus of CBT often invalidated the lived experiences and suffering of many of her clients. This led to poorer therapeutic alliance and higher attrition rates due to the inability of the therapist to meet the full spectrum of the client's needs. While CBT addressed immediate concerns (e.g., self-harm, dissociation, substance abuse, etc.), the profound sense of invalidation led to other client therapy-interfering behaviors (e.g., missed appointments, unwillingness to do homework, verbal attacks on the therapist for his/her lack of sensitivity to their pain). These observations highlighted the importance of acceptance-based strategies, including strategic use of validation. DBT is a third-wave CBT, which extends and deviates from traditional CBT and moves beyond treating a list of problem behaviors exclusively in favor of holistic and principle-driven approach incorporating both acceptance and mindfulness as key components (Hayes, 2004; Forman & Herbert, 2009).

The reliance on behavioral science within a biosocial approach, combined with the inclusion of acceptance and dialectics, as well as Eastern and Western contemplative practices, constitute the major philosophical underpinnings represented within DBT (see Linehan, 1993a; or Neacsiu, Bohus, & Linehan, 2014). Behavioral science informs the development of skills and change-based strategies that exist within DBT while at the same time normalizing and validating the clients' high-risk behaviors to promote more effective and adaptive coping behaviors. DBT strongly emphasizes a biosocial model where individuals with biological vulnerabilities (e.g., high emotion sensitivity/reactivity and slow return to baseline) interact with an invalidating environment resulting in a transaction that has the potential to increase emotion dysregulation and decreased sense of self. When viewing behaviors within this context, it becomes clear high-risk behaviors and other symptoms are attempts to increase emotion regulation as well as to communicate distress to the environment.

The inclusion of Western and Eastern contemplative practices within DBT are a primary means of highlighting the importance of self-acceptance as well as non-judgmental awareness, a process characterized by mindfulness (Hayes, Follette, & Linehan, 2011; Kabat-Zinn, 1994; Linehan, 1994; Marlatt, 1994). Mindful awareness within DBT draws from dialectical philosophy in that clients use non-judgmental awareness to move towards a synthesis of seemingly opposing viewpoints. This supports clients and therapists in moving away from polarized perspectives in order to develop a more complex understanding of being, avoiding conflict, and preventing being "stuck" or entering into power struggles within the therapeutic relationship. The central dialectic in DBT is the balance between acceptance and change, moving towards the middle path of Wise Mind and forming a synthesis between Emotion Mind and Reasonable Mind. DBT therapists seek to find a Wise Mind balance between acceptance and change strategies by the integration of a "technical cognitive behavioral skills set, heightened acceptance and awareness, and capacity to improvise with DBT's change, acceptance, and dialectical philosophy – to alter entrenched behavioral patterns and 'get the patient out of hell'" (Swenson, 2016, p. 23).

DBT is recognized as the gold standard for treatment for individuals diagnosed with borderline personality disorder (National Institute for Health and Care Excellence, 2015; U.S. Department of Health & Human Services, 2009), is supported by over 36 peer-reviewed published randomized control and comparative trials (Linehan Institute, n.d.), and has significant cost benefits to treatment as usual (American Psychiatric Association, 1998; Linehan & Heard, 1999). Previous research indicates that DBT is associated with a reduction of NSSI disorder and suicidal behaviors, depression, hopelessness, anger, disordered eating, substance use, impulsiveness, as well as increases in overall functioning and social adjustment, self-concept and self-esteem, and lower rates of attrition among clients (Iverson, Shenk, & Fruzzetti, 2009; Linehan et al, 2006; McMain, Sayrs, Dimeff, & Linehan, 2007; Rathus & Miller, 2002; Roepke et al, 2011; Safer, Telch, & Agras, 2001; van Dijk, Jeffrey, & Katz, 2013; Verheul, van den Bosch, Koeter, van den Brink, & Stijn, 2003). A number of adaptations focusing on specific populations, topics, and settings also exist (Dimeff & Koerner, 2007). DBT strategies have been adapted for clients within relationships and families

(Fruzzetti, 2006; Fruzzetti, Santisteban, & Hoffman, 2007), persons with intellectual disabilities (Brown, 2015), adolescents (Mehlum et al., 2014; Miller, Rathus, & Linehan, 2007), caregiver burnout (Drossel, Fisher, & Mercer, 2011), as well as adult and juvenile forensic populations (McCann, Ivanoff, Schmidt, & Beach, 2007). Adaptations have also focused on specific topics and settings. Comtois, Kerbrat, Atkins, Harned, and Elwood (2010) examined the effectiveness of DBT related to transitioning into work and school from psychiatric disability. Other adaptations have generalized DBT strategies to substance use (e.g., reducing urges and craving, McMain et al., 2007), examined outcomes and social functioning among college students (Pistorello, Fruzzetti, MacLane, Gallop, & Iverson, 2012), and explored emotional problem solving with adolescents in school settings (Mazza, Dexter-Mazza, Miller, Rathus, & Murphy, 2016).

Programmatic structure and features of DBT

The standard outpatient comprehensive DBT program consists of four modes of treatment (a) individual psychotherapy, (b) group skills training, (c) telephone coaching and consultation and (d) consultation meetings for therapists. Moreover, ancillary treatments (e.g., inpatient psychiatric, pharmacotherapy) may be used in addition to the standard modes. These modes of treatment function to enhance capabilities, improve motivation, and provide opportunities for the generalization and application of knowledge and skills to other settings. Furthermore, they guide and support the structuring of the environment by the individual, and enhance the motivation and abilities of therapists to provide effective treatment (Chapman, 2006).

To assist in developing a treatment plan based on the client's severity and chronicity of their problem behavior, DBT is organized into four stages of treatment with specific goals and sets of targets delineated at each stage (Linehan, 1993a, 2010). It is important to note the hierarchical nature of the targets. The first set treated in therapy is related to life-threatening behavior and it is only after the client is able to exert behavioral control that the therapy moves onto therapy-interfering behaviors, and, finally, quality of life-interfering behaviors (see Table 3.1).

Mindfulness as the "what" and "how" of Wise Mind

Mindfulness is defined as "the act of consciously focusing the mind in the present moment without judgment and without attachment to the moment" (Linehan, 2014b, p. 151). Within DBT, mindfulness skills are core practices learned in Stage 1 of treatment, they are consistently re-introduced and connected to other core skills, and continue to be expanded upon while clients progress in treatment. The DBT set of mindfulness skills consists of psychological and behavioral versions of Eastern and Western spiritual and contemplative practices, which clients learn in order to manage dysregulation associated with self, cognitions, general psychological distress, and emotions. Linehan (1993a) views fostering Wise Mind through mindfulness as an active strategy that balances Reasonable Mind, defined as logical, intellectual, concrete, and problem-focused, and Emotion Mind, which is mood-dependent, propulsive, and reactive. Much like the "You are here" dot on a map, Wise Mind provides a bird's eye view of one's current location and where one wants to go while maintaining awareness of the thoughts and emotions that may act as a barrier to arriving at the destination.

Within the skills training component of DBT, Linehan (1993b, 2014a, 2014b) provides a set of mindfulness skills, categorized into "What" and "How" skills, which work as "vehicles

Table 3.1 DBT stages, goals, and behavioral targets

Stage	Goal	Behavioral Targets
1 Severe behavioral dyscontrol	Gaining behavioral control	Decrease imminent life-threatening, therapy-interfering, and quality of life-interfering behaviors; increasing behavioral skills and self-management
2 Quiet desperation	Regulating emotional experiencing	Resolving earlier trauma, enhancing capacity to fully experience painful negative emotions
3 Experiencing ordinary problems of living	Experiencing ordinary happiness, effectively balancing problems, building self-respect	Addressing ordinary problems in living, simple mental health disorders, improving capacity to achieve individual life goals, and/or enhancing self-respect, enhance feelings of peace and well-being
4 Profound feeling of emptiness and incompleteness	Experiencing joy, freedom, enlightenment, spirituality, connectedness, and meaning	Address individual goals of fulfillment, which might focus on spirituality and sense of meaning, as well as having a larger capacity for joy and freedom

for balancing Emotion Mind and Reasonable Mind . . . and other extreme sets of mind and action to achieve wise mind and wise action" (p. 153). The "What" skills are specific behavioral practices, and consist of (a) Observe, (b) Describe, and (c) Participate. The "Observe" skill focuses on increasing attentional awareness of events, self, emotions, and behavioral responses without reacting, labeling, or engaging with the prompting or inciting event. The "Describe" skill refers to the process of non-judgmentally and factually describing a stimulus. "Participate" skills relate to throwing oneself into the current moment without self-awareness, fully entering the "flow", and moving away from cognitions, which exist outside of happenings and events in the current moment.

The "How" skills pertain to the intentions associated with engaging in the practice of the "What" skills. The "How" skills consists of having a (a) Non-Judgmental stance, (b) being of One-Mindfulness, and (c) engaging Effectively. When practicing a Non-Judgmental stance clients (and therapists) bring attention to describing their reactions and environment using non-judgmental language, and when judgments arise observing and labeling these judgments rather than judging themselves for having judgments. The practice of One-Mindfulness refers to doing one specific activity with full awareness in the moment, rather than attempting to multitask or dividing one's attention. Effectiveness requires one to maintain a focus on one's long-term goals, and move skillfully towards these goals rather than focusing on what is perceived as "wrong" or "right."

Mindfulness skills exist to increase access to Wise Mind as well as to complement and facilitate the practice of the remaining core skillsets (Emotion Regulation, Distress

Tolerance, and Interpersonal Effectiveness). Without the acquisition of mindfulness skills and the ability to identify Wise Mind, successful application of these skill sets would be difficult, if not impossible. Emotion Regulation skills focus on increasing awareness and accurate labeling of emotions, reducing the impact of negative emotions and suffering that comes with being more aware of emotional experiences, and at the same time, increasing opportunities for experiencing positive emotions that allow for broadening experiences and changing emotions. Distress tolerance skills allow clients to normalize, depathologize, and validate their emotional experiences while focusing on behavioral skills (e.g., self-soothing, pros and cons) and acceptance skills (e.g., validation of experience, half-smile) to tolerate pain without suffering or making the pain worse. Interpersonal effectiveness skills offer tools for the balancing of meeting goals and objectives, the relationship with the other person, and maintaining self-respect and integrity with other individuals present in the life of the client.

Mindfulness practice exercises from DBT

The integration of behavioral principles with acceptance and mindfulness perspectives in DBT allows for the conceptualization, teaching, and practice of mindfulness as a set of discrete behavioral skills. Within the DBT skills training component, skills trainers lead clients through behavioral practices meant to demonstrate the six core mindfulness skills (Observe, Describe, Participate, Non-Judgmentally, One-Mindfully, and Effectively) and elicit new behaviors from clients in the skills group. These practices incorporate the use of analogies, and examples of how skills leaders have used skills and experiential exercises in order to demonstrate the skill. The section below provides specific strategies and examples of mindfulness training used in skills training in order to assist clients in the program in learning, practicing, and generalizing mindfulness skills and the cultivation of Wise Mind to multiple environments during Stage 1 treatment. The following exercises are derived from suggestions for mindfulness practice outlined by Linehan (2014a, 2014b).

Bringing attention to the present moment

It is essential to draw attention to the one moment in which the client currently exists. At the same time, when one is dysregulated, drawing attention to the one moment without a process to do this is akin to telling an individual to keep their eye on one leaf of a tree in a windstorm. The Mindfulness 5-5-5 exercise uses the Describe skill, and has the goal of using factual labels to draw attention to the present moment, rather than interpreting or judging the moment, which act as a barrier to direct awareness and mindfulness of the moment. When teaching this skill (as with all skills) a therapist may instruct their clients to notice when they become distracted and move away from the skill. When this occurs, the suggestion is made for clients to "return to their home" and try the practice again, thus teaching the principle of Wise Mind being a "home" to which clients return in order to be skillful. In addition, the instruction to "return home" demonstrates the principle that the goal is not to exist in Wise Mind 100% of the time, but to notice when one has moved away from Wise Mind, and to return when possible. Specific instructions for the Mindfulness 5-5-5 exercise are as follows:

Take a moment to look around your surroundings. Describe aloud 5 things that you see, using just the facts of what you can observe, rather than judgments or interpretations of the object. Instead of "The weather outside is horrible" you could state, "I notice rain falling faster than I can count the raindrops." Instead of "I see the best book" you might say, "I observe a book that I recognize and have positive judgments about." In addition, be sure not to interpret what you see – just stick to the facts. For example, stating "I see a glass of water on the table" is an interpretation – you do not know for sure there is water in the glass, and a factual observation would be "there is a hollow cylinder in front of me with a clear liquid in it." Using the same principles, factually describe out loud 5 things you hear and then factually describe out loud 5 things you feel. Moving on, use the same principles again to describe out loud 4 things you see, 4 things you hear, and 4 things you feel, then factually describe out loud 3 things you see, 3 things you hear, and 3 things you feel, then factually describe out loud 2 things you see, 2 things you hear, and 2 things you feel. Finally, factually describe aloud 1 thing you see, 1 thing you hear, and 1 thing you feel.

Connecting to the deep well within

Linehan (2014a, 2014b) suggests the analogy of a deep well as a way of explaining Wise Mind. The deep well within holds our deepest wisdom and knowledge as well as provides connection to other humans and creatures, allowing for compassion and understanding. One must be careful to cultivate this connection, since it is easy to think one is connected to the deep water when in reality, the well is blocked and one can mistake connection for the experience of emotion dysregulation or re-experiencing of traumatic events as deepest wisdom and Wise Mind. For example, emotions such as intense anger can feel congruent and powerful in the moment and may seem like a Wise Mind state, while in reality the intensity of the anger is associated with rigid thinking or the inability to see situations from multiple perspectives. Moving past and around these blockages allows for increased connection to Wise Mind and the ability to see the wisdom of one's own goals. For many people who have had their environment consistently tell them their emotions are incorrect or cannot be trusted, the concept of Wise Mind on its own can be overwhelming and difficult to grasp. Providing a specific practice such as focusing on the breath allows clients consistent place to anchor their experience to, in that the practice is both a starting point for mindfulness practice and core skill to return to repeatedly. Specific instructions for this practice are as follows:

Sit in a comfortable position you can hold for a few minutes, and bring attention to your breath. Follow your breath without attempting to change it. When you notice you are judging your breathing, wishing it was different, or become distracted, gently bring yourself back to your home, where you are noticing your breathing as it is, without judgment or distraction. When you are ready, focus on your Wise Mind by bringing the word "Wise" to your attention when taking a breath in, and the word "Mind" when exhaling. Repeat this practice to link your mind and body together and find the state of being where your Wise Mind resides and remember it is your home. When your attention wanders, return to your home, pairing your inhalation with the word "Wise" and your exhalation with the word "Mind."

Describing without judgment

As humans, we use judgment on a consistent basis. These judgments may have been things we have learned over the years, and they may be terms we use to provide a "short cut" to explain something. We may often judge ourselves, or our own behaviors, as "bad" or "wrong" or "crazy" since we have heard these judgments before. These judgments lead to increased self-invalidation (e.g., "I shouldn't be this way") and often are not an accurate description of a situation (e.g., what one individual thinks of, as "bad coffee" could be what another individual thinks of as "good coffee"). Our goal is to use non-judgmental terminology to describe ourselves, others, and the world around us. This mindfulness practice applies the Non-Judgmental skill to practice moving from judgmental terminology we may be used to using to more mindful, non-judgmental terminology. Specific instructions for a sample nonjudgmental practice are as follows:

Bring to mind a person you know well. Set a timer, and for two minutes write down all of the judgmental thoughts about this person. When you notice your mind wander, or you start to judge your judgments, bring yourself back to the task of writing down every judgment you can think of. When the timer goes off, set it for another two minutes. This time, write down all of the non-judgmental thoughts you can think of about this person. This may require you to see things from the other person's perspective, or to find a way to describe, in a factual way, a behavior you historically have judged. Describe it well enough that a person who does not know this individual could understand the behavior you are referring to. Again, when you notice you are moving from facts to judgments, bring yourself back to your home and return to describing this individual using non-judgmental facts.

Observing your conveyor belt of thoughts

One of the most difficult mindfulness skills to learn is the Observe skill. As humans, we seek to understand and label the world around us, and it is very difficult to observe something in our world without moving towards naming the object or event. At the same time, we are prone to over attaching to a label or event, and then not noticing other experiences around us. This mindfulness skill is to practice the Observing, and then Describing of a thought, without attaching to the thought. At the same time, it is common to become distracted by focusing on and following a thought rather than noticing the thought and letting it go. If this happens, notice that you have become distracted, and move yourself back to your home where you will wait for the next thought to arise.

Imagine there is a conveyor belt coming out of your forehead. On this belt, each of your thoughts is placed. You are watching the end of the belt, and your job is just to sort the thoughts into buckets. On a piece of paper, draw four boxes, and label the boxes "Emotions", "Judgments", "Distractions", and "Other Experiences". While emotions are thoughts associated with physical sensations or feelings associated with emotion experiences (e.g., sadness, anger, anxiety), judgments refer to evaluations of the experience (e.g., "this is a stupid exercise" or "I should be doing a better job at this"). Distractions refer to thoughts or sensations that draw your attention away from the exercise (e.g., having an itchy nose, thinking "what's that squirrel doing outside the window?") while other experiences pertain to anything else that does not fit in the other three boxes. When you notice a thought, put a mark in the box where the thought belongs, and then allow yourself to step back and wait for the next thought. It is likely you will at first notice you have too many thoughts to count, or that your mind goes blank. When this happens, return to your Wise Mind home, and focus on looking for the next thought. Do not try to block thoughts, and do not try to hold onto thoughts and follow them. Instead, allow yourself to notice the thought, mark the box, and then detach from the thought. This often takes practice, and when you notice you have held onto a thought, or are judging the thought, or are distracted, again observe your experience without judgment and return to your Wise Mind home to look for the next thought.

Conclusion

The primary and overarching goal of DBT is to build a life worth living, which includes the experience of ordinary and transformative happiness, connection, meaning, and a sense of purpose through skillful means. A necessary and essential component of this transformation is the cultivation of and connection to Wise Mind. Existing at the overlap of "Reasonable Mind" and "Emotion Mind", "Wise Mind" grows out of deliberate behavioral practice (as well as generalization) of mindfulness skills that are rooted in the "What" and "How" skills taught during DBT skills training. While "What" skills act as ingredients of experience to be practiced, "How" skills guide the process allowing mindfulness to be practiced and integrated within an individual's everyday experiences to enhance awareness and engagement. As Linehan (2014a) states, Wise Mind is "that part of each person that can know and experience truth. It is where a person knows something to be true or valid. It is where the person knows something in a centered way" (p. 170). Mindfulness skills are the central skills introduced to clients during DBT and are a key acceptance-based strategy, which balances with change-based strategies, such as those found in traditional CBT. The supplementation of change-based strategies with mindfulness and acceptance strategies allows for better generalization and integration of skills use through increased connection to one's life and accuracy of information collected from one's experiences in the moment.

Additional information and resources on mindfulness within DBT

- **The Linehan Institute/Behavioral Tech DBT Mindfulness Resources** (http://behavioraltech.org/resources/mindfulness.cfm) is an archive of sample mindfulness exercises, instructions on teaching mindfulness, and general handouts to use when learning, doing, or giving instruction on mindfulness.
- **Walking Like a Buffalo** (http://behavioraltech.org/products/details.cfm?pc=CD02 is a 57-minute audio containing step-by-step instructions for learning mindfulness skills and also discusses differences between meditation and mindfulness, provides an overview of core mindfulness skills, including the "What" and the "How" skills, as well as strategies for creating a formal mindfulness practice.
- **National Education Alliance for Borderline Personality Disorder** (www.borderline-personalitydisorder.com) has a variety of resources for practitioners, clients, and family members that include mindfulness practices.
- **Twenty-Two Mindfulness Exercises** (https://positivepsychologyprogram.com/mindfulness-exercises-techniques-activities/) provides a comprehensive overview by a Positive Psychology Program on learning and teaching mindfulness skills, with video, audio, and text examples as well as ideas for how to use mindfulness for different life demands.
- **The Mindfulness Solution for Intense Emotions: Take Control of Borderline Personality Disorder with DBT** (see www.cedarkoons.com) is a text, workbook, and mindfulness practice manual that includes an accompanying online companion site with registration that features guided meditations by the author, Cedar Koons.

References

American Psychiatric Association. (1998). Gold Award: Integrating dialectical behavior therapy into a community mental health program. *Psychiatric Services, 49*(10), 1338–1340. http://dx.doi.org/10.1176/ps.49.10.1338

Brown, J. F. (2015). *The emotion regulation skills system for cognitively challenged clients: A DBT-informed approach.* New York, NY: Guilford Press.

Chapman, A. (2006). Dialectical behavior therapy: Current indications and unique elements. *Psychiatry, 3*(9), 62–68.

Comtois, K. A., Kerbrat, A. H., Atkins, D. C., Harned, M. S., & Elwood, L. (2010). Recovery from disability for individuals with borderline personality disorder: A feasibility trial of DBT-ACES. *Psychiatric Services, 61*(11), 1106–1111. http://dx.doi.org/10.1176/ps.2010.61.11.1106

Dimeff, L., & Koerner, K. (2007). *DBT in clinical practice: Applications across disorders and settings.* New York, NY: Guilford Press.

Drossel, C., Fisher, J. E., & Mercer, V. (2011). A DBT skills training group for family caregivers of persons with dementia. *Behavior Therapy, 42*(1), 109–119. http://dx.doi.org/10.1016/j.beth.2010.06.001

Forman, E. M., & Herbert, J. D. (2009). New directions in cognitive behavior therapy: Acceptance-based therapies. In W. O'Donohue & J. E. Fisher (Eds.), *General principles and empirically supported techniques of cognitive behavior therapy* (pp. 102–114). Hoboken, NJ: Wiley.

Fruzzetti, A. E. (2006). *The high conflict couple: A dialectical behavior therapy guide to finding peace, intimacy, and validation.* Oakland, CA: New Harbinger.

Fruzzetti, A. E., Santisteban, D. A., & Hoffman, P. D. (2007). Dialectical behavior therapy with families. In L. A. Dimeff & K. Koerner (Eds.), *Dialectical behavior therapy in clinical practice: Applications across disorders and settings* (pp. 22–244). New York, NY: Guilford Press.

Hayes, S. C. (2004). Acceptance and commitment therapy and the new behavior therapies: Mindfulness, acceptance and relationship. In S. C. Hayes, V. M. Follette, & M. Linehan (Eds.), *Mindfulness and acceptance: Expanding the cognitive behavioral tradition* (pp. 1–29). New York, NY: Guilford Press.

Hayes, S. C., Follette, V. M., & Linehan, M. M. (2011). *Mindfulness and acceptance: Expanding the cognitive-behavioral tradition.* New York, NY: Guilford Press.

Iverson, K. M., Shenk, C., & Fruzzetti, A. E. (2009). Dialectical behavior therapy for women victims of domestic abuse: A pilot study. *Professional Psychology: Research and Practice, 40*(3), 242–248. http://dx.doi.org/10.1037/a0013476

Kabat-Zinn, J. (1994). *Wherever you go, there you are: Mindfulness meditation in everyday life.* New York, NY: Hyperion.

Linehan, M. M. (1993a). *Cognitive behavioral treatment of borderline personality disorder.* New York, NY: Guilford Press.

Linehan, M. M. (1993b). *Skills training manual for treating borderline personality disorder.* New York, NY: Guilford Press.

Linehan, M. M. (1994). Acceptance and change: The central dialectic in psychotherapy. In S. C. Hayes, N. S. Jacobson, V. M. Follette, & M. J. Dougher (Eds.), *Acceptance and change: Content and context in psychotherapy* (pp. 73–86). Reno, NV: Context Press.

Linehan, M. M. (2010). *The house of DBT.* Seattle: Behavioral Tech Research, Inc.

Linehan, M. M. (2014a). *DBT skills training handouts and worksheets* (2nd Ed.). New York, NY: Guilford Press.

Linehan, M. M. (2014b). *DBT skills training manual* (2nd Ed.). New York, NY: Guilford Press.

Linehan, M. M., Comtois, K. A., Murray, A. M., Brown, M. Z., Gallop, R. J., Heard, H. L., Korslund, K. E., Tutek, D. A., Reynolds, S. K., & Lindenboim, N. (2006). Two-year randomized trial + follow-up of dialectical behavior therapy vs. therapy by experts for suicidal behaviors and borderline personality disorder. *Archives of General Psychiatry, 63*(7), 757–766. http://dx.doi.org/10.1001/archpsyc.63.7.757

Linehan, M. M., & Heard, H. L. (1999). Borderline personality disorder: Costs, course, and treatment outcomes. In N. Miller & K. Magruder (Eds.), T*he cost effectiveness of psychotherapy: A guide for practitioners* (pp. 291–305). New York, NY: Oxford University Press.

Linehan Institute. (n.d.). *Summary of DBT data to date*. Retrieved on April 30, 2016 from www.linehan institute.org/research/data-to-date.php

Marlatt, G. A. (1994). Addiction, mindfulness, and acceptance. In S. C. Hayes, N. S. Jacobson, V. M. Follette, & M. J. Dougher (Eds.), *Acceptance and change: Content and context in psychotherapy* (pp. 175–197). Reno, NV: Context Press.

Mazza, J. J., Dexter-Mazza, E. T., Miller, A. L., Rathus, J. H., & Murphy, H. E. (2016). *DBT skills in schools skills training for emotional problem solving for adolescents*. New York, NY: Guilford Press.

McCann, R. A., Ivanoff, A., Schmidt, H., & Beach, B. (2007). Implementing dialectical behavior therapy in residential forensic settings with adults and juveniles. In L. A. Dimeff & K. Koerner (Eds.), *Dialectical behavior therapy in clinical practice: Applications across disorders and settings* (pp. 112–144). New York, NY: Guilford Press.

McMain, S., Sayrs, J. H., Dimeff, L. A., & Linehan, M. M. (2007). Dialectical behavior therapy for individuals with borderline personality disorder and substance dependence. In L. A. Dimeff & K. Koerner (Eds.), *Dialectical behavior therapy in clinical practice: Applications across disorders and settings* (pp. 145–173). New York, NY: Guilford Press.

Mehlum, L., Tormoen, A. J., Ramberg, M., Haga, E., Diep, L. M., Laberg, S., Larsson, B. S., Stanley, B. H., Miller, A. L., Sund, A. M., & Groholt, B. (2014). Dialectical behavior therapy for adolescents with repeated suicidal and self-harming behavior: A randomized trial. *Journal of the American Academy of Child & Adolescent Psychiatry*, *53*(10), 1082–1091. http://dx.doi.org/10.1016/j.jaac.2014.07.003

Miller, A. L., Rathus, J. H., & Linehan, M. (2007). *Dialectical behavior therapy with suicidal adolescents*. New York, NY: Guilford Press.

National Institute for Health and Care Excellence. (2015). *Surveillance review of CG78: Borderline personality disorder: Treatment and management*. Retrieved from www.nice.org.uk/guidance/CG78/documents/cg78-borderline-personality-disorder-bpd-surveillance-review-decision-january-20153

Neacsiu, A. D., Bohus, M., & Linehan, M. M. (2014). Dialectical behavior therapy: An intervention for emotion dysregulation. In J. J. Gross (Ed.), *Handbook of emotion regulation* (2nd Ed., pp. 491–507). New York, NY: Guilford Press.

Pistorello, J., Fruzzetti, A. E., Maclane, C., Gallop, R., & Iverson, K. M. (2012). Dialectical behavior therapy (DBT) applied to college students: A randomized clinical trial. *Journal of Consulting and Clinical Psychology*, *80*(6), 982–984. http://dx.doi.org/10.1037/a0029096

Rathus, J. H., & Miller, A. L. (2002). Dialectical behavior therapy adapted for suicidal adolescents. *Suicide and Life-Threatening Behaviors*, *32*(2), 146–157. doi: 10.1521/suli.32.2.146.24399

Roepke, S., Schroder-Abe, A. S., Jacob, G., Dams, A., Vater, A., Ruter, A., Merkl, A., Heuser, I., & Lammers, C. H. (2011). Dialectic behavioural therapy has an impact on self-concept clarity and facets of self-esteem in women with borderline personality disorder. *Clinical Psychology and Psychotherapy*, *18*(2), 145–158. http://dx.doi.org/10.1002/cpp.684

Safer, D. L., Telch, C. F., & Agras, W. S. (2001). Dialectical behavior therapy for bulimia nervosa. *American Journal of Psychiatry*, *158*(4), 632–634. http://dx.doi.org/10.1176/appi.ajp.158.4.632

Swenson, C. (2016). *DBT principles in action: Acceptance, change, and dialectics*. New York, NY: Guilford Press.

U.S. Department of Health and Human Services, Substance Abuse and Mental Health Administration. (2009). *Report to Congress on borderline personality disorder* (HHS Publication No. SMA-11–4644). Retrieved from https://store.samhsa.gov/shin/content/SMA11-4644/SMA11-4644.pdf

Van Dijk, S., Jeffrey, J., & Katz, M. R. (2013). A randomized, controlled, pilot study of dialectical behavior therapy skills in a psychoeducational group for individuals with bipolar disorder. *Journal of Affective Disorders, 145*(3), 386–393. doi: 10.1016/j.jad.2012.05.054

Verheul, R., Vad Den Bosch, L. M., Koeter, M. W., DeRidder, M. A., Stijnen, T., & Van Den Brink, W. (2003). Dialectical behaviour therapy for women with borderline personality disorder: 12-month, randomised clinical trial in The Netherlands. *British Journal of Psychiatry, 182*, 135–140. http://dx.doi.org/10.1192/bjp.182.2.135

Chapter 4

Mindfulness-Based Stress Reduction

Theory, practice and evidence base

Diane Reibel and Donald McCown

Introduction

Mindfulness-Based Stress Reduction (MBSR) was conceived by Jon Kabat-Zinn in 1979 as a way to teach patients with chronic medical conditions how to live fuller, healthier, more adaptive lives. MBSR is currently offered in over 700 medical centers in the U.S. and around the world. More than 35 years of research has shown physical and mental health benefits of MBSR, including reduced anxiety, depression, and pain, as well as improved cognitive, brain, and immune function. The evidence base for MBSR has helped to expand its use beyond patient populations into educational, corporate, and community settings.

MBSR is a formalized and well-structured group intervention that is participant-centered, experiential, and educational. The core of the 8-week program involves intensive training in mindfulness meditation and its applications for daily living and coping with stress, pain, and illness. Mindfulness meditation cultivates moment-to-moment awareness that is intentionally non-reactive and non-judgmental.

Kabat-Zinn defines mindfulness operationally "as the awareness that arises by paying attention on purpose, in the present moment and non-judgmentally." (Kabat-Zinn, 2003, p. 145) This operational definition has been further described by Shapiro and colleagues who suggest that mindfulness contains three axioms: intention, attention, and attitude (Shapiro, Carlson, Astin, & Freedman, 2006). These three axioms are not sequential but engaged simultaneously throughout the process of cultivating mindfulness. The **intention** – what motivates the participant to engage in the program and the practices – has been shown to shift along a continuum "from self-regulation, to self-exploration, and finally to self-liberation." The **attention** is trained in two capacities: the ability to maintain focused attention, and the ability to have flexibility of focus. The **attitude** is one of non-judgment and of having an accepting, open, and kind curiosity towards experience. The cultivation of these axioms of mindfulness increases one's ability for self-regulation and self-management, allowing one to identify and then choose to override habitual reactions and respond with more balance and greater skill.

MBSR is an 8-week program comprising 9 sessions, in which participants attend 2-1/2 hour sessions once a week, and one full-day (7-hours) class between the sixth and seventh sessions. Class time each week is divided between formal meditation practice, small and large group discussions, didactic presentations (including on stress physiology and the role that perception plays in the shaping of one's experience), and dialogical inquiry with individuals into their present-moment experiences.

Formal practices include body scan meditation, sitting meditation (with focus on the breath), mindful Hatha yoga, sitting meditation (expanding awareness to objects of attention beyond the breath, to open awareness of the present moment), walking meditation, and eating meditation. Class discussions focus on group members' experiences in the formal meditation practices and the application of mindfulness in day-to-day life. Home practice is an integral part of MBSR. In Kabat-Zinn's original program (Kabat-Zinn, 2013) participants are asked to commit to formal practice, supported by audio recordings of guided meditations, for 45 minutes a day, 6 days per week.

The basic curriculum

The original MBSR curriculum changes somewhat based on the specific population and setting in which it is taught. However, the integrity of the MBSR program is typically maintained through the continuity of basic themes and practices. The outline below describes themes, expected learnings, and specific practices introduced in each session. The themes and practices are reinforced and built upon in each succeeding week.

Session One: The theme for the first session is that "There is more right with you than wrong with you, no matter what challenges you are facing." Participants find that it is possible to turn towards their difficulties and that the MBSR program provides a supportive environment for working with challenges. The foundation for learning is cultivating awareness of the present moment – of body sensations, thoughts, and emotions – because it is only in the present that one can learn, grow, and change. The instructor explains what mindfulness is, and the formal practices provide direct experience of present-moment awareness. Practices include the raisin-eating exercise (mindful eating), abdominal breathing, and the body scan meditation, in which participants are instructed to notice sensations in each part of their body with curiosity and non-judgement.

Session Two: The theme of session two, "Perception and creative responding," shows participants that how they see (or don't see) what is happening in their lives determines how they will react or respond. The class discussion relates this to how people see the stress and pressures in their lives and to the understanding that it is not the stressors themselves, but how they handle them that determines if stress will negatively impact their mind and body. Exercises in perception followed by class dialogue illustrate that it is possible to see differently – that things are not necessarily what they seem. The body scan meditation is reinforced. A form of sitting meditation is introduced, which is a practice of focusing attention on the breath and, when the attention wanders, bringing it back – again and again.

Session Three: With the theme, "The pleasure and power of being present," participants begin to explore how the immediate assignment of pleasant or unpleasant labels to experience is limiting. A formal dialogue around the moment-by-moment unfolding of pleasant events in the body, mind, and emotions helps deepen understanding and present-moment awareness, while potentially revealing that it is possible to have pleasant moments even in the midst of stress or pain. The body scan and sitting meditations are reinforced and mindful yoga, a practice of bringing non-judgmental attention to the moving of the body in simple standing and lying down postures, is introduced.

Session Four: The theme for session four is "Stress reactivity and the role of mindfulness." Participants explore how automatic stress reactivity negatively impacts the body and mind and how being mindful can reduce stress reactivity and its effects. The physiological and psychological bases of the stress reaction (fight/flight, or freeze) is discussed and helps participants understand the mechanisms involved with the short- and long-term effects of stress on the body and mind. Body scan and mindful yoga are reinforced; sitting meditation expands its focus from awareness of breath to include sensations in the whole body.

Session Five: The theme for week five is "Responding versus reacting," and participants explore "Finding the space for making choices." The focus of experiential activities and dialogue is to show how mindfulness can shape perception, appraisal, and choice in critical moments. Participants find the possibilities of observing thoughts as events in the mind, reinforcing that "You are not your thoughts." Mindful yoga practice is reinforced; sitting meditation includes expanding awareness beyond breath, body sensations to hearing, to observing thoughts, emotions, and whatever arises in the present moment ("choiceless awareness"). Consciously shifting attention to different objects in this way strengthens flexibility of focus, and expanding to choiceless awareness strengthens one's ability to mindfully be with whatever is happening moment to moment.

Session Six: The theme is "Working with difficult situations, including stressful communication," and the participants experiment with and engage in dialogue about recognizing their automatic patterns of relating and finding options to those patterns in stressful situations, while staying centred in body, mind, and emotions. There is formal teaching on mindful communication and exercises in mindful communication to explore bringing mindfulness to interpersonal relationships. "Choiceless awareness" is reinforced in the sitting meditation. Walking meditation – attending to the body's movement and the environment when walking – is introduced. This practice offers the opportunity once again to engage mindfully in an activity often done automatically without awareness.

All-Day Session: For this day of practice in silence, participants are invited to "Dive in!" and cultivate mindfulness over a 7-hour period. This may reveal participants' habits of mind, deepening self-knowledge. It also allows participants to keep their experience in awareness for a longer time than ever before, offering opportunities for insight into the impermanence of pleasant and unpleasant body-mind-states. All meditations from prior sessions are engaged in again, and two new ones are introduced. One new practice, a "mountain" meditation, uses guided imagery of the sitting body as a mountain – able to sit in stillness with stability and majesty through the storms and glories of days and years. Sitting like a mountain through all kinds of changing weather patterns and changing seasons is a metaphor for mindfulness meditation practice – and life. The second new practice, loving-kindness meditation, guides participants in offering well-wishes to themselves, their loved ones, and increasingly wider circles of people, to include at last all beings. This meditation helps people recognize the inherent human qualities of friendliness, compassion, and connection that are available and capable of being cultivated.

Session Seven: The theme is "Integrating mindfulness practice more fully and personally into daily life." The learnings from this session include how to cultivate a disposition of generosity and compassion in formal meditation practice so that it may arise more readily in our day-to-day life. Participants are asked to reflect on lifestyle choices that are adaptive and self-nourishing, and on those that are maladaptive and self-limiting. There is also reflection and discussion on how mindfulness can support wise and healthy choices. Expanding awareness and loving-kindness meditations are reinforced.

Session Eight: The theme for the last class is "The eighth week is the rest of your life." This class begins with the body scan, the first formal practice introduced in the first class. This gives participants the opportunity to observe and discuss any changes that have taken place through mindfulness practice over the course of the program. Participants are offered a range of resources for continuing and supporting their ongoing learning and meditation including a mindfulness bibliography, lists of downloadable recordings and apps, and information on advanced courses and free all-day sessions. A closing circle includes a meditation and time for participants to offer final reflections.

MBSR participant learnings

Experiencing new possibilities: "Beginner's mind" is one of the "attitudinal foundations" in MBSR introduced in the very first class. Kabat-Zinn (2013, p. 35) explains,

> Too often we let our thinking and our beliefs about what we "know" prevent us from seeing things as they really are. We tend to take the ordinary for granted and fail to grasp the extraordinariness of the ordinary. To see the richness of the present moment, we need to cultivate what had been called "beginner's mind," a mind that is willing to see everything as if for the first time.

In the first class, the curriculum emphasizes new possibilities in two particularly directed exercises (Kabat-Zinn, 2013). First is the mindful eating of a raisin. Through a guided encounter with one raisin at a time, participants are helped to suspend their "preconceived ideas" and to investigate the "facts" of the encounter in the present moment. By exploring the raisin with all the senses, new information challenges familiar ways of thinking.

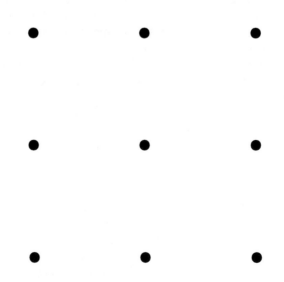

Figure 4.1 The nine dots: a puzzle.

Note: Without lifting the pencil from the paper, draw four lines so that all of the dots are connected by having a line passing through them. (Solution is revealed at end of chapter.)

Through such a contemplative approach to an ordinary undertaking which is often done on "automatic pilot," participants can gain understanding of habitual thought patterns. A participant in a recent class noted, "I always thought I didn't like the taste of raisins so I don't eat them. But this raisin tasted sweet and delicious. I really enjoyed eating it. Who would have thought?" Another exercise that often exemplifies seeing new possibilities is the nine-dot puzzle, often given as homework after the first class. To struggle with the problem, and then to see the "out of the box" solution, can be an "aha" moment, the power of experiencing new possibilities.

Discovering embodiment: This learning involves sensing into bodily experience and connecting with the wisdom of the body. Beginning with the first class, participants in MBSR are invited to "be with" or "be in" whatever experience is arising in the domain of body sensation, without judgment. The teacher's guidance attempts to bring participants to their own experience of their bodies – to "discovering embodiment."

The guidance of the body scan provides permission for *any* experience to be present; for example, calling the participant's attention to their feet, and offering language that names a range of experiences, from variations in temperature, to tingling, itching, pressure, to "nothing at all" – with an emphasis that "nothing at all" is a possible, acceptable experience. Further, initial guidance helps participants to parse immediate experience from stories *about* experience, to separate anticipation or opinion from the direct present-moment experience. Insights are often experienced and expressed such as, "I always thought that my pain was constant but I see that it actually comes and goes" and "I thought it was going to be my right foot that started hurting, but it was my left!"

The understanding of embodiment deepens as classes and practices unfold. Movement, such as the gentle mindful Hatha yoga presented in the curriculum is easily accessible as an embodiment practice. Participants can often make connections to their bodies quickly with mindful movement. Central to the presentation of movement is the permissiveness with which it is presented. It is offered for the purpose of exploration of the interrelationship of body and mind, without expectations of meeting a standard of "performance." Participants who are physically challenged are encouraged to adapt the offered postures to their capabilities, or to practice through imagination – noticing the possibility for connection with the body in that way.

The exploration of embodiment is a key to participant learning across the entire 8 weeks: helping participants to see their thoughts *as* thoughts and to focus on direct sensory experience is a gateway into the present moment and to experiencing new possibilities.

Cultivating observation: In the formal mindfulness practices, such as the body scan and sitting meditation, participants learn to work *with* rather than *against* the "wandering mind." They are guided to simply notice whenever the mind wanders and to gently bring the mind back to the object of attention (body part, breath). The "wandering mind" is natural and not to be judged. By observing thoughts as objects of attention rather than being unconsciously lost in the stream of thoughts, one can open to present-moment experience rather than to being confined by conditioned conceptions about experience.

Moving towards acceptance: In MBSR, this attitude points to a warmth that has its roots in non-judgment, and that flowers into "an affectionate, compassionate quality . . . a sense of openhearted, friendly presence and interest" (Kabat-Zinn, 2003, p. 145). The teacher's ability to build a safe, open, non-judgmental class environment is an important ingredient in MBSR (McCown, Reibel, & Micozzi, 2010, 2016; Santorelli, 1999) and supports the co-creation of mindfulness of the group. It is in this co-created space where these warm compassionate qualities can blossom and support individuals in moving towards acceptance in their own lives (McCown et al., 2010).

Growing compassion: Compassion is implicit in the formal and informal mindfulness practices introduced in the early weeks of the course, as guidance suggests being kind, non-judgmental, and accepting. During the all-day session, a specific practice of loving-kindness meditation is introduced, which supports participants' growing compassion. This meditation practice involves offering wishes for happiness, safety, well-being, and ease to oneself and others. It provides a link that helps many participants see how the benefits of their personal practice can be of benefit to others. They discover the potential impact of their growing compassion for their family, friends, workplace, and larger community.

MBSR research

Early studies: Jon Kabat-Zinn published the first scientific paper on MBSR research in 1985 (Kabat-Zinn, Lipworth, & Burney, 1985), studying the effects of MBSR for the self-regulation of chronic pain. Ninety chronic pain patients participated in what was then a 10-week MBSR program. Statistically significant reductions were observed in measures of present-moment pain; reduction of physical activity by pain; mood disturbance; and psychological symptomatology, including anxiety and depression. Pain-related drug utilization decreased and activity levels increased. At follow-up, the majority of the improvements observed during the meditation training were maintained up to 15 months following meditation training.

Another early study on MBSR by Kabat-Zinn and colleagues demonstrated that participants with generalized anxiety or panic disorders experienced clinically and statistically significant improvements in symptoms of anxiety and panic after completing an 8-week MBSR program (Kabat-Zinn et al., 1992). A three-year follow-up study of the same group of participants showed maintenance of the gains obtained in anxiety and depression (Miller, Fletcher, & Kabat-Zinn, 1995).

Chronic pain: The results of these early studies were extremely promising and led the way for a burgeoning of interest in MBSR research.

More recent studies on MBSR have shown improvements in quality of life and psychological symptoms of distress in patients with a variety of chronic pain conditions (Rosenzweig et al., 2010) including back pain (Cherkin et al., 2017), fibromyalgia (Grossman, Tiefenthaler-Gilmer, Raysz, & Kesper, 2007; Schmidt et al., 2011), arthritis (Rosenzweig et al., 2010), and chronic headache/ migraines (Bakhshani, Amirani, Amirifard, & Shahrakipoor, 2016).

Results of a meta-analysis of thirty-eight randomized control trials with chronic pain patients (21 studies utilizing MBSR) found that mindfulness training is associated with a decrease in pain compared with all types of control groups (Hilton et al., 2017) and with statistically significant improvements in depression and quality of life.

Other medical conditions: Numerous studies have documented health benefits of MBSR in other patient populations as well (Cramer, Lauche, Paul, & Dobos, 2012; Goyal et al., 2014; Grossman, Niemann, Schmidt, & Walach, 2004; Reibel, Greeson, Brainard, & Rosenzweig, 2001). Patients with Type 2 diabetes participating in MBSR showed significant improvements in blood glucose control and blood pressure (Rosenzweig et al., 2007; Gross & Reibel, 2014). Patients with coronary heart disease participating in MBSR showed decreases in blood pressure and body mass index, as well as symptoms of stress (Parswani, Sharma, & Iyengar, 2013).

In addition to improvements in psychological symptoms in patients with cancer participating in MBSR (Carlson, Speca, Patel, & Goodey, 2003; Cramer et al., 2012), improved immune function (Carlson et al., 2003) and cognitive function (Johns et al., 2016) have also been reported. MBSR has also resulted in improved immune function in patients with HIV (Creswell, Myers, Cole, & Irwin, 2009).

Healthy Individuals: The effects of MBSR have also been studied in non-clinical populations. In a meta-analysis of 29 studies with over 2500 healthy individuals (Khoury, Sharma, Rush, & Fournier, 2015), results showed significant reductions in stress, anxiety, depression, distress, and burnout with improvements in quality of life.

Neuroscience findings: Research on brain science and the effects of mindfulness has grown exponentially in the past decade. A study with healthy employees in a corporate setting, demonstrated that participation in the 8-week MBSR class resulted in electrical changes in the brain with a shift toward increased activity in the left pre-frontal cortex (Davidson et al., 2003), which has been shown to be associated with positive affect. The degree of change in electrical activity in the brain with MBSR was found to be proportional to improvements in immune function in these healthy individuals.

In addition to changes in the electrical activity in the brain, researchers have found that participating in the 8-week MBSR program results in structural changes in the brain including increases in gray matter in the prefrontal cortex. Increased gray matter has been found in areas of the brain associated with executive functioning such as planning, problem solving and emotion regulation as well as areas associated with learning and memory (Hölzel et al., 2011).

Research suggests that mindfulness training is associated with improvements in various aspects of cognitive function (Jha, Krompinger, & Baime, 2007; Johns et al., 2016; Lenze, 2014; Raffone, & Srinivasan, 2017).

Brain studies have also shown that the amygdala decreases in brain cell volume after mindfulness practice (Hölzel et al., 2010). The amygdala is involved in the fight, flight, or freeze response and is activated in stress reactions. This decrease in the size of the amygdala has been associated proportionately with a reported reduction in perceived stress level (Hölzel et al., 2010).

A recent systematic review of 21 studies looking at brain function indicates that the emotional and behavioral changes observed in people after participating in MBSR are related to both functional and structural changes in the brain (Gotink, Meijboom, Vernooij, Smits, & Hunink, 2016).

Conclusion: Research on the physical and mental benefits of MBSR and mindfulness training in general continues to grow by leaps and bounds. The current emphasis is on large randomized controlled trials examining the effectiveness of the program and the psychological, biochemical, and neural mechanisms underlying the positive changes that prior research has demonstrated.

It may be that reading this section has helped you to see that MBSR and its practices could be valuable in your own life. In this next section, we've included two sample practices that you can easily guide yourself through to get a taste of the program.

A preliminary exploration of MBSR practices

It's been said that in MBSR you simply learn things you already know, like breathing, sitting, lying down, walking, and eating – but you learn them as if they were new. It's that application of "beginner's mind" that matters. Below are instructions for two sample practices that can help you get a sense – literally – of the practice of mindfulness in an MBSR course. They are broken down into steps marked with numbers, so that you can easily keep your place as you guide yourself through them.

Mindful eating

The mindful eating of a raisin is the very first guided practice in the basic MBSR curriculum (if you prefer you can use some other food to do this mindful eating practice). It's simple to follow, and often pays off in insights. What's more, it's not a one-time practice. You can take what you learn and apply it – not only to any meal, but also to any experience of the senses that you choose.

1. You might approach this practice as if you have never seen raisins before and don't know what they are and therefore are very curious to explore them in depth.
2. Take two raisins, and put them in your palm, and close your hand. Humans get the vast majority of our information about the world through vision, so maybe, for the sake of beginner's mind, you can start with a different sense – touch. How do the raisins feel in the palm of your hand? Can you feel that they have weight? Now, pick up one of the raisins between your thumb and forefinger and notice the texture, feeling any softness, smoothness, coarseness, and ridges. Perhaps squeeze gently. What sensations do you notice now?
3. Bring the raisin up to your ear. Yes, you read that right. We don't automatically think of sound and dried fruit together. Yet, in the interest of beginner's mind, we can override such preconceived ideas and explore. As you bring it to your ear, what happens if you roll the raisin between your thumb and finger? Do you hear any sound coming from it? Perhaps yes, perhaps no.
4. Now bring the raisin beneath your nose and breathe in, opening to the sense of smell. Is there a scent that you notice and is there anything happening in your mouth or stomach as you do this?
5. Now use your sense of sight to explore the raisin. Place the raisin back in your palm. What do you see when you look now at the raisin? Notice the size, shape, color, and texture. Are you noticing thoughts arise like "I don't like how this raisin looks" or "This practice is odd"? Simply notice what your thoughts may be, letting them go as much as possible and allowing the primary focus of your attention to be on the direct exploration of the raisins. Right now, on their size, shape, color. . .
6. Next, slowly bring the raisin towards your mouth, noticing how it feels to be raising your arm, perhaps noticing if your mouth is watering. Place the raisin in your mouth – first allowing it to simply rest on your tongue. Perhaps you are noticing sensations of taste or texture. When you are ready, intentionally take one bite and pause, noticing the flavor that is released. Continue to chew slowly, being aware of changes in consistency and taste. When you are ready, consciously choose to swallow and notice the sensations in the throat. After swallowing, pay attention to any taste that remains in your mouth.
7. Check in and notice your body as a whole and how you are feeling after eating one raisin mindfully.
8. Perhaps, choose to eat a second raisin mindfully at your own pace.
9. Inquiry: How was this different from your normal way of eating? What did you notice during the exercise? Any thoughts about how these principles might apply to eating or other areas of your life?

Mindfulness-Based Stress Reduction 37

Mindful walking

For the formal practice of mindful walking, choose an indoor or outside walking path about ten to twenty paces long. The intention of the walking practice is not to reach a specific destination, "to get somewhere," but rather to be present with each step that you take.

1. Start by simply standing still and sensing the weight of your body at your feet, feeling the support of the ground beneath you. Allow your feet to be hip-width apart and your weight equally distributed. Feel the whole body as you stand in this way.
2. Keep your eyes open with a soft gaze. To begin walking, slowly shift your weight onto one leg and feel the sensations of this shifting. Then, lift the other foot up and step forward. Feel the foot as it touches down on the ground or floor. Notice how the weight now shifts to this leg. Continue moving at a slow pace and notice with each step the sensations of *shifting* the weight, *lifting* the foot forward and *placing* the foot on the ground.
3. Sense each step fully as you walk in a relaxed way to the end of the path you have chosen. When you arrive, pause and stand still. Feel your whole body standing and allow your senses to be open – to sights, smells, and sounds. When you have the impulse to move, slowly and mindfully – turn to face in the other direction and begin walking again. Paying attention to each step as you walk mindfully back and forth on your chosen path.

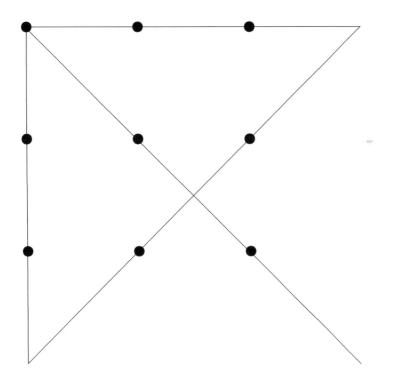

Figure 4.2 The nine dots: solution.

Note: The "box" shape of the dots suggests that the solution is found inside the confines or boundaries of the dots. It is only when you see that you can think "outside the box" that solutions become possibilities.

4   At some point, you may choose to walk at a quicker pace, more like everyday walking. At this speed, it may be easier for you to focus your attention on the movement of the legs, the swing of the arms, or the movement of the body as a whole.
5   As you walk, you will probably notice that your attention wanders at times, which is quite natural. When you notice your mind has wandered, simply note where it has gone (planning, worrying, etc.) and gently bring your attention back to the sensations of taking a step.
6   Inquiry: How was this different from the way you usually walk? Is it possible to bring more awareness to walking in your daily life? Perhaps choosing a path where you walk every day (i.e., from house to car, car to work, parking lot to store) and commit to walking that distance mindfully, being present step by step.

MBSR resources

To find MBSR teachers in your location

www.umassmed.edu/cfm/mindfulness-based-programs/mbsr-courses/find-an-mbsr-program/
or
Google MBSR in your location

Centers with long-standing MBSR programs

Center for Mindfulness-University of Massachusetts Medical School
Worcester, Mass
www.umassmed.edu/cfm/

Center for Mindfulness- University of California San Diego Medical Center
San Diego, California
https://health.ucsd.edu/specialties/mindfulness/

Duke Integrative Medicine-MBSR
Durham, North Carolina
www.dukeintegrativemedicine.org/programs-training/public/mindfulness-based-stress-reduction/

Mindful Living Programs
Chico and Mountain View California
www.mindfullivingprograms.com

Mindfulness Institute, Myrna Brind Center of Integrative Medicine
Thomas Jefferson University Hospitals
Philadelphia, PA
www.jefferson.edu/mindfulness
University of Wisconsin-Integrative Health

Madison, Wisconsin
www.uwhealth.org/alternative-medicine/mindfulness-based-stress-reduction

Online MBSR programs

MBSR Online – Sounds True
www.SoundsTrue.com/MBSR

MBSR Online – umassmed.edu
umassmed.edu/cfm/mindfulness-based-programs/mbsr-courses/mbsr-online

MBSR Online – Mindful Living Programs
www.mindfullivingprograms.com/mbsr_online_schedule.php

Online MBSR – Palouse (free)
https://palousemindfulness.com

Guided free downloadable audio files of MBSR practices

UCSD Center for Mindfulness https://health.ucsd.edu/specialties/mindfulness/programs/mbsr/Pages/audio.aspxss

Insight LA
http://inside.insightla.org/mbsraudio/

MaineHealth Learning Resource Center
www.mainehealthlearningcenter.org/mbsr/

Palouse Mindfulness
https://palousemindfulness.com/guidedmeditations.html

Mindfulness Practices Guided by Jon Kabat – Zinn
www.mindfulnesscds.com

Books on MBSR

Goldstein, E., & Stahl, B. (2015). *MBSR every day: Daily practices from the heart of mindfulness-based stress reduction.* Oakland, CA: New Harbinger.
Kabat-Zinn, J. (1994). *Wherever you go, there you are: Mindfulness meditation in everyday life.* New York, NY: Hyperion.
Kabat-Zinn, J. (2013). *Full catastrophe living: Using the wisdom of your body and mind to face stress, pain and illness* (Revised Ed.). New York, NY: Bantam Books.
Lehrhaupt, L., & Meibert, P. (2017). *Mindfulness-based stress reduction: The MBSR Program for enhancing health and vitality.* Novato, CA: New World Library.
Rosenbaum, E. (2017). *The heart of mindfulness-based stress reduction: A MBSR guide for clinicians and clients.* Eau Claire, WI: PESI Publishing & Media.
Santorelli, S.(1999). *Heal thy self: Lessons on mindfulness in medicine.* New York, NY: Bell Tower.

Stahl, B., & Goldstein, E. (2010). *Mindfulness-based stress reduction workbook*. Oakland, CA: New Harbinger.

Stahl, B., Meleo-Meyer, F., & Koerbel, L. (2014). *A mindfulness-based stress reduction workshop for anxiety*. Oakland, CA: New Harbinger.

References

Bakhshani, N. M., Amirani, A., Amirifard, H., & Shahrakipoor, M. (2016). The effectiveness of mindfulness-based stress reduction on perceived pain intensity and quality of life in patients with chronic headache. *Global Journal of Health Science*, 8(4): 142–151.

Carlson, L. E., Speca, M., Patel, K. D., & Goodey, E. (2003). Mindfulness-based stress reduction in relation to quality of life, mood, symptoms of stress, and immune parameters in breast and prostate cancer outpatients. *Psychosomatic Medicine*, 65: 571–581.

Cherkin, D. C., Anderson, M. L., Sherman, K. J., Balderson, B. H., Cook, A. J., Hansen, K. E., & Turner, J. A. (2017). Two-year follow-up of a RCT of MBSR vs CBT or usual care for chronic low back pain. *Journal of American Medical Association*, 317(6): 642–644.

Cramer, H., Lauche, R., Paul, A., & Dobos, G. (2012). Mindfulness-based stress reduction for breast cancer: A systematic review and meta-analysis. *Current Oncology*, 19(5): 343–352.

Creswell, J. D., Myers, H. F., Cole, S. W., & Irwin, M. R. (2009). Mindfulness meditation training effects on CD4+ T lymphocytes in HIV-1 infected adults: A small randomized controlled trial. *Brain, Behavior, and Immunity*, 23: 184–188.

Davidson, R. J., Kabat-Zinn, J., Schumacher, J., Rosenkranz, M., Muller, D., Santorelli, S., . . . Sheridan, J. (2003). Alterations in brain and immune function produced by mindfulness meditation. *Psychosomatic Medicine*, 65(4): 564–570.

Gotink, R., Meijboom, R., Vernooij, M., Smits, M., & Hunink, M. (2016). 8-week mindfulness-based stress reduction induces brain changes similar to traditional long-term meditation practice: A systematic review. *Brain and Cognition*, 108: 32–41.

Goyal, M., Singh, S., Sibinga, E., Gould, N., Rowland-Seymour, A., Berger, Z., . . . Haythornthwaite, J. (2014). Meditation programs for psychological stress and well-being: A systematic review and meta-analysis. *JAMA Internal Medicine*, 174(3): 357–368.

Gross, C., & Reibel, D. (2014). Mindfulness: A non-pharmacological approach to diabetes management. In Ie, A., Ngnoumen, C. T., & Langer, E. J. (eds.), *Handbook of Mindfulness*. Oxford, UK: Wiley-Blackwell.

Grossman, P., Niemann, L., Schmidt, S., & Walach, H. (2004). Mindfulness-based stress reduction and health benefits: A meta-analysis. *Journal of Psychosomatic Research*, 57: 35–43.

Grossman, P., Tiefenthaler-Gilmer, U., Raysz, A., & Kesper, U. (2007). Mindfulness training as an intervention for fibromyalgia: Evidence of post intervention and 3-year follow-up benefits in well-being. *Psychotherapy and Psychosomatics*, 76: 226–233.

Hilton, H., Hempel, S., Ewing, B. A., Apaydin, E., Xenakis, L., Newberry, S., . . . Maglione, M. (2017). Mindfulness meditation for chronic pain: Systematic review and meta-analysis. *Annals of Behavioral Medicine*, 51(2): 199–213.

Hölzel, B. K., Carmody, J., Evans, K. C., Hoge, E. A., Dusek, J. A., Morgan, L., . . . Lazar, S. W. (2010). Stress reduction correlates with structural changes in the amygdala. *Social Cognitive and Affective Neuroscience*, 5(1): 11–17.

Hölzel, B. K., Carmody, J., Vangel, M., Congelton, C., Yerramsetti, S., Gard, T., & Lazar, S. (2011). Mindfulness practice leads to increases in regional brain gray matter density. *Psychiatry Research: Neuroimaging*, 191(1): 36–43.

Jha, A. P., Krompinger, J., & Baime, M. J. (2007). Mindfulness training modifies subsystems of attention. *Cognitive Affective and Behavioral Neuroscience*, 7(2): 109–119.

Johns, S. A., Von Ah, D., Brown, L. F., Beck-Coon, K., Talib, T. L., Alyea, J. M., . . . Giesler, R. B. (2016). Randomized controlled pilot trial of mindfulness-based stress reduction for breast and colorectal cancer survivors: Effects on cancer-related cognitive impairment. *Journal of Cancer Survivorship*, 10: 437–448.

Kabat-Zinn, J. (2003). Mindfulness-based interventions in context: Past, present, and future. *Clinical Psychology: Science and Practice*, 10: 144–156.

Kabat-Zinn, J. (2013). *Full catastrophe living: Using the wisdom of your body and mind to face stress, pain and illness*. New York, NY: Bantam Books.

Kabat-Zinn, J., Lipworth, L., & Burney, R. (1985). The clinical use of mindfulness meditation for the self-regulation of chronic pain. *Journal of Behavioral Medicine*, 8: 163–190.

Kabat-Zinn, J., Massion, A. O., Kristeller, J., Peterson, L. G., Fletcher, K. E., Pbert, L., . . . Santorelli, S. F. (1992). Effectiveness of a meditation-based stress reduction intervention in the treatment of anxiety disorders. *American Journal of Psychiatry*, 149: 936–943.

Khoury, B., Sharma, M., Rush, S., & Fournier, C. (2015). Mindfulness-based stress reduction for healthy individuals: A meta analysis. *Journal of Psychosomatic Research*, 78(6): 519–528.

Lenze, E. J., Hickman, S., Hershey, T., Wendleton, L., Ly, K., Dixon, D., . . . Wetherell, J. L. (2014). Mindfulness-based stress reduction for older adults with worry symptoms and co-occurring cognitive dysfunction. *International Journal of Geriatric Psychiatry*, 29: 991–1000.

McCown, D., Reibel, D., & Micozzi, M. (2010). *Teaching mindfulness: A practical guide for clinicians and educators*. New York, NY: Springer.

McCown, D., Reibel, D., & Micozzi, M. (eds.) (2016). *Resources for teaching mindfulness: An international handbook*. New York, NY: Springer.

Miller, J., Fletcher, K., & Kabat-Zinn, J. (1995). Three-year follow-up and clinical implications of a mindfulness-based stress reduction intervention in the treatment of anxiety disorders. *General Hospital Psychiatry*, 17: 192–200.

Parswani, M. J., Sharma, M. P., & Iyengar, S. (2013). Mindfulness-based stress reduction program in coronary heart disease: A randomized control trial. *International Journal of Yoga*, 6: 111–117.

Raffone, A., & Srinivasan, N. (2017). Mindfulness and cognitive functions: Toward a unifying neurocognitive framework. *Mindfulness*, 8(1): 1–9.

Reibel, D. K., Greeson, J. K., Brainard, G. C., & Rosenzweig, S. (2001). Mindfulness-based stress reduction and health-related quality of life in a heterogeneous patient population. *General Hospital Psychiatry*, 23: 183–192.

Rosenzweig, S., Greeson, J., Reibel, D. K, Green, J., Jasser, S., & Beasley, D. (2010). Mindfulness-based stress reduction for chronic pain conditions: Variation in treatment outcomes and role of home meditation practice. *Journal of Psychosomatic Research*, 68: 29–36.

Rosenzweig, S., Reibel, D. K., Greeson, J. M., Edman, J. S., Jasser, S. A., McMearty, K. D., & Goldstein, B. J. (2007). Mindfulness-based stress reduction is associated with improved glycemic control in type 2 diabetes mellitus: A pilot study. *Alternative Therapies in Health and Medicine*, 13(5): 36–39.

Rouleau, C. R., Garland, S. N., & Carlson, L. E. (2015). The impact of mindfulness-based interventions on symptom burden, positive psychological outcomes, and biomarkers in cancer patients. *Cancer Management and Research*, 7: 121–131.

Santorelli, S. (1999). *Heal thy self, lessons on mindfulness in medicine*. New York, NY: Bell Tower.

Schmidt, S., Grossman, P., Schwarzer, B., Jena, S., Naumann, J., & Walach, H. (2011). Treating fibromyalgia with mindfulness-based stress reduction: Results from a 3-armed randomized controlled trial. *Pain*, 152: 361–369.

Shapiro, S., Carlson, L., Astin, J., & Freedman, B. (2006). Mechanisms of mindfulness. *Journal of Clinical Psychology*, 62: 373–386.

Shellekens, M. P., van den Hurk, D. G., Prins, J. B., . . . Speckens, A. E. (2017). MBSR added to care as usual for lung cancer patients and/or their partners: A multi-centre randomized controlled trial. *Psycho-oncology*, March 23. doi: 10.1002/pon.4430

Chapter 5

Mindfulness-Based Positive Behavior Support

Nirbhay N. Singh, Giulio E. Lancioni, Jeffrey Chan, Carrie L. McPherson, and Monica M. Jackman

Introduction

In our research and clinical work, we encounter caregivers – families, paid support staff, teachers, and clinicians – who provide treatment and care for people with a wide range of disabilities. Regardless of the love and compassion they may have for the people in their care, they are often stressed and burned out in their role as caregivers. For some, this is due to the nature of the caregiving itself that produces psychological stress and emotional exhaustion. For others, the stresses and strains of caregiving are compounded not only by the challenging behaviors (e.g., physical and verbal aggression, property destruction, defiance, bullying) of the people in their care but also the interventions prescribed to treat their behaviors.

In the field of intellectual and developmental disabilities, for example, caregivers provide services to people with serious and persistent behavioral challenges, particularly physical aggression and property destruction. Typical treatments involve psychopharmacological, behavioral, and cognitive-behavioral strategies. While these treatment modalities can be effective in reducing the frequency and intensity of challenging behaviors, they pose risks as well. For instance, psychopharmacological treatments produce unintended side effects that may cause functional, cognitive, or social impairments (Deb, 2016). Under ideal conditions, behavioral interventions are effective when the behavior support plans (i.e., intervention plans) are developed and implemented by trained professionals. However, when caregivers implement similar plans in real life contexts, the treatment often degenerates into reactive and restrictive interventions for controlling rather than treating people (Feldman, Atkinson, Foti-Gervais, & Condillac, 2004). Implementing the often lengthy and complex behavior support plans adds to the stress of caregivers (Neece, Green, & Baker, 2012).

In our experience, this situation exists across diverse groups of people, such as people with intellectual disabilities, autism spectrum disorders, Alzheimer's disease, and dementia, and across multiple contexts, such as in institutions, nursing homes, community group homes, schools, and regular family homes. Thus, over the past 20 years, we have developed and systematically evaluated a program that targets the two cardinal issues that have affected caregivers' wellbeing. First, we realized that the people needing care in all of these settings exhibit behaviors that challenge the skills and patience of their caregivers, and that the caregivers find it enormously difficult and stressful to consistently implement the required behavioral treatments with any degree of fidelity. Thus, there was a need to make the process of developing and implementing behavior support plans less stressful, and more efficient and effective. Second, we noticed that caregivers experience stress and emotional exhaustion due to the context of service provision itself. Thus, a second need was to teach skills to caregivers so that they could respond mindfully with more equanimity in their caregiving role.

These considerations gave rise to the development of Mindfulness-Based Positive Behavior Support (MBPBS), a program designed to streamline behavior support plans and to deliver these supports more mindfully, thereby enhancing personal the wellbeing of the caregivers and those in their care (Singh et al., 2014a). MBPBS training is ideal for anyone who provides services to people with challenging behaviors, regardless of their disorder or disability, gender, age, and race. It is also intended for caregivers of people with a diverse range of behavioral challenges, including those with intellectual and developmental disabilities, early stage Alzheimer's disease or dementia, multiple sclerosis, psychiatric disorders, and medical conditions that may give rise to aggressive, destructive, or disruptive behaviors secondary to these conditions.

Theoretical background

The MBPBS course has two major components: positive behavior support and mindfulness practice. Caregivers need to have a good grounding in positive behavior support because it gives them the basis for assisting people to change their behavior. They also need to have a disciplined mindfulness meditation practice that will enable them to provide the services mindfully without being psychologically stressed, emotionally exhausted, and burned out.

Positive behavior support

Positive Behavior Support (PBS) is, "an applied science that uses educational and systems change methods to enhance quality of life and minimize problem behavior" (Carr et al., 2002, p. 4). Behavior therapists use the technology of applied behavior analysis to develop PBS plans that primarily increase positive functional behaviors and secondarily decrease socially undesirable behaviors. Ideally, the PBS plans blend behavior change principles with the values and rights of people being served. Their focus is on enriching people's lifestyle and wellbeing rather than on eliminating challenging behaviors. Although there are no standardized templates for designing PBS plans (Morris & Horner, 2016), there are general process guidelines for customizing PBS plans for specific individuals (e.g., Bambara & Knoster, 2009).

In our experience, caregivers often state that behavior therapists take too long (i.e., on average about two months) to undertake functional behavior assessment and develop PBS plans, and that the plans have too many interventions and are too long (i.e., often upwards of 15 to 20 pages). They also state that the interventions are too complex and are written in behavioral jargon. In addition, caregivers complain that implementing these plans for serious and persistent problem behaviors is very stressful due to the effort involved in reading, interpreting and implementing the plans, which often detracts from their ability to spend quality time with clients. It is well documented that caregivers experience stress and burnout due to their work with people with challenging behaviors (Smyth, Healy, & Lydon, 2015). In addition to teaching caregivers specific skills that reduce the emotional burden of care, an adjunctive approach to enhancing their wellbeing is to reduce the work demands in a meaningful way without compromising the care provided to people with challenging behaviors. The stepped care model of services provides one evidence-based approach for achieving this (O'Donohue & Draper, 2011).

Stepped care provides a practical process for matching the complexity of the PBS plan to the treatment needs of the individual (Bower & Gilbody, 2005). Caregivers can use a three-step process: (1) *Primary Care*: Recognize an emergent behavioral issue, assess and observe its progress, and keep an eye on the behavior to see if an intervention is necessary. Often problem behaviors arise and fade away with minor adjustments in the individual's environment. (2) *Low Intensity Care*: If the behavior persists or threatens to escalate in severity, use a low intensity PBS plan. (3) *High Intensity Care*: If the low intensity intervention does not meet the desired outcomes, then step up the PBS plan to a high intensity intervention. This model enables caregivers to observe and respond in the context of quality of life changes for the individual by beginning with observation of the problem behavior and tweaking of the individual's environment, using low intensity PBS interventions, stepping up to high intensity interventions if needed, stepping down to less intensive intervention as appropriate, and stepping out when the intervention is effective.

We incorporated stepped care for delivering PBS interventions in the MBPBS model. The caregivers are taught the three-step process for behavioral intervention, with most of the emphasis being placed on the first two steps, the primary care and the low intensity care. In terms of staff training and performance, we use what is akin to a spiral curriculum (Bruner, 1960) which requires caregivers to learn and apply the same PBS principles but at greater depth and complexity as they step up the level of care. The curriculum includes the following components: (1) guiding principles of PBS, (2) goals for the PBS team, (3) information gathering, functional behavior assessment, and developing function-based hypotheses for target behaviors, and (4) designing PBS plans. There are five components of PBS plans: (1) modify antecedents and setting events; (2) function-based modifications; (3) teach alternative skills – replacement, general, and coping skills; (4) change the consequences; and (5) provide long-term supports to increase quality of life.

The client's support team is required to assess and develop the PBS plan and to periodically review and revise the plan based on outcome data (McKevitt & Braaksma, 2004). In our model, we place much greater emphasis on direct caregivers than on the professional staff on the individual's support team. Once the direct caregivers (and other team members) are trained in our PBS curriculum, for each new referral for a low intensity PBS plan, the caregivers meet with the rest of the individual's support team and develop the plan. At this meeting, each direct caregiver completes two assessments, (1) the Questions About Behavior Function (QABF) rating scale with language modified from the Singh et al. (2006a) version, although any preferred alternative scale can be used, and (2) the Behavioral Assessment Interview Questions (see Table 5.1) adapted from Miltenberger, Bloom, Sanchez, and Valbuena (2016). Following a discussion of the assessment findings, the direct caregivers develop a one- or two-page PBS plan. They develop the plan by responding to a series of prompts across the five areas that are mandated for PBS plans (see Table 5.2).

Tables 5.1 Behavioral assessment interview questions

1 Which challenging behavior affects his/her quality of life the most?
2 For this behavior, define how it is performed, how often it occurs, and how long it lasts.
3 When, where, and with whom is the behavior most likely? Least likely?
4 What activity is most likely to produce the behavior? Least likely?
5 Does the behavior typically occur when the individual is alone or around others?

6 What does the person get as a consequence of the behaviors?
7 What does the person avoid or escape from as a consequence of the behavior?
8 What expressive communication strategies does the person use?
9 What events, activities, objects, or people (staff, peers, family members) does the person appear to enjoy?
10 What appropriate behaviors or skills does the person perform or can be strengthened that could occur in place of the behavior?

Source: Adapted from Miltenberger et al. (2016).

Table 5.2 Prompts for designing PBS plans

1 Antecedent and setting-event modifications
  a How can the triggering antecedent or setting events be changed so that problem situations can be prevented?
  b What can be added to this person's daily routines to make desired behaviors more likely and situations more pleasant for this person?
2 Teaching alternative skills
  a When a problem situation arises, what alternative skill could this person use that would serve the same function as the challenging behavior (replacement skill)?
  b What general skills (e.g., social, communication, leisure) might help this person prevent challenging situations?
  c What skills are needed to help this person cope with potentially difficult or frustrating situations that cannot be changed (coping or tolerating skills)?
3 Consequence interventions
  a How will you reinforce this person's use of alternative skills so that he/she might become more effective and efficient than the challenging behavior?
  b How will you teach this person that the challenging behavior is no longer effective, efficient, or desirable?
  c What can be done to de-escalate crisis situations and protect this person and others (staff, peers) from harm?
4 Long-term supports
  a What lifestyle factors could be improved for a more gratifying quality of life for this person?
  b What supports are needed to maintain and generalize positive outcomes for this person across settings?
5 Quality of life outcomes
  a What lifestyle outcomes will be behaviorally evident?
  b How will we know that this person's quality of life is better?

The PBS plan is realistic and applicable immediately because the staff that will implement the plan essentially develops it. Once developed, reviewed, and approved by the individual's support team, the PBS plan is implemented from the next day. The entire process may take up to four hours at a single meeting, and the individual's remaining support staff are trained in the plan by the support staff that developed the plan. No peer review or other approvals are needed because the entire plan is learning based and without any aversive or punishment contingencies. The individual's support team meets periodically to review progress and outcomes, make adjustments based on the data, step it up to the next level if needed, and eventually step out of the program once the desired outcomes are achieved. Families and schools use the same process, with minimal contextual adjustments to the process.

Mindfulness

Mindfulness is the translation of *sati*, the Pali term used to describe, "lucid awareness of present happenings" in the context of impermanence and interdependence of all experiences (Bodhi, 2011, p. 25). Kabat-Zinn (2003) defined mindfulness as "the awareness that emerges through paying attention on purpose, in the present moment, and nonjudgmentally to the unfolding of experience" (p. 145). Mindfulness is present in all humans, but it invariably requires strengthening and this can be achieved in a number of ways, most notably through mindfulness meditation. In MBPBS, mindfulness meditation is paired with other meditation practices to provide caregivers a broad set of skills that they can use to alleviate their stress and suffering and enhance their wellbeing, thereby also contributing to the alleviation of suffering of those in their care. The theoretical bases of mindfulness in the MBPBS program have been explicated in several papers and need not be repeated here (see Hwang & Singh, 2016; Singh et al., 2014b, 2016c). The key issue is that mindfulness may reduce stress by modulating attention and emotion regulation, with downstream effects on caregiver reactivity when confronted with the challenging behaviors of clients. In effect, MBPBS is the seamless braiding of two evidence-based approaches, with mindfulness focused on the wellbeing of the caregiver and PBS on the wellbeing of the client.

Research support for MBPBS

Research support from MBPBS comes from a number of studies with paid caregivers, parents and teachers. Singh et al. (2004) reported that teaching mindfulness-based practices to caregivers increased wellness in people with intellectual and developmental disabilities in the absence of explicit programming for their wellness. Singh et al. (2006a) found that the addition of mindfulness-based practices to behavioral training considerably enhanced the ability of the group home caregivers to effectively treat aggressive behavior and to enhance the learning of individuals with intellectual disabilities. Singh et al. (2009) reported that mindfulness-based training enabled caregivers to substantially reduce the use of physical restraints and emergency medications for aggressive and destructive behavior of people with intellectual disabilities. Singh et al. (2015) replicated these findings with caregivers who were trained in MBPBS and, in addition, reported reduced staff stress and turnover, and elimination of staff and peer injuries. Singh et al. (2016a, 2016b) showed that MBPBS was effective in enabling caregivers to manage their perceived psychological stress, and in reducing the use of physical restraints and emergency medications for aggressive behavior of the individuals in their care.

These findings were replicated and extended in a series of studies with parents and teachers of children with intellectual and developmental disabilities. For example, Singh et al. (2006b) reported that following a mindfulness-based course for parents, there was a sustained decrease in their children's aggression, non-compliance, and self-injury and an increase in the mothers' satisfaction with their parenting and interactions with their children. Similar results were obtained in a follow-up study with the additional finding that parental stress was greatly reduced following the mindfulness-based training (Singh et al., 2007). In an extension of these studies, Singh et al. (2010) reported that compliance to parental requests increased in children with Attention Deficit/Hyperactivity Disorder when their parents were provided training in mindfulness-based practices. In a further extension, MBPBS training for mothers of adolescents with Autism Spectrum Disorder showed that the adolescents' challenging behaviors decreased and compliance behaviors increased in addition to statistically significant reductions in the mothers' stress levels (Singh et al., 2014a). Finally, training teachers of preschool children in mindfulness-based practices resulted in significant decreases in the children's challenging behaviors and increases in their compliance with teacher requests (Singh et al., 2013). In addition, the children decreased their negative social interactions and increased independent play.

Structure of the MBPBS program

The MBPBS program comes in three formats, depending on the level of intensity of the program. According to the three-step process described above, the seven-day program is the High Intensity Care, the eight-week program is the Low Intensity Care and the one-day program is the Primary Care version of MBPBS.

The seven-day intensive MBPBS program

In the seven-day MBPBS program, the first day of the training is a month prior to and the last day is a month following the five-day intensive training. Each eight-hour day includes instructions and meditation practice. The caregivers are taught three basic meditations in a group format during the first day of training. First, they receive instructions and practice on the fundamentals of meditation posture for Samatha meditation as in Singh et al. (2015, p. 929): "sit comfortably with a straight spine, without slouching or stretching the shoulders; head tilted slightly forward; eyes slightly open; tip of the tongue lightly touching the upper palate; right hand resting over the left hand on the lap, with thumbs just touching; and breathing evenly (Buksbazen, 2002)." They are taught to focus on their breathing as the object of their meditation, without deliberately changing the length of each breath. They learn to count an inhalation and exhalation as one breath until they reach ten breaths, before restarting the counting cycle. They are taught to simply observe their discursive thoughts and emotions, without interacting with them or trying to suppress them. That is, they are required to focus their awareness on whatever takes place in their mind without judgment or engagement.

Second, they are taught Kinhin meditation (Buksbazen, 2002). Kinhin is a walking meditation that enables a person to be in the present moment while walking slowly and mindfully. We use Kinhin meditation between sessions of Samatha meditation because it helps the participants to stretch their legs, which may have gone to sleep or caused some pain during sitting meditation. Third, they are taught Vipassanā (Insight) meditation (McDonald, 2005) to gain insight into the true nature of reality through mindfulness of breathing, thoughts, feelings, and actions (Shonin, Van Gordon, & Singh, 2015). This is followed by instruction on the five hindrances (sensual desire, ill will or anger, sloth and torpor, restlessness and worry, and doubt) (Anālayo, 2013). Following the end of the first day of training, the caregivers are instructed to develop a personal meditation practice, beginning with a few minutes each day and incrementally increasing it until they reached between 20 and 30 minutes of daily practice. They master the first meditation before moving on to the second, and then the third. In addition, they are taught to log their daily meditation practice.

The caregivers practice the three foundational meditations for four weeks. During the fifth week, they receive the five-day intensive MBPBS training. The training format for the five-day training is the same as for the first day of training. The training includes meditation practice, instructions and practice in the four immeasurables (lovingkindness, compassion, joy, and equanimity) and the three poisons (attachment, anger, and ignorance) (Kyabgon, 2004), beginner's mind, being in the present moment, Shenpa and Compassionate Abiding (Chödrön, 2010; Kongtrül, 2008), and Meditation on the Soles of the Feet (Singh et al., 2011).

In addition, caregivers are given explicit instructions on the guiding principles of PBS, functional behavior assessment, and designing and implementing PBS plans within the context of mindfulness practices. Essentially, caregivers practice their mindfulness skills with the clients and use specific mindfulness practices such as observing the client with a beginner's mind when the client engages in challenging behaviors and reacting to such behavior with equnimity. By the end of the five-day training, the caregivers are expected to be familiar with the five components of standard PBS plans, as specified above. In addition, they are given instructions on mindful observation of the individual's behavior, mindful communication (with a focus on mindful prompting and feedback), mindful pause between requests and prompts, and use of reinforcement contingencies that focus on the rate, quality, magnitude, delay, and specificity of the reinforcement delivered by the support staff (Singh et al., 2016a).

Following the five-day training, the caregivers are asked to skillfully apply their newly acquired mindfulness practices and PBS principles for four weeks with the individuals in their care. In addition, they continue to develop their personal daily meditation practice. Following the four weeks of practice, the caregivers meet with the trainer for the final one-day training to review their meditation practices and use of MBPBS procedures, discuss three ethical precepts (see Table 5.3), and provide feedback on the training program. Any questions that may have arisen during their four weeks of practice are fully answered by the trainer. Table 5.3 presents the MBPBS program and a brief outline of each day's training.

Table 5.3 Outline of the 7-day MBPBS program

PART I	
Day 1 (1st one-day training)	Samatha meditation Kinhin meditation Vipassanā meditation Five hindrances – sensory desire, ill will, sloth and torpor, restlessness and remorse, and doubt Daily logs and journaling
PART II	
Day 2 (1st day of five-day intensive training)	Review of meditation practice Introduction to the Four Immeasurables (*Brahmavihara*: *metta* – lovingkindness; *karuna* – compassion; *mudita* – empathetic joy; *upekkha* – equanimity) Equanimity meditation Beginner's mind Guiding principles of PBS
Day 3	Review of Day 2 instructions and practices Further instructions on the Four Immeasurables Equanimity meditation Lovingkindness meditation Being in the present moment Goals for the PBS support team

Day 4	Review of Days 2 and 3 instructions and practices
Further instructions on the Four Immeasurables
Equanimity meditation
Lovingkindness meditation
Compassion meditation
The three poisons – attachment, anger, and ignorance
Information gathering for PBS plans, functional behavior assessment, and developing function-based hypotheses for target behaviors
Day 5	Review of Days 2 to 4 instructions and practices
Further instructions on the Four Immeasurables
Equanimity meditation
Lovingkindness meditation
Compassion meditation
Joy meditation
Attachment and anger – shenpa and compassionate abiding meditations
Designing and implementing PBS plans
Day 6	Review of Days 2 to 5 instructions and practices
Review and practice Samatha, Kinhin and Vipassanā meditations
Review of the Four Immeasurables
Practice equanimity, lovingkindness, compassion and joy meditations
Attachment and anger – meditation on the soles of the feet
Braiding of mindfulness and PBS practices
Review of the MBPBS training program
PART III	
Day 7
(2nd one-day training)	Review of the meditation instructions and practices (daily logs)
Review and practice Samatha, Kinhin, and Vipassanā meditations
Review of the Four Immeasurables
Practice equanimity, lovingkindness, compassion, and joy meditations
Emotion regulation and anger – meditation on the soles of the feet
Instructions for practicing three ethical precepts – refrain from (1) harming living beings, (2) taking that which is not given, and (3) incorrect speech
Mindfulness and PBS practice
Review of the seven-day MBPBS training program

The eight-week MBPBS program

The eight-week course has a similar content to the seven-day intensive although with less actual meditation practice during the training because of the restricted time available. This course begins with a two-hour pre-training session followed by two-hour training sessions one day a week for eight consecutive weeks. Originally, the eight-week course was offered one day a week for eight weeks (Singh et al., 2016b), but this was reduced to two hours a day for eight weeks because it is now the low-intensity program.

The three-day MBPBS program

In the three-day MBPBS program, the first day focuses on mindfulness meditation training and includes the following components: what is mindfulness, open presence, Samatha meditation, Kinhin meditation, body scan, beginner's mind, impermanence, thoughts, self-compassion, and informal mindfulness practices. The second and third days are devoted to instructions and practice in developing positive behavior support plans and includes the following components: guiding principles, goals for the plan, functional assessment, development of hypotheses, designing a PBS plan, plan implementation and revisions, and phasing out of the PBS plan.

In sum, the MBPBS program is an emerging research-informed mindfulness-based program for caregivers of people with a diverse range of behavioral challenges. MBPBS was developed to address the need for a holistic intervention that targets the caregiver-client dyad, and the interconnectedness and transactional nature of their behavior. Not only does MBPBS teach caregivers therapeutic skills, but it also provides a means of personal transformation that may decrease their perceived stress, enhance their ability to serve people with challenging behaviors with lovingkindness, and to respond to changes in their own life and the lives of the people in their care (and all sentient beings, in general) with equipoise and equanimity.

References

Anālayo. (2013). *Perspectives on Satipaṭṭhāna*. Cambridge, UK: Windhorse Publications.
Bambara, L. M., & Knoster, T. P. (2009). *Designing positive behavior support plans* (2nd ed.). Washington, DC: American Association on Intellectual and Developmental Disabilities.
Bodhi, B. (2011). What does mindfulness really mean? A canonical perspective. *Contemporary Buddhism, 12*(1), 19–39.
Bower, P., & Gilbody, S. (2005). Stepped care in psychological therapies: Access, effectiveness and efficiency. *British Journal of Psychiatry, 186*, 11–17.
Bruner, J. S. (1960). *The process of education*. Cambridge, MA: Harvard University Press.
Buksbazen, J. D. (2002). *Zen meditation in plain English*. Boston, MA: Wisdom Publications.
Carr, E. G., Dunlap, G., Horner, R. H., Koegel, R. L., Turnbull, A. P., Sailor, W., . . . Fox, L. (2002). Positive behavior support: Evolution of an applied science. *Journal of Positive Behavior Interventions, 4*(1), 4–16.
Chödrön, P. (2010). *Taking the leap: Freeing ourselves from old habits and fears*. Boston, MA: Shambhala.
Deb, S. (2016). Psychopharmacology. In N. N. Singh (Ed.), *Handbook of evidence-based practices in intellectual and developmental disabilities* (pp. 347–381). New York, NY: Springer.
Feldman, M. A., Atkinson, L., Foti-Gervais, L., & Condillac, R. (2004). Formal versus informal interventions for challenging behavior in persons with intellectual disabilities. *Journal of Intellectual Disabilities Research, 48*, 60–68.
Hwang, Y-S., & Singh, N. N. (2016). Mindfulness. In N. N. Singh (Ed.), *Handbook of evidence-based practices for individuals with intellectual and developmental disabilities* (pp. 311–346). New York, NY: Springer.
Kabat-Zinn, J. (2003). Mindfulness-based interventions in context: Past, present, and future. *Clinical Psychology: Science and Practice, 10*, 144–156.
Kongtrül, D. (2008). *Light comes through: Buddhist teaching on awakening to our natural intelligence*. Boston, MA: Shambhala.

Kyabgon, T. (2004). *Mind at ease: Self-liberation through Mahamudra meditation*. Boston, MA: Shambhala.

McDonald, K. (2005). *How to meditate: A practical guide*. Boston, MA: Wisdom Publications.

McKevitt, B., & Braaksma, A. (2004). Best practices in developing a Positive Behavior Support system at the school level. In A. Thomas & J. Grimes (Eds.), *Best practices in school psychology V* (pp. 735–748). Bethesda, MD: National Association of School Psychologists.

Miltenberger, R. G., Bloom, S. E., Sanchez, S., & Valbuena, D. A. (2016). Functional assessment. In N. N. Singh (Ed.), *Handbook of evidence-based practices in intellectual and developmental disabilities* (pp. 69–97). New York, NY: Springer.

Morris, K. R., & Horner, R. H. (2016). Positive behavior support. In N. N. Singh (Ed.), *Handbook of evidence-based practices in intellectual and developmental disabilities* (pp. 415–441). New York, NY: Springer.

Neece, C. L., Green, S. A., & Baker, B. L. (2012). Parenting stress and child behavior problems: A transactional relationship across time. *American Journal on Intellectual and Developmental Disabilities, 117*, 48–66.

O'Donohue, W. T., & Draper, C. (2011). *Stepped care and e-health*. New York, NY: Springer.

Shonin, E., Van Gordon, W., & Singh, N. N. (2015). *Buddhist foundations of mindfulness*. New York, NY: Springer.

Singh, N. N., Lancioni, G. E., Karazsia, B. T., Chan, J., & Winton, A. S. W. (2016a). Effectiveness of caregiver training in Mindfulness-Based Positive Behavior Support (MBPBS) vs. training-as-usual (TAU): A randomized controlled trial. *Frontiers in Psychology, 7*, 1549.

Singh, N. N., Lancioni, G. E., Karazsia, B. T., & Myers, R. E. (2016b). Caregiver training in Mindfulness-Based Positive Behavior Supports (MBPBS): Effects on caregivers and adults with intellectual and developmental disabilities. *Frontiers in Psychology, 7*, 98.

Singh, N. N., Lancioni, G. E., Manikam, R., Latham, L. L., & Jackman, M. M. (2016c). Mindfulness-based positive behavior support in intellectual and developmental disabilities. In I. Ivtzan & T. Lomas (Eds.), *Mindfulness in positive psychology: The science of meditation and wellbeing* (pp. 212–226). East Sussex, UK: Taylor and Francis.

Singh, N. N., Lancioni, G. E., Karazsia, B. T., Myers, R. E., Winton, A. S. W., Latham, L. L., & Nugent, K. (2015). Effects of training staff in MBPBS on the use of physical restraints, staff stress and turnover, staff and peer injuries, and cost effectiveness in developmental disabilities. *Mindfulness, 6*, 926–937.

Singh, N. N., Lancioni, G. E., Winton, A. S. W., Curtis, W. J., Wahler, R. G., Sabaawi, M., Singh, J., & McAleavey, K. (2006a). Mindful staff increase learning and reduce aggression by adults with developmental disabilities. *Research in Developmental Disabilities, 27*, 545–558.

Singh, N. N., Lancioni, G. E., Winton, A. S. W., Fisher, B. C., Wahler, R. G., McAleavey, K., Singh, J., & Sabaawi, M. (2006b). Mindful parenting decreases aggression, noncompliance and self-injury in children with autism. *Journal of Emotional and Behavioral Disorders, 14*, 169–177.

Singh, N. N., Matson, J. L., Lancioni, G. E., Singh, A. N., Adkins, A. D., McKeegan, G. F., & Brown, S. W. (2006c). Questions About Behavioral Function in Mental Illness (QABF-MI): A behavior checklist for functional assessment of maladaptive behavior exhibited by individuals with mental illness. *Behavior Modification, 30*(6), 739–751.

Singh, N. N., Lancioni, G. E., Winton, A. S. W., Karazsia, B. T., Myers, R. E., Latham, L. L., & Singh, J. (2014a). Mindfulness-Based Positive Behavior Support (MBPBS) for mothers of adolescents with Autism Spectrum Disorder: Effects on adolescents' behavior and parental stress. *Mindfulness, 5*, 646–657.

Singh, N. N., Lancioni, G. E., Winton, A. S. W., Singh, J., Singh, A. N. A., & Singh, D. A. (2014b). Mindful caregiving and support. In J. K. Luiselli (Ed.), *Children and youth with Autism-Spectrum Disorders (ASD): Recent advances and innovations in assessment, education and intervention* (pp. 208–221). New York, NY: Oxford University Press.

Singh, N. N., Lancioni, G. E., Winton, A. S. W., Karazsia, B. T., & Singh, J. (2013). Mindfulness training for teachers changes the behavior of their preschool students. *Research in Human Development, 10*(3), 211–233.

Singh, N. N., Lancioni, G. E., Winton, A. S. W., Singh, A. N., Adkins, A. D., & Singh, J. (2009). Mindful staff can reduce the use of physical restraints when providing care to individuals with intellectual disabilities. *Journal of Applied Research in Intellectual Disabilities, 22*, 194–202.

Singh, N. N., Lancioni, G. E., Winton, A. S. W., Singh, J., Curtis, W. J., Wahler, R. G., & McAleavey, K. M. (2007). Mindful parenting decreases aggression and increases social behavior in children with developmental disabilities. *Behavior Modification, 31*, 749–771.

Singh, N. N., Lancioni, G. E., Winton, A. S. W., Wahler, R. G., Singh, J., & Sage, M. (2004). Mindful caregiving increases happiness among individuals with profound multiple disabilities. *Research in Developmental Disabilities, 25*, 207–218.

Singh, N. N., Singh, A. N., Lancioni, G. E., Singh, J., Winton, A. S. W., & Adkins, A. D. (2010). Mindfulness training for parents and their children with ADHD increases the children's compliance. *Journal of Child and Family Studies, 19*, 157–166.

Singh, N. N., Singh, J., Singh, A. D. A., Singh, A. N. A., & Winton, A. S. W. (2011). *Meditation on the soles of the feet for anger management: A trainer's manual.* Raleigh, NC: Fernleaf. www.fernleafpub.com.

Smyth, E., Healy, O., & Lydon, S. (2015). An analysis of stress, burnout, and work commitment among disability support staff in the UK. *Research in Developmental Disabilities, 47*, 297–305.

Chapter 6

Mindfulness-Based Mind Fitness Training (MMFT)

Mindfulness training for high-stress and trauma-sensitive contexts

Kelsey L. Larsen and Elizabeth A. Stanley

Introduction

As evidenced in this handbook, there is considerable empirical evidence of the benefits of mindfulness-based interventions (MBIs) in both clinical and healthy populations (for reviews, see Chiesa & Serretti, 2009; Creswell, 2017). However, high-stress environments – where individuals are subjected to prolonged stress and trauma, often by virtue of serving in high-demand occupations like the military, law enforcement, firefighting, medicine, and first response – come with distinct challenges that many traditional MBIs are not designed to address. These populations typically bear heavy allostatic loads from prolonged stress and trauma exposure, frequent legacies of childhood adversity, stressful professional training regimens, and culturally ingrained coping strategies, all of which demand a more robust approach.

Mindfulness-Based Mind Fitness Training (MMFT)® was explicitly designed to offer such an approach. Originally conceived for implementation with the U.S. military, MMFT draws from two lineages – mindfulness training and body-based trauma therapies – to address the complex constellation of stressors that accompany these high-stress, high-demand roles. As this chapter will show, MMFT tackles the powerful effects of prolonged stress and trauma exposure – with the goal of training participants to achieve better functioning during stressful experiences and more complete recovery afterwards.

Intended population and targets of MMFT

Unlike many other MBIs, MMFT is explicitly intended for individuals working in high-stress occupations, who frequently have high allostatic loads – i.e., large cumulative effects of stress on the mind-body system – due to the many environmental stressors of their work. Evidence of high allostatic loads can be seen in elevated rates of mood and anxiety disorders, sleep disorders, substance use/misuse, and suicidal ideation and behavior across these professions (see Berger et al., 2012; Bray et al., 2009; Carey, Al-Zaiti, Dean, Sessanna, & Finnell, 2011; Denhof & Spinaris, 2013; Institute of Medicine, 2014; Nock et al., 2014; Stanley, Hom, & Joiner, 2016).

Several common stressors across these professions may contribute to this higher allostatic load. For instance, sleep deprivation and/or variable sleep patterns due to shift work are common, with evidence of cognitive, emotional, and motor impairments among such cohorts (Barger, Lockley, Rajaratnam, & Landrigan, 2009; Rajaratnam et al., 2011), and demonstrated negative effects on decision-making and risk assessment capacity (Vila, Morrison, &

Kenney, 2002). Additionally, these individuals must cope with threats to individual safety and mortality, exposure to the injury/death of others, and sometimes the need to inflict harm (Adler, McGurk, Stetz, & Bliese, 2003; Kavanagh, 2005). Managing such mortality concerns not only consumes self-regulation capacity, but also, in doing so, further increases vulnerability to disturbing thoughts and feelings about death (Gailliot, Schmeichel, & Baumeister, 2006). Additionally, individuals in high-stress environments often employ emotional labor to align with organizational objectives – masking already-developed emotions or manufacturing new emotions to align with role expectations and improve overall performance – which may increase psychological strain, deplete mental resources, and detract energy from additional cognitive tasks (see Hülsheger & Schewe, 2011 for a review).

Furthermore, these professions engage in stressful occupational training – stress inoculation training (SIT) – to habituate members to the stressors they are likely to encounter during "real-world" missions and thereby improve their performance (Kavanagh, 2005; Larsen & Stanley, in press). Yet, while SIT may help members adaptively function during stress, its intensity and lack of focus on recovery (Larsen & Stanley, in press) may exacerbate temporal impairment and depletion of executive functioning – thereby contributing to difficulties with physiological and emotion regulation (Heatherton & Wagner, 2011; Hofmann, Schmeichel, & Baddeley, 2012). Indeed, evidence from internal medicine residency training (Gohar et al., 2009), firefighter live-fire drills (Baumann, Gohm, & Bonner, 2011), military field training (Kavanagh, 2005; Lieberman et al., 2005), military survival training (Morgan, Doran, Steffian, Hazlett, & Southwick, 2006; Morgan et al., 2004; Morgan et al., 2002), and military pre-deployment training (Jha, Witkin, Morrison, Rostrup, & Stanley, 2017; Jha et al., 2015; Jha, Morrison, Parker, & Stanley, 2016; Jha, Stanley, Kiyonaga, Wong, & Gelfand, 2010) significantly links inoculation training regimens to mood disturbances and cognitive degradation, including problem-solving deficits, attention deficits, and declines in working memory capacity.

Meanwhile, these populations are often characterized by culturally-sanctioned and deeply-socialized suppressive coping mechanisms. In particular, because suppression of emotions and physical pain can be adaptive in the short-term and increase the team's likelihood of survival (Bonanno, 2004), managing distress through "suck it up and drive on" techniques is a cultural expectation reinforced in high-demand roles (see Berg, Hem, Lau, & Ekeberg, 2006; Braswell & Kushner, 2012; Bryan, Jennings, Jobes, & Bradley, 2012). Yet, when employed habitually and continually, such suppression may have maladaptive effects, including higher rates of depression, self-destructive behaviors, and suicide (Braswell & Kushner, 2012). Cultural norms may deny the trauma of challenging experiences, stigmatize psychological injury as "weakness," and prevent individuals from seeking help (Berg et al., 2006; Bryan et al., 2012; Stanley et al., 2016). This undermined ability to access social support may also extend to personal relationships, resulting in disrupted communication and increased isolation (Butler et al., 2003; Gross & John, 2003), and contributing to decreased marital satisfaction, increased intention to divorce, and increased self-reported spousal abuse (Hoge, Castro, & Eaton, 2006; Teten et al., 2010). This distress may also lead to maladaptive coping strategies, like heavy alcohol consumption and illicit drug use (Bray et al., 2009; Institute of Medicine, 2014; Violanti, Marshall, & Howe, 1985); increased tobacco use (Biggs et al., 2010); and inappropriate aggressive behavior, violent outbursts, or the abuse/harassment of others (Braswell & Kushner, 2012; Hoge et al., 2006; Nillni et al., 2014; Teten et al., 2010).

Finally, it bears noting that a large subset of individuals in these populations were exposed to adverse childhood experiences (ACEs) – such as sexual, physical, and emotional abuse;

physical and emotional neglect; and/or childhood family dysfunction – which have been shown to increase the risk for many mental and physical health problems in adulthood (Bruffaerts et al., 2010; Felitti, 2009; Kessler et al., 2010; Mann & Currier, 2010; Neigh, Gillespie, & Nemeroff, 2009). ACE exposure is significantly linked with early-life developmental alterations in neurobiological systems, leading to life-long dysregulation and sensitization of the hypothalamic-pituitary-adrenal (HPA) axis and autonomic nervous system (Neigh et al., 2009). In the U.S. military, there is evidence that service members during the All-Volunteer Force era are disproportionately likely to come from such backgrounds (Blosnich, Dichter, Cerulli, Batten, & Bossarte, 2014), and many other high-stress professions draw from veteran pools. Empirical research in these professions shows links between ACE exposure and significantly larger physiological and emotional responses after stressful occupational experiences – as well as significantly higher risk of PTSD and other mood disorders – compared with colleagues without ACE exposure, including among paramedics (Maunder, Halpern, Schwartz, & Gurevich, 2012), police (Pole et al., 2007), and the military (Cabrera, Hoge, Bliese, Castro, & Messer, 2007; Fritch, Mishkind, Reger, & Gahm, 2010; Sareen et al., 2013).

Though some exceptions exist (e.g., Dialectical Behavioral Therapy, DBT; Linehan, 1993), most MBIs were not designed to accommodate and/or re-regulate such deep-seated mind-body dysregulation. However, without complementary skills to re-regulate the nervous system, mindfulness alone may actually flood the mind-body system with heightened attention on the stress response – which, paradoxically, may worsen the ability to self-regulate and thereby exacerbate symptoms of dysregulation (Stanley, in press). Indeed, some MBIs note their contraindication for individuals actively suffering from post-traumatic stress or trauma. For instance, the University of Massachusetts' Center for Mindfulness states that mindfulness-based stress reduction (MBSR) is not advised during active PTSD or other mental illness, suggesting that individuals seek other training or treatment if they have "a history of substance or alcohol abuse with less than a year of being clean or sober, thoughts or attempts of suicide, recent or unresolved trauma," or if they are "in the middle of major life changes" (Center for Mindfulness in Medicine, 2014; Santorelli, 2014). Importantly, *all* of these criteria are quite common in high-stress environments.

Overview of MMFT

Given the complex stressors typically encountered by MMFT's intended populations, MMFT was designed with two overarching goals in mind: to widen individuals' windows of tolerance for stress arousal, and to do so in a trauma/dysregulation-sensitive manner. Thus, MMFT seeks to improve functioning before and during stressful experiences – as well as provide for more effective recovery afterwards – with special attention given to the fact that varying levels of pre-existing chronic stress and trauma exposure may exist among training cohorts.

MMFT has three parts: (1) mindfulness skills training; (2) an understanding of the neurobiology of stress and resilience, and body-based self-regulation skills training to regulate the autonomic nervous system; and (3) concrete applications of both types of skills to participants' personal and professional lives. This blend of mindfulness skills training with body-based self-regulation skills is crucial for increased psychological and physiological resilience and enhanced performance in high-stress situations. It also facilitates individuals widening their windows of tolerance for stress arousal, so that they can interact more effectively with their complex external environments. Thus, a major goal of MMFT is to improve individuals' self-regulation and resilience, at both the micro- and macro-levels.

At the micro-level, this means improving individual self-regulation in the mind-body system – with better functioning during stress and more complete recovery back to "baseline" afterwards. As individuals learn to direct their attention in ways that support discharging the effects of prior stress arousal, they may facilitate their mind-body system returning to a functioning allostasis and thereby decrease both their allostatic load and cognitive, emotional, and/or physiological symptoms of dysregulation. As allostatic functioning improves, individuals may actively redirect focus from inner symptoms towards the outward environment. Thus, awareness, physiological and emotional self-regulation, and impulse control – hallmarks of self-regulation at the micro-level – each pave the way for more successful, connected, and supportive interpersonal interactions and more agile and adaptive decisions in complex environments – hallmarks of self-regulation at the macro-level (Stanley, in press).

Conversely, it is not surprising that ineffective micro-level self-regulation has shown cascading negative effects in the external environment. For instance, police officers suffering from a sleep disorder – a common symptom of micro-level mind-body dysregulation – were significantly more likely to display uncontrolled anger towards citizens and suspects, and significantly more likely to have citizen complaints filed against them (Rajaratnam et al., 2011; see also Shermer, 2015). Likewise, U.S. troops who screened positive for mental health problems after deployments in Iraq and Afghanistan were almost three times more likely to report having engaged in unethical behavior while deployed, such as unnecessarily damaging property or insulting, harming, or killing noncombatants (Office of the Surgeon Multi-National Force-Iraq, 2006).

To achieve its tailored goals, MMFT draws from two lineages: mindfulness training and body-based trauma therapies for re-regulating the nervous system and survival brain after trauma, such as sensorimotor psychotherapy (Ogden & Fisher, 2015; Ogden, Minton, & Pain, 2006), Somatic Experiencing (Levine, 1997; Payne, Levine, & Crane-Godreau, 2015), and the Trauma Resilience Model (Leitch, Vanslyke, & Allen, 2009). This integration of mindfulness skills with body-based self-regulation skills sets MMFT apart from other mindfulness training programs. Using these diverse lineages, MMFT aims to cultivate two core skills: *attentional control* and *tolerance for challenging experience*. Attentional control is the ability to direct and sustain attention deliberately on a chosen target over time. Tolerance for challenging experience is the ability to pay attention to, track, and stay with such experience without needing for it to be different. Such challenging experiences can be external (e.g., harsh environmental conditions or difficult people) or internal (e.g., physical pain, stress activation, intense emotions, distressing thoughts, nightmares, or flashbacks). These core skills undergird other competencies needed for agile and adaptive decision-making in high-stress environments, such as situational awareness, emotion regulation, impulse control, and mental agility (Stanley, in press).

Theoretical background of MMFT

In cultivating these core skills, MMFT emphasizes the gradual development of interoception, "the process through which the brain monitors and updates the body about its overall physical state, including its ability to recognize bodily sensations, be aware of emotional states, and maintain physiological homeostasis" (Johnson et al., 2014, p. 844). Some authors argue that the insula cortex and anterior cingulate cortex (ACC) – brain regions implicated in interoception, emotion regulation, and impulse control – may provide top-level control to the subcortical processes that regulate stress and negative emotions (Critchley et al., 2003; Critchley, Wiens, Rotshtein, Öhman, & Dolan, 2004; Garfinkel & Critchley, 2013). By improving the functioning of this regulatory loop through attention to interoception rather than cognition, it may be possible to improve subcortical functioning regarding stress and emotions. Indeed, non-intervention studies among military and civilian "elite performers" demonstrate insula and ACC activation patterns consistent with more efficient interoceptive processing during stress, relative to healthy controls (Paulus et al., 2012; Paulus et al., 2010; Simmons et al., 2012; Thom et al., 2014). In contrast, compromised interoceptive functioning has been shown to play a critical role in the development of mood and anxiety disorders (Avery et al., 2014; Domschke, Stevens, Pfleiderer, & Gerlach, 2010; Paulus & Stein, 2010) and addiction (Paulus & Stewart, 2014).

As previously noted, there are several reasons why individuals in high-stress environments may suffer from declines in executive functioning, which could compromise the effectiveness of top-down self-regulation techniques (Heatherton & Wagner, 2011; Hofmann et al., 2012). In contrast, interoceptive awareness may help counteract already depleted states. For example, a recent study (Friese, Messner, & Schaffner, 2012) found that individuals experiencing self-regulatory depletion were able to counteract the effects of that depletion with a brief period of mindfulness practice – demonstrating similar performance on a subsequent task requiring self-control as a control group not experiencing self-regulatory depletion. In contrast, a third group, in a state of self-regulatory depletion without mindfulness practice, showed the expected performance impairment on the subsequent task requiring self-control.

Thus, mind-body skills training to improve interoceptive processes – such as MMFT – may facilitate improved responses to both stress and emotions, even in high-stress contexts characterized by depleted executive functioning. For this reason, MMFT emphasizes building interoceptive awareness, but in a gradual manner so as not to flood the mind-body system and exacerbate dysregulation. Indeed, troops who received MMFT showed altered brain activation post-training indicative of improved interoceptive functioning during stress (Haase et al., 2016; Johnson et al., 2014), similar to the pattern observed among "elite performers" in earlier studies (Paulus et al., 2012; Paulus et al., 2010; Simmons et al., 2012; Thom et al., 2014).

Structure of the MMFT program

Research has tested different MMFT variants, ranging from 8–24 hours of classroom instruction delivered over eight weeks. Arguably the most effective variant is 20 hours of classroom instruction, which includes eight 2-hour sessions, a short individual practice interview in the third week, and a 4-hour practicum in the sixth week to refine mindfulness and self-regulation skills. The first four 2-hour sessions occur in the first two weeks, to front-load the neurobiology context for skills taught in the course. The other four 2-hour sessions are taught in the fourth, fifth, seventh, and eighth weeks. (In addition to this 8-week format, MMFT has also been taught as a week-long intensive course, or through introductory subsets of course material as part of daylong or weekend workshops. In these formats, participants learn the didactic context intensively and then complete the 8-week exercise sequence afterwards, on their own.)

As noted, a major goal of MMFT is self-regulation at the micro- and macro-levels. Thus, the first half of MMFT focuses on micro-level self-regulation, providing the scientific foundation of the neurobiology of stress and resilience and teaching the basic exercises for self-regulation in the mind-body system. The second half focuses on macro-level self-regulation, providing didactic content about habitual reactions, decision-making, emotions, interpersonal interactions, and conflict, and teaching more advanced exercises for self-regulation in relationship to others (Stanley, in press).

MMFT's efficacy may come from its unique developmental sequence of exercises, specifically designed to move someone from dysregulation to regulation. This is particularly important for high-stress environments, where participants are often dysregulated from prior exposure to chronic stress or trauma without adequate recovery. Participants are asked to complete daily at least 30 minutes of mindfulness and self-regulation skills exercises, divided into several practice periods throughout the day. MMFT's exercises range from 5 to 30 minutes – which is notably (and deliberately) shorter than practices in many other MBIs. Participants initially use audio tracks to guide the exercises, but over time are able to do them without audio support. Some exercises are conducted while sitting quietly or lying down, some while stretching, and some are designed for integration into daily-life tasks.

The first exercise in the sequence is the Contact Points Exercise. By developing the ability to notice the physical sensations of contact between their body and their surroundings, participants gain a portable grounding skill. By directing attention to sensations of contact, participants may not only develop attentional control, but also cue the survival brain and nervous system towards a neuroception of safety (Porges, 2011), even during stress activation or dysregulation. In contrast, when someone is activated or dysregulated, breathing sensations may not be neutral stimuli, and awareness of breathing may inadvertently create more stress activation. This is why interoceptive awareness needs to be developed gradually, to protect a dysregulated individual from flooding and re-traumatizing their mind-body system. For these reasons, the ability to bring steady awareness to the contact points is a fundamental skill, on which all other MMFT exercises build (Stanley, in press).

To try Contact Points yourself, find a comfortable place to sit, preferably with your back towards a solid wall. Sit with your feet shoulder-width apart and flat on the ground. If it feels comfortable to you, you can close your eyes; if not, simply direct your gaze softly at the ground in front of you. Sit so that your spine is both upright yet relaxed. Allow yourself to notice the feeling of being supported by the chair and ground. Aim for the *felt sense* of this support, in your body, rather than trying to *think about* or analyze this support. Notice the physical sensations of contact between the body and your surroundings, such as pressure, hardness or softness, heat or coolness, tingling, numbness, sweatiness or dampness. Notice these sensations at three different places: (1) between your legs or lower back with the chair; (2) between your feet with the ground; and (3) between your hands touching your legs or each other. Select the place where you can notice sensations of contact most strongly; this one contact point will now be your target object of attention. Anytime you notice your attention wandering, simply choose to begin again without judgment – redirecting your attention back to the sensations at your chosen contact point. In the beginning, aim to practice for 5 minutes. To conclude the exercise, widen your attention to take in the whole body seated in the chair. Notice if anything has changed in your mind-body system from having done this exercise. Over time, you can build up to practicing Contact Points for 10–20 minutes (Stanley, in press; Stanley & Schaldach, 2011).

Research About MMFT

One of MMFT's strengths is that it has been tested through rigorous neuroscience and stress physiology research – through four studies, funded by the U.S. Department of Defense and other foundations, with results published in peer-reviewed journals. U.S. combat troops preparing to deploy to Iraq and Afghanistan who received variants of the 8-week MMFT course showed significant benefits on several outcome measures, including improved cognitive performance, better regulation of negative emotions, and better physiological self-regulation and resilience during stressful pre-deployment training. These findings are notable because pre-deployment training is a form of SIT, which previous empirical research has associated with declines in mood, self-regulation capacity, and cognitive performance (for a review, see Kavanagh, 2005; Larsen & Stanley, in press).

In terms of cognitive performance, compared with control groups, troops trained in MMFT saw significant improvements in sustained attention (Jha et al., 2015; Jha et al., 2016), protection against working memory degradation (Jha et al., 2017), and improvements in working memory capacity, which was significantly linked to decreased negative emotions (Jha et al., 2010). In terms of self-regulation, compared with controls, MMFT participants demonstrated significantly more efficient physiological stress arousal before and during combat drills, followed by more complete recovery afterwards, as indexed by blood-plasma levels of neuropeptide Y and by heart-rate and breathing-rate during the drills (Johnson et al., 2014). They also showed significantly more efficient activation under stress of the insula cortex and ACC, as indexed with fMRI during restricted breathing (Haase et al., 2016) and emotional face processing (Johnson et al., 2014) tasks. Moreover, MMFT participants reported significant improvements in sleep quality – including longer sleep duration and decreased use of over-the-counter and prescription sleep aids – which was significantly correlated with higher blood-plasma levels of insulin-like growth factor, a biomarker of health produced during restful sleep (Sterlace et al., 2012). Finally, MMFT participants reported significant improvements in their perceived stress levels (Stanley, Schaldach, Kiyonaga, & Jha, 2011) and mood (Jha et al., 2010), even during the increasing demands of the pre-deployment interval.

In sum, this research suggests that MMFT may provide greater cognitive, emotional, and physiological resources to widen an individual's window of tolerance and facilitate adaptive functioning before, during, and after high-stress and high-demand contexts.

References

Adler, A. B., McGurk, D., Stetz, M. C., & Bliese, P. D. (2003). *Military occupational stressors in garrison, training, and deployed environments.* Paper presented at the NIOSH/APA Symposium Modeling Military Stressors: The WRAIR Occupational Stress Research Program, Toronto, ON.

Avery, J. A., Drevets, W. C., Moseman, S. E., Bodurka, J., Barcalow, J. C., & Simmons, W. K. (2014). Major depressive disorder is associated with abnormal interoceptive activity and functional connectivity in the insula. *Biological Psychiatry, 76*(3), 258–266.

Barger, L. K., Lockley, S. W., Rajaratnam, S. M., & Landrigan, C. P. (2009). Neurobehavioral, health, and safety consequences associated with shift work in safety-sensitive professions. *Current Neurology and Neuroscience Reports, 9*(2), 155–164.

Baumann, M. R., Gohm, C. L., & Bonner, B. L. (2011). Phased training for high-reliability occupations live-fire exercises for civilian firefighters. *Human Factors, 53*(5), 548–557.

Berg, A. M., Hem, E., Lau, B., & Ekeberg, Ø. (2006). An exploration of job stress and health in the Norwegian police service: A cross sectional study. *Journal of Occupational Medicine and Toxicology*, *1*(26), 115–160.

Berger, W., Coutinho, E. S. F., Figueira, I., Marques-Portella, C., Luz, M. P., Neylan, T. C., . . . Mendlowicz, M. V. (2012). Rescuers at risk: A systematic review and meta-regression analysis of the worldwide current prevalence and correlates of PTSD in rescue workers. *Social Psychiatry and Psychiatric Epidemiology*, *47*(6), 1001–1011.

Biggs, Q. M., Fullerton, C. S., Reeves, J. J., Grieger, T. A., Reissman, D., & Ursano, R. J. (2010). Acute stress disorder, depression, and tobacco use in disaster workers following 9/11. *American Journal of Orthopsychiatry*, *80*(4), 586–592.

Blosnich, J. R., Dichter, M. E., Cerulli, C., Batten, S. V., & Bossarte, R. M. (2014). Disparities in adverse childhood experiences among individuals with a history of military service. *JAMA Psychiatry*, *71*(9), 1041–1048.

Bonanno, G. A. (2004). Loss, trauma, and human resilience: Have we underestimated the human capacity to thrive after extremely aversive events? *American Psychologist*, *59*(1), 20–28.

Braswell, H., & Kushner, H. I. (2012). Suicide, social integration, and masculinity in the US military. *Social Science & Medicine*, *74*(4), 530–536.

Bray, R., Pemberton, M., Hourani, L., Witt, M., Olmsted, K., Brown, J., . . . Scheffer, S. (2009). *2008 Department of Defense survey of health related behaviors among active duty military personnel*. Research Triangle Park, NC: RTI International.

Bruffaerts, R., Demyttenaere, K., Borges, G., Haro, J. M., Chiu, W. T., Hwang, I., . . . Nock, M. K. (2010). Childhood adversities as risk factors for onset and persistence of suicidal behaviour. *The British Journal of Psychiatry*, *197*(1), 20–27.

Bryan, C. J., Jennings, K. W., Jobes, D. A., & Bradley, J. C. (2012). Understanding and preventing military suicide. *Archives of Suicide Research*, *16*(2), 95–110.

Butler, E. A., Egloff, B., Wilhelm, F. H., Smith, N. C., Erickson, E. A., & Gross, J. J. (2003). The social consequences of expressive suppression. *Emotion*, *3*(1), 48–67.

Cabrera, O. A., Hoge, C. W., Bliese, P. D., Castro, C. A., & Messer, S. C. (2007). Childhood adversity and combat as predictors of depression and post-traumatic stress in deployed troops. *American Journal of Preventive Medicine*, *33*(2), 77–82.

Carey, M. G., Al-Zaiti, S. S., Dean, G. E., Sessanna, L., & Finnell, D. S. (2011). Sleep problems, depression, substance use, social bonding, and quality of life in professional firefighters. *Journal of Occupational and Environmental Medicine*, *53*(8), 928–933.

Center for Mindfulness in Medicine, Health Care, and Society. (2014). *FAQ – Stress reduction*. Retrieved from www.umassmed.edu/cfm/stress-reduction/faqs/

Chiesa, A., & Serretti, A. (2009). Mindfulness-based stress reduction for stress management in healthy people: A review and meta-analysis. *The Journal of Alternative and Complementary Medicine*, *15*(5), 593–600.

Creswell, J. (2017). Mindfulness interventions. *Annual Review of Psychology*, *68*, 491–516.

Critchley, H. D., Mathias, C. J., Josephs, O., O'Doherty, J., Zanini, S., Dewar, B. K., . . . Dolan, R. J. (2003). Human cingulate cortex and autonomic control: Converging neuroimaging and clinical evidence. *Brain*, *126*, 2139–2152.

Critchley, H. D., Wiens, S., Rotshtein, P., Öhman, A., & Dolan, R. J. (2004). Neural systems supporting interoceptive awareness. *Nature Neuroscience*, *7*(2), 189–195.

Denhof, M., & Spinaris, C. (2013). *Depression, PTSD, and comorbidity in United States corrections professionals: Prevalence and impact on health functioning*. Florence, CO: Desert Waters Correctional Outreach.

Domschke, K., Stevens, S., Pfleiderer, B., & Gerlach, A. L. (2010). Interoceptive sensitivity in anxiety and anxiety disorders: An overview and integration of neurobiological findings. *Clinical Psychology Review*, *30*(1), 1–11.

Felitti, V. J. (2009). Adverse childhood experiences and adult health. *Academic Pediatrics*, *9*(3), 131–132.

Friese, M., Messner, C., & Schaffner, Y. (2012). Mindfulness meditation counteracts self-control depletion. *Consciousness and Cognition, 21*(2), 1016–1022.

Fritch, A. M., Mishkind, M., Reger, M. A., & Gahm, G. A. (2010). The impact of childhood abuse and combat-related trauma on postdeployment adjustment. *Journal of Traumatic Stress, 23*(2), 248–254.

Gailliot, M. T., Schmeichel, B. J., & Baumeister, R. F. (2006). Self-regulatory processes defend against the threat of death: Effects of self-control depletion and trait self-control on thoughts and fears of dying. *Journal of Personality and Social Psychology, 91*(1), 49–62.

Garfinkel, S. N., & Critchley, H. D. (2013). Interoception, emotion and brain: New insights link internal physiology to social behaviour. Commentary on: 'Anterior insular cortex mediates bodily sensibility and social anxiety' by Terasawa et al. (2012). *Social Cognitive and Affective Neuroscience, 8*(3), 231–234.

Gohar, A., Adams, A., Gertner, E., Sackett-Lundeen, L., Heitz, R., Engle, R., . . . Bijwadia, J. (2009). Working memory capacity is decreased in sleep-deprived internal medicine residents. *Journal of Clinical Sleep Medicine, 5*(3), 191–197.

Gross, J. J., & John, O. P. (2003). Individual differences in two emotion regulation processes: Implications for affect, relationships, and well-being. *Journal of Personality and Social Psychology, 85*(2), 348–362.

Haase, L., Thom, N. J., Shukla, A., Davenport, P. W., Simmons, A. N., Stanley, E. A., . . . Johnson, D. C. (2016). Mindfulness-based training attenuates insula response to an aversive interoceptive challenge. *Social Cognitive and Affective Neuroscience, 11*(1), 182–190.

Heatherton, T. F., & Wagner, D. D. (2011). Cognitive neuroscience of self-regulation failure. *Trends in Cognitive Sciences, 15*(3), 132–139.

Hofmann, W., Schmeichel, B. J., & Baddeley, A. D. (2012). Executive functions and self-regulation. *Trends in Cognitive Sciences, 16*(3), 174–180.

Hoge, C. W., Castro, C. A., & Eaton, K. M. (2006). *Impact of combat duty in Iraq and Afghanistan on family functioning: Findings from the Walter Reed Army Institute of Research Land Combat Study*. Paper presented at the Human Factors and Medicine Panel Symposium (HFM-134) on Human Dimensions in Military Operations: Military Leaders' Strategies for Addressing Stress and Psychological Support, Neuilly-sur-Seine, France.

Hülsheger, U. R., & Schewe, A. F. (2011). On the costs and benefits of emotional labor: A meta-analysis of three decades of research. *Journal of Occupational Health Psychology, 16*(3), 361–389.

Institute of Medicine. (2014). *Preventing psychological disorders in service members and their families: An assessment of programs*. Washington, DC: The National Academies Press.

Jha, A. P., Morrison, A. B., Dainer-Best, J., Parker, S., Rostrup, N., & Stanley, E. A. (2015). Minds 'at attention': Mindfulness training curbs attentional lapses in military cohorts. *PloS One, 10*(2), e0116889.

Jha, A. P., Morrison, A. B., Parker, S. C., & Stanley, E. A. (2016). Practice is protective: Mindfulness training promotes cognitive resilience in high-stress cohorts. *Mindfulness*, 1–13.

Jha, A. P., Stanley, E. A., Kiyonaga, A., Wong, L., & Gelfand, L. (2010). Examining the protective effects of mindfulness training on working memory capacity and affective experience. *Emotion, 10*(1), 54–64.

Jha, A. P., Witkin, J., Morrison, A., Rostrup, N., & Stanley, E. (2017). Short-form mindfulness training protects against working memory degradation over high-demand intervals. *Journal of Cognitive Enhancement, 1*(2), 154–171.

Johnson, D. C., Thom, N. J., Stanley, E. A., Haase, L., Simmons, A. N., Pei-an, B. S., . . . Paulus, M. P. (2014). Modifying resilience mechanisms in at-risk individuals: A controlled study of mindfulness training in Marines preparing for deployment. *American Journal of Psychiatry, 171*(8), 844–853.

Kavanagh, J. (2005). *Stress and performance a review of the literature and its applicability to the military*. Santa Monica, CA: RAND Corporation.

Kessler, R. C., McLaughlin, K. A., Green, J. G., Gruber, M. J., Sampson, N. A., Zaslavsky, A. M., . . . Williams, D. R. (2010). Childhood adversities and adult psychopathology in the WHO World Mental Health Surveys. *The British Journal of Psychiatry, 197*, 378–385.

Larsen, K. L., & Stanley, E. A. (in press). Conclusions: The way forward. In K. Hendricks Thomas & D. Albright (Eds.), *Bulletproofing the psyche: Preventing mental health problems in our military and veterans*. Santa Barbara, CA: Praeger.

Leitch, M. L., Vanslyke, J., & Allen, M. (2009). Somatic experiencing treatment with social service workers following Hurricanes Katrina and Rita. *Social Work, 54*(1), 9–18.

Levine, P. A. (1997). *Waking the tiger: Healing trauma: The innate capacity to transform overwhelming experiences*. Berkeley, CA: North Atlantic Books.

Lieberman, H. R., Bathalon, G. P., Falco, C. M., Kramer, F. M., Morgan, C. A., & Niro, P. (2005). Severe decrements in cognition function and mood induced by sleep loss, heat, dehydration, and undernutrition during simulated combat. *Biological Psychiatry, 57*(4), 422–429.

Linehan, M. M. (1993). *Cognitive-behavioral treatment of borderline personality disorder*. New York, NY: Guilford Press.

Mann, J. J., & Currier, D. M. (2010). Stress, genetics and epigenetic effects on the neurobiology of suicidal behavior and depression. *European Psychiatry, 25*(5), 268–271.

Maunder, R. G., Halpern, J., Schwartz, B., & Gurevich, M. (2012). Symptoms and responses to critical incidents in paramedics who have experienced childhood abuse and neglect. *Emergency Medicine Journal, 29*(3), 222–227.

Morgan, C. A., Doran, A., Steffian, G., Hazlett, G., & Southwick, S. M. (2006). Stress-induced deficits in working memory and visuo-constructive abilities in special operations soldiers. *Biological Psychiatry, 60*(7), 722–729.

Morgan, C. A., Hazlett, G., Doran, A., Garrett, S., Hoyt, G., Thomas, P., . . . Southwick, S. M. (2004). Accuracy of eyewitness memory for persons encountered during exposure to highly intense stress. *International Journal of Law and Psychiatry, 27*(3), 265–279.

Morgan, C. A., Rasmusson, A. M., Wang, S., Hoyt, G., Hauger, R. L., & Hazlett, G. (2002). Neuropeptide-Y, cortisol, and subjective distress in humans exposed to acute stress: Replication and extension of previous report. *Biological Psychiatry, 52*(2), 136–142.

Neigh, G. N., Gillespie, C. F., & Nemeroff, C. B. (2009). The neurobiological toll of child abuse and neglect. *Trauma, Violence & Abuse, 10*(4), 389–410.

Nillni, Y. I., Gradus, J. L., Gutner, C. A., Luciano, M. T., Shiperd, J. C., & Street, A. E. (2014). Deployment stressors and physical health among OEF/OIF veterans: The role of PTSD. *Healthy Psychology, 33*(11), 1281–1287.

Nock, M. K., Stein, M. B., Heeringa, S. G., Ursano, R. J., Colpe, L. J., Fullerton, C. S., . . . Schoenbaum, M. (2014). Prevalence and correlates of suicidal behavior among soldiers: Results from the Army Study to Assess Risk and Resilience in Servicemembers (Army STARRS). *JAMA Psychiatry, 71*(5), 514–522.

Office of the Surgeon Multi-National Force-Iraq, O. o. t. C. S., & Office of The Surgeon General United States Army Medical Command. (2006). *Mental Health Advisory Team (MHAT)-IV—Operationa Iraqi Freedom 05–06: Iraq*. Washington, DC.

Ogden, P., & Fisher, J. (2015). *Sensorimotor psychotherapy: Interventions for trauma and attachment*. New York, NY: WW Norton & Company.

Ogden, P., Minton, K., & Pain, C. (2006). *Trauma and the body: A sensorimotor approach to psychotherapy*. New York, NY: WW Norton & Company.

Paulus, M. P., Flagan, T., Simmons, A. N., Gillis, K., Potterat, E. G., Kotturi, S., . . . Davenport, P. W. (2012). Subjecting elite athletes to inspiratory breathing load reveals behavioral and neural signatures of optimal performers in extreme environments. *PloS One, 7*(2), e29394.

Paulus, M. P., Simmons, A. N., Fitzpatrick, S. N., Potterat, E. G., Van Orden, K. F., Bauman, J., & Swain, J. L. (2010). Differential brain activation to angry faces by elite warfighters: Neural processing evidence for enhanced threat detection. *PloS One, 5*(4), e10096.

Paulus, M. P., & Stein, M. B. (2010). Interoception in anxiety and depression. *Brain Structure and Function, 214*(5–6), 451–463.

Paulus, M. P., & Stewart, J. L. (2014). Interoception and drug addiction. *Neuropharmacology, 76*, 342–350.

Payne, P., Levine, P. A., & Crane-Godreau, M. A. (2015). Somatic experiencing: Using interoception and proprioception as core elements of trauma therapy. *Frontiers in Psychology, 6*, 1–18.

Pole, N., Neylan, T. C., Otte, C., Metzler, T. J., Best, S. R., Henn-Haase, C., & Marmar, C. R. (2007). Associations between childhood trauma and emotion-modulated psychophysiological responses to startling sounds: A study of police cadets. *Journal of Abnormal Psychology, 116*(2), 352–361.

Porges, S. W. (2011). *The Polyvagal Theory: Neurophysiological foundations of emotions, attachment, communication, and self-regulation (Norton Series on Interpersonal Neurobiology)*. New York, NY: WW Norton & Company.

Rajaratnam, S. M., Barger, L. K., Lockley, S. W., Shea, S. A., Wang, W., Landrigan, C. P., . . . Cade, B. E. (2011). Sleep disorders, health, and safety in police officers. *Journal of the American Medical Association, 306*(23), 2567–2578.

Santorelli, S. (2014). *Mindfulness-based Stress Reduction (MBSR): Standards of practice*. Worcester, MA: The Center for Mindfulness in Medicine and Society, University of Massachusetts Medical School.

Sareen, J., Henriksen, C. A., Bolton, S. L., Afifi, T. O., Stein, M. B., & Asmundson, G. J. G. (2013). Adverse childhood experiences in relation to mood and anxiety disorders in a population-based sample of active military personnel. *Psychological Medicine, 43*(1), 73–84.

Shermer, M. (2015). Outrageous. *Scientific American, 313*(1), 77.

Simmons, A. N., Fitzpatrick, S., Strigo, I. A., Potterat, E. G., Johnson, D. C., Matthews, S. C., . . . Paulus, M. P. (2012). Altered insula activation in anticipation of changing emotional states: Neural mechanisms underlying cognitive flexibility in Special Operations Forces personnel. *Neuroreport, 23*(4), 234–239.

Stanley, E. A. (in press). *Widen the window: Training the brain and body to thrive during stress, uncertainty, and change*. New York, NY: Avery Books.

Stanley, E. A., & Schaldach, J. (2011). *Mindfulness-based mind fitness training course manual, Second Edition*. Alexandria, VA: Mind Fitness Training Institute.

Stanley, E. A., Schaldach, J., Kiyonaga, A., & Jha, A. P. (2011). Mindfulness-based mind fitness training: A case study of a high-stress predeployment military cohort. *Cognitive and Behavioral Practice, 18*(4), 566–576.

Stanley, I. H., Hom, M. A., & Joiner, T. E. (2016). A systematic review of suicidal thoughts and behaviors among police officers, firefighters, EMTs, and paramedics. *Clinical Psychology Review, 44*, 25–44.

Sterlace, S. R., Plumb, T. N., El-Kara, L., Van Orden, K. A., Thom, N. J., Stanley, E. A., . . . Johnson, D. C. (2012). *Hormone regulation under stress: Recent evidence from warfighters on the effectiveness of Mindfulness-Based Mind Fitness Training in building stress resilience*. Society for Neuroscience Poster Presentation.

Teten, A. L., Schumacher, J. A., Taft, C. T., Stanley, M. A., Kent, T. A., Bailey, S. D., . . . White, D. L. (2010). Intimate partner aggression perpetrated and sustained by male Afghanistan, Iraq, and Vietnam veterans with and without posttraumatic stress disorder. *Journal of Interpersonal Violence, 25*(9), 1612–1630.

Thom, N. J., Johnson, D. C., Flagan, T., Simmons, A. N., Kotturi, S. A., Van Orden, K. F., . . . Paulus, M. P. (2014). Detecting emotion in others: Increased insula and decreased medial prefrontal cortex activation during emotion processing in elite adventure racers. *Social Cognitive and Affective Neuroscience, 9*(2), 225–231.

Vila, B., Morrison, G. B., & Kenney, D. J. (2002). Improving shift schedule and work-hour policies and practices to increase police officer performance, health, and safety. *Police Quarterly, 5*(1), 4–24.

Violanti, J. M., Marshall, J. R., & Howe, B. (1985). Stress, coping, and alcohol use: The police connection. *Journal of Police Science & Administration, 13*(2), 106–110.

Chapter 7

Mindfulness-Based Emotional Balance

History of development, curriculum, and research

Margaret Cullen, Gonzalo Brito-Pons, and Robert W. Roeser

History and development

Program background

The Mindfulness-Based Emotional Balance (MBEB) program has evolved under various names (Cultivating-Emotional Balance (CEB), **S**tress-**M**anagement **a**nd **R**elaxation **T**raining (SMART)-in-Education Program, M-Power Teacher Program, and the Mindfulness-based Attentional Training (MBAT) for-Spouses Program). Many people, across long periods of time, have contributed to its current form. With each iteration in the development of the MBEB program, we have attempted to bring together the twin themes of mindfulness and emotion in a deeper and more integrated way.

The MBEB program sits squarely in the lineage of Western Buddhist teachers/teachings (Kabat-Zinn, 2003); the Mindfulness-based Stress Reduction (MBSR) program of Jon Kabat-Zinn (1990); and the emergence of secular mindfulness-based interventions (Cullen, 2011). In 2002, at the suggestion of her mentor Jon Kabat-Zinn, Cullen participated as the "emotion trainer" on an intervention-focused research study of the Cultivating Emotional Balance (CEB) program. This study was the brainchild of Dr. Paul Ekman, who developed the idea with others after participating in a Mind and Life dialogue with the Dalai Lama on Destructive Emotions (Goleman, 2003). At this meeting, contemplatives and scientists discussed the different approaches taken in Buddhism and in Western psychology towards the management of difficult emotions. The Dalai Lama challenged the group to combine tools from the contemplative traditions and science and to make them available to a wider audience.

With the help of Buddhist scholar, teacher and translator, Alan Wallace, Ekman began to work on creating a program for teachers that was also based on his research on emotion. The focus on teachers was chosen because, not only do teachers experience high degrees of stress, but their ability to manage their emotions has a direct impact on their students. From the contemplative side, Wallace focused on teaching a meditation approach called Tamatha (focused attention/quieting), as well as a set of practices around prosocial qualities called "The Four Immeasurables."

In the CEB program, in addition to teaching the didactic emotion component of CEB, Cullen's role was to address the challenge of integrating the emotion training with the contemplative practice component of the program. This proved challenging for several reasons.

For instance, in Ekman's taxonomy of universal emotions, feelings such as shame, envy and compassion were not considered universal emotions (Ekman, 2003). In addition, Wallace chose to teach the Four Immeasurables (e.g., loving kindness, compassion, sympathetic joy, and equanimity). These immeasureables resemble emotions, but they are not well understood in modern psychological science. Compassion, for example, could be taught from the "contemplative" side, but couldn't be included on the "emotion" side because compassion did not meet the criteria that defined emotions in science at the time (see Ekman, 2008).

Another example of the complexity of integrating emotion into contemplative practices, Wallace also taught the four foundations of mindfulness, a framework and related set of practices that don't specifically include emotions in their purview (Cullen, 2011). Thus, emotions themselves, ironically, were never the object of formal meditation in the CEB program.

Emergence of the Mindfulness-Based Emotional Balance program

The next stage in the development of the MBEB program occurred in 2006 when Ulco Visser (Impact Foundation), a social entrepreneur interested in education, invited Cullen to teach CEB in Denver, Colorado, to teachers. Visser was determined to develop a model that could be both scalable and financially self-sustaining and, in 2007, he invited Cullen to develop her own curriculum integrating emotion training and contemplation.

Having trained in MBSR in 1995 with Kabat-Zinn, Cullen had been aware of the knowledge and skill bank that MBIs were accumulating as more and more programs were offered, specific cohorts were targeted, data was collected, and instructors honed their skills (McCown, Reibel, & Micozzi, 2010). Kabat-Zinn's original vision had been road tested by hundreds of teachers and much had been learned, not only about how to "language" contemplative practices in mainstream settings, but also how to facilitate this type of program (e.g., embodiment of mindfulness, facilitating inquiry, and creating a safe container). The new program Cullen created drew from MBSR and from Ekman's theory and techniques for developing emotional literacy. She also drew on her work with cancer patients and their families to incorporate "forgiveness" because she had learned from this community that forgiveness practice was foundational to emotional balance. Forgiveness was a novel and somewhat radical addition as it didn't have a clear precedent in either emotion training or in contemplative training.

It was at this juncture that the program was called "Mindfulness-based Emotional Balance" (MBEB) by Cullen and the SMART (Stress Management and Relaxation Training)-in-Education program by Visser and the Impact Foundation. In 2009, Cullen, Linda Wallace, and Betsy Hedberg co-wrote a complete SMART-in-Education teacher manual based on Cullen's program. Visser and the Impact Foundation gave the US rights to the SMART program and manual to Passageworks, located in Colorado and the Canadian rights to University of British Columbia in Kelowna, Canada. In 2015, a workbook based on MBEB was published (Cullen & Brito Pons, 2015), which has also been published in Spanish. In 2017 the first two international MBEB Teacher Training programs are underway through the Center for Mindfulness at UC San Diego and the Australian Psychological Society.

In summary, the MBEB program has been refined and studied over time, a manual has been published, the training of MBEB instructors has begun, and lines of research in education and the military using variants of MBEB are currently underway. Before describing the program and the research on MBEB in slightly more depth, we discuss the nature of this challenge a bit more theoretically.

Central theoretical and practical challenge: integrating mindfulness and emotion

Over the course of the development of the MBEB program, we confronted several challenges when attempting to create a mindfulness program that focused on emotions. First, what we call emotions don't have exact equivalences in Tibetan, Sanskrit, or Pali, the languages in which Buddhist philosophy is mainly written. Most mindfulness trainings draw heavily on the Satipaṭṭhāna Sutta (The Discourses on the Establishing of Mindfulness) from the Pali Canon. These four foundations parse experience into categories that are particularly fruitful places to investigate with mindful awareness into the nature of reality. Traditionally, emotions simply don't fit neatly into any of the four foundations. They are experienced in both the body *and* the mind, yet the Sutta separates the body into the first foundation and the mind into the third foundation. They are sometimes placed in the second foundation which is awareness of *vedana* or feeling tones (Gunaratana, 2012), but many scholars limit this foundation strictly to awareness of the qualities of pleasant, unpleasant, or neutral that accompany all experience (Thera, 1965; Analayo, 2003; Wallace, 2011). Of the two principal Vipassana teachers in the West, Jack Kornfield places emotions in the second foundation (Kornfield, 2013), while Joseph Goldstein places emotions in the third foundation (Goldstein, 2002). The second foundation is intended to bring insight into the tendency of mind to react to these feeling tones of pleasant, unpleasant, and neutral by clinging, pushing away or "checking out," which can lead to liberating insight into the nature of mind but does not necessarily allow for insight into the nature of emotional experience. The third foundation is designed to provide insight into the way mental states affect the nature of mind, but doesn't include awareness of the physical correlates of emotion.

What was clear from the beginning of CEB, was that Ekman's maps of emotions and the Buddhist map of the four foundations could neither fully integrate, nor could they fully address the lived reality of our 21st-century participants. As beautiful as these maps are, they are not, in fact, the territory. Our lived experience of emotions is complex, multi-faceted and defies strict categorization.

Even with the approval and support of highly respected teachers and mentors, it is a bold leap to suggest that the maps provided by two thousand plus years of Buddhist scholars cannot literally be followed if they are to address the emotional lives of 21st-century Westerners. At the same time, if they aren't deeply honored and respected within the contexts in which they evolved, mindfulness programs risk getting reduced to simple "stress reduction." Like all good scientists, Ekman continues to revise and update his theories and his ideas influence new generations of thinkers which, in turn, have influenced MBEB (Davidson, 2012; Barrett, 2017; Gilbert, 2009).

In developing and teaching MBEB, our intention was to remain open to useful contemplative and scientific maps on emotional experience, while remaining aware that not only the map is not the territory, but that an attachment to maps can become an obstacle to communicate the radically experiential nature of the practice in an original and authentic way, an embodiment of the "real curriculum."

Reflecting on the importance of honoring the tradition while keeping an open mind to find new ways to convey the depth of contemplative practices, Kabat-Zinn (2011) wrote:

> It can be hugely helpful to have a strong personal grounding in the Buddhadharma and its teachings. . . . Yet little or none of it can be brought into the classroom *except in essence*. And if the essence is absent, then whatever one is doing or thinks one is doing, it is certainly not mindfulness-based in the way we understand the term.

This means that we cannot follow a strict Theravadan approach, nor a strict Mahayana approach, nor a strict Vajrayana approach, although elements of all these great traditions and the sub-lineages within them are relevant and might inform how we, as a unique person with a unique dharma history, approach specific teaching moments in both practice, guided meditations, and dialogue about the experiences that arise in formal and informal practice among the people in our class. But we are never appealing to authority or tradition, only to the richness of the present moment held gently in awareness, and the profound and authentic authority of each person's own experience, equally held with kindness in awareness.

(p. 299)

The program

The eight-week version of MBEB follows the general structure of MBSR and other MBIs, including eight two-and-a-half hour classes and a silent daylong between weeks 6 and 7. Each class in the program focuses on a different theme (see below) following a progression that goes from developing basic mindfulness skills during the first half of the program to applying these skills for enhancing emotional awareness and developing more adaptive emotional patterns during the second half of the program. Throughout the course of the eight weeks, participants are asked to dedicate 30 minutes a day to formal meditation practice using downloadable audio guides. Informal practices ("field observations" and "experiments") are also used to investigate and deepen the understanding of each theme in a way that is immediately relevant in daily life.

Each class in the program includes:

- guided meditation,
- inquiry about the previous week's formal and informal practice,
- experiential and dialogical pedagogy on the theme of the class,
- introduction and practice of the meditation for the coming week, and
- home assignments (formal and informal practices).

The pedagogy of the themes typically involves individual or relational exercises and experiments to explore the topic experientially, after which participants reflect on their experience in small groups or in the large group. The instructor uses the inquiry process to introduce key teaching points based on emotion theory, scientific research, and contemplative wisdom related to the topic of the week.

The themes and practices of the program are designed and organized to enhance participants' nonjudgmental awareness about their emotional processing, emotional patterns, and reactions, and to gain insight about the relationship between emotions and related phenomena such as attention, intention, thoughts, and behavior. From this enhanced awareness, difficult emotional states such as fear, anger, jealousy, envy, and shame are approached from the perspective of mindfulness, normalizing and de-shaming the experience of these emotions, thus preventing the proliferation of these states through self-criticism and aversion. Finally, health-supportive and prosocial emotional states including forgiveness, love, kindness, and compassion are cultivated and strengthened through meditation and informal practices. Table 7.1 presents a summary of the main themes and formal practices of the program week by week.

Table 7.1 Mindfulness-Based Emotional Balance (MBEB) protocol

Week	Mindfulness-Based Emotional Balance (MBEB)
1	**Introduction to mindfulness** What mindfulness is and how it relates to emotional balance. The role of intention in emotional balance is explored and setting intentions is introduced as a practice. Awareness of breath is presented as a foundational practice that helps develop a basis of nonreactivity and equanimity from which to explore emotions. Formal practice: awareness of breath
2	**Feelings: pleasant, unpleasant, neutral** Key aspects of emotion theory from a psychological and evolutionary perspective are introduced (universal and personal triggers, automatic appraisers, refractory period, etc.). Learning to recognize feeling tones (pleasant, unpleasant, and neutral), habitual reactions to them, and the relationship between these reactions and emotional patterns. Formal practice: awareness of breath and feelings
3	**Mindfulness of thoughts** Learning to recognize thoughts as mental events. Understanding the link between thoughts, emotions, and moods, and how different thoughts stimulate different emotional systems (threat, drive, soothing-affiliative) that can generate and feed loops between the body, emotions, and thoughts. Formal practice: mindfulness of breath and thoughts
4	**Forgiveness** Forgiveness is explored as a trainable skill supportive of emotional balance and consisting of letting go of resentment toward self and others without condoning or minimizing harmful actions. Through guided discovery, participants explore blocks and misconceptions about forgiveness and learn a process to practice forgiveness for self, from others, and for others. Formal practice: forgiveness meditation
5	**Love and kindness** Learning to recognize love and kindness when it arises naturally in relation to loved ones, and how this appreciation and commitment to other's wellbeing can be trained and expanded beyond the immediate circle of close ones. Taking joy in other's happiness, versus feeling jealousy and envy affect the body and mind in ways that nourish or undermine emotional balance. Formal practice: loving-kindness meditation
6	**Defensive emotions: anger and fear** Anger and fear are explored as evolutionarily derived emotions that protect us by helping to remove obstacles and avoid threat. Normalizing and de-shaming the experience of having these emotions as normal functions of the human "tricky brain." Participants recognize and do exercises to embody defensive emotions and explore personal anger and fear triggers. Participants learn to identify and map their anger profiles. Formal practice: mindfulness of breath, thoughts, and emotions
	MBEB silent day of practice This day of practice is designed to deepen the participants' experience with the core practices and themes of the program in the context of shared silence. The day combines guided mindfulness meditations (mindful breathing, awareness of feelings, awareness of thoughts, and emotions) and guided generative practices (forgiveness, loving-kindness, compassion), along with mindful walking and movement practices.

Week	Mindfulness-Based Emotional Balance (MBEB)
7	**Compassion** Learning to develop qualities such as greater self-acceptance, tenderness, nonjudgment, and caring in self-to-self and self-to-other relations. Participants begin to cultivate compassion for all beings by moving from focusing on the self to focusing on a loved one to focusing on a neutral person, then on a difficult person, and finally on all beings. Relevant psychological blocks and obstacles to self- and other- compassion are explored, including shame, guilt, grief, and self-criticism. Formal practice: compassion meditation
8	**Integrated practice and continuation** The essential elements of the program are combined into an integrated meditation practice that can continue to be done daily by participants. The group explores strategies to develop habits of the heart, mind, and body that support emotional balance and resilience after the program. Formal practice: integrated meditation

For a detailed idea of the contents and strategies used in MBEB, you can explore the workbook and the audio guided meditations in the accessories webpage for the workbook version of this program (Cullen & Brito Pons, 2015) at www.newharbinger.com/mindfulness-based-emotional-balance-workbook/accessories.

Finally, we would like to share two exercises that are used in the program:

1. **Exploring forgiveness**. A key pedagogical strategy in MBEB consists in exploring the (often unconscious) beliefs and assumptions that participants hold about specific emotional processes. One example of this is the use of Socratic dialogue and guided discovery in class four to explore participants' beliefs and assumptions about what forgiveness is. Please write your responses to each question in your journal, taking a moment to reflect on what you truly believe.

    - Who benefits from forgiveness?
    - Is forgiveness the same as reconciliation? If not, what's the difference?
    - Does the act of forgiveness condone or minimize behavior? Why or why not?
    - Is forgiveness a sign of weakness or strength? Why or why not?
    - Does forgiveness require an apology?
    - Is forgiveness a process, or does it happen in a moment? Can it be forced?
    - What's the difference between forgiving and forgetting?

2. **Exploring envy and empathetic joy**. In this guided visualization used in week five (love and kindness) participants use an imaginary situation to explore the physiological, mental, and emotional correlates of joy versus envy as possible responses to others' happiness. Read the following instructions to try this exercise on your own, taking some time with each bullet point before moving to the next (and try to resist the temptation to read ahead):

    - Sit in meditation posture, in a comfortable yet alert position, with your hands resting calmly and your eyes gently closed. Check in with your body, feeling the places where it contacts the chair or floor.

- Take some deep breaths, completely filling the torso with air, then completely releasing the breath.
- Now, imagine or remember a time when something wonderful happened to a loved one, perhaps a dear friend or a family member. Envision and experience what happened, and notice the bodily sensations, the thoughts, and emotions that arise when you imagine or remember this. For a few moments, allow the feeling to get as strong as possible.
- Now, imagine a competitor making a great accomplishment, receiving acknowledgment, and enjoying success. Again, notice how that feels in the body and in your mind, allowing yourself to feel whatever arises.
- Compare the sensations, emotions, and thoughts that arose in these two scenarios. If you felt envy arising, how did it feel in the body? What kind of thoughts came up?
- After acknowledging the envy as a very human emotional reaction, try this thought experiment in which you choose to do something rather unusual: imagine how would it feel to choose to be happy for this person.
- Just for a few minutes, consider this thought: "What if their happiness posed no threat to me?" Knowing that you can return to envy at any time, see if it is possible to participate in and celebrate their happiness for even just one minute.

If you followed the previous steps, reflect on this exercise. From your own experience, what did you observe?

It is important to remember that these two exercises are embedded in an eight-week program that intentionally and systematically supports both an inner and outer environment in which to safely experiment with potentially triggering subjects like forgiveness and envy.

For participants as well as institutions, the growing body of research validating this program as "evidence-based" plays a key role in the intellectual "buy-in" that is necessary before engaging with challenging and potentially transforming programs such as MBEB.

Research on the program

Beginning in 2009, Dr. Robert Roeser, with many collaborators and colleagues, began to undertake a systematic line of research on the teacher and classroom effects of the MBEB program (under the name SMART-in-Education program) in primary and secondary school settings (see Roeser et al., 2013). The work began in Vancouver, British Columbia, Canada, with Drs. Kimberley Schonert-Reichl and Amishi Jha as collaborators. MBEB was first piloted in Vancouver with district staff, principals, and administrators, and then with groups of primary and secondary school teachers in a randomized-control scientific trial. The program was then implemented and studied in successive cohorts of parents and educators in Boulder, Colorado; Ann Arbor, Michigan; Berkeley, California; and Portland, Oregon, with various collaborators (see research summary below). Although the program was initially offered to educators, it was designed to be readily and easily translated for any sector: education, health care, parenting, business, sports, and so forth. The program is viewed as transferrable in this way because, we posit, it has both a non-directive approach to "outcomes," and, due to the nature of each group served, a structured approach that allows for the organic emergence of shared experience and dialogue around how the transfer of mindfulness skills to one's various life settings (e.g., the classroom) can occur in the service of various ends (e.g., better relationships with students). Indeed, studying the processes of transfer from this kind of non-directive teacher program to changes in teachers' classroom practice has been a main focus of this entire line of research (see Roeser, 2016).

For a series of research projects beginning in 2013 in the Northwest United States called Empowering Educators through Mindfulness Training, Roeser enlisted Cullen to continue offering the MBEB program for his research projects under the name "M-Power Program for Teachers." More recently, neuroscientist Amishi Jha at University of Miami hired Cullen to adapt MBEB for military spouses. Under the name Mindfulness-Based Attention Training (MBAT)-Spouse, Cullen and colleagues delivered several iterations of MBEB to military spouses at army and air force bases around the US and a teacher training at Joint Special Operations Command. These military setting programs have been studied by Jha's lab. We briefly review this work below.

Research and theory of change on MBEB in education

Several randomized-control research trials using mixed methods of investigation have been conducted on the MBEB program in education with parents and teachers of special needs students (e.g., Benn, Akiva, Arel, & Roeser, 2012) and with primary and secondary school teachers (Crain, Schonert-Reichl, & Roeser, 2016; Taylor et al., 2016; Roeser, 2016; Roeser, Mashburn, & Skinner, in preparation; Roeser et al., 2013). These studies are summarized in Table 7.2.

Table 7.2 Study modalities or findings for MBEB program in education with parents and teachers of special needs students

Treatment modality	Explanation
Self-care and home therapies	Self care techniques; Psychoeducation; CAM; massage, yoga, placental encapsulation.
Individual psychotherapy	Proven therapies include Interpersonal therapy, Cognitive therapies, Psychoanalytic therapy. Limited to AD only in military facilities.
Pharmacotherapy	Medications including antidepressants, mood stabilizers or antipsychotics. Studies have shown many women prefer non-medication treatments and perceive medication as "giving up."
Community support: network	MOPS international; PSI support groups in community, PSI international warm-line.
Partner or dyadic therapies	Marriage therapies and parent-infant therapies not generally available to military. Referred to network or obtains marital counseling from chaplains.
Home-health therapies	Home-visiting programs such as New Parents support/ civilian equivalent. NPSP is only model available to military families.
Group therapies	Found to be overall beneficial in civilian communities. Usually consist of support groups/education groups. Only group study in military is Mothers in Transition Program at Camp Pendleton. Two studies presented at APA conference on postpartum support group or mother-infant group therapy.
Parent-infant therapies	Mother-infant therapy, usually in conjunction with visit to therapist. NPSP has parent-child interaction therapy.

The research studies on the MBEB program in education have been guided by a theory of change of intended program effects on teachers, classrooms, and students (see Figure 7.1 – Roeser, Skinner, Beers, & Jennings, 2012). The theory begins with the **fidelity of implementation** of the MBEB program in terms of adherence to the curriculum and the acceptability and feasibility of the program to teacher participants. Given high quality implementation of MBEB, we hypothesized that the MBEB program would have **teacher effects**, first in terms of teachers' strengthening of mindfulness-related skills and dispositions (e.g., self-compassion); and then secondly, in terms of increasing teachers' occupational health, wellbeing and prosocial dispositions (e.g., forgiveness, compassion). By helping teachers to be less exhausted, more engaged, and more prosocial, the MBEB program is hypothesized to have **classroom effects**. Specifically, teachers who feel less stress, greater wellbeing, and greater prosociality are hypothesized to create more emotionally-supportive and well-managed classrooms. Finally, the theory of change postulates **student effects** – specifically that students will be more motivated and engaged in classrooms that they perceive as emotionally-supportive, safe, and well-managed; and where they have emotionally closer relationships with their teachers, because such classrooms address their needs for autonomy, belonging, and competence (Eccles & Roeser, 2016). To date, research studies provide empirical support for the hypothesized teacher and classroom effects of MBEB in education, though more research is needed to further establish the validity of these findings.

Summary of research studies in education

In 2009 and 2010, Roeser and colleagues conducted the first randomized control trials of a nine-week, 36-hour version of MBEB for public school teachers in Western Canada and in the Western United States (see Crain, Schonert-Reichl, & Roeser, 2016; Roeser et al., 2013; Taylor et al., 2016). The sample included 113 public elementary (50%) and secondary school teachers. Results published in several papers document that teachers found the program feasible and acceptable, were able to attend most program sessions, and completed the

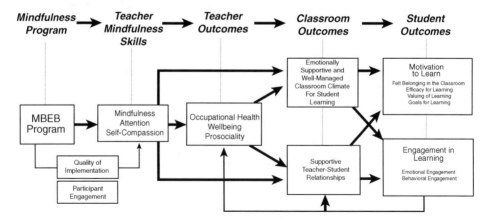

Figure 7.1 Theory of change.

Note: Hypothesized effects of the MBEB program on teachers, classrooms, and students.

daily 15 minutes of home practice. In addition, teachers receiving MBEB showed significant increases in mindfulness, self-compassion, and an objective measure of attention and memory; in empathy and forgiveness, and in sleep quality and quantity. Teachers receiving the training also showed significant reductions in occupational stress, burnout, and symptoms of anxiety and depression. No effects on biological measures of stress were found. Greater teacher mindfulness and self-compassion in the MBEB group after the training mediated longer-term reductions in occupational stress and burnout and anxiety and depression at follow-up during a new school year.

In 2010, Benn, Akiva, Arel, & Roeser (2012) conducted a randomized control trial in the Midwest examining the feasibility and efficacy of a five-week, 34-hour summertime version of the SMART program for parents and educators of children with special needs. The sample included 37 special educators (10 teachers, 11 teaching assistants, and 16 other professional staff) and 23 parents of children with special needs. The research results showed that parents and teachers were able to attend most sessions and reported enjoying and deriving benefit from the program. Furthermore, those receiving MBEB showed significant increases in mindfulness and self-compassion; significant increases in in empathy and forgiveness; and significant reductions in stress and anxiety. Greater parent and teacher mindfulness in the MBEB group after the training mediated longer-term reductions in stress and anxiety at follow-up two months later.

In 2012, Roeser (2016) and colleagues conducted a pre-post, uncontrolled process study in the Western US of the nine-week 36-hour version of MBEB program for 16 educators in K-12 settings. The goal of this study was to "look inside the black box" of the MBEB program to document specific processes by which MBEB might be effecting teacher outcomes. Results showed that teachers reported increases in mindfulness and decreases in stress and depressive symptoms from pre- to post-program. Process study results showed that there were specific activities and ways of teaching employed by the mindfulness instructor (M. Cullen) that help participants to learn the skills of mindfulness and compassion. These activities and acts included the largely practice-focused, experiential, and dialogic nature of the program; a consistent focus on autonomy-supportive language and practice; and the embodiment of the qualities being taught to the teachers on the part of the mindfulness instructor (e.g., mindfulness, kindness, clarity, trustworthiness).

From 2014 to 2016, Roeser, Mashburn, and Skinner (in preparation) conducted a randomized control trial in the Northwest examining the feasibility and efficacy of a nine-week 28-hour summertime version of the SMART program for parents and educators of children with special needs. The sample included 58 middle school teachers. Results showed that teachers found the program feasible and acceptable, were able to attend most program sessions, and completed the daily 15 minutes of home practice. In addition, teachers receiving MBEB showed significant increases in mindfulness and self-compassion, but not an objective measure of attention and memory. Teachers receiving the training also showed significant reductions in occupational stress, burnout, and symptoms of anxiety and depression. No effects on biological measures of stress were found. This study also examined classroom effects. Results showed that participation in MBEB was not associated with increases in classroom emotional support or management/organization right after the program ended, but teachers who participated in the program did show more productive and better organized classrooms climates four months later at the beginning of a new school year.

In summary, results from these research trials provide evidence of program feasibility and efficacy for educator and parent outcomes, and evidence of promise for how the MBEB teacher program can help middle teachers to create more productive and better managed classroom environments for student learning. More research is needed that includes: (a) active control groups; (b) non-self report measures of outcomes; (c) more diverse geographic samples of teachers; (d) additional measures of teacher behavior in the classroom and (e) student outcomes. We can say at this point that this program shows promising evidence in terms of improving teachers' mindfulness, self-compassion, occupational health, and wellbeing, as well as preliminary evidence in relation to improving middle school classroom climates for student learning.

Summary of research studies in military settings

Another line of research is examining the implementation of MBEB in military settings. One recent study compared the effects of two different-length versions of the MBEB program adapted for military spouses on attention and wellbeing outcomes (Brudner et al., 2016). The study included 95 military spouses recruited from three military bases. The study compared program effects on spouses allocated to one of three conditions (control, four-week/eight-hour MBEB, eight-week/27-hour MBEB). Both the four- and eight-week versions of the program improved subjective reports of increased mindfulness and improved psychological wellbeing. Participants in the eight-week, but not the four-week program, showed improvements on an objective measure of attention regulation.

Conclusion and acknowledgments

For fifteen years, MBEB has been evolving. The experience of every participant in every iteration has, in some way, influenced this evolution, not only through their participation in the scientific research, but through their comments in class and engagement with the materials. The history of MBEB begins with the key contributions of Wallace and Ekman. Wallace was the first to bring the four immeasurables into a secular contemplative training. Ekman's theories on emotion could be operationalized in a way to make our emotional lives more "user friendly." Collaborators have emerged at key moments to shape the direction of MBEB in profound ways. Kabat-Zinn was a tireless champion of MBEB, and a paragon of courage in his own determination to teach from the territory, not the map. Roeser brought not only a uniquely collaborative approach to research, but also a depth of understanding of emotion in the context of human development. Brito Pons brought the combination of years of intensive practice, clinical training, and in-depth training with Paul Gilbert. Jha contributed the bold vision of bringing mindfulness and emotion training into the military. It is our expectation that MBEB will continue to evolve, shaped by research outcomes, teacher trainings, future collaborators, and individual experience. And it is our hope that MBEB will continue to support the emotional wellbeing of our participants in the actuality of their lives.

References

Analayo. (2003). *Sattipatthana: The Direct Path to Realization*. Birmingham: Windhorse.
Barrett, L.F. (2017). *How Emotions Are Made: The Secret Life of the Brain*. New York, NY: Houghton Mifflin Harcourt.
Benn, R., Akiva, T., Arel, S., & Roeser, R.W. (2012). Mindfulness training effects for parents and educators of children with special needs. *Developmental Psychology, 48*, 1476–1487.

Brudner, E.G., Ramos, N., Denkova, E., Morrison, A.B., Cullen, M., MacAulay, J., & Jha, A.P. (2016). *The Influence of Training Program Duration on Cognitive and Psychological Benefits of Mindfulness and Compassion Training in Military Spouses*. Poster presented at the biennial meeting of the International Symposium on Contemplative Studies, San Diego, CA.

Crain, T., Schonert-Reichl, K., & Roeser, R.W. (2016). Cultivating teacher mindfulness: Effects of a randomized-controlled trial on work, home, and sleep outcomes. *Journal of Occupational Health Psychology, 22*(2), 138–152.

Cullen, M. (2011). Mindfulness-based interventions: An emerging phenomenon. *Mindfulness, 2*, 186–193.

Cullen, M., & Brito Pons, G. (2015). *The Mindfulness-Based Emotional Balance Workbook: An Eight-Week Program for Improved Emotion Regulation and Resilience*. Oakland, CA: New Harbinger.

Davidson, R. (2012). *The Emotional Life of Your Brain: How Its Unique Patterns Affect the Way You Think, Feel, and Live*. New York, NY: Hudson.

Eccles, J.S., & Roeser, R.W. (2016). School and community influences on human development. In M.H. Boorstein & M.E. Lamb (Eds.), *Developmental Psychology: An Advanced Textbook, Seventh Edition*. Hillsdale, NJ: Erlbaum.

Ekman, P. (2003). *Emotions Revealed*. New York, NY: Holt.

Ekman, P. (2008). *Emotional Awareness: Overcoming the Obstacles to Psychological Balance and Compassion*. New York, NY: Holt.

Gilbert, P. (2009). *The Compassionate Mind*. Oakland, CA: New Harbinger.

Goldstein, J. (2002). *One Dharma*. San Francisco, CA: Harper.

Goleman, D. (1997). *Healing Emotions*. Boston, MA: Shambhala.

Goleman, D. (2003). *Destructive Emotions: A Scientific Dialogue with the Dalai Lama*. New York, NY: Bantam.

Gunaratana, B. (2012). *The Four Foundations of Mindfulness in Plain English*. Somerville, MA: Wisdom.

Kabat-Zinn, J. (1990). *Full Catastrophe Living: Using the Wisdom of Your Body and Mind to Face Stress, Pain, and Illness*. New York, NY: Delta Trade.

Kabat-Zinn, J. (2003). Mindfulness-based interventions in context: Past, present and future. *Clinical Psychology: Science and Practice, 10*, 144–156.

Kabat-Zinn, J. (2011). Some reflections on the origins of MBSR, skillful means, and the trouble with maps. *Contemporary Buddhism, 12*, 281–306.

Kornfield, J. (2013, December 13). *Four principles for mindful transformation*. Retrieved May 15, 2017, from http://www.oprah.com/own-super-soul-sunday/Jack-Kornfield-Four-Principles-for-Mindful-Transformation/3

McCown, D., Reibel, D., & Micozzi, M. (2010). *Teaching Mindfulness*. New York, NY: Springer.

Roeser, R.W. (2016). Processes of teaching, learning and transfer in mindfulness-based interventions (MBIs) for teachers: A contemplative educational perspective. In K. Schonert-Reichl & R.W. Roeser (Eds.), *Handbook of Mindfulness in Education: Theory, Research, Practice and Future Directions*. New York, NY: Springer.

Roeser, R.W., Mashburn, A.J., & Skinner, E.A (in preparation). Teacher and classroom impacts of mindfulness training for middle school teachers. *Mixed Methods Results from a Randomized-Control Trial*.

Roeser, R.W., Schonert-Reichl, K.A., Jha, A., Cullen, M., Wallace, L., Wilensky, R., Oberle, E., Thomson, K., Taylor, C., & Harrison, J. (2013). Mindfulness training and reductions in teacher stress and burnout: Results from two randomized, waitlist-control field trials. *Journal of Educational Psychology, 105*, 787–804. doi: 10.1037/a0032093

Roeser, R.W., Skinner, E., Beers, J., & Jennings, P.A. (2012). Mindfulness training and teachers' professional development: An emerging area of research and practice. *Child Development Perspectives, 6*, 167–173.

Taylor, C., Harrison, J., Haimovitz, K., Oberle, E., Thomson, K., Schonert-Reichl, K., & Roeser, R.W. (2016). Examining ways that a mindfulness-based intervention reduces stress in public school teachers: A mixed-methods study. *Mindfulness*, 1–15.

Thera, N.T. (1965). *The Heart of Buddhist Meditation*. Boston, MA: Weiser.

Wallace, B.A. (2011). *Minding Closely: The Four Applications of Mindfulness*. Ithaca, NY: Snow Lion.

Section II

Mindfulness programs in families

Chapter 8

Mindfulness-Based Childbirth and Parenting
Preparing a new generation for birthing and beyond

Nancy Bardacke and Larissa G. Duncan

Mindfulness-Based Childbirth and Parenting (MBCP) (Barrack) is a nine-week childbirth education program that offers expectant parents the opportunity to learn mindfulness skills for working with the stresses of pregnancy, the pain, fear, and potentially unexpected events that can occur during childbirth, and to have these inner skills in place for the intense adjustment of early parenting. The potential exists that in learning mindfulness skills during this profound time of change, expectant parents will build a foundation for more attuned, compassionate parenting.

MBCP is a formal adaptation of the Mindfulness-Based Stress Reduction (MBSR; Kabat-Zinn, 2013) program founded in 1979 by Jon Kabat-Zinn, Ph.D. at the University of Massachusetts (UMASS) Medical Center. Nancy Barrack, CNM, MA, the founder of the MBCP program, began formally adapting the MBSR program to the needs of expectant families in the San Francisco Bay Area in California in 1998. In 2007 Nancy was invited to bring MBCP to the University of California, San Francisco (UCSF) Osher Center for Integrative Medicine, where she was joined by Larissa Duncan, Ph.D. who began a research program to systematically investigate the potential benefits of this approach. This close clinical-research partnership has continued for more than a decade through Nancy's not-for-profit organization, the Mindful Birthing and Parenting Foundation (MBPF) as well as through Larissa's work as a faculty member at UCSF and now at the University of Wisconsin-Madison.

Intended population

The intended population for the MBCP program is expectant parents (those who are pregnant and their partners of all genders) who are seeking what is commonly referred to as "childbirth education". The majority of participants who attend the nine-week course are couples in the second half of pregnancy who are expecting their first baby Expectant parents who have previously given birth, including those who have had a less than optimal childbirth experience also attend. Women and their partners who anticipate a childbirth needing special medical attention such as delivering twins/multiples or a planned Cesarean delivery are also welcomed, as are expectant women without partners. Though not essential, women without partners are encouraged to attend with a family member, friend, support person, or birthing professional, such as a doula.

Deeper intentions informing the MBCP program

In addition to offering mindfulness skills for decreasing stress during pregnancy, for working with pain in childbirth, and for the stresses of early parenting, the MBCP program, offers a way to strengthen a couple's relationship by bringing mindful awareness to their communication patterns. It also provides an opportunity to build a community among expectant parents. This community aspect of the MBCP program may prove to be important in the prevention of postpartum depression (PPD), as isolation is a significant contributing factor to PPD.

Another key intention for the MBCP program is to foster healthy attachment relationships between new parents and their infant. It is well known that poor attachment between parents and their children can have important consequences for the mental health of the developing child, possibly through impacts on the developing brain (Schore, 2001). It is perhaps here, in nurturing the capacity for attentional presence through mindfulness practice during pregnancy that intergenerational patterns of suffering may be interrupted.

In addition, it is a deep intention of the MBCP program to bring mindfulness skills to highly stressed populations. The burden of stress on those of low socioeconomic status, communities of color, and immigrant populations living in majority white societies is already quite large. We know that this stress ripples outward into physical and mental suffering for pregnant women and their babies. An example of this is the intergenerational link between experiencing racism and the increased risk for preterm birth and/or low birth weight babies born to African American women in the United States. This is seen even among African American women who have attained high levels of income and education (Kramer & Hogue, 2009). Bringing mindfulness skills to highly stressed expectant parents, ideally by members of these vulnerable populations who can offer the program in culturally relevant ways may prove to significantly improve the quality of life for parents and their children. It also offers skills that may be protective for withstanding current difficult conditions while the work of uprooting the systems that undergird economic, racial, and other social inequities moves forward.

And finally, it is an intention of the MBCP program to foster mindfulness skills among perinatal healthcare providers. Caring for expectant women and families, particularly during the unpredictable birthing process is both an extremely rewarding and highly stressful calling. MBCP instructors are commonly midwives, obstetricians, nurses, or doulas who care for families in the perinatal period as well as psychiatrists and psychologists who focus on supporting maternal, newborn, and family mental health in this vulnerable period. The instructors find that in learning mindfulness skills for teaching MBCP, they are deeply contributing to their own health and well-being, as well as bringing greater joy, satisfaction, and meaning to their work.

The MBCP course begins with a phone call

The nine-week MBCP program begins with a phone conversation between the expectant parents and the MBCP course instructor. During the conversation the expectant parents ask questions about the course and the instructor learns about any specific concerns or challenges the expectant parents may have, such as existing or past physical or mental health conditions, difficulties conceiving, a perinatal loss, a previous traumatic birth experience, or a pregnancy considered "high risk". In addition, the instructor shares that the mindfulness skills the couple will learn are fundamentally life skills that will also serve them well in parenting. During the interview the instructor also clearly states the expectation that each parent will make a commitment to a formal mindfulness practice of half an hour per day, six days per week for the duration of the program, using the guided audio meditations that will be provided as part of the course materials.

Class 1: all we know is now

In Class 1 the instructor briefly reviews the history of MBCP and its relationship to MBSR, and introduces many of the themes that are interwoven throughout the course, such as the reality that the future is uncertain and all that can be truly known is the present moment. Participants are introduced to the notion that present moment awareness is a universal capacity of the human mind that can be cultivated through meditation practice, that change, such as the profound life change they are currently experiencing, can be quite stressful and the capacity to be mindful is a skill that can increase one's resilience. Learning mindfulness is presented as an eminently practical thing to learn right now.

Uncertainty about the future is exemplified by the reality that expectant parents don't know exactly when their baby will be born and this example becomes a way of teaching about how the mind can get caught in worries about the future and thoughts of the past rather than being in the present moment, the only moment there really is to be alive, to give birth, and to parent. The link between mindfulness and parenting is made by pointing out how much babies and children live in the present moment and that in truth, what we call parenting is actually a process of present-moment interactions between parents and children. Partners, who often have the notion that "childbirth education" is predominantly for the pregnant woman, are reminded that they too will be having a birth experience and becoming a parent and that practicing mindfulness is important for their own birthing and parenting – and life. The experiences of pregnancy, childbirth, and becoming a parent are thereby framed for both expectant parents as wonderful opportunities for learning and growing in awareness and wisdom in this time of change.

The process of creating a community of safety and connection begins as each expectant parent shares their name, where they live, when and where they expect to deliver, and one thing that has changed in their life since they or their partner became pregnant. This community aspect of MBCP is reinforced each week during the inquiry process and the snack break, a time for socializing and relationship building among class participants. This is an essential element of the MBCP program.

The Raisin Meditation, followed by a formal Awareness of Breathing practice, are taught in Class 1. Awareness of Breathing is the home assignment for the week ahead.

Class 2: being in the body

Community connection deepens in Class 2, as participants share their experience of a guided reflection known as the "Stone in the Well", which poses the question "Why are you here?" In addition, expectant parents are asked to share something about their name, allowing for a brief sharing of personal and family history. Participants then practice a Body Scan, which in the MBCP program is guided from the head to the feet, in harmony with the downward movements of the baby through the pelvis and outward through the vagina.

It is important to note that throughout the MBCP course it is emphasized that mindfulness practice is about learning a life skill rather than about "natural childbirth" or any particular way of giving birth. In fact, there is an emphasis on not becoming attached to a particular way of giving birth, as the future is unknown and an attachment to a "birth plan" can easily become a recipe for immense self-judgment and suffering if reality does not match the imagined future. Mindfulness skills are offered as a way to support both the normal physiologic process of giving birth *and* skills for working with whatever may come to pass during the birth process itself.

Home practices include a Body Scan, Mindfulness of the Activities of Daily Living, and "Being with Baby", a mindfulness practice for expectant women to use the sensations of the movements of the baby she feels throughout her day as a way to come into the present moment.

Class 3: reframing childbirth pain

Fundamental to the MBCP program are the pain practices developed for working with the pain of childbirth. A foundational teaching is offered in Class 3, with a presentation using a white board to illustrate how labor is a moment-to-moment process of intense, intermittent sensations commonly called pain arising and passing that are interspersed with very real moments of calm and ease. In a synthesis learning to this point, it becomes abundantly clear to participants how the untrained mind caught in aversive reactivity regarding worries and fears of future pain and the attendant stress physiology of fight or flight, or becoming caught in the memory of past pain, is eminently unhelpful during childbirth itself. By learning to train the mind to work with unpleasant sensations in the present moment and fostering a decreased resistance to things as they are, participants can promote a mind and body that is in harmony with the normal physiological processes of childbirth. With this teaching, participants come to understand how, with mindfulness practice, it is possible to uncouple the physical sensations of contractions in the body from the suffering (thoughts and emotions) that arise in the mind. The result is a liberating and confidence building shift in perception regarding the process of childbirth itself.

The two diagrams in Figure 8.1 illustrate this teaching.

Home practice includes the Body Scan, a short Awareness of Breathing, Activities of Daily Living, and an Awareness of Pleasant Events Calendar.

Class 4: pain is in the body, suffering is in the mind

Class 4 includes a 30-minute yoga sequence that is appropriate for both the pregnant body and a partner's non-pregnant body and a series of mindfulness practices for being with physical pain. Using ice cubes as a way to simulate pain or unpleasant body sensations arising and passing, expectant women and their partners are given the opportunity to use present moment awareness while holding ice cubes for 60 seconds *and* continuing to be present for the 90 seconds of pleasant moments of ease and peace that are invariably present between labor contractions. This is a direct application of the shift in perception experienced in Class 3 and allows participants to understand *from their own direct experience* the difference between pain and suffering and reacting or responding to physical pain.

It is emphasized throughout the MBCP course that each person has a different mind, a different body, a different nervous system, and a different history in relation to physical pain and that that there is no one "right way" to be with physical pain, or one "right way" to give birth. What is offered is the possibility that each woman and her partner can find their own way, separately and together, to work with the arising and passing of intense physical sensations called pain during childbirth. The variety of pain coping practices offered in the MBCP are framed as "tools in a toolbox", tools that can be used during the labor process as needed. Experimentation and improvisation are encouraged.

Home practice includes alternating the yoga sequence with the Body Scan, formal pain practice, awareness of stressful events or "the contractions of life", continued Activities of Daily Living, Being with Baby practice, and keeping an Awareness of Unpleasant Events Calendar.

Mindfulness-Based Childbirth and Parenting 83

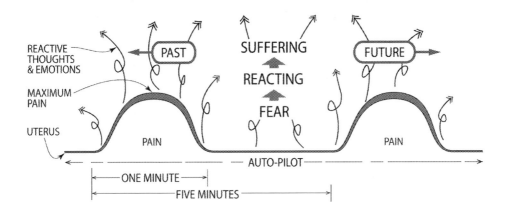

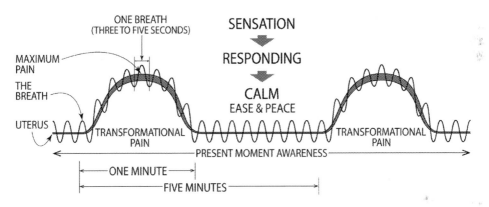

Figure 8.1 Teachings from *Mindful Birthing: Training the Mind, Body and Heart for Childbirth and Beyond* by Nancy Bardacke, CNM.

Source: Copyright © 2012 by Nancy Bardacke. Image copyright © 2012 by Logan Granger. Courtesy of HarperCollins Publishers.

A pain practice for the reader

Preparation

Gather together the following items: a large bowl half-filled with ice cubes, a hand towel, and a timer or stop watch. Though the practice described here can be done on one's own, it can be quite helpful to have someone time the "contractions" for you.

The practice

When you are ready, set the timer for one minute and pick up a handful of ice.

As you hold the ice in your hand for 60 seconds, allow yourself to strongly resist the sensations. Complain loudly about how much your hand hurts, how the pain is moving up your arm, how much you don't like the experience, perhaps asking aloud in a tone of distress "when will this be over?" Let out sounds of pain and resistance, such as cries of "owww!!" or "noooo!" or "I don't like this!" or "When will this be over?" When the timer signals 60 seconds, put down the ice. Dry and comfort your hand.

This is an experience of ordinary mind as it reacts to and resists painful or unpleasant sensations in the body.

Now setting the timer once again for one minute, pick up a handful of ice as before, in the other hand. This time the instruction is to bring your absolute and complete attention to the breath, paying attention to the breath as if your life depended on it. Maintaining the focus on the breath . . . being with the breath. And each time the mind wanders, as it most likely will do, returning the attention to the breath.

When the timer indicates that a minute has passed, put down the ice and *return the attention to the breath* for 90 seconds. *It is as important to come back to the breath during this time of ease as it is to focus on the breath during the times when sensations are present.*

Being with the breath during the "ice contractions" is the most basic of the pain practices. Many participants are quite surprised by their perception that the first experience of resisting the ice seemed much longer than the second experience, when the breath is used as an anchor to the present moment. Of course the point is that though nothing has changed in relation to the time spent holding the ice, as both experiences were 60 seconds in duration, the *choice* about where to focus the mind changed.

Following this initial experience, you are now encouraged to experiment with a variety of ways to work with unpleasant sensations while holding ice in your hand for 60 seconds and being with the breath for the moments of ease between the sensations for 90 seconds. This entire practice series takes approximately 15 minutes.

Once again, set the timer for 60 seconds.

Now, picking up the ice, allow the attention to move directly to the sensations in the hand. Notice, with an attitude of curiosity, where the sensations are most intense; where the sensations are least intense. Notice the edges of the sensations . . . and perhaps the drops of water from the ice as it melts from the warmth of your hand.

When the timer sounds at 60 seconds, set the ice down, set the timer for 90 seconds, and return the attention to the breath. Stay with the breath for 90 seconds . . . remembering, as best you can, to return the attention to the breath, with gentleness and kindness, whenever the mind wanders.

When the timer sounds at 90 seconds, set the timer once again for 60 seconds and pick up the ice.

This time, you are invited to experiment with counting the breaths . . . counting one on the in-breath, two on the out-breath, three on the in-breath, four on the out-breath, and so on. If you get lost or confused, just start over, counting the breaths from the number one again.

When the timer sounds at 60 seconds, put down the ice and once again set the timer to 90 seconds . . . allowing the attention to be with the breath for these moments . . . the sensations of breathing . . . right here, right now.

When the timer sounds at 90 seconds, set the timer again to 60 seconds and pick up the ice.

Now expand your awareness to the body as a whole . . . noticing that there are many areas of the body that are not in pain, areas that in fact are quite comfortable. Noticing perhaps the left foot, sensations of contact or pressure on the left foot. Or noticing the right leg . . . noticing that as you hold the body as a whole in awareness, there is only one part of the body, the hand, with intense sensations.

When the timer sounds at 60 seconds, once again put down the ice, and set the timer to 90 seconds ... bringing attention to the breath ... the sensations of breathing ... right here, in this very moment.

And when the timer sounds at 90 seconds, set the timer again to 60 seconds, and pick up some ice. This time, bring attention to the corners of the mouth ... allowing the corners of the mouth to turn up ever so slightly ... and each time the mind wanders away from the corners of the mouth, bringing the attention back to the slight tension in the muscles at the corners of the mouth. Notice what this does to the mind.

And when the timer sounds at 60 seconds, once again, put down the ice, setting the timer for 90 seconds, and come back to the breath ... letting the sensations of breathing be an anchor to the present moment.

When the timer sounds at 90 seconds, sett the timer again to 60 seconds, and pick up the ice. This time, allow an image of a baby to arise in the mind's eye. This is an imaginary baby. See if you can explore this baby in the mind's eye ... noticing the baby's hair ... is it curly or straight? Light or dark? Notice the baby's soft pink cheeks, tiny fingers ... the little toes ... the curve of the belly, the buttocks.

When the timer sounds at 60 seconds, put down the ice and once again set the timer for 90 seconds ... coming back to the breath ... the sensations of breathing ... right here, right now.

And when the timer sounds at 90 seconds, gently open the eyes. Allowing light to enter into your eyes, notice how you feel ... perhaps calm ... or at ease ... whatever is present for you, right in this very moment.

****

These are some of the ways offered in MBCP to mindfully work with childbirth pain. When participants are asked to briefly respond to the question "How is your labor going?" the most common responses are "manageable", "I can do this", "surprising", "peaceful", "interesting", "empowering", and "okay".

What words would you use to describe your experience of intermittently holding ice cubes as you mindfully worked with unpleasant sensations in your hands arising and passing, as well as being with moments of ease and peace when you had put down the ice cubes?

Class 5: more mindfulness practices for being with pain

Class 5 begins with sitting meditation. Following inquiry, the MBCP instructor demonstrates the mechanisms of labor using life-size models of a baby and pelvis. Positions for labor and birth are also demonstrated and a description of how mindful pooping can be a way to prepare for pushing or the second stage of labor is described. A Three-Step Breathing Space practice is also taught.

The remainder of the class is devoted once again to pain practice, adding the modality of touch between partners while holding ice. With the intention of cultivating compassion through direct experience, as well as teaching the universal life skill of working with physical pain, partners also have a turn being touched while intermittently holding ice.

Home practice includes continuing to alternate the yoga sequence with the Body Scan, practicing an ice-pain sequence, "being with" moments of reactivity in daily life, and continuing the practices assigned in previous weeks.

Class 6: causes and conditions, navigating what is

Class 6 begins with sitting meditation, followed by a teaching on Causes and Conditions. The demystification of the notion of control – both in childbirth and in life – reinforces the truth that life is indeed uncertain and unpredictable, and that the process of childbirth can be an opportunity to understand this truth on a deep level, growing in wisdom and compassion for oneself and others. Through this teaching, participants begin to see that while there are a great many factors in the birth process that cannot be controlled, they are not passive recipients of conditions but an integral part of the causes and conditions arising in any moment. Rather than trying to control external conditions, which is impossible, participants are encouraged to see that the real locus of "control" is *internal* – that "control" resides in the attitudes they have been cultivating in mindfulness practice toward whatever is happening in the present moment. In this way, participants come to a deeper understanding of how to be with things as they are and that awareness is big enough to hold anything and everything.

During pain practice in Class 6, participants are encouraged to experiment with still more options for working with pain, such as open-throated vowel sounds, gentle rocking, and various positions such as standing or child's pose while having one or both hands fully immersed in ice water. With this increase in intensity of unpleasant physical sensations participants often come to understand that they have an inner strength that can be drawn upon that perhaps may have never been understood or used before now.

The home practice assignments for this week are sitting meditation, pain practice, and informal practices.

A day of silence: going deeper

A day of silent practice occurs on the weekend between Classes 6 and 7. All the formal meditations offered to date are practiced. Walking meditation is taught, and practiced, along with a suggestion to use this practice during early labor or when comforting a fussing or crying baby. In addition, couples are guided through a Speaking and Listening practice on fear and joy. Using the form of a repeated request, couples have an opportunity to step out of ordinary "conversational", reactive speech and be more deeply present for each other as each shares anticipated fears and joys regarding the upcoming labor, birth, and their life together as new parents. This practice is often cited as one of the highlights of the MBCP course.

Classes 7, 8, and 9: life after birth

Class 7 shifts from focusing on preparing for childbirth to preparing for living life mindfully as parents of a newborn. Loving-kindness practice is introduced and participants are encouraged to begin the practice by first directing the phrases of Loving-kindness to the baby within. This practice of well-wishing for the baby often becomes a core practice for participants for the remainder of the course and continues well into parenting.

A teaching on the biological, social, and emotional needs of the newborn are encapsulated in a teaching on the moment-to-moment repeated sleep/hunger/feeding/wake cycles that make up the moments of daily life with an infant. There is encouragement to see their baby as their "mindfulness teacher", and suggestions for how to continue mindfulness practice in the postpartum period are offered – such as feeding, diaper changing, and bathing the baby mindfully. Their social and emotional needs as newly birthed parents are reviewed and participants are encouraged to begin thinking about who they can turn to for the physical and emotional support they will need as "baby parents". This class also covers symptoms of postpartum depression in both new mothers and fathers and how to get help if needed.

Home practice assignments include alternating sitting meditation with either yoga or the Body Scan, incorporating Loving-kindness into their practice, a mindful Speaking and Listening Practice about the ways they were parented, and previous informal mindfulness practice assignments.

Class 8 begins with a substantial period of formal practice followed by a teaching on the normal physiology of breastfeeding and how mindfulness practice supports that physiology, just as it supports the normal physiology of childbirth. It is acknowledged that breastfeeding is a substantial topic and that the focus of this class is to outline the optimal conditions for beginning the breastfeeding relationship in the early days after birth. Participants are encouraged to begin reading a book about breastfeeding and to take a short class on breastfeeding if they are particularly curious or concerned about breastfeeding. The teaching emphasizes the importance of knowing how to contact a lactation consultant or a breastfeeding clinic before giving birth so that information is available should the need arise.

In preparation for the course ending, there is a conversation about whether participants would like to set up an online group or email list to facilitate their continued connection.

For home practice, participants are encouraged to experiment with practicing without the guided meditations, practicing whichever meditation most supports their learning, and continuing their informal practice.

In Class 9, after a formal sitting practice, two couples from a previous MBCP course share how they used their mindfulness practice for birthing and how they are continuing to use their practice as new parents. While the birthing and postpartum experiences described may be quite variable, all describe how mindfulness practice was incredibly helpful for working with whatever arose during childbirth and for living now in their new life.

After a snack break, participants gather in a circle one last time before their babies are born. A closing or "graduation ceremony" is facilitated during which key learning points regarding mindfulness practice and its application to childbirth and parenting are reviewed. After another "Stone in the Well" guided reflection, participants share something of what they learned in the MBCP course and what they are taking with them for the days, weeks, months, and years ahead.

MBCP reunion

The bonds of friendship formed between expectant parents during the MBCP course can be quite strong, with some classes having maintained their connections for a decade or longer. The result is that there is a particular kind of excitement that is brought to the Reunion gathering; participants are happy to be together again. After a brief awareness of breathing, parents introduce their new babies, identify their particular joys and challenges of early parenting, and offer appreciation of oneself and one's partner.

A guided reflection regarding what was learned in the process of giving birth or by being with their partner as their partner gave birth is followed by deep and often deeply moving sharing. Interwoven throughout the gathering are descriptions about the use of formal and informal mindfulness practice in parenting with an emphasis on Loving-kindness and compassion for self and others. The MBCP instructor is sensitive to potential or existing postpartum depression or post-traumatic stress syndrome in either parent and referrals are made as appropriate.

During the Reunion, the supportive connections and sense of community that formed during the nine-week course are enlivened and participants often make plans to meet again to nurture and learn from each other as they grow into parenthood.

The evidence for MBCP

In 2008, we recruited participants who had already enrolled (self-selected) in an MBCP course into an observational research study (Duncan & Bardacke, 2010). We asked them to complete self-report questionnaires at the beginning of MBCP (the "pre-test"), at the end of the nine-week course (the "post-test"), and again after giving birth. We also recorded the narrative stories they shared at the post-birth reunion, which added additional qualitative data to our initial investigation on the impact of MBCP. We learned that in the San Francisco Bay Area, parents choosing this form of childbirth education and able to access it were predominantly white (88%) and highly educated (over 50% with a graduate degree), with above area median income, and high rates of prior experience with meditation or yoga (over 90%). They were also somewhat older (mean age 34.61; SD = 4.22) than usual first-time parents, about a third had experienced a prior pregnancy loss, one-fifth reported a medical problem during the current pregnancy, and 70% had experienced a stressful life event (e.g., a move, job loss, death in the family) during the pregnancy. Analysis of quantitative measures showed that mothers who participated in MBCP experienced statistically significant reductions in pregnancy-related anxiety, depression symptoms, and negative affect, and increases in the frequency and intensity of positive affect and dispositional mindfulness (nonreactivity and nonjudging subscales of the Five Facet Mindfulness Questionnaire: FFMQ; Baer et al., 2008). Fathers/partners demonstrated a similar pattern of effects, but changes for them did not reach statistical significance in this small sample (n = 27 families). In coding the qualitative data, we uncovered several important themes that served as the foundation for our hypotheses in later studies.

Noting how many MBCP participants found a space of rest and ease between contractions during labor very helpful, we sought to better understand the impact of this training on labor-related pain and fear. With pilot funding, we were able to recruit a racially/ethnically and socioeconomically diverse community sample of first-time parents in the third trimester. Participants were randomly assigned to an intensive weekend workshop based on the skills taught in the nine-week MBCP program entitled the *Mind in Labor (MIL): Working with Pain in Childbirth* or an active comparison of traditional childbirth education (treatment as usual; TAU). TAU controls selected a childbirth course from a list of hospital and community-based childbirth education classes that we screened to ensure they did not contain an emphasis on mindfulness. In this study, named the Prenatal Education About Labor Stress (PEARLS) randomized controlled trial (RCT) (N=30) (Duncan et al., 2017), MIL participants reported a significant reduction in depression symptoms post-course that was maintained post-birth. In contrast, TAU participants experienced an increase in depression symptoms that continued to increase post-birth. This difference in depression symptom trajectory between groups was statistically significant, as was the increase in childbirth self-efficacy among the mindfulness participants. We also saw improvements in mindful body awareness as measured with the Multidimensional Assessment of Interoceptive Awareness (MAIA; Mehling et al., 2012), but not dispositional mindfulness as measured with the FFMQ (Baer et al., 2008), suggesting that the MIL weekend workshop impacts childbirth-specific and childbirth-relevant functioning, but that the longer MBCP course may be needed to establish a formal meditation practice that can impact general mindfulness in daily life. In addition, although both groups used epidurals at similarly high rates, the MIL participants were marginally less likely to use other forms of pain medication (i.e., opioid/narcotic analgesia) during labor. We have published these early postnatal (approximately six weeks post-birth, on average) results and are now analyzing follow-up data that carries into the second year of the child's life, as well as examining potential mechanisms of the effect on depressions symptoms.

To align with our intentions to offer MBCP skills in accessible and culturally relevant ways for communities of color, immigrant populations, and those suffering from poverty, we partnered with Sharon Rising, MSN, CNM, FACNM. Sharon is the developer of the CenteringPregnancy Model and founder of the Centering Healthcare Institute. CenteringPregnancy (CP) is a well-known, evidence-based model of group prenatal care that has been shown to reduce risk of preterm birth (Ickovics et al., 2007). Working with Sharon, we developed an enhanced CenteringPregnancy with Mindfulness Skills (CPMS; Bardacke & Duncan, 2016) course that draws on the mindfulness practices from Nancy's MBCP curriculum and Larissa's mindful parenting theory and curricula. We carried out a series of curriculum development and feasibility studies followed by a quasi-experimental trial of CP compared to CPMS with very low income, predominantly racial/ethnic minority women receiving care at the San Francisco General Hospital Outpatient Midwifery Service and the Homeless Prenatal Program.[1] We learned a great deal about our study participants' experiences of pregnancy, prenatal care, and birth (Liu et al., 2016) and found that CPMS was both feasible to deliver and acceptable to participants (Duncan et al., 2016). As of the time of this writing, we are analyzing the primary study outcomes.

In the future, our aim is to conduct full-scale RCTs of both the MIL weekend workshop and MBCP. While we expect MIL to influence obstetrical outcomes, we were unable to accurately assess this due to budget limitations and low participant numbers that meant the study was underpowered to detect statistically significant effects in the PEARLS pilot study. We anticipate that the full nine-week MBCP course delivered prenatally will prove beneficial for: a) reducing stress and enhancing parental physical and mental health and well-being during pregnancy, including decreased anxiety regarding the childbirth process itself; b) coping with the childbirth experience along parameters such as the use of pain medication, length of labor, and greater satisfaction with the birth experience regardless of outcome; c) supporting greater parental resilience during the lived experience of adjusting to the profound life change that comes with caring for a newborn in the postpartum period; d) supporting sensitive responsiveness in parent-child interactions in early life; and e) enhancing both the behavioral and neural development of children.

In our future work with CP and the CPMS innovation, we anticipate that mindfulness training may improve CP providers' skill in "facilitative leadership", a foundational component for that program's benefits in reducing the risk of preterm birth. To develop professional training for CPMS providers, who so often offer this model of care in communities of color at greater risk for adverse birth outcomes, we will seek consultation from people and organizations with expertise in this area who are themselves deeply skilled in bringing much-needed cultural relevance to the field of mindfulness (Watson, Black, & Hunter, 2016).

We are also partnering on MBCP clinical trials being conducted at the Chinese University of Hong Kong and the University of Amsterdam in the Netherlands (Veringa et al., 2016). These trials will begin to reveal the cross-cultural relevance of the MBCP program when delivered outside the United States.

Conclusion

Since the publication of *Mindful Birthing: Training the Mind, Body and Heart for Childbirth and Beyond* (Bardacke, 2012) and the recent PEARLS study results, interest in this way of preparing parents for childbirth has grown worldwide. Professionals from a wide variety of disciplines, who sense or recognize that more might be offered to expectant parents to prepare them for childbirth and parenting, are finding their way to the Mindful Birthing and Parenting Foundation's MBCP Teacher Training Program (www.mindfulbirthing.org). Though still early in the development of a full MBCP Certification Program, to date, MBCP Instructors from 16 countries are currently at various stages along the training pathway. Our original intention remains: to facilitate the dissemination the MBCP program with integrity to the model and to rigorously investigate how the MBCP program may benefit expectant parents and those yet to be born so that a transformative way to prepare for childbirth and beyond is available for generations to come.

For information regarding Mindfulness-Based Childbirth and Parenting (MBCP), **see www.mindfulbirthing.org.**

Note

1 This study was made possible in part by a K01 Career Development Award to Larissa Duncan from the National Institutes of Health/National Center for Complementary and Integrative Health (Duncan K01 AT005270) and funding from the Mt. Zion Health Fund administered by UCSF Medical Center.

References

Baer, R. A., Smith, G. T., Lykins, E., Button, D., Krietemeyer, J., Sauer, S., Walsh, E., Duggan, D., & Williams, J. M. G. (2008). Construct validity of the five facet mindfulness questionnaire in meditating and nonmeditating samples. *Assessment, 15*(3), 329–342.

Bardacke, N. (2012). *Mindful Birthing: Training the Mind, Body, and Heart for Childbirth and Beyond*. New York, NY: HarperCollins.

Bardacke, N., & Duncan, L. G. (2016). CenteringPregnancy with mindfulness skills: Enhancing the thread of presence. In S. S. Rising & C. Quimby (eds.), *The CenteringPregnancy® Model: The Power of Group Health Care*. New York, NY: Springer Publishing Co.

Coatsworth, J. D., Duncan, L. G., Greenberg, M. T., & Nix, R. L. (2010). Changing parents' mindfulness, child management skills and relationship quality with their youth: Results from a randomized pilot intervention trial. *Journal of Child and Family Studies, 19*, 203–217.

Duncan, L. G., & Bardacke, N. (2010). Mindfulness-based childbirth and parenting education: Promoting family mindfulness in the perinatal period. *Journal of Child and Family Studies, 19*, 190–202.

Duncan, L. G., Coatsworth, J. D., & Greenberg, M. T. (2009a). A model of mindful parenting: Implications for parent – child relationships and prevention research. *Clinical Child and Family Psychology Review, 12*(3), 255–270.

Duncan, L. G., Coatsworth, J. D., & Greenberg, M. T. (2009b). Pilot study to gauge acceptability of a mindfulness-based, family-focused preventive intervention. *Journal of Primary Prevention, 30*, 605–618.

Duncan, L. G., Cohn, M. A., Chao, M. T., Cook, J. G., Riccobono, J., & Bardacke, N. (2017). Benefits of preparing for childbirth with mindfulness training: A randomized controlled trial with active comparison. *BMC Pregnancy & Childbirth, 17*(1), 140.

Duncan, L. G., Cook, J. G., Santana, T., Castro-Smyth, L., Hutchison, M., Jurkiewicz, L., Mallareddy, D., Rising, S. S., & Bardacke, N. (2016, June). *Prenatal Mindfulness Training as Primary Prevention of Maternal Anxiety: Reaching Underserved Pregnant Women Through CenteringPregnancy with Mindfulness Skills Group Medical Visits*. Paper presented at the 24th annual meeting of the Society for Prevention Research, San Francisco, CA.

Folkman, S. (1997). Positive psychological states and coping with severe stress. *Social Science & Medicine, 45*(8), 1207–1221.

Fredrickson, B. L. (1998). What good are positive emotions? *Review of General Psychology, 2*, 300–319.

Ickovics, J. R., Kershaw, T. S., Westdahl, C., Magriples, U., Massey, Z., Reynolds, H., & Rising, S. S. (2007). Group prenatal care and perinatal outcomes: A randomized controlled trial. *Obstetrics and Gynecology, 110*(2 Pt 1), 330–339.

Kabat-Zinn, J. (2013). *Full Catastrophe Living, Revised Edition: How to Cope with Stress, Painand Illness Using Mindfulness Meditation*. New York, NY: Bantam.

Kramer, M. R., & Hogue, C. R. (2009). What causes racial disparities in very preterm birth? A biosocial perspective. *Epidemiologic Reviews, 31*(1), 84–98.

Lazarus, R. S., & Folkman, S. (1984). *Stress, Appraisal, and Coping*. New York, NY: Springer Publishing Co.

Liu, R., Chao, M. T., Jostad-Laswell, A., & Duncan, L. G. (2016). Does 'CenteringPregnancy' group prenatal care affect the birth experience of underserved women? A mixed methods analysis. *Journal of Immigrant and Minority Health, 19*(2), 415–422.

Mehling, W. E., Price, C., Daubenmier, J. J., Acree, M., Bartmess, E., & Stewart, A. (2012). The multidimensional assessment of interoceptive awareness (MAIA). *PLoS One, 7*(11), e48230.

Schore, A. N. (2001). Effects of a secure attachment relationship on right brain development, affect regulation, and infant mental health. *Infant Mental Health Journal, 22*, 7–66.

Veringa, I. K., de Bruin, E. I., Bardacke, N., Duncan, L. G., van Steensel, F. J. A., Dirksen, C. D., & Bögels, S. M. (2016). 'I've changed my mind', Mindfulness-Based Childbirth and Parenting (MBCP) for pregnant women with a high level of fear of childbirth and their partners: Study protocol of the quasi-experimental controlled trial. *BMC Psychiatry, 16*, 377.

Watson, N. N., Black, A. R., & Hunter, C. D. (2016). African American women's perceptions of mindfulness meditation training and gendered race-related stress. *Mindfulness*, 1–10.

Chapter 9

Coping with the stress of parenting
The mindful parenting program

Lisa-Marie Emerson and Susan Bögels

Our interests in mindful parenting originate from personal experiences: of being parented as a child; of parenting children while developing a career; of developing partner and co-parenting relationships; of post-divorce; and from working with parents in child and adult health care settings. We often wondered how life would have been different if our parents had participated in a mindful parenting course when they were suffering from parenting stress, and if I (SB) would have participated in a mindful parenting course when I needed it most. The first version of the mindful parenting course was developed in 2000 for youth with ADHD, autism, and/or oppositional-defiant and conduct disorder. I (SB) felt that at least one of their parents or other caregiver should be involved in the process by participating in their own parallel mindful parenting group course. Based on the transformations we witnessed in these first mindful parenting groups, the mindful parenting course has since been adapted to the needs of parents in multiple contexts (e.g. parents of younger children, babies; adoptive or foster parents; parents with their own mental and somatic disorders). Over the years, we continued to observe the profound changes in mothers' and fathers' parenting experiences and parenting behaviours, and in the relationship with their children and their partner and/or co-parent. While we continue to learn and grow on this path, this chapter gives an overview of where we are now.

The Mindful Parenting program (Bögels & Restifo, 2014) is an eight-week training course for parents, which applies the principles of mindfulness in the context of parenting stress. The course is designed for parents who are experiencing stress, due to the demands of parenting, which is having an adverse effect on their parenting and relationship with their child. The Mindful Parenting program aims to reduce the stress associated with parenting, by training parents in mindfulness and self-care practices. In addition, an open, nonjudgmental and accepting attitude toward their child, the parent-child interaction, and themselves as a parent is cultivated through the course. The course is based on the foundations set by Mindfulness-Based Stress Reduction (MBSR; Kabat-Zinn, 1990) and Mindfulness-Based Cognitive Therapy (MBCT; Segal, Williams, & Teasdale, 2002, 2012), with specific adaptations made for parents.

Theoretical context: parenting stress

The Mindful Parenting program was originally developed to address the heightened stress that parents of children with additional needs (e.g. mental health diagnoses; neurodevelopmental problems) can experience (Deater-Deckard, 1998). However, stress is also an inherent part of parenting for many individuals. Parents often have an idealised view of themselves as a parent, influenced by social norms, which can create an impossible standard and fails to acknowledge the ubiquitous nature of parenting stress. The comparison of the idealised parent-self with actual parent-self can create conflict and stress, as well as negative emotions, such as guilt and shame (Liss, Schiffrin, & Rizzo, 2013).

Siegal and Hartzell (2004) suggest that under stress parents revert to a survival response: fight, flight, freeze. This survival response takes a short route through the brain, bypassing the prefrontal cortex, which is the centre of wise decision-making and problem-solving, resulting in over-reactive parenting. These faster reactions to threat make evolutionary sense; in the case of acute danger, such as a child almost being attacked by a dangerous animal, they help preserve the life of the child and therefore the future of their genes. Modern society poses very different threats, which are less immediately life-threatening, but can trigger the same survival response in parents, often with negative effects on parenting behaviour. In the Mindful Parenting program, this concept of the survival response and the impact on parenting is explored in an experiential way with parents in the initial session (see Box 1: Morning stress exercise).

Increased parenting stress is known to adversely impact parenting behaviour and the parent-child relationship. Parents experiencing heightened stress show increased negative parenting behaviours (Leinonen, Solantaus, & Punamäki, 2003), and decreased positive parenting behaviours (Assel, Landry, Swank, Steelman, Miller-Loncar, & Smith, 2002). Increased parent and child difficulties can be explained by an increase in negative parenting behaviour (Leinonen, Solantaus, & Punamäki, 2003), thus a cycle of cause and effect may ensue.

The Mindful Parenting program aims to decrease parenting stress and increase levels of mindful parenting, which can benefit parenting behaviour and subsequently parent and child mental health (Bögels, Lehtonen, & Restifo, 2010). Increasing levels of mindful parenting allows parents to self-regulate their emotional and automatic reactions in the parenting context, which reduces reactivity (Smith & Dishion, 2013). Indeed, research has shown that parents who report higher levels of mindful parenting also report lower levels of parenting stress, less negative parenting behaviour and more adaptive parenting behaviour (Gouveia, Carona, Canavarro, & Moreira, 2016).

Becoming a parent involves a shift in priorities away from the self, and toward another. The protection and thus survival of the child becomes paramount for many parents. The reality of this change in priorities for parents is a reduction in self-nourishing. In the context of a child with additional difficulties, additional demands are placed on parenting, which contributes to this neglect of the self. Negative emotions toward the self, such as guilt and shame, can also be commonplace. Feelings of shame can lead to parents isolating themselves from other parents, resulting in reduced emotional and practical support. At best, parents may experience neglect in terms of self-nourishing, and at worst can become self-critical.

The Mindful Parenting program aims to provide parents with a way to nourish themselves, finding time for their own needs and setting limits in their relationship with their child and partner so that they can care for themselves. In addition, compassion elements within the program aim to cultivate self-kindness as an antidote to feelings of guilt and shame. The development of self-compassion is later used as a foundation from which to direct compassion toward the child and partner.

> **Box 9.1   Morning stress exercise**
>
> All participants are asked to sit comfortably, close their eyes, and imagine the following situation as if it were happening to them now:
>
> > *It's 8.20am. The children have to be at school at 8.30am. You've already received a warning from the principal that your daughter has been late too often. Your daughter is taking her time, doing her hair and changing her clothes again. "Come on now, hurry up or we'll be late", you say, several times, but she doesn't come down from her room. You walk into your child's room, urging her to come, but she throws herself on the floor screaming: "I'm not going to school!"*
>
> Participants are then asked to open their eyes.
>   On a flipchart, the facilitator then writes the following:
>
> > *Sensations   Emotions   Thoughts   Action tendencies*
>
> The facilitator asks for contributions from the group about what they noticed, starting with body sensations. Initial emphasis on body sensations helps parents to learn to ground themselves in the here and now through the body. The facilitator moves on through emotions and thoughts, noting the distinction between these. Finally, parents' initial reactions are discussed, their action tendencies, not necessarily what they would do, but their first impulse. In this way, it is important to allow openness to discuss all action tendencies without judgment, acknowledging that as parents sometimes we do things we don't intend to.
>   The facilitator goes on to explain how these responses relate to the survival response. The first column is the physical manifestation of stress. The responses in the final column can usually be divided into fight, flight, freeze reactions: our automatic reactions to stress. We can step out of this automatic reaction by becoming aware of our bodily sensations. This allows us to use the longer route in the brain, which engages the prefrontal cortex to help with problem-solving and decision-making.

The Mindful Parenting program

Structure

The Mindful Parenting program follows a similar structure to the MBSR and MBCT programs, with eight weekly group sessions, followed by a ninth follow-up session (see Table 9.1 for an overview). The course is delivered in a group context, with group size ranging from eight to sixteen parents, who attend as singles or couples. Each weekly session is approximately three hours long, with a mid-point 15-minute tea break scheduled. The beginning of each session follows a similar structure: an initial experiential mindfulness practice precedes a review of home practice. From the second session onwards, home practice is discussed in pairs toward the beginning of each session. A group discussion may follow paired discussions to draw out

Table 9.1 Overview of the 8-week Mindful Parenting program

Week	Title	Themes	Core and unique elements	Home practices
1	Automatic pilot parenting	Aims of course Automatic pilot parenting Experience of mindfulness	• *Mindful eating – raisin* • Course rationale: morning stress • *Bodyscan*	• Bodyscan • Child as raisin • Mindful routine activity • Mindful first bite
2	Beginner's mind parenting	Beginner's mind parenting Self-kindness in parenting	• *Bodyscan* • Observation of your child • Morning exercise – a friend's perspective • *Mindful seeing* • Gorilla video • *Gratitude practice* • *Breathing meditation*	• Bodyscan • Sitting meditation: breath • Mindful routine activity
3	Reconnecting with our body as a parent	Awareness of body in parenting	• *Breath and body* • *three-minute breathing space* • *Yoga (lying down)* • Observing the body during parenting • *Self-kindness*	• Yoga (lying) • Sitting meditation: breath and body • *three-minute breathing space* • Mindful activity with child
4	Responding versus reacting to parenting stress	Automatic reactions to parenting stress	• *Breathing meditation: Sounds and thoughts* • *three-minute breathing space under stress* • *Imagination: Awareness and acceptance* • Standing yoga	• Yoga (standing) • Sitting meditation: breath, body and thoughts • *three-minute breathing* • Autobiography
5	Parenting patterns and schemas	Experiences of parenting and being parented Self-compassion	• *Breathing meditation: emotions* • Reactive parenting and schema modes • 3min breathing space • *Walking meditation* • Imagination: holding your emotions	• Sitting meditation: breath, body, sounds, and thoughts and emotions • Walking meditation • *three-minute breathing space* • Parenting stress calendar + schema mode recognition
6	Conflict and parenting	Rupture and repair with compassion	• *Choiceless awareness* • *Walking meditation* • Perspective taking, repair	• Choice of 40-min practice • Rupture and repair • Breathing space • Mindfulness day

(Continued)

Table 9.1 Continued

Week	Title	Themes	Core and unique elements	Home practices
7	Love and limits	Compassion Setting limits as "ruthless compassion"	• *Loving-kindness meditation* • *Imagination: Limits* • Role play: Limits	• Choice of 40min practice • Mindful limit setting • Loving-kindness
8	A mindful path through parenting	Reflections on the journey thus far	• *Bodyscan* • Gratitude practice • *Meditation on learning* • Setting intentions for next 8weeks • Reflection on process • *Loving-kindness meditation*	• Choice of practice

core themes from home practice or for the current session. The main body of each weekly session includes experiential practices, such as formal meditations and imagination exercises. Toward the end of each weekly session, the home practice for the upcoming week is discussed. Most sessions are closed with a further brief experiential practice, poem or story. In this way the group sessions are bookended with mindfulness experiences.

The mid-point tea break is a key part of the session structure; it provides an opportunity for parents to connect with one another, exchange information and experiences. We provide tea and biscuits for this break, and an invitation to drink and eat mindfully. Within the context of freely accessible health services, the provision of sustenance is our opportunity as facilitators to show an act of kindness and caring for the parents attending the group. This kindness also serves as an acknowledgement for their "showing up", physically and emotionally, to the course.

The follow-up session is scheduled for eight weeks after the end of the main course with two main functions. First, having a follow-up session acts as a reminder regarding parents' intentions to maintain their own mindfulness practice, which they can practice for a period as long as the period of the course. Secondly, the follow-up session is a booster for the skills and attitude cultivated through the course. It is an opportunity to revisit some of the mindfulness practices learned during the eight-week course, and to discuss ongoing challenges and benefits in sustaining a mindfulness practice.

Content

The content of the Mindful Parenting program focuses on core themes that relate mindfulness to parenting. These themes are developed progressively over the eight-week course, and explored through experiential practice (meditations, imagination exercises), discussion, and demonstrations. In the first half of the course, core themes of mindfulness (e.g. automatic pilot) are utilised from the standard MBSR and MBCT programs, and set as a foundation to understanding key concepts. These themes are applied specifically to the task of parenting, through examples and practices. Core meditation practices are applied in a progressive manner over the eight-week duration of the course, and linked to the role of parenting. In the latter half of the course, unique themes of mindful parenting are developed, with the aim of increasing awareness of parenting stress, and the impact this has on parenting. The foundation of mindfulness developed earlier in the course serves as a springboard to exploring more challenging aspects of parenting, such as conflict and setting limits, and how mindfulness can help. A series of imagination exercises and compassion practices allows parents to explore these mindful parenting elements.

We discuss the themes of the Mindful Parenting program below, including a description of the key practices referred to. Each of the practices are adapted from Bögels and Restifo (2014), which can be referred to for a complete description of the Mindful Parenting program.

Core mindfulness themes and practices

The theme of automatic pilot parenting is introduced in session 1 of the Mindful Parenting program. Discussion of the morning stress exercise (Box 1) is related to the idea that we all experience times of heightened parenting stress, and at these times the tendency can be to parent in an automatic manner, through habit or routine. The idea of automatic pilot is then expanded to include times when we engage in routine activities with little awareness of what we're doing: driving to work, or school, brushing our teeth, washing the dishes. This idea is applied specifically to parenting, and the many tasks or activities that are routine and automatic. The concepts of "being" and "doing" modes are drawn out through examples of these activities, and the suggestion that they could be carried out in being mode with little sacrifice on time and potential benefits to the parent-child relationship. Awareness of body and breath is cultivated through the bodyscan, mindfulness of breath, and breath and body meditations. Mindful eating is introduced in the first session to compliment the theme of automatic pilot parenting. The standard practice of eating a raisin is then applied to parenting through home practice of observing the child as a raisin. Within this practice, the same principles of beginner's mind experienced through mindful eating are applied to the practice of observing the child as though for the first time, without judgment and preconceptions.

In session 2, the theme of beginner's mind parenting is explored. Parents will have experienced observing their child through the home practice (child as raisin); the discussion of their experiences is used to introduce the idea of beginner's mind parenting. We discuss what parents noticed about their child and their experience, highlighting instances of expanding awareness. Often problem behaviour or a particular label or diagnosis has coloured parents' experiences of their child, and may have created a bias toward that problem so that awareness of the child's other qualities is reduced. Through beginner's mind parenting, we aim to become aware how previous experiences with our child can colour our interpretation of current experiences, and to practice expanding awareness to see the whole child.

The theme of beginner's mind is supported by the practice of mindful seeing, and complimented by showing the invisible gorilla video (www.youtube.com/watch?v=vJG698U2Mvo). In this short film, viewers are invited to watch a basketball game during which a person in a gorilla costume wanders through. Many people miss seeing the gorilla because it is unexpected. We link this experience back to the effect of labelling, bias and judgment in parenting.

Throughout the eight-week course, and highlighted in session 3, is the theme of reconnecting with the body. We explore the idea that our bodies are our best way to connect with the present moment, and to return to being mode. Reconnecting with the body is a way of tuning into our own experience, and begin to understand our limits so that we may take better care of ourselves. Formal meditation practices are taught from the beginning of the course to help parents connect with the breath and body (e.g. bodyscan, mindfulness of breathing). From session 3 onwards, mindful movement practices (e.g. yoga and mindful walking) are also used to cultivate an attitude of acceptance and understand our limits. Parents learn to return to the body in stressful interactions with their child or partner in order to ground themselves in the present moment, and create a pause before reacting. Parents are invited to inhabit their body through pleasant and challenging parenting situations.

We focus on the core theme of responding versus reacting in relation to parenting in session 4. The idea of the survival response (fight, flight, freeze) is revisited to highlight our tendency to react to stressful parenting situations in a habitual manner, our automatic reactions to parenting stress. We develop this idea further by looking at the contribution of our thoughts to our experience of parenting stress, which often serve to compound the problem. Formal meditation of sounds and thoughts increases awareness of the activity of the mind in labelling and judging experiences. We explore how mindfulness can create the possibility for alternatives to our habitual reactions in parenting situations. Mindfulness creates the space needed to see new possibilities. The three-minute breathing space is introduced as a way to connect with the present moment during stressful parenting situations, and create the pause that allows us to observe and respond. Nonreactivity to thoughts and feelings is considered a key component in allowing us to engage in responding rather than reacting.

Self-kindness is a theme that runs throughout the eight-week course. We begin by creating awareness of our critical thoughts as parents (of ourselves and our child), and the tendency to respond with kindness to a friend but not ourselves. Formal self-compassion practices are utilised from session 3 onwards to practice directing kindness to the self, particularly at times of parenting stress. The practice of self-compassion culminates toward the end of the course with the practice of loving-kindness. The embodiment of nonjudgment and acceptance in the facilitator is an essential part of conveying kindness and models the attitude that we hope parents can cultivate toward themselves. The idea of self-compassion is built upon further through the experience of self-compassion in relation to parenting stress: an in-session meditation practice (see Box 9.2).

Box 9.2 Self-compassion during parenting stress

Sitting comfortably, letting your eyes close. Imagine, as vividly as possible, a difficult or stressful parenting interaction which you feel did not go well. Who is there, what are they saying or doing, what are you saying or doing? (*The facilitator asks those who don't have a situation yet to raise their hands, and if there are any hands raised then allows a few moments more*). When you have a clear picture, bringing your attention to this moment, checking in: how are you right now? Noticing whatever comes up. Are there bodily sensations? Emotions? Thoughts? Tension? Say to yourself: whatever it is I am feeling, it is ok, let me feel it. Just notice whatever comes up . . . are there critical or judgmental thoughts? Feelings of sadness? Anger? Guilt? Tension in the body? (*Allow a couple of minutes.*)

> And now, see if you can bring an attitude of kindness and compassion for yourself, the way you would toward a friend. Recognise this is a moment of suffering for you. Comfort yourself, for example, by saying to yourself "this is really hard" or "you try so hard to be a good parent, but sometimes it's so hard". If you like, experiment with comforting yourself physically by placing both hands over your heart, feeling the warmth of your hands on your chest (*allow a few moments*). Or hug yourself by placing your arms around your shoulders (*allow a few moments*). Or try stroking yourself wherever it feels comfortable for you, arms, face. . . .
>
> And now, can you remind yourself that all parents struggle, make mistakes, or feel that they have failed their children at times? Perhaps remember other parents who struggle or regret things that they've done. Remind yourself that making mistakes is part of being human, and connects us with all other parents who struggle to do their best and yet make mistakes along the way.

Unique themes and practices

Parenting patterns and schemas are explored in session 5: we aim to develop insight into the way our childhood experiences of being parented affect our parenting, and particularly our parental overreactivity. Parents investigate examples of reactive parenting patterns with their child and look for parallels with how they have been parented. They learn to recognise their own angry and vulnerable inner child modes and their own punitive or demanding internalised parent states, which may arise during emotionally intense interactions with their child. Parents are invited to bring self-compassion and acceptance to their child modes when these difficult emotional states are triggered.

Mindfulness is related to the theme of conflict and parenting in session 6, with the aim of exploring the process of repairing the parent-child relationship following rupture. Conflict is a common part of family life; negative emotions that arise can be barriers to reconciliation. As parents we tend to avoid the repair process following conflict with our child. This avoidance may be driven by our own guilt or shame, or harbouring of negative emotions toward our child. The process of repair is key to maintaining the parent-child relationship, as is for parents to be perceived as a "safe base". When parents take the lead in the repair process, they are also modelling to the child how loved ones can experience conflict and resolve those difficulties. Parents are taught to use mindfulness and self-compassion to create a pause during or after conflict, in order to reconnect with their body, reflect on what has been triggered in them (schema modes), and take the perspective of their child. This perspective taking is an essential part of repair, and is practiced in-session and at home through the rupture and repair exercise imagination exercise (see Box 9.3).

Toward the end of the course, compassion becomes one part of a central theme of the Mindful Parenting program: love and limits. Self-compassion is visited by the formal introduction of the loving-kindness meditation, which is a springboard to explore our own blocks to directing kindness toward the self, such as negative feelings (e.g. unworthiness and shame). From a foundation of mindfulness and self-compassion, parents become aware of their own limits, recognising these within their bodies. From this inside-out perspective, parents approach the task of limit-setting for their child. Through imagination and role play

> **Box 9.3 Rupture and repair imagination exercise**
>
> Adopting a comfortable sitting posture, and directing your attention to how your body feels, notice where the body makes contact with the chair, cushion, and ground. Let a situation in which you were very angry with your child and in which you were not happy about your own behaviour, for example, because you exploded or felt out of control, come to mind. Imagine the conflict as vividly as you can, as if it were happening to you right now. Who were you with? What were you doing/saying? What was the other person doing/saying? What were you feeling? What did you notice in your body? What thoughts ran through your mind? What action tendencies did you notice?
>
> When you have a vivid image of the conflict situation, shift your attention to the here and now. What bodily sensations, feelings, thoughts are you aware of, right now? Can you be compassionate toward yourself? Say to yourself, "whatever I feel, it is ok, let me feel it", welcoming any emotion coming up, whether it is fear, sadness, anger, pain.
>
> Then bring your attention to your breath, the movement of the breath in the body . . . following three breaths with full awareness . . . widening the attention to your body as a whole, in this sitting position . . . becoming aware of any tension.
>
> And then, when you are ready, on the next outbreath, shifting your attention as best you can to your child. How are they feeling? What emotions may they experience? What bodily sensations? Thoughts? Action tendencies? Desires? Can you allow yourself to feel what you are feeling, and to allow the other person to feel what he or she is feeling? Can you allow him or her to feel angry . . . sad . . . hurt . . . afraid? Can you tell him or her that whatever it is they are feeling it is ok?
>
> Can you understand your child from their perspective? Can you feel compassion toward them in the now?
>
> What would you want to say to your child from this position of understanding and compassion? Could you let go of your pride and – really from yourself – apologize for what you did wrong?

exercises (see Box 9.4 for example), parents decide on limits from a sense of their own values and what they would like to teach their child. Limit-setting serves two functions in mindful parenting: it provides necessary structure for the child, and addresses parents' tendency to neglect their own needs.

Home practice

As with MBSR and MBCT, home practice is a core part of the Mindful Parenting program. Each week, parents are directed to engage in regular experiential practice between sessions, as well as additional exercises relating to parenting. The home practice element enables parents to develop a regular formal mindfulness practice home, and find a means to integrate mindfulness into the task of parenting. Formal meditations include core practices, such as bodyscan, as well as parenting-specific practices, such as the child as raisin. Informal practice of daily mindfulness is encouraged through home practice that involves a choice of activity

Box 9.4 Limits imagination exercise

Call to mind an interaction with your child which was difficult, and where you felt your limits were crossed, or a particular behaviour of your child which you feel you need to set more effective limits on (such as temper tantrums, hitting, or not cleaning up). Seeing if you can imagine it as vividly as possible: who is there? What is happening? Who is saying or doing what?

Now, see if you can remember how your body felt, your feelings and thoughts, what you felt like saying or doing. Did you notice a mindstate? Such as anger, sadness or fear? Were you aware of a childlike part of yourself that was triggered by this interaction? Angry or vulnerable child? Punitive or demanding parent? Notice also what you are experiencing now. What is coming up for you in your body? Your thoughts? And your feelings? What action tendencies can you notice?

And now, letting go of the situation, and taking a three-minute breathing space (*facilitator guides a three-minute breathing space*), see if you can direct self-compassion toward your own suffering. You can imagine saying kind words to yourself, putting both hands on your heart, or stroking yourself, giving yourself a hug, or simply feeling compassion for yourself as a parent. If you feel the presence of your vulnerable or angry child, you can comfort him or her.

Did you recognise your own limits before or after your child went over them? What is it like for you when you try to set a limit? What would you avoid by not setting a limit? What do you want to do now?

Now, open your eyes. Discuss in pairs or trios what you experienced.

to practice bringing mindful awareness to; this activity progresses through the course to an activity with their child. Parents are also encouraged to continue cultivating self-care and compassion through home practice of in-session exercises, such as limit-setting, and rupture and repair. Home practice is reviewed within group sessions; sharing experiences in this manner becomes an integral part of learning about mindfulness in the context of parenting.

Research and future developments

The effectiveness of the Mindful Parenting program has been assessed in a number of published and ongoing empirical studies. Two published studies have been conducted at the University of Amsterdam; a summary of these can be found in Table 9.2. In both studies, parents participated in the Mindful Parenting program and completed self-report measures before and after the group, and at a two-month follow-up. The findings demonstrate that mindful parenting effectively achieves the goal of reducing parenting stress, as parents reported a reduction in stress from before to after the group. Parent and child psychopathology also improved across both studies. All main effects were maintained at follow-up, demonstrating potential sustained effects of the mindful parenting program beyond participating in the course.

In study 2, the mechanism underlying improved parent and child psychopathology was also investigated. The results showed specificity of the effects, such that improvements in

Table 9.2 Overview of research assessing the effectiveness of the eight-week Mindful Parenting Program

	Study 1 – Bögels et al. (2010)	Study 2 – Meppelink et al. (2016)
Participants	86 parents across 10 groups	70 parents across 10 groups
Outcomes		
Parent	Parent psychopathology (Young Adult Self-report)	Parent psychopathology (Adult Self-report)
	Parenting stress (Parent Stress Index)	Mindfulness (Five Facet Mindfulness Questionnaire)
Parenting	Parenting (Rearing Behaviour Inventory; Co-parenting Scale)	Mindful Parenting (Interpersonal Mindfulness in Parenting)
Child	Child psychopathology (Child Behaviour Checklist)	Child psychopathology (Child Behaviour Checklist)
Main findings		
Parent	Improved psychopathology	Improved psychopathology
	Decreased internalising (medium effect size)	Decreased internalising (medium effect size)
	Decreased externalising (medium effect size)	Decreased externalising (small effect size)
	Decreased stress (medium effect size)	Increased mindful awareness (medium-large effect sizes)
Parenting	Improved parenting behaviour and practices (small-medium effect sizes)	Increased mindful parenting (medium-large effect sizes)
	Increased autonomy encouragement	
	Decreased overprotection	
	Decreased rejection	
Child	Improved psychopathology	Improved psychopathology
	Decreased internalising (medium effect size)	Decreased internalising (small effect size)
	Decreased externalising (small effect size)	Decreased externalising (small effect size)
		Decreased attention problems (small effect size)

Note:

Parent measures: Young Adult Self-report (Achenbach, 1997); Adult Self-report (Achenbach & Rescorla, 2003); Parent Stress Index (De Brock, Vermulst, Gerris, & Abidin, 1992); Five Facet Mindfulness Questionnaire (Baer, Smith, Hopkins, Krietemeyer, & Toney, 2006)

Parenting measures: Rearing Behaviour Inventory (Bögels & van Melick, 2004); Co-parenting Scale (McHale, 1997); Parenting Scale (Arnold, O'Leary, Wolff, & Acker, 1993); Interpersonal Mindfulness in Parenting (Duncan, Coatsworth, & Greenberg, 2009)

Child measures: Child Behaviour Checklist (Achenbach & Rescorla, 2001)

parents' general mindful awareness (but not mindful parenting) predicted change in parent psychopathology. Conversely, improvements in mindful parenting (but not general mindful awareness) predicted changes in child psychopathology.

Improvements in parenting behaviour and practices were also demonstrated in study 1, including a reduction in negative parenting behaviour (e.g. overprotection, rejection and overreactivity) known to contribute to child psychopathology, as well as increased positive parenting (e.g. autonomy granting). Study 2 confirmed that the Mindful Parenting program improved self-reported mindful parenting, which confirms that the program has the predicted specified effect.

Ongoing implementation and future directions

The Mindful Parenting program has been adapted to the mindful with your baby (mothers with babies from birth to 18 months) and mindful with your toddler training (mothers with toddlers aged 18 to 48 months), for mothers experiencing parenting stress. Both courses incorporate insights from the infant mental health (IMH) movement; the nine sessions are facilitated by a mindfulness trainer and an IMH-specialist. A number of the sessions are delivered in the presence of the babies (seven of nine) or toddlers (five of nine), with the aim of facilitating "on-the-job-training" and generalization of learning: to become aware of the mothers' own experience even while the baby/toddler is there, to focus a friendly, open attention on the baby/toddler and their signals, and to apply mindfulness in stressful situations. Preliminary research findings have demonstrated positive findings for both programs, including improvements in maternal mindfulness, mindful parenting, self-compassion, psychopathology, well-being, parenting stress, lack of confidence, warmth, responsivity and hostility toward the baby (Potharst, Aktar, Rexwinkel, Rigterink, & Bögels, 2017). Infants also seem to benefit from the intervention, as was shown by improved positive affectivity (Potharst et al., 2017).

The next step in the evaluation of the Mindful Parenting program appears to be a replication of the positive effects through a randomised controlled trial within secondary mental health care settings. A comparison with established parenting programs (e.g. behavioural) would also provide an indication as to which may be appropriate for whom, when, and under what circumstances. Future research should also aim to determine the mechanisms of the Mindful Parenting program, for example, developing an understanding of the effects on the parent-child relationship, parenting and coping, as a means to explain positive outcomes for parenting stress, parent and child psychopathology.

The Mindful Parenting program has recently been implemented in unique ways across services in the United Kingdom. The Mindful Parenting Community Project has implemented the Mindful Parenting program with adoptive and foster parents. Sheffield Children's Hospital has piloted the Mindful Parenting program, offering the course to parents of children on the waitlist for mental health services. Preliminary findings demonstrate positive effects on parents' report of their own stress. Further work is ongoing to provide a larger-scale assessment of the acceptability, feasibility and effects of implementing the Mindful Parenting program in this manner.

Future implementation of the Mindful Parenting program would be appropriate in other settings where parenting stress is an identified need and may be a legitimate target for intervention. Emerson and Bögels (2017) highlight the need to address parenting stress in pediatric settings, where often a child's physical health condition has an impact on parental well-being. Indeed, diabetic adolescents of parents with higher levels of mindful parenting are found to have better control of their diabetes (Serkel-Schrama et al., 2016). Future work should focus on the implementation and evaluation of Mindful Parenting in Pediatric settings.

References

Achenbach, T.M. (1997). *Manual for the Youth Self-Report and Young Adult Behavior Checklist*. Burlington, VT: University of Vermot Department of Psychiatry.

Achenbach, T.M., & Rescorla, L.A. (2001). *Manual for the ASEBA School-Age Forms & Profiles*. Burlington, VT: University of Vermont, Research Center for Children, Youth, and Families.

Arnold, D.S., O'Leary, S.G., Wolff, L.S., & Acker, M.M. (1993). The parenting scale: A measure of dysfunctional parenting in the discipline situations. *Psychological Assessments*, 5, 137–144.

Assel, M.A., Landry, S.H., Swank, P.R., Steelman, L., Miller-Loncar, C., & Smith, K.E. (2002). How do mothers' childrearing histories, stress and parenting affect children's behavioural outcomes? *Child: Care, Health and Development*, 28, 359–368.

Baer, R., Smith, G.T., Hopkins, J., Krietemeyer, J., & Toney, L. (2006). Using self-report assessment methods to explore facets of mindfulness. *Assessment*, 13, 27–45.

Bögels, S.M., Lehtonen, A., & Restifo, K. (2010). Mindful parenting in mental health care. *Mindfulness*, 1, 107–120.

Bögels, S.M., & Restifo, K. (2014). *Mindful Parenting: A Guide for Mental Health Practitioners*. London: Norton.

Bögels, S.M., & Van Melick, M. (2004). The relationship between child-report, parent self-report, and partner report of perceived parental rearing behaviors and anxiety in children and parents. *Personality and Individual Differences*, 37, 1583–1596.

Deater-Deckard, K. (1998). Parenting stress and child adjustment: Some old hypotheses and new questions. *Clinical Psychology: Science and Practice*, 5, 314–332.

De Brock, A., Vermulst, A.A., Gerris, J.R.M., & Abidin, R.R. (1992). *Nijmeegse Ouderlijke Stress Index: Handleiding experimentele versie* [Nijmeegse Ouderlijke Stress Index: Manual]. Lisse: Swets & Zeitlinger.

Duncan, L.G., Coatsworth, J.D., & Greenberg, M.T. (2009). A model of mindful parenting: Implications for parent-child relationships and prevention research. *Clinical Child & Family Psychology Review*, 12, 255–270.

Emerson, L-M., & Bögels, S. (2017). A systemic approach to pediatric chronic health conditions: Why we need to address parental stress. *Journal of Child and Family Studies*, 26, 2347. https://doi.org/10.1007/s10826-017-0831-4

Gouveia, M.J., Carona, C., Canavarro, M.C., & Moreira, H. (2016). Self-compassion and dispositional mindfulness are associated with parenting styles and parenting stress: The mediating role of mindful parenting. *Mindfulness*, 7, 700–712.

Kabat-Zinn, J. (1990). *Full Catastrophe Living*. New York, NY: Bantam Doubleday Dell.

Leinonen, J.A., Solantaus, T.S., & Punamäki, R-L. (2003). Parental mental health and children's adjustment: The quality of marital interaction and parenting as mediating factors. *Journal of Child Psychology and Psychiatry*, 44, 227–241.

Liss, M., Schiffrin, H., & Rizzo, K. (2013). Maternal guilt and shame: The role of self-discrepancy and fear of negative evaluation. *Journal of Child and Family Studies*, 22, 1112–1119.

McHale, J.P. (1997). Overt and covert coparenting processes in the family. *Family Process*, 36, 183–201.

Potharst, E.S., Aktar, E., Rexwinkel, M., Rigterink, M., & Bögels, S.M. (2017). Mindful with your baby: Feasibility, acceptability, and effects of a Mindful Parenting group training for mothers and their babies in a mental health context. *Mindfulness*. DOI: https://doi.org/10.1007/s12671-017-0699-9

Segal, Z., Williams, J.M.G., & Teasdale, J. (2002; 2012). *Mindfulness-based Cognitive Therapy for depression: A New Approach to Preventing Relapse*. New York, NY: Guilford Press.

Serkel-Schrama, I.J., de Vries, J., Nieuwesteeg, A.M., Pouwer, F., Nyklíček, I., Speight, J., . . . & Hartman, E.E. (2016). The association of mindful parenting with glycemic control and quality of life in adolescents with type 1 diabetes: Results from diabetes MILES – The Netherlands. *Mindfulness*, 7, 1227–1237.

Siegal, D.J., & Hartzell, M. (2004). *Parenting from the Inside out*. New York, NY: Penguin.

Smith, J.D., & Dishion, T.J. (2013). Mindful parenting as a transdiagnostic family process in the development and maintenance of youth psychopathology. In J.T. Ehrenreich-May & B.C. Chu (eds.), *Transdiagnostic Mechanisms and Treatment for Youth Psychopathology*. New York, NY: Guilford Press.

Chapter 10

Mindfulness-Based Relationship Enhancement for couples

Nathan Bohy and James W. Carson

Maintaining the health and longevity of a committed romantic relationship presents a variety of complex challenges. A satisfying long-term partnership requires the coordination of two people's unique personalities, needs, expectations, skills, and imperfections. In an individualistic society like the United States, this task has proven to be increasingly difficult, and a wide variety of programs have been proposed to support couples in their efforts toward a thriving partnership. As the popularity of mindfulness-based techniques has grown steadily among mental health and wellness professionals in a variety of settings, a number of programs have sought to apply mindfulness specifically to strengthening romantic relationships. This chapter will describe one such program, Mindfulness-Based Relationship Enhancement, as well as provide an overview of the research informing its design and assessing its benefits to participants.

Mindfulness has been described as the ability to accept and remain focused on the reality of the present moment, without becoming distracted by elaborative thoughts or emotional reactions to temporary situations (Kabat-Zinn, 1990). Consistent mindfulness practice appears to develop greater patience and tolerance for stressful stimuli, which in turn supports healthier and more skillful responses (Germer, Siegel, & Fulton, 2005; Kornfield, 2008). Practitioners of mindfulness have frequently reported a deeper sense of personal well-being, including enhanced feelings of compassion and patient understanding toward both themselves and others. Because mindfulness has such powerful potential to increase the capacity for self-soothing in stressful interpersonal interactions, it was only a matter of time before these skills were studied and adapted specifically to benefit couples.

In the context of romantic relationships, mindfulness has been correlated with increased stress coping ability, relationship satisfaction, and constructive conflict outcomes (Burpee & Langer, 2005; Barnes, Brown, Krusemark, Campbell, & Rogge, 2007). Mindfulness contributes to connectedness and sexual intimacy in couples (Kabat-Zinn, 1990), and mindful "attunement" between partners encourages neurobiological activity that supports a felt sense of openness and safety (Siegel, 2007). Mindfulness promotes couples' attentiveness and emotionally intelligent sensitivity to subtle signals of communication (Goleman, 2006; Wachs & Cordova, 2007), encouraging couples to "see each other more clearly, regard each other more nonjudgmentally, behave more responsibly toward each other, and navigate the emotionally challenging waters of intimacy more gracefully" (Wachs & Cordova, 2007).

Mindfulness-Based Relationship Enhancement

Noting that the majority of previous clinical interventions designed for couples had focused on strategies for repairing relationships already in distress, Carson and colleagues at the

University of North Carolina at Chapel Hill created Mindfulness-Based Relationship Enhancement (MBRE), "a novel intervention... designed to enrich the relationships of relatively happy, non-distressed couples" (Carson, Carson, Gil, & Baucom, 2004). The theoretical design of the MBRE program is based on four outcomes frequently attributed to previous mindfulness-based interventions, which are particularly relationship-enhancing (Carson, Carson, Gil, & Baucom, 2006). First, the practice of non-judgmental self-observation often generates insights into the causes and consequences of previously automatic patterns of thinking. These insights allow practitioners to respond to situations in ways that are more carefully considered and constructive than their previous automatic reactions (Kabat-Zinn, 1990; Teasdale et al., 2000). Increasing an individual's ability to respond with a more thoughtful and wise perspective clearly has vast potential for improving interactions with other people. A person who is more mindful is less likely to be reactive, self-centered, and defensive when challenged, and more likely to consider another person's viewpoint, as well as what would be most mutually beneficial. Second, mindfulness practice appears to strengthen both self-acceptance and empathy. As mindfulness practice strengthens the ability to observe one's own thoughts and emotions non-judgmentally, compassion and calm acceptance for oneself and others tend to naturally arise (Shapiro, Schwartz, & Bonner, 1998). Third, mindfulness practice tends to strengthen the relaxation response (Kabat-Zinn, 1990; Carson, Carson, Gil, & Baucom, 2004), which is the ability to self-induce feelings of calm in response to stress-related hyperarousal (Benson, 1975). The ability to soothe oneself in this way during times of stress has been identified as a significant factor in enhancing the health of relationships (Gottman, 1993; Bodenmann, Charvoz, Cina, & Widner, 2001). Fourth, mindfulness meditators have frequently reported an experience of expansion of the sense of self, with accompanying feelings of increased compassion and connectedness with others. Couples that participate in mutually-shared activities that are exciting and self-expanding in this way are typically rewarded with increased relationship satisfaction (Aron & Aron, 1997, as cited in Carson, Carson, Gil, & Baucom, 2006).

Much of the MBRE program's format and content were adapted from Mindfulness-Based Stress Reduction (MBSR), a formalized eight-week program that teaches foundational mindfulness practices such as meditation and gentle yoga exercises, which has demonstrated success in reducing stress indicators in a variety of both clinical and non-clinical populations (Kabat-Zinn, 1982, 1990, 1993, 2003; Baer, 2003). Given the success of the MBSR program in reducing stress, and the established connection between stress management and relationship health (Gottman, 1993; Gottman, Coan, Carrere, & Swanson, 1998), the MBRE program's targeting improvement in dyadic stress coping abilities, "was a logical next step" (Carson, Carson, Gil, & Baucom, 2006). When MBRE was developed, its authors suggested that the qualifications for its program instructors should mirror those of MBSR instructors, as summarized at the time in the MBSR program's treatment manual (Kabat-Zinn & Santorelli, 1999). Similar to the MBSR program standards at that time, the recommended instructor qualifications for MBRE included the following: possession of an advanced degree in a health science field, at least three years experience of daily mindfulness practice, ongoing participation in official MBSR training and retreats, at least two years experience teaching stress reduction and yoga techniques in a group setting, proven ability to teach mindfulness in an accessible way, and experience facilitating groups of diverse clients (Carson & Carson, 2001).

MBRE was designed to deliver and build upon the skills taught in MBSR, while modifying their delivery to be couple-focused. These couple-focused adaptations include loving-kindness meditations focusing specifically on compassion toward one's partner, increased emphasis on mindful communication skills, and the inclusion of yoga exercises in which partners support each other in performing pleasurable and therapeutic postures (Carson, Carson, Gil, & Baucom, 2006). Participating couples are also guided through more intensive shared mindfulness activities, such as compassionate eye-gazing exercises and mindful massage, as well as a discussion of the applications of mindful touch to physical intimacy (Carson, Carson, Gil, & Baucom, 2006). Mirroring the MBSR program's design, the MBRE program consists of eight weekly 2.5-hour sessions plus one all-day "retreat," and couples are assigned daily homework to complete between sessions. A discussion portion of each MBRE group meeting focuses the participating couples' current relationship functioning, emphasizing their efforts to integrate mindfulness skills into their shared activities, as well as how they handle their disagreements (Carson, Carson, Gil, & Baucom, 2006). The topics covered in each of the MBRE program sessions are outlined below, followed by an overview of two sample program activities that exemplify mindfulness-enhancing activities for couples.

Box 10.1 Main topics of Mindfulness-Based Relationship Enhancement intervention sessions

Session 1: Welcome and guidelines, loving-kindness meditation with partner focus, brief personal introductions, introduction to mindfulness, body-scan meditation, homework assignments (body scan, and mindfulness of a shared activity)

Session 2: Body-scan meditation, group discussion of practices and homework, introduction to sitting meditation with awareness of breath, homework assignments (body scan plus sitting meditation, and pleasant events calendar including shared activities)

Session 3: Sitting meditation, group discussion of practices and homework with didactic focus on pleasant experiences, individual yoga, homework assignments (alternating body scan with yoga plus meditation, and unpleasant events calendar including shared events)

Session 4: Sitting meditation, group discussion of practices and homework with didactic focus on stress and coping, dyadic eye-gazing exercise and discussion, homework assignments (alternating body scan with yoga plus meditation, and stressful communications calendar including communications with partner)

Session 5: Sitting meditation, taking stock of program half over, group discussion of practices and homework with didactic focus on communication styles, dyadic communication exercise, homework assignments (alternating sitting meditation with yoga, and attention to broader areas of life [e.g. work] that impact relationships, exploration of options for responding with mindfulness under challenging conditions)

Session 6: Partner yoga, sitting meditation, group discussion of practices and homework with didactic focus on broader areas of life [e.g. work] that impact relationships, homework assignments (alternating sitting meditation with yoga, and attention to obstacles and aids to mindfulness)

All-Day Session: Multiple sitting meditations and walking meditations, individual and partner yoga, mindful movement and touch exercise, dyadic and group discussions

Session 7: Sitting meditation, group discussion of experiences during full day session, discussion of obstacles and aids to mindfulness, loving-kindness meditation, mindful touch exercise and discussion, homework assignments (self-directed practice)

Session 8: Partner yoga, sitting meditation, group discussion/review of program focusing on lessons learned, personal and relationship-related changes, and wrap-up

Source: (Carson, Carson, Gil & Baucom, 2004)

Box 10.2 Overview of two sample activities from Mindfulness-Based Relationship Enhancement

A) *Partner-Focused Loving-Kindness Meditation (20 minutes)*

Emphasizing love and forgiveness, this silent meditation exercise invites practitioners to generate compassionate thoughts and feelings toward themselves and their partners. With guidance from the group facilitators, the participants focus their attention on their breathing and other bodily sensations. Next, they are asked to visualize a mental image of their partners, and are encouraged to focus on any felt sense of positive emotions that arise while their partners are being visualized. They are then guided to direct positive intentions toward their partner, such as, "May my partner be at ease, joyful, healthy, safe and secure. . ." Next, these wishes for health and happiness are directed inward, toward the practitioners themselves. Finally, these same wishes for well-being are directed toward a mental image of someone the practitioner has had difficulty with, or someone they feel negative emotions toward. Utilizing this exercise, the participating couples learn to direct mindful effort toward amplifying compassion and positive emotions in the service of their relationships. The participants are also provided with an audio CD, which guides them through practicing this exercise together at home.

B) *Partner Eye-Gazing Exercise (15 minutes)*

During this exercise, partners are seated facing one another. The couples are encouraged to take a curious and "experimental" attitude toward this exercise, including any stressful thoughts or feelings that arise during prolonged eye contact, which they may not be accustomed to. Mutual eye-gazing is then used to directly engage with each other's physical presence, with guidance to calmly observe any inner sensations that arise while doing so. The group facilitators acknowledge that the urge to divert eye contact may feel almost irresistible at times, but having previously practiced maintaining mindful concentration on their breathing, practitioners are now encouraged to utilize the same skills to hold their partner steadily in their mutual gaze. Particular attention is paid to any tightening in the abdomen and any accompanying restriction in the flow of breath, which is often a cue from the body that may signal, "I feel threatened, I feel under stress." While maintaining mindful awareness of these physical cues, the participants practice experimenting with consciously choosing to "let go" and simply observe or accept the situation, rather than reacting impulsively. In closing, partners continue eye-gazing while being encouraged to recognize and welcome the "deep-down goodness" and shared commonality in each other. Once the exercise is complete, a group discussion is facilitated about the experience, including any guardedness, vulnerability, or other feelings that may have arisen, as well as any implications this shared experience may have for their relationships going forward.

Source: (Carson & Carson, 2001)

The initial clinical trial for MBRE produced encouraging results among the twenty-two couples that participated, in multiple domains of relationship health. In comparison to a wait-listed control group, the participating couples demonstrated significant improvements on measures of the following domains: relationship satisfaction, relationship distress, daily relationship happiness, daily relationship stress, autonomy, relatedness, acceptance of partner, and closeness (Carson, Carson, Gil, & Baucom, 2004). As individuals, this group's participants demonstrated measured benefits in the areas of spirituality, relaxation, optimism, daily stress coping efficacy, and reduced psychological distress, with these positive changes attributed to participation in the program and maintained at a three-month follow-up (Carson, Carson, Gil, & Baucom, 2004). MBRE participants have frequently described the program's all-day "retreat" session, which is conducted largely in silence, as an experience of powerfully heightened awareness and surprising closeness with their partners (Carson, Carson, Gil, & Baucom, 2006). In a follow-up study of MBRE's contributions to relationship improvements, its creators posited that its guided mindfulness meditation and yoga exercises stimulate participants to discover new and exciting aspects of themselves and their partners, and this quality of "self-expansion" was found to be the most significant mediating variable tested (Carson, Carson, Gil, & Baucom, 2007).

The MBRE program has also been examined with qualitative research methods, with the intention of better understanding its contributions to strengthening committed relationships. Bohy (2010) examined MBRE through the lens of relationship resilience indicators established by John Gottman and colleagues to predict relationship health and longevity (Gottman & Levenson, 1992, 2000), and analyzed the subjective experiences of participating couples via in-depth interviews before and after the eight-week program, including their perceived benefits from participation. Additional context was provided by audio recordings of all group sessions and weekly consultation with the group's facilitators, who were the program's developers and are a married couple themselves. Analysis of the participating couples' interviews indicated a number of significant contributions to established indicators of relationship resilience, including more ability to manage stress and difficult emotions, less defensive communication, increased flexibility and acceptance, increased ability to soothe each other and repair disagreements, and increased feelings of intimacy and closeness (Bohy, 2010).

MBRE integrates established mindfulness techniques and research into an eight-week program that strengthens the health and longevity of couples' relationships in a number of valuable ways. As awareness of the MBRE program and the number of qualified facilitators continues to grow, it holds enormous potential to strengthen the intimate relationships that are among our society's most vulnerable and valuable.

References

Baer, R. (2003). Mindfulness training as a clinical intervention: A conceptual and empirical review. *Clinical Psychology*, 10, 125–143.

Barnes, S., Brown, K., Krusemark, E., Campbell, W., & Rogge, R. (2007). The role of mindfulness in romantic relationship satisfaction and responses to relationship stress. *Journal of Marital and Family Therapy*, 33, 482–500.

Benson, H. (1975). *The relaxation response*. New York, NY: HarperCollins.

Bodenmann, G., Charvoz, L., Cina, A., & Widner, K. (2001). Prevention of marital distress by enhancing the coping skills of couples: 1-year follow-up study. *Swiss Journal of Psychology*, 6, 3–10.

Bohy, N. (2010). *A qualitative study of mindfulness-based relationship enhancement and its contributions to relationship resilience*. Doctoral dissertation. Available from ProQuest Dissertations and Theses database (UMI# 3411566).

Burpee, L.C., & Langer, E.J. (2005). Mindfulness and marital satisfaction. *Journal of Adult Development*, 12, 43–51.

Carson, J.W., & Carson, K.M. (2001). *Treatment manual for mindfulness-based relationship enhancement*. Unpublished Manuscript, University of North Carolina.

Carson, J.W., Carson, K.M., Gil, K.M., & Baucom, D.H. (2004). Mindfulness-based relationship enhancement. *Behavior Therapy*, 35, 471–494.

Carson, J.W., Carson, K.M., Gil, K.M., & Baucom, D.H. (2006). Mindfulness-based relationship enhancement in couples. In R. Baer (Ed.), *Mindfulness-based treatment approaches: Clinician's guide to evidence base and applications* (pp. 309–331). Amsterdam: Elsevier.

Carson, J.W., Carson, K.M., Gil, K.M., & Baucom, D.H. (2007). Self-expansion as a mediator of relationship improvements in a mindfulness intervention. *Journal of Marital and Family Therapy*, 33, 517–528.

Germer, C.K., Siegel, R.D., & Fulton, P.R. (2005). *Mindfulness and psychotherapy*. New York, NY: Guilford Press.

Goleman, D. (2006). *Social intelligence: The new science of human relationships*. New York, NY: Bantam.

Gottman, J.M. (1993). A theory of marital dissolution and stability. *Journal of Family Psychology*, 7, 57–75.

Gottman, J.M., Coan, J., Carrere, S., & Swanson, C. (1998). Predicting marital happiness and stability from newlywed interactions. *Journal of Marriage and the Family*, 60, 5–22.

Gottman, J.M., & Levenson, R.W. (1992). Marital processes predictive of later dissolution: Behavior, physiology, and health. *Journal of Personality and Social Psychology*, 63, 221–233.

Gottman, J.M., & Levenson, R.W. (2000). The timing of divorce: Predicting when a couple will divorce over a 14-year period. *Journal of Marriage and the Family*, 62, 737–745.

Kabat-Zinn, J. (1982). An outpatient program in behavioral medicine for chronic pain patients based on the practice of mindfulness meditation: Theoretical considerations and preliminary results. *General Hospital Psychiatry*, 4, 33–47.

Kabat-Zinn, J. (1990). *Full catastrophe living: Using the wisdom of your body and mind in everday life*. New York, NY: Delacorte.

Kabat-Zinn, J. (1993). Mindfulness meditation: Health benefits of an ancient Buddhist practice. In D. Goleman & J. Garin (Eds.), *Mind/Body Medicine*. New York, NY: Consumer Reports.

Kabat-Zinn, J. (2003). Mindfulness-based interventions in context: Past, present, and future. *Clinical Psychology: Science and Practice*, 10, 144–156.

Kabat-Zinn, J., & Santorelli, S.F. (1999). *Mindfulness-based stress reduction professional training resource manual*. Shrewbury, MA: Center for Mindfulness in Medicine, Health Care, and Society.

Kornfield, J. (2008). *The wise heart: A guide to the universal teachings of Buddhist psychology*. New York, NY: Bantam Dell.

Shapiro, S.L., Schwartz, G.E., & Bonner, G. (1998). Effects of mindfulness-based stress reduction on medical and premedical students. *Journal of Behavioral Medicine*, 21, 581–599.

Siegel, D.J. (2007). *The mindful brain: Reflection and attunement in the cultivation of well-being*. New York, NY: Norton & Company.

Teasdale, J.D., Segal, Z.V., Williams, J.M., Ridgeway, V.A., Soulsby, J.M., & Lau, M.A. (2000). Prevention of relapse/ recurrence in major depression by mindfulness-based cognitive therapy. *Journal of Consulting and Clinical Psychology*, 68, 615–623.

Wachs, K., & Cordova, J. (2007). Mindful relating: Exploring mindfulness and emotional repertoires in intimate relationships. *Journal of Marital and Family Therapy*, 33, 464–481.

Chapter 11

Mindful Mamas
Mindfulness-based yoga for depressed women entering motherhood

Laurel M. Hicks, Barbara Brookens-Harvey, and Maria Muzik

Pregnancy can be a transformative time, both physically and emotionally. Pregnancy is often thought of as a happy and joyful time, however, stress and symptoms of mental illness commonly prevail. Symptoms of mental illness during pregnancy can place infants at risk for negative biological and psychosocial outcomes (Gentile, 2015). Fifteen to twenty percent of women experience antenatal depression (Ashley, Harper, Arms-Chavez, & LoBello, 2016; Marcus, 2009) and 25% report high levels of anxiety (Hall et al., 2009). This places the mother and infant at psychosocial and medical risk including postpartum depression (Biaggi, Conroy, Pawlby, & Pariante, 2016), poor infant development (Junge et al., 2016), preterm birth (Marcus, 2009; Staneva, Bogossian, Pritchard, & Wittkowski, 2015), and low birth weight (Blackmore et al., 2016). Furthermore, up to 50% of women decline pharmacological treatment for perinatal mental health concerns due to fear of damage to the infant in-utero or during breastfeeding (Goodman, 2009). These fears often remain despite advice and consultation from a trained health professional. Effective treatment during pregnancy is crucial to prevent the deleterious effects of untreated mental illness (Muzik & Hamilton, 2016). The combination of yoga and mindfulness (M-Yoga) is a low-cost treatment that is reported to successfully reduce symptoms in clinically depressed pregnant women (Muzik, Hamilton, Rosenblum, Waxler, & Hadi, 2012) and women often consider it an acceptable complementary or alternative therapy to pharmacological treatment.

This chapter reviews results of research studies, theoretical foundations regarding the potential importance of yoga in pregnancy, and most importantly, guidelines and recommendations for teaching mindfulness-based yoga to pregnant women, especially those experiencing symptoms of mental illness. These guidelines are intended for prenatal yoga teachers and pregnant women who are interested in improving their personal wellbeing during pregnancy.

Overview of the program

Traditionally, all yoga includes an element of mindfulness: the emphasis to be in the present moment, to observe and notice in a nonjudgmental way. As yoga expands and grows in the Western world, sometimes the emphasis in a class may be solely on the postures or other philosophies of yoga. A mindfulness-based prenatal yoga class ensures that the attributes of mindfulness, as taught by Jon Kabat-Zinn, are woven throughout every class. The teacher assumes a nonjudgmental, curious, and compassionate stance and encourages the student to cultivate similar attributes. Language is shifted to aid in reduction of any striving that may be present for the student to change their current experience, therefore, phrases such as "feel your shoulders relax" are replaced with, "notice the sensation in the shoulders as you breathe, perhaps they soften, maybe you notice tightness". By offering suggestions in this way, the student is then encouraged to be curious about what they actually notice instead of striving towards something they think they should be achieving, such as relaxation.

Mindfulness-based prenatal yoga is suitable for women in all trimesters. Women are expected to gain their doctor or midwife's approval prior to beginning the yoga program. The yoga teacher should complete a specialized training in prenatal women (the gold standard is completion of an 85-hour training with a registered prenatal yoga school). This training ensures that the teacher is prepared to safely modify the yoga postures for a variety of common discomforts. The M-Yoga program was studied in a group of clinically depressed women; however, any woman may participate in this program. When teaching a group of depressed women, care should be taken to ensure the yoga classes are trauma-informed due to the high comorbidity between depression and trauma (Silverstein, Feinberg, Sauder, Egbert, & Stein, 2010). The prenatal yoga training program developed by Dr. Hicks, Mindful Mamas™, includes information necessary to teach a mindfulness-based, trauma-informed class that is suitable for women experiencing symptoms of mental illness.

A mindfulness-based prenatal yoga class is often a parallel process to what is experienced during the transition from pregnancy to parenthood, which may be especially challenging if the woman is suffering from elevated depression symptoms or other mental health concerns. Expectant women often arrive at yoga class with worries, concerns, uncertainty, excitement, and/or fear. Frequently, the idea of birthing a child and feeling the potential discomfort of childbirth, or the idea of future sleepless nights, is met with resistance, and a need to change the experience. The practice of mindful yoga guides the woman to be *with* the emotional or physical discomfort, to move through it and notice how it may change and shift, often breath by breath. For example, mindfulness practice can teach an individual to notice, with compassion and curiosity, what bodily sensations are present and the connection to emotion or thoughts. While practicing yoga, a woman may notice some slight physical discomfort, such as lower back discomfort, or rising anxiety, they may then begin to be curious about the experience and ask herself questions. Where exactly is the discomfort? What else does she notice? Is there anything else present? Is she judging or striving to change the experience? By allowing the pause, the woman may then begin to perceive the experience differently. Perhaps she decides to then move her body differently, if so, this is a choice made out of awareness instead of an automatic reaction.

Similarly, during birth, a woman may notice discomfort and want to push the feeling away, to change it somehow. Ideally, her mindful yoga practice can then move off the mat and into the birth experience reminding the woman to breathe, notice with deep curiosity and acceptance what the moment holds, and potentially connect with compassion towards herself and her experience. The birth experience can then morph into a different, potentially calmer experience. This metaphor can continue throughout parenthood, to include the discomfort of hearing a baby cry, or dealing with a challenging toddler. Nancy Bardacke, the developer of the evidence-based program Mindfulness-Based Childbirth and Parenting Education, lovingly names these difficulties "the contractions of life" (Bardacke, 2012; Bardacke & Duncan, 2014).

Theoretical foundations and research

It is widely accepted that early relationships between a mother and infant are crucial for healthy infant development and behavior. This relationship between mother and baby begins while the baby is in utero as the mother begins to develop an internal representation of her relationship with her baby. Prenatal representations are reported to be linked to later parenting behaviors (Dayton, Levendosky, Davidson, & Bogat, 2010). Mindful prenatal yoga may begin to cultivate the mother-infant relationship in a supportive, loving and compassionate way and may, in turn, affect the way mothers parent their infants during the postpartum period. This relationship can often be disrupted by depression symptoms (Lefkovics, Baji, & Rigo, 2014), although some research suggests that increased mindfulness may buffer the relationship between prenatal depression and bonding with the unborn child (Hicks, Dayton, Brown, Muzik, & Raveau, under review)

For many, pregnancy also brings anxiety, worry and stress, especially if a parent struggles with mental illness, lives in poverty, or is exposed to violence, trauma, or racial oppression (Åsenhed, Kilstam, Alehagen, & Baggens, 2014; Deave, Johnson, & Ingram, 2008). Unfortunately, this is the reality for many expectant parents during pregnancy, and stress may reach toxic levels (Frodl & O'Keane, 2013; Lupien, Ouellet-Morin, Herba, Juster, & McEwen, 2016; Shonkoff et al., 2012). *Toxic* stress is broadly defined as the stress that is incurred from frequent, intense, or lengthy activation of the body's physical stress response system (Shonkoff et al., 2012). Typically, during a stressful event, the nervous system reacts to respond with either fight, flight or freeze reaction, then, after a stressful event is over, the body settles back into homeostasis. For parents living with chronic stress, stressors such as the experience of coping with psychopathology (e.g., depression, anxiety, and trauma), financial distress, and exposure to violence may culminate in toxic stress.

The long-term consequences of exposure to toxic stress or depression symptoms, especially during times of developmental vulnerability, constitute a significant health concern. In pregnancy, for example, toxic stress or high symptoms of depression experienced by the mother are linked to poorer birth outcomes for the infant and can trigger a physiological signal to the fetus' developing brain, defined as *fetal programming*, which is believed to be linked to health (Entringer, Buss, & Wadhwa, 2012), behavior (Buss, Entringer, & Wadhwa, 2012), and developmental concerns (Davis & Sandman, 2010; DiPietro, Matthew, Costigan, Atella, & Reusing, 2006) for the infant throughout the lifespan. Prenatal yoga may help to mitigate the effects of stress on the mother's neuroendocrine system, as participation in weekly prenatal yoga is linked to lower cortisol levels in expectant mothers (Chen et al., 2017; Field, Diego, Delgado, & Medina, 2013).

Women who suffer from mood disorders during pregnancy may also experience less positive feelings towards their infant and lack the ability to effectively mirror their infant's emotional states (Bialy, 2006). This could lead to poorer self-regulation and attunement within the mother-infant dyad. Additionally, symptoms of mood disorders may lead to pregnant women experiencing a decreased ability to cope with stress in an adaptive way (Folkman, 1997; Lazarus & Folkman, 1984).

Empirical support

Research identifies mindfulness-based interventions (MBI) as an effective method to reduce symptoms of depression, anxiety in pregnancy. Yoga practiced mindfully was shown to reduce depressive symptoms in non-depressed (Beddoe, Paul Yang, Kennedy, Weiss, & Lee, 2009) and clinically depressed women (Field et al., 2013; Muzik et al., 2012), as well as increase maternal-fetal attachment (Muzik et al., 2012), anxiety (Beddoe et al., 2009; Field et al., 2013) and pain (Beddoe et al., 2009).

A number of mindfulness group interventions have been adapted for pregnancy from the heavily empirically researched interventions Mindfulness-Based Stress Reduction and Mindfulness-Based Cognitive Therapy (MBCT). These include Mindfulness-Based Childbirth and Parenting, Mindful Motherhood, and CALM pregnancy. All follow the basic structure of mindfulness-based stress reduction, an eight-week group program, two to two-and-a-half hours in length with a six-hour-long silent retreat day. Participants complete exercises including mindful eating, walking, meditating and yoga as well as weekly homework assignments. The interventions add exercises that invite mothers to focus mindfully on their baby, as well as on fears of pregnancy and birth.

A decrease in negative affect (Duncan & Bardacke, 2010; Vieten & Astin, 2008), anxiety (Goodman et al., 2014; Vieten & Astin, 2008), pregnancy-related anxiety (Duncan & Bardacke, 2010) and depression (Duncan et al., 2017; Goodman et al., 2014; Muzik et al., 2012) were reported in Mindfulness-Based Childbirth and Parenting Education, Mindful Motherhood, CALM interventions. The above interventions unveiled similar themes. Women enjoyed the social support and connectedness that emerged from the group setting and expressed greater insight to their own emotions. The women found mindfulness to be an effective coping skill that they utilized in the stresses of their daily life. The CALM intervention found the majority of women who participated were no longer diagnosed with generalized anxiety disorder (93%) and major depressive disorder (100%) (Goodman et al., 2014).

Prenatal M-Yoga was studied in a small sample of clinically depressed pregnancy women. The women were invited to participate in a 90-minute, weekly mindful prenatal yoga class over a ten-week program. After the program, women reported lower levels of depressive symptoms, higher levels of mindfulness and greater maternal-infant attachment (Muzik et al., 2012). The increase in maternal-infant attachment suggests that women who completed the intervention were more comfortable being in a mother role, they also reported more pleasure interacting with the fetus and were more likely to participate in healthy behaviors due to the pregnancy.

Structure of the program

The M-Yoga program is offered by a trained prenatal yoga teacher in 90-minute weekly sessions, over a ten-week period. The overall class included an introduction/ check-in, seated meditation, seated, kneeling, standing, restorative postures, and a mindfulness reading.

Introduction and check-in

Class begins quietly. The teacher and pregnant women sit in a circle. Many women require props to allow for comfort with their daily changing body. We begin by checking in. This allows the teacher to customize the class based on current symptoms. For example, many women experience breathlessness in pregnancy. If this is present, the teacher can encourage students to lengthen the sides of the body, creating more space around the chest and ribs. Instructions can include bringing compassion towards oneself as their baby grows and begins to occupy more space. Each woman shares their name, how many weeks into this pregnancy they are, what new joys, discomforts, and challenges have they noticed, and how their baby grown. Each woman is provided time to talk and the group responds with acknowledgement, acceptance and support. A sense of community is created through this shared experience. (Ten to fifteen minutes.)

Seated meditation on the breath

Awareness then shifts from each other to themselves, towards their center, and to their babies. The breath is introduced: "Notice your breath, feel it come in through the nose, through the throat, feel it expand the lungs, push the diaphragm. Exhale and notice the breath leave through the mouth or nose. The breath may be shallow or deep, just notice. Bring awareness to your baby, snug in your womb, riding the wave of the breath. How does your body respond to this breath, how does your baby respond within your womb?" As the class is led through the opening meditation, many bodies soften, hands move across the abdomen, women gently hold their babies. A stillness settles in the room. (Two to five minutes.)

Seated postures

These postures build awareness of the relationship between the pelvis and spine while in a seated posture. (Ten to fifteen minutes.)

1. Sukhasana/Simple Cross-Legged Pose: Sit on the floor with the sit bones (ischial tuberosity) on the edge of a blanket or bolster to allow for a neutral pelvic position. The shoulders and ears are positioned over the hips. Legs are crossed. Shoulder and chest stretches can be added. A gentle twist can be offered, with the belly button facing forward and the upper back emphasized in the movement. Benefits: Encourages healthy alignment of spine and pelvis. Increases mobility and health of the spine.
2. Baddha Konasana/Bound Angle Pose: Sit on the floor with a blanket or bolster under the sit bones to allow for greater ease in the hips. Bring the soles of the feet together and knees out to the side. Gently move the knees in the direction of the floor. Lengthen upwards from the tail bone through the crown of the head. The hands can be placed on the lower back for more support. Think of hugging baby towards you and away from the pelvic floor. Open the chest and breathe deeply for four breaths. Women with pubic symphysis can practice this with the legs crossed or together. Benefits: Grounding to the earth. Accessible to women throughout pregnancy. Allows for ease with deep breathing. Relaxes and tones the pelvic floor, tones the abdominal muscles, and helps to position the pelvis for birthing process.
3. Upavistha Konasana I/Wide Angle Seated Pose: Open the legs wide out to the side. Place the arms behind your back, palms to the floor or bolster to support the spine. Press the arms downward. Continue to sit up lengthening the spine and opening the chest. Press the quadriceps down and flex the feet. If hamstrings are tight, the knees can remain slightly bent. Engage the abdominal muscles and lift upwards. Add side stretches by reaching the right arm up alongside the right ear. Inhale to reach up and exhale to reach the arm to the left, opening the right rib cage. Hold for four breaths. Repeat on the left side. Women with pubic symphysis can practice this with the legs together. Benefits: Strengthens the spine, opens the hips, tones the pelvic floor, creates space for the baby by broadening the sides of the body and the pelvis. Eases labor and delivery if practiced consistently throughout pregnancy.
4. Janu Sirsasana/Head to Knee Pose: Extend the right leg forward. Bend the left knee out to the side and place the left foot on the inner thigh of the right leg. Place a yoga strap around the ball of the right foot. Hold the strap in each hand pulling back to lift the spine and open the chest. Press the left knee and the right quadriceps down towards the floor. If

hamstrings are tight, the knee should remain slightly bent. Hug baby towards you to help tone the abdominal muscles. Benefits: Stretches the hamstrings, strengthens the pelvic floor, opens the hips.

Kneeling postures

These positions may relieve lower back pain, improve spine mobility, increase circulation to legs, reduce swelling, encourage ideal fetal positioning, and create space for deeper breathing. (Ten to fifteen minutes.)

5   Cat/Cow: Begin on hands and knees. Shoulders are over wrists and hips over knees. Inhale to slightly lower the belly towards the floor and gaze forward, move the shoulders back and down. Exhale round the back, draw baby towards you and drop the chin to your chest. Repeat several rounds, gently rocking your baby. Gentle hip swaying or circling can also be beneficial. Benefits: Eases low back pain, strengthens the abdominal muscles. Encourages your baby to move. May encourage baby to be in an anterior position.
6   Balasana/Supported Wide Leg Child's Pose: Place a bolster in front of you. Sit on the floor with knees wide and sit bones on top of your heels. Lengthen the spine. Inhale, lift arms up to the ceiling. Exhale, reach the arms forward bringing the torso to the bolster. Allow room for your baby. Arms can wrap around the front of the bolster. Turn the head to one side and take four breaths. Turn the head to the opposite side for four breaths. Benefits: Eases tension from the back. Opens the hips. Allows attention to move inward, brings a sense of connection to the earth and surrender to the process of your baby's growth and your transition to mother. Child's pose is a great position for the body and mind to rest between contractions during labor.

Standing postures

These positions can increase energy, circulation, allow for rib cage expansion to facilitate deeper breathing, develop strength, stamina, and flexibility. An increase of strength in the legs and hips can lessen the stress on the lower back and position the pelvis to support the increasing weight in the body. The positions can also empower women to feel confident in the body's abilities. (Fifteen to twenty minutes.)

7   Adho Mukha Svanasana/Downward Facing Dog: Downward dog can be considered a standing pose or a gentle inversion. Begin on hands and knees. Exhale, lift the hips up to the sky and press the torso back towards the thighs. Separate the feet wide enough to accommodate the baby. Lengthen the arms and press into the floor with the palms, fingers are spread wide. Rotate the inner thighs towards each other and press through the heels towards the floor. Start with the knees bent. If hamstrings are very flexible, the heels can move towards the ground. If doing this causes rounding in the spine, keep knees bent and spine long. Do not practice if you have uncontrolled high blood pressure or experience heart burn, nausea, dizziness, or too much pressure in the head. Benefits: Stretches and lengthens all muscles, strengthens the arms, relieves tension in the neck and shoulders.
8   Tadasana/Mountain Pose: Stand with feet hip width distance apart. Bring shoulders up to the ears and roll back and down. Allow the arms to lengthen toward the floor. Engage

the abdominal muscles in and up and send the tail bone towards the floor. Feel the feet firmly press into the ground and notice the earth securely underneath you. Stand tall and strong. Place hands on baby and take five deep breaths. You may think of breathing in energy, love, and peace to you and your child. Benefits: Builds awareness while standing. Builds, supports and maintains good posture to prevent back pain. Encourages a sense of confidence.

9   Virabhadrasana B/Warrior B: Stand with legs about three to four feet apart, facing the long edge of your mat. Turn the front foot to face the front of the mat. Turn the back foot to point towards the front corner of the mat. Bend the front knee so the knee is above or behind the ankle. Bring arms to a "T" shape, a shoulder height. Gaze to your front fingers. Shoulders are over hips. Breathe deeply for four to five breaths. Switch sides. Benefits: Strengthens the legs, opens the hips, builds a sense of strength and confidence.

10 Utthita Trikonasana/Extended Triangle: Stand with legs three to four feet apart. Turn the front foot to face the front of the mat. Turn your back foot in to point approximately to the front corner of the mat. Reach your arms out in a "T" position at shoulder height. Reach your arms and torso to the right while moving your hips to the left. Slide the front arm down to your front leg and reach the back arm up, fingers to the ceiling. Gaze down to the mat if you want more stability or up at your top fingers. Hug baby in and notice the spine lengthen. You may use a block or chair under your bottom hand for stability. Take a few deep breaths and then lift the torso up, rest your arms at your side. Repeat on the other side. Benefits: Strengthens legs and pelvic floor. Creates space in sides of the body. May relieve back discomfort.

11 Malasana/Squat: Stand with your feet wide apart. Place block or bolster underneath to sit on. Bend the knees deeply and slowly bring your sits bones to the bolster or block. Heels remain on the floor. If heels can remain on the floor with the bottom hovering just above the ground, then you may remove the props. The bottom moves back and chest lifts. Knees move out to the sides and the belly is between the inner thighs. Hug baby in. Bring the hands together in front of your chest in prayer position. Hold and breathe for four or five deep breaths. For women with varicosities, do not hold for long to ensure good circulation. Women with placenta praevia should only do this position with clearance from their midwife or doctor. Women with breech babies (after 34 weeks) may choose to avoid this position so baby's bottom doesn't engage in the birth canal. Benefits: Opens the hips and brings mobility to the hip joints. Tones and strengthens pelvic floor. Widens the space of the pelvic area which may aid in engagement of baby in the birth canal in preparation for birthing. Common birthing position.

Restorative positions

Classes ended with a 15–20 minute restorative pose, including a full-body relaxation exercise, along with a reading about mindfulness. A significant feature of the intervention is being "mindful" of the baby, to observe its unique identity, which in turn facilitates the attachment process.

12 Savasana/Final Resting Pose: A reclined chair can be made by resting a bolster, lengthwise on a block. Lie back onto the bolster. Add a blanket under the head to support the head and neck. A rolled blanket can be placed under the knees to support the legs. Place the arms on either side of the hips or directly on the belly, connecting to baby. If lying on

your back is uncomfortable, lie on your left side with a blanket or block underneath the head and a bolster or blanket between the knees. Notice the parts of the body touching the ground, perhaps some muscles soften. Breathe softly and slowly. Connect inward to your own body and to your baby. Send compassion and gratitude to your body for creating and growing this child. A reading from a text such as *Everyday Blessings: The Inner Work of Mindful Parenting* (M. Kabat-Zinn, 2009) is then shared out loud with the class. (Fifteen to twenty minutes.)

Language

Throughout the yoga class, the teacher embodies and describes the seven qualities of mindfulness as described by Jon Kabat-Zinn (J. Kabat-Zinn, 2003): allowing presence, non-judging of the experience, patience, a beginner's mind, non-striving, acceptance and letting go. The following are examples of how this may be worded by the teacher.

- Move your awareness and focus inward to your breath.
- Watch the in breath and the out breath, there is no need to change it, just simply observe.
- Allow the inhalation to bring an extension of the spine.
- As you exhale, you may notice the shoulders soften, you may not.
- Observe your posture as you stand in mountain pose. What parts of the feet touch the ground? Perhaps you notice your balance shifting from the front of the foot to the rear. Maybe you can feel all four corners of the feet on the ground.
- Gently escort your awareness to your breath and to your center where your baby always is. The breath is your constant companion in this practice, as is your baby.
- Observe if you need to come out of a position, doing so with the same awareness and attention that we had during the position.
- Start the position afresh as we repeat it on the second side. Notice what is similar, what is different.
- Observe the breath and body, if you find yourself judging or analyzing, perhaps just say to yourself, "hmm, my mind is judging right now", and then bring your awareness back to your breath or to your baby.
- If you feel your baby move within, perhaps wonder with curiosity what your baby is doing, how are they moving, what may they be experiencing in this practice.
- Notice whatever arises, whether it's thinking, a feeling, or a physical sensation.
- Just notice this moment, just as it is.

Conclusion

Pregnancy is both an exciting and vulnerable time that may be accompanied by stress, depression, or anxiety. Many women and health providers look to alternatives to pharmacology to decrease symptoms of mood disorders. Prenatal M-Yoga is a widely accepted and effective treatment to improve wellbeing. Not only does practicing prenatal M-Yoga improve mood, but it also creates a supportive, accepting, and loving community for the expectant woman to transition throughout her pregnancy. The safe haven that the yoga class provides allows the woman to explore difficult emotions and sensations in a space that encourages exploration and curiosity. The yoga mat may be a safe place for the woman to connect both to herself, emotionally and physically, as well as to her developing baby.

Further resources

- Mindful Mamas™: Mindfulness-Based Prenatal Yoga Teacher Training www.mindfulmamasyoga.com
- Mindful Birthing: Mindfulness-Based Childbirth and Parenting Training www.mindfulbirthing.org
- Mindful Motherhood: Practical Tools for Staying Sane During Pregnancy and Your Child's First Year www.mindfulmotherhood.org

References

Åsenhed, L., Kilstam, J., Alehagen, S., & Baggens, C. (2014). Becoming a father is an emotional roller coaster – an analysis of first-time fathers' blogs. *Journal of Clinical Nursing, 23*(9–10), 1309–1317.

Ashley, J. M., Harper, B. D., Arms-Chavez, C. J., & LoBello, S. G. (2016). Estimated prevalence of antenatal depression in the US population. *Archive of Women's Mental Health, 19*(2), 395–400. doi:10.1007/s00737-015-0593-1

Bardacke, N. (2012). *Mindful Birthing: Training the Mind, Body, and Heart for Childbirth and Beyond.* London: HarperOne.

Bardacke, N., & Duncan, L. G. (2014). Mindfulness-based childbirth and parenting: Cultivating inner resources for the transition to parenthood and beyond. In Baer, R. A. (ed.), *Mindfulness-Based Treatment Approaches: Clinician's Guide to Evidence Base and Applications* (pp. 213–237). Cambridge, MA: Academic Press.

Beddoe, A. E., Paul Yang, C. P., Kennedy, H. P., Weiss, S. J., & Lee, K. A. (2009). The effects of mindfulness-based yoga during pregnancy on maternal psychological and physical distress. *Journal of Obsteteric, Gynecology, & Neonatal Nursing, 38*(3), 310–319. doi:10.1111/j.1552–6909.2009.01023.x

Biaggi, A., Conroy, S., Pawlby, S., & Pariante, C. M. (2016). Identifying the women at risk of antenatal anxiety and depression: A systematic review. *Journal of Affective Disorders, 191*, 62–77. doi:http://dx.doi.org/10.1016/j.jad.2015.11.014

Bialy, L. (2006). Impact of stress and negative mood on mother and child: Attachment, child development and intervention (unpublished doctoral dissertation). San Francisco, CA: California Institute of Integral Studies.

Blackmore, E. R., Putnam, F. W., Pressman, E. K., Rubinow, D. R., Putnam, K. T., Matthieu, M. M., . . . O'Connor, T. G. (2016). The effects of trauma history and prenatal affective symptoms on obstetric outcomes. *Journal of Traumatic Stress, 29*(3), 245–252. doi:10.1002/jts.22095

Buss, C., Entringer, S., & Wadhwa, P. D. (2012). Fetal programming of brain development: Intrauterine stress and susceptibility to psychopathology. *Science Signaling, 5*(245).

Chen, P-J., Yang, L., Chou, C-C., Li, C-C., Chang, Y-C., & Liaw, J-J. (2017). Effects of prenatal yoga on women's stress and immune function across pregnancy: A randomized controlled trial. *Complementary Therapies in Medicine, 31*, 109–117. doi:http://dx.doi.org/10.1016/j.ctim.2017.03.003

Davis, E. P., & Sandman, C. A. (2010). The timing of prenatal exposure to maternal cortisol and psychosocial stress is associated with human infant cognitive development. *Child Development, 81*(1), 131–148. doi:10.1111/j.1467–8624.2009.01385.x

Dayton, C. J., Levendosky, A. A., Davidson, W. S., & Bogat, G. A. (2010). The child as held in the mind of the mother: The influence of prenatal maternal representations on parenting behaviors. *Infant Mental Health Journal, 31*(2), 220–241. doi:10.1002/imhj.20253

Deave, T., Johnson, D., & Ingram, J. (2008). Transition to parenthood: The needs of parents in pregnancy and early parenthood. *BMC Pregnancy and Childbirth, 8*(1), 30.

DiPietro, J. A., Matthew, F. S. X. N., Costigan, K. A., Atella, L. D., & Reusing, S. P. (2006). Maternal psychological distress during pregnancy in relation to child development at age two. *Child Development, 77*(3), 573–587. doi:10.1111/j.1467–8624.2006.00891.x

Duncan, L. G., & Bardacke, N. (2010). Mindfulness-based childbirth and parenting education: Promoting family mindfulness during the perinatal period. *Journal of Child and Family Studies*, *19*(2), 190–202. doi:10.1007/s10826-009-9313-7

Duncan, L. G., Cohn, M. A., Chao, M. T., Cook, J. G., Riccobono, J., & Bardacke, N. (2017). Benefits of preparing for childbirth with mindfulness training: A randomized controlled trial with active comparison. *BMC Pregnancy and Childbirth*, *17*(1), 140. doi:10.1186/s12884-017-1319-3

Entringer, S., Buss, C., & Wadhwa, P. D. (2012). Prenatal stress, telomere biology, and fetal programming of health and disease risk. *Science Signaling*, *5*(248), pt. 12.

Field, T., Diego, M., Delgado, J., & Medina, L. (2013). Yoga and social support reduce prenatal depression, anxiety and cortisol. *Journal of Bodywork and Movement Therapies*. doi:10.1016/j.jbmt.2013.03.010

Folkman, S. (1997). Positive psychological states and coping with severe stress. *Social Science & Medicine*, *45*(8), 1207–1221.

Frodl, T., & O'Keane, V. (2013). How does the brain deal with cumulative stress? A review with focus on developmental stress, HPA axis function and hippocampal structure in humans. *Neurobiology of Disease*, *52*, 24–37. doi:10.1016/j.nbd.2012.03.012

Gentile, S. (2015). Untreated depression during pregnancy: Short- and long-term effects in offspring: A systematic review. *Neuroscience*. doi:10.1016/j.neuroscience.2015.09.001

Goodman, J. H. (2009). Women's attitudes, preferences, and perceived barriers to treatment for perinatal depression. *Birth*, *36*(1), 60–69. doi:10.1111/j.1523–536X.2008.00296.x

Goodman, J. H., Guarino, A., Chenausky, K., Klein, L., Prager, J., Petersen, R., . . . Freeman, M. (2014). CALM pregnancy: Results of a pilot study of mindfulness-based cognitive therapy for perinatal anxiety. *Archives of Women's Mental Health*, *17*. doi:10.1007/s00737-013-0402-7

Hall, W., Hauck, Y., Carty, E., Hutton, E., Fenwick, J., & Stoll, K. (2009). Childbirth fear, anxiety, fatigue, and sleep deprivation in pregnant women. *Journal of Obsteterics, Gynecology & Neonatal Nursing*, *38*. doi:10.1111/j.1552–6909.2009.01054.x

Hicks, L., Dayton, C. J., Brown, S., Muzik, M., & Raveau, H. (under review). Mindfulness moderates depression and quality of prenatal bonding in expectant parents. *Mindfulness*.

Junge, C., Garthus-Niegel, S., Slinning, K., Polte, C., Simonsen, T. B., & Eberhard-Gran, M. (2016). The impact of perinatal depression on children's social-emotional development: A longitudinal study. *Maternal and Child Health*, 1–9. doi:10.1007/s10995-016-2146-2

Kabat-Zinn, J. (2003). Mindfulness-based interventions in context: Past, present, and future. *Clinical Psychology (New York, N.Y.)*, *10*(2), 145.

Kabat-Zinn, M. (2009). *Everyday Blessings: The Inner Work of Mindful Parenting*. London: Hachette.

Lazarus, R. S., & Folkman, S. (1984). *Stress, Appraisal and Coping*. New York, NY: Springer.

Lefkovics, E., Baji, I., & Rigo, J. (2014). Impact of maternal depression on pregnancies and on early attachment. *Infant Mental Health*, *35*(4), 354–365. doi:10.1002/imhj.21450

Lupien, S., Ouellet-Morin, I., Herba, C., Juster, R., & McEwen, B. (2016). From vulnerability to neurotoxicity: A developmental approach to the effects of stress on the brain and behavior. In *Epigenetics and Neuroendocrinology* (pp. 3–48). New York, NY: Springer.

Marcus, S. M. (2009). Depression during pregnancy: Rates, risks and consequences – Motherisk Update 2008. *Canadian Journal of Clinical Pharmacology*, *16*(1), e15–22.

Muzik, M., & Hamilton, S. E. (2016). Use of antidepressants during pregnancy? What to consider when weighing treatment with antidepressants against untreated depression. *Maternal and Child Health Journal*, 1–12. doi:10.1007/s10995-016-2038-5

Muzik, M., Hamilton, S. E., Rosenblum, K. L., Waxler, E., & Hadi, Z. (2012). Mindfulness yoga during pregnancy for psychiatrically at-risk women: Preliminary results from a pilot feasibility study. *Complementary Therapies in Clinical Practice*, *18*(4), 235–240. doi:10.1016/j.ctcp.2012.06.006

Shonkoff, J. P., Garner, A. S., Siegel, B. S., Dobbins, M. I., Earls, M. F., McGuinn, L., . . . Care, D. (2012). The lifelong effects of early childhood adversity and toxic stress. *Pediatrics*, *129*(1), e232-e246.

Silverstein, M., Feinberg, E., Sauder, S., Egbert, L., & Stein, R. (2010). Comorbid posttraumatic stress symptoms in an urban population of mothers screening positive for depression. *Archives of Pediatrics & Adolescent Medicine, 164*(8), 778–779.

Staneva, A., Bogossian, F., Pritchard, M., & Wittkowski, A. (2015). The effects of maternal depression, anxiety, and perceived stress during pregnancy on preterm birth: A systematic review. *Women and Birth, 28*(3), 179–193. doi:10.1016/j.wombi.2015.02.003

Vieten, C., & Astin, J. (2008). Effects of a mindfulness-based intervention during pregnancy on prenatal stress and mood: Results of a pilot study. *Archives of Womens Mental Health, 11*(1), 67–74. doi:10.1007/s00737-008-0214-3

Chapter 12

A ceremony of losses
Mindfulness for elders and caregivers

Lucia McBee and Antonella Buranello

The Buddha's final words before dying were: "Things fall apart. Tread the path with care." (Mahaparinibbana sutta, translation from Higgins, 2016). This core Buddhist teaching reminds us that everything changes, "things fall apart." It is most clearly apparent in the process of aging. Our bodies and minds change, as do our living circumstances and the choices available to us. Mindfulness-Based Interventions (MBIs) originate with Buddha's teaching and include formal and informal practices that help us "proceed with care." In this chapter, we will describe ways that MBIs can provide essential pathways for navigating aging as well as for caregivers to those experiencing the aging process. The trajectory of aging takes infinite varieties. For this reason, there is no formula for adapting the teaching of mindfulness for elders. On the other hand, there are general guidelines and suggestions that we will review. In addition, frailer elders are dependent on caregivers, and caregivers themselves may be highly stressed. Therefore, it is essential to include both professional and informal caregivers when considering MBIs for frail elders. And finally, elders often live in assisted living, long-term care, and rehabilitation facilities, previously modeled on hospitals. MBIs can offer keys to shifting to care that is more home-like and person centered.

Bringing MBIs to elders: a personal story (AB)

A lot has changed in the last 15 years, since I began to work in the elder care sector and in the psychology of aging. I'm a psychotherapist, and I'm always looking for ways to improve people's wellbeing as they age and when they are family or professional caregivers of persons living with dementia or other chronic conditions. Something that I realized quite early on was the difficulty of facing the suffering of the aging and of their caregivers.

Telling and teaching how to age well or to have good communication with the elderly and their relatives, or to be empathetic, or to work in a team, didn't seem to be enough when based only on giving them instructions and information. I felt frustrated because I found that I was not able to help grow the "being" part of the fundamental concepts of training: "knowing, doing, and being." I was so affected by the suffering of others, and mine, and also so determined to relieve that suffering – going beyond the knowing and the doing – that I attended hours of training in aging psychology and other branches of psychology.

And I was not alone. My colleagues in the nursing home and the administration were constantly searching for ways to improve the quality of care and of life. In 2004 we began a collaboration with Padua University for a Master's degree in the Psychology of Aging and later with the Italian Psychology of Aging Society. We worked in a multidisciplinary team and exchanged ideas and expertise in a context where the values pursued were the centrality of the person, the relationships, the respect, the dignity, and self-determination of the elderly. It was what made the difference.

The population

Global demographics provide an important rationale for investigating multiple, non-pharmacological interventions for the aging population. By 2020 it is expected that adults over 65 will exceed their younger counterparts, and that this will exponentially increase over time. Lower birth rates combined with advances in medicine both contribute to this demographic. In addition, the fastest growing segment of the over-65 population will be those over 80, "oldest-old" (NIA.NIH, 2017). While we are living longer, we are also living with more chronic conditions, cognitive as well as physical disability, and pain, often with the need for caregiving assistance. In a review of 44 studies in North America, Europe and Australia, researchers describe multimorbidity, the presence of more than one health condition, as the norm for those over 65 (Violan, 2014).

In this chapter, we use elder, traditionally a term of respect, to describe the population. The definition of an elder can vary from those over 50, in less developed countries, to those over the age of 60–65, for instance those who are pensionable in Western countries (WHO, 2017). The experience of aging varies greatly, however. Some elders continue to work, travel and function independently into late life, while others experience significant disability. Highly functioning elders mirror their younger peers in most ways, thus MBIs offered to the general population will be appropriate. Elders with physical and cognitive disabilities differ significantly from their peers, and adaptations of MBIs for this population will be our chapter's focus.

Caregiving for dependent elders is provided by both unpaid family and friends (informal caregivers) or paid professionals (formal caregivers). Caregivers may offer minimal assistance, such as shopping, bill paying or even just checking in regularly with the elder. At the other end of this spectrum, caregivers may provide 24-hour support for frail, confused or vulnerable elders. Paid-direct caregivers often find their work satisfying, but also demanding and underpaid. Both paid and unpaid caregivers are at risk of physical injury and emotional distress.

Many elders continue to live in their homes, perhaps with physical adaptations and caregivers. Other elders may move to assisted living, housing that provides both physical and caregiving support. The frailest elders may reside in long-term care institutions, traditionally modeled on hospitals.

Mindfulness-based elder care program intentions

MBIs for elders and caregivers have demonstrated to be an acceptable and beneficial companion for medical interventions (McBee, 2008). Older adults suffer disproportionately from chronic conditions, loss of physical and cognitive functioning and disability. While the experience of aging varies, one common factor is the experience of loss. Elders are more likely to lose physical and cognitive functioning and abilities, leading to dependence on others and possible relocation. In addition, elders may experience dramatic identity and role changes in retirement. Loss of hearing, vision and even taste and touch diminishment, can lead to isolation and reduced enjoyment of sensations. As one ages, friends and family are more likely to die, move or become frail, adding to the loss of identity and support for an elder.

These multiple factors clearly impact each other often leading to sadness, mourning and even depression. While there are some circumstances here that could be cured or positively changed, most of them are conditions and situations that are lasting changes for the elder. Despite these losses, many elders report increased happiness or life satisfaction as they age (Sorrell, 2009). MBIs may offer ways for elders and caregivers to further ameliorate the effects of loss.

Mindfulness-Based Stress Reduction (MBSR), the first widely popularized and replicated MBI, was initially designed by Jon Kabat-Zinn to help people learn to live as fully as possible with chronic pain. It represented a paradigm shift from the goals of fixing, curing or eradicating found in conventional Western medicine. MBSR is an eight-week series of two-and-a-half to three-hour classes with an all-day retreat and homework expectations. This model often requires adaptation for frail elders while maintaining the integrity of the practices. Mindfulness-Based Elder Care (MBEC) is not a specific intervention, but a range of suggested adaptations based on MBSR.

Research on MBIs for elders and caregivers

The most significant characteristic of research on MBIs is the holistic nature of identified benefits. These benefits align with the complex, overlapping and systemic biopsychosocial issues facing elders. As we learn more about the underlying factors in disease process, it appears that chronic inflammation is at the core of most or all physical and cognitive disease, and that stress is related to inflammation (Egger, 2012; McGeer & McGeer, 2004). A small 2013 study (Creswell et al.) offered MBSR to a group of non-frail elders and found that participants reported a reduction in loneliness (often associated with health problems in elders) and also reduced pro-inflammatory gene expression. There is also an increasing body of evidence on MBIs specifically for elders and caregivers including applications for chronic conditions and pain, cognitive loss, mood disorders and quality of life. Selected examples are listed below.

Older adults with distress, anxiety and vulnerability to stress are at increased risk of poor cognition, Alzheimer's Disease (AD) and more rapid decline in global cognition (Stawski, Sliwinski & Smyth, 2006; Wilson et al, 2011). Cognitive loss is a significant concern for the aging population and to date, medical interventions have had little impact. The World Health Organization (WHO) currently reports that 47.5 million people worldwide have dementia, including approximately 60–70% with AD, with 7.7 million new cases reported yearly. In 2011, Holzel et al. reported regeneration or growth of the brain's "grey matter" following an eight-week MBSR course, giving hope of regeneration in the areas of the brain damaged in the process of dementia. This finding was replicated in 2013 (Wells et al.) for older adults with mild cognitive loss who took the eight-week course with their caregivers. Other studies have demonstrated improvements in cognition and functioning using adapted MBIs (Larouche, Hudon & Goulet, 2015; Quintana et al, 2013). A review of 12 studies investigating the effects of a variety of meditation techniques confirmed that teaching meditation to elders, even those with cognitive loss, was both feasible and beneficial in offsetting cognitive decline and even potentially increasing cognitive capabilities (Gard, Holzel & Lazar, 2014). A 2016 review of benefits of meditation for elders (Acevedo, Pospos & Lavretsky) found that meditation impacts areas of the brain connected to awareness, attention, memory, and emotion regulation. This meta-analysis included seven MBIs and six active-type meditation interventions, finding overall positive benefits for elders in cognition, mood and physical disorders.

Researchers on aging also confirm findings on the benefits of MBIs for the chronic pain and physical conditions that disproportionately impact elders. Lunde, Nordhus and Pallesen (2009) reviewed 12 studies of cognitive behavioural treatments (CBT) for pain in elders (including MBIs) and found minimal, but promising results. Their recommendations included further research of the "third wave" of CBT interventions, like MBIs, that focus on acceptance. Marone et al (2008) studied 37 community-dwelling, cognitively intact older adults with chronic lower back pain. The findings reported positive results for participants of an eight-week course based on MBSR (with no yoga) in functioning and pain acceptance for the experimental group, and that these results were sustained in a three-month follow up. While the Marone study focused on community-dwelling, cognitively intact elders, one chapter author (LM) offered a similar modified MBSR program for nursing home residents finding a significant improvement in mood, and a trend towards less pain (2004). Clearly the chronic conditions impacting elders are interwoven, complex and often immutable. For this reason, MBIs can be especially effective in offering ways to "tread the path with care" or live with what cannot be fixed or changed. Oken et al (2016) found that compared to a wait list, a yoga practice can improve quality of life and physical measures for older adults. For many, mindfulness meditation offers a spiritual experience that may or may not be connected to religious affiliation (Greeson et al, 2011).

Caregivers experience a high degree of stress, and thus are susceptible to the physical, emotional and psychological conditions related to stress. Caregiving for persons with dementia is one of the most difficult scenarios due to erratic or dangerous behaviour. Caregivers clearly know they are stressed, yet may not know helpful ways to reduce their stress. MBIs may offer some ways in helping to reduce their stress. Whitebird et al (2013) found that an MBSR program for families caring for a relative with dementia at home reduced depression scores and stress, and improved overall mental health, as compared to an educational group. Hou et al (2014) taught MBSR to caregivers whose family member had a chronic condition and also found MBSR feasible and beneficial as compared to an educational group. In addition, one chapter author (LM) taught MBSR to caregivers whose family member was in long-term care, also finding positive results (Epstein-Lubow, McBee, Darling, Armey & Miller, 2011).

MBIs for elders and caregivers

In this section, we will review programs offered by one chapter author (LM) in a large urban US long-term care facility. These programs were introduced as discrete supplements for inpatient elders and their caregivers. We will also describe a program in Treviso, Italy (AB), a small city that integrates mindfulness as a foundational principle for eldercare throughout the community, supportive housing and long-term care. While discrete programs offering MBIs have been beneficial for both caregivers and elders, introducing mindfulness throughout the range of services and entire community may offer the best option as each segment can reinforce the other.

Mindfulness-based elder care (LM)

Beginning in 1994, I began offering adaptations of MBSR initially to frail elderly nursing home residents, eventually expanding to include residents on the specialized dementia unit, community-dwelling elders, and professional and family caregivers. Programs were developed based on adaptations of MBSR, my knowledge of frail elders and caregivers, available literature on group and individual work with this population, and trial and error.

MBEC for nursing home elders

When working with frail elders individually or in groups, a few basic principles emerged:

- Shorten the activity and group length; eliminate the retreat
- Treat groups as single sessions rather than ongoing groups
- Use simple, concrete language; repeat as indicated
- Communicate both verbally and non-verbally
- Less silence and more instruction
- Slower pace, ensuring comprehension; allow time to respond
- Limit discussion, eliminate dyad activities; remember that even passive engagement can be beneficial
- Adapt movement for limitations including cane, walker, chair and bed
- Focus on informal application of skills if homework assigned
- Include caregivers with elder groups when appropriate and possible

In groups for frail elders with mild cognitive loss, I taught the basic practices of MBSR with modifications described above, and at length in my book *Mindfulness Based Elder Care* (McBee, 2008). Eating meditation was practiced with crackers to prevent swallowing problems; the body scan was shortened and simplified; yoga was modified for chair positions; and walking meditation became wheeling meditation. Compassion and kindness were emphasized. Homework was not specifically assigned, but group discussion strategized on how to use mindfulness skills in the many stressful situations elders encountered, especially pain and dependency. Additionally, because the groups were held in the communal dining room, I used soft music and aromatherapy to create a therapeutic milieu.

I also individualized skills for isolated elders who were bedbound, and taught in groups for elders with dementia and behaviour problems such as agitation. In these groups, the emphasis was on repetition and nonverbal communication. Staff reported a decrease in agitation with elders following these groups (Lantz, Buchalter & McBee, 1997).

Returning to the core definitions and practices of mindfulness and MBSR, and then considering how they could be communicated to frail elders, was essential in all programs. The most important ingredient became my embodiment of the principles of awareness and compassion. Inquiry and discussion can emphasize abilities and empowerment, rather than limitations and disability. Elders reported finding peace, feeling empowered and less lonely (McBee, 2008).

MBEC for community and assisted living dwelling elders

I also taught MBEC to elders outside long-term care. In these populations, groups with similar or lesser adaptations were possible. For isolated homebound elders, I offered a telephone six-week class modelled on MBSR (McBee, 2008).

MBEC for caregivers

Both formal and informal caregivers can find the caregiving experience stressful and can benefit from learning skills to reduce stress. I taught both groups (separately) an MBSR class with positive results. I also found it helpful to teach shorter sessions, as many caregivers are reluctant to take the time for a class. This may be a realistic evaluation of their available time, and it also may indicate an inability or unwillingness to care for themselves rather than their care receiver. Often, the first step may be to remind the caregiver of the importance of self-care. A brief discussion on the short- and long-term mental and physical effects of stress will engage some. For others, a reminder that "stress is contagious" and can impact the care receiver, is helpful.

In addition, teaching simple stress reduction skills that can be incorporated into busy lives is important, and can introduce caregivers to longer practices. Some practices/methods I found helpful are listed below:

- Identify locations and times that work for caregivers
    - For family caregivers:
        - Use meeting time to teach the practices
        - Demonstrate use of the skills when they are providing care
        - Introduce these skills at group meetings for family caregivers
    - For staff caregivers,
        - Consider break time, or charting time on the unit
        - Use part of staff or team meetings to teach the practices
- Teach simple, brief practices that can be used throughout the day, with specific suggestions:
    - Deep breathing was the most well received of practices I taught
    - Seated or standing mountain pose (from yoga pis an attainable and feasible practice for most
    - Indicating specific applications can be important. For example, suggest using standing mountain pose while waiting in line or deep breathing when in a stressful meeting.
- Provide short handouts with simple instructions to remind caregivers of skills taught
    - Include a list of community resources for caregivers interested in follow-up
- Teach skills that can be practiced while providing care
    - If the care receiver is demanding and confused, I suggest caregivers try a deep breath
    - Simple stretches and deep breathing can be practiced by caregiver and care receiver together
    - Audio resources available online can be played and benefit both caregiver and care receiver
- Provide group sessions that include both care receivers and care givers

Reducing caregiver stress is important and feasible with adapted mindfulness skills. Ultimately, teaching caregivers may be the most important way we can bring mindfulness to frail elders. The programs and practices above proved helpful to both elders and caregivers within the challenging context of institutional living. As I argued in my book, however, a systemic approach would offer a more seamless environment supporting mindfulness for elders and caregivers (McBee, 2008).

Mindfulness at ISRAA (AB)

The Istituto per Servizi di Ricovero e Assistenza agli Anziani (ISRAA) is the public care provider for elders in a small Italian city, Treviso, where I've been working since 2002. I've been practicing mindfulness since 1996, after reading the book written by Jon Kabat-Zinn, *Wherever You Go, There You Are* (Kabat-Zinn, 1994). I was interested in how the mind causes suffering and how to relieve that suffering. Buddhist psychology together with Gestalt psychotherapy training gave me a very supportive and nourishing framework for my personal and professional growth. The goal at ISRAA is to improve or maintain wellbeing and quality of life of the elderly by promoting health and preventing disease. ISRAA supports programs for elders and caregivers across the spectrum of aging using approaches based on mindfulness including Kitwood's Person-Centered Care (Kitwood, 1997); person and family-centered care; the role of attachment styles in aging and caring; the Alzheimer Café (a day program for elders with dementia, Miesen & Jones, 2004) support groups; the impact of ambiguous loss (Boss, 2011) on dementia caregivers; and emotional intelligence for the leadership and the team. ISRAA also supports elders and caregivers in their homes, in the community, in day programs for elders with dementia and in long term care.

At ISRAA, we utilized the Mindfulness-Based Living Course (MBLC) (www.london.samye.org). According to Rob Nairn (Nairn, 2001), founder of MBLC, "Mindfulness can be defined as knowing what is happening while it is happening, without preference." Nairn has developed a unique secular training in mindfulness, which takes us on a step-by-step journey into a deepening experience of being present and accepting ourselves as we are. The training includes teachings in Western psychological language that provide a context for understanding what is happening in our minds as we practice, and working with obstacles that arise. He suggests three stages to training in mindfulness. First, training ourselves to be present in the moment with what is there, second, developing the attitude of self-acceptance so that whatever arises is OK, thus coming to terms with ourselves, and third, abandoning all goals. He clarified this third stage further by stating that "if we let go of the idea of getting anywhere we come to see that we are already there. There is nowhere to go" (Nairn, 2001).

It is an eight-week course consisting of eight classes, which are typically two hours long, preceded by an introductory class before the eight-week course begins and concluded by a follow-up class after the eight-week course ends.

The weekly themes are as follows:

Introductory Session – What is Mindfulness and Why Practice It?
Week 1 – Start Where We Are
Week 2 – The Body as a Place to Stay Present
Week 3 – Introducing Mindfulness Support
Week 4 – Working with Distraction
Week 5 – Exploring the Undercurrent

Week 6 – Attitude of the Observer
Week 7 – Self-acceptance
Week 8 – A Mindfulness-Based Life
Follow-Up Day of Practice – The Rest of Your Life

Working with elders in assisted living

Casa Albergo is ISRAA's assisted living for elders who need some care but also have a good level of autonomy. The elder's self-determination and the involvement of the family are important aspects of our person-centered care approach. A yoga program was well received by residents, and we decided to study the efficacy of mindfulness-based training on the affective and cognitive factors of aging. We investigated the effect of an eight-week mindfulness-based program on nine elder women aged 85 to 92 years compared to a similar, wait-listed population. The Cognitive and Affective Mindfulness Scale (Feldman, Hayes, Kumar, Greeson & Laurenceau, 2007), Resilience Scale (Wagnild & Young, 1993), and D2 Test of Attention (Bates & Lemay, 2004) were employed. The content of the program included introduction to mindfulness, mindful eating exercise, introduction to sitting meditation, body scan, mindful breathing, introduction to yoga, mindful walking and loving-kindness meditation. Formal and informal mindfulness practices were proposed as well as a pleasant and unpleasant events diary.

This data showed that there was a statistically significant improvement in the experimental group only in the dimension of attention, with trends towards improvement in the other dimensions. Our research findings shed light on how mindfulness-based training could improve working memory capacity and have a positive effect both on cognitive tasks and self-regulation of emotional expression (Borella, Marigo & Cirà Madonna, 2015; Buranello, Marigo & Madonia, 2016).

Furthermore, the recorded subjective experiences of the participants during the intervention and upon completion were very positive. Maria, a 90-year-old participant, suffering from chronic disease, told us about her changing attitude towards pain and reported a general improvement in her global functioning. She said, "There is a need to learn at all ages."

Participants were very impressed by the practice of body and sensation awareness and mindful breathing, and asked for additional similar training. We are currently integrating

Table 12.1 Study data

Tools	Group	Mean	Standard Deviation	T-test value	p
Cognitive and Affective Mindfulness Scale	Experimental	0.00	0.18	0.68	=0.50
	Control	−0.05	0.20	0.68	
Resilience Scale	Experimental	−0.01	0.03	−0.64	=0.52
	Control	0.01	0.11	−0.64	
D2 test of Attention	Experimental	0.35	0.42	2.82	=0.01
	Control	−0.06	0.12	2.82	

some mindfulness practice into other activities, such as the Cognitive Stimulation Lab, offered to the elders in our nursing homes. The Cognitive Stimulation Lab is a nonpharmacological intervention designed to improve cognitive skills and quality of life for people with dementia through activities such as categorization, word association and discussion of current affairs.

During the Cognitive Stimulation Lab we start with some mindful breathing. An anecdotal finding of the mindfulness-based training for elders living at Casa Albergo was a very calm atmosphere among participants. The MBLC trainer, Cinzia Marigo, told me that it could be possible because of an improvement in the attitude of self-acceptance and welcoming at any level of cognition (Borella, Marigo & Cirà Madonna, 2015). In a setting like a independent living facility where sometimes is difficult to manage relational conflicts, this is a very remarkable finding.

Even if further research is needed to define the benefits of MBIs for the institution-dwelling elderly, we are confident in the efficacy of these trainings to promote the elder's wellbeing.

Working with professional caregivers

As described above, mindfulness for frail elders in the nursing home is integrated into some of their activities. For frail elders, however, it is especially important to consider support for their caregivers. There are cultural considerations. For example, in Italy, moving into a nursing home is a difficult choice for families because there are strong beliefs that it is a family's duty to care for elders. Families are expected to provide assistance to the elderly, often with the help of private aides with no professional training. And when a family cannot provide the necessary care, the decision to find a place where the elder's needs will be met is often accompanied by conflicts among children, and a sense of guilt. Sometimes, for the nursing home's helping professionals, it is difficult to change their negative and judgmental attitudes towards the family. For some families, it can be difficult to change their negative view of nursing homes. This attitude may also be reflected in the behaviours of some professional caregivers in the nursing homes of ISRAA, which can even lead to misunderstanding and relational suffering.

After Rob Nairn visited our facilities in 2013, we decided to introduce our staff to MBLC and investigate the benefits. A variety of studies have suggested that the introduction of mindfulness and compassion-based interventions should be an integral part of a healthcare professional's training, continued professional development and ongoing self-care program (Irving, Dobkin & Park, 2009; Shapiro, Astin, Bishop & Cordova, 2005; Shapiro, Brown & Biegel, 2007). This research shows that mindfulness confers significant benefits on health, wellbeing and quality of life in general. This in turn has significant benefits and implications for people's performance in the workplace, either in terms of their reduced levels of stress and increased productivity, or in terms of the qualities of interpersonal relationships. Chaskalson (2011) lists the characteristics of a more mindful workplace: lower levels of stress and illness-related absenteeism; more employee engagement; less conflict; higher levels of job satisfaction; lower levels of employee turnover; higher levels of creativity and innovation; and greater productivity.

In 2016 we conducted a study on MBLC training for the helpers working at ISRAA, and 82 agreed to participate on a voluntary basis. Of these, 15 women were selected for the training, and 15 similar participants were wait-listed.

Table 12.2 Second study data

	Experimental group N= 15		Control group N = 15	
	M	SD	M	DS
Age	45.87	10.281	46.67	10.417
Education	12.67	3.519	12.67	3.519
Years of work	14.73	7.126	15.33	10.702

Three self-report questionnaires were chosen. Baseline and post-intervention measures were taken from each questionnaire and analyzed. Participants completed self-report questionnaires on-site to simplify delivery and to maximize questionnaire return. To control for the impact of mindfulness practice on questionnaire responses, baseline questionnaires were given out and completed at the beginning of the first session and again completed at the end of the last session of the eight-week program. Pre- and posttests included Perceived Stress Scale, Cohen-Katz et al (2005); Self-Compassion Scale (Neff, 2003); Emotion Regulation Questionnaire – EQR; and the Resilience Scale – RS (Wagnild & Young, 1993).

Statistical analysis was carried out on each of the three self-report measures with the Statistical Package for Social Science (SPSS). A two-way ANOVA was used to determine statistically significant differences between the experimental and control groups. Data analysis for the experimental group on the posttest revealed the following:

- There is a negative correlation (that is a relationship between two variables in which one variable increases as the other decreases, and vice versa) between the perceived stress and the cognitive reappraisal subscale;
- There is a positive correlation between resilience and self-compassion.

The posttest scores showed a statistically significant reduction in perceived stress for the experimental group and a statistically significant increase of the same aspects for the control group. We supposed that this increased level of stress at work for the control group could be found because of care environment complexity improvement. The increasing involvement of elderly families in the residential long-term care requires the development of cooperative communication skills. The staff sometimes feel families complain excessively – they're too demanding. On the flip side, families sometimes feel that staff aren't sufficiently caring, that staff are rude to them. Furthermore the importance of the volunteers in providing informal care involves for staff to accept them on board.

Another finding of our study was that there were no statistically significant differences between the two groups on self-compassion. A hypothesis for these data on self-compassion could be the ceiling effect on the baseline. In other words, the healthcare staff who decided to participate in the training had high scores on the self-compassion test on the pretest. We think that they were motivated to attend to MBLC because of their awareness on the impact of psychological wellbeing in caregiving. With this specific group, we can meet the need for stress reduction employing MBLC. The study raises further questions. What can we do to reach the whole care staff and improve compassion (*that is, a sensitivity to suffering in self and others with a commitment to try to alleviate and prevent it*; Gilbert, 2009) in our facilities, and in the community around them? How can we design effective training for improving the elderly and caregivers health? What steps are needed to help people living well with chronic conditions?

How can we foster capacity building in our community to promote an age friendly environment supporting people as they age in a sustainable and inclusive way? We think that empowering people to age in a good health, enhancing the solidarity between generations, encouraging the social engagement of the community and promoting a mindful ageing could be a promising line of development for our country.

Working with dementia

ISRAA also provides services for community-dwelling elders with dementia and their professional and family caregivers in a day program called the Alzheimer's Cafe. What kind of support can we give to caregivers that isn't based only on information about how to deal with dementia behaviors and teach them how to be empathetic towards elders and others? With this goal in mind, we needed to change the training programs for our staff and the way we delivered it to the support groups for caregivers. ISRAA helping professionals were all well trained according to the national guidelines, but they began to show dissatisfaction with the lack of continued learning. The caregivers of the Alzheimer's Café meetings who have been attending for years began to ask for something in addition to how to deal with dementia.

My colleagues and I started to integrate mindfulness-based practices into the training program for professionals and into the Alzheimer Café groups. For us, it was the missing piece for our elder care model. Why mindfulness-based training for healthcare professionals and family caregivers? Because mindfulness is a practice, not simply information, or a knowing, or a way of fixing problems. It is a practice that leads to acceptance of the present moment with a non-judgmental attitude. It opens the mind, the heart and the will. A lot of caregivers suffer from stress and the decline of emotional and physical wellbeing due to rumination, anticipatory loss and grief. Furthermore, caring for someone who has dementia may mean experiencing the "ambiguous loss" (Boss, 2011) of having a person both here and not here, physically present, but psychologically absent. With dementia, absence and presence coexist, and we need to embrace this ambiguity and find the middle ground instead of falling into absolute thinking. Dealing with dementia means finding a sort of koan, the paradox to be meditated upon that is used to train Zen Buddhist monks to abandon ultimate dependence on reason and to encourage them into gaining intuitive enlightenment.

During our first mindfulness-based programs for healthcare professionals, we integrated the following principles through practice and discussion:

- Responding versus reacting to our triggers
- Developing a flexible (beginner's) mind, and learning to tolerate some discomfort
- Using mindfulness and grounding practices during times of extreme stress
- Awareness of interconnection: we are hardwired to connect with one another
- Radical Acceptance (Brach, 2004): acceptance doesn't mean resignation but acknowledging the reality of what is happening, while it's happening, without preferences (Nairn, 2001)
- Ambiguous loss, complicated loss and grief, and the myth of closure (Boss, 2011):
- Embracing the mode of *being*, as well as *doing*

Participants reported an increased perception of self-efficacy in listening, managing conflicts, and decision-making. We collected positive feedback on the use of some simple practices during team meetings, such as the three-minute breathing space. What impressed more was the ability to pause and to prevent pushing out of the window of tolerance. One of our unit care coordinators told us that:

> Before the training I often felt overwhelmed and overloaded at work. I was unaware of my mind spinning with all the tasks. My listening skills were deteriorating. The more I tried to fix the situation, the more I failed. The climate of my team was toxic. I began to be dissatisfied and demotivated at work. I didn't attend the whole training on mindfulness as my team did. I thought I was too busy for training. What happened was that the psychologist of the interdisciplinary team, started to pause when all of us began to be pushed out of our windows of tolerance during our meetings. I began to be aware of what triggered me in the fight or flight response. I became an observer of my mind. And I began to listen to my team. I recognized the importance of training the mind for not causing suffering in others an in myself. So I asked for help, and I had some individual sessions with a mindfulness trainer. Now I'm practicing mindfulness at work, and even if I'm still having some resistance in formal mindfulness practice, I warmly support these kinds of training for helping professions.

After these positive qualitative results with staff, we began to introduce some of the contents of the mindfulness-based programs for healthcare professionals in the Alzheimer's Café groups and in psychological support. The result are well represented by one of the family caregiver's feedback, as below:

> Now when I have a shower, I simply have a shower. I learned how to stay in the present moment, and when my mind wanders, I intentionally come back to the present moment using my body sensations or breathing as a support. And I'm aware when I'm criticizing myself, and so I can let go of this story, remind me that thoughts are not facts. Now when I suffer because of some challenging situations or frustrations caused by dementia disease, I try to feel the connection with other people who are suffering for the same reason. I don't feel alone.

Working with pain

On March 15th, 2010, Italy adopted Law no. 38, "Disposizioni per garantire l'accesso alle cure palliative e alla terapia del dolore" (Provisions aimed at ensuring access to palliative care and pain therapy). The aim of pain therapy is to enable patients with chronic diseases to achieve pain control. In 2011, the Dolomite project was established at ISRAA to remove the barriers to pain relief in older adults. (The Dolomites comprises a mountain range in the northern Italian Alps, and is a World Heritage Site. In the Italian language, "dolore" means pain and "mite" means "mild").

The lack of adequate education of healthcare professionals and the ageist belief that pain is a normal part of aging were only some of the limits in assessing and treating the pain of the elders. We started thinking how to integrate nonpharmacological treatments in the relief of chronic pain. We improved the use of massage (nurturing touch) and of the Snoezelen Room (a controlled multisensory environment) with elder people experiencing chronic pain. And we also began MBEC training for the residents of one of our facilities, following the indications and adaptations of LM's work.

In addition, we wondered how to provide more compassionate care for the elderly, with the help and supervision of the Mindfulness Association and Innersight (the Italian provider of MBI interventions). We conducted the two studies on mindfulness-based training described above, one for the elderly and the other for caregiving staff.

Summary

How we take care of our elders matters. At ISRAA values matter. A compassionate community, based on solidarity and social inclusion, can create the conditions for the development of a sustainable and resilient environment where people can age well. For these reasons, we are designing two paths of an integrated care model: one for the coordinators of our facilities and the other for the community of our city, Treviso.

The *first path*: a commitment of the ISRAA leadership in Mindfulness and Compassion in action. At ISRAA there are more than 20 coordinators (unit care coordinators, facility coordinators, administrative coordinators, and a general manager). Some of these coordinators participated at the MBLC. We have a lot of self-reported feedback from the participants of MBLC that told us how Mindfulness practice leads to a change in attitude. Most reported that:

> "Mindfulness is a wonderful training, but . . . we don't have time to practice, to attend such a long training."

For us Mindfulness is not *only* sitting in meditation. We aim to integrate Mindfulness and Compassion practice into our eldercare model through a project now called *One Mindful Step* (from the Zen passage "A journey of a thousand miles begins with one step" Lao Tzu). We will help coordinators with individual and group coaching sessions based on their identified need. In one care unit the main issue may be pain management; in another, the relationship with the family of the elderly or accompanying the dying. We will figure out how Mindfulness and Compassion could be beneficial. There could be a balance between doing, caring and being. We hope that taking *One Mindful Step* could bring more mindful and compassionate decision-making to the coordinators. Learning to pause mindfully could help coordinators step out of reactivity and become more compassionate and emotionally intelligent leaders. We want to help the leaders of our facilities to focus on three aspects: self-awareness; awareness of others, and of the context (Goleman & Senge, 2014). When a leader focuses on an issue, his/her team will make choices based on their perception of what matters to him/her. This ripple effect gives leaders an extra load of responsibility. Sometimes "doing the right thing" in the elder care could mean "doing nothing" and only being present. For example, it may be more ethical not to overtreat an elderly person who is dying, or not to exercise restraints that limit the autonomy and freedom of the elderly. We can plant seeds for wisdom and compassion in our nursing homes and in the community for the benefit of all.

Furthermore, we realize that it is important that the leaders of the nursing homes become more aware of the importance of community care. Raising the awareness of our leaders and care staff on the importance of the interconnection with the community and openness to the city has led to the second path of the integrated care model.

The second path: engagement of the community in caring for the elderly. It is important that no old person is alone, and similarly that the caregivers are not alone. As the old saying says "It takes a village to raise a child" and we can add "and to age well." Aging and living well with all the chronic conditions or situations are responsibilities of the whole community. Currently, ISRAA is designing training to connect elders with the larger community, giving an important role to compassion, mindful communication and presence, and to attitudinal changes that can lead to respect and acceptance of others, and of aging as a normal part of life. For us this means to integrate mindfulness and compassion in community care. This is what Einstein called "widening the circle of compassion" (as cited in Ricard & Thuan, 2009).

With a world population that is living longer, and often with chronic conditions, cognitive loss and pain, MBIs can offer a path to relieve suffering. Buddha's teachings "things fall apart, tread the path with care" remain relevant and true, as do the practices of mindfulness that enable all to work with these truths. Here we have described a few ways to adapt the teachings for elders and caregivers. For those wishing to bring mindfulness to these populations, our final recommendation is to begin with your own practice of meditation and mindfulness. The most important intervention is our presence, conveying authentic connection, warmth and acceptance.

References

Acevedo, B. P., Pospos, S., & Lavretsky, H. (2016). The neural mechanisms of meditative practices: Novel approaches for healthy aging. *Current Behavioral Neuroscience Report, 3*, 328–339. doi:10.1007/s40473–016–0098-x

Aggs, C., & Bambling, M. (2010). Teaching mindfulness to psychotherapists in clinical practice: The mindful therapy programme. *Counselling and Psychotherapy Research, 10*(4), 278–286.

Bates, M. E., & Lemay, E. P. (2004). The d2 test of attention: Construct validity and extensions in scoring techniques. *Journal of the International Neuropsychological Society, 10*(3), 392–400.

Borella, E., Marigo, C., & Cirà Madonna, J. (2015). *L'efficacia di un training di mindfulness con un gruppo di anziani sugli aspetti emotivo-motivazionali (The effectiveness of mindfulness training for the elderly on the emotional and motivational aspects)*. Master's Dissertation in Aging, Padua University, Italy.

Boss, P. (2011). *Loving someone who has dementia: How to find hope while coping with stress and grief*. San Francisco, CA: Jossey-Bass.

Brach, T. (2004). *Radical acceptance: Embracing your life with the heart of a Buddha*. London: Bantam.

Buranello, A., Marigo, C., & Madonia, V. (2016). *Prendersi cura di chi si prende cura: percorso di mindfulness per operatori socio sanitari (Caring for the caregivers: A mindfulness path for nursing assistants)*. Master's Dissertation in Aging, Padua University, Italy.

Chaskalson, M. (2011). *The mindful workplace: Developing resilient individuals and resonant organizations with MBSR*. Hoboken, NJ: Wiley-Blackwell.

Cohen-Katz, J., Wiley, S., Capuano, T., Baker, D. M., Deitrick, L., & Shapiro, S. (2005). The effects of mindfulness-based stress reduction on nurse stress and burnout: A qualitative and quantitative study, part III. *Holistic Nursing Practice, 19*(2), 78–86.

Didonna, F. (2009). *Clinical handbook of mindfulness*. New York, NY: Springer.

Egger, G. (2012). In search of a germ theory equivalent for chronic disease. *Preventing Chronic Disease, 9*, 110301.

Epstein-Lubow, G., McBee, L., Darling, E., Armey, M., & Miller, I. W. (2011). A pilot investigation of mindfulness-based stress reduction for caregivers of frail elderly. *Mindfulness, 2*(2), 95–102.

Feldman, G., Hayes, A., Kumar, S., Greeson, J., & Laurenceau, J. P. (2007). Mindfulness and emotion regulation: The development and initial validation of the Cognitive and Affective Mindfulness Scale-Revised (CAMS-R). *Journal of Psychopathology and Behavioral Assessment, 29*(3), 177.

Gard, T., Holzel, B. K., & Lazar, S. W. (2014). The potential effects of meditation on age-related cognitive decline: A systematic review. *The Annals of the New York Academy of Sciences, 1307*, 89–103. doi:10.1111/nyas.12348

Germer, C. (2009). *The mindful path to self-compassion*. New York, NY: Guilford Press.

Gilbert, P. (2009). *The compassionate mind*. London: Constable & Robinson.

Goldman, D. (2015). *Focus: The hidden driver of excellence*. New York, NY: Harper Press.

Goleman, D., & Senge, P. (2014). The triple focus. *Reflections, 14*(1).

Greeson, J. M., Webber, D. M., Smoski, M. J., Brantley, J. G., Ekblad, A. G., Suarez, E. C., & Wolever, R. Q. (2011). Changes in spirituality partly explain health-related quality of life outcomes after Mindfulness-based Stress Reduction. *Journal of Behavioral Medicine, 34*(6), 508–518.

Hall, D. (2012). Out the window: The view in winter. *The New Yorker*, January 23.

Hesse, H. (2011). *Seasons of the soul*. Berlin, Germany: Suhrkamp Verlag.

Higgins, W. (2016). Treading the path with care. *Tricycle*, Winter, 39–41.

Hou, R. J., Wong, S. Y. S., Yip, B. H. K., Hung, A. T., Lo, H. H. M., Chan, P. H., . . . & Mercer, S. W. (2014). The effects of mindfulness-based stress reduction program on the mental health of family caregivers: A randomized controlled trial. *Psychotherapy and Psychosomatics, 83*(1), 45–53.

Irving, J. A., Dobkin, P. L., & Park, J. (2009). Cultivating mindfulness in health care professionals: A review of empirical studies of mindfulness-based stress reduction (MBSR). *Complementary Therapies in Clinical Practice, 15*(2), 61–66.

Kabat-Zinn, J. (1994). *Wherever you go, there you are*. New York, NY: Hyperion.

Kabat-Zinn, J. (2004). *Full catastrophe living*. London: Piatkus.

Kitwood, T. (1997). *Dementia reconsidered: The person comes first*. Buckingham, UK: Open University Press.

Lantz, M. S., Buchalter, E. N., & McBee, L. (1997). The wellness group: A novel intervention for coping with disruptive behavior in elderly nursing home residents. *The Gerontologist, 37*(4), 551–557.

Larouche, E., Hudon, C., & Goulet, S. (2015). Potential benefits of mindfulness-based interventions in mild cognitive impairment and Alzheimer's disease: An interdisciplinary perspective. *Behavioral Brain Research, 276*, 199–212.

Lunde, L-H., Nordhus, I. H., & Pallesen, S. (2009). The effectiveness of cognitive and behavioural treatment of chronic pain in the elderly: A quantitative review. *Journal of Clinical Psychology in Medical Settings*, September, *16*(3), 254–262.

McBee, L. (2008). *Mindfulness Based Elder Care*. New York: Springer.

McBee, L., Westrich, L., & Likourzos, A. (2004). A psychoeducational relaxation group for pain and stress management in the nursing home. *Journal of Social Work in Long-Term Care, 3*(1).

Mccollum, E. E., & Gehart, D. R. (2010). Using mindfulness mediation to teach beginning therapists therapeutic presence: A qualitative study. *Journal of Marital and Family Therapy, 36*(3), 347–360.

McGeer, P. L., & McGeer, E. G. (2004). Inflammation and the degenerative diseases of aging. *Annals of the New York Academy of Sciences, 1035*(1), 104–116.

Miesen, B., & Jones, G. (2004). *Care-giving in dementia: Research and applications, Volume 4*. New York, NY: Routledge.

Moss, A., Reibel, D., & Thapar, A. (2013). *Quantitative and qualitative assessment of MBSR for elderly in in long term care*. Presentation 11th Annual International Scientific Conference of the Center for Mindfulness in Medicine, Healthcare and Society. Norwood MA, USA.

Moynihan, J. A., Chapman, B. P., Klorman, R., Krasner, M. S., Duberstein, P. R., Brown, K. W., & Talbot, N. L. (2013). Mindfulness-based stress reduction for older adults: Effects on executive function, frontal alpha asymmetry and immune function. *Neuropsychobiology, 68*(1), 34–43. doi:10.1159/000350949

Nairn, R. (2001). *Diamond mind.* Boston, MA: Shambhala.
Nairn, R. (2008). *Lecture on mindfulness.* Tara Rokpa Centre, South Africa, November 3.
National Institute on Aging, National Institute of Health. (2017). *World popultation aging.* Retrieved April 12, 2017 from http://www.nia.nih.gov/research/dbsr/world-population-aging
National Institute on Aging, National Institute of Health. (2017). *Why population aging matters: A global perspective. Trend 3: Rising numbers of the oldest old.* Retrieved April 12, 2017 from www.nia.nih.gov/publication/why-population-aging-matters-global-perspective/trend-3-rising-numbers-oldest-old
Neff, K. D. (2003). The development and validation of a scale to measure self-compassion. *Self and Identity, 2*(3), 223–250.
Oken, B. S., Fonareva, I., Haas, M., Wahbeh, H., Lane, J. B., Zajdel, D. P., & Amen, A. M. (2010). Pilot controlled trial of mindfulness meditation and education for dementia caregivers. *Journal of Alternative and Complementary Medicine, 16,* 1031–1038.
Oken, B. S., Wahbeh, H., Goodrich, E., et al. (2016). Meditation in stressed older adults: Improvements in self-rated mental health not paralleled by improvements in cognitive function or physiological measures. *Mindfulness,* 1–12. doi:10.1007/s12671-016-0640-7
Pomykala, K. L., Silverman, D. H., Geist, C. L., et al. (2012). A pilot study of the effects of meditation on regional brain metabolism in distressed dementia caregivers. *Aging Health, 8*(5), 509–516.
Quintana, H. D., Miró, B. M., Ibáñez, F. I., Del Pino, A. S., García, R. J., & Hernandez, J. R. (2013). Effects of a neuropsychology program based on mindfulness on Alzheimer's disease: Randomized double-blind clinical study. *Revista española de geriatría y gerontología, 49*(4), 165–172.
Ricard, M. & Thuan T. X. (2009). *The quantum and the lotus: A journey to the frontiers where science and Buddhism meet.* Portland, OR: Broadway Books.
Rigg, I. (2013). *The effects of the 8-week mindfulness based living course (mblc) when delivered to a mixed group of health care staff: A prospective pilot Study* (unpublished master's thesis). Aberdeen University, UK.
Shapiro, S. L., Astin, J. A., Bishop, S. R., & Cordova, M. (2005). Mindfulness-based stress reduction for health care professionals: Results from a randomized trial. *International Journal of Stress Management, 12*(2), 164–176.
Shapiro, S. L., Brown, K. W., & Biegel, G. M. (2007). Teaching self-care to caregivers: Effects of mindfulness-based stress reduction on the mental health of therapists in training. *Training and Education in Professional Psychology, 1*(2), 105.
Siegel, D. (2007). *The mindful brain: Reflection and attunement in the cultivation of well-being.* New York, NY: Norton & Company.
Sorrell, J. M. (2009). Aging toward happiness. *Journal of Psychosocial Nursing and Mental Health Services, 47*(3), 23–26.
Violan, C., Foguet-Boreu, Q., Flores-Mateo, G., Salisbury, C., Blom, J., Freitag, M., . . . Valderas, J. M. (2014). Prevalence, determinants and patterns of multimorbidity in primary care: A systematic review of observational studies. *PloS one, 9*(7), e102149.
Wagnild, G., & Young, H. (1993). Development and psychometric. *Journal of Nursing Measurement, 1*(2), 165–178.
WeDO European project. (2010–2012). *European quality framework for long term services.* Bruxelles, Belgium: European Partnership for the Wellbeing and Dignity of Older People.
Wells, R. E., Yeh, G. Y., Kerr, C. E., Wolkin, J., Davis, R. B., Tan, Y., . . . Kong, J. (2013). Meditation's impact on default mode network and hippocampus in mild cognitive impairment: A pilot study. *Neuroscience Letters, 556,* 15–19.
Whitebird, R. R., Kreitzer, M., Crain, A. L., Lewis, B. A., Hanson, L. R., & Enstad, C. J. (2013). Mindfulness-based stress reduction for family caregivers: A randomized controlled trial. *The Gerontologist, 53*(4), 676–686.

Wilson, R. S., Begeny, C. T., Boyle, P. A., Schneider, J. A., & Bennett, D. A. (2011). Vulnerability to stress, anxiety, and development of dementia in old age. *The American Journal of Geriatric Psychiatry*, *19*(4), 327–334. doi:10.1097/JGP.0b013e31820119da

World Health Organization. (2007). *Global age-friendly cities: A guide*. World Health Organization. Retrieved 4/1/17 from: www.who.int/healthinfo/survey/ageingdefnolder/en/

Section III

Mindfulness programs in health-care

Chapter 13

Promoting healing through mindful medical practice

Patricia Lynn Dobkin

Overview of the mindful medical practice program

Mindfulness-Based Stress Reduction (MBSR), developed by Kabat-Zinn and colleagues at the University of Massachusetts Medical Center, spans eight weeks and consists of weekly 2.5-hour-long classes and a retreat day of practice in silence after the sixth class. Participants are taught various types of meditation practices that they apply in class and to routine activities during daily life. Key elements of the program include: (a) group format; (b) emphasis upon a non-striving orientation; (c) expectation of relief; (d) sense of active engagement in the process and responsibility for outcomes; (e) demand characteristics (a significant time commitment and amount of home practice); (f) variation of meditation techniques; (g) didactic material (e.g. how the mind and body are connected); (h) finite duration (long enough to learn skills, yet short enough not to become dependent upon group); and (i) a long-term perspective (continued practice is encouraged after the program is terminated).

The Mindful Medical Practice (MMP) program is closely modeled after MBSR. It differs in how it adds weight to self-care and communication practices. For example, MMP includes exercises on interpersonal mindfulness aimed at helping clinicians integrate mindfulness into their work (Dobkin, Hickman, & Monshat, 2014). Participants are given a home practice manual and CDs/MP3s created by the instructor to teach the following meditation practices: body-scan, sitting meditation, and yoga. At the end of each class, participants are asked to complete specific home practice exercises. Group discussions throughout the course focus on the practice itself and how it was being integrated into the participants' daily lives and work (for a narrative description of week-to-week experiences the reader is directed to Dobkin, 2016).

Table 13.1 outlines MMP themes and exercises for each class. Rather than provide a manual for the program which would mislead the reader into believing one simply needs to follow procedures to teach the course, I will explain how various exercises may help heal the participant and help him to create a healing environment. It is critical that the reader understand that the way the course is taught has more to do with who the instructor is, how his own practice informs his teaching, and his skill in conducting inquiry, than following methods in a ridged manner. He must be attuned to each person and the group as a whole in order to teach skilfully. He needs to listen deeply to participants, help them gain insight from their experiences, while embodying key attitudes, such as beginner's mind, curiosity, non-judgment, non-striving, acceptance, and kindness (see Chapter 7, Dobkin & Hassed, 2016c for a full discussion on educating the teachers).

Table 13.1 Mindful Medical Practice: outline of the program

Class 1: Being present to yourself

Introduction	Guidelines for working together
	Two brief meditations
	Contemplation: why are you here now?
Raisin exercise	Coming home to our senses
Body scan meditation	Being with and accepting the body as it is, here and now

Class 2: Perception and creative responding

Body scan meditation	Class exercise and discussion of home practice
Perceptual exercise	Thinking and acting "outside the box"
Self-care exercise	Work in dyads: making space for one's self in life
Awareness of breath meditation	Informal practice introduced; using the breath throughout the day to be in the present moment

Class 3: Joy and sorrow – both are part of life

Yoga	Meditation in movement
Pleasant events	Review homework in groups of four
Artwork exercise	Work in dyads using patients' artwork to highlight different ways of perceiving pain
Sitting meditation	Guided, including various objects of awareness (not only breath)

Class 4: Stress and coping

'Choiceless' awareness meditation	Sitting with no object, simply with what arises
Unpleasant events	Review homework in groups of 4 (choose different people)
Stressors and stress responses	Use home practice manual – section on stressors and reaction versus responding
Teaching tools	STOP and Triangle of Awareness

Class 5: Mindful communication

"Soundscape" meditation	Listening to sounds and noticing what emerges
Mid-way questionnaire	Work in groups of three – home practice manual
Satir's communication stances	Mindful congruence: self-other-context
Role play	Unresolved clinical situation
Walking meditation	Mindful movement

Class 6: Interpersonal mindfulness

Yoga	
Insight dialogue: roles at work/ roles in one's personal life	1 Pause – calls forth awareness
	2 Relax – calls forth tranquility and acceptance
	3 Open – calls forth relational availability and spaciousness
	4 Trust Emergence – calls forth flexibility and letting to
	5 Listen Deeply – calls forth receptivity and attunement
	6 Speak the Truth – involves integrity and care
Communication Exercise	Work in dyads
Sitting meditation	

Retreat

Practice in silence	Seamless practice, including a silent lunch
	Debrief at the end: what did I learn? What was challenging? What surprised me?

Class 7: Healing/being whole

Loving kindness meditation
Insight Dialogue
Rumi exercise
Walking meditation

Compassion towards the self and others
Work in dyads: theme = suffering
Welcoming "uninvited guests"

Class 8: Ending and integrating

Body scan meditation
Follow-up questionnaire
Letter writing
Ending...

Overview of course, what was learned, etc.
What do you want to take with you? Recall?
1 What did you want/hope for?
2 What did you learn?
3 What aspect was most helpful?
4 How do you feel about the program ending?

Maintaining practice
Closing ceremony

Home practice is assigned after each class.

Theoretical background

Promoting healing in the self and the other

When an ill person knocks on a clinician's door she may be suffering physically, mentally, and spiritually. The social contract between the clinician and patient is that the former will assist the latter with the tools available to him: knowledge about disease and experience treating it with medicines, procedures and lifestyle recommendations. The patient comes to a medical encounter with previous experiences of illness (e.g. hers or another's) beliefs about its causes and treatments, habits (e.g. smoking, diet), and feelings (e.g. hope, fear, anger, sadness). The clinician harbors thoughts and feelings as well (e.g. "Why do the most difficult patients always show up at the end of the day? I'm running on empty.") – although these may not be conscious. Bringing them into awareness enables the clinician to meet the person in a space that promotes healing (Dobkin, 2009, 2011; Scott et al., 2008). But first, he must face his own *woundedness* so that he can be available and authentic in offering service to the person in his care (Remen, 2008; Santorelli, 1999).

Hutchinson and Dobkin (2015) propose that this can be done when a clinician is mindful and congruent. Congruent means taking into consideration the self (clinician), the other (patient) and the context. And this occurs within the clinician-patient relationship, or what Buber (1970) would call the equilibrium between the *I-thou* and *I-It* relational space (Scott et al., 2009). *I-It* relationships are characterized by experiencing and using objects. They are one way. *I-Thou*, on the other hand, are two-way relationships based in dialogue. One encounters another with mutual awareness. Buber calls this *presentness* – not bound by time. One is enabled to experience a relational event from the standpoint of oneself and the other simultaneously. Thus, a clinician can discern his impact on the patient based not on empathy, but from a stance Buber calls *inclusion* – by this he means combining presence with connection to "suffer with" the other, rather than simply "be in her shoes."

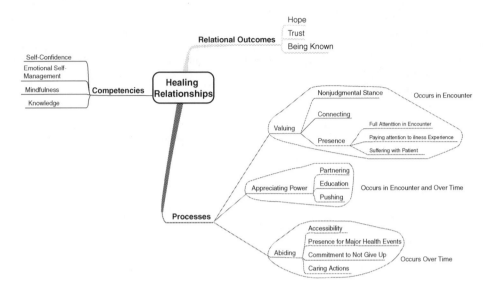

Figure 13.1 Healing Relationship Model.
Source: Scott et al. 2008, 2009.

Mindfulness as part of patient-centered care

The Healing Relationship Model developed by Scott et al. (2008, 2009) is depicted in Figure 13.1. It will be used herein to provide a rationale for MMP. Rather than focus on high rates of burnout and compassion-fatigue in health care professionals as the impetus for giving or taking a mindfulness-based course, I will examine how mindfulness is one "competency," among others, that contributes to fostering wellness in the healer and healee. Other clinician attributes are: self-confidence, emotional self-management, and knowledge. Research has consistently shown that mindfulness practice helps a person regulate their emotions. A grounded, emotionally stable clinician who is self-aware can help the patient gain hope, feel trust and experience "being known" (Relational Outcomes in Figure 13.1) or what Siegel (2010) calls attunement (i.e. understanding and responding appropriately to another person emotionally).

How is this done? According to this model, attitudes such as being non-judgmental, offering presence, and connecting with the other person, all occur during the encounter (Valuing in Figure 13.1). These are taught explicitly in the MMP course.

Healing Relationship Model

An important aspect of being a participant in a MBSR or MMP course is called "common humanity" (Neff, 2003). Participants come to understand that we all get sick, age and eventually die. This enables health care professionals to "pay attention to the illness experience" and "suffer with the patient" (Presence in Figure 13.1). Cohn (2001), in her examination of Existential Medicine from a Buber's perspective, suggests that it is possible to strike a balance in the dialectic between the *I-Thou* (subjective, reciprocal) and *I-It* (objective, detached) spheres. By doing so, the inherent power differential between the professional and person seeking care would lessen (Appreciating Power in Figure 13.1), allowing for partnering, educating, and pushing (e.g. being firm about changes that are in the patient's best interest in the face of resistance).

Developing competencies

As shown in Figure 13.1, we consider emotional regulation and mindfulness as clinician competences. Exercises that may lead to their development include various forms of meditation (e.g. body scan, sitting, walking, yoga) – as the literature on MBSR and Mindfulness-Based Cognitive Therapy (MBCT) indicate (see Chapter 2, Dobkin & Hassed, 2016 for a review of the scientific evidence). Informal practices, that is, being present in the moment while engaging in everyday activities are encouraged throughout the MMP and MBSR courses, as are brief Awareness-of-Breath exercises that may last from moments to minutes.

Two teaching tools used in MMP and MBSR to change reactivity into responding are the Triangle of Awareness (Figure 13.2) and STOP. Together, they help a person choose a skilful way of dealing with a stressful situation or an interpersonal interaction. By bringing awareness to how thoughts, emotions, and body sensations are interconnected he can begin change conditioned patterns. For example, a clinician may notice his fatigue, frustration about working overtime, and thoughts about how unfair the situation is, and then gain insight into how

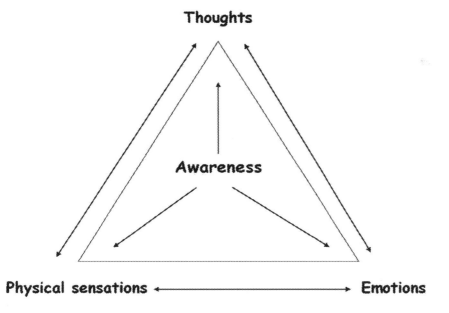

Figure 13.2 Triangle of Awareness.
Source: Dobkin 2016.

these factors impact her attitudes (e.g. impatience) and behaviours (e.g. interrupting when a patient is speaking) while working in a busy outpatient clinic. The person can use: STOP: S=slow down/stop; T=take a breath; O=observe (use the Triangle of Awareness); P=proceed (respond rather than react).

One exercise used in MMP that promotes *self-compassion* (which may contribute to *self-confidence*) includes a self-care exercise. Participants are paired up and encouraged to explore this issue together. Instructions include that each person speak their truth and listen deeply to what emerges, without commenting or interrupting when the other is exploring the answer to the question posed.

> First: Pick a partner (A and B) – decide who is A and who is B.
> Second: A asks B, "What is the one thing you notice when you DO NOT make space for yourself in your work life?"
> Third: B responds, then A says, "Thank you."
> Fourth: A repeats the question – for a few minutes.
> Fifth: A and B switch roles and the exercise is repeated.
> Sixth: the exercise is changed to:
> A asks B, "What is the one thing you notice when you DO make space for yourself in your work life?" following the same sequence as the first round.
> Then B asks A the same question.
> A and B are mirrors for each other.

Other means of supporting self-care and mindfulness

Yoga practice is a form of self-care that enables those who care for others' bodies to notice and take care of their own. It is woven into the course and included as home practice. Loving Kindness Meditation helps participants become self-compassionate. It is introduced towards the middle of the program.

Processes: valuing-during the medical encounter

Nonjudgmental stance

Healing relationships processes include maintaining a nonjudgmental stance (see Figure 13.1). Throughout the course the teacher models this attitude and helps participants, who are often their own harsh critics, adopt a kinder attitude towards themselves and others. Many doctors and allied health care professionals maintain high standards, perfectionistic tendencies, and critical minds. This appears to be an advantage in their high-stakes, high-risk work environment but, these habits of mind may backfire when held too tightly and lead to emotional exhaustion and beliefs that they are not performing well enough. These are both aspects of burnout (Irving et al., 2014). Meditation instructions ask the participant to accept all that arises without holding onto what is pleasant or rejecting what is unpleasant.

Another exercise used to promote acceptance and openness towards experiences involves reading this poem, then asking participants to consider "uninvited guests" (e.g. anger, injury) in their lives.

The Guest House

This being human is a guest-house.
Every morning a new arrival.

A joy, a depression, a meanness,
some momentary awareness comes
as an unexpected visitor.

Welcome and entertain them all!
Even if they're a crowd of sorrows,
who violently sweep your house
empty of its furniture,
still, treat each guest honorably.
He may be clearing you out
for some new delight.

The dark thought, the shame, the malice,
Meet them at the door laughing,
and invite them in.

Be grateful for whoever comes,
because each has been sent
As a guide from beyond.
     Jalaluddin Rūmī (1995)

Participants write a short narrative about an "uninvited guest." What was your reaction? What did you notice in your mind and body? What emotions were triggered?

Connecting

Next healing relationships process is connecting, as depicted in Figure 13.1. Hutchinson and Dobkin (2015) define congruence as full presence to oneself, to the other person, and to the context. The MMP course includes role plays where participants act out real clinical scenarios to become aware of mindful congruence (or lack thereof). For example, a doctor may be placating (leaving the self out) with a patient with chronic pain who complains continually. While focusing exclusively on the patient's needs, he may lose sight of boundaries and limits – going overtime during medical visits, ruminating about the patient after hours. When he becomes aware of this automatic reaction (attempting to please the other; wishing to be appreciated) he may stop trying so hard, feel more balanced, and leave room for the patient to take responsibility for certain aspects of his health care (e.g. pace activities, adhere to medications). This may result in less frustration as the doctor and patient *partnering* (Appreciate Power in Figure 13.1) while working together.

Presence

Last, but not least process in the valuing part of healing relationships is presence (see Figure 13.1). There are different ways to teach participants how to be fully present with a patient. I use Insight Dialogue developed by Kramer (2007), which is a form of interpersonal mindfulness. Participants learn to be with another person fully by following a sequence of steps in dyads, led by the teacher. Given the nature of their work I start with the concept suffering. I ask them to contemplate first one then the other question. Participants work in dyads, much like during the self-care exercise. The questions are:

1   Who am I in the face of suffering?
2   What do I know about listening to myself and others' suffering?

Then the steps are introduced with "an explanation" of what they entail:

> *Pause* "interrupts automatic reactions and opens the door to another way of relating. It is not about time. We can pause at any moment and become are of the mind and body just as they are. One learns to appreciate silence. Stillness meets reactivity."
> *Relax* "the body and mind. Become aware of the body as a whole, let go of tension, move into ease. Release resistance."
> *Open* "awareness extends beyond the body to the world, including other people, around us. Open allows us to move beyond ME. The subject/object split disappears. There is no boundary between inside/outside; you/me."
> *Trust Emergence* "letting go of preconceived ideas of what the answer to the question 'should' be, allowing what arises to do so without controlling what unfolds. Practice without a goal or outcome in mind. Meet others in the spirit of not-knowing; be curious. Engage the beginner's mind. It is not about trusting others *per se*, we are trusting ourselves to meet the unknown with mindfulness and acceptance. We recognize that nothing is permanent and go with the flow of change."
> *Listen Deeply* "be a receptive field; listen with kindness; let the words enter your heart. See if you are having a conversation with yourself at the same time. Notice if you are thinking about you rather than being open to the other. Offer a sustained presence. What do you see in addition to hear? Do you notice the quality of voice, pauses, speed of speech etc. What is the energy level of the person speaking?"
> *Speak the Truth* "express what emerges; do not say what is not useful; speak with kindness. Be aware of the body parts needed to speak. Notice thoughts before they are voiced. To speak the truth, you must first know it; one must listen internally first and discern it. If you find yourself speaking out of habit, PAUSE to interrupt the flow."

Another exercise used to help participants see where they are "stuck" in poor communication patterns is the following: First, participants are given colored pens and paper and asked to draw a pattern of a relationship that is problematic. They do this individually for about ten minutes, then choose a partner, preferably one they have not worked with previously. The teacher is careful to guide the exercise in such a way that they continue to drop into silence in between steps so that they do not simply have a conversation.

> Speaker 1: Tell the Listener about the pattern
> Listener 1: Listen without nodding or commenting in any way; then reflect the words
> Speaker 1: Tell more
> Listener 1: Listen, then reflect the body language
> Speaker 1: Repeat, adding dialogue
> Then, switch speakers.

Next, they all share with the larger group. They respond to these questions: What was it like to be the speaker? What was it like to be listened to in this way?

Presence: paying attention to the illness experience

Artwork exercise

Working in dyads, each person in the dyad receives the same copy of artwork created by a patient with chronic pain. They sit with it in silence. Then, one person describes what emerges for him as he looks at it. The other person listens. They switch, and the second person describes what emerges for him. Next, they both read what was written by the patient who created the artwork. Often the three perspectives differ, and this is the focus of the ensuing discussion.

The other components of the MMP course are like MBSR. Stress management is taught in a didactic manner as is coping with challenges, especially those that are common in clinical settings, such as top-down directives in a changing health care system, power issues embedded in the hierarchical structure of the work setting, heavy patient loads, lack of work-life balance, and burnout. While the focus is on stressors in the workplace, participants often generalize what they are discovering to their personal lives.

Participants

Selected quotes from students and clinicians in practice provide a glimpse into why they take a MMP course and/or what they gain from it.

Medical students

While taking a MMP course during his 4th year of medical school, Garneau stated:

> This greater awareness (of the self and others) was accompanied by the emergence of personal discomforts, doubts, sadness, empathy, frustration, and happiness. We [the students] were encouraged to express our emotions and experiences in the class; something as simple as "my back hurt when I was doing the sitting meditation, so I could not concentrate" to other more revealing observations such as, "I felt mediocre and inferior when the health care professionals said that to me." One of the means of disentangling certain experiences that were deemed difficult at work was to contemplate them with a nonjudgmental stance. We were able to share with our fellow medical students in an open, safe setting exactly what we felt and perceived. Under the tutelage of a medical doctor and clinical psychologist [the teachers] we learned to explore our inner lives, listen to what was on our minds, and understand via meditation the workings of our own minds.
> (Garneau, Hutchinson, Zhao and Dobkin, 2013)

Residents

From a second-year family medicine resident:

> My awareness of this tension grew throughout my first year of residency training. Various instances – encounters in the hospital, with patients, and with myself – would bring out this constricted feeling in my throat. At this level of training I often felt unsettled.

> I carried with me some knowledge from medical school and my various life experiences. And I also carried with me the knowledge of not knowing – that is, the knowledge that I really did not know how to fit into this world of doctors. To me, the role of the intern (another name for first year resident physicians) is not so well defined. On one hand, I was the low person on the very tall totem pole of the medical hierarchy – looking to my seniors for wisdom and approval. On the other hand, I was being listed as the primary care physician of a couple hundred patients, feeling that people were looking to me, expecting me to find the cure for their diabetes and depression. In the midst of this confusing role, this knowing and not-knowing, I lost my voice.
>
> (Minichiello, 2015)

Physicians

From a pediatric psychiatrist:

> My intention for taking the MBSR training stemmed mainly from curiosity and the apparent opportunity to improve the quality of my attention when with patients. As a pediatric psychiatrist I sometimes felt overwhelmed by stressful situations, especially those related to child abuse. I hoped the program would give me a break and help me relax somehow during the 60-hour-work-week-rush. Prior to taking the course, I had only a vague notion about mindfulness. I had heard about it from other physicians and a few of my patients' parents. I had even tried to follow one of my Parisian colleague's audiobooks but stopped after a week as I could not find time for regular practice. It seemed then that MBSR was a trendy relaxation technique or some novel type of psychotherapy. Yet, after the first couple of weeks, with practice, I realized that it is neither a technique nor a form of psychotherapy. Gradually meditation began to transform my life.
>
> (Dobkin, Bagnis & Spodenkiewicz, 2015)

A family physician said post-MBSR:

> I am much more attuned to listening. I put a mental stopwatch in my head. I [now] have a heightened awareness and sensitivity to people's conversation. I look at my own communication and pay much more attention to that. I pay much more attention in general.
>
> (Beckman et al., 2012)

Psychologists

From a clinical psychologist:

> There was just no way was I going to "fix" him, so I didn't really even try to. My intention changed from problem solving and fixing to being, connecting, understanding and sharing what I knew. It took the pressure off me as a junior psychotherapist; I could simply be myself in the encounter. I didn't have to "pretend" to be an expert. Being me was good enough for Stephen, in fact it was just what he needed. Applying the attitudes of acceptance, non-judging and letting go to myself, Stephen and our relationship was liberating and ultimately healing for us both.
>
> (Carlson, 2015)

Nurses

When nurses who had taken the MBSR program participated in focus groups they mentioned the following benefits: increased relaxation/calmness; self-acceptance/self-compassion; self-awareness; feeling more self-reliant; decreased physical pain; improved sleep. One nurse said: "As a result of this course, I've more to give to others. That "more" is patience, presence, and caring" (Cohen-Katz et al., 2005).

Social workers

After taking an MBSR program, a social worker said:

> I'm able to go deeper with clients, and my practice also positively affects my relationship with my clients. Only when I can love wholeness in myself, can I hold unconditional friendly space for clients and their difficulties. My clients and I collaborate, and we learn from each other. I am not an expert; just a curious guide. We are all in this human life together.
>
> (Jensen, 2016)

Multidisciplinary groups

A nurse practitioner said:

> Personally, I especially appreciated that we were all from different backgrounds and disciplines. It was interesting, because as much as it can be logical to yes have only doctors together to observe things, to go further, to dig deeper . . . it's also good for the doctors to realize that what it boils down to is a human being in front of another human being. That's the base, that's the common denominator here, it's more fundamental than having a PhD, or being a psychologist, a nurse, an acupuncturist, etc. . . . so yes that's good too. I really wanted to say that I found it enriching and pleasant.
>
> (Irving et al., 2014)

MBSR and MMP: empirical results

Given that the literature supporting the benefits of mindfulness for clinicians derives from studies of both MBSR and MMP, both will be examined here. Irving, Dobkin and Park (2009) published a review of quantitative and qualitative studies regarding MBSR for health care professionals at the early stage of development of MMP. At the time, there were few high-quality studies. Results suggested that the program helped reduce stress, but there was a paucity of information on positive outcomes (such as self-compassion) or adverse effects (such as increased depression post-MBSR). Irving followed up with a qualitative study that examined how health care professionals (half were physicians) thought the MMP course contributed to changes in them and if mindfulness influenced their practices (Irving et al., 2014).

The model derived from the data demonstrated that participants echoed similar themes to those described by clinical populations (Dobkin, 2008; MacKenzie, Carlson, Munoz, & Speca, 2007) who took MBSR, such as the salience of the group experience and support, discovery of acceptance, and the realization that some degree of frustration and/or distress is part of learning and establishing a mindfulness practice. Themes identified were becoming aware of perfectionism and the automaticity of "other-focus" and the "helping or fixing mode." Findings illustrated the unique and multifaceted change processes undertaken by participants, who attributed them to enhancement in awareness of cognition, emotion, and interpersonal and behavioral tendencies and patterns to mindfulness practice through participation in the group program. Participants indicated that these changes had implications across multiple domains: for themselves, family members, colleagues, as well as the patients they serve.

Studies from around the world have shown that health care professionals benefit from MBSR or a variant of the program tailored to them. Asuero et al. (2014) working with primary care physicians in Spain; Moody et al. (2013) working with pediatric oncologists in Israel and New York; Lovas, Lovas and Lovas (2008) working with dentists in Canada all point to the benefits of training physicians to be able to handle stress and their emotions better, as well as communicate with more awareness. For example, a modified and extended MBSR program for primary physicians offered by Krasner et al. (2009) resulted in self-reported improvements on mindfulness, burnout, empathy, and responsiveness to psychosocial aspects of patients' problems, mood disturbance, conscientiousness and engagement at work, and more emotional stability.

Quantitative pre-post-program data pertaining to 126 clinicians who took the MMP course at McGill Programs in Whole Person Care are shown in Figures 13.3 and 13.4. The sample consisted of: 79% women; 54% medical doctors. Ten percent screened positive for depression before the course; attendance was 90%. There were significant reductions in stress, increases in mindfulness, and self-compassion. There were significant decreases for depersonalization and emotional exhaustion and increases in a sense of personal accomplishment (three aspects of burnout).

In a multisite, observational study of 45 clinicians (mostly physicians) caring for HIV-positive patients Beach et al. (2013) asked the clinicians to complete a mindfulness scale and then audiotaped their medical visits. The audiotapes were coded by independent raters blinded to the mindfulness scores. Patients independently rated the encounter following the medical visit. Data from the audiotapes indicated that clinicians who scored high on

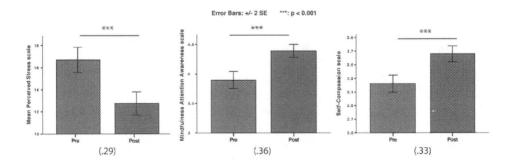

Figure 13.3 Changes in stress, mindful awareness, self-compassion pre- and post-MMP (effect sizes).

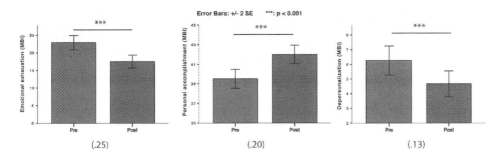

Figure 13.4 Changes in burnout subscales pre- and post- MMP (effect sizes).

mindfulness were more likely to engage in patient-centered communication (e.g. discussed psychosocial issues, built rapport) and they displayed more positive emotional tone with patients. Patients reported better communication with the more mindful physicians and they were more satisfied with their care. While promising, the results were based on a cross-sectional data which cannot determine causality.

As an extension to Beach et al.'s cross-sectional findings, a longitudinal cohort study conducted in Paris with 27 clinicians showed similar benefits (Dobkin, Bernardi, & Bagnis, 2016). Pre-and post-MBSR online questionnaires assessed: burnout, depression, stress, meaningfulness, and mindfulness. Patients independently rated their clinicians using the Rochester Communication Rating Scale (RCRS) after a clinical encounter before and after their clinician took the MBSR course. Nine medical doctors audio-recorded consultations pre- and post-MBSR; the tapes were coded and analyzed by an independent team using the Roter Interaction Analyses System (the same as in the Beach et al. study).

Significant reductions in stress and burnout were found, as well as increases in mindfulness and meaningfulness. As seen in Table 13.2, a decrease in stress correlated with less judgmental attitudes and less reactivity – facets of mindfulness. The decrease in emotional exhaustion correlated with more acting with awareness and less judgmental attitudes – facets of mindfulness. Patients' perceptions of the clinical encounter suggested that patient-centered care improved post-MBSR. Decreased depersonalization was significantly associated with the

Table 13.2 Correlations between changes in mindfulness, stress, and burnout

Clinicians (n = 25)	Stress	Exhaustion	Depersonalization	Accomplishment
Act with awareness	−0.254	−0.444[*]	−0.314	0.264
Non reactivity	−0.485[*]	−0.304	−0.297	0.152
Non judgment	−0.651[***]	−0.512[**]	−0.333	0.112

Values represent the non-parametric correlation coefficients for the correlations between changes in mindfulness scores (FFMQ) and changes in stress (PSS) and burnout (MBI) following MBSR.

For the two subscales of non-judgment and non-reactivity, a higher score indicates lower attitudes.

[*]p < 0.05;
[**]: p < 0.01;
[***]: p < 0.001.

Rochester Communication Rating Scale subscale, "understanding of the patient's experience of illness." At both time periods doctors dominated the exchange and were patient-centered. The findings indicate the MBSR may help clinicians become more resilient and offer excellent service without succumbing to compassion-fatigue, burnout, or vicarious trauma when working with chronically ill people (Dobkin et al, 2016).

Ongoing reflections

Epstein (2014) states mindful practice has a moral dimension, encompassing the intention for compassion towards the self and others and prosocial behaviors (e.g. respect for persons, beneficence, and justice). It takes place within a social context where there is a need to achieve consensus while managing uncertainty and emotional situations. But if the work environment does not support this way of being, good intentions may be subjugated to the institutional demands (Ward & Outram, 2016). If there is not support from decision and policy makers then it will be hard for a clinician to act mindfully or compassionately (Brewster, 2016). Young doctors, accustomed to working with technology, may rely more on data from laboratory tests than the story told by the patient believing that this is more efficient and accurate. One way to overcome these obstacles is to demonstrate that practicing mindfully increases the quality of care (Knowles, 2008), reduces errors, and protects the health care professionals from burnout. It is possible to change the culture of medicine, which can be harsh (e.g. doctors go to work sick because they cannot find anyone to cover for them) but it takes buy-in from the top. One success story of making fundamental changes at the institutional level is described by Frolic (2016) and another can be found in Suchman, Sluyter and Williamson (2011). There are several medical schools that have integrated mindfulness training in their curriculums (see Chapter 4 in Dobkin & Hassed, 2016b), which shows that is possible to integrate mindfulness into medical training.

But there are barriers to overcome. While working with physicians I have come to appreciate that most enjoy patient contact and rarely point to patient care as a major source of stress. Instead, they relate how technology has encroached on their ability to be in the *I-Thou* relationship they value. For example, many are now required to use electronic records while working with a patient; computer screens are situated in between them and the people they wish to make eye contact with (Lowen & Rodriguez, 2012). Smartphone alerts distract clinicians during examinations. Patients take phone calls during examinations. Recently I shared the angst of a family doctor who told me that her patient had audiotaped their medical encounter without telling her. In another situation, a pediatrician related that her colleague's medical visit was videotaped and posted on social media without his consent.

Despite these challenges hope is kindled by the fact that increasingly health care professions around the world recognize the value of mindfulness in the workplace. While I and others are concerned about "McMindfulness" i.e. the commercialization and oversimplification of what it means to live a mindful life, I recall how things were when I began to practice yoga 20 years ago. At that time, it was viewed as marginal; certainly, medical students were not practicing it in between their exams and doctors were not recommending it to their patients. Over time recognition of its value has rendered it mainstream. It is possible that a similar trajectory awaits MMP.

References

Asuero, A.M., Queraltó, J.M., Pujol-Ribera, E., Berenguera, A., et al. (2014). Effectiveness of a mindfulness education program in primary health care professionals: A pragmatic controlled trial. *Journal of Continuing Education in the Health Professions*, *34*(1), 4–12. doi: 10.1002/chp.21211.

Beach, M.C., Roter, D., Korthuis, P.T., Epstein, R.M., Sharp, V., Ratanawongsa, N., et al. (2013). A multicenter study of physician mindfulness and health care quality. *Annals of Family Medicine*, *11*(5), 421–428.

Beckman, H.B., Wendland, M., Mooney, C., Krasner, M.S., Quill, T.E., Suchman, A.L., Epstein, R.M. (2012). The impact of a program in mindful communication on primary care physicians. *Academic Medicine*, *87*(6), 815–819. doi: 10.1097/ACM.0b013e318253d3b2.

Brewster, L. (2016). Resilience, respite and general practice: Taking a mindful approach to cultural change [Editorial]. *Family Practice*, *33*(2), 119–120.

Buber, M. (1970). *I and Thou*. (Kaufman, W., trans.). New York, NY: Charles Scribner's Sons.

Carlson, L.E. (2015). Mindfulness in oncology: Healing through relationship. In P.L. Dobkin (Ed.), *Mindful Medical Practice: Clinical Narratives and Therapeutic Insights* (pp. 71–74). Switzerland: Springer International Publishing.

Cohen-Katz, J., Wiley, S., Capuano, T., Baker, D.M., Deitrick, L., Shapiro, S. (2005). The effects of MBSR on nurse stress and burnout: A qualitative and quantitative study, part III. *Holistic Nursing Practice*, *19*(2), 78–86.

Cohn, F. (2001). Existential medicine: Martin Buber and physician-patient relationships. *Journal of Continuing Education in the Health Professions*, *21*, 170–181.

Dobkin, P.L. (2008). Mindfulness-based Stress Reduction: What processes are at work? *Complementary Therapies in Clinical Practice*, *14*(1), 8–16.

Dobkin, P.L. (2009). Fostering healing through mindfulness in the context of medical practice [Guest Editorial]. *Current Oncology*, *16*(2), 4–6.

Dobkin, P.L. (2011). Mindfulness and whole person care. In T.A. Hutchinson (Ed.), *Whole Person Care: A New Paradigm for the 21st Century* (pp. 69–82). New York, NY: Springer.

Dobkin, P.L. (2015). Mindful attitudes open hearts in clinical practice. In P.L. Dobkin (Ed.), *Mindful Medical Practice: Clinical Narratives and Therapeutic Insights* (pp. 155–160). Switzerland: Springer.

Dobkin, P.L. (2016). Mindfulness-based medical practice: Eight weeks *en route* to wellness. In I. Ivtzan & T. Lomas (Eds.), *Mindfulness in Positive Psychology: The Science of Meditation and Wellbeing* (pp. 193–211). London: Taylor & Francis/Routledge.

Dobkin, P.L., Bagnis, C.I., Spodenkiewicz, M. (2015). Being human in medicine: Beyond hierarchy. *The International Journal of Whole Person Care*, *2*(1), 38–49.

Dobkin, P.L., Bernardi, N.F., Bagnis, C.I. (2016). Enhancing clinicians' well-being and patient-centered care through mindfulness. *Journal of Continuing Education in the Health Professions*, *36*(1), 11–16.

Dobkin, P.L., Hassed, C.S. (2016a). Scientific underpinnings and evidence pertaining to mindfulness. In *Mindful Medical Practitioners: A Guide for Clinicians and Educators* (pp. 9–31). Switzerland: Springer.

Dobkin, P.L., Hassed, C.S. (2016b). How mindfulness has been integrated into three medical school curriculums. In *Mindful Medical Practitioners: A Guide for Clinicians and Educators* (pp. 43–64). Switzerland: Springer.

Dobkin, P.L., Hassed, C.S. (2016c). Educating teachers. In *Mindful Medical Practitioners: A Guide for Clinicians and Educators* (pp. 89–104). Switzerland: Springer.

Dobkin, P.L., Hickman, S., Monshat, K. (2014). Holding the heart of MBSR: Balancing fidelity and imagination when adapting MBSR. *Mindfulness*, *5*(6), 710–718. doi: 10.1007/s12671-013-0225-7.

Dobkin, P.L., Lucena, R.J.M. (2016). Mindful medical practice and the therapeutic alliance. *The International Journal of Whole Person Care*, *3*(1), 34–45.

Epstein, R. (2014). What will it take for physicians to practice mindfully? Promoting quality of care, quality of caring, resilience and well-being. In A. Ie, C.T. Ngnoumen & E.J. Langer (Eds.), *The Wiley Blackwell Handbook of Mindfulness* (pp. 584–607). Chicester, UK: John Wiley & Sons, Ltd.

Frolic, A.N. (2016). Pilgrims together: Leveraging community partnerships to enhance workplace resilience. *International Journal of Whole Person Care*, *3*(1), 46–62.

Garneau, K., Hutchinson, T., Zhao, Q., Dobkin, P. (2013). Cultivating person-centered medicine in future physicians. *European Journal for Person Centered Healthcare*, *1*(2), 468–477.

Hutchinson, T.A., Dobkin, P.L (2015). Discover mindful congruence. *Le Spécialiste*, *17*(1), 31–32.

Irving, J.A., Dobkin, P.L., Park, J. (2009). Cultivating mindfulness in health care professionals: A review of empirical studies of Mindfulness-Based Stress Reduction (MBSR). *Complimentary Therapies in Clinical Practice*, *15*(2), 61–66.

Irving, J.A., Dobkin, P.L., Williams, G., Chen, A., Park, J. (2012). Mindfulness-Based Medical Practice (MBMP): A mixed-methods study exploring benefits for physicians enrolled in an 8-week adapted MBSR program. *AMA-CMA-BMA International Conference on Physician Health*, 25–27, Montreal, Quebec, Canada.

Irving, J.A., Park-Saltzman, J., Fitzpatrick, M., Dobkin, P.L., et al. (2014). Experiences of health care professionals enrolled in Mindfulness-based Medical Practice: A grounded theory model. *Mindfulness*, *14*(5), 60–71.

Jensen, A.K. (2016). *What is the meaning of mindful practice among practitioners?* Master of Social Work Clinical Research Papers. Paper 603. http://sophia.stkate.edu/msw_papers/603.

Knowles, P. (2008). What is trying to happen here? Using mindfulness to enhance the quality of patient encounters. *Permanente Journal*, *12*(2), 55–59.

Kramer, G. (2007). *Insight Dialogue: The Interpersonal Path to Freedom*. Boston, MA: Shambhala Publications, Inc.

Krasner, M.S., Epstein, R.M., Beckman, H., Suchman, A.L., Chapman, B., Mooney, C.J., Quill, T.E. (2009). Association of an educational program in mindful communication with burnout, empathy, and attitudes among primary care physicians. *Journal of American Medical Association*, *302*(12), 1284–1293. doi: 10.1001/jama.2009.1384.

Lovas, J.G., Lovas, D.A., Lovas, P.M. (2008). Mindfulness and professionalism in dentistry. *Journal of Dental Education*, *72*(9), 998–1009.

Lowen, B.A., Rodriguez, D. (2012). Lost in translation? How electronic health records structure communication, relationships, and meaning. *Academic Medicine*, *87*(4), 392–394.

Mackenzie, M.J., Carlson, L.E., Munoz, M., Speca, M. (2007). A qualitative study of self-perceived effects of mindfulness-based stress reduction (MBSR) in a psychosocial oncology setting. *Stress Health*, *23*(1), 59–69. doi: 10.1002/smi.1120.

Minichiello, V.J. (2015). Finding my voice in residency: Reflections on integrative family medicine. *International Journal of Whole Person Care*, *2*(2), 37–40.

Moody, K., Kramer, D., Santizo, R.O., Magro, L., et al. (2013). Helping the helpers: Mindfulness training for burnout in pediatric oncology – A pilot program. *Journal of Pediatric Oncology Nursing*, *30*(5), 75–84. doi: 10.1177/1043454213504497.

Neff, K. (2003). The development and validation of a scale to measure self-compassion. *Self and Identity*, *2*, 223–250.

Rūmī, J. (1995). *The Essential Rumi* (translated by Coleman Barks with John Moyne, A. J. Arberry, Reynold Nicholson). New York, NY: HarperCollins Publishers.

Santorelli, S. (1999). *Heal Thy Self: Lessons on Mindfulness in Medicine*. London: Bell Tower.

Scott, J.G., Cohen, D., DiCicco-Bloom, B., Miller, W., Stange, K.C., Crabtree, B.F. (2008). Understanding healing relationships. *Annals of Family Medicine*, *6*(4), 315–322.

Scott, J.G., Scott, R.G., Miller, W.L., Stange, K.C., Crabtree, B.F. (2009). Healing relationships and the existential philosophy of Martin Buber. *Philosophy, Ethics, and Humanities in Medicine*, *4*, 11. doi: 10.1186/1747-5341-4-11.

Siegel, D.J. (2010). *The Mindful Therapist: A Clinician's Guide to Mindsight and Neural Integration*. New York, NY: W. W. Norton & Company, Inc.

Suchman, A.L., Sluyter, D.J., Williamson, P.R. (2011). *Leading Change in Healthcare: Transforming Organizations Using Complexity, Positive Psychology and Relationship-Centered Care*. London: Radcliffe Publishing Ltd.

Ward, S., Outram, S. (2016). Medicine: In need of culture change. *Internal Medicine Journal*, *46*(1), 112–116. doi: 10.1111/imj.12954.

Chapter 14

Mindfulness-Based Cancer Recovery
An adaptation of MBSR for people with cancer and their caregivers

Linda E. Carlson, Erin Zelinski, Kirsti Toivonen, and Michelle Flynn

Program overview

The MBCR program was developed at our institution in 1997 by three of our counsellors as a response to the ongoing suffering they witnessed in their clients: people diagnosed with cancer alongside their families and support persons. While individual counselling and traditional support groups were available, there was recognition that more existential approaches based on acceptance and emotional coping were also needed. As it turned out, these professionals each had a deep personal practice of meditation and/or yoga, and felt these approaches had helped them in their own personal crises, hence offering these approaches to their clients made sense. They developed the predecessor to the current MBCR program, which was further adapted by Carlson and Speca to incorporate components of MBSR in 1998, resulting in the current hybrid program (Carlson & Speca, 2010).

The intention of the program is to help people living with cancer (both patients and their families) cope with the difficulties inherent in this experience, including an immediate life threat, uncertainty about the future, loss of control, fear of cancer recurrence, and symptoms including depression, anxiety, stress, worry, pain, fatigue and sleep loss. The MBCR program is appropriate for almost anyone diagnosed with cancer and their support persons, including those both on and off treatment and into survivorship and palliation. The program can be adapted for people with functional limitations and we have developed an online version for those who are unable to attend in person. We have offered this program year-round since 1998 and have led between three to nine groups of 15–20 diverse participants each year.

Theoretical Background

Psychotherapeutic mindfulness programs have been used in clinical practice for several decades, but their history is considerably older. Mindfulness is oft touted as the core of Buddhist and Taoist traditions, but the psychotherapeutic interpretation incorporates modern ideologies regarding emotional regulation, physiological responses, and principles from various models of psychotherapy (Shapiro & Carlson, 2009). Current practices in mindfulness are predominantly secular, but Buddhist concepts of mindfulness retain much of their utility and serve as the epistemological predecessors of the Westernized, psychotherapeutic concept of mindfulness (Shapiro & Carlson, 2009). Hence, the current Westernized concept of mindfulness carries with it a central focus on developing consciousness and purposeful attention, retained from its Buddhist origins. One of the earliest psychotherapeutic mindfulness programs – MBSR – was developed as a general tool to relieve suffering that could be adapted to various contexts such as prisons, hospitals or corporate settings (Kabat-Zinn, 1990).

MBSR provided tools to allow patients to identify, consider and define ways of coping in order to provide relief from suffering (Kabat-Zinn, 1990). It was conceptualized as a training paradigm that used the mind-body connection to relieve emotional and physical suffering. From the outset, MBSR was designed as a model that could be adapted to more specific challenges of circumstances following principles of affectionate, openhearted friendliness (Kabat-Zinn, 1990).

One such challenge is cancer. Cancer diagnosis, treatment, and survival are associated with periods of heightened emotions – including distress and anxiety (Carlson, Waller, Groff, Giese-Davis, & Bultz, 2011). Poorer prognoses are often observed for individuals experiencing increased negative emotional arousal during cancer treatment and recovery than among individuals who are coping more effectively (Giese-Davis et al., 2011). Still, even cancer patients with good prognosis can experience lingering fears and changes in appearance, ability and lifestyle that can be distressing (Ganz, 2009). MBCR and other MBSR-adaptations are programs that have been increasingly widely used to help individuals cope with their anxieties and have been shown effective (Piet, Wurtzen, & Zachariae, 2012; Zhang et al., 2015).

MBCR is an adaptation of MBSR in response to the unique constellation of challenges faced by cancer patients. The focus of MBCR is on training participants to develop a mindfulness meditation practice that enhances their capacity for coping through acceptance and improvements in emotion-focused coping, by learning strategies to deal with difficult emotions in uncontrollable situations (Carlson & Speca, 2010). Emotion-focused coping is distinguished from problem-focused coping; whereas the latter is useful in situations where action can be taken to solve a problem, emotion-focused coping is required in situations that are upsetting but largely uncontrollable, like living with the fear of cancer recurrence. Improvements in emotion-focused coping enhance people's ability to embrace the unknown and continue to function well when faced with uncertainty. A common theme that emerges in MBCR classes is the fear that every ache and pain represents cancer recurrence along with the belief that the increased stress associated with these aches and pains also increases the likelihood of cancer recurrence. MBCR training provides real tools that cancer patients can use to help them cope more effectively with difficult emotions, thereby improving their capacity to address challenges.

Mindfulness interventions are useful in a variety of settings, but they are especially effective in coping with cancer because they provide the ability to accept a problem rather than try to resolve it – which can be an impossible task when faced with a chronic or serious health issue. Another mechanism by which MBCR can be helpful is the idea that by attending to the present moment and "slowing down", our ability to detect fluctuations in experience and sensation is improved, which provides opportunities to challenge beliefs about pain or suffering being constant and immutable. This realization often provides relief because it teaches patients that their experiences are not permanent.

Most often delivered in a group setting over the course of several weeks, MBCR introduces participants to various forms of meditation including gentle Hatha yoga. In addition to learning various forms of meditative practice including body scans, seated and walking meditation, and guided imagery exercises, the group setting provides opportunities for reflection, problem solving, social support, and didactic instruction. The core tool gained through MBCR is kind, stable attention and acceptance through training that focuses on directing kind, curious, and nonjudgmental awareness to the present.

The achievement of mindful attention is garnered through the development of skill along three main axioms: intention, attention and attitude. Intention provides the spotlight or direction of attention through extensive group and home practices targeting the participant's ability to repeatedly direct attention toward the present moment. Perhaps most importantly, intention and attention are trained with an attitude of nonjudgmental curiosity and kindness. Bringing awareness to the role of attitude can help patients leverage their emotional resources by teaching them to recognize patterns of thinking that are more or less helpful. The recognition and modification of patterns of behavior allow patients to adjust their thinking to ways that better serve them. Mindfulness training enables behavioral modification because it provides the emotional space to approach oneself safely. The didactic instruction that accompanies the MBCR program helps train participants to recognize and adapt non-functional constructs.

Research results

The empirical evaluation of MBCR has been underway for nearly 20 years. The first study evaluating MBCR was published in 2000 (Speca, Carlson, Goodey, & Angen, 2000). Eighty-nine patients were randomized to either receive MBCR immediately, or to join a waitlist. Various stages and types of cancer (including breast, ovarian, prostate, non-Hodgkins lymphoma, melanoma, endometrial, colon, and cervical) were represented among those who participated in MBCR. Patients who received MBCR improved significantly more on mood states and symptoms of stress than those on the waitlist, experiencing large improvements of approximately 65% on mood and around 35% on stress symptoms. More specifically, these patients reported a wide range of benefits, including less tension, depression, anger, concentration problems, anxiety/fear, and emotional instability; fewer physical manifestations of stress (e.g., tingling in hands and feet), cardiopulmonary symptoms (e.g., hyperventilation, heart racing), central neurologic symptoms (e.g., faintness, dizziness), habitual stress patterns (e.g., overeating, smoking), gastrointestinal symptoms (e.g., diarrhea, upset stomach); and more vigor. Patients of all ages and both men and women reported these positive outcomes. A second study followed these patients after all participants, including those in the original waitlist, had completed the program (Carlson, Ursuliak, Goodey, Angen, & Speca, 2001). Similar benefits were seen among all patients and, importantly, these benefits were maintained at follow-up six months later, demonstrating that the program was effective in decreasing mood disturbance and stress symptoms for months beyond program completion.

A next logical step in MBCR's empirical evaluation was determining *how* this program brings about such beneficial outcomes. Mackenzie, Carlson, Munoz, and Speca (2007) attempted to answer this question by completing in-depth interviews and a focus group with nine cancer patients. These patients had participated in the eight-week MBCR program and continued to attend weekly drop-in MBCR sessions for between one and six years. Five themes emerged – opening to change, self-control, shared experience, personal growth, and spirituality – which were used to develop a specific theory regarding how MBCR works for these patients. This theory posits that initial participation in MBCR is the beginning of an ongoing self-discovery process. At the time of their diagnoses, patients felt isolated and unsure of what to do, and the MBCR program helped them to feel less isolation in their journeys. MBCR also taught these patients concrete tools for self-regulation and offered an introduction to looking at the world in new ways, resulting in fewer stress symptoms and lower levels of mood disturbance. Continuing practice in the drop-in group allowed patients to deepen their sense of social support and learn to be less reactive across a variety of life circumstances. Patients who continued to practice in the drop-in sessions also reported broader pro-social outcomes, such as personal transformation, feeling part of a larger whole, developing positive qualities of personal growth and positive health, growing spirituality, finding meaning and purpose in one's life, feeling increasingly interconnected with others, and qualities of gratitude, compassion, and equanimity.

Over the past 20 years, numerous studies investigating MBCR's efficacy have been published most of which replicate the results of the first study, finding that MBCR reduces symptoms of stress and mood disturbance. There is now a growing body of literature supporting its efficacy in improving a range of other psychological and biological outcomes for patients with various types and stages of cancer including:

- Improvements in self-reported sleep in terms of better overall sleep quality, increased hours of sleep per night, increased sleep efficiency (i.e., how much time in bed is spent sleeping), decreased sleep latency (i.e., the time it takes to fall asleep), and less daytime dysfunction

    (Carlson & Garland, 2005; Garland, Rouleau, Campbell, Samuels, & Carlson, 2015)

- Less fatigue

    (Carlson & Garland, 2005)

- Decreased rumination (i.e., tendency towards self-attentiveness and recurrent, repetitive, primarily past-oriented thinking; habitual thinking which frequently results in depressed mood) and better self-regulation of emotions

    (Campbell, Labelle, Bacon, Faris, & Carlson, 2012; Labelle, Campbell, & Carlson, 2010; Labelle, Campbell, Faris, & Carlson, 2015)

- Increased ability to be mindful, increased mindfulness

    (Garland, Tamagawa, Todd, Speca, & Carlson, 2012; Labelle et al., 2010)

- Improved overall global quality of life

    (Carlson, Speca, Patel, & Goodey, 2003)

- Greater meaning and purpose in life, connections with something larger than oneself

    (Garland, Carlson, Cook, Lansdell, & Speca, 2007)

In addition, several improvements in biological outcomes have been found, including:

- Shifts in an immune profile from one typically associated with depression symptoms, to one representing a healthier profile (specifically, increases in T cell production of stimulated IL-4, an anti-inflammatory cytokine, and decreases in interferon gamma and NK cell production of IL-10)

    (Carlson et al., 2003)

- Persistent reductions in pro-inflammatory cytokines over one year of follow-up

  (Carlson, Speca, Patel, & Faris, 2007)

- Pre- to post-intervention shifts in cortisol profiles, with fewer evening cortisol elevations and some normalization of abnormal daily salivary cortisol profiles

  (Carlson, Speca, Patel, & Goodey, 2004)

- Decreases in overall cortisol levels that persisted over a year of follow-up as a result of further decreases in evening cortisol levels

  (Carlson et al., 2007)

- Decreases in systolic blood pressure over the course of the program in women with elevated blood pressure compared to those in a waitlist group

  (Campbell et al., 2012)

Numerous reviews and meta-analyses over the last decade complement the several individual studies in the research literature and provide additional support for MBCR's efficacy in improving the aforementioned outcomes for patients and survivors with various types and stages of cancer (Carlson, 2012; Cramer, Lauche, Paul, & Dobos, 2012; Matchim, Armer, & Stewart, 2011; Musial, Bussing, Heusser, Choi, & Ostermann, 2011; Piet et al., 2012; Shennan, Payne, & Fenlon, 2011; Zainal, Booth, & Huppert, 2013; Zhang, Xu, Wang, & Wang, 2016).

Recent studies

While support for MBCR's efficacy can be found in numerous studies and continues to grow, important research questions regarding MBCR's processes and applications remain and recent studies have attempted to address some of these gaps in the research literature. For example, many earlier studies compared those who participated in MBCR to those on a waitlist rather than to another active intervention. Addressing this gap, Carlson et al. (2016) compared MBCR to another active psychosocial intervention (Supportive Expressive Therapy or SET). Women with breast cancer were randomized to either MBCR or SET or a minimal intervention control group (one day stress management seminar) and completed questionnaires about their mood, stress symptoms, quality of life, social support, spirituality (i.e., feelings of peace, meaning in life), and post-traumatic growth (i.e., appreciation for life and ability to see new possibilities) before and after the interventions, as well as at six- and 12-month follow-up. Women who participated in the MBCR group reported greater benefits (e.g., reduced mood disturbance and stress symptoms; improved quality of life, social support, spirituality, and post-traumatic growth) than those who participated in SET. Importantly, most benefits were maintained at 12-month follow-up.

On the same sample and data set, Schellekens et al. (Schellekens et al., 2016) investigated the claim that nonspecific therapeutic factors (e.g., social support) rather than mindfulness contribute to the positive effects of mindfulness-based interventions. The researchers found that increased social support (but not increased mindfulness) was partially responsible for the impact of MBCR versus SET on mood disturbance and stress symptoms, suggesting that social support plays a more important role in enhancing the outcomes of MBCR than previously believed.

Another aspect of the research literature on MBCR that warrants further attention is avenues to increase MBCR's (and other evidence-based psychosocial programs') accessibility. One means of increasing accessibility is increasing online availability of interventions. Zernicke et al. (Zernicke et al., 2014; Zernicke et al., 2016) assessed the effects of cancer patient participation in online MBCR in their study called the eCALM trial. Participants completed questionnaires before and after participating in the online MBCR program. The researchers found that the cancer patients reported improvements over time on measures of mood, stress, spirituality, post-traumatic growth, and mindfulness. Younger participants showed greater improvements in stress symptoms and spirituality than older participants, and women's post-traumatic growth increased more over time than men's. The results of this study are promising in terms of lending support to an accessible online MBCR approach. Future research may allow greater understanding and tailoring of the program to improve accessibility and ease of use.

Program structure and content

The MBCR program content is described in detail in our book, including guided meditation exercises (Carlson & Speca, 2010). The format was initially 8 classes plus an individual or small group orientation session before classes began, and a 6-hour weekend retreat; we recently switched to 9 classes plus the retreat because many people were missing the orientations and we had to repeat material in the first class. Hence, now the first class incorporates orientation material and some of the original first session practices; the rest are spread out over the following 8 sessions. Each class includes group discussion, teaching, and practice. Typically, about half of the class is devoted to discussion about participants' past experiences and successes or challenges with home practice and didactic discussion of the topic to be introduced for the week. The latter half is practice of yoga followed by meditation. The course is cumulative – each new topic that is introduced builds upon prior material – and is taught in a secular manner. The specific content of each week follows.

Week 1: introduction and orientation

The first session consists of a general introduction to MBCR as well as the overarching goal: to teach individuals how to be more mindful and apply the principles of mindfulness to everyday life to help cope with stress and illness. The concept of "mindfulness" is introduced as the practice of being aware of one's inner state and surroundings during the present moment, without judgement or evaluation. The course format (described above) is presented to participants as well as an outline for the topics to be discussed in the weeks ahead, and a review of logistics (e.g., parking). The "group principles" are described: attendance, commitment, confidentiality, self-responsibility and safety. Participants introduce themselves to the group in the first class and continue to wear nametags to subsequent sessions. They are typically asked to share where they are at in their cancer journey (as much or little as they like), whether they have any experience with these practices, and what they are hoping to gain from attending the group. They are given a book with printed session materials for each week and homework logs, as well as an audio CD with recordings to guide the meditation and yoga, a DVD of the yoga postures, and links to download the audio and video tracks if they prefer.

At the end of the first session, the group is led through a body scan meditation, lasting 30 minutes. This activity consists of participants comfortably lying down on their backs while being directed to pay attention to sensations in successive body parts (e.g., the big toe in the right leg to the crown of the head). Individuals are assigned the body scan as homework to complete once daily, and they are asked to track their practice as well as any comments in the homework log.

Week 2: mindfulness and breath awareness

The second group session delves deeper into the concept of mindfulness and introduces diaphragmatic breathing, which is meant to deepen and lengthen the breath, resulting in stress reduction and relaxation. The group is led through a mindful breathing exercise and is taught about using breathing as a focus of attention to anchor oneself into the present moment. Yoga is also introduced to the program, beginning with a series of gently lying-down poses from the book Full Catastrophe Living (Kabat-Zinn, 1990). It is emphasized that yoga is a form of meditation or "mindful movement", and that one should be aware of maintaining a mindful disposition while practising yoga. Participants learn the rest pose on their backs and they are taught to move in synchronization with the breath, returning to rest pose between movements. The pace is very slow and people are encouraged to pay close attention to the feeling of the movements in the body, reconnecting with a changed body and repairing the relationship they have with their body that may have suffered over the course of cancer diagnosis and treatment. We talk about "re-friending" the body as an ally.

Following the yoga, another body scan is practiced and assigned as homework again, along with a short yoga practice (DVDs as well as guided audio and diagrams are provided for the yoga practices).

Week 3: mindfulness attitudes

The third session places more emphasis on the attitudes of mindfulness meditation, beginning with the raisin exercise, which involves mindfully eating a raisin. Participants slowly examine a raisin with different sensory modalities: they are instructed to carefully look at the raisin (e.g., notice colour, shape, ridges, lighting), smell the raisin, listen to the raisin (i.e., put it against the ear and notice if there is sound, then squeeze it with fingers and notice if there is sound), feel the raisin, taste the raisin (i.e., place it in the mouth but without chewing immediately, then slowly chewing it), and swallowing the raisin with intention "at a moment of their choosing". The raisin exercise is an example of applying the attitude of "beginner's mind" and promotes paying attention to the act and sensations involved in eating food, as well as having an appreciation for its source. The primary attitudes presented and discussed, including *non-judging, patience, beginner's mind, trust, non-striving, acceptance,* and *letting go*, are based on the descriptions from Full Catastrophe Living (Kabat-Zinn, 1990).

Sitting meditation is introduced, and time spent demonstrating how to sit in various postures, including on a chair, with cushions, on a meditation bench and/or with various other props and blankets (lying down is also an option for those who are uncomfortable in a seated position). Once comfortable, participants are instructed to maintain full awareness of their breathing and "simply be" in the moment while applying the mindfulness attitudes outlined above. They are reminded that arising thoughts and discomforts do not indicate failure – when one notices their thoughts have strayed, they should gently guide their attention back to the breath. Home practice assignments include practising mindfulness attitudes throughout the day and completing a "pleasant events log" (recording positive events and the thoughts and feelings that accompanied them) in addition to daily sitting meditation and yoga, and eating at least one meal mindfully throughout the week.

Week 4: mind-body wisdom and healing

The fourth session includes information about the mind-body connection and the effects of stress on the body, emphasizing the difference between automatically reacting to perceived stressful events and mindfully responding. The lemon exercise is introduced before the discussion of stress symptoms. This exercise entails having participants close their eyes and visualize a highly detailed description about feeling, holding, cutting open and tasting a lemon. For most individuals, vividly picturing a lemon will stimulate salivation, resulting in a powerful first-hand demonstration of how thoughts alone can trigger a physical response. Participants are then asked to consider symptoms of stress they have experienced over the past week, including physical (e.g., headaches, stomach aches, back pain), behavioral (e.g., smoking, compulsive eating, excessive drinking), emotional (e.g., crying, nervousness, anger), cognitive (e.g., forgetfulness, indecisiveness, worry), spiritual (e.g., emptiness, doubt, loss of meaning), or relational (e.g., loneliness, resentment, lack of intimacy) symptoms. The idea is to identify one's own "stress fingerprint", which can serve as a trigger to mindfully pay attention to thoughts and feelings that have set off the stress reaction.

The class is then taught about the biological systems involved in the body stress response (e.g., the hypothalamus-pituitary-adrenal axis), the physiological consequences of both acute and long-term stress, and the bi-directional relationship between psychological and physical problems. Mindfulness is positioned as a way to short-circuit the potentially harmful effects of the stress reaction going unchecked, allowing us to respond more intentionally. Assigned homework includes daily sitting meditation, lying yoga, and completion of an "unpleasant events log" (recording negative experiences and corresponding thoughts and feelings).

Week 5: balance in the autonomic nervous system

The fifth week includes information about the components of the autonomic nervous system: the sympathetic (which promotes arousal and activity) and the parasympathetic (which promotes rest and relaxation); and teaches a variety of diaphragmatic breathing exercises that are meant to differentially activate the autonomic nervous system. There are three 'balanced' breathing exercises: 1) counting down from 10, fully inhaling and exhaling with each number, 2) counting from one to four for each inhalation and counting from four to one for each exhalation, repeated several times, and 3) inhaling, pausing, exhaling, pausing, and repeating. As heart rate increases with inhalation and decreases with exhalation, a breathing technique involving inhaling, exhaling, and pausing is used for promoting relaxation, while a technique involving inhaling, pausing, and exhaling is used for promoting arousal. A breathing technique involving alternating breathing through the nostrils is also taught as a way to balance the effects of the dominant and non-dominant nostril (activating when the right nostril, relaxing when the left nostril). A sided breathing exercise to promote sleep by enhancing relaxation is also taught.

These breathing exercises are called "minis" and the class brainstorms about where and when they may be usefully applied. Sitting meditation with deeper focus on bare or choiceless awareness is practiced and the standing yoga postures are introduced. Daily homework of sitting meditation, standing yoga, and the "mini" breathing exercises is assigned.

Week 6: mindful coping

The sixth session provides psychoeducation about how our thoughts can affect our feelings and how different habitual ways of thinking that can lead to difficult feelings. Such patterns include: *labeling* (overgeneralizing and seeing some people or situations as fixed and unchanging), *jumping to conclusions* (making an interpretation despite lack of evidence), *magnification/catastrophizing* (exaggerating the importance or likelihood of a negative event), *minimization* (minimizing the importance or likelihood of a negative event), *emotional reasoning* (believing something is true because it is felt or feared), *mental filters* (picking out a limited aspect of a situation and letting it color your whole perception of it), *all-or-nothing thinking* (seeing everything in "black and white" categories), *personalization* (interpreting an event as being about oneself without considering other possibilities), and "*musterbation*" (believing that you must or should do a certain thing/behave a certain way). Participants are encouraged to use their mindfulness skills to identify the stories they tell using these heuristics, and pay attention to the consequences when they do so.

Walking meditation is also introduced, which involves very slow, deliberate walking during which individuals are instructed to pay close attention to the sensations in their bodies (e.g., noticing the feeling of the heel making contact, noticing the shifting and transfer of the weight), and standing yoga is also introduced. Assigned homework consists of alternating between walking and sitting meditation, standing yoga, and completion of a thought monitoring record where individuals record situations and thoughts, identify cognitive distortions and consider alternative thoughts.

Week 7: cultivating beneficial states of heart and mind

Week seven introduces imagery and loving-kindness meditation. Imagery involves a vivid and detailed description of a setting (e.g., mountain, lake) that participants listen to and immerse themselves in to help emphasize some quality of themselves they wish to amplify. For example, while imagining a mountain as majestic, rooted and solid, and not bothered by the changing weather and able to see the long view, individuals imagine themselves as the mountain and as embodying these mountain-like qualities themselves. The imagery is most effective when all sensory modalities beyond just visual are evoked (i.e., encouraging people to imagine sounds, tastes, and smells).

Loving-kindness or "metta" meditation is meant to elicit feelings of love and compassion for oneself and others. Initially, it typically involves conjuring thoughts about another person whom the individual already has loving feelings toward. Over time, individuals direct these feelings towards themselves and eventually to individuals whom they may have neutral feelings towards or even dislike. This exercise is meant to serve as a reminder of the universality of human suffering and enhance feelings of connectedness and shared humanity. Homework includes imagery meditation, loving-kindness meditation, and standing yoga. Individuals also attend a one-day retreat between the seventh and eighth session.

Weekend retreat: a day of silence

The weekend retreat is a one-day, six-hour session that includes practices that have been learned over the MBCR program, such as body scan, sitting and walking meditation, lake meditation, loving-kindness and both lying and standing yoga. Individuals are asked to keep "noble silence" throughout the day, in which they refrain from communicating with each other during the retreat to emphasize individual self-reflection and personal exploration, as well as to conserve energy for focusing and concentrating on the tasks of the day. Everyone packs a lunch and eats their meal mindfully and in silence as part of the retreat.

Week 8: deepening and expanding

The eighth session of MBCR works on expanding beyond breath awareness/concentration type meditation to a bare awareness/open awareness practice. People are encouraged to expand their awareness to other experiences such as sensations, emotions, and passing thoughts. An eventual outcome of expanding awareness to other facets of experience is for insight to develop. Insight is an understanding or awareness of fundamental truths about oneself or the world that were previously unknown or outside of conscious awareness. Insight often develops rapidly as an "ah-ha" moment, or can increase gradually over time. A discussion of personal and collective insight highlights the process by which meditation can lead to further awareness of interconnectedness and the root causes of suffering.

A series of yoga postures coordinated with breathing called the "sun salutation" is introduced as a practice that can improve strength and flexibility with regular practice, with adaptations using a chair first taught as a gentler alternative to the standard sequence. Homework for the next week is sitting meditation, standing yoga or sun salutations, and making plans for continued practice after the end of the program.

Week 9+: moving into the world

The final week of the program is an opportunity to reflect on where people imagined they would be at the end of the program and revisit the goals they stated in their introductions in week 1, with consideration given to what their actual experience was over the course of the program. We ask them to share the plans they have made for continued practice and incorporating mindfulness into daily life. We discuss resources in the form of books, magazines, websites and local groups, as well as several ways in which individuals can continue their practice (e.g., continuing home practice with CDs, joining a yoga class) and incorporate mindfulness into everyday life (e.g., practicing mindful speech, respecting the environment). Individuals are encouraged to maintain what they have learned over the course, as it is expressed that "the ninth week is the rest of your life".

Materials and resources

Book: Carlson, L. E., & Speca, M. (2011). *Mindfulness-based cancer recovery: A step-by-step MBSR approach to help you cope with treatment and reclaim your life.* Oakland, CA: New Harbinger.
Facebook page: Mindfulness-Based Cancer Recovery

Access to program audio-tracks: www.cancerbridges.ca/resources/local-resources/calgary/calgary-area/guided-mindfulness-meditation/
Twitter: @Linda_E_Carlson

References

Campbell, T. S., Labelle, L. E., Bacon, S. L., Faris, P., & Carlson, L. E. (2012). Impact of mindfulness-based stress reduction (MBSR) on attention, rumination and resting blood pressure in women with cancer: A waitlist-controlled study. *Journal of Behavioral Medicine, 35*(3), 262–271. doi:10.1007/s10865-011-9357-1

Carlson, L. E. (2012). Mindfulness-based interventions for physical conditions: A narrative review evaluating levels of evidence. *ISRN Psychiatry, 2012*, Article ID 651583, 21.

Carlson, L. E., & Garland, S. N. (2005). Impact of mindfulness-based stress reduction (MBSR) on sleep, mood, stress and fatigue symptoms in cancer outpatients. *International Journal of Behavioral Medicine, 12*, 278–285.

Carlson, L. E., & Speca, M. (2010). *Mindfulness-based cancer recovery: A step-by-step MBSR approach to help you cope with treatment and reclaim your life.* Oakville, CA: New Harbinger.

Carlson, L. E., Speca, M., Patel, K. D., & Faris, P. (2007). One year pre-post intervention follow-up of psychological, immune, endocrine and blood pressure outcomes of mindfulness-based stress reduction (MBSR) in breast and prostate cancer outpatients. *Brain, Behavior, and Immunity, 21*(8), 1038–1049. doi:10.1016/j.bbi.2007.04.002

Carlson, L. E., Speca, M., Patel, K. D., & Goodey, E. (2003). Mindfulness-based stress reduction in relation to quality of life, mood, symptoms of stress, and immune parameters in breast and prostate cancer outpatients. *Psychosomatic Medicine, 65*(4), 571–581.

Carlson, L. E., Speca, M., Patel, K. D., & Goodey, E. (2004). Mindfulness-based stress reduction in relation to quality of life, mood, symptoms of stress and levels of cortisol, dehydroepiandrosterone sulfate (DHEAS) and melatonin in breast and prostate cancer outpatients. *Psychoneuroendocrinology, 29*(4), 448–474.

Carlson, L. E., Tamagawa R., Stephen, J., Drysdale, E., Zhong, L., & Speca, M. (2016). Randomized-controlled trial of mindfulness-based cancer recovery versus supportive expressive group therapy among distressed breast cancer survivors (MINDSET): Long-term follow-up results. *Psycho-Oncology, 25*, 750–759.

Carlson, L. E., Ursuliak, Z., Goodey, E., Angen, M., & Speca, M. (2001). The effects of a mindfulness meditation based stress reduction program on mood and symptoms of stress in cancer outpatients: Six month follow-up. *Supportive Care in Cancer, 9*, 112–123.

Carlson, L. E., Waller, A., Groff, S. L., Giese-Davis, J., & Bultz, B. D. (2011). What goes up does not always come down: Patterns of distress, physical and psychosocial morbidity in people with cancer over a one year period. *Psycho-Oncology*. doi:10.1002/pon.2068; 10.1002/pon.2068

Cramer, H., Lauche, R., Paul, A., & Dobos, G. (2012). Mindfulness-based stress reduction for breast cancer – A systematic review and meta-analysis. *Current Oncology, 19*(5), e352.

Ganz, P. A. (2009). Survivorship: Adult cancer survivors. *Primary Care, 36*(4), 721–741. doi:10.1016/j.pop.2009.08.001

Garland, S. N., Carlson, L. E., Cook, S., Lansdell, L., & Speca, M. (2007). A non-randomized comparison of mindfulness-based stress reduction and healing arts programs for facilitating post-traumatic growth and spirituality in cancer outpatients. *Supportive Care in Cancer, 15*(8), 949–961. doi:10.1007/s00520-007-0280-5

Garland, S. N., Rouleau, C. R., Campbell, T., Samuels, C., & Carlson, L. E. (2015). The comparative impact of mindfulness-based cancer recovery (MBCR) and cognitive behavior therapy for insomnia (CBT-I) on sleep and mindfulness in cancer patients. *Explore (New York, N.Y.), 11*(6), 445–454. doi:10.1016/j.explore.2015.08.004

Garland, S. N., Tamagawa, R., Todd, S. C., Speca, M., & Carlson, L. E. (2012). Increased mindfulness is related to improved stress and mood following participation in a mindfulness-based stress reduction program in individuals with cancer. *Integrative Cancer Therapies*. doi:10.1177/1534735412442370

Giese-Davis, J., Collie, K., Rancourt, K. M., Neri, E., Kraemer, H. C., & Spiegel, D. (2011). Decrease in depression symptoms is associated with longer survival in patients with metastatic breast cancer: A secondary analysis. *Journal of Clinical Oncology: Official Journal of the American Society of Clinical Oncology, 29*(4), 413–420. doi:10.1200/JCO.2010.28.4455

Kabat-Zinn, J. (1990). *Full catastrophe living: Using the wisdom of your body and mind to face stress, pain and illness*. New York, NY: Delacourt.

Labelle, L. E., Campbell, T. S., & Carlson, L. E. (2010). Mindfulness-based stress reduction in oncology: Evaluating mindfulness and rumination as mediators of change in depressive symptoms. *Mindfulness, 1*(1), 28–40.

Labelle, L. E., Campbell, T. S., Faris, P., & Carlson, L. E. (2015). Mediators of mindfulness-based stress reduction (MBSR): Assessing the timing and sequence of change in cancer patients. *Journal of Clinical Psychology, 71*(1), 21–40. doi:10.1002/jclp.22117

Mackenzie, M. J., Carlson, L. E., Munoz, M., & Speca, M. (2007). A qualitative study of self-perceived effects of mindfulness-based stress reduction (MBSR) in a psychosocial oncology setting. *Stress and Health: Journal of the International Society for the Investigation of Stress, 23*(1), 59–69.

Matchim, Y., Armer, J. M., & Stewart, B. R. (2011). Mindfulness-based stress reduction among breast cancer survivors: A literature review and discussion. *Oncology Nursing Forum, 38*(2), 61. doi:10.1188/11.ONF.E61-E71

Musial, F., Bussing, A., Heusser, P., Choi, K. E., & Ostermann, T. (2011). Mindfulness-based stress reduction for integrative cancer care: A summary of evidence. *Forschende Komplementarmedizin (2006), 18*(4), 192–202. doi:10.1159/000330714; 10.1159/000330714

Piet, J., Wurtzen, H., & Zachariae, R. (2012). The effect of mindfulness-based therapy on symptoms of anxiety and depression in adult cancer patients and survivors: A systematic review and meta-analysis. *Journal of Consulting and Clinical Psychology, 80*(6), 1007–1020.

Schellekens, M. P., Tamagawa, R., Labelle, L. E., Speca, M., Stephen, J., Drysdale, E., . . . Carlson, L. E. (2016). Mindfulness-based cancer recovery (MBCR) versus supportive expressive group therapy (SET) for distressed breast cancer survivors: Evaluating mindfulness and social support as mediators. *Journal of Behavioral Medicine*. doi:10.1007/s10865-016-9799-6

Shapiro, S. L., & Carlson, L. E. (2009). *The art and science of mindfulness: Integrating mindfulness into psychology and the helping professions*. Washington, DC: American Psychological Association Publications.

Shennan, C., Payne, S., & Fenlon, D. (2011). What is the evidence for the use of mindfulness-based interventions in cancer care? A review. *Psycho-Oncology, 20*(7), 681–697.

Speca, M., Carlson, L. E., Goodey, E., & Angen, M. (2000). A randomized, wait-list controlled clinical trial: The effect of a mindfulness meditation-based stress reduction program on mood and symptoms of stress in cancer outpatients. *Psychosomatic Medicine, 62*(5), 613–622.

Zainal, N. Z., Booth, S., & Huppert, F. A. (2013). The efficacy of mindfulness-based stress reduction on mental health of breast cancer patients: A meta-analysis. *Psycho-Oncology, 22*(7), 1457–1465. doi:10.1002/pon.3171; 10.1002/pon.3171

Zernicke, K. A., Campbell, T. S., Speca, M., McCabe-Ruff, K., Flowers, S., & Carlson, L. E. (2014). A randomized wait-list controlled trial of feasibility and efficacy of an online mindfulness-based cancer recovery program: The eTherapy for cancer applying mindfulness trial. *Psychosomatic Medicine, 76*(4), 257–267. doi:10.1097/PSY.0000000000000053; 10.1097/PSY.0000000000000053

Zernicke, K. A., Campbell, T. S., Speca, M., McCabe, K. M., Flowers, S., Tamagawa, R., & Carlson, L. E. (2016). The eCALM trial: eTherapy for cancer applying mindfulness. exploratory analyses of the associations between online mindfulness-based cancer recovery participation and changes in mood, stress symptoms, mindfulness, posttraumatic growth, and spirituality. *Mindfulness, 7*, 1071. doi:10.1007/s12671-016-0545-5

Zhang, J., Xu, R., Wang, B., & Wang, J. (2016). Effects of mindfulness-based therapy for patients with breast cancer: A systematic review and meta-analysis. *Complementary Therapies in Medicine, 26,* 1–10. doi:10.1016/j.ctim.2016.02.012

Zhang, M. F., Wen, Y. S., Liu, W. Y., Peng, L. F., Wu, X. D., & Liu, Q. W. (2015). Effectiveness of mindfulness-based therapy for reducing anxiety and depression in patients with cancer: A meta-analysis. *Medicine, 94*(45), 897. doi:10.1097/MD.0000000000000897

Chapter 15

Mindful Sport Performance Enhancement (MSPE)

Keith A. Kaufman, Carol R. Glass, and Timothy R. Pineau

Intended population and targets of the program

Mindful sport performance enhancement (MSPE) is a mindfulness-based mental training program for athletes and coaches (Kaufman, Glass, & Pineau, 2018). The program can be tailored for use with any sport of focus or with mixed groups representing multiple sports, and is applicable for sport performers at any level, from recreational to elite. While MSPE is intended to be a group-based intervention, it can also be implemented with a single athlete or coach, and could even be adapted for performing artists (such as dancers, actors, or musicians) or others working and performing in high-pressure roles.

There are numerous potential benefits for those in athletics when they learn about and practice mindfulness. As the name of the program suggests, one of the primary targets of MSPE is performance enhancement. Taking on a mindful way of being could facilitate the achievement of peak-performance experiences, perhaps by providing a way through the self-criticism, anxiety, attentional lapses, and rumination that so often accompany sport endeavors. It should be noted that we view MSPE as a holistic training that not only targets experiences in sport, but also daily life beyond athletics. As such, the benefits that any MSPE participant may get can manifest across a range of domains (e.g., school, work, relationships, and psychological well-being).

MSPE overview

There is growing recognition that certain internal states (e.g., *flow;* Csikszentmihalyi, 1990) and mental skills (e.g., self-regulation of attention and emotions), which are considered crucial to attaining peak performance and well-being in athletics, are theoretically consistent with the concept of mindfulness and can be strengthened through mindfulness practice. This recognition has contributed to an explosion of interest in applications of mindfulness within sport and performance psychology, and several high-profile examples have emerged of championship-winning athletes and coaches incorporating mindfulness successfully into their training regimens (e.g., Delehanty, 2014; Jackson, 2013).

MSPE was created in 2005, just as mindfulness was first starting to gain traction in athletics as an alternative to conventional psychological skills training. The primary goal of the program is to systematically train athletes and coaches to participate in their sport with mindful awareness and acceptance, to maximize both their performance and enjoyment. Rooted in the traditions of Kabat-Zinn's (1990) mindfulness-based stress reduction (MBSR) and Segal, Williams, and Teasdale's (2002, 2013) mindfulness-based cognitive therapy (MBCT),

MSPE defines mindfulness as a way of paying attention that involves intentionally tuning in to the present moment and allowing things to be just as they are without judgment (e.g., Kabat-Zinn, 1994). It employs various meditations as core building blocks of the program, with adaptations that make it unique and specific to athletic and other performance populations. Consultation with Jon Kabat-Zinn and former Olympian, Bruce Beall, who had collaborated on what appears to be the first formal application of mindfulness to sport (Kabat-Zinn, Beall, & Rippe, 1985), was instrumental to this adaptation process.

Over the last decade, several studies have indicated MSPE's potential as an effective intervention, including a recent randomized controlled trial. MSPE was originally designed as a four-session group program, shorter than many existing mindfulness protocols for physical- and mental-health concerns, in order to accommodate the often-demanding schedules of those in athletics. However, early research suggested that lengthening the program could be advantageous, so it was expanded to its current format of six sessions. Additionally, session content has been further refined based on quantitative and qualitative findings from earlier work (see Kaufman et al., 2018 for the complete, up-to-date MSPE protocol).

Each MSPE session contains educational, discussion, and experiential components, guiding participants through a structured, easy-to-follow protocol that allows them to learn about mindfulness through their own experience and the experiences of peers. Exercises are taught in an intuitive sequence that moves progressively from sedentary practice to mindfulness in motion, culminating in a sport-specific exercise in which participants apply the mindfulness techniques from MSPE directly to core skills in their sport (e.g., swing for golfers). Additionally, emphasis is placed on incorporating mindfulness *informally* into workouts, practices, and competitions, as well as daily life beyond sport. The intention of this dual focus on formal and informal mindfulness practice is to instill the fundamentals of this powerful way of paying attention, as well as to integrate it into real-world training and competitive routines.

Theoretical background

While mindfulness- and acceptance-based interventions have been found to be effective in the treatment of various physical and psychological issues, the question remains, "Why should those in *athletics* learn mindfulness?" This is a fair question and, in response, we like to reference Gordhamer's (2014) contention that, "The benefits of mindfulness practice as applied to sports are almost blindingly obvious. Focus, awareness, clarity of thought, and the ability to stay in the present moment are basic skills for any great athlete – and meditator." Similarly, Birrer, Röthlin, and Morgan (2012) highlighted a range of factors that are fostered by mindfulness and conducive to peak sport performance (e.g., attention, acceptance and non-judgment, emotion regulation). In addition to enhancing these important skills, taking a mindful perspective to one's inner experience may also help to resolve the performance deficits caused by the "ironic processes of mental control" (Wegner, 1994), in which attempts to suppress or eliminate an internal experience (e.g., thought, feeling) actually intensify that experience (Gardner & Moore, 2004).

Beyond these broad arguments for mindfulness in sport, we believe that the unique content and user-friendly structure of MSPE can maximize what any athlete or coach gets out of mindfulness training, so that capacities like present-moment focus and non-judgmental acceptance can translate into peak sport performance. As we propose below, this outcome effect happens through the *core performance facilitators* taught in MSPE – which enhance certain self-regulatory capacities that ultimately set the stage for flow.

Mindfulness and flow

Csikszentmihalyi's (1990) concept of flow, what many athletes call being "in the zone," is a psychological state defined by the complete, non-self-conscious engagement in and enjoyment of an activity, typically resulting in optimal performance. Flow is thought to consist of nine elements (Csikszentmihalyi, 1990; Jackson & Eklund, 2002): (1) a balance between a challenge faced and the skills required to meet it, (2) having clear goals, (3) receiving unambiguous feedback on the pursuit of those goals, (4) a merging of action and awareness such that the activity almost feels automatic, (5) total concentration on the task at hand, (6) a sense of control, (7) a loss of self-consciousness (lack of self-scrutiny), (8) the transformation of time (e.g., speeding up or slowing down), and (9) autotelic experience (i.e., intrinsic enjoyment). The first three elements are considered prerequisite conditions for flow, with the state then characterized by some or all of the other six elements (Swann, Keegan, Piggott, & Crust, 2012).

There is a significant theoretical connection between mindfulness and flow (Gardner & Moore, 2004; Kaufman, Glass, & Arnkoff, 2009; Pineau, Glass, & Kaufman, 2014; Salmon, Hanneman, & Harwood, 2010), as both explicitly involve a present-moment focus. In fact, the elements of flow that athletes have reported experiencing most frequently are concentration on the task at hand and merging of action and awareness (Swann et al., 2012), both of which are strongly related to mindfulness practice (Chiesa, Calati, & Serretti, 2011; Hölzel & Ott, 2006). Importantly, these theoretical connections have strong empirical support, as flow has been found to be positively related to mindfulness in athletes (Cathcart, McGregor, & Groundwater, 2014; Kaufman et al., 2009; Kee & Wang, 2008; Pineau, Glass, Kaufman, & Bernal, 2014; Scott-Hamilton, Schutte, Moyle, & Brown, 2016), while athletes who receive mindfulness training exhibit increases in their propensity to experience flow (Aherne, Moran, & Lonsdale, 2011; Kaufman et al., 2009; Schwanhausser, 2009; Scott-Hamilton, Schutte, & Brown, 2016).

We believe that primary characteristics of mindfulness (awareness and acceptance) cultivated through MSPE contribute to flow experiences for participants through the enhancement of crucial self-regulatory capacities. Those capacities are the regulation of attention and emotion, both of which are considered main mechanisms through which mindfulness practice enacts change (Hölzel et al., 2011), as well as essential for optimal sport performance (e.g., Boutcher, 2008; Hanin, 2000). Evidence of the links between such self-regulation and sport performance abound. For instance, superior attentional capacity has been found to differentiate more successful from less successful athletes (Hunt, Rietschel, Hatfield, & Iso-Ahola, 2013), while athletes' attempts to suppress negative emotions (reflective of the aforementioned ironic processes of mental control) have been found to lead to poorer performance (Wagstaff, 2014).

Being able to regulate attention and emotion has clear connections to achieving flow, given that "prolonged effortless concentration of attention" is considered a principal characteristic of flow (Dormashev, 2010, p. 306), and that athletes' emotional states can facilitate or hinder flow (Jackson, Kimiecik, Ford, & Marsh, 1998; Koehn, 2013). It is also important to highlight that improvements in these self-regulatory capacities have not only been observed in self-reports of mindfulness practitioners, but also through neuroplastic brain changes. As we detail elsewhere (Kaufman et al., 2018), brain regions known to govern attention and emotion regulation have been shown to change, both structurally and functionally, in response to mindfulness practice (e.g., Fox et al., 2014; Hölzel et al., 2007). And, as Marks (2008) pointed out in his review of the neural correlates of mindfulness and sport psychology, these self-regulatory abilities are "skills that allow for effective athletic training and make peak performance possible" (p. 220).

Learning to self-regulate in these ways is no easy feat, but MSPE attempts to make the process as straightforward and tangible as possible through the identification of five core performance facilitators, which are acceptance- and/or awareness-based skills targeted by the training. It is through the repeated practice of these facilitators that participants strengthen their capacities to manage their attention and emotions, potentially establishing conditions for flow.

Core performance facilitators

Drawing on and adapting the work of Kabat-Zinn et al. (1985), the five core performance facilitators emphasized in MSPE are concentration, letting go, relaxation, establishing a sense of harmony and rhythm, and forming key associations, which we will briefly describe in turn.

Concentration

Most definitions of mindfulness include an emphasis on directing attention (Carmody, 2014), and Ivtzan and Hart (2016) pointed out that the ability to regulate attention is integral to all different forms of meditation. As such, each MSPE exercise contains at least one present-moment attentional anchor that participants direct and then redirect their minds to once attention invariably wanders. These anchors become increasingly applied to the sport(s) of focus as the training progresses, ultimately reinforcing the capacity to concentrate on the athletic task at hand.

Better concentration within the often distraction-rich sport environment can allow athletic performers to minimize the mistakes that can result from lapses in focus, and get more out of their training and competitive experiences through a more deliberate engagement with the activity. The importance of deliberate practice (i.e., intentionally directing attention to the task at hand) in the development of expertise has been well documented (Ericsson, 2006), and so performers who can maintain concentration when practicing and competing are more likely to learn and improve from those experiences. Toner and Moran (2015) suggested that even after developing expertise to the point that certain skills have become automatic, it is only through this kind of intentional present-moment focus that continued improvement is possible.

Letting go

Mindfulness embraces a Buddhist approach to the arising and cessation of suffering, where *reactions* to experiences, rather than the experiences themselves, are seen as most responsible for distress. Thus, MSPE training emphasizes learning to identify and let go of the expectations and attachments that underlie these reactions. Didactic explanations and meditation exercises illustrate for participants how reactions can hijack attention from the present moment (the only time at which one can make choices about performance) and further, how mindful acceptance (e.g., letting go) can help with detaching from these reactions and returning attention to the task at hand. Over time, this simple act of letting go of thoughts, feelings, and sensations in order to redirect attention to a present-moment anchor helps to build an accepting and nonjudgmental attitude toward all experiences, allowing performers to reduce the self-imposed limitations that are often created in response to feelings like fatigue, boredom, and pain that commonly arise during sports participation.

Relaxation

In MSPE, relaxation refers to the absence of *unnecessary* tension, as we recognize that some degree of tension and arousal is necessary for sport performance. But, too much tension can waste energy, interfere with coordination, and increase anxiety, all of which may negatively impact performance. Additionally, Fitzgerald (2010) explained that a lack of bodily awareness is particularly problematic for athletes, since this poor communication between the brain and the muscles can actually make it more difficult for athletes to even notice when they are tense, let alone to let that tension go. While not synonymous with relaxation, meditation practices have long been connected to the relaxation response (e.g., Benson, 1975). As MSPE participants explicitly focus attention on their muscles in several of the formal exercises, they enhance their ability to observe when and where they are carrying tension, and over time, to then choose to release that tension. This intentional use of relaxation can help to regulate anxiety and arousal, which, as noted above, is essential for optimal performance. For instance, Sime (2003) suggested that optimal control of muscle tension can help athletes improve skill execution and conserve energy.

Establishing a sense of harmony and rhythm

Successful sport performance requires a degree of coordination across multiple levels, e.g., intrapersonal, interpersonal, and extrapersonal (Millar, Oldham, & Renshaw, 2013). Take rowing as an example, where the specific motions of an athlete's legs, back, and arms need to be highly coordinated to produce efficient rowing technique (intrapersonal). At the same time, each athlete is working to synchronize those movements with the other rowers in the boat (interpersonal), all the while processing important environmental factors (e.g., chop of the water, wind) to make the appropriate technical adjustments to maximize boat speed (extrapersonal). Recognizing and experiencing the interdependence of coordination at all of these levels can create a sense of harmony and rhythm that may be crucial for sport performance. As MacPherson, Collins, and Obhi (2009) noted, "feeling the rhythm or temporal structure of a movement may be the only necessary strategy when attempting to produce peak performance" (p. 58). MSPE encourages participants to become more attuned to these interconnections, as they come to see that it is the integration of concentrating on the task at hand, letting go of distractions, and releasing excess tension (i.e., the first three performance facilitators) that allows the natural rhythm of a performance to emerge effortlessly. Or, as Kabat-Zinn et al. (1985) described, it allows for "one's performance to unfold out of the stillness of mind, from a cultivated state of detached observation, beyond fatigue, pain, and fear." Importantly, this kind of mindset entails a sense of openness to one's experience that has been associated with enhanced creativity, which in turn has been tied to superior sport performance (Memmert, 2007) and flow (Csikszentmihalyi, 1996).

Forming key associations

Unlike the other performance facilitators, which help MSPE participants understand *how* to put the mindfulness characteristics of awareness and acceptance into practice, forming key associations helps them know *when*. Participants are asked to choose or create environmental cues, both in and out of their sport, which can serve as reminders throughout the day to practice mindfulness. A focus in MSPE is helping sport performers get off of "automatic pilot" so that they can intentionally reengage with their lives. However, outside of the explicit discussion of this topic in MSPE sessions, it can often be difficult to recognize being on automatic pilot (after all, it is lack of awareness that characterizes this state).

MSPE participants thus are taught to use these key associations to reinforce their regular mindfulness practice (both formal and informal), as some studies have shown that the amount of time spent practicing mindfulness can impact the effectiveness of mindfulness training (e.g., Carmody & Baer, 2008; Crane et al., 2014). It is this kind of regular practice, as well as the integration of practice and daily life, that ultimately moves MSPE participants toward training, competing, and living in a mindful way.

Pathways to peak performance

In our book (Kaufman et al., 2018), we pulled all of these components together into a theoretical model of how MSPE optimizes performance. To reiterate, the model proposes that the intentional deployment of specific skills (i.e., core performance facilitators), reflecting central characteristics of mindfulness (e.g., awareness and acceptance), helps to strengthen the self-regulation of attention and emotion, which are essential capacities to the achievement of flow. While the actual pathway may be more complex, the connections among the facets of the model are clear, and highlight the potential mechanisms underlying the program.

As important as this model is in explaining *why* MSPE works, it is equally important to consider the practical aspects of *how* MSPE can be integrated into a regular training regimen – because athletes and coaches can't benefit from mental training if they aren't practicing what they learn. There is ample evidence that psychological, not physical, factors are primarily responsible for day-to-day sport performance fluctuations (Weinberg & Gould, 2015). Yet, despite this knowledge, mental training continues to be a lower priority for many athletes and coaches (if it's a priority at all) than physical and tactical training (Vealey, 2007). We call this phenomenon the "mental training paradox," which is perpetuated by a variety of factors including athletes' and coaches' perceived time constraints, lack of knowledge about how to conduct mental training, and distrust of both outsiders and unfamiliar training techniques (Kaufman et al., 2018).

This paradox is a significant impediment to any sport performers who are looking to take their training and performance to the next level, as it may preclude them from exploring strategies that systematically train the mind. While MSPE has a strong theoretical rationale and a growing evidence base, no mental training program (no matter how theoretically or empirically sound) can have maximum impact without overcoming this paradox. As such, MSPE has evolved over the past decade to present mindfulness in a way that clearly and directly addresses the factors sustaining this phenomenon. For instance, from our experience leading MSPE groups, we've learned the importance of gradually increasing the amount of home practice throughout the workshop, consistently drawing direct parallels between mental and physical training, providing detailed suggestions for integrating mindfulness practice in sport (and daily life), and encouraging the active involvement of MSPE group leaders in other team activities (e.g., attending games or practices). We hope that, with these strategies, MSPE can begin to challenge hurdles like perceived time constraints and lack of "how to" knowledge around mental training, so that athletes and coaches can make space for a new way of understanding their experience that is not simply brought in by an outsider, but rather, is generated from a sense of intrinsic motivation and personal significance that promotes a mindful team culture.

Program structure

The structure described here includes the content of six 90-minute sessions, delivered weekly to groups of athletic performers. However, leaders of an MSPE training can use their knowledge of sport psychology, mindfulness, and the participants to tailor the intervention to address specific needs. For instance, sessions can be shortened due to time constraints, meeting frequency can be adjusted, and/or the training can be adapted for use with a single performer in a sport or other performance activity. While MSPE leaders have access to a detailed protocol, including transcripts for all MSPE exercises (see Kaufman et al., 2018), we also encourage the infusion of personal style into the discussions and exercises to help the content fully come alive for participants.

MSPE cultivates mindfulness skills in a deliberate sequence. It is not assumed that participants have any background in mindfulness, so the first two sessions include the largest didactic components. During these initial sessions, mindfulness is defined, a rationale for the application of mindfulness to sport is presented (Session 1), and the training mechanisms (performance facilitators) are explained using sport-specific examples (Session 2). New concepts are introduced throughout the training, but once a foundational understanding of mindfulness is established, more time is devoted to experiential practice and discussion in the subsequent sessions. Thus, there is a gradual increase in the formal mindfulness practice load over the course of MSPE, both within and between sessions.

Formal mindfulness practice in MSPE involves doing various meditations. As the program progresses and the training becomes more experiential, the practice transitions from sedentary meditations to movement-based ones. This progression culminates with a highly applied, sport-specific meditation, which uses core movements in the sport(s) of focus as present-moment anchors for attention. Attentional anchors are used throughout the training to help participants build connections between their formal mindfulness practice and daily activities, especially their sport performance. The bridge between mindfulness and sport performance is further solidified through extensive guidance in bringing mindfulness more informally into game preparation, competitions, and everyday life.

Session 1: building mindfulness fundamentals

The main objectives of Session 1 are introducing group members and going over ground rules, defining elements of mindfulness (e.g., non-judgment of present-moment experience), explaining the theoretical basis for MSPE as a performance-enhancement program (e.g., links to flow), presenting how mindfulness training can be beneficial in participants' sport(s) (e.g., incorporating comments or perspectives from notable figures in these sports), and providing a first taste of formal and informal mindfulness practice. At the outset, it is important for participants to understand the science behind what they will be learning and doing in MSPE, as well as the significance of committing to this form of mental training. Making such a commitment might feel strange or unfamiliar given the typical prioritization of physical and tactical preparation in sport, but emphasizing the necessity of this commitment to mental training is an important step in addressing the mental training paradox. Sport-specific parallels between mental and physical training may be useful in this discussion, illustrating how, like the body, the mind benefits from versatile, systematic exercise of increasing intensity, with MSPE providing the structure to train the mind in this way.

Formal mindfulness practice commences in this session using food and then the breath as initial attentional anchors. First is the candy exercise, which was inspired by the raisin exercise, a mindfulness training staple (e.g., Kabat-Zinn, 1990). During this approximately ten-minute exercise, participants receive two pieces of candy and are asked to eat them one at a time while paying attention to what they are doing and experiencing, moment by moment. This practice gives a sense of what it is like to function mindfully and how rich and complex even the most familiar activities actually are.

Participants learn about using the breath as an anchor through two exercises: 3 minutes of diaphragmatic breathing and then a sitting meditation with a focus on the breath (which lasts around 10 minutes). Diaphragmatic breathing is taught separately because it is such a valuable skill, and the instructions provided are inherently change-focused (i.e., there is a "correct" way to breathe), which, in some ways, does not fit the acceptance-based nature of mindfulness practice. Conversely, the sitting meditation asks participants to simply observe the process of breathing, whatever it might be in a given moment. Group discussion of participants' experiences follows every formal practice exercise in MSPE.

The first session concludes with the assignment of home practice for the week, which includes daily practice of the diaphragmatic breathing exercise or the sitting meditation with a focus on the breath. Additionally, the concept of informal practice is described, and participants are invited to *s*top, *t*ake a diaphragmatic breath, *o*bserve, and *p*roceed (S.T.O.P.; Stahl & Goldstein, 2010) during daily activities both in and out of their sport. Finally, there is a short discussion of the power and freedom available during an experience when mindfully taking oneself off of "automatic pilot."

Session 2: strengthening the muscle of attention

Session 2 continues to emphasize the importance of attention, and dives deeper into the performance-enhancing aspects of MSPE. This session, and each subsequent one, begins with a centering diaphragmatic breathing practice where participants can let go of whatever was consuming their attention before arrival. Then, there is a discussion of the week's home practice, which often involves reviewing some common obstacles to building a new mindfulness routine. This discussion transitions into an explanation of the performance-enhancement mechanisms underlying MSPE. Specifically, the five performance facilitators described above (concentration, letting go, relaxation, establishing a sense of harmony and rhythm, and forming key associations) are explained, along with sport-specific examples to emphasize the impact that each facilitator may have on performance.

An introduction to the body scan and review of the sitting meditation with a focus on the breath comprise the formal mindfulness practice in this session. The MSPE body scan lasts for approximately 30 minutes and is designed to strengthen concentration, attentional flexibility, mind-body communication, and letting go, as focus is directed sequentially around various body regions. Participants are asked to practice the body scan and the sitting meditation with a focus on the breath for home practice, and they are reminded to incorporate informal mindfulness practice into their daily lives. This session also includes the first emphasis on the fifth performance facilitator, forming key associations. Participants are encouraged to choose or create the environmental cues that they will use throughout the training and beyond, and this remains a point of focus in the home practice discussions throughout the rest of the program. Session 2 concludes with another physical training parallel by noting the mental "reps" involved with this kind of practice, in which participants notice when their minds have wandered and then non-judgmentally reengage their attention with the present moment.

Session 3: stretching the body's limits mindfully

Movements are incorporated into the practice in Session 3, with an emphasis on connecting, with awareness and acceptance, to the sensations (and limits) of the body in motion. This session starts with the centering diaphragmatic breathing exercise and a discussion of the past week's home practice. During this discussion, participants are encouraged to recognize the presence and power of *expectations*, in this context meaning beliefs about what an experience should or needs to be. Distress often occurs when expectations of what should be do not match what is happening, and the performance-detracting implications of this process are highlighted.

Formal practice in this session includes a mindful yoga exercise and an expanded version of the sitting meditation. The MSPE yoga routine lasts for approximately 40 minutes and was developed in consultation with a 500-hour certified yoga instructor. It involves basic stretches intended for a yoga beginner, and represents the first chance participants have to practice being mindful while doing active bodily movements, with the physical sensations themselves serving as attentional anchors. Participants are encouraged to notice when their bodies encounter limits and to respond to such observations non-judgmentally. The expanded sitting meditation (about 15 minutes) includes a new portion that extends attention beyond the breath to the body as a whole. Participants are asked to practice the yoga and the expanded sitting meditation during the week, and are again reminded to find opportunities for informal practice. Session 3 concludes with a discussion of using connection to the body as a route to present-moment awareness.

Session 4: embracing "what is" in stride

Session 4 builds on the theme of paying attention mindfully while the body is in motion. It begins with the centering diaphragmatic breathing exercise and a discussion of home practice over the past week. During this discussion, references are made back to the concept of expectations, with *attachments* identified as the factors that give expectations their power. Attachments refer to underlying beliefs about what is "good," "bad," "right," or "wrong," which can generate rigid expectations regarding what "should" be. Participants are encouraged to consider where attachments might exist for them, and how the mindfulness skills being nurtured through MSPE can facilitate separation from these often-limiting beliefs.

In this session, the formal practice includes a review of the mindful yoga routine and an introduction to the walking meditation. The approximately ten-minute-long MSPE walking meditation continues the progression of incorporating more and more movement into mindfulness practice and involves using the sensations generated by walking as attentional anchors. The process of walking, rather than the destination, is the identified focus, illustrating the concept of *non-striving*. Participants are asked to practice the walking meditation, yoga, and body scan during the week, and again are reminded to seize opportunities for informal mindfulness practice. This session ends with a discussion of the nature of present-moment acceptance, in particular differentiating it from resignation, which is based on assumptions about the future.

Session 5: embodying the mindful performer

This session focuses on the full integration of mindfulness into sport performance. It starts with the centering diaphragmatic breathing exercise and a discussion of the past week's home practice. The complex idea of non-striving is further explored in this discussion, as participants are asked to consider whether they have been working to accept present-moment experience in order to change it (e.g., meditating to relieve stress), a common misconception in a training like MSPE which may perpetuate unexamined attachments to outcomes. Maintaining such attachments can perhaps ironically impede progression toward desired goals.

Formal practice in this session introduces the sport meditation and a further expanded sitting meditation. The sport meditation is the culmination of formal mindfulness practice in MSPE, and involves using the physical sensations generated through core motions in participants' sport(s) of focus as attentional anchors. In other words, this exercise is a chance to practice actually participating in a sport in a mindful way. MSPE leaders may wish to select anchors for this exercise in advance, or in-session in collaboration with participants. To illustrate, one set of anchors for the action of throwing a baseball might be: stance, rotation back, rotation forward, release, and follow through. Participants can be guided through these motions and prompted to simply *observe* the sensations generated by moving through these steps in the throw. Introducing this exercise presents an important opportunity to highlight the differences between observing oneself in action and micromanaging or unnecessarily self-instructing one's actions, as mindfulness practice encourages the former, whereas the very attachments that mindfulness helps to address (e.g., needing to do things "right") can perpetuate the latter long after an action is well-learned. Since this exercise involves literally executing a sport skill, space and safety should be considered. The further expanded sitting meditation lasts about 20 minutes and moves attention beyond the breath and body as a whole to include environmental stimuli (e.g., sounds), as well as a period of silence to give the opportunity for unguided practice.

Home practice for the week includes doing the sport meditation (the one done in session and/or one created independently) and the further expanded sitting meditation. Participants are also again reminded to find ways to practice mindfulness more informally during daily activities. This session wraps up with a discussion on how mindfulness concepts like awareness, acceptance, and non-striving can provide participants with the choice to promote self-care.

Session 6: ending the beginning

The final MSPE session is an opportunity for reflection on the program and consideration of how an ongoing mindfulness practice can be established. It begins with the centering diaphragmatic breathing exercise and a discussion of the practice done outside of sessions both over the past week and throughout the entire training. No new formal practice exercises are introduced in this session. Rather, the body scan is reviewed with an emphasis on how experiences of the exercise may have evolved since first attempting it, and the sport meditation is repeated, using either the same or a new set of movement anchors.

MSPE concludes with a discussion of overall experiences in the training and a brief summary of the major concepts learned. The training is framed as just the beginning of a journey in mindfulness, and recommendations are offered for building a sustained practice, such as finding a reliable time, making a reasonable commitment, creating a literal (e.g., a room) and figurative (i.e., beyond an existing daily routine) space, and personalizing the practice.

Empirical support for MSPE

Research on mindfulness in sport is still in its infancy, but a growing number of studies suggest MSPE's promise as a sport-specific, mindfulness-based intervention. Early support for MSPE was obtained with adult recreational athletes in individual sports, while more recent research has focused on collegiate athletes, either using intact teams or mixed-sport groups. Other studies have examined the feasibility of conducting MSPE training with younger student-athletes, in both high school and elementary school settings.

Initial studies with community athletes

MSPE for archers and golfers

For our initial study of MSPE (Kaufman et al., 2009), we chose to focus on athletes from two sports requiring significant concentration and fine-motor coordination. Seven archers and 14 golfers, who were recruited from local clubs, received a four-week MSPE training. They met in groups separated by sport for approximately two and a half hours weekly, and completed questionnaires both before and immediately after the training. Significant increases in trait mindfulness, sport optimism, state mindfulness (openness to experience), and state flow were found. No significant changes in sport performance were noted, which was perhaps unsurprising given the brevity of the training and challenges in this study with determining a standardized performance metric for the archers. Nonetheless, approximately three-quarters of the athletes who responded to open-ended feedback questions indicated expectations that MSPE would lead to greater performance enjoyment and/or quality in the future.

MSPE for long-distance runners

Our second MSPE study was conducted with 22 recreational long-distance runners (De Petrillo, Kaufman, Glass, & Arnkoff, 2009). MSPE is designed to be tailorable to any sport(s) of focus, so adjustments to the four-session protocol were made to suit this endurance sport. Significant decreases were found in aspects of sport anxiety and perfectionism, with increases found in mindfully attending to the present moment. No significant changes in running performance were reported, but 81% of the runners who provided post-training feedback expected that continued mindfulness practice would lead to future performance improvements.

One-year follow-up

Athletes from these initial studies were invited to participate in a follow-up assessment a year after their MSPE training (Thompson, Kaufman, De Petrillo, Glass, & Arnkoff, 2011).

Approximately 92% of the archers and golfers and 77% of the runners who chose to participate reported at least occasional mindfulness practice during the year. Significant reductions in cognitive interference (both task-irrelevant thoughts and task-related worries) were found. Compared to both before and immediately after the training, significant increases in mindfulness were also noted, and sport anxiety decreased significantly since the conclusion of the program. Additionally, the archers showed a near-significant trend towards improvement in their outdoor shooting scores, golfers reported significantly better scores compared to post-training, and runners reported best-mile times that were significantly faster than those reported both prior to MSPE training and at post-test. Responses to open-ended questions revealed enhanced understanding of mental aspects of their sport, along with increased confidence and relaxation, which a large number of the athletes attributed to mindfulness and related mental strategies. Over half of the athletes also mentioned benefits of mindfulness skills for stress and/or anxiety reduction outside of sport, as well as improved ability to focus.

Studies with collegiate athletes

MSPE for a university cross-country team

Although our intention when developing MSPE was to keep it brief, post-training feedback from participants in the community studies suggested that four weeks was not sufficient time to learn and apply a new mental skill set. Pineau (2014) thus expanded the program to six weekly 90-minute sessions, cultivating more specific themes and content for each session, and creating original scripts for all exercises as well as audio recordings to guide home practice. Two NCAA Division I cross-country teams were recruited to participate, with one receiving MSPE and the other serving as an assessment control.

Unexpected (and in most cases uncontrollable) methodological issues resulted in a lack of significant findings, but critical lessons were learned that strengthened our later work. For example, there was limited contact with the team outside of scheduled sessions, coaches could not be involved in the groups, and these in-season athletes were adding MSPE training to a day already filled with classes and practice. Additionally, we lacked a private space to hold the groups so that sessions faced frequent distractions and interruptions, and the treatment team lost funding as a varsity sport during our study, likely impacting athletes' motivation.

MSPE for NCAA Division III college student athletes

Because our previous published studies were open trials with same-sport community athletes, the extent to which MSPE was effective for mixed-sport groups was unknown. In the first randomized controlled trial of MSPE, athletes represented a range of interactive (e.g., baseball, lacrosse, field hockey) and coactive sports (e.g., swimming, tennis), and were recruited with the support of the university's athletics department. Forty-nine university student-athletes (eight men and 41 women) attended at least one session, either initially assigned to six-week MSPE training or serving as wait-list controls (Glass, Spears, Perskaudas, & Kaufman, 2017). For this study, additional content was added to the MSPE protocol regarding the incorporation of informal mindfulness into home practice and into daily life, as well as sport. All participants completed online measures both before and after the first round of groups, after the wait-list athletes completed the program, and at a five-to-six-month follow-up at the end of the school year.

A significant condition by time interaction revealed that whereas athletes in the control group reported significantly increased depressive symptoms over time, those in the MSPE group reported less depression. After wait-list participants had received the training, comparisons of pre- and post-intervention scores revealed that athletes showed significant improvement in sport anxiety (worry) and in overall dispositional flow as well as three flow dimensions (challenge-skill balance, merging of action and awareness, and loss of self-consciousness). Furthermore, treatment "completers" (who attended at least five sessions) additionally demonstrated significant increases in life satisfaction, self-rated sport performance, and facets of mindfulness (observing and nonreactivity to inner experience).

At the time of the follow-up assessment, all of the gains found at post-test were maintained, with near-significant trends for further increases in mindfulness and self-rated athletic performance. Finally, associations between outcomes and both the frequency and enjoyment of mindfulness practice were found. It was also gratifying that the university's athletics program achieved its highest-ever overall ranking that year, and was named the best athletics program in the conference. As the university's Athletic Director shared with us, "You all helped a number of our coaches and student-athletes recalibrate themselves to produce an even higher level of performance. That's got to go into your summary somewhere. . . . It WORKED!" (S. Sullivan, personal communication, May 22, 2015).

Qualitative coding of responses to open-ended questions after MSPE training found that the athletes generally characterized it as a positive experience, liked the specific mindfulness skills and techniques they had been taught as well as the group discussions, and felt they had experienced many of their expected benefits (Mistretta et al., 2017). They reported it had been helpful for their sport by promoting relaxation and anxiety reduction, improving athletic performance, and benefiting their mindsets (e.g., more focus, awareness, self-confidence, and ability to let go of negative emotions). It was also notable that athletes reported similar benefits in their daily lives, in addition to being better able to stay in the moment and collect their thoughts.

Around three-quarters of the athletes were at least somewhat sure they would continue to practice mindfulness. A recent email from one of the participants, who had a breakout season a year after MSPE training and was one of only 48 student-athletes in the country in Division III of the NCAA to be honored recently as an All-American in her sport, shed additional light on how MSPE can benefit sport performance. She described playing with a "more mindful attitude on the field," and that the meditations she practiced had given her a good sense of what it felt like to be "focused and in the zone," which she was able to channel into her play. This athlete also reported feeling "less anxious on the field," and that she was "able to have more success because I was focused and not worrying about my mistakes nor unrelated issues."

Adapting MSPE for college teams

Pineau (2016) provided six one-hour MSPE sessions to two intact teams of university athletes. This adaptation of MSPE for teams was done with the consent of the university athletics program and in collaboration with both teams' coaches, who did the training along with their athletes and incorporated mindfulness into team practices and workouts. The 32 athlete-participants showed significant increases in most dimensions of flow, trait mindfulness and the refocusing aspect of sport-related mindfulness, and self-rated performance, as well as decreases in experiential avoidance, and sport-related anxiety.

At a post-season follow-up several months later, nearly all gains were maintained and significant increases were found in coach-rated performance and total sport mindfulness. Both teams had losing records the previous year, but had winning seasons following MSPE, with one team having the best season in its history, while the other had its best season in over a decade. It was also notable that one of these teams (which continued to receive MSPE follow-up sessions over the next year) went on to win their regional conference championship the following season for the first time in program history. The coach of this team credited the integration of mindfulness into their team culture as a significant contributing factor to their success, stating "Our program was able to achieve our ultimate goal and MSPE helped us immensely all along the way."

Studies with youth athletes

MSPE for high school teams

A large local school district interested in offering MSPE training to boost student-athlete wellness worked with Keith Kaufman to offer a pilot program to 12 female field hockey and soccer players. Significant improvements were found in overall sport mindfulness (and specifically in awareness), emotion regulation (especially acceptance of emotions), and the clear goals and challenge-skill balance dimensions of flow (Mistretta, Kaufman, Glass, & Spears, 2016). These were striking findings given the small sample size and that weather-related school closings forced consolidation of the protocol into five sessions.

The True Athlete Project

The True Athlete Project is a non-profit organization whose goal is to change the culture of youth sport through the practice of mindfulness (Cook, 2015). The Project conducted a pilot MSPE program for 47 elementary school children, with modifications to make the content developmentally appropriate for these participants. Analyses revealed that the children's levels of anxiety decreased significantly, while acceptance and mindfulness scores increased significantly (personal communication, S. Parfitt, March 27, 2016).

Future research

It is crucial that additional research be conducted by other investigators, who now can have access to the full MSPE protocol (Kaufman et al., 2018). Such studies could employ larger samples, and be randomized controlled trials comparing MSPE to other active treatments such as CBT-based psychological skills training or other mindfulness-based interventions for athletes (e.g., the mindfulness-acceptance-commitment (MAC) approach, Gardner & Moore, 2007). They can also include checks for treatment adherence, long-term follow-up, objective measures of performance, and potentially brain or psychophysiological assessment. It is also important to further investigate the moderators of change in MSPE (i.e., who benefits the most, the role of formal meditation practice), and to answer questions regarding best practice in program delivery. Additionally, testing our conceptualization of the role of the five core performance facilitators discussed earlier in this chapter will help to fine-tune our MSPE model.

It is notable that prior studies have indicated benefits of MSPE within both sport and daily life. Further work with youth and young-adult student-athletes might offer MSPE as a preventive measure for reducing the likelihood of clinical distress and promoting resilience in the face of stressors such as overtraining, sports-related injuries, and failing to live up to athletic expectations (Glass et al., 2018). A "mental training program for athletes" like MSPE could be less stigmatizing and thus more acceptable for many at-risk students than traditional counseling. Such research could be conducted within high school and college athletic departments, with coaches involved not only as participants in the training, but also as collaborators in helping their athletes to apply MSPE skills during practice and competition. Finally, the potential for expanding MSPE to musicians, dancers, and actors is an exciting future direction for research (see Kaufman et al., 2018), and it is our hope that MSPE evolves to provide an easy-to-follow framework for mindfulness training for any high-pressure performers.

Online materials for further resources and information relating to the program

The most comprehensive resource available to learn more about MSPE, as well as the state of the field regarding mindfulness interventions for sport performers, is our recent book published by the American Psychological Association, *Mindful Sport Performance Enhancement: Mental Training for Athletes and Coaches* (Kaufman et al., 2018). Additional information about MSPE, including audio recordings of all exercises, can also be found on our website, mindfulsportperformance.org.

References

Aherne, C., Moran, A. P., & Lonsdale, C. (2011). The effect of mindfulness training on athletes' flow: An initial investigation. *The Sport Psychologist, 25*(2), 177–189.
Benson, H. (1975). *The relaxation response*. New York, NY: Morrow.
Birrer, D., Röthlin, P., & Morgan, G. (2012). Mindfulness to enhance athletic performance: Theoretical considerations and possible impact mechanisms. *Mindfulness, 3*, 235–246.
Boutcher, S. H. (2008). Attentional processes and sport performance. In T. S. Horn (Ed.), *Advances in sport psychology* (3rd ed., pp. 325–338). Champaign, IL: Human Kinetics.
Carmody, J. (2014). Eastern and western approaches to mindfulness: Similarities, differences, and clinical implications. In A. Ie, C. Ngnoumen, & E. Langer (Eds.), *The Wiley Blackwell handbook of mindfulness* (Vol. I, pp. 48–57). Chichester, UK: John Wiley & Sons.
Carmody, J., & Baer, R. A. (2008). Relationships between mindfulness practice and levels of mindfulness, medical and psychological symptoms and well-being in a mindfulness-based stress reduction program. *Journal of Behavioral Medicine, 31*, 23–33.
Cathcart, S., McGregor, M., & Groundwater, E. (2014). Mindfulness and flow in elite athletes. *Journal of Clinical Sport Psychology, 8*, 119–141.
Chiesa, A., Calati, R., & Serretti, A. (2011). Does mindfulness training improve cognitive abilities? A systematic review of neuropsychological findings. *Clinical Psychology Review, 31*, 449–464.
Cook, D. (2015, June 7). Float like a butterfly, play like a kid. *TimesFreePress.com*. www.timesfreepress.com/news/opinion/columns/story/2015/jun/07/flobutterfly-play-kid/308320/
Crane, C., Crane, R. S., Eames, C., Fennell, M. J. V., Silverton, S., Williams, J. M. G., & Barnhofer, T. (2014). The effects of amount of home meditation practice in mindfulness based cognitive therapy on hazard of relapse to depression in the Staying Well after Depression Trial. *Behaviour Research and Therapy, 63*, 17–24.

Csikszentmihalyi, M. (1990). *Flow: The psychology of optimal experience.* New York, NY: Harper & Row.

Csikszentmihalyi, M. (1996). *Creativity: Flow and the psychology of discovery and invention.* New York, NY: Harper Collins.

Delehanty, H. (2014, December). The game changer. *Mindful,* 45–53.

De Petrillo, L. A., Kaufman, K. A., Glass, C. R., & Arnkoff, D. B. (2009). Mindfulness for long-distance runners: An open trial using Mindful Sport Performance Enhancement (MSPE). *Journal of Clinical Sport Psychology, 3,* 357–376.

Dormashev, Y. (2010). Flow experience explained on the grounds of an activity approach to attention. In B. Bruya (Ed.), *Effortless attention: A new perspective in the cognitive science of attention and action* (pp. 287–333). Cambridge, MA: Massachusetts Institute of Technology Press.

Ericsson, K. A. (2006). The influence of experience and deliberate practice on the development of superior expert performance. In K. A. Ericsson, N. Charness, P. Feltovich, & R. R. Hoffman (Eds.), *Cambridge handbook of expertise and expert performance* (pp. 685–706). New York, NY: Cambridge University Press.

Fitzgerald, M. (2010). *Run: The mind-body method of running by feel.* Boulder, CO: Velo Press.

Fox, K. C. R., Nijeboer, S., Dixon, M. L., Floman, J. L., Ellamil, M., Rumak, S. P., . . . Christoff, K. (2014). Is meditation associated with altered brain structure? A systematic review and meta-analysis of morphometric neuroimaging in meditation practitioners. *Neuroscience and Biobehavioral Reviews, 43,* 48–73.

Gardner, F. L., & Moore, Z. E. (2004). A mindfulness-acceptance-commitment-based approach to athletic performance enhancement: Theoretical considerations. *Behavior Therapy, 35,* 707–723.

Gardner, F. L., & Moore, Z. E. (2007). *The psychology of enhancing human performance: The Mindfulness-Acceptance-Commitment (MAC) approach.* New York, NY: Springer.

Glass, C. R., Spears, C. A., Perskaudas, R., & Kaufman, K. A. (2018). Mindful sport performance enhancement: Randomized controlled trial of a mental training program with collegiate athletes. *Journal of Clinical Sport Psychology,* 1–34.

Gordhamer, S. (2014, March 5). Mindfulness: The Seattle Seahawks' sports psychologist shares why it matters. *Huffington Post.* Retrieved from www.huffingtonpost.com

Hanin, Y. L. (Ed.). (2000). *Emotions in sport.* Champaign, IL: Human Kinetics.

Hölzel, B. K., Lazar, S. W., Gard, T., Schuman-Olivier, Z., Vago, D., & Ott, U. (2011). How does mindfulness meditation work? Proposing mechanisms of action from a conceptual and neural perspective. *Perspectives on Psychological Science, 6,* 537–559.

Hölzel, B. K., & Ott, U. (2006). Relationships between meditation depth, absorption, meditation practice, and mindfulness: A latent variable approach. *The Journal of Transpersonal Psychology, 38,* 179–199.

Hölzel, B. K., Ott, U., Hempel, H., Hackl, A., Wolf, K., Stark, R., & Vaitl, D. (2007). Differential engagement of anterior cingulate and adjacent medial frontal cortex in adept meditators and non-meditators. *Neuroscience Letters, 421,* 16–21.

Hunt, C. A., Rietschel, J. C., Hatfield, B. D., & Iso-Ahola, S. E. (2013). A psychophysiological profile of winners and losers in sport competition. *Sport, Exercise, and Performance Psychology, 2,* 220–231.

Ivtzan, I., & Hart, R. (2016). Mindfulness scholarship and interventions: A review. In A. L. Baltzell (Ed.), *Mindfulness and Performance* (pp. 3–28). New York, NY: Cambridge University Press.

Jackson, P. (2013). *Eleven rings: The soul of success.* New York, NY: Penguin Books.

Jackson, S. A., & Eklund, R. C. (2002). Assessing flow in physical activity: The Flow State Scale-2 and Dispositional Flow Scale-2. *Journal of Applied Sport & Exercise Psychology, 24,* 133–150.

Jackson, S. A., Kimiecik, J. C., Ford, S. K., & Marsh, H. W. (1998). Psychological correlates of flow in sport. *Journal of Sport & Exercise Psychology, 20,* 358–378.

Kabat-Zinn, J. (1990). *Full catastrophe living: Using the wisdom of your body and mind to face stress, pain, and illness.* New York, NY: Delta.

Kabat-Zinn, J. (1994). *Wherever you go, there you are: Mindfulness meditation in everyday life.* New York, NY: Hyperion.

Kabat-Zinn, J., Beall, B., & Rippe, J. (1985, June). *A systematic mental training program based on mindfulness meditation to optimize performance in collegiate and Olympic rowers.* Poster session presented at the World Congress in Sport Psychology, Copenhagen, Denmark.

Kaufman, K. A., Glass, C. R., & Arnkoff, D. B. (2009). Evaluation of mindful sport performance enhancement (MSPE): A new approach to promote flow in athletes. *Journal of Clinical Sport Psychology, 3*, 334–356.

Kaufman, K. A., Glass, C. R., & Pineau, T. P. (2018). *Mindful sport performance enhancement: Mental training for athletes and coaches.* Washington, DC: American Psychological Association.

Kee, Y. H., & Wang, C. K. J. (2008). Relationships between mindfulness, flow dispositions and mental skills adoption: A cluster analytic approach. *Psychology of Sport and Exercise, 9*, 393–411.

Koehn, S. (2013). Effects of confidence and anxiety on flow state in competition. *European Journal of Sport Science, 13*, 543–550.

MacPherson, A. C., Collins, D., & Obhi, S. S. (2009). The importance of temporal structure and rhythm for the optimum performance of motor skills: A new focus for practitioners of sport psychology. *Journal of Applied Sport Psychology, 21*(S1), 48–61.

Marks, D. R. (2008). The Buddha's extra scoop: Neural correlates of mindfulness and clinicalsport psychology. *Journal of Clinical Sport Psychology, 2*, 216–241.

Memmert, D. (2007). Can creativity be improved by an attention-broadening training program? An exploratory study focusing on team sports. *Creativity Research Journal, 19*, 281–291.

Millar, S-K., Oldham, A. R., & Renshaw, I. (2013). Interpersonal, intrapersonal, extrapersonal? Qualitatively investigating coordinative couplings between rowers in Olympic sculling. *Nonlinear Dynamics, Psychology and Life Sciences, 17*, 425–443.

Mistretta, E. G., Glass, C. R., Spears, C. A., Perskaudas, R., Kaufman, K. A., & Hoyer, D. (2017). Collegiate athletes' expectations and experiences with mindful sport performance enhancement. *Journal of Clinical Sport Psychology, 11*, 201–221.

Mistretta, E. G., Kaufman, K. A., Glass, C. R., & Spears, C. A. (2016, April). *Mindful sport performance enhancement for high school athletes.* Mid-Atlantic Regional Conference of the Association for Applied Sport Psychology, Philadelphia, PA.

Pineau, T. R. (2014). *Effects of mindful sport performance enhancement (MSPE) on running performance and body image: Does self-compassion make a difference?* Doctoral dissertation. Available from ProQuest Dissertations and Theses database. (UMI No. 364138).

Pineau, T. R. (2016). *Evaluation of mindful sport performance enhancement (MSPE) in a naturalistic university setting.* Manuscript in preparation.

Pineau, T. R., Glass, C. R., & Kaufman, K. A. (2014). Mindfulness in sport performance. In A. Ie, C. T. Ngnoumen, & E. J. Langer (Eds.), *The Wiley Blackwell handbook of mindfulness* (Vol. II, pp. 1004–1033). Chichester, UK: John Wiley & Sons.

Pineau, T. R., Glass, C. R., Kaufman, K. A., & Bernal, D. R. (2014). Self- and team efficacy beliefs of rowers and their relation to mindfulness and flow. *Journal of Clinical Sport Psychology, 8*, 142–158.

Salmon, P., Hanneman, S., & Harwood, B. (2010). Associative/dissociative cognitive strategies in sustained physical activity: Literature review and proposal for a mindfulness-based conceptual model. *The Sport Psychologist, 24*, 127–156.

Schwanhausser, L. (2009). Application of the Mindfulness-Acceptance-Commitment (MAC) protocol with an adolescent springboard diver. *Journal of Clinical Sport Psychology, 3*, 377–395.

Scott-Hamilton, J., Schutte, N. S., & Brown, R. F. (2016). Effects of a mindfulness intervention on sports-anxiety, pessimism, and flow in competitive cyclists. *Applied Psychology: Health and Well-Being, 8*, 85–103.

Scott-Hamilton, J., Schutte, N. S., Moyle, G. M., & Brown, R. F. (2016). The relationships between mindfulness, sport anxiety, pessimistic attributions and flow in competitive cyclists. *International Journal of Sport Psychology, 47*, 103–121.

Segal, Z. V., Williams, J. M. G., & Teasdale, J. D. (2002). *Mindfulness-based cognitive therapy for depression: A new approach to preventing relapse*. New York, NY: Guilford Press.

Segal, Z. V., Williams, J. M. G., & Teasdale, J. D. (2013). *Mindfulness-based cognitive therapy for depression* (2nd ed.). New York, NY: Guilford Press.

Sime, W. E. (2003). Sport psychology applications of biofeedback and neurofeedback. In M. S. Schwartz & F. Andrasik (Eds.), *Biofeedback: A practitioner's guide* (3rd ed., pp. 560–588). New York, NY: Guilford Press.

Stahl, B., & Goldstein, E. (2010). *A mindfulness-based stress reduction workbook*. Oakland, CA: New Harbinger Publications, Inc.

Swann, C., Keegan, R. J., Piggott, D., & Crust, L. (2012). A systematic review of the experience, occurrence, and controllability of flow states in elite sport. *Psychology of Sport and Exercise, 13*, 807–819.

Thompson, R. W., Kaufman, K. A., De Petrillo, L. A., Glass, C. R., & Arnkoff, D. B. (2011). One year follow-up of mindful sport performance enhancement (MSPE) for archers, golfers, and runners. *Journal of Clinical Sport Psychology, 5*, 99–116.

Toner, J., & Moran, A. (2015). Enhancing performance proficiency at the expert level: Considering the role of 'somaesthetic awareness'. *Psychology of Sport and Exercise, 16*, 110–117.

Vealey, R. S. (2007). Mental skills training in sport. In G. Tenenbaum & R. Eklund (Eds.), *Handbook of sport psychology* (3rd ed., pp. 287–309). Hoboken, NJ: John Wiley & Sons.

Wagstaff, C. R. D. (2014). Emotion regulation and sport performance. *Journal of Sport & Exercise Psychology, 36*, 401–412.

Wegner, D. M. (1994). Ironic processes of mental control. *Psychological Review, 101*, 34–52.

Weinberg, R. S., & Gould, D. (2015). *Foundations of sport and exercise psychology* (6th ed.). Champaign, IL: Human Kinetics.

Chapter 16

Mindfulness-Based Eating Awareness Training (MB-EAT)

Jean L. Kristeller

Overview of the program

We all eat – and we all eat mindlessly at times (Wansink, 2007). Engaging mindfulness while eating not only deepens our relationship with food and our body. It can go beyond that, as it also connects us with the experience of mindfulness many times each day. The Mindfulness-Based Eating Awareness Training (MB-EAT) program helps people engage a sense of flexible balance in relation to their eating and food – and themselves. It does this by cultivating both "inner wisdom" and "outer wisdom". Inner wisdom entails a greater awareness of physical hunger, fullness and taste, along with more awareness of non-nutritive triggers for eating. "Outer wisdom" means making more balanced use of nutritional information, attuned to one's personal needs and preferences. Cultivating and then drawing on this greater sense of personal "wisdom" is a core unifying theme across all elements of the program.

MB-EAT is delivered as a group program, with 12 sessions, as evaluated in National Institutes of Health-funded clinical trials (Kristeller & Wolever, 2011; Kristeller, Wolever, & Sheets, 2013), and is adaptable to varying populations and contexts. The program includes practices in mindfulness meditation, mindful eating exercises, and other guided meditations to deepen self-acceptance, manage anger, and clarify personal values (Kristeller & Wolever, in press).

MB-EAT has been used with people with a wide range of issues, from milder levels of eating issues, experienced at times by most individuals, to the extreme levels of dysfunction suffered by those with binge eating disorder, the most common eating disorder, regardless of age (Kristeller, 2016). It has also been adapted for use with individuals with type II diabetes, for those preparing for bariatric surgery, and for overweight adolescents and children. At the same time, virtually all practices are suitable to be used by almost anyone seeking to gain a higher quality experience of eating and making food choices, while letting go of undue anxiety around weight and dieting (Kristeller, 2016).

Goals of the program

The overall intent of the MB-EAT program is to help individuals create a healthier, more balanced, and more satisfying relationship to their eating, to food, and to their body. MB-EAT is NOT designed to produce rapid or significant weight change in the short term, but rather focuses on helping people create sustainable ways to be in better balance with their eating and food choices. All elements of the program are subsumed under cultivating greater "inner wisdom" and "outer wisdom". Inner wisdom goals focus on deepening interoceptive awareness of physical hunger, feelings of fullness, and experiences of taste satisfaction/satiety; and awareness of thoughts and emotions as they relate to eating choices. Related goals include enhancement of self-acceptance/compassion and self-awareness regarding personal values related to eating and weight, as appropriate, which are generally so missing for individuals struggling with these issues, yet so responsive to mindfulness practices (Gilbert, 2009). Outer wisdom goals focus on replacing the rigid, highly self-judgmental attitudes and behaviors associated with structured diets and rapid weight loss with a sense of curiosity regarding nutritional values of food, flexibility, and internalizing food choices consistent with personal health needs. If weight loss is a reasonable, healthy goal for an individual, then guidelines are explored to reduce caloric intake and increase physical activity in non-judgmental sustainable ways, and always from a non-dieting perspective.

Personal story

The development of MB-EAT has woven together many strands from both my personal background and professional interests. I became intrigued with the power of meditation practice first through Transcendental Meditation in the early 1970s and then to various Buddhist traditions, both as spiritual practices and for their psychological astuteness (Kristeller, 2003; Kristeller & Rapgay, 2013). During my training as a psycho-physiologist and clinical psychologist, I became intrigued with understanding mind-body connections related to meditation practice, in both research and clinical application (Cuthbert, Kristeller, Simons, Hodes, & Lang, 1981; Kristeller, 1977). I also drew on my own struggles with weight and eating issues, classically similar to those of millions of women: my concern with being thinner had led to over-dieting and a sense of constant struggle with eating and weight, as I alternated over-restriction and over-eating.

In the late 1970s, I began developing treatment components that would become part of the MB-EAT program: use of meditation to quiet both the mind and body; practices that encouraged deeper awareness of hunger, fullness, and taste; eating-related practices that countered compulsive over-eating, yet fostered a sense of self-acceptance. Though I had been integrating these into work with clients both individually and in groups, the MB-EAT program itself started to coalesce after I began working with Jon Kabat-Zinn at the University of Massachusetts Medical School in the mid-1980s. Personally experiencing the Mindfulness-Based Stress Reduction (MBSR) program and then joining his research team led to a greater appreciation of brief guided mindfulness practices, delivering a mindfulness-based program that contained many focused elements, and the receptivity of the general public to such practices.

Theoretical background and research

MB-EAT reflects the convergence of several theoretical lines, further informed by research by myself and others over the last 35 years. As noted above, development of the program reflects the merging of several decades of research on mindfulness-based interventions, interoceptive awareness, and self-regulation theory (Schwartz, 1975; Shapiro & Schwartz, 2000), merging with models of food intake regulation that have also emphasized the interplay of psychological and physiological control processes (Rodin, 1981). Such self-regulation models differ markedly from will-power or even self-control models more typically associated with dieting and weight loss, by positing that when appropriate feedback mechanisms are engaged and then internalized, there is far less need for ongoing vigilance or sense of struggle (Carver & Scheier, 2011). It also incorporates body acceptance practices, broader self-awareness practices, and engagement with interpersonal challenges.

Mindfulness theory and MB-EAT

Neuroscience continues to support meditation practice as a path toward re-regulation (Davidson & Goleman, 2017), especially when complex cognitive-emotional-behavioral interactions need to be brought into better balance with physiological functioning. The external regulation of structured diets, by imposing rigid food guidelines and greatly reduced caloric intake, further disconnects individuals from the internal regulatory systems integral to our physical functioning. *Integrated regulation*, as laid out in Ryan and Deci's (2000) Self-Determination Theory, addresses the ways by which intrinsic processes link with external factors for improved self-regulation. From early in the development of MB-EAT, the "relaxation" effects of meditation practice, although useful for managing some aspects of stress-related eating, are intended to be secondary to cultivating these more complex self-regulation process. Rather, mindfulness practice cultivates self-awareness of internal experience and external triggers for eating, powerfully turning mindless reactivity into "wise" response (Kristeller & Wolever, 2014).

The MB-EAT program includes both open and guided meditations, extended practice and very brief practice ("mini-meditations"), all of which have extensive basis in meditative traditions, yet play distinct roles in self-regulatory processes (Kristeller, 2007). Also core to traditional meditation practice is the concept of "wisdom", or insight. Contemporary definitions of wisdom, from a psychological perspective, involve exercising good judgment in complex or uncertain situations (Sternberg, 1990). From a neuroscience perspective, mindfulness practice facilitates both access to, and integration of, the complexity of past experience and knowledge that each person already carries within (Kristeller, 2003; Meeks, Cahn, & Jeste, 2012). In MB-EAT, the term "wisdom" is introduced within this context, whether in relation to making apparently simple, but often challenging – or mindless – decisions about food choice ("do I eat one more bite – or not?"), or larger decisions about longer term eating patterns. The term resonates with participants, as they stop for a moment, at any time during the day, and access their 'wise' mind, in the face of long-standing patterns and temptations. A wisdom meditation later in the program deepens these experiences. Meditation is also traditionally grounded in spiritual engagement, and even relatively short practice can deepen such experience, as found for the MBSR program (Carmody, Reed, Kristeller, & Merriam, 2008). We have found similar increases in spiritual well-being in the MB-EAT program, correlated with improvement in eating regulation (Kristeller & Jordan, 2018).

Eating regulation theory and MB-EAT

The interplay between physiological hunger and satiety cues, and social, environmental and emotional triggers to eat (or stop eating) is highly complex (Drewnowski, 1996). Wansink, in his wide-ranging work on "mindless eating" (2007), found that individuals, on average, make 200–300 food decisions per day regarding when and what to eat, and when to stop (Wansink & Sobal, 2007). People also vary considerably in their general patterns of eating in regard to emotional eating, eating without being physically hungry, and compulsive overeating (Drewnowski, 1996; Kristeller & Rodin, 1989). Such issues are more extreme in individuals who are heavier, and who have issues with compulsive overeating; these individuals show higher sensitivity to external cues and internal "non-nutritive" cues, such as emotions or cravings, and lower sensitivity to internal cues of hunger and satiety (Sysko, Hildebrandt, Wilson, Wilfley, & Agras, 2010). While biological variation (genetic or epigenetic) undoubtedly contributes (Appelhans, 2009), most individuals can become "disconnected" from internal experience and over-sensitized to non-nutritive triggers, whether emotions, thoughts, or external triggers, creating habitual patterns of mindless – and often compulsive – overeating. Cultivating mindfulness to address compulsive or binge eating has parallels with using mindfulness for management of alcohol problems (Bowen, Chawla, & Marlatt, 2011), such as "surfing the urge" and avoiding the "abstinence violation effect" (or as referred to in MB-EAT: the "I've blown it" effect).

Recognizing the differences between physical hunger and all the other triggers for eating is particularly challenging. Many individuals confuse simply wanting some food with physical need; others, often from lower socioeconomic status (SES) backgrounds, have been taught to avoid even mild levels of hunger. Drawing on the science of psychophysics (Bartoshuk, 1978), participants learn to rate their awareness of physical hunger on a scale of 1 to ten, "mindfully" observing the feelings they associate with each number, from "no hunger" to "as hungry as they've ever felt", and then learning to distinguish these feelings from other triggers, such as stress.

Yet the relationship between eating and stress is complex. Although individuals with binge eating disorder (BED) are more likely to eat when stressed (Goldfield, Adamo, Rutherford, & Legg, 2008), it is greatly oversimplifying the stress-eating relationship to make this the primary foundation for mindfulness-based interventions. Indeed, the potential value of mindfulness practice is much broader. Tuning into such triggers, including mundane ones as simply having food available, thoughts ("just one won't matter"; "I've already blown it so I might as well keep going"; "I have to clear my plate"), or emotions, whether stress, anger, depression – or joy, is also heightened through mindful self-awareness. Individuals may note that they eat "for comfort", but rather than deriving comfort from the pleasure of the food, guilt kicks in so quickly that little comfort is derived. We encourage them, instead, to tune into this desire for comfort, a normal use of eating for many people (Kristeller & Rodin, 1989) – but with smaller, rather than large quantities.

Mindful eating involves not only knowing when to start eating, but also knowing when to stop. Many individuals, including those with BED, are not only poorly-attuned to physical hunger, but they pay little attention to satiety cues, or signals from the body that they've eaten "enough". The program brings mindful awareness to three different types of satiety: sensory-specific satiety; experiences of stomach fullness; and what we refer to as "body satiety", or the absorption of nutrients. Sensory-specific satiety (SSS) happens remarkably quickly. SSS, referred to within MB-EAT as "taste satiety", is the process by which food loses its appeal as the taste buds in our mouths habituate to specific combinations of flavors (Remick, Polivy, & Pliner, 2009). Yet individuals continue to eat, "chasing the flavor", hoping to get back the pleasure of those first few bites. SSS may indeed be disrupted in individuals with obesity and/or binge eating (Raynor & Epstein, 2001), but evidence suggests that SSS functions more normally when awareness is brought to the process (Brondel et al., 2007). Therefore, mindfulness can also be applied to heightening the enjoyment from eating, thereby shifting the focus of that pleasure from "quantity" to "quality", as a 1–10 "taste satisfaction meter" is applied to changing experiences. This process is very counter to addictive models of compulsive eating (Grosshans, Loeber, & Kiefer, 2011), in which the solution offered is usually abstinence, rather than counter-balancing this addictive aspect. Although further research is needed, in our experience, those foods considered most vulnerable to addictive type consumption (sugar, fats, and salt) respond the most quickly to the processes involved in SSS.

Stomach fullness comes on more gradually, yet may also not be attended to by heavier individuals and those with BED. They will note that they often eat to a "10" on the 1–10 scale, tolerating very high levels of fullness and discomfort (Sysko, Devlin, Walsh, Zimmerli, & Kissileff, 2007). They often also note that they experience considerable social pressure within their family or social network to continue eating "until the food is gone". Learning how to stop for a moment and politely decline food in social situations is another opportunity for mindful awareness. "Body satiety" is more subtle; it can occur quite quickly, for example, within a few minutes of eating a calorically dense sugared snack in the face of physical hunger, during a meal when your mind-body says "enough!", or at an intense level an hour after an overly large meal, when you don't want to even move.

These elements of interoceptive awareness related to eating are introduced in the first half of the program (see below for details). For each one – physical hunger, taste satiety, fullness, and body satiety – individuals mindfully observe their inner experiences with guided practices, and then extend them during the week to all their meals and snacks. When mindfully observed, individuals learn to tune in surprisingly quickly to rather subtle differences in these experiences.

Research and empirical support

Initial research with MB-EAT focused on treatment of individuals with BED. The first pilot study (Kristeller & Hallett, 1999), used an extended baseline/extended follow-up design in a small sample of women (N=18; ages 25–62; avg. = 46.5) weighing on average 239 lbs. (BMI = 40). Many also struggled with depression and anxiety. We productively used this design in our research on MBSR and anxiety disorders (Kabat-Zinn et al., 1992). It allows for individual analysis if relatively few individuals respond, but if consistent enough, group data can be used. We found significant decreases in frequency and size of binges, compulsive overeating, depression and anxiety, and increases in awareness of hunger and satiety. Notably, reduction in compulsive overeating correlated with amount of mindfulness practice at home, particularly guided eating-related meditations (r = .66, p < .01).

Given these results, National Institutes of Health (NIH) funding was obtained for a multisite randomized clinical trial, comparing MB-EAT to a modified cognitive-behavioral CBT) intervention and a wait-list control (Kristeller et al., 2013), enrolling 150 men and women, again with clinical or sub-clinical binge eating disorder, and similar in age and weight level to the pilot study. The focus was again on improving patterns of eating and emotional stability (cultivating "inner wisdom"), with little focus on weight change *per se*. The results largely replicated and extended the pilot research. Although improvement for the two active treatment groups were similar on many variables, more individuals in the MB-EAT group no longer met criteria for BED than in the CBT group, and when binges occurred, they were significantly smaller, indicating a greater ability to self-regulate even after some loss of control. The men who enrolled responded in comparable ways. Meditation practice again correlated with improvement with a number of variables indicative of better eating regulation in the MB-EAT group. At the end of treatment, participants reported over two hours of sitting meditation per week and about 30 minutes of 'mini-meditations'. Notably, there was no significant weight loss in either group, with some individuals losing 10 lbs. or more and others gaining weight. In the MB-EAT group, overall mindfulness practice (a combination of sitting practice, guided eating meditations and mini-meditations) significantly predicted weight loss (r = −.33, p < .05). It may be that some individuals gaining weight heard the message that it was acceptable to eat more freely, without balancing that adequately with mindful eating and mindful choices.

With that in mind, in a subsequent NIH-funded trial, the "outer wisdom" components were further developed in order to facilitate weight loss, but with a strong commitment to maintaining a non-dieting approach (Kristeller, Jordan, & Bolinskey, in preparation). This included attending to nutritional and caloric values of food, but with a non-restrictive, explorative attitude, finding sustainable ways to reduce daily food intake through portion size or frequency of preferred high caloric foods. Gradually increasing physical activity was also introduced. To accommodate these components, the length of sessions was increased and another session added, resulting in the current model of MB-EAT. This study also evaluated the intervention for heavier individuals (BMI > 34) without BED, randomizing 117 men and women (26% with BED) to MB-EAT or to a Wait List control. Results were consistent with those from our previous research, and highly comparable for those with and without BED. Furthermore, a weight loss of about 7 lbs. at immediate post was evident regardless of BED status, with no one showing any appreciable weight gain at one month follow-up. This was approximately one pound per week from when participants began a self-guided non-dieting caloric reduction as part of the program (the "500 Calorie Challenge" described below). Also consistent with engaging "outer wisdom" was a significant increase on a measure of "healthy restraint" both for those with BED and those without, maintained into follow-up. For example, one man, who'd been on many diets, losing and then regaining the weight, decided that he would decrease his soda intake from three per day to one, accounting for about half of his 500 calorie goal. But after a few weeks, as he began to find highly sweet foods less appealing, he cut out all sodas. Previously, this was a food he'd always gone back to after dieting, and now realized he didn't even like very much, and wouldn't miss.

Several other clinical trials have been conducted, modifying and extending the original MB-EAT program for different populations, including individuals with type II diabetes (Miller, Kristeller, Headings, & Nagaraja, 2014) and high school students (Barnes, Kristeller, & Johnson, 2016). Other research has added components specifically addressing stress-related eating along with a stronger weight-loss focus (Daubenmier et al., 2016; Mason et al., 2016); this study demonstrated that reducing reward-driven eating accounted for about half of weight loss six months after intervention ended, but change in psychological stress did not relate to weight change (Mason et al., 2016).

Structure and content of the program

The core components of the MB-EAT program are delivered in ten weekly group sessions, with two follow up sessions spaced about a month apart. Session 9 and 10 are separated by two weeks, to decrease dependency on group support.

See Table 16.1 for an outline of the structure of the program addressing conceptual aspects cultivating mindful self-regulation in four areas: general mindfulness; mindful eating; emotional balance; and self-acceptance. As noted above, a unifying theme is how mindfulness helps with tuning into both "inner wisdom" and "outer wisdom". Each weekly session is 2.5 hours long, and contains general mindfulness practice, time for questions and inquiry, and targeted practices, promoting both inner and outer wisdom. Prior to the first session, during an assessment/orientation meeting, participants fill out the "KEEP in Balance" scale,

Table 16.1 Components of MB-EAT: principles and related exercises

Concept/Principle	Component	Session	Exercise
Cultivating Mindfulness			
Cultivate capacity to direct attention, be aware, disengage reactivity, and be non-judgmental.	Mindfulness meditation practice.	1–10	Sitting practice in session. Meditation homework. Discussion.
Cultivate capacity to bring mindfulness into daily experience, including eating.	"Mini-meditations" General use of mindfulness.	2–10	"Mini-meditation" use. Brief practice in all sessions.
Cultivating/engaging "inner wisdom" and "outer wisdom/ spiritual growth.	Meditation practice/ mindfulness in daily life	All sessions	Encouragement of insight. Wisdom meditation (Session 10)
Cultivating Mindful Eating			
Bring mindful attention and awareness to eating experience. Recognizing mindless eating.	Meditation practice. "Mini-meditations" Chain reaction model.	1–10	Wide range of practices (see below for specifics).
Cultivate taste experience/ savoring and enjoying food.	Mindfully eating raisins. All mindful eating experiences.	1, 2, 4, 6, 7, 9	Raisins; cheese and crackers; chocolate; fruit and veggies; "favorite food"; pot luck/buffet homework.
Cultivate awareness of hunger experience.	Awareness of physical vs. other hunger experience vs. craving.	3, 8	Hunger meditation; craving meditation. Homework; discussion.
Awareness and cultivation of sensory-specific (taste) satiety/taste satisfaction.	Training in taste satiety, in and out of session.	4, 7	Taste satisfaction "meter". Pot luck/buffet homework.
Making mindful food choices, based on both "liking" and health.	"Inner wisdom" and "outer wisdom" in regard to food. Mindful decrease in calories.	2–7	Choice: Chips or cookies. Mindful use of nutrition info. Quality Over Quantity Challenge. Managing social influences.
Awareness and cultivation of fullness experience.	Mindfully ending a meal.	5, 7	Fullness awareness/ratings Pot luck/buffet homework
Awareness of negative self-judgment regarding eating. Cultivate non-judgmental awareness of eating experience.	Eating challenging foods. Identifying cognitive distortions.	2–6, 9–10.	Identifying "black and white" thinking; "surfing the urge"; abstinence violation effect. "KEEP in Balance" self-assessment.

(Continued)

Table 16.1 Continued

Concept/Principle	Component	Session	Exercise
Cultivating Emotional Balance			
Cultivate awareness of emotions and emotional reactivity.	Learn to identify and tolerate emotional triggers.	3–5, 9, 10	Mindfulness practice; chain reaction model; mini-meditation.
Meeting emotional needs in healthy ways.	Behavior substitution; modifying comfort eating.	Most sessions	Emotional eating visualization. Savoring food.
Cultivating Self-Acceptance			
Acceptance and non-self-judgment of body/self-regulation/gentle exercise.	Relationship to the body.	1, 3–5, 8	Breathe awareness; body scan practice; healing self-touch; chair yoga; pedometers; mindful walking.
Recognition of anger at self and others. Acceptance of self/others.	Exploring feeling and thoughts toward self and others.	4, 5, 10	Loving kindness meditation. Forgiveness meditation. Discussion.
Recognizing/engaging capacity for growth. Self-empowerment.	Cultivating "inner wisdom"/values; spiritual strength.	All, 9, 10	Wisdom meditation. Values practice. Discussion all sessions.

Source: Adapted from Kristeller and Wolever (in press).

which contains 40 items related to different aspects of mindless/mindful eating (five items relate to physical activity), which are self-scored by frequency of occurrence from "never" to "multiple times/day" (e.g., I waited to eat until I felt physically hungry enough.). This "self-assessment" is used throughout the program to help individuals move away from an "all-or-nothing" attitude to their eating and food, so pervasive within a "dieting" perspective; to help them focus on manageable goals to increase mindful eating; and to incorporate both self-acceptance and meaningful challenges. When people review their baseline patterns at the end of the program, they are usually amazed at the shifts they have been able to make in their eating and relationship to food, activity levels, and to themselves.

"Inner wisdom" practices include general mindfulness meditation, mindful eating, body awareness/acceptance, and scripted practices on forgiveness, values, and deepening wisdom. Mindfulness meditation is introduced in Session 1 using breath awareness, rather than the body scan, as is the case for MBSR, due to both the extreme self-consciousness many participants have about their bodies, and also to the physical challenge of moving onto the floor for heavier individuals. "Mini-meditations" – or pausing for just a few moments when faced with a challenging choice or experience – are introduced in Session 2, and used throughout. Both sitting practice and use of "minis" are encouraged for daily practice. Core elements related to interoceptive awareness include a focus on physical versus other types of hunger, fullness, and taste satisfaction/satiety. These are introduced separately and then woven into mindful eating experiences, and of course, encouraged for practice at meals and snacks between sessions.

The first session begins with mindfully eating raisins, as in the MBSR program, but a fourth raisin has been added to highlight mindful choice: people are asked to decide for themselves whether to eat this fourth raisin or not. And to the surprise of many, including those who would describe themselves as "addicted" to food, they realize that they do not want this raisin, as they truly tune into the taste experience. The foods used in mindful eating experiences over the sessions increase in challenge: from raisins, to cheese and crackers, chocolate, mindfully choosing between chips and cookies ("Which do you really want right now? Something salty and crunchy, or sweet and chewy?"), finally culminating in a carry-in/pot luck meal. They can be adapted to the background of participants, and reflect foods that might often be overeaten. The mindful choice practice cultivates mindfully pausing for a moment to check into what food might be more appealing in the moment, rather than mindlessly grabbing something. Another source of surprise is a shift in taste preferences; it is not unusual that someone will find that they don't actually like some of the foods offered, when they had perceived them previously as highly desirable and even "addictive" (such as corn chips or chocolate). As mindful eating skills develop, more challenging practices include the concept of "chaining", drawn from CBT and Dialectical Behavior Therapy (DBT) (Wisniewski & Kelly, 2003), in which attention is to brought to the complexity of conditioned links among thoughts, feelings and behaviors, communicating the point that mindful engaging can be used at any point – even in the middle of a binge – to step back and break the chain of reactivity. Various body practices, although not the core focus, are used to assist individuals to cultivate non-judgmental awareness and self-acceptance.

"Outer wisdom" elements, as noted above, entail a gradual introduction to making healthier nutritional choices, keeping an eye on serving sizes, checking on caloric level of food from a place of curiosity rather than anxiety, and gradually increasing physical activity, with a focus on using a pedometer to walk about ten percent more each week. All of these practices are framed as ways to support both weight management and also general health. For example, beginning with the cheese-and-crackers practice, the group is challenged to identify the number of calories in a piece that they've just eaten. The surprise comes when they find they are overestimating the calories in a small piece by two- to three-fold, and that indeed they could savor and enjoy small amounts of these foods without overeating them.

Counter to usual approaches to weight loss that require reduced caloric goals in the range of 1200 calories, a highly restrictive and unsustainable amount for virtually anyone, an alternative non-diet approach to reducing calories is introduced in Session 2. Originally referred to as the "500 Calorie Challenge", but now renamed the "Quality Over Quantity Challenge" (the QOQ) to make it more broadly applicable, the QOQ, rather than restricting individuals to a predetermined caloric level, encourages them to identify foods from their usual pattern of eating to consider removing, reducing in quantity, and/or replacing with healthier choices in sustainable and flexible ways. Choices often include reduction of sugary beverages, fried foods, sweets and reducing serving sizes. The original target of 500 calories was chosen for several reasons: 1) for individuals in the obese range, this amount reflects a level of reduction consistent with long term goals; 2) 500 calories over the course of a week (7 days) equals 3500 calories, a recommended level to lose about 1 lb per week; 3) 500 divided by 5 – three meals and two snacks – equals 100 calories, and seems manageable to most heavier individuals as a goal for reducing usual meal/snack intake. Although the "500 Calorie Challenge" has been misperceived by some as a "diet" type formulation, it was intentionally designed as quite the opposite. The term "diet" implies a structured, short-term approach, virtually always in a total caloric range (1200–1500 calories) that would not be feasible to sustain indefinitely, and which does not include even small portions of someone's special foods. Further, a "diet" is "prescriptive", rather than self-designed. While MB-EAT introduces nutritional guidelines and healthier foods into the mindful eating practices, consistent with the "outer wisdom" messages, these are intended to help with the "Quality Over Quantity Challenge", rather than being exclusive of any food choices, thereby promoting flexibility and sustainability. If someone does not wish to lose weight, then they would be encouraged to identify ways to cut back on less healthy foods, while adding healthier ones. Thin, healthy people may occasionally drink sugared beverages, eat rich desserts, or have a rich cream sauce with their meal, and the message is strongly communicated that they approach their own decisions with a frame of acceptance and curiosity. Two more challenges are introduced later in the program: a pot luck meal as part of Session 7, and having a meal at an all-you-can-eat buffet. For the pot luck meal, individuals bring in two dishes, one a healthier one they would like to eat more of, and one less healthy, but that they wish to continue to eat. Going to the buffet restaurant is often anxiety-provoking, but participants are surprised by how differently they experience it, as they choose small amounts of food to taste, go back for seconds of those most appealing – and realize they can leave food on their plate.

Body acceptance is engaged throughout. Most individuals come into the program with substantial concerns about their appearance, desiring to lose weight yet also disengaged from their body. Throughout the program, chairs rather than cushions, are used, with body practices adapted for that. The body scan, introduced in Session 3, is done seated, and then augmented the following session with a healing self-touch practice,[1] in which participants direct warm loving energy from their hands into their muscles and bones. Chair yoga is also introduced, as is mindful walking, both as a means to increase physical activity ("outer wisdom") and as a way to become more comfortable in their bodies.

Self-acceptance and loving kindness practices, including a forgiveness meditation and a values practice, are woven into the program. The forgiveness practice, although primarily focused on moving past their own feelings of anger toward themselves and their weight, weaves in mention of forgiveness toward others. Many women in the program have noted that this has helped with resolving anger towards parents or husbands, feelings that they acknowledged were often binge triggers. The values practice presents a challenge designed to help those individuals who place undue focus on weight and eating concerns. It asks them to identify what proportion of their thoughts during the day drifts toward such concerns (a response of 75% is not uncommon), and then to reflect whether this is in balance with their overall priorities of family, work, and other time commitments. The concept of wandering mind (Smallwood & Schooler, 2015) frames the value of bringing mindfulness to all aspects of experience. By the time this is brought into the program (Session 9), people realize how many resources they have to draw on, including their skills in mindfulness.

In summary

MB-EAT, the effects of which are now well supported by substantial evidence for a range of individuals, provides a mindfulness-based alternative to the obsessive concern and dieting mentality that preoccupies so many individuals. Its overarching intention is to assist individuals in creating a new flexible and sustainable relationship to eating and food that heightens enjoyment, reinforces both the health and social value of food, and cultivates self-acceptance and self-awareness.

Online materials and Resources

www.mb-eat.com: My personal website with training announcements, access to publications, both professional and popular press, and selected guided meditations.

www.TCME.org: The website for The Center for Mindful Eating, a virtual professional resource center, that publishes a newsletter, lists trainings, and hosts various online discussions. Membership brings access to further resources.

Note

1 The healing self-touch exercise was developed by Sasha Loring, MS, Med, at Duke Integrative Medicine.

References

Appelhans, B. M. (2009). Neurobehavioral inhibition of reward-driven feeding: Implications for dieting and obesity. *Obesity, 17*(4), 640–647.

Barnes, V., Kristeller, J., & Johnson, M. H. (2016). Impact of mindfulness-based eating awareness on diet and exercise habits in adolescents. *International Journal of Complementary and Alternative Medicine, 3*(2), 70.

Bartoshuk, L. M. (1978). The psychophysics of taste. *American Journal of Clinical Nutrition, 31,* 1068–1077.

Bowen, S., Chawla, N., & Marlatt, G. A. (2011). *Mindfulness-based relapse prevention for addictive behaviors: A clinician's guide*. New York, NY: Guilford Press.

Brondel, L., Romer, M., Van Wymelbeke, V., Walla, P., Jiang, T., Deecke, L., et al. (2007). Sensory-specific satiety with simple foods in humans: No influence of BMI? *International Journal of Obesity, 31*(6), 987–995.

Carmody, J., Reed, G., Kristeller, J., & Merriam, P. (2008). Mindfulness, spirituality, and health-related symptoms. *Journal of Psychosomatic Research, 64*(4), 393–403.

Carver, C. S., & Scheier, M. F. (2011). Self-regulation of action and affect. In K. D. Vohs & R. F. Baumeister (Eds.), *Handbook of self-regulation* (2nd ed., pp. 3–21). New York, NY: Guilford Press.

Cuthbert, B., Kristeller, J., Simons, R., Hodes, R., & Lang, P. J. (1981). Strategies of arousal control: Biofeedback, meditation, and motivation. *Journal of Experimental Psychology: General, 110*(4), 518–546.

Daubenmier, J., Moran, P. J., Kristeller, J., Acree, M., Bacchetti, P., Kemeny, M. E., et al. (2016). Effects of a mindfulness-based weight loss intervention in adults with obesity: A randomized clinical trial. *Obesity, 24*(4), 794–804.

Davidson, R., & Goleman, D. (2017). *Altered States: Science reveals how meditation changes your mind, brain, and body*. New York, NY: Random House.

Drewnowski, A. (1996). The behavioral phenotype in human obesity. In E. D. Capaldi (Ed.), *Why we eat what we eat: The psychology of eating*. Washington, DC: American Psychological Association.

Gilbert, P. (2009). *The compassionate mind*. London: Constable & Robinson.

Goldfield, G. S., Adamo, K. B., Rutherford, J., & Legg, C. (2008). Stress and the relative reinforcing value of food in female binge eaters. *Physiology & Behavior, 93*(3), 579–587.

Grosshans, M., Loeber, S., & Kiefer, F. (2011). Implications from addiction research towards the understanding and treatment of obesity. *Addiction Biology, 16*(2), 189–198.

Kabat-Zinn, J., Massion, A. O., Kristeller, J. L., Peterson, L. G., Fletcher, K. E., Pbert, L., et al. (1992). Effectiveness of a meditation-based stress reduction program in the treatment of anxiety disorders. *The American Journal of Psychiatry, 149*(7), 936–943.

Kristeller, J. (1977). Meditation and biofeedback in the regulation of internal states. In S. Ajaya (Ed.), *Meditational therapy*. Glenview, IL: Himalayan International Institute Press.

Kristeller, J. (2003). Finding the buddha/finding the self: Seeing with the third eye. In S. Segal (Ed.), *Encountering Buddhism* (pp. 109–130). Albany, NY: State University New York Press.

Kristeller, J. (2016). *The joy of half a cookie: Using mindfulness to lose weight and end the struggle with food*. New York, NY: Penguin Books.

Kristeller, J., Jordan, K., & Bolinskey, K. (in preparation). A mindful eating intervention in moderately to morbidly obese individuals.

Kristeller, J., & Rapgay, L. (2013). Buddhism: A blend of religion, spirituality, and psychology. In K. I. Pargament, J. J. Exline, J. W. Jones, K. I. Pargament, J. J. Exline, & J. W. Jones (Eds.), *APA handbook of psychology, religion, and spirituality (vol 1): Context, theory, and research* (pp. 635–652). Washington, DC: American Psychological Association.

Kristeller, J., & Wolever, R. (2014). Mindfulness-based eating awareness training: Treatment of overeating and obesity. In R. A. Baer (Ed.), *Mindfulness-based treatment approaches* (2nd ed., pp. 119–139). San Diego, CA: Elsevier.

Kristeller, J., & Wolever, R. (in press). *Mindfulness-based eating awareness training (MB-EAT): A treatment manual*. New York, NY: Guilford Press.

Kristeller, J. L. (2003). Mindfulness, wisdom and eating: Applying a multi-domain model of meditation effects. *Journal of Constructivism in the Human Sciences, 8*, 107–118.

Kristeller, J. L. (2007). Mindfulness meditation. In P. M. Lehrer, R. L. Woolfolk, & W. E. Sime (Eds.), *Principles and practice of stress management* (3rd ed., pp. 393–427). New York, NY: Guilford Press.

Kristeller, J. L. (2016). The struggle continues: Addressing concerns about eating and weight for older women's well-being. *The Journal of Women & Therapy, 39*, 1–11.

Kristeller, J. L., & Hallett, C. B. (1999). An exploratory study of a meditation-based intervention for binge eating disorder. *Journal of Health Psychology, 4*(3), 357–363.

Kristeller, J. L., & Jordan, K. D. (2018). Spirituality and meditative practice: Research opportunities and challenges. *Psychological Studies, 63*(2), 130–139.

Kristeller, J. L., & Rodin, J. (1989). Identifying eating patterns in male and female undergraduates using cluster analysis. *Addictive Behaviors, 14*, 631–642.

Kristeller, J. L., & Wolever, R. Q. (2011). Mindfulness-based eating awareness training for treating binge eating disorder: The conceptual foundation. *Eating Disorders: The Journal of Treatment & Prevention, 19*(1), 49–61.

Kristeller, J. L., Wolever, R. Q., & Sheets, V. (2013). Mindfulness-based eating awareness training (MB-EAT) for binge eating: A randomized clinical trial. *Mindfulness, 4*, 282–297.

Mason, A. E., Epel, E. S., Aschbacher, K., Lustig, R. H., Acree, M., Kristeller, J., et al. (2016). Reduced reward-driven eating accounts for the impact of a mindfulness-based diet and exercise intervention on weight loss: Data from the shine randomized controlled trial. *Appetite, 100*, 86–93.

Mason, A. E., Epel, E. S., Kristeller, J., Moran, P. J., Dallman, M., Lustig, R. H., et al. (2016). Effects of a mindfulness-based intervention on mindful eating, sweets consumption, and fasting glucose levels in obese adults: Data from the shine randomized controlled trial. *Journal of Behavioral Medicine, 39*(2), 201–213.

Meeks, T. W., Cahn, B. R., & Jeste, D. V. (2012). Neurobiological foundations of wisdom. In C. K. Germer, & R. D. Siegel (Eds.), *Wisdom and compassion in psychotherapy: Deepening mindfulness in clinical practice* (pp. 189–201). New York, NY: Guilford Press.

Miller, C. K., Kristeller, J. L., Headings, A., & Nagaraja, H. (2014). Comparison of a mindful eating intervention to a diabetes self-management intervention among adults with type 2 diabetes: A randomized controlled trial. *Health Education & Behavior, 41*(2), 145–154.

Raynor, H. A., & Epstein, L. H. (2001). Dietary variety, energy regulation, and obesity. *Psychological Bulletin, 127*(3), 325–341.

Remick, A. K., Polivy, J., & Pliner, P. (2009). Internal and external moderators of the effect of variety on food intake. *Psychological Bulletin, 135*(3), 434–451.

Rodin, J. (1981). Current status of the internal-external hypothesis for obesity: What went wrong? *American Psychologist, 36*, 361–372.

Ryan, R. M., & Deci, E. L. (2000). Self-determination theory and the facilitation of intrinsic motivation, social development, and well-being. *American Psychologist, 55*(1), 68–78.

Schwartz, G. E. (1975). Biofeedback, self-regulation, and the patterning of physiological processes. *American Scientist, 63*(3), 314–324.

Shapiro, S. L., & Schwartz, G. E. (2000). The role of intention in self-regulation: Toward intentional systemic mindfulness. In M. Boekaerts, P. R. Pintrich, & M. Zeidner (Eds.), *Handbook of self-regulation* (pp. 253–273). San Diego, CA: Academic Press.

Smallwood, J., & Schooler, J. W. (2015). The science of mind wandering: Empirically navigating the stream of consciousness. *Annual Review of Psychology, 66*, 487–518.

Sternberg, R. J. (1990). *Wisdom: Its nature, origins, and development*. New York, NY: Cambridge University Press.

Sysko, R., Devlin, M. J., Walsh, B. T., Zimmerli, E., & Kissileff, H. R. (2007). Satiety and test meal intake among women with binge eating disorder. *International Journal of Eating Disorders, 40*(6), 554–561.

Sysko, R., Hildebrandt, T., Wilson, G. T., Wilfley, D. E., & Agras, W. S. (2010). Heterogeneity moderates treatment response among patients with binge eating disorder. *Journal of Consulting and Clinical Psychology, 78*(5), 681–690.

Wansink, B. (2007). *Mindless eating: Why we eat more than we think*. New York, NY: Bantam Books.

Wansink, B., & Sobal, J. (2007). Mindless eating: The 200 daily food decisions we overlook. *Environment and Behavior, 39*(1), 106–123.

Wisniewski, L., & Kelly, E. (2003). The application of dialectical behavior therapy to the treatment of eating disorders. *Cognitive and Behavioral Practice, 10*(2), 131–138.

Chapter 17

Mindfulness-Based Therapy for Insomnia

Jason C. Ong and Rachel Manber

Introduction and overview of MBTI

Sleeplessness is a highly prevalent health problem with about one-third to one-half of adults reporting difficulty falling asleep or staying asleep (Ohayon, 2002). When acute sleep disturbance goes untreated, it can evolve into a chronic insomnia disorder consisting of sleep-specific symptoms (e.g., difficulty falling or staying asleep) associated with significant waking distress or impairment that occurs on a regular basis for at least three months. Chronic insomnia is the most widespread sleep disorder, occurring in about 10% to 18% of adults (Jansson-Frojmark & Linton, 2008; LeBlanc et al., 2009; Ohayon, 2002). Moreover, it is associated with impaired cognitive functioning, compromised immune functioning, and comorbid medical and psychiatric conditions (Fernandez-Mendoza et al., 2010; Ford & Kamerow, 1989; Irwin, 2015; Shekleton et al., 2014; Taylor et al., 2007).

In addition to sleeplessness, individuals with chronic insomnia report psychological and physiological hyperarousal (Bonnet & Arand, 2010; Hantsoo, Khou, White, & Ong, 2013; Kuisk, Bertelson, & Walsh, 1989; Riemann et al., 2010) that includes preoccupation with the inability to sleep when desired, anxiety about the ability to function the next day, physiological tension in bed, and a tendency to experience intrusive thoughts about life when trying to sleep. This state of hyperarousal is incompatible with sleep and with repeated occurrences in bed, the bed becomes associated with hyperarousal rather than sleepiness. Putting forth more effort to sleep only compounds the problem, thus perpetuating the sleep disturbance and leading to a cycle of chronic insomnia.

Sleep medications are the most common intervention for insomnia. These medications might increase the probability of falling and staying asleep but do not directly address the cognitive hyperarousal or increased effort for sleep that perpetuates chronic insomnia. Cognitive-Behavior Therapy for Insomnia (CBT-I) is an empirically-supported treatment package consisting of techniques for regulating sleep/wake patterns, re-associating the bed with sleepiness, and changing maladaptive sleep-related thoughts (Perlis, Jungquist, Smith, & Posner, 2005). CBT-I is now the recommended treatment for chronic insomnia disorder (Qaseem et al., 2016) but remission is only achieved in about 30% to 50% of patients (Morin et al., 2009; Wu, Appleman, Salazar, & Ong, 2015). Furthermore, some patients find it difficult to tolerate some components of CBT-I, such as limiting time in bed or getting out of bed during prolonged wakefulness. As a result, some patients do not fully engage in CBT-I.

Mindfulness-Based Therapy for Insomnia (MBTI) is an eight-week group program intended for people with chronic insomnia disorder who have persistent difficulty falling or staying asleep (Ong, 2017). We developed this program as an alternative to CBT-I with a focus on helping people reduce their struggles with insomnia and on reducing hyperarousal. Rather than trying harder to solve the sleep problem, MBTI uses the principles of mindfulness and the practice of meditation to reduce hyperarousal by teaching people with insomnia how to become aware of the brain's signals for sleepiness and making shifts in how they relate to their experience of sleeplessness. Through meditation practice, insomnia patients learn how their own thoughts, feelings, and sensations can guide taking thoughtful actions that are compatible with their current state of mind. In this manner, patients can see the problem of insomnia from a different perspective rather than repeatedly trying harder to sleep, thus creating the space that is needed to allow sleep to occur effortlessly.

Although MBTI uses techniques that might be considered cognitive and behavioral in nature, it is distinct from CBT-I in several ways. First, the focus of MBTI is on mindfulness principles and meditation practice. While CBT-I might include relaxation exercises as a component, MBTI uses meditations to cultivate awareness and to make metacognitive shifts. Second, the behavioral strategies in MBTI are delivered from a patient-centered perspective rather than a prescriptive perspective that is typical of CBT-I. Finally, MBTI does not focus on changing thought content (i.e., cognitive restructuring), which is the focus on the cognitive component of CBT-I. Instead, MBTI focuses on shifting metacognitions (i.e., thinking about thinking) or changing the relationship with thoughts rather than the content of the thoughts.

This chapter provides an overview and summary of the MBTI program, including the theoretical background, the structure of the program, and the emerging research evidence to support its use for people with chronic insomnia. Important themes and key activities are highlighted to provide the reader an understanding of the program and the research that has been conducted thus far.

Theoretical background of MBTI

Clinical observation of insomnia patients reveals a strong attachment to solving the sleep problem. These patients often make statements such as "If only I could figure out how to sleep better, my whole life would be much better." This and similar statements reveal a strong attachment to the need for sleep to happen a certain way and an absorption with solving the sleep problem. Ironically, many patients with insomnia are quite resistant to making changes to their sleep behaviors. For example, it is common for those with insomnia to spend excessive amounts of time in bed in an attempt to get more sleep. Furthermore, they often become resistant to changing this behavior even when their sleep is not improving. They hold rigidly to thoughts and behaviors that functionally serve to maintain rather than resolve their sleep difficulties.

The rationale for using a mindfulness-based approach to the problem of insomnia is described in a conceptual paper (Ong, Ulmer, & Manber, 2012) in which we proposed a metacognitive model of insomnia (see Figure 17.1). This conceptual model posits that there are two levels of arousal. Primary arousal consists of the content of sleep-related thoughts that directly prevent the ability to sleep. Examples include thoughts about the amount of time left to sleep or concerns about the next-day functioning if sleep is inadequate. Secondary arousal consists of metacognitions about sleep that includes absorption in the problem, rigidity in sleep-related beliefs, and attachment to the idea that one needs a certain amount of sleep. In the model, secondary arousal is hypothesized to amplify the negative emotion or create attentional bias for cues that reflect threat to sleep (such as environmental noise) or consequences of insufficient sleep (such as diminished work performance).

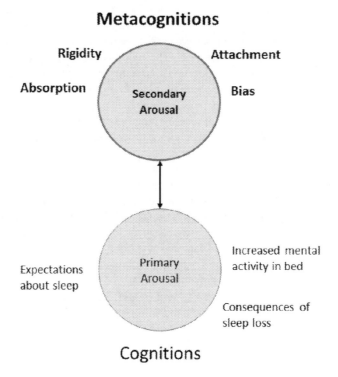

Figure 17.1 In the metacognitive model of insomnia, primary arousal refers to the thoughts and mental activities that interfere with sleep, while secondary arousal consists of the relationship with thoughts and behaviors (i.e., metacognitions) as opposed to the actual thoughts themselves.

Source: Adapted from Ong, Ulmer, & Manber (2012).

Conceptualizing insomnia using this metacognitive model leads to the idea that mindfulness principles can be used to reduce secondary arousal and that this could have downstream effects on reducing primary arousal and lead to the reduction in the symptoms of insomnia. A key to cultivating mindfulness is the meditation practice, in which a person is intentionally paying attention to the present experience with an attitude that is accepting and non-judging (Shapiro, Carlson, Astin, & Freedman, 2006). Through regular practice of applying mindfulness principles and meditation, there develops an increase in *awareness* of the mental and physical states that arise when experiencing insomnia symptoms during the night and during the day; this then promotes *shifting* metacognitions to reduce secondary arousal. Ultimately, mindfulness practice facilitates adopting a *mindful stance* when experiencing symptoms of insomnia resulting in reduced sleep effort and hyperarousal (Ong et al., 2012).

The process of cultivating awareness, metacognitive shifting, and embodying a mindful stance is usually not a linear progression; it is an iterative process that involves patience and practice of the mindfulness principles. It involves letting go of the attachment to certain beliefs about sleep, increasing flexibility in the response to insufficient sleep, and accepting alternative pathways to well-being. It should be noted that letting go of the problem is not the same as giving up on sleeping better. Instead, letting go and acceptance is an *active* process – it is an intentional choice to see the problem differently and to make metacognitive shifts. In contrast, giving up is a passive process that is dominated by despair and hopelessness. Taking a mindful stance also involves re-establishing or re-connecting with important personal values other than the need for sleep. In trying to solve the sleep problem, many insomnia patients neglect important life goals and/or social activities. Re-connecting with these values is seen as an act of self-compassion and an important aspect of reducing secondary arousal. It allows the patient to put sleep in a larger context and perspective.

Structure of the MBTI program

The MBTI program is delivered in a group format and integrates mindfulness-based stress reduction (MBSR; (Kabat-Zinn, 1990) and mindfulness-based cognitive therapy (MBCT; (Segal, Williams, & Teasdale, 2002) with behavioral therapy for insomnia. Similar to MBSR and MBCT, MBTI is designed as eight weekly sessions plus an optional meditation retreat that is typically held between the sixth and seventh sessions. During each session, patients are led through guided formal meditations, a period of discussion of one or more mindfulness principles, and insomnia-related activities and didactics. The specific content of each session is described in Table 17.1. In addition to activities in session, patients are assigned home meditation practice, starting from the first session, as well as specific sleep related recommendations to be followed. The home practice includes formal quiet and movement meditations along with informal meditations and are based on the guided meditations taught

Table 17.1 Key themes and activities of MBTI

Phase	Session	Theme	Key Activities
Phase 1: Fundamentals of Mindfulness and Insomnia	1	Introduction and overview of program	Provide overview of the program and patient expectations; introduce the concept of mindfulness and model of insomnia; lead patients through first formal mindful practice
	2	Stepping out of automatic pilot	Begin with formal meditation and inquiry; discuss relevance of meditation for insomnia
Phase 2: Synchronizing Sleep Behaviors	3	Paying attention to sleepiness and wakefulness	Begin with formal meditation and inquiry; discuss sleepiness, fatigue, and wakefulness; provide instructions for sleep consolidation
	4	Working with sleeplessness at night	Begin with formal meditation and inquiry; discuss questions about sleep consolidation and make adjustments; provide instructions for sleep reconditioning
Phase 3: Taking a Mindful Stance with Insomnia	5	The territory of insomnia	Begin with formal meditation and inquiry; introduce the territory of insomnia and discuss metacognitive shifts

(Continued)

Table 17.1 Continued

Phase	Session	Theme	Key Activities
	6	Acceptance and letting go	Begin with formal meditation and inquiry; explain the relevance of acceptance and letting go for working with thoughts and feelings in the territory of insomnia
	7	Revisiting the relationship with sleep	Begin with formal meditation and inquiry; discuss patients' relationship with sleep and taking a mindful stance with insomnia; discuss informal meditations during everyday life
	8	Living mindfully after MBTI	Begin with formal meditation and inquiry; set up an action plan for future episodes of insomnia; discuss ways to continue mindfulness meditation beyond this program

Source: Adapted from Ong (2017).

during the session that week. Recommendations for the home meditation practice are for 30 minutes per day. Digital media with guided meditations are provided to help facilitate the home meditation practice. The MBTI program can be roughly divided into three phases: 1) acquiring fundamentals of mindfulness and insomnia, 2) synchronizing sleep behaviors with signals from the brain, and 3) taking a mindful stance with insomnia. The key themes and activities for each phase are described below.

Phase 1: fundamentals of mindfulness and insomnia (Sessions 1 and 2)

During the first two sessions of MBTI, the patient is oriented to mindfulness principles and practices using concepts and exercises that are directly borrowed from MBSR (Kabat-Zinn, 1990). These include a discussion of the seven principles of mindfulness – beginner's mind, non-striving, letting go, non-judging, acceptance, trust, and patience – and the importance of these principles to approaching the problem of insomnia in a different way. To reinforce this discussion, meditations are introduced as an activity to cultivate and practice mindfulness. Similar to MBSR, the raisin exercise is used as the first guided meditation to introduce the concepts of mindfulness. This informal meditation provides a real-world example of how mindfulness is relevant to everyday experiences.

Trainspotting is another meditation introduced in Phase 1 of MBTI that can be used to explain the concept of metacognitive shifts (Ong, 2017). In this meditation, patients are asked to imagine that the mind is a train station and that trains represent the thoughts that come in and out of the mind. Most people who are in a train station are used to being passengers, waiting to board the train and then using the train to travel to their destination. Using this context as a metaphor, people typically engage in thoughts (i.e., enter the train), analyze them, and expect it to help them solve or answer a question (i.e., reach a destination), often without full awareness of this process. In contrast to being a passenger on a train, a trainspotter is one who observes trains or takes photographs of trains passing by because of a curiosity and interest in the train itself. A trainspotter is more interested in the qualities of the train – the type of train, how fast it is going, and how full it is – than the destination of the train. In the meditation, patients are asked to be a "trainspotter of the mind." Rather than being a passenger who steps on the train and uses it as a mode of transportation, patients are asked to remain on the platform of the train station and just watch the trains go by. By practicing this stance, patients will find that it is possible to observe the thoughts in the mind without following them to their destination. This is a metacognitive shift from an outcome-oriented mode (i.e., thoughts which lead to problem solving) to a process-oriented mode (i.e., observing the thoughts themselves). Phrases such as "stepping off the train" and "becoming a trainspotter" can provide an expression for patients to describe their experiences in observing thoughts without attachment to outcomes.

In addition to these concepts and activities, patients are taught quiet meditations, including sitting with the breath and the body scan. They are asked to practice these meditations at home and to begin establishing a regular time and place for a meditation practice. The overall goal of the first two sessions is to understand the principles of mindfulness and to establish a regular meditation practice at home.

The discussion of the mindfulness principles is integrated with the provision of information about sleep regulation and includes an explicit reference to the application of these principles directly to the experience of chronic insomnia. For example, many people with chronic insomnia lose trust in their own ability to sleep. They can learn how to regain trust in their ability to sleep by cultivating awareness of when their body is ready for sleep. This is aided by learning about how the body regulates sleep and how sleepiness can be interpreted as a sign that the brain is ready for sleep. This information is then integrated into specific activities during Phase 2.

Phase 2: synchronizing sleep behaviors (sessions 3 and 4)

Sessions 3 and 4 build upon the fundamental of mindfulness and the meditation practice as patients are taught how to use awareness of mental and physical states to work with the problem of insomnia (see Table 17.1). Particular emphasis is given to recognizing thoughts, feelings, and physical sensations that can discern the state of sleepiness at bedtime from other states such as fatigue or the attachment to a particular rule about when one ought to go to sleep. During mindfulness meditation practice at home, awareness can be directed to discern sensations associated with sleepiness from fatigue or other states of wakefulness. By identifying the sensations associated with sleepiness, patients are able to connect with the brains signals indicating readiness for sleep and synchronize their behaviors with these signals, thus increasing the likelihood that sleep will occur when they attempt it.

Based on discerning the state of sleepiness, the behavioral strategies for insomnia are also introduced in Sessions 3 and 4. These strategies include stimulus control (Bootzin, 1972) and sleep restriction (Spielman, Saskin, & Thorpy, 1987), two core behavioral components of CBT-I. Stimulus control is based on operant conditioning, whereby the failure to discriminate the bed or bedroom as a stimulus for sleep leads to decreased likelihood of sleep onset and increased likelihood of arousal (Bootzin, 1972). The goal of stimulus control is to re-establish the bed and bedroom as a stimulus for sleep to occur by not going to bed until feeling sleepy and getting out of bed after a period of not being able to sleep. In MBTI, stimulus control is referred to as "sleep reconditioning" and it is introduced with a focus on awareness of sleepiness to guide when to be in bed and the idea that states of sleepiness and alertness change over time.

Sleep restriction (Spielman et al., 1987) is a method of mobilizing the homeostatic pressure for sleep, which accumulates during wakefulness, reaches a maximum around bedtime, and is subsequently reset during sleep by the dissipation of slow wave activity (Borbely & Achermann, 1999). This pressure for sleep is associated with the sensation of sleepiness and is an important factor in the regulation of normal sleep/wake patterns. In sleep restriction, the time in bed is limited to a specific time frame (e.g., 12:00 a.m. to 6:00 a.m.) that is based on the average amount of sleep over the past week. After keeping the new time frame for at least one week, subsequent adjustments are made by increasing or reducing time in bed by 15 minutes based upon the average percent of time asleep relative to the time spent in bed as recorded by the patient daily in a sleep diary. This approach aims to regulate the sleep schedule and prevent compensation for poor sleep by spending extra time in bed. In MBTI, sleep restriction is referred to as "sleep consolidation."

Importantly, the effective implementation of both sleep reconditioning and sleep consolidation requires an understanding of the state of sleepiness. In CBT-I, this is usually explained by the therapist in conceptual terms but in MBTI the meditation practices are used as opportunities for the patient to gain first-hand experience of the sensations of sleepiness. This experiential approach is consistent with a patient-centered framework by allowing patients to discover sleepiness in their own way. Also in the patient-centered framework, after hearing an explanation of sleep regulation and the role of the homeostatic sleep drive, MBTI patients are given the opportunity to set their own time in bed schedules rather than being asked to adhere to a therapist-prescribed schedule that is typical of CBT-I. By the end of Phase 2, patients should be practicing specific tools that use mindfulness principles to regulate sleep-related behaviors.

Phase 3: taking a mindful stance with insomnia (Sessions 5 to 8)

During Phase 3 of MBTI, the meditation practice and the tools that were introduced during the first two phases of MBTI are reinforced and the focus turns towards taking a mindful stance with insomnia. A mindful stance uses the principles of mindfulness to guide mindful action to regulate sleep and wakefulness through sleep reconditioning and sleep consolidation. These techniques are reviewed during Session 5 through Session 7 with discussions about the application of these techniques at home led by the instructor. A mindful stance also involves making metacognitive shifts and maintaining personal values even when symptoms of insomnia are present. The discussions and didactics in Phase 3 broaden to include examination of aspects of daytime functioning and life values that are relevant to chronic insomnia.

One way to encourage metacognitive shifting to a broader perspective is through the concept of the territory of insomnia (Ong, 2017). This concept is similar to the territory of depression that is used in MBCT (Segal et al., 2002) to encourage patients to examine thought patterns that lead to a depression relapse. In MBTI, the territory of insomnia is used to develop awareness of other aspects of insomnia beyond sleeplessness. This might include specific thoughts (e.g., "I cannot function on less than 6 hours of sleep"), metacognitions (e.g., "I am very absorbed with getting more sleep"), or changes in value (e.g., "I have stopped going out in the evening so I can keep my sleep schedule"). By helping patients become aware of how these reactions and changes in personal values can contribute to sleep-related arousal, MBTI instructors can reinforce the use of metacognitive shifting to approach the symptoms of insomnia from a mindful stance and therefore reduce sleep-related arousal.

Daytime fatigue is another symptom of insomnia that can persist even when sleep reconditioning and sleep consolidation are effectively reducing wakefulness at night. One useful activity for working with fatigue and low energy is the nurturing/depleting exercise that has been used in MBCT (Segal et al., 2002). In this exercise, patients examine their daily lives and develop awareness of the type of activities that are nurturing and the types of activities that are depleting. They first create a list of activities they do during a typical day and then rate each activity as being nurturing or depleting based on whether the activity cultivates energy or reduces energy. They then tally the number of nurturing activities and the number of depleting activities. This yields a ratio that provides an indication of the energy balance across the day. If there are more depleting than nurturing activities, there is a net reduction in energy for that day. This would indicate a need to engage in more nurturing activities during the day rather than dwelling in a fatigued state. Awareness of the energy transactions for their usual daily activities can help patients cope with fatigue after several nights of poor sleep by mindfully choosing how to channel their limited energy, using self-compassion rather than self-pity. By creating a list of their daily activities, patients might also discover they are no longer engaging in some activities they used to do but employing an avoidance strategy due to a perceived inability to initiate the activity. By distinguishing between the energy it takes to initiate the activity and the nurturing/depleting value after having engaged in it, patients can take a mindful stance by re-engaging in some activities with net positive energy outcome, particularly when these activities support their life values. As a result, they can learn to let go of the perceived constraints of fatigue and reduce catastrophizing about the negative impact of insufficient sleep.

The final MBTI session includes a discussion of the episodic nature of insomnia and creation of a relapse prevention plan. This plan includes continued meditation practice after the MBTI program ends and a list of elements of the program that have been helpful and could therefore be used in the future when poor sleep remerges. This discussion emphasizes responding to future bouts of sleep disturbance, especially during periods of stress, with a mindful stance. Having an action plan ready to serve as a reminder of the MBTI tools can be particularly helpful if the recurrence of insomnia happens in the future after the MBTI program ends. In addition, strategies and resources for maintaining their meditation practice are discussed, including meditation groups in the community, on-line resources, and peer support from other group members. MBTI concludes with a period of sharing by each patient regarding what they learned during the program.

Meditation retreat

In addition to the eight weekly sessions, an all-day retreat is scheduled between the fifth and seventh sessions of MBTI. As is the case with MBSR, this retreat provides an opportunity to experience a deeper level of meditation practice with an extended period of meditation practice lasting about six hours. Patients generally find the retreat to be a positive experience that enhances their understanding and practice of mindfulness.

Research findings

We have conducted a series of studies as we developed MBTI. Our first study (Ong, Shapiro, & Manber, 2008) was an uncontrolled study that evaluated an earlier six-week version of MBTI that combined a mindfulness component with the behavioral components for insomnia. At this stage, the goal was to gather data on the feasibility and acceptability of using mindfulness for insomnia. We tested this first prototype of MBTI on 30 patients and found significant pre-to-post treatment improvements on several sleep parameters, significant decreases in maladaptive thoughts about sleep, and a significant decrease in sleep-related arousal. We also found indications of clinically significant benefits, with 87% of the sample no longer reported taking more than 30 minutes to fall asleep or being awake for more than 30 minutes in the middle of the night and 50% of the sample reported a reduction of 50% or greater from baseline on the total amount of time awake in bed. Qualitative data from this study revealed strong interest from patients in learning about mindfulness and suggestions to increase the amount of meditations being taught. As a result, we revised the MBTI program to an eight-week program featuring mindfulness and increasing the amount attention to meditation, thus increasing the similarity of the format to other mindfulness-based interventions. We also enhanced the integration between mindfulness principles and the behavioral components for insomnia by connecting the concepts of awareness with the instructions for stimulus control and sleep restriction. We then conducted a pilot tested the revised eight-week version of MBTI in a small group (Ong & Sholtes, 2010).

Our first randomized controlled trial for MBTI was conducted on 54 adults who met the criteria for chronic insomnia, and were randomized into one of three groups: MBTI, MBSR, or a self-monitoring control condition in which patients monitored their sleep using daily diaries (Ong et al., 2014). We found that patients in both the MBTI and MBSR groups reported significantly greater reduction in insomnia symptom severity using the Insomnia Severity Index (Bastien, Vallieres, & Morin, 2001) from baseline to post-treatment compared to the control group. MBTI was also associated with a greater reduction in insomnia symptom severity from baseline to the six-month follow-up compared to MBSR. In terms of clinical significance, using validated cut-offs for remission and response, MBTI had remission rates rising from 33.3% at post-treatment to 50% at six-month follow-up and response rates increased from 60% at post-treatment to 78.6% at six-month follow-up in MBTI. In contrast, MBSR had remission rates of 46.2% at post-treatment, 38.5% at three months, and 41.7% at six months and a response rates between 38.5% and 41.7%. MBTI was also associated with favorable secondary outcomes, including measures of cognitive-emotional arousal. Specifically, there were significant and large effect sizes for reduction in sleep effort, maladaptive sleep-related cognitions, and hyperarousal which were superior to the control group and non-inferior to behavior therapy for insomnia, which was received by patients in the control group after they completed the self-monitoring portion of their participation (Ong, Xia, Smith, & Manber, under review). Collectively, the findings from this randomized controlled trial indicates that both MBSR and MBTI are effective at reducing nocturnal symptoms of insomnia but MBTI is also effective at reducing cognitive-emotional symptoms of insomnia and appears to have more enduring effects on global symptoms of insomnia.

Beyond MBTI, the evidence base for other mindfulness-based interventions (MBSR, MBCT) in treating insomnia has grown considerably over the past five years. In general, the evidence from these studies indicates that the largest effect sizes were found on self-reported global measures of insomnia (Ong & Smith, 2017). Also, stronger effects have been found on subjectively measured sleep parameters (e.g., sleep diary data) compared to objectively-measured sleep (e.g., polysomnography, actigraphy). This pattern is generally consistent with other treatments for insomnia. The accumulating evidence indicates that mindfulness-based interventions can serve as a viable treatment option for people with chronic insomnia, although it is not yet clear if any particular version is superior.

Conclusions and future directions

MBTI is a mindfulness-based intervention for chronic insomnia. It is focused on promoting mindful awareness and metacognitive shifting to reduce sleep-related arousal and sleeplessness at night. Current research evidence from relatively small studies, indicates that MBTI has significant benefits for reducing the symptoms of insomnia with remission rates that are comparable to those previously found for CBT-I.

Further research is needed to build upon these promising initial findings. First, large-scale studies are needed to confirm the effectiveness of MBTI. If confirmatory evidence is found, then efforts will be needed to disseminate MBTI. This could include training practitioners to deliver MBTI as well as internet- or mobile-based delivery of the intervention. Research is also needed to identify which patients are most likely to benefit from a mindfulness-based approach, such as MBTI versus a more traditional approach, such as CBT-I. Importantly, additional research of the mechanisms underlying how MBTI works could support better dissemination and promote understanding for whom it will work best. Specific mechanisms to consider include changes in awareness and metacognitive shifts, and the possibility that MBTI works by reducing hyperarousal. For readers interested in learning more about MBTI, Table 17.2 provides a list of resources that have been published on MBTI. In the future, it is

Table 17.2 Published resources on MBTI

Reference	Description
Ong, J. C. (2017). *Mindfulness-Based Therapy for Insomnia*. Washington, DC: American Psychological Association.	This book includes session-by-session guidelines and the theoretical background for delivering MBTI.
Ong, J. C., & Manber, R. (2010). Mindfulness-based therapy for insomnia. In M. L. Perlis (Ed.), *Behavioral Sleep Medicine Treatments* (pp. 133–141). London: Elsevier.	This book chapter provides an example of using the mindfulness principles of acceptance and letting go in MBTI.
Ong, J. C., Manber, R., Segal, Z., Xia, Y., Shapiro, S. L., & Wyatt, J. K. (2014). A randomized controlled trial of mindfulness meditation for chronic insomnia. *Sleep, 37*, 1553–1563.	This paper presents the main outcomes for a randomized controlled trial using MBTI.
Ong, J. C., Ulmer, C. S., & Manber, R. (2012). Improving sleep with mindfulness and acceptance: A metacognitive model of insomnia. *Behaviour Research and Therapy, 50*, 651–660.	This paper describes the metacognitive model of insomnia and how mindfulness and acceptance can improve sleep.
Ong, J., & Sholtes, D. (2010). A mindfulness-based approach to the treatment of insomnia. *Journal of Clinical Psychology: In Session, 66*, 1175–1184.	This paper provides a case example of a participant receiving MBTI.

(Continued)

Table 17.2 Continued

Reference	Description
Ong, J. C., Shapiro, S. L., & Manber, R. (2008). Combining mindfulness meditation with cognitive-behavior therapy for insomnia: A treatment-development study. *Behavior Therapy*, 39, 171–182.	This paper presents data from the first pilot study on MBTI.
Ong, J. C., Shapiro, S. L., & Manber, R. (2009). Mindfulness meditation and CBT for insomnia: A naturalistic 12-month follow-up. *Explore: The Journal of Science and Healing*, 5, 30–36.	This paper presents the 12-month follow-up data from the pilot study on MBTI.
Cvengros, J. A., Crawford, M., Manber, R., & Ong, J. C. (2015). The relationship between beliefs about sleep and adherence to behavioral treatment combined with mindfulness meditation for insomnia. *Behavioral Sleep Medicine*, 13, 52–63.	This paper examines predictors of adherence to the components of MBTI.

our hope that courses and workshops will also be available to train practitioners interested in delivering MBTI.

References

Bastien, C. H., Vallieres, A., & Morin, C. M. (2001). Validation of the Insomnia Severity Index as an outcome measure for insomnia research. *Sleep Medicine*, 2(4), 297–307.

Bonnet, M. H., & Arand, D. L. (2010). Hyperarousal and insomnia: State of the science. *Sleep Medicine Reviews*, 14(1), 9–15.

Bootzin, R. R. (1972). *Stimulus control treatment for insomnia*. Paper presented at the 80th Annual Convention of the American Psychological Association.

Borbely, A. A., & Achermann, P. (1999). Sleep homeostasis and models of sleep regulation. *Journal of Biological Rhythms*, 14(6), 557–568.

Fernandez-Mendoza, J., Calhoun, S., Bixler, E. O., Pejovic, S., Karataraki, M., Liao, D., . . . Vgontzas, A. N. (2010). Insomnia with objective short sleep duration is associated with deficits in neuropsychological performance: A general population study. *Sleep*, 33(4), 459–465.

Ford, D. E., & Kamerow, D. B. (1989). Epidemiologic study of sleep disturbances and psychiatric disorders: An opportunity for prevention? *Journal of American Medical Association*, 262(11), 1479–1484.

Hantsoo, L., Khou, C. S., White, C. N., & Ong, J. C. (2013). Gender and cognitive-emotional factors as predictors of pre-sleep arousal and trait hyperarousal in insomnia. *Journal of Psychosomatic Research*, 74(4), 283–289.

Irwin, M. R. (2015). Why sleep is important for health: A psychoneuroimmunology perspective. *Annual Review of Psychology*, 66, 143–172. doi:10.1146/annurev-psych-010213-115205

Jansson-Frojmark, M., & Linton, S. J. (2008). The course of insomnia over one year: A longitudinal study in the general population in Sweden. *Sleep*, 31(6), 881–886.

Kabat-Zinn, J. (1990). *Full catastrophe living: Using the wisdom of your body and mind to face stress, pain, and illness*. New York, NY: Delacorte Press.

Kuisk, L. A., Bertelson, A. D., & Walsh, J. K. (1989). Presleep cognitive hyperarousal and affect as factors in objective and subjective insomnia. *Perceptual and Motor Skills*, *69*(3 Pt 2), 1219–1225.

LeBlanc, M., Merette, C., Savard, J., Ivers, H., Baillargeon, L., & Morin, C. M. (2009). Incidence and risk factors of insomnia in a population-based sample. *Sleep*, *32*(8), 1027–1037.

Morin, C. M., Vallieres, A., Guay, B., Ivers, H., Savard, J., Merette, C., . . . Baillargeon, L. (2009). Cognitive behavioral therapy, singly and combined with medication, for persistent insomnia: A randomized controlled trial. *Journal of American Medical Association*, *301*(19), 2005–2015. doi:10.1001/jama.2009.682

Ohayon, M. M. (2002). Epidemiology of insomnia: What we know and what we still need to learn. *Sleep Medicine Reviews*, *6*(2), 97–111.

Ong, J., & Sholtes, D. (2010). A mindfulness-based approach to the treatment of insomnia. *Journal of Clinical Psychology*, *66*(11), 1175–1184.

Ong, J. C. (2017). *Mindfulness-based therapy for insomnia*. Washington, DC: American Psychological Association.

Ong, J. C., Manber, R., Segal, Z., Xia, Y., Shapiro, S., & Wyatt, J. K. (2014). A randomized controlled trial of mindfulness meditation for chronic insomnia. *Sleep*. doi:10.5665/sleep.4010

Ong, J. C., Shapiro, S. L., & Manber, R. (2008). Combining mindfulness meditation with cognitive-behavior therapy for insomnia: A treatment-development study. *Behavior Theraphy*, *39*(2), 171–182.

Ong, J. C., & Smith, C. E. (2017). Using mindfulness for the treatment of insomnia. *Current Sleep Medicine Reports*, *3*(2), 57–65.

Ong, J. C., Ulmer, C. S., & Manber, R. (2012). Improving sleep with mindfulness and acceptance: A metacognitive model of insomnia. *Behavioral Research and Therapy*, *50*(11), 651–660. doi:10.1016/j.brat.2012.08.001

Ong, J. C., Xia, Y., Smith, C. E., & Manber, R. (under review). *A randomized controlled trial of mindfulness meditation for chronic insomnia: Effects on cognitive-emotional arousal and daytime functioning*.

Perlis, M., Jungquist, C., Smith, M., & Posner, P. (2005). *Cognitive behavioral treatment of insomnia: A session-by-session guide*. New York, NY: Springer.

Qaseem, A., Kansagara, D., Forciea, M. A., Cooke, M., Denberg, T. D., & Clinical Guidelines Committee of the American College of Physicians. (2016). Management of chronic insomnia disorder in adults: A clinical practice guideline from the American college of physicians. *Annals of Internal Medicine*, *165*(2), 125–133. doi:10.7326/M15–2175

Riemann, D., Spiegelhalder, K., Feige, B., Voderholzer, U., Berger, M., Perlis, M., & Nissen, C. (2010). The hyperarousal model of insomnia: A review of the concept and its evidence. *Sleep Medicine Reviews*, *14*(1), 19–31.

Segal, Z. V., Williams, J. M. G., & Teasdale, J. D. (2002). *Mindfulness-based cognitive therapy for depression: A new approach to preventing relapse*. New York, NY: Guilford Press.

Shapiro, S. L., Carlson, L. E., Astin, J. A., & Freedman, B. (2006). Mechanisms of mindfulness. *Journal of Clinical Psychology*, *62*(3), 373–386.

Shekleton, J. A., Flynn-Evans, E. E., Miller, B., Epstein, L. J., Kirsch, D., Brogna, L. A., . . . Rajaratnam, S. M. (2014). Neurobehavioral performance impairment in insomnia: Relationships with self-reported sleep and daytime functioning. *Sleep*, *37*(1), 107–116. doi:10.5665/sleep.3318

Spielman, A. J., Saskin, P., & Thorpy, M. J. (1987). Treatment of chronic insomnia by restriction of time in bed. *Sleep*, *10*(1), 45–56.

Taylor, D. J., Mallory, L. J., Lichstein, K. L., Durrence, H. H., Riedel, B. W., & Bush, A. J. (2007). Comorbidity of chronic insomnia with medical problems. *Sleep*, *30*(2), 213–218.

Wu, J. Q., Appleman, E. R., Salazar, R. D., & Ong, J. C. (2015). Cognitive Behavioral Therapy for insomnia comorbid with psychiatric and medical conditions: A meta-analysis. *JAMA Internal Medicine*, *175*(9), 1461–1472. doi:10.1001/jamainternmed.2015.3006

Section IV

Mindfulness programs in education

Chapter 18

Cultivating Awareness and Resilience in Education

The CARE for teachers program

Patricia A. Jennings, Anthony A. DeMauro, and Polina Mischenko

Overview

Cultivating Awareness and Resilience in Education (CARE) for Teachers is a professional development program designed to provide teachers with the skills they need to manage the social and emotional demands of teaching. Recently, teacher stress and attrition have become recognized as serious problems that have negative impacts on education quality (Greenberg, Brown, & Abenavoli, 2016), particularly among high-poverty schools where stress and attrition levels are highest (Alliance for Excellent Education, 2014; Hoglund, Klingle, & Hosan, 2015). The demands teachers face have increased over the past several decades with more children coming to school unprepared, and with unmet needs (Children's Defense Fund, 2014). Furthermore, teachers face mounting pressures to be accountable for their students' standardized test scores (Valli & Buese, 2016). Indeed, teachers reported rising occupational stress and decreasing job satisfaction. A survey of 1,000 U.S. K-12 public school teachers found that 59% reported being under great stress, a significant increase from 35% in 1985 (Markow, Macia, & Lee, 2013). Teachers' job satisfaction dropped from 62% in 2008 to 39% in 2012, the largest drop since 1984 when the survey began.

It is no wonder that teachers report high levels of stress. Unlike many professions, teachers are constantly exposed to emotionally challenging situations such as student-student conflicts and misbehavior. Furthermore, they must manage strong emotions while they are teaching, often under time pressure to cover academic content. For example, when a student interrupts a lesson, especially when the teacher is constrained by time, it is only natural for the teacher to feel frustration. However, her expressions of frustration can interfere with her teaching and behavior management, and her students' learning. Unlike other work environments, she cannot excuse herself to calm down in private, but must stay in the classroom with the students and continue to teach.

Research has shown that this need to manage strong negative emotions while teaching is a primary work stressor for teachers (Carson, Weiss, & Templin, 2006; Montgomery & Rupp, 2005; Sutton & Wheatley, 2003). Emotion reactivity can impair teachers' cognitive functioning. When emotionally triggered, a teacher can lose track of her lesson, negatively impacting the quality of her teaching (Emmer & Stough, 2001). Constantly coping with strong negative emotions can impair teachers' motivation and eventually lead to burnout (Chang, 2009).

When teachers have to regulate strong emotions while they are teaching, it can interfere with their classroom management causing a deterioration of the classroom environment. This can result in emotional exhaustion and trigger a "burnout cascade" (Jennings & Greenberg, p. 492). When exhausted emotionally, teachers may develop a callous, cynical attitude toward their students, students' parents, and colleagues and eventually grow to feel they are ineffective teachers. In contrast, research suggests that teachers who cultivate more positive emotions may be more resilient, intrinsically motivated, and better able to cope with the complex social and emotional demands of teaching (Gu & Day, 2007; Sutton & Wheatley, 2003). Additionally, developing adaptive coping strategies may support teachers' well-being and performance (Chang, 2013). A study examining the combined results of 65 studies of teacher stress identified the strengthening of emotion regulation as key to preventing teacher stress (Montgomery & Rupp, 2005).

Teachers who experience high levels of stress and strong negative emotions may transmit these to students via "stress-contagion" (Wethington, 2000, p. 234). One recent study involving a large, nationally representative sample of first grade children ($N = 10,700$) found that those children in classrooms with teachers reporting higher levels of stress were more likely to be assessed with emotional disorders (Milkie & Warner, 2011). Another study involving 406 elementary school children and their teachers (N = 17) found that teachers' burnout was associated with students' biological stress regulation processes, such that teachers with higher levels of burnout had students with more dysregulated biological stress responses (Oberle & Schonert-Reichl, 2016). Although more research will be required to assess the causal direction of these associations, these studies show evidence of the "contagious" nature of stress in the classroom.

Mindful awareness practices (MAPs) may help teachers build the social and emotional competencies they need to manage stress and the growing demands of teaching. MAPs involve cultivating present moment awareness with an attitude of openness and curiosity. Examples of such practices include mindfulness meditation, mindful movement practices such as yoga or tai chi, and mindfully engaging in activities such as mindful eating and mindful listening. MAPs appear to promote adaptive emotion regulation and coping ability, which may reduce burnout and promote psychological distress regulation (Corcoran, Farb, Anderson, & Segal, 2010). As a result, teachers may experience more energy and self-regulatory resources (e.g., greater job satisfaction, improved well-being) that can then be invested in supportive teacher-student interactions that promote student learning (Roeser, 2016; Roeser, Skinner, Beers, & Jennings, 2012; Skinner & Beers, 2016).

Recognizing the potential benefits of MAPs for addressing the social, emotional, and cognitive demands of teaching and the importance of teachers' emotional support for student learning, a team of contemplative practitioners with backgrounds as teachers and teacher educators (Jennings, Turksma, & Brown, 2015) developed CARE for Teachers with the support of the Garrison Institute. The program was developed to support the social and emotional competencies teachers need to manage these demands and to effectively create and maintain supportive learning environments.

The first author had previously worked on the Cultivating Emotional Balance (CEB) project that was developed in response to calls for such research by the 14th Dalai Lama during a Mind and Life Dialog in 2001, one of a series of meetings organized by the Mind and Life Institute to promote communication and collaboration between Buddhist practitioners and scholars and scientists (see Goleman, 2003 for documentation of this meeting). At the meeting, a team of researchers and contemplative teachers decided to create a program designed to reduce destructive emotions that combined emotion skills instruction and contemplative practices. The team decided to examine the program's efficacy in a randomized trial involving teachers, given they experience a great deal of stress and that it can have an impact on their students' learning. The first author served as project director of this study and attended all the CEB trainings delivered as part of the trial. While CEB exhibited promise for reducing teachers' stress and supporting emotion regulation (Kemeny et al., 2012), a pilot study showed no impact on teachers' emotional supportiveness (Jennings, Foltz, Snowberg, Sim, & Kemeny, 2011). Thus, the CARE for Teachers team concluded that to impact classroom and student outcomes, the emotion skills and contemplative practices would need to be contextualized in terms of the specific stressors that teachers typically face, and they embarked on a process to adapt CEB to achieve this goal.

Theoretical background

The CARE for Teachers program is grounded in the Prosocial Classroom Model that proposes that teachers' well-being and social and emotional competencies play a critical role in their ability to build supportive relationships with their students, manage their classrooms effectively, and teach social and emotional competencies (SEC) to their students through direct instruction, coaching, and modeling (Jennings & Greenberg, 2009). The model further articulates how these three elements of the model promote a classroom climate conducive to desirable student academic and behavioral outcomes. Social and emotional competencies can be organized into five domains: self-awareness and self-management are two intrapersonal competencies; social awareness and relationship skills are two interpersonal competencies; and the last, responsible decision making, involves the application of the other four. These competencies form the basis of social and emotional learning as articulated by the Collaborative for Academic, Social and Emotional Learning (CASEL, 2013). The competencies develop continuously across the lifespan and can be context dependent. For example, the SEC required to be a teacher is different than that required to be a police officer. No one would expect the average adult to have the social and emotional skills required for either of these professions without specific training. However, until recently, this was not recognized, and to this day, teachers (or police for that matter) rarely receive training to manage the intense social and emotional demands of their professions. The CARE program was designed to help teachers build the specific SEC required to create and maintain a supportive learning environment.

Program structure

Unlike many mindfulness-based programs that are delivered across seven to eight short weekly classes and one retreat day, CARE for Teachers is delivered over the course of several full days. CARE for Teachers is offered as both a field-based in-service professional development program and as a week-long intensive summer retreat at the Garrison Institute in Garrison, New York and the 1440 Multiversity in Northern California. The field-based program typically entails four daylong sessions spread across four to five weeks of the school year with an additional daylong booster session delivered several months thereafter (totaling 30 hours of in-person training). Between the sessions, CARE facilitators provide coaching for teachers by phone and email on using the new skills and practices inside and outside the classroom. The summer retreats are delivered as five-day intensives with no standardized follow-up coaching. A program workbook as well as a take-home audio CD/MP3 of mindfulness practices is provided to all participants in either program. While the field-based programs typically serve teachers from a single district or school, the retreats are open to the public and serve teachers and educators from around the world. The Garrison Institute offers a limited number of need-based scholarships to those who would otherwise not be able to partake in the program.

Program components

The CARE for Teachers program follows best practices for adult learning by introducing material sequentially and blending didactic instruction with experiential and interactive learning activities (Garet, Porter, Desimone, Birman, & Yoon, 2001; Guskey, 2003). At the beginning of the program, facilitators clarify that participants are invited, not obliged, to participate in the practices presented, and that they are free to choose which practices they wish to engage in. Additionally, facilitators offer support outside of sessions if participants encounter challenges or discomfort with any of the program practices.

Self-care

The CARE for Teachers program is based on the premise that to be empathic and compassionate toward others it is important to develop these qualities toward oneself, and that caring for others, requires self-care. At the beginning of the program, participants are given the opportunity to explore their current self-care routines and to see whether they have a balanced set of practices that support their physical, emotional, intellectual, and psychological/spiritual development. They are also invited to identify and reflect on the gaps in their self-care routines in relation to these areas of personal growth and development. Toward the end of the program, participants are guided to develop a feasible self-care plan that integrates MAPs and other practices learned throughout the program.

Intention setting

Another introductory practice that participants learn at the beginning of the program and repeatedly revisit is intention setting. To introduce the practice, participants are invited to recall their reason for becoming a teacher and the values they hold that underlie this decision. After reflecting on this, participants are invited to imagine their "best self," develop a vision for what their ideal classroom would look like, and set an intention based on this vision. This involves focusing on the intention using words or their imagination for a few moments. Participants explore the difference between a goal and an intention, and learn how intention setting can help to orient one's thoughts and actions to align with their values and vision, without carrying with it the pressure and fear of failure that often comes with goal-setting. Finally, participants are given a moment of silence to set an intention for the particular day. To help them stay on track with their intention, participants are invited to share their intention with an "intention buddy" and are encouraged to periodically check-in and remind each other of their intention. Periodically, participants are given the opportunity to reflect on their intention to see how they are doing and to modify it if needed. Participants are also guided on how to continue their intention setting practice when they return to the school setting.

Emotion skills instruction

Given the high emotional demands of teaching, CARE for Teachers aims to share with participants the latest neuropsychological findings on the role of emotions and the brain in teaching and learning. A sequential model of emotional mastery is introduced called The Four Rs (respect, recognition, regulation, responsiveness). The first "R" is respect because having respect for the power of our emotions is an important first step in developing emotional mastery; along with respect for our biological inheritance that evolved to help us survive. The next "R" is recognition because in order to master our emotions, we must be able to recognize the sensations, thoughts and behaviors that are associated with them. Regulation, the next "R," is the ability to monitor and adjust the intensity level of emotional experience and expression. Typically, this may involve reducing the intensity of strong uncomfortable emotions, such as anger, but it can also involve increasing the intensity of any emotion, depending upon the situation. Finally, the culmination of this process is the fourth "R," responsiveness. When we master our emotions, we can respond to situations more skillfully and thoughtfully rather than reacting impulsively in ways we may later regret.

Through a series of mini-lectures, participants learn about the parts of the brain involved in the fight, flight, or freeze response and the role of the prefrontal cortex in helping humans engage their higher order thinking capacities to appropriately manage behavioral reactions during strong emotions. Experiential activities, such as reflections and role-plays, are used to help participants explore their own habitual emotion response patterns, also called "scripts," and learn to re-appraise emotionally challenging situations. These activities are designed to normalize the emotional experience and to help teachers understand and build mastery of their emotions. Although some emotions, such as anger or fear, may be more uncomfortable to experience than others, they evolved to support our survival and are thus important experiences not to be ignored or suppressed. CARE for Teachers emphasizes that all emotions have a purpose and are neither "bad" nor "good." Nevertheless, participants are introduced to the benefits of and science behind the self-induction of pleasant emotions, such as joy and gratitude, as a way to build resilience and well-being (Cohn, Brown, Fredrickson, Milkels, & Conway, 2009). Finally, participants learn how mindfulness can help them become more efficient in recognizing the signals of emotional onset and more effective in choosing to respond thoughtfully, rather than automatically, to emotionally-triggering situations.

Mindful awareness practices

In CARE for Teachers, participants learn to cultivate mindfulness through basic secular MAPs. One of the first practices that is introduced is mindful awareness of the breath. In this practice participants are asked to bring their attention to the breath, to notice when their attention wanders away from the breath, and to acknowledge the thoughts or other distractions that arise before gently redirecting their attention back to the breath. This MAP can help participants become aware of habitual thought patterns and improve their ability to respond compassionately and calmly to emotional evocations that may arise. It facilitates an awareness that we do not necessarily need to identify with the thoughts, emotions, desires, and other phenomena that capture our attention. Participants are typically invited to engage in this practice for five to fifteen minutes. Depending on the comfort-level of participants, this practice may be increased to twenty minutes toward the end of the program.

Other MAPs in the program emphasize the development of body awareness. Participants learn that body awareness involves recognizing how different emotions are expressed in the body as sensations associated with psychophysiological reactions. They also learn that developing body awareness can help them more swiftly recognize the subtle sensations associated with the onset of emotions, giving them the opportunity to recognize and regulate the emotions before they overwhelm the mind. One such practice is the body scan. During the body scan the participants are guided to direct their attention sequentially to different parts of the body, noticing any sensations they experience. Similar to the breath awareness practice, participants are asked to redirect their attention back to the point of focus (in this case a specific body part) if they notice that their mind has wandered.

Other body awareness practices involve standing or moving. In one practice, referred to as a *centering* practice, participants are invited to stand with their feet parallel and focus on the connection between their body's center of gravity and their base of support as they work together to support the weight of the body and keep the body balanced and upright. Mindful walking is an extension of this practice in which participants are invited to focus their attention on the soles of their feet, noticing the weight shift from the heel, to the ball, to the toe with each step. As in all MAPs, participants are instructed to notice when their mind wanders and gently bring their attention back to the point of focus, which in this case is the sensations of the feet as they transfer the weight of the body from one foot to the other.

Throughout the program, participants are invited to envision how they can incorporate mindfulness into their daily lives both formally and informally. Thus, the practices presented are simple, short, and aligned with normal daily activities (i.e., sitting, lying down, standing, and walking) to point out that mindfulness does not have to be a separate activity, but can be integrated into everyday experiences. One MAP that illustrates this point well is mindful eating. In the mindful eating activity, participants are invited to slow down and engage their senses, one by one, in experiencing and savoring a piece of fruit. Participants reflect on the process and also learn to apply this approach to eating in their daily lives to promote greater enjoyment, gratitude and healthy eating habits.

Caring and listening practices

A crucial element of the program is learning how to cultivate empathy and compassion for self and others. One of the key practices that participants learn in the program is the *caring practice*, which is an adapted and secularized version of the Buddhist *metta* (loving-kindness) practice. This practice entails silently generating feelings of loving-kindness and care by offering well-being, happiness, and peace to oneself and others. Research has shown that this practice, done regularly, can promote positive emotions and reductions in illness and depressive symptoms (Fredrickson, Coffey, Pek, Cohn, & Finkel, 2008). Another related practice involves recalling experiences associated with pleasant emotions (e.g., joy, gratitude) to develop one's ability to recall and cultivate these emotions, especially when one feels depleted, in order to build resilience and prevent burnout (Cohn et al., 2009).

Mindful listening is another key component of CARE for Teachers and an important practice for cultivating care and compassion. There are several activities in which participants engage in mindful listening through partner work and role plays and reflect on their thoughts, emotions and personal scripts or mental schema associated with emotions. In one exercise, partners take turns being the speaker and the listener for three to five minutes as one of the partners talks about a challenging situation they have experienced while the other partner listens. As the listener, the participant is invited to offer his or her full open-hearted presence to the speaker and to decline from engaging in the conversation by nodding, aligning their facial expressions to the speaker, or making statements such as, "I see" and "I understand." In fact, partners are asked to sit beside each other instead of facing each other in order to avoid any signs of *active listening*. The idea is that this approach allows for both individuals to fully focus on their listening or speaking task – the listener does not need to expend energy thinking of ways to express engagement and understanding, and the speaker is not influenced by the listener's reactions to what they share. Participants are given the opportunity to reflect on their experiences as listener and speaker. Typically, participants report becoming more aware of their internal experiences (e.g. thoughts, emotions, scripts, physical sensations) when listening and speaking, as well as noticing how much more in-tune they are to the other person's emotions when they listen to them mindfully.

Another activity presented later in the program explores situations that involve emotional triggers to discover scripts and how these scripts may interfere with their understanding of their students' needs and behavior and their ability to provide support. As an example, during one workshop a teacher participant expressed frustration about a student who came late to school each day. The second-grade girl came into class 30–40 minutes late, disrupting her class by giggling and acting silly. In response, this teacher scolded her and had her sit for time out as a punishment. During the training, she realized that she had never asked the child why she was coming late and that as a child she had learned that being late was very bad and disrespectful and that this script triggered her strong frustration in this situation. When she asked the child why she was late, she learned that the girl's mother worked at night and she had to get to school without any help. Learning this completely transformed the teacher's feelings about this child from frustration to compassion and she realized that the giggling and acting out was embarrassment. The teacher changed her approach to warmly welcome the girl while working to find ways to help her get to school on time. As a result, the girl's disruptive behavior stopped and she began to thrive in school (Jennings, 2015).

This is one of many anecdotes that provide evidence that CARE for Teachers can help teachers manage the social and emotional demands of teaching and provide better support to their students. Next we review the extensive quantitative and qualitative research that has provided empirical evidence as well.

CARE for Teachers research

Research on CARE for Teachers began with Jennings, Snowberg, Coccia, and Greenberg's (2011) two small pilot studies. The first delivered CARE to a sample of 31 urban elementary school teachers and assessed teachers at pre- and post-program completion on measures of depressive symptoms, time urgency, physical symptoms, approach to motivating students, teaching efficacy, mindfulness, and interpersonal mindfulness in teaching. At post-test, participants reported significantly reduced task-related hurry and marginally reduced general hurry. Participants also showed significant increases in mindfulness and interpersonal mindfulness. Significant changes were not observed on the other measures.

The second pilot study randomly assigned 39 teachers and student teachers in suburban/semi-rural schools to receive CARE for Teachers or waitlist control. This study found no significant changes on self-report measures of affect, depressive symptoms, hurry/time pressure, physical symptoms, teaching efficacy, and mindfulness. The second pilot also included pre-post observational assessments of classroom quality, but no significant changes were observed on this measure. Results led the researchers to conclude that CARE for Teachers may be more useful for teachers working in high-risk settings due to the significant findings only in the sample of urban teachers.

Building upon the pilot studies, Jennings, Frank, Snowberg, Coccia, and Greenberg (2013) conducted a randomized controlled trial (RCT). Fifty pre-K–12 teachers in a northeast metropolitan area were randomly assigned to receive CARE for Teachers or waitlist control. At post-test, treatment teachers reported significantly higher levels of mindfulness, teacher efficacy, and reappraisal (a dimension of emotion regulation), along with reductions in daily physical symptoms, general hurry, and the personal accomplishment dimension of burnout compared to controls. Significant effects were not found on measures of positive/negative affect, depressive symptoms, and other dimensions of time pressure and burnout. The findings demonstrated the program's promise in improving teachers' mindfulness and emotion skills, while also reducing experiences of stress and burnout. Researchers also collected qualitative data from program participants to better understand what aspects of the program led to these outcomes.

Schussler, Jennings, Sharp, and Frank (2016) conducted focus groups with a total of 44 head classroom teachers and six assistant teachers who received CARE in order to explain results from Jennings et al.'s (2013) RCT. Participants described how CARE helped them develop an enhanced awareness of both their physical and emotional responses to stress, along with strategies to regulate their emotions more effectively. Teachers across all four focus groups described similar processes of taking a moment to breathe and calm down during difficult situations, allowing them to respond versus emotionally react to them. One participant shared, "I take a minute and calm myself down before I try to take care of the situation" (Schussler et al., 2016, p. 137).

Similar themes were found by Sharp and Jennings (2016), who also studied participants of the CARE for Teachers trial. Conducting in-depth interviews with eight treatment teachers, they found numerous teachers discussing a generally enhanced emotional awareness, along with gaining emotional regulation skills and becoming less reactive. Quantitative findings from the RCT showed effects on the reappraisal dimension of an emotion regulation survey, and teachers in this study repeatedly described this process of shifting their perspectives on events to regulate emotional reactions (i.e. experiencing less frustration from a difficult situation with a parent after considering the event from the parent's point of view). Findings from these studies began to suggest CARE for Teachers was beneficial for teachers beyond just their own well-being, as many teachers described how it changed the way they interacted with students. This idea was a critical point of exploration in the ensuing study.

The most recent CARE for Teachers trial provided the largest and most rigorous study of an MBI for teachers to date and investigated its efficacy for both teachers' well-being and the quality of their classroom interactions. Performing a cluster RCT, Jennings et al. (2017) randomized 224 teachers to receive CARE for Teachers or a waitlist control. Using hierarchical linear modeling to account for nesting of teachers within schools, outcomes showed that treatment teachers' mindfulness and adaptive emotion regulation improved, along with reductions in psychological distress and time urgency compared to controls. Moreover, blind observers rated the quality of teachers' classroom interactions at pre- and post-test using the Classroom Assessment Scoring System (CLASS; Pianta, La Paro, & Hamre, 2008), and results showed significant positive impacts on teachers' emotional support and two sub-dimensions of emotional support: positive climate (the teacher's warmth and ability to establish relationships with students) and teacher sensitivity (the teacher's awareness and responsiveness to students' needs). Results also showed a marginally significant positive impact on the classroom organization domain, with a significant impact on the sub-dimension of productivity (how efficiently the classroom operates). There were no significant impacts on the instructional support domain of the CLASS, but researchers did not hypothesize such changes would occur because CARE for Teachers does not involve training related to delivery of academic instruction.

This study provided strong evidence that an MBI can have positive impacts beyond teachers' own well-being by applying a rigorous observational measurement strategy. Considering that CLASS scores have shown predictive validity for student achievement (Bill & Melinda Gates Foundation, 2012, 2013), the study also has implications that MBIs for teachers may benefit students. The first report on main outcomes did not include follow-up assessments. However, future reports are in preparation that examine follow-up/growth models, participant interview data, and impacts on student achievement.

On social validity assessments of CARE for Teachers, participants have consistently reported positive experiences with the program. In each of the trials, more than 80% of participants felt the program improved their self-awareness and well-being. More than 75% of teachers reported they were better able to establish and maintain supportive relationships with students and better able to manage classroom behaviors effectively and compassionately following the program. Additionally, more than 87% of participants strongly agreed or agreed that this type of program should be integrated into preparation and in-service training for all teachers.

Open-ended evaluation surveys further illustrated participants' satisfaction and takeaways from the program. One teacher described CARE for Teachers as "the most valuable, personally rewarding and important class that [she has] ever taken" (Jennings, 2016, p. 139). Following completion of the program, another teacher stated, "Now I have the tools to stay calm, reflective, appreciative, joyful and grateful every day, which will help me interact positively with my students and colleagues" (p. 140). These quotes demonstrate both the value teachers found in CARE for Teachers and the ways in which the training enhanced their teaching experiences.

Conclusion

The body of evidence supporting the effectiveness of mindfulness-based interventions for teachers, such as CARE for Teachers, is growing, as are the number of teachers and schools reaching out for these professional development opportunities. Thus far, more than 1000 teachers and educators have benefitted from the CARE program since its founding in 2006.

Overall, the program is well received by teachers and has promise to address the problems of teacher stress and the effects of stress on teaching and learning. Evidence indicated CARE for Teachers can reduce psychological distress and time urgency and promote mindfulness and adaptive emotion regulation. Furthermore, CARE for Teachers has significant positive impacts on teacher-student interactions. Nevertheless, additional research is needed to better understand the mechanisms involved in making MAPs effective tools for improving teachers' well-being and their capacity to effectively support student learning.

There is a need for further qualitative research to understand the processes that underlie the positive impacts demonstrated in research involving quantitative methods. Further research is also required to determine whether the positive impacts on classroom interactions translate into significant positive impacts on student behavior and achievement. The most recent large-scale study collected school administrative data and teacher reports on these student outcomes from a sample of 5200 students enrolled in the teachers' classrooms. Papers reporting on these outcomes are currently in preparation. Finally, research is required to examine whether programs like CARE for Teachers can boost the effectiveness of mindfulness-based programs designed for students such as MindUp (Schonert-Reichl et al., 2015). It is likely that if teachers receive the CARE for Teachers program prior to beginning instruction in programs like MindUp, students may show greater gains in prosocial behavior and learning. Teachers who know how to cultivate mindful awareness may be better prepared to teach such practices to their students.

The CARE for Teachers team hopes to continue addressing these research gaps within its capacity in order to continue improving the program and benefitting more teachers in the most effective way possible.

References

Alliance for Excellent Education. (2014). *On the path to equity: Improving the effectiveness of beginning teachers* [Press release]. Retrieved from http://all4ed.org/press/teacher-attrition-costs-united-states-up-to-2-2-billion-annually-says-new-alliance-report/

Bill & Melinda Gates Foundation. (2012). *Gathering feedback from teaching: Combining high-quality observations with student surveys and achievement gains*. Seattle, WA: Author. Retrieved from http://files.eric.ed.gov/fulltext/ED540960.pdf

Bill & Melinda Gates Foundation. (2013). *Have we identified effective teachers? Validating measures of effective teaching using random assignment*. Seattle, WA: Author. Retrieved from http://files.eric.ed.gov/fulltext/ED540959.pdf

Carson, R. L., Weiss, H. M., & Templin, T. J. (2010). Ecological momentary assessment: A research method for studying the daily lives of teachers. *International Journal of Research & Method in Education, 33*, 165–182. http://dx.doi.org/10.1080/1743727X.2010.484548

Chang, M. L. (2009). An appraisal perspective of teacher burnout: Examining the emotional work of teachers. *Educational Psychology Review, 21*, 193–218. http://dx.doi.org/10.1007/s10648-009-9106-y

Chang, M. L. (2013). Toward a theoretical model to understand teacher emotions and teacher burnout in the context of student misbehavior: Appraisal, regulation and coping. *Motivation and Emotion, 37*, 799–817. http://dx.doi.org/10.1007/s11031-012-9335-0

Children's Defense Fund. (2014). *The state of America's children*. Retrieved from www.childrensdefense.org/library/state-of-americas-children/2014-soac.pdf

Cohn, M. A., Brown, S. L., Fredrickson, B. L., Milkels, J. A., & Conway, A. M. (2009). Happiness unpacked: Positive emotions increase life satisfaction by building resilience. *Emotion, 9*, 361–368.

Collaborative for Academic, Social, and Emotional Learning. (2013). *2013 CASEL guide: Effective social and emotional learning programs – Preschool and elementary school edition*. Chicago, IL: Author.

Corcoran, K. M., Farb, N., Anderson, A., & Segal, Z. V. (2010). Mindfulness and emotion regulation: Outcomes and possible mediating mechanisms. In A. M. Kring & D. M. Sloan (Eds.), *Emotion regulation and psychopathology: A transdiagnostic approach to etiology and treatment* (pp. 339–355). New York, NY: Guilford Press.

Emmer, E. T., & Stough, L. M. (2001). Classroom management: A critical part of educational psychology, with implications for teacher education. *Educational Psychologist, 36*, 103–112. http://dx.doi.org/10.1207/S15326985EP3602_5

Fredrickson, B. L., Coffey, K. A., Pek, J., Cohn, M. A., & Finkel, S. M. (2008). Open hearts build lives: Positive emotions, induced through loving-kindness meditation, build consequential personal resources. *Journal of Personality and Social Psychology, 95*, 1045–1062.

Garet, M. S., Porter, A. C., Desimone, L., Birman, B. F., & Yoon, K. S. (2001). What makes professional development effective? Results from a national sample of teachers. *American Educational Research Journal, 38*(4), 915–945.

Goleman, D. (2003). *Destructive emotions*. New York, NY: Bantam.

Greenberg, M. T., Brown, J. L., & Abenavoli, R. M. (2016). *Teacher stress and health effects on teachers, students, and schools*. Issue Brief. Retrieved from Robert Wood Johnson Foundation website: www.rwjf.org/content/dam/farm/reports/issue_briefs/2016/rwjf430428

Gu, Q., & Day, C. (2007). Teachers' resilience: A necessary condition for effectiveness. *Teaching and Teacher Education, 23*, 1302–1316. http://dx.doi.org/10.1016/j.tate.2006.06.006

Guskey, T. R. (2003). What makes PD effective? *Phi Deltan Kappan, 84*, 748–750.

Hoglund, W. L. G., Klingle, K. E., & Hosan, N. E. (2015). Classroom risks and resources: Teacher burnout, classroom quality and children's adjustment in high needs elementary schools. *Journal of School Psychology, 53*, 337–357. http://dx.doi.org/doi.org/10.1016/j.jsp.2015.06.002

Jennings, P. A. (2015). *Mindfulness for teachers: Simple skills for peace and productivity in the classroom*. New York, NY: W. W. Norton.

Jennings, P. A. (2016). CARE for teachers: A mindfulness-based approach to promoting teachers' well-being and improving performance. In K. Schonert-Reichl & R. Roeser (Eds). *The handbook of mindfulness in education: Emerging theory, research, and programs* (pp. 133–148). New York, NY: Springer-Verlag.

Jennings, P. A., Brown, J. L., Frank, J. L., Doyle, S., Oh, Y., Tanler, R., Rasheed, D., DeWeese, A., DeMauro, A. A., Cham, H., & Greenberg, M. T. (2017). Impacts of the CARE for Teachers program on teachers' social and emotional competence and classroom interactions. *Journal of Educational Psychology*. Advance online publication. http://dx.doi.org/10.1037/edu0000187

Jennings, P. A., Foltz, C., Snowberg, K. E., Sim, H., & Kemeny, M. E. (2011). *The influence of mindfulness and emotion skills training on teachers' classrooms: The effects of the cultivating emotional balance training*. ERIC online submission. Retrieved from www.eric.ed.gov/contentdelivery/servlet/ERICServlet?accno=ED518584

Jennings, P. A., Frank, J. L., Snowberg, K. E., Coccia, M. A., & Greenberg, M. T. (2013). Improving classroom learning environments by cultivating awareness and resilience in education (CARE): Results of a randomized controlled trial. *School Psychology Quarterly, 28*, 374–390. http://dx.doi.org/10.1037/spq0000035

Jennings, P. A., & Greenberg, M. T. (2009). The prosocial classroom: Teacher social and emotional competence in relation to student and classroom outcomes. *Review of Educational Research, 79*, 491–525. http://dx.doi.org/10.3102/0034654308325693

Jennings, P. A., Snowberg, K. E., Coccia, M. A., & Greenberg, M. T. (2011). Improving classroom learning environments by cultivating awareness and resilience in education (CARE): Results of two pilot studies. *Journal of Classroom Interactions, 46*, 27–48.

Jennings, P. A., Turksma, C., & Brown, R. (2015). *Cultivating Awareness and Resilience in Education (CARE for Teachers) facilitators manual*. Garrison, NY: Garrison Institute.

Kemeny, M. E., Foltz, C., Cavanagh, J. F., Giese-Davis, J., Jennings, P. A., Rosenberg, E. L., . . . Ekman, P. (2012). Contemplative/emotion training reduces negative emotional behavior and promotes prosocial responses. *Emotion, 12*, 338–350. http://dx.doi.org/10.1037/a0026118

Markow, D., Macia, L., & Lee, H. (2013). *The MetLife survey of the American teacher: Challenges for school leadership*. New York, NY: Metropolitan Life Insurance Company.

Milkie, M. A., & Warner, C. H. (2011). Classroom learning environments and the mental health of first grade children. *Journal of Health and Social Behavior, 52*, 4–22. http://dx.doi.org/10.1016/j.cpr.2013.05.00510.1177/0022146510394952

Montgomery, C., & Rupp, A. A. (2005). A meta-analysis for exploring the diverse causes and effects of stress in teachers. *Canadian Journal of Education/Revue Canadienne De L'Éducation, 28*, 458–486.

Oberle, E., & Schonert-Reichl, K. A. (2016). Stress contagion in the classroom? The link between classroom teacher burnout and morning cortisol in elementary school students. *Social Science and Medicine, 159*, 30–37. http://dx.doi.org/10.1016/j.socscimed.2016.04.031

Pianta, R. C., La Paro, K., & Hamre, B. K. (2008). *Classroom assessment scoring system (CLASS) manual: K-3*. Baltimore, MD: Paul H. Brookes Publishing Company.

Roeser, R. W. (2016). Processes of teaching, learning, and transfer in mindfulness-based interventions (MBIs) for teachers: A contemplative educational perspective. In K. Schonert-Reichl & R. Roeser (Eds.), *The handbook of mindfulness in education: Emerging theory, research, and programs* (pp. 133–148). New York, NY: Springer-Verlag.

Roeser, R. W., Skinner, E., Beers, J., & Jennings, P. A. (2012). Mindfulness training and teachers' professional development: An emerging area of research and practice. *Child Development Perspectives, 6*, 167–173. doi: 10.1111/j.1750–8606.2012.00238.x

Schonert-Reichl, K. A., Oberle, E., Lawlor, M. S., Abbott, D., Thomson, K., Oberlander, T. F., & Diamond, A. (2015). Enhancing cognitive and social-emotional development through a simple-to-administer mindfulness-based school program for elementary school children: A randomized controlled trial. *Developmental Psychology, 51*, 52–66. doi: 10.1037/a0038454

Schussler, D. L., Jennings, P. A., Sharp, J. E., & Frank, J. L. (2016). Improving teacher awareness and well-being through CARE: A qualitative analysis of the underlying mechanisms. *Mindfulness, 7*, 130–142. doi: 10.1007/s12671-015-0422-7

Sharp, J. E., & Jennings. P. A. (2016). Strengthening teacher presence through mindfulness: What educators say about the Cultivating Awareness and Resilience in Education (CARE) program. *Mindfulness, 7*, 209–218. doi: 10.1007/s12671-015-0474-8

Skinner, E., & Beers, J. (2016). Mindfulness and teachers' coping in the classroom: A developmental model of teacher stress, coping, and everyday resilience. In K. Schonert-Reichl & R. Roeser (Eds.), *The Handbook of mindfulness in education: Emerging theory, research, and programs* (pp. 133–148). New York, NY: Springer-Verlag.

Sutton, R. E., & Wheatley, K. F. (2003). Teachers' emotions and teaching: A review of the literature and directions for future research. *Educational Psychology Review, 15*, 327–358. doi: 10.1023/A:1026131715856

Valli, L., & Buese, D. (2016). The changing roles of teachers in an era of high-stakes accountability. *American Educational Research Journal, 44*, 519–558.

Wethington, E. (2000). Contagion of stress. *Advances in Group Processes, 17*, 229–253.

Chapter 19

"Wellness Works in Schools"
The practice and research of a mindfulness program in urban middle schools

Cheryl T. Desmond, Wynne Kinder, Laurie B. Hanich, and Obioram C-B Chukwu

Youth in underserved, urban communities may be at risk for a host of negative achievement and psychosocial outcomes. This may include, but not be limited to, social-emotional difficulties, behavior problems, and poor academic performance that are the byproduct of chronic environmental stressors. Mindfulness has the potential to lessen anxiety, promote social skills, and improve academic performance through the use of meditation, coping, and mindful awareness strategy instruction. Recent research has shown a convergence of findings from correlational studies, clinical interventions, and experimental studies of mindfulness which show that mindfulness is positively associated with cognitive outcomes, socio-emotional skills and psychological well-being (Keng, Smoski, & Robins, 2011). Yet, much of the research to date has been limited to adults or youth in suburban schools.

Wynne Kinder begins this chapter with a discussion of Wellness Works in Schools (WWiS), a mindfulness-based program in Lancaster, Pennsylvania, United States, which is designed to motivate, educate, and support students, teachers, and families in developing the mental, emotional, physical, and social competencies needed to handle life's challenges. In the rest of the chapter, the research team of Desmond, Hanich, and Chukwu reports on their investigation of the effectiveness of WWiS, specifically with urban youth from a public school, grades 6–8, in 2008 through 2011. Ninety percent of the children of the school received free or reduced lunch (to qualify, the annual income of a family of four must fall below $24,500), over 90 per cent were Latino or African American, 24 per cent required special needs' services; approximately 30 per cent were identified as English language learners; and approximately seven percent were identified as homeless (Council of Chief State School Officers, 2009).

Description of Wellness Works in Schools (WWiS)

"Why didn't you tell me your parents taught classes that help people manage stress?" asked my school principal on Monday morning after she attended a weekend mindful awareness training at our local hospital. Midge and Rick Kinder, had led adult programming in the community for years under the name of Mindful Yoga. At the time, I, Wynne Kinder, their daughter, was teaching fifth grade in a large urban school on the south side of Lancaster, Pennsylvania.

My answer to her first question was, "Well, they have been coming in as volunteers and working with me and then with some of my students in small groups. I just figured their volunteering was based on student need and was big as it would get."

Her follow-up question set the mindfulness in education field in Lancaster, Pennsylvania, into motion. "Can they come here and work with whole classrooms of students too?"

"Sure." I made the call.

Out of that brief inquiry, as well as a professional discussion about the needs of students and teachers (and administrators) at our school, came a shift to prioritize instructional time for self-care practices. Until then mindful awareness practices (MAPs) were typically only offered as an intervention for adults wanting to manage stress. In 2001 Kinder Associates established Wellness Works in Schools (WWiS), a MAPs program designed as a developmentally- appropriate and comprehensive series for urban intermediate students (ages 9–12). The weekly classroom sessions included attention training (chimes), sensory experiences (noticing breath and subtleties in the body), mindful movement (increasing regulation and releasing stress), balance practice, and guided rest. The thread that tied session concepts together were tools (mindful in nature and self-care in relevance).

The urban school district then hired WWiS to provide MAPs instruction each week for 50-minute lessons in each of the fourth- and fifth-grade elementary classrooms. Teachers, including myself, were encouraged to sit near the front and fully participate with the students. The outcomes were both small and significant that first year. Teachers would informally survey the cafeteria in an attempt to identify which groups had participated in WWiS during the morning. A few of us would gather in the middle of the large space and look for a chilled-out teacher with a calm-looking class. We often chose accurately.

While such anecdotal evidence was exciting, it wasn't until that spring when both fourth- and fifth-grade students took standardized tests that we had formal evidence. Fourth graders scored significantly higher than in previous years and fifth graders helped the school reach its state goal of annual yearly progress (AYP). There was little doubt among staff members that MAPs had contributed to these optimistic outcomes.

While the program initially targeted stressed out students and staff in an urban elementary school, it has expanded over the years. This work has moved into the wider central Pennsylvania community and has been adapted for a broader range of students' needs. In fact it grew so quickly that the Kinders needed support to meet the weekly demands in local schools. I didn't hesitate to provide assistance.

My personal practice had supported me through years of challenging moments in my own classroom. It made sense to shift my 15-year teaching career to a new phase. I believed that I could make a difference by taking WWiS into other children's lives as well. I retired as a teacher in the school district and joined my parents as a full time WWiS instructor in 2004.

Our avenues into schools were opening notably within the special needs community. "Special needs" defined in a more traditional sense, refers to students who may "require a special setting or supports." We have spent much of our time in school-based classrooms: learning support, emotional support, autistic support and multiple-disability settings, during instructional time. Additionally, we have worked with a great many other special-needs populations who require accommodations and adaptations that are more specific to their needs, settings and backgrounds. These groups may include, but are not limited to school-to-work program, night school /summer school, life skills, visual, auditory, sensory, social skills, speech and language support, traumatic brain injury (tbi), anti-bullying program, sexual assault recovery, LGBTQIA youth, and refugee support.

As of 2016, the number of students and teachers reached 11,000 young people and 1,500 teachers and staff since inception of the program. Educational foundations, special education departments, school improvement budgets, local, state and federal grants, and community partners supported our efforts in the schools. Measurement of its impact came through a venture grant from the Lancaster Osteopathic Health Foundation, and from an eager middle school staff and Millersville University. In 2008, we, the Kinders, approached Cheryl Desmond, professor and researcher at Millersville University, to act as the grant evaluator. She had taken mindfulness classes with my parents in 2004–2005 and was knowledgeable about our work.

Having observed my own students as nervous fifth graders and having moved onto the middle school with trepidation, I knew that sixth-grade students are in a critical phase of life and school experience. We received training to support them through the daunting transition to the middle grades. Success over time requires learning a new means of independence and an increased responsibility during their next six years in secondary school. While the transition from the more nurturing approach of the elementary school culture comes naturally, for so many more it causes stress. Sixth grade was the perfect target group for the intervention.

For the WWiS program we created a curriculum called The Mindful Tool Kit (MTK), introducing concepts and skills in metaphors that represent what intrinsic tools students might already possess. The MTK has grown out of 16 years of teaching mindfulness and recognizing that we all have tools inside to fix or strengthen our responses to life. WWiS uses actual "tools" as tangible metaphors to represent the mindful skills that are teachable, learnable and practicable. Young people can begin to grasp the meaning of metaphors around fourth grade; so the MTK is accessible to fourth- through eighth-grade students. The formal program is anticipated that it will be published in the near future. There will also be a high school version ready for teachers to teach in their classrooms in 2018.

The developmentally appropriate content in Table 19.1 is based on the MTK.

Samples practices are included in Table 19.2

Table 19.1 The Mindful Tool Kit

Lesson Name and Tool	Tangible Metaphor	Description of Tool
Mindful Tool Kit	Tool Kit	We introduce the concept that personal tools are inside each of us and the purpose of these tools is to assist us in taking really good care of ourselves. This weekly program teaches us all about our own tools, the skills/tools we can practice using and the strength we gain by practicing together as well as on our own.
Strength of Mind	Flashlight/ Chimes	Our quality of attention can determine our ability to manage ourselves as well as the world around us. Our attention can change and in fact get stronger over time. We explore the science of attention, the habits of our own attention and the possibilities of using attention to increase awareness. The *flashlight of attention* helps us recognize what attention might look like (scattered, settled, wandering, focused), the chimes add an auditory expression of attention.
Posture Outside – Emotions Inside	Posture Cards	Our posture can express how we feel, affect how we feel, and possibly even change how we feel. We use two opposite seated postures (slumped and alert) drawn on cards to inspire discussion and understanding of what we see and feel when sitting in certain ways. Then we practice mindful movement that enhances our awareness of how the body affects emotions.

(Continued)

Table 19.1 (Continued)

Lesson Name and Tool	Tangible Metaphor	Description of Tool
Power of the Breath	Expanding Sphere	Specific ways of breathing can have an immediate impact on thoughts and emotions. We can assess our own internal landscape just by noticing breath patterns. We can also shift that landscape with the breath. The expanding sphere (breathing ball) allows us to experience (feel and see) that we can regulate our breath and notice regulation inside.
Self-regulation	Faucet	An invaluable tool at every age and stage is one's ability to transition from one activity to another, from one emotion to another, based on what we notice in ourselves and in our environment. A group-generated story related to water faucets and the ways that each of us responds to situations helps us to better understand a given situation and to value regulating our own behavior.

Table 19.2. Sample practices

Attention Training and Mindful Movement	Purpose or Goal of Practice	Guided Instruction
Belly Breath	Somatically take note of attention focusing on sensations in the core of the body while breathing.	Both open palms rest on belly (near navel). As the body breathes, notice the subtle sensations present in the lower core. In breath and out breath generate different movement. Notice that, without judgment, just notice.
Bobble Head	With attention on our own bodies, we can move, stretch and pause, based purely on what we notice, for ourselves. Practice choosing what's best for ourselves, in each moment.	Sit tall. Be still and relaxed there, like a mountain. Practice choice -based on what your body tells you to do. Lift and lower chin, as much or as little as you choose. As slow or as quickly as you choose. Pause or stop whenever you choose. Turn side to side, then tilt and finally, gently circle – as you choose. Stop and rest.
Lifting Breath	Practice regulating our own movement. Match movement with our own breath and pace, in our own way.	Your body can be tall like a building – strong and calm at the same time. Palms can be up with backs of hands on tops of thighs. Raise one hand with inhale, maybe fill to shoulder height (or so), pause when full. Flip hand to slowly exhale down again. Repeat with other hand. Try both as well. Repeat a few times with natural breath. Maybe one more time with slow-motion exhale. Rest when finished.

Miss, I was in those classes at the middle school back in the day. You brought a tool box, bells and a flashlight. Remember? We learned that elevator thing (mindful movement with breath) to use when we needed to get control again. I remember.

Jose, age 19, working at local restaurant

Research on the Wellness Works in Schools program

When Midge and Wynne Kinder asked me to serve as the grant evaluator for the WWiS program that Wynne was teaching in an urban school, I, Cheryl Desmond was intrigued and interested. My own university research and teaching background in urban education and my personal experience taking mindful yoga with the Kinders prompted me to accept their request.

As I observed WWiS's classes, I saw how the children used interactive speech as a tool to understand their behaviors and used physical-mindfulness movements to learn new responses to stressful situations. I realized that Vygotsky's social-cognitive theory was applicable to their instruction. Vygotsky believed that children developed within an influential social-historical context and that speech played an essential role in their adaption to, and their control of, that environment (Vygotsky, 1978). The MTK, implemented by the WWiS teachers, provided activities for the children to interpret and express their emotions and their responses to conflicts verbally and to engage in physical movements to practice their new behaviors. I was also impressed by the teachers' use of actual tools as metaphors to support the children's changes in behaviors.

For the grant evaluation, I created a numerical, observational rating scale that monitored the individual changes in physical, social, and emotional behaviors of six children in grades 6–8 that I observed during two sets of seven to nine MTK lessons over a six-month period, October 2008 through early May 2009. Wynne Kinder and a second WWiS teacher taught the lessons. (This research with the rating scale is documented in the unpublished Osteopathic Foundation report and is available electronically upon request.)

The two classrooms in the urban middle school in the district where Wynne had previously taught at the elementary level, included children with special needs who each were identified through the district's psychologists' testing as either a child with emotional-behavioral needs or a child with academic learning needs. Three students in each of the two different classrooms participated in the study. The first classroom consisted of 17–20 students who were identified as learning support students. The second classroom consisted of 11 students who were a combined group of students identified as emotional-behavioral support students and learning support students. I had initially observed each classroom once to script the teaching instruction and students' behaviors I observed. From this observation, I developed the rating scale, based on this observation and young adolescent behavioral characteristics (Caskey & Anfara, 2007). I decided that I could observe three children in each class and designed the scale as a checklist to note each student's behaviors.

The rating scale identified seventeen behaviors: five behaviors that were identified as cognitive responses; eight behaviors as physical responses; and four behaviors, as social responses. The behavior indicators were generalized to allow for observations of different lessons. At timed intervals of two to three minutes, a student received a check mark on his/her individual rating instrument for the behaviors that I had observed. Fifteen of the seventeen behaviors were indicators of a positive self-regulating behavior and two were indicators of a negative behavior I had observed in the previous WWiS classes I observed. The negative behaviors were subtracted from each student's total number of checkmarks, and became the individual child's frequency rating for each lesson. The scale also included a section to note other specific behaviors that were not on the scale, for instance, nail biting.

Two of the learning support students consistently received the highest number of positive checkmarks. The third student, who received emotional support, showed scores that improved significantly from the first to the second lesson observation. She maintained high frequencies of positive responses for the remainder of the observations. The fourth student, also an emotional support student, showed a high need for social interaction with her peers; her nervous habits of nail biting and nametag chewing interfered at times with her ability to perform at a high level of frequency ratings for her social behaviors. Her cognitive and physical behaviors maintained high ratings throughout the observations. The fifth student, a learning support student, showed measurable improvement in his number of positive behavior check marks over the course of six months. By my last observation, he was able to attend to directions and respond to the teacher directions and tasks. The sixth student, an emotional support student, whose negative behaviors in his regular classroom required the presence of a therapeutic support person throughout his school day and had resulted in a number of school suspensions demonstrated the most improvement in the rating of his behaviors over the six months. By observation eight, he was the model student for the class and was actively and positively engaged in all aspects of the lesson. His frequency ratings for cognitive, physical, and social behaviors were at the highest point value on the rating scale for the last lesson.

For each of the six students observed, the MTK lessons provided the opportunity to sustain/reinforce or improve their skills of self-regulation and self-awareness. The WWiS teachers offered calming practices and their nonjudgmental, quiet redirecting or assistance with the instructional tasks provided the opportunity for a student to redirect and discontinue negative behaviors. For the sixth student, the changes in behavior were most dramatic. His substantial improvement supported research findings by Flook et al (2010), which concluded that the strongest changes in self-regulation occur in students who have the most difficulty when they begin directed lessons on MAPs. Nonetheless, my research was limited by the small sample of students I had observed, by the potential of my biases regarding student behaviors, and by the absence of data on whether the changes in students' self-regulation transferred to their behaviors in the special needs classroom with their full-time teachers.

Considering the encouraging results in the first study, I decided that a randomized, control study would be much stronger and more scientifically reliable and valid research. In summer 2009, Midge Kinder, gave me copies of two unpublished articles by Smalley et al (2009) and Flook et al. (2010) on MAPs and executive function that she had received through Kaiser-Greenland, one of the co-authors of both papers. Both studies used the externally validated Behavior Rating Inventory on Executive Functions (BRIEF). I decided to ground my research in their methodology and to do so, I began extensive research on executive functions from both scientists' and educators' research on brain behaviors.

As defined by Gioia, Isquith, Guy, & Kenworthy (2000) and Gioia & Isquith (2004) in the BRIEF manual, executive functions are a collection of processes that are responsible for guiding, directing and managing cognitive, emotional, and behavioral functions, particularly during active novel problem solving. Psychometric properties of the BRIEF are strong (internal consistencies .80-.98). The BRIEF assesses eight domains of EF: 1) inhibiting, 2) shifting, 3) emotional control, 4) initiating, 5) working memory, 6) planning and organizing, 7) organizing of materials, and 8) monitoring. Two broad composites are also totaled across the eight domains: The Behavioral Regulation Index and Metacognition Index; these two indices are then combined to yield an overall Global Executive Composite. The Behavioral Regulation Index is comprised of inhibit, shift, and emotional control subscales and the Metacognition Index is comprised of the initiate, working memory, plan/organize, organization, and monitor subscales. Lower t-scores on the BRIEF are measures of higher levels of EF behaviors.

For the second study on the effects of WWiS's MKT instruction with urban young adolescents, I designed a randomized control study on the executive functions (EF) of 52 sixth-grade students, ages 11–12 years, in the same urban, middle school as in the previous study. I asked my colleague, Laurie Hanich, to assist with the analysis of the BRIEF's quantitative data. The second study investigated whether a student's behaviors developed in the WWiS sessions transferred to the behaviors observed by a student's teacher in the regular classroom whereas the previous study had been conducted solely in the WWiS classroom.

From a numerically coded list of the 52 sixth-grade students, ages 11–12, whose parents had provided permission to participate in the study, the school principal blindly and randomly assigned 26 students to the experimental group and 26 students to the control group. The experimental group of students received WWiS instruction for 45 minutes, once a week, for a total of ten weeks over a period of three months, beginning the first week in November 2009 and finishing in mid-January 2010. The school district had limited the funding for ten weeks of WWiS instruction due to district finances. Fifteen students persisted in the experimental group and completed all sessions of the ten-week study. The other eleven students in the initial experimental group attended six or fewer treatment sessions due to tardiness, absenteeism, or participation in specials such as chorus, and so forth.

The 26 control students had ten sessions of independent reading supervised by a teacher but received no direct instruction. The core (communication arts, mathematics, science, and social studies) classroom teachers released both groups of students from their respective homeroom periods to participate in the WWiS class or the independent reading class, but were not informed as to which group a student was assigned.

The core classroom-homeroom teachers (n = 8) for each of the 52 children's core content areas completed two BRIEF instruments for each of the control and experimental students who were in their respective homeroom classrooms, immediately before and following the ten-week period. On the BRIEF teacher form, items were scored on a three-point scale indicating whether the behavior was observed "never (3)," "sometimes (2)," or "often (1)." Raw scores on the BRIEF scale were converted in the BRIEF manual to t-scores prior to our data analysis.

The primary data analytic procedures used repeated measures analysis of variance (RMANOVA) and multiple regression. A common problem for intervention studies that require participants to undergo multiple treatment sessions is the potential loss of participants over time. We used an imputation procedure to include the data for eleven students in the experimental group who attended six or fewer treatment sessions due to tardiness and absenteeism to garner all available data. Using SPSS version 18, we computed twenty imputations for each of the BRIEF variables.

First, Laurie, conducted independent t-tests to determine that there were not any significant differences between the experimental and control groups on initial baseline measures of EF. Results indicated comparable levels of performance between the experimental and control group participants on all subscales of the BRIEF on pre-test measures ($p > .05$). Next, Laurie did multivariate analysis of variance (MANOVA) with group as a between-subjects factor (experimental and control), including the eight domains of executive functions as defined by the BRIEF and time as a within-subjects factor were conducted to examine group by time effects. None of the analyses revealed a significant main effect of group, with the exception of the shift subscale, $F(1,39) = 5.46$, $p < .05$, nor a significant main effect of time. There was no significant time by group interactions (all $p > .05$). There were also no significant interaction terms for any of the outcome variables with regard to the Index or Composite measures. Interaction terms among the eight domains that measure EF behaviors were examined. Significant interaction between Global Executive Composite pre-test score and group membership for predicting EF difference scores occurred for Shift ($\beta = -0.83$, $p < .05$); $\beta = -0.83$, $p < .05$); that is, children in the experimental group showed greater improvement in their EF skill, shifting or transitioning from one task to another, than children in the control group. The other subscales did not yield significant group by time interactions: Inhibit ($\beta = 0.14$, $p > .05$), Emotional Control ($\beta = -0.43$, $p > 05$), Initiate ($\beta = 0.13$, $p >. 05$), Working Memory ($\beta = -0.43$, $p > .05$), Plan/Organize ($\beta = -0.28$, $p > .05$), Organization of Materials ($\beta = -0.27$, $p > .05$), and Monitor ($\beta = 0.26$, $p >. 05$).

In addition to the significant interaction that occurred for Shift for children in the experimental group, the pre and post mean t-scores on the BRIEF for the experimental group, however, did show a small decline in t-scores for the metacognitive index and for the global executive composite as compared to the control group's t-scores. The scores for the experimental group did not show as a great an increase in the mean t-scores for the behavioral regulation index as the control group (see Figure 19.1). As noted earlier, lower t-scores indicate higher functioning of EF skills. We could hypothesize from this that the control group over the ten weeks of school began to exhibit fewer skills in inhibiting, emotional control and initiating as well as in shifting.

We can conclude that participation in the WWiS program does hold promise for improvements in EF skills to transfer from the MTK classroom to behaviors in the core classrooms as based on the teacher reporting. Since the MTK instruction only occurred once a week for ten weeks, it is possible that regular weekly MTK instruction for the experimental group would result in additional significant BRIEF findings similar to the Flook et al. study and found in the exploratory study that lasted six months.

Chukwu (2015), Desmond's doctoral student, conducted a third quantitative study utilizing Desmond and Hanich's shelf data (2014) and examined teacher ratings on the BRIEF at the item level for each of the urban middle school students. Chukwu's findings confirmed the statistical outcomes of the study. However, in his analysis of the item ratings by the teachers of the pre and post raw scores for the experimental and control groups, he concluded that the entire BRIEF scales may not have been the best test of EF, in that they also included work habits in the classroom. He postulated that if a similar study were to be repeated, it would be better to hypothesize which of the BRIEF items were likely to reflect change and use those raw scores for the study. His findings did show that some BRIEF scales indicated that school interventions can have a positive impact on students' EF.

Conclusions

All three studies contributed to the growing body of research on MAPs for children and youth, and in particular, for children in economically disadvantaged urban middle schools with high populations of ethnic and racial minorities of English language learners and of children with special needs.

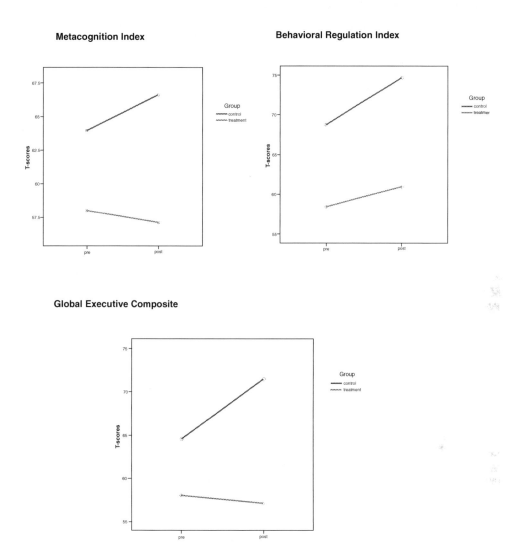

Figure 19.1 Mean t-scores by group and time point (pre and post) for the Metacognition Index, Behavioral Regulation Index and the Global Executive Composite.

Note: Lower t-scores are measures of higher levels of EF behaviors.

Since 2001, Kinders Associates' WWiS program with its MTK has expanded extensively. Several school districts have provided the funding for the program, a testimony to districts' and teachers' field observations that the WWiS's mindfulness instruction has improved children's behaviors.

Future research should also continue to explore other potential applications of MAPs in the classroom and examine practical issues concerning the delivery, implementation, and evaluation of mindfulness-oriented interventions.

Wellness works in schools – resources

Kinder, W. & Kinder, M. (2017). *Peace work: Mindful lessons in self-regulation for a child's early years*. Nashville: Spring House Press.

Kinder, W. (2017). *Mindful choices: A mindful, social emotional learning program for grades 6–8*. Lancaster: Kinder Associates LLC.

Kinder, W. (2017). *Mindful moods: A mindful, social emotional learning program for grades 3–5*. Lancaster: Kinder Associates LLC.

Mindful, Educational Videos by GoNoodle.com – Channels include: *FLOW, Think About It, Maximo, and Blazer Fresh (SEL)* globally reaching millions for students and teachers.

Kinder, W., & Coscia, C. (2015). Mindfulness with special needs children. In C. Willard & A. Saltzman (Eds.), *Teaching mindfulness skills to kids and teens* (pp. 54–67). New York, NY: Guilford Press.

Best Practices for Teaching Yoga in Schools. (2015), contributing editor

Mindful Audio Practices: for the ADHD Mind at MindfullyADD.com

For further information regarding publications/trainings: www.WellnessWorks in Schools.com

References

Caskey, M., & Anfara, V.A. (2007). Research summary: Developmental characteristics of young adolescents. *Association of Middle Level Education*. Retrieved from pdxscholar.library.edu

Chukwu, O.C. (2015). *Analysis of teacher ratings on the Behavior Rating Inventory of Executive Functions (BRIEF) at the item level for urban middle school students included in a study of the effectiveness of a mindful awareness program*. Doctoral dissertation.

Council of Chief State School Officers. (2009). *School matters*. Washington, DC: Council of Chief State School Officers.

Desmond, C.T. (2009). *The effects of mindful awareness teaching practices in the Wellness Works in Schools Program on cognitive, physical and social behaviors of students with learning and emotional disabilities in an urban, low income middle school*. Lancaster, PA: Lancaster Osteopathic Health Foundation. Unpublished report.

Desmond, C.T., & Hanich, L.B. (2014, April). *The effects of a mindful awareness program on the executive functions of early adolescents in an urban middle school*. Paper presented at the annual meeting of the American Educational Research Association, Philadelphia, PA.

Flook, L., Smalley, S.L., Kitil, M.J., Galla, B.M., Kaiser-Greenland, S., Locke, J., Ishijima, E., & Kasari, C. (2010). Effects of mindful awareness practices on executive functions in elementary school children. *Journal of Applied School Psychology*, 26(1), 70–95.

Gioia, G.A., & Isquith, P.K. (2004). Ecological assessment of executive function in traumatic brain injury. *Developmental Neuropsychology*, 25, 135–158.

Gioia, G.A., Isquith, P.K., Guy, S.C., & Kenworthy, L. (2000). *BRIEF behavior rating of inventory of executive function, Professional Manual*. Lutz, FL: Psychological Assessment Resources, Inc.

Keng, S., Smoski, M.J., & Robins, C.J. (2011). Effects of mindfulness on psychological health: A review of empirical studies. *Clinical Psychological Review*, 31(6), 1041–1056.

Smalley, S.L., Flook, L., Kitil, J., Dang, J., Cho, J., Kaiser-Greenland, S., Locke, J., & Kasari, C. (2009). *A mindful awareness practice in pre-k children improves executive function*. Unpublished manuscript. Department of Psychiatry and Biobehavioral Sciences, University of California, Los Angeles, Los Angeles, CA.

Vygotsky, L.S. (1978; 1930). *Mind in Society: The development of higher psychological processes*. Cambridge, MA: Harvard University Press.

Chapter 20

Mindfulness for adolescents
A review of the learning to BREATHE program

Jennifer L. Frank, Kimberly M. Kohler, Lamiya Khan, and Patricia C. Broderick

Program overview

Learning to BREATHE (L2B) (Broderick, 2013) is a mindfulness-based universal prevention program for adolescents designed to be integrated into typical educational settings. The program includes instruction in the practice of mindful awareness and provides opportunities for adolescents to practice skills and discuss experiences in a group setting. L2B is "manual-guided" and includes adaptable lesson plans and instructional materials. The program is organized according to a specific scope and sequence of themes built around the "BREATHE" acronym (*Body, Reflections, Emotions, Attention, Tenderness/Take it As It Is, Habits for a Healthy Mind*, leading to *Empowerment*) and can be delivered in 6, 12, 18, or more sessions by expanding each thematic unit. Each lesson follows a predictable lesson-plan format beginning with a brief mindfulness practice and introduction to the topic, followed by experiential activities to engage students in lesson content and illustrate key ideas, and ending with an opportunity for in-class mindfulness practice. L2B content includes coverage of the core practices of Mindfulness-Based Stress Reduction (MBSR) (Kabat-Zinn, 1990) including body scan, awareness of thoughts and feelings, mindful movement, and loving kindness practice, developmentally adapted for children and adolescents. Although the target audience of the L2B curriculum includes children in the developmental periods of late childhood and adolescence (grades 5–12), the L2B curriculum has also been successfully modified for use with students in their first year of college (Dvořáková et al., 2017).

A unique feature of the L2B program is the fact that instructional objectives have been explicitly linked to some specific learning standards (e.g., in health education and counseling), and thus are designed to be readily integrated with existing school health and social-emotional learning content. As of 2015, the L2B curriculum has been recognized as only one of four mindfulness programs meeting research criteria as an effective supplement to formal Social-Emotional Learning (SEL) programs by the Collaborative for Academic, Social, and Emotional Learning (CASEL, 2015).

The cumulative goal of L2B is to provide developmentally appropriate mindfulness instruction designed to enhance adolescents' emotion regulation, strengthen attentional capacity, reduce stress, cultivate compassion and gratitude, and help students integrate mindfulness as a way to approach experiences in their daily lives. The L2B curriculum, conceptualized by Dr. Patricia Broderick, arose out of a personal interest in the role of rumination and mental stress as risk factors during students' transition from elementary to middle/high school years. Drawing from her formal training in Mindfulness-Based Stress Reduction (MBSR) and a personal mindfulness practice, Dr. Broderick began to implement MBSR practices in a range of school settings, using a small group, targeted approach with varying populations of students. Noting that everyone experiences stress to differing degrees, the critical need for programs to work within the situational demands of the school, and the potential marriage of skills and concepts of MBSR with the social and emotional learning model, Dr. Broderick developed the foundations of L2B as a universal intervention in educational settings. The goal was to acknowledge the role that emotions, attention, self-awareness, and self-management play in student well-being and success during adolescence as well as support and empower adolescents during this transition through mindfulness practice.

L2B is designed to be implemented by a variety of school-based professionals including classroom teachers, school psychologists, counselors, and social workers. Formal introductory and intensive professional development in L2B program implementation is available from program trainers (see http://learning2breathe.org/) and personal instruction in mindfulness practice is widely available from many sources. Mindfulness is more than cognitive understanding. It is a practice of orientating to all experience with openness and compassion, which the teacher needs to embody. Since embodiment of mindfulness is of critical importance for teachers of adult mindfulness programs, it seems reasonable that this is also important when working with children and youth. Although little is known about this from a research perspective, L2B teachers are advised to engage students and build connections through facilitating a supportive classroom environment which focuses on present moment experience, curious investigation, "being" mode rather than "doing" mode, and kindness toward self and others, especially in the face of difficult experiences. To best meet the developmental needs of students, manage classroom behavior, and guide group discussions, program developers recommend that potential implementers also have a strong background and prior experience working with the age/grade of students in the target population. Overall, anecdotal evidence from observations of L2B lessons suggests that greater implementation success is demonstrated when program facilitators have an ongoing personal mindfulness practice, established relationships with students, developmental understanding of students, and training in the L2B program.

Theoretical background

Adolescence is a time of significant physical and cognitive growth, particularly in the area of logical reasoning capacity (American Psychological Association, 2002). It can also be a developmentally challenging time during which heightened emotionality, sensitivity to social information, and underdeveloped emotion regulation skills combine to create a period of heightened risk for development of emotional and/or behavioral problems (Andersen & Teicher, 2008; Dahl, 2004). Adolescents' capacity to cope with stressful events becomes particularly salient during this period, as youth begin to grapple with ill-defined problems of personal identity, romantic relationships, sexual identity, and emerging social value systems. Research has shown that adolescent decision-making is compromised when situations are perceived to be stressful and personal control and agency is limited (Arnsten & Shansky, 2004; Smith, Chein, & Steinberg, 2013); therefore, young people who are better equipped to manage these developmentally normative sources of stress have a distinctive advantage over those who are not. We have argued elsewhere (Broderick & Frank, 2014) that the mindfulness practices taught within the L2B curriculum may exert their effect by helping adolescents cultivate *distress tolerance*, or the general capacity to persist in goal directed behavior despite experiencing psychological distress (Daughters, Sargeant, Bornovalova, Gratz, &

Lejuez, 2008) during this pivotal time period. Through engagement in mindfulness practices, students learn to be more attentive to present moment experiences, which include awareness of both pleasant and unpleasant emotions as they arise. This awareness, if accompanied by attitudes of nonjudgment, openness, and acceptance, is a first step towards the cultivation of distress tolerance for difficult emotions like anger and sadness. These skills build resilience and, in turn, serve as key emotion regulation strategies which can be used to moderate affective experiences to meet the demands of different situations and achieve personal and learning goals during times of heightened stress (Campos, Frankel, & Camras, 2004; Eisenberg & Spinrad, 2004; Op't Eynde & Turner, 2006). Over time, the resulting greater levels of awareness and control over emotional responsiveness may lead to a decrease in negative affect and reductions to rumination and somatic symptoms. Together, these benefits may help to protect adolescents against the potential risks of developing internalizing and externalizing problems linked to emotion regulation deficits, and reduce overall reactivity to stress known to impair executive functions including attentional control, working memory, and problem-solving capacity (Blair, 2002; Arnsten, 1998; Liston, McEwen, & Casey, 2009).

Summary of research on effectiveness

The effectiveness of L2B on outcomes relevant to student learning and social-emotional well-being have been established across several empirical studies. The earliest pilot study of L2B conducted by Broderick and Metz (2009) with 12th-grade students found significant reductions in negative affect and concurrent increases in perceived sense of calm, relaxation, and self-acceptance among adolescents who participated in L2B compared to controls. Within the treatment group, substantial improvements in self-reported emotion regulation skills and reductions in somatic symptoms (e.g., aches/pains, overtiredness) were noted as well.

A matched-control study conducted by Metz et al. (2013) found that a universal sample of general education high school students who participated in L2B reported significantly lower levels of perceived stress, somatic complaints, and higher levels of perceived self-regulatory efficacy as compared to controls. Specifically, program participants reported improvements on several dimensions of emotion regulation including overall emotional awareness, access to emotion regulation strategies, emotional clarity, and overall capacity for regulation.

A randomized control study of ethnically diverse at risk youth in an alternative school setting (Bluth, Campo, Pruteanu-Malinici, Reams, Mullarkey, & Broderick, 2016) explored the feasibility and acceptability of the L2B program as compared to an active control group (substance abuse class). Both intervention and control conditions groups met once per week with non-school personnel as facilitators. Results indicated significant post-intervention decreases in depressive symptoms for students in the L2B program as compared to students in the substance abuse class. On measures of acceptability, students initially rated the L2B program as less credible than the substance abuse class and demonstrated a great deal of resistance (i.e., significant behavioral and discipline issues, apathy toward mindfulness and practices). However, as the semester progressed and important adaptations were made (e.g., change to a non-classroom setting, incorporation of more yoga and body scan practices, addition of school personnel during lessons, L2B facilitator participation in other school activities), student rated credibility of L2B increased and surpassed that of the active control, which decreased overall. Qualitative measures showed students wished to continue with L2B as they felt mindfulness helped to alleviate their levels of stress.

Fung, Guo, Jin, Bear, and Lau (2016) examined the efficacy of L2B among ethnic minority Latino and Asian American students in a wait-list randomized controlled trial. Compared to wait-list controls, ethnic minority students reported significant reductions in youth reported internalizing problems and use of expressive suppression in addition to parent-reported reductions in externalizing problems. Eva and Thayer (2017) studied the effectiveness of a six-week L2B course with 17 20-year-old male students of color at risk for school failure. Significant improvements were found at posttest on measures of self-reported self-esteem and perceived stress. Qualitative focus group data identified positive changes in participants' attention-awareness, self-regulation, and positive thinking as important post-intervention outcomes potentially driving quantitative changes.

Two unpublished pilot studies were conducted with fifth-grade students and high school aged males. Flook and Pinger (2011, unpublished) found that fifth-grade participants demonstrated significant within group improvements after L2B in spatial working memory, social competence, and internal locus of control combined with reductions in internalizing symptoms. In another small pilot study with secondary school males in two settings (urban and rural), Potek (2012, unpublished) showed reductions in anxiety for both groups who participated in L2B compared to comparison group students.

More recently, researchers have investigated the efficacy of the L2B program as a potential strategy for mitigating the risk of type II diabetes among female adolescents by reducing depressive symptoms and improving insulin resistance (Shomaker et al., in press). Participants were randomly assigned to either L2B or Cognitive Behavioral Therapy (CBT). Both groups reported increased mindfulness at post-treatment; however, L2B participants were more mindful at the one year follow-up. Participants in the L2B group experienced a greater reduction in depressive symptoms at post-treatment and 6 months as well as a greater decrease in insulin resistance at post-treatment and one year follow-up compared to CBT participants.

Presently, the L2B program is part of a three-year Institute of Education Sciences (IES) RCT study examining the integration of L2B into a public high school health curriculum. Students received either L2B or their regular health classes as part of this study. Overall program-related changes on student self-report measures were not significantly different from control group students. However, those students most at risk for depression, anxiety and substance use did show significant improvement on these variables after L2B compared to similar students in the regular heath classes. Results from measures of executive functioning did show that L2B participants overall exhibited increased attention to task demands and ability to resist distractions, decreased tendency to take risks, increased capacity to resist reflexive responding to stimuli, and greater maintenance of goal-directed behavior compared to students who participated in the regular health classes.

Program structure and organization

Through activities, discussion, and practices, students gain greater understanding of the role that thoughts and emotions play in their lives and learn tools to help manage their day to day emotions and stress. L2B can be used as a stand-alone program or as part of an established curriculum (e.g., health class, advisory periods). Each lesson follows a common format encompassing three main elements: (a) introductory mindfulness practice, brief review of past concepts, and presentation of the new lesson theme; (b) activities that facilitate understanding of the lesson theme; and (c) in-class mindfulness-based practice.

"Scripted," lessons should be presented in a guided discovery format, using approaches that foster inquiry and experiential learning to best meet the developmental and academic needs of students. Throughout the program, adolescent participants are continually engaged in the process of investigating experience, and teachers seek to use student comments and observations, rather than didactic methods, to scaffold understanding. Students participating in the L2B program receive workbooks containing reference content, additional activities, reflective opportunities, and "Tips to Take Away" as well as access to audio files with guided L2B mindfulness practices to foster additional practice outside of the classroom setting.

The setting in which L2B sessions are conducted cannot be overlooked. It is important for facilitators to create a calm environment that supports engagement and attention. Creating such a space in a school setting can be extremely challenging. However, care should be taken to create a space that is as quiet and inviting to students as possible, whether it be within a classroom, library, or auditorium. If at all possible, seating (e.g., chairs, floor cushions, yoga mats) should be configured in a circle, with space to lie down for specific mindful awareness practices.

With the exception of the introductory lesson, each L2B session begins with a short mindful awareness practice (i.e., breath awareness) to help students "check in" with their bodies and orient to the present moment. As students progress through the curriculum, other mindful awareness practices such as mindful movement or a brief body scan may be used as well.

The L2B curriculum covers six central themes, which comprise the BREATHE acronym: (a) **B**ody; (b) **R**eflections (Thoughts); (c) **E**motions; (d) **A**ttention; (e) **T**enderness/Take it as it is; (f) **H**abits for a healthy mind, all leading to **E**mpowerment or gaining the "inner **E**dge" (Broderick, 2013).

The overarching goal of the B or "Body" theme is to encourage students to stop and listen, through mindful awareness practices, to what their body is trying to tell them. During Theme B lessons, students learn through "hands on" activities what mindfulness (versus mindlessness) is, its application in everyday life (e.g., mindful eating, mindful listening) and its potential impact on their health and well-being. Through experiential practices, students begin to recognize the way their bodies hold stress and tension and practice greater awareness of the breath and the body. Breath awareness is a core practice in the L2B curriculum, as students are reminded that the breath is always with them and something they can return to at any time. Students are guided through breath awareness practices, focusing on the benefits of "complete" or deep, belly breathing instead of "shallow" breathing. Another mindful awareness practice used to relax and foster greater attention on the body as a whole is the *Body Scan*. During this practice, students are invited to sit or lie down, following the facilitator's instructions as best they can through the entire practice. The practice begins by inviting students to focus their attention on their breath, then moving attention to throughout the body.

Theme R or "Reflections" introduces how thoughts (or reflections) are just thoughts. Students learn how our minds are filled with "inner self-talk" and how this chatter impacts attention and performance. The relationship between thoughts and feelings is introduced, including how feelings can be experienced as pleasant, unpleasant, or neutral. Students learn how our brains often "retell stories," allowing us to think about and feel the emotions of an event far after it has ended. Students experience how mindfulness can be used to notice and observe thoughts and then let them go instead of getting stuck in thoughts. *Mindfulness of Thoughts* is a practice that cultivates present moment attention. Through this practice, students "see" that although we cannot stop thinking, we can be patient and allow our thoughts to float by like clouds in the sky, water in a stream, or snow in a snow globe. We can simply observe our thoughts and not react to them. The practice begins by focusing on the sensations of their breath. If students are distracted by their thoughts, the breath is used as an anchor as students return to present moment awareness. Some example instructions from the *Mindfulness of Thoughts* practice are as follows:

> *As you sit here watching your breath, you may find yourself thinking about something you did or something you need to do, something that happened to you or something that is going to happen. These are the kinds of thoughts that occur spontaneously in our minds all the time.*
>
> (Broderick, 2013, p. 53, emphasis in original)

> *Your mind is like a revolving door . . . with thoughts moving in and thoughts moving out while you just sit observing them as they come and go . . . bringing your attention back to your breath.*
>
> (Broderick, 2013, p. 54, emphasis in original)

"Emotions" or Theme E focuses on our emotional experience. Students learn how emotions impact our balance, resilience, and general well-being. Through experiential practices, students discover how they can pay attention to and be mindful observers of their feelings, allowing emotions to come and go without acting on them immediately or covering them up. "*Surfing the Waves*," is a practice that allows students to experience unpleasant feelings (i.e., boredom, restlessness) and pleasant feelings (i.e., gratitude) in their body and mind. Students are invited to "sit" with their feelings by observing them rather than reacting to them or covering them up. This practice highlights the importance of being aware of the range of emotions we experience as well as how emotions change in intensity and duration, just like the waves of the ocean. Students learn to "surf" their waves by becoming mindful of their emotions as they build up and fade away, letting go of any that may be harmful by practicing self-compassion. The practice begins by asking students to focus on their breath and any sensations in their body as they sit in silence for two to three minutes. As restlessness and boredom set in, students are invited to explore these experiences without resisting them.

> *Let the feelings of restlessness or boredom be like the waves coming and going. Don't try to block them or get rid of them. Don't try to hold on to them or keep them. See if you can approach them with curiosity. Notice that you don't need to act on them. They are just a kind of energy in the body and mind that you can be curious about. Just focus on the breath. See if you can ride the waves of restlessness or boredom, and notice whether they change. Say to yourself inwardly. . . . I can feel these feelings without covering them up.*
>
> (Broderick, 2013, p. 67, emphasis in original)

The second part of this activity invites students to experience pleasant feelings through the cultivation of gratitude. Just as in the first part of this activity, students are guided to notice how their emotions are like surges of energy that can be observed in their body. By being mindful, students can simply observe their pleasant and unpleasant emotions without judging them (as good or bad) or reacting in some way.

Theme A or "Attention" allows students to see how stress may greatly impact their lives. Students learn important concepts about stress and its effects on the body and mind through various activities. This theme offers the opportunity for teachers to introduce content about stress physiology, if the teacher finds it useful. However, the main goal is for students to begin to understand how bringing awareness to all experiences can help alleviate the impact of chronic stress and foster greater well-being. The practices from themes B, R, and E may be considered focused attention practice. Alternately, the *Mindful Movement* in theme A is an open awareness practice, wherein students are invited to be aware of any thoughts, feelings, and body sensations that come and go during the movement. It is important for students to understand that the movements are not "exercises" or a competition between students, but a means to fully become aware of all experience. Therefore, facilitators should encourage students to be gentle with themselves (i.e., practice non-judgement) as they engage in the movements. Both seated and standing movement practices are provided for use in the classroom as space and time allow. Images of the movements are given in the student workbook for additional reference. The following text illustrates one seated L2B *Mindful Movement* practice:

Seated Tree

Sit with your feet flat on the floor and your hands in your lap. Feel your neck and head balanced on your spine. Your back is straight but not rigid. Inhale and raise both arms above your head, interlacing your fingers together. Exhale slowly and you bend to the right without moving your hips. Breathe deeply while holding the posture as you notice sensations in your body, the movement of your breath, and any thoughts or feelings that might arise. (Repeat on the other side.)

(Broderick, 2013, p. 82, emphasis in original)

Mindful Mini-Movements are also included in the manual for in-between session practice.

"Tenderness" or "Take It As It Is" (Theme T) explores the importance of kindness and compassion for self and others. Students learn how the mind is trainable and how it can help support happiness and well-being. Additionally, students learn how mindful awareness practices nurture greater resilience, health, and wellbeing so that we can take better care of ourselves and those around us. One core practice of this theme is a loving-kindness practice, which offers adolescents a way to practice being kind to themselves and others. Students direct loving-kindness to themselves while inwardly repeating wishes that they be strong, balanced, happy, and peaceful. These wishes are also directed to others through this practice. *A Person Just Like Me* is a variation on a loving-kindness that helps students cultivate compassionate awareness of others in the class by considering their connectedness to others. Six shorter versions of *A Person Just Like Me* are available for use at the end of each theme. These shorter versions apply core themes of each letter to the *Person Just Like Me* practice. An example for the "B" lesson follows:

Before we leave today, let's check in one more time, closing eyes if that's comfortable, and taking a moment to consider each and every person in this class. Whether we shared anything in the group today or not, we all practiced being mindful together. Now bring to mind the image of someone in this room. It could be someone who is a friend or someone you don't know very well.

Consider that:

> *This person, from time to time, has been mindless and on "automatic pilot" in their day to day life . . .*

just like me.

> *This person has felt tension, fatigue, and restlessness in their body . . .*

just like me.

> *So, I wish that this person may be mindful of the simple things in life that can bring them joy. I wish that they be free of tension, fatigue, and discomfort, as much as possible. Because this person is a fellow human being, just like me.*
> (Broderick, 2017, unpublished, emphasis in original)

Theme H or "Habits" explores ways in which students can integrate mindfulness into their daily lives in order to reduce feelings of stress and increase resilience. During Theme H sessions, facilitators review content and practices from previous themes, emphasizing ways students can use them in their day to day experience. This theme also includes various "wrap up" activities, including constructing a mindful quilt, and a closing circle wherein students practice mindful speaking and listening as they share experiences in the L2B course. The workbook page of tips for this lesson offers students "Mindfulness Cues" as an easy reference for ongoing integration of mindful awareness practices. Some tips for students are as follows:

- *Ride in a car or walk with the music turned off to notice your surroundings.*
- *Practice taking a mindful breath before responding to an email or text message, or before answering a question.*
- *When you talk to a friend, really listen. Gently let go of your own thoughts and ideas, and tune in to what the person is saying.*
- *Practice kindness to yourself and others at least once a day.*

(Broderick, 2013, p. 248, emphasis in original)

Summary

Learning to BREATHE is a promising mindfulness-based curriculum for adolescents that provides training in key mindful awareness skills designed to strengthen emotion regulation, inter and intra-personal compassion, distress tolerance, and executive functioning that support classroom learning. The core curriculum provides developmentally appropriate training in several of core practices including body scan, awareness of thoughts and feelings, mindful movement, and loving-kindness/compassion practice. The program itself is manual-guided but designed to be implemented in a flexible manner that is responsive to participant needs. L2B was created from the ground up to be compatible with the routines and practices of authentic school settings, and is intended to be integrated in a complimentary fashion with existing health and/or social-emotional learning programming. Evidence for the potential effectiveness of L2B on student cognitive and social-emotional related outcomes has been established across multiple independent studies. There is converging evidence for the promise of L2B to decrease negative affect and enhance emotion regulation among adolescents of various ethnic backgrounds, to increase some executive functions, to reduce social-emotional risk status, and to improve the physical and psychological health for certain at-risk groups. Although promising, L2B has yet to be subjected to a large randomized control group trial necessary to fully establish evidence for effectiveness. Important empirical questions remain related to the required dosage to achieve program effects, optimal implementation environments, training requirements for facilitators, inter and intra-personal mediators of intervention effects, and program impact on the daily lives and decisions of adolescents.

Suggested online material and resources

Learning to BREATHE Curriculum

Broderick, P.C. (2013) *Learning to Breathe: A mindfulness for adolescents*. Oakland, CA: New Harbinger.

Learning to BREATHE Website:

http://learning2breathe.org/

Schedule of Learning to BREATHE Trainings and Workshops:

http://learning2breathe.org/presentations-and-workshops

Learning to BREATHE Facebook Page:

www.facebook.com/Learning-to-Breathe-274148185959391/

References

Andersen, S. L., & Teicher, M. H. (2008). Stress, sensitive periods and maturational events in adolescent depression. *Trends in Neuroscience, 31*, 183–191.

Arnsten, A. F. T. (1998). Catecholamine modulation of prefrontal cortical cognitive function. *Trends in Cognitive Science, 2*, 436–447.

Arnsten, M. F. T., & Shansky, R. M. (2004). Adolescence: Vulnerable period for stress-induced prefrontal cortical function? *Annals of the New York Academy of Science, 1021*, 143–147.

Blair, C. (2002). School readiness: Integrating cognition and emotion in a neurobiological conceptualization of children's functioning at school entry. *American Psychologist, 57*, 111–127.

Bluth, K., Campo, R. A., Pruteanu-Malinici, S., Reams, A., Mullarkey, M., & Broderick, P. C. (2016). A school-based mindfulness pilot study for ethnically diverse at-risk adolescents. *Mindfulness, 7*, 90–104.

Broderick, P. C. (2013). *Learning to breathe: A mindfulness for adolescents*. Oakland, CA: New Harbinger.

Broderick, P. C., & Frank, J. L. (2014). Learning to BREATHE: An intervention to foster mindfulness in adolescence. *New Directions in Youth Development, 142*, 31–44.

Broderick, P. C., & Metz, S. (2009). Learning to BREATHE: A pilot trial of a mindfulness curriculum for adolescents. *Advances in School Mental Health Promotion, 2*, 35–46.

Campos, J. J., Frankel, C. B., & Camras, L. (2004). On the nature of emotion regulation. *Child Development, 75*, 377–394.

Collaborative for Academic and Social Emotional Learning. (2015). *2015 CASEL Guide: Effective Social and Emotional Leaning Programs – Middle and High School Education*. Retrieved from http://secondaryguide.casel.org/casel-secondary-guide.pdf

Dahl, R. E. (2004). Adolescent brain development: A period of vulnerabilities and opportunity. *Annals of the NY Academy of Science, 1021*, 1–22.

Daughters, S. B., Sargeant, M. N., Bornovalova, M. A., Gratz, K. L., & Lejuez, C. W. (2008). The relationship between distress tolerance and antisocial personality disorder among male inner-city treatment seeking substance users. *Journal of Personality Disorders, 22*, 509–524.

Dvořáková, K., Kishida, M., Li, J., Elavsky, S., Broderick, P. C., Agrusti, M. R., & Greenberg, M. T. (2017). Promoting healthy transition to college through mindfulness training with first-year college students: Pilot randomized controlled trial. *Journal of American College Health, 11*, 1–9.

Eisenberg, N., & Spinrad, T. L. (2004). Emotion-related regulation: Sharpening the definition. *Child Development, 75*, 334–339.

Eva, A. L., & Thayer, N. M. (2017). Learning to BREATHE: A pilot study of a mindfulness-based intervention to support marginalized youth. *Journal of Evidence-Based Complementary & Alternative Medicine*. http://dx.doi.org/10.1177/2156587217696928

Flook, L., & Pinger, L. (2011). *Unpublished pilot study*. Madison, WI: University of Wisconsin, Center for Investigating Healthy Minds.

Fung, J., Guo, S., Jin, J., Bear, L., & Lau, A. (2016). A pilot randomized trial evaluating a school-based mindfulness intervention for ethnic minority youth. *Mindfulness, 7*, 819–828.

Kabat-Zinn, J. (1990). *Full catastrophe living: Using the wisdom of your body and mind to face stress, pain and illness*. Delacorte, NY: Delta Trade.

Liston, C., McEwen, B. S., & Casey, B. J. (2009). Psychosocial stress reversibly disrupts prefrontal processing and attentional control. *Proceedings of the National Academy of Sciences, 106*, 912–917.

Metz, S., Frank, J. L., Reibel, D., Cantrell, T., Sanders, R., & Broderick, P. C. (2013). The effectiveness of the learning to BREATHE program on adolescent emotion regulation. *Research in Human Development, 10*, 252–272.

Op't Eynde, P., & Turner, J. E. (2006). Focusing on the complexity of emotion-motivation issues in academic learning: A dynamical component systems approach. *Educational Psychology Review, 18*, 361–376.

Potek, R. (2012). *Mindfulness as a school-based prevention program and its effect on adolescent stress, anxiety and emotion regulation*. New York, NY: New York University, ProQuest, UMI Dissertations Publishing.

Shomaker, L., Bruggink, S., Pivarunas, B., Skoranski, A., Foss, J., Chaffin, E., Dalager, S., Annameier, S., Quaglia, J., Brown, K., Broderick, P., & Bell, C. (in press). Pilot randomized controlled trial of a mindfulness-based group in adolescent girls at risk for type 2 diabetes with depressive symptoms. *Complementary Therapies in Medicine*.

Smith, A., Chein, J., & Steinberg, L. (2013). Impact of socio-emotional context, brain development, and pubertal maturation on adolescent decision-making. *Hormones and Behavior, 64*, 323–332.

Chapter 21

Audio-guided Mindful-Based Social Emotional Learning (MBSEL) training in school classrooms

The inner explorer program

Jutta Tobias Mortlock

Overview

What if in one generation we could break the vicious cycle of living in despair or poverty, feeling depressed or anxious, abusing drugs or each other in repeated, destructive cycles? Imagine a world where people have awareness and compassion, for themselves and others. Imagine a world where children learn these skills as part of their school education.

For decades, school interventions have included social and emotional learning (SEL) programs, designed to help pupils develop self-management and interpersonal skills such as listening, following instructions, reciprocating collaborative behaviors, and overcoming disagreements (Collaborative for Academic, Social and Emotional Learning, 2005). A particular type of SEL programs in particular, namely those drawing on individuals' ability to pay attention to the here and now with curiosity and kindness (Kabat-Zinn, 2003), have been shown to positively impact children's self-regulation skills (Zoogman et al., 2014) and reduce the negative effects of stress on wellbeing and achievement outcomes (Biegel, 2009; Broderick & Metz, 2009; Mendelson et al., 2010). Such "mindful-based social emotional learning" (MBSEL; Bakosh et al., 2015) interventions have shown promise in helping pupils develop emotion management and social competencies (Kaiser-Greenland, 2010).

In 2011, after nearly two decades of personal mindfulness practice and teaching, Laura Bakosh and lifelong friend, Janice Houlihan, co-founded the non-profit organization Inner Explorer (IE) in the United States to bring daily mindfulness practices to children in schools in time and resource efficient ways. Laura and Janice decided then that they wanted to contribute to laying a mindfulness-based foundation for breaking the vicious cycle of despair, violence, and underachievement.

The audio-guided MBSEL training program featured in this chapter is based on Laura and Janice's work at IE and on Laura's PhD dissertation work researching the effectiveness of audio-guided approaches to mindfulness training. To date, Inner Explorer has been implemented in almost 7000 classrooms in almost 1000 schools across 45 U.S. states, enabling over 180,000 pupils to practice mindfulness during their daily school routine.

How this story began

Laura began practicing mindfulness in 1993 while working for GE Healthcare, as a way to manage the stress of work and travel. In 2001 while working at GE Headquarters in Wisconsin in the United States, she decided to bring in a Mindfulness-Based Stress Reduction (MBSR) trainer to offer classes for her team and provide tools for daily practice. Over the next several years, as individuals engaged in regular mindfulness practice, Laura and other members of the GE leadership team observed that business results soared, along with team productivity and morale.

Witnessing the beneficial effect of daily mindfulness practice in a workplace context, Laura decided to investigate whether mindfulness could be taught to children with similar success. Laura trained as an MBSR instructor at the University of Massachusetts, Center for Mindfulness in 2007. She began teaching an adapted MBSR program in classrooms and after school centers, while in graduate school to get a PhD investigating effective ways to bring mindfulness to schools. Janice joined Laura in her quest to bring technology-enabled mindfulness training to school children, focusing on program development using her expertise in Education and as a MBSR trainer.

Through their initial mindfulness training experience in schools, it emerged that daily practice was the single biggest predictor of positive outcomes, yet this was also the most difficult to foster with the traditional approach to teaching mindfulness. Weekly or biweekly training did not provide enough formal practice time for children to integrate and sustain these skills and aptitudes. In addition, Laura and Janice found that the majority of children exposed to mindfulness training were unable to commit to a regular practice on their own.

These insights led Laura and Janice to create a series of audio-guided programs that require only five to ten minutes a day. Through a series of scientific experiments, Laura and her team demonstrated that participating in these programs is linked to significantly higher grades and test scores and fewer behavior events (cf. Bakosh et al., 2015).

How this MBSEL program brings benefits to school classrooms

We provide an outline of the program as well as a summary of the empirical research examining its effectiveness below. In addition, we argue in this chapter that this MBSEL program is innovative in two additional ways.

First, the design of such brief mindfulness practices make it possible for mindfulness training to fit into a normal school day without extending or amending the class curriculum. Second, the automated and pre-recorded delivery mode requires very little teacher training, thus dramatically lowering the human and financial resource constraints required traditionally for implementing a mindfulness program in schools.

Based on the evidence we present in this chapter, we propose that this MBSEL program can significantly predict an increase in student achievement in schools, delivered in a curriculum-neutral and teacher-independent way. In the sections that follow, we outline each of these points in detail.

Program structure

MBSEL program purpose and content

Inner Explorer's MBSEL programs are designed for children and student audiences in school settings. The underlying assumption for creating these programs was that students who practice audio-guided mindfulness exercises each school day would become more mindful, and thus experience increased emotional regulation, which in turn promotes academic attainment, as has been shown in both student and adult studies (Huppert & Johnson, 2010).

Thus, the goals of the program are to enhance social and behavioral aptitude, advance academic performance, improve classroom behavior, and ultimately help close the achievement gap between students from mainstream social groups and their counterparts from minority and disadvantaged backgrounds.

The MBSEL programs are an audio-guided series of mindfulness practices with four age- and-stage appropriate training courses, delivered by short audio-guided mindfulness training tracks and offering students and teachers from a diverse participant population the opportunity to consistently participate in mindfulness practices each school day without impacting teaching operations.

All four programs are based on the extensively researched and world-renowned MBSR protocol originally developed by Jon Kabat-Zinn and colleagues at the Center for Mindfulness at the University of Massachusetts Medical School.

Each program contains 90 audio-guided practices. The age stages have been designed in the context of the United States state school system:

- Exploring Me (Pre-K/1st grade) – Available in English and Spanish
- Exploring Originality – (elementary school 2nd–4th grades) – Available in English and Spanish
- Exploring Potential (middle school 5th–7th grades) – Available in English
- Exploring Relevance (high school 8th–12th grades) – Available in English

Each track is five to ten minutes long, dependent on age, and includes a one-minute song for the younger students and two-minute journaling integration exercise for the older students.

The content closely follows MBSR, however has been adapted to a child audience, and begins with direct instruction and lessons that reflect and encourage the competencies associated with SEL. While the MBSEL program was modeled on the MBSR protocol, the guided audio tracks facilitate a daily formal mindful awareness practice. With the MBSEL audio format, basic didactic information is included throughout the series, covering how to sit, why to practice, and what to expect from the practice.

Consistent with MBSR, concepts including awareness of senses, thoughts, and emotions are integrated into the daily recordings, as well as periods of silence, relaxation, and breathing practices. Through the series, students are guided to practice both focused-awareness and open-awareness exercises. Focused-awareness exercises include sequences on the five senses, relaxation, and body scan, as well as identifying and labeling thoughts and emotions. A mindful movement component is included in several tracks throughout the series, but all movements are done while students are seated. Open-awareness exercises included sequences on identifying and noticing how thoughts and emotions come into and then leave the field of awareness, and the subsequent flow of this process.

Also consistent with both MBSR and SEL, self-awareness, self-control, and social awareness concepts are woven within the 90 tracks, as well as responsible decision making and core values including kindness and gratitude (Collaborative for Academic, Social and Emotional Learning, 2005; Kabat-Zinn, 2003).

The program is designed to allow students to consistently explore what is happening inside themselves so they become familiar with their inner experiences. As an example, a student who has consistently experienced how it feels to be angry and has brought awareness to how the body and thought patterns respond to this emotion may be more likely to identify anger when it comes up, and choose productive ways to respond. The language and examples were developed specifically for children in the relevant age group.

The audio-guided series includes:

(1) breathing and focusing practices meant to help students attend to their direct experiences, leading to self-awareness;
(2) relaxation and sense awareness practices that reduce the flight-or-fight response – interrupting auto-pilot reactivity, leading to improved self-management;
(3) thought and emotion awareness practices that create space between the stimulus and response, fostering responsible decision-making;
(4) gratitude, kindness and forgiveness practices, towards self and others, connects students to the larger community.

How the program is implemented in schools

The learning environment for Inner Explorer's program begins when teachers view a 30-minute training video or participate in in-person training or a webinar; yet they aren't required to prepare or present any portion of the mindfulness training lessons to their pupils.

To run the program, the teacher needs to access the pre-recorded audio materials. If the classroom has internet access and a sound system, then teachers can simply log on to the IE secure website and press "play" for a prerecorded audio-guided practice that leads both teacher and students in a daily lesson.

If the classroom has no internet access, then teachers need a classroom kit including a preloaded iPod MP3 player with 90 MBSEL program tracks, a docking station with speakers, Teachers' Guide, student journaling notebooks, and a few additional classroom tools to use in support of the program, for example a gazing stone.

The teachers are in control of when to run the MBSEL program track, either during transition time or during a regular daily slot, such as directly after lunch. Because the program tracks are short and designed to be run between normal classroom sessions, the teachers are invited to take part in each session as well as the pupils and practice mindfulness with their class.

This is a relatively straightforward process, because the series of mindfulness training tracks include various sitting and breathing practices as well as awareness of senses (sound, touch, taste, smell, and sight, along with kinesthetic, balance and others), thoughts, emotions, cause and effect, connection, and so forth.

The program also includes "Body Scan" practices, as well as "Comfortably Quiet" practices where students and teachers participate in increasing times of silence (with limited narration). This helps both pupils and teachers experience mindfulness without the support of the audio-guided program, making it more likely that they can "take it with them" wherever they are – so they can become grounded in self-awareness and self-control.

Each series is played sequentially from Practice 1 through Practice 90. The series can be repeated throughout the year, simply by starting again at Practice 1 after Practice 90 has been played.

During the last two minutes of each ten-minute recording for the older students, participants are instructed, while still quiet, to take out their journals and write or draw about their experience with the practice that day in order to integrate any insights. This is done specifically to keep the overall time within the ten-minute target in place of group sharing that forms part of the standard MBSR protocol.

According to teachers who have already participated in the program, a journaling time of two minutes was adequate on most days for students to complete the exercise. On the few occasions when students requested more time, the classroom teachers could decide if another minute or two could be accommodated given the curriculum schedule that day.

What makes this program innovative?

Because of its technology-based design and de livery format, several unique features of this program make it particularly innovative.

First, unlike traditional MBSR training programs, the mindfulness training outlined here is brief, yet it fosters daily mindfulness practice, deemed by many mindfulness experts as an essential part of mindfulness training and critical for the development of mindfulness skills and aptitudes.

Second, the program is designed to deliver mindfulness training to students, so that it can be used each school day in all classrooms during normal transition times, for instance, after lunch or in between two challenging subjects. It was designed specifically so that the program can be consistently operationalized into the normal school day, without changing the existing curriculum, thus serving as a curriculum-neutral method of delivering mindfulness to improve student wellbeing and performance. The ultimate goal of this is to leverage technology in order to enable more schools to benefit from the potential that mindfulness represents for their students and teachers, including those that may not have access to the funds required for investing in high-quality face-to-face mindfulness teachers or teacher training.

Finally, unlike traditional mindfulness in schools programs, this mindfulness training program is unique in that teachers are participants alongside with the pupils. In other words, teachers can experience the same benefits as the pupils and The program could hence be considered teacher-independent in that teachers do not need to spend extensive time training to become mindfulness teachers, which again may be a challenge in resource-constrained state school settings.

Empirical research conducted on this MBSEL program

In this section, we provide a summary of the scientific research conducted by Laura and her colleagues to evaluate the effectiveness of IE's MBSEL program. This section focuses in particular on the program's impact on participating pupils' academic achievement as well as on implementing the program within existing curricula and teaching resources.

Theoretical background

Extensive research targeting clinical and at-risk student populations has shown that mindfulness interventions can facilitate improved academic performance, as well as decreased anxiety, stress and negative self-assessment, reduced clinical symptoms, and increased attention, cognitive function, and self-esteem (e.g., Bogels et al., 2008; Zylowska, 2008).

Short, technology driven interventions such as the present MBSEL program are supported by an increasing base of research showing positive outcomes associated with brief (Moore et al., 2012) or technology-facilitated interventions (Krusche et al., 2012; Querstret et al., 2017). These results suggest that it may be plausible for schools to run mindfulness-based programs each day from classroom to classroom and across student sub-populations through the use of technology, without requiring any change to the existing curriculum nor extensive training, scheduling, or cost.

However, while mindfulness training and other types of SEL may appear to be a simple and effective antidote against mind wandering and other types of reduced attention capacity in schools, there are several concrete obstacles that currently work against fully incorporating mindfulness training into the normal school day has to date not been practical for many schools, for two main reasons.

The need for curriculum changes

First, most mindfulness programs in schools extend or replace existing curricular activity. Many SEL and especially the vast majority of face-to-face MBSEL programs amend or interrupt the planned curriculum flow. Generally, these programs are implemented over a set period of time, for instance 30 to 45 minutes once a week for eight weeks (Kuyken et al., 2013). With the current regulatory environment and time constraints, many schools may struggle to add a mindfulness training intervention to a curriculum that is already busy.

The need for thorough mindfulness teacher training

Second, most mindfulness training programs are delivered by mindfulness experts whose expertise has developed over several years of practice. Many world-leading mindfulness experts emphasize that a mindfulness program must be taught with fidelity to the underlying principles and foundations to be successful (Crane et al., 2011; Kabat-Zinn, 2003). In other words, to become a mindfulness teacher, a person needs to go through extensive training over several months or years to become sufficiently proficient to pass on mindfulness skills to others.

This requirement is at odds with the reality that many classroom teachers face today, unable to find the time to become proficient in mindfulness as a competency, or invest resources in hiring external expert mindfulness teachers capable of training their pupils in mindfulness.

Inner Explorer's MBSEL program offers an alternative approach to minimize both previously stated obstacles because it can be seamlessly integrated in the existing school curriculum and classroom operations without extensive upfront investment.

Empirical research conducted to date

Following a non-randomized pilot study conducted in eight U.S. classrooms with 191 primary school students, which demonstrated that ten minutes per day of MBSEL significantly enhanced quarterly grades in reading and science (Bakosh et al., 2015), a Randomized Controlled Trial (RCT) was conducted in 18 classrooms in two elementary schools.

RCT in 18 classrooms

The RCT assessed the effect of running the MBSEL program over a ten-week period on student grades as well as impact on curriculum and fidelity of daily implementation. A total of 383 students participated in the study, amounting to eight classrooms and 177 students in School A, and ten classrooms with 103 students in School B. Teachers in both schools had been invited to participate in the study, and the randomized selection of assigning the participating teachers' classrooms into intervention or waitlist control group occurred after that.

Student academic attainment was operationally defined as students' Grade Point Average (GPA), an average of quarterly term grades, which served as the dependent variable. This academic data was already being collected by each school as a part of its normal operations. Each classroom teacher or the school administrator completed a grades tracker at the start and the conclusion of the study. The tracker was used to document student grades in each of six subject areas, including reading, math, science, written language, spelling, and social studies for School A, and reading, math, science, written language, verbal communication, and social studies for School B. Each student was assigned a numerical identifier to be used throughout the study. No student names were disclosed.

Program efficacy data were collected daily throughout the study. Participating teachers reported if they were able to run the program each day, if they participated in the program with students, if they accomplished the planned curriculum and if there were any issues related to the program, including student participation. This information was used to assess the practical feasibility of running the program every day without changing the planned curriculum, as well as the fidelity of operation from teacher to teacher.

The intervention classrooms participated in the ten-minute-per-day audio-guided mindfulness program, from the 90-track series. Each day, the classroom teacher selected and played one track, in sequential order, using the preloaded MP3 player and speaker system in the classroom. Teachers were encouraged to pick a normal transition time to run the program of their own choosing. They were encouraged to stay with the selected time throughout the study. Teachers were encouraged to participate in the program, along with students, by sitting and listening to the recording each day, while either closing their eyes or looking at the gazing stone. Teachers filled out the program tracker each day. The control classrooms simply continued with the existing curriculum.

Results

MBSEL program impact on grade performance

The effect of mindfulness practices on students' grade performance, operationally defined as their term GPA, was analyzed in several ways. First, an independent samples t-test was conducted to compare overall GPA grade changes for the mindfulness intervention and control groups in each school (see Table 21.1). Second, subject-specific independent samples t-tests and effect sizes were calculated to measure the effect of the MBSEL program on specific academic subjects (see Tables 21.2 and 21.3).

Table 21.1 Schools A and B: independent samples t-test comparing overall GPA grade changes by intervention and control groups

	n	M	SD	t	p-value	d
School-A 1st-grade Intervention	22	.171	.312	5.48	< .001	.96
School-A 1st-grade Control	24	.115	.165			
School-A 2nd–5th-grade Intervention	64	2.80	3.13			
School-A 2nd–5th-grade Control	67	.045	2.61			
School-B All grades Intervention	103	.038	.065			
School-B All grades Control	103	.010	.126	1.91	.058	.27

Table 21.2 School A: independent samples t-test comparing subject grades changes for intervention and control groups

	n	M	SD	t	p-value	d
Reading Intervention	64	4.64	6.61	1.61	.110	
Reading Control	67	2.51	8.42			
Writing Intervention	64	2.58	6.44			
Writing Control	67	2.08	6.98	.429	.669	.89
Spelling Intervention	64	–.188	6.50	.547	.585	.72
Spelling Control	67	–.701	4.01	5.08	<.001	1.00
Math Intervention	64	.953	3.10	4.15	<.001	
Math Control	67	–2.66	4.81	5.75	<.001	
Science Intervention	64	4.25	6.95			
Science Control	67	–.209	5.26			
Social Studies Intervention	64	4.56	5.49			
Social Studies Control	67	–.746	5.09			

Table 21.3 School B: independent samples t-test comparing subject grade change scores for intervention and control groups

	n	M	SD	t	p-value	d
Reading-Treatment	103	.031	.146	.815	.416	
Reading Control	103	.013	.170			
Writing Treatment	103	.034	.181			
Writing Control	103	.021	.245	.427	.670	.52
Verbal Comm. Treatment	103	.027	.129	.1.37	.173	
Verbal Comm. Control	103	–.002	.177	3.70	< .001	
Math Treatment	103	.053	.184	1.28	.203	
Math Control	103	–.060	.250	–1.31	.190	
Science Treatment	103	.036	.137			
Science Control	103	.003	.218			
Social Studies Treatment	103	.034	5.49			
Social Studies Control	103	.079	5.09			

Note. Comm. = Communication.

In school A, for first-grade students, (total n = 46), with a grading scale of 1–3, there was no significant effect, most likely due to a small sample size of two classrooms, and the potential for only a two-point difference in the grading scale. However, for second- through fifth-grade students (total n = 131), with a grading scale of 1–100, there was a significant difference in GPAs between the intervention (N = 64, M = 2.80, SD = 3.13), and control (N = 67, M = .045, SD = 2.61) groups; t(129) = 5.48, p < .001 (two-tailed), 95% CI [1.76, 3.75], d = .96.

In school B, for first- through fourth-grade students, (total n = 206), on a grading scale of 1–4, there was a near significant mindfulness intervention effect on GPAs between the intervention (N = 103, M = .038, SD = .065) and control (N = 103, M = .010, SD = .126) group; t(204) = 1.91, p = .058 (two-tailed), 95% CI [–.001, .054], d = .27.

These results suggest that overall grade performance tended to increase significantly for the intervention groups.

Next, by-subject independent samples t-tests and effect size calculations (using Bonferroni's correction) were conducted to determine which academic subjects were influenced by the MBSEL program. Effect sizes were calculated using Cohen's d (Cohen, 1988). Tables 21.2 and 21.3 present a by-subject comparison of the mean grade changes, standard deviations, p-values and Cohen's d, for students in the intervention and control groups in School A and School B, respectively.

In School A, with over 74% Hispanic students, using a grading scale of 1–100, there was a significant difference in the change of math grades for intervention ($N = 64$, $M = .953$, $SD = 3.10$) and control ($N = 67$, $M = -2.66$, $SD = 4.81$) groups; $t(129) = 5.08$, $p < .001$ (two-tailed), 99% CI [2.20, 5.01], $d = .89$. There was a significant difference in the change of science grades for intervention ($N = 64$, $M = 4.25$, $SD = 6.95$) and control ($N = 67$, $M = -.209$, $SD = 5.26$) groups; $t(129) = 4.15$, $p <. 001$ (two-tailed), 99% CI. [2.33, 6.58], $d = .72$. Finally, there was a significant difference in the change of social studies grades for intervention ($N = 64$, $M = 4.56$, $SD = 5.49$) and control ($N = 67$, $M = -.746$, $SD = 5.09$) groups; $t(129) = 5.746$, $p < .001$ (two-tailed), 99% CI [3.48, 7.14], $d = 1.00$. These by-subject effect sizes, represented by Cohen's d-values, suggest that in School A, mindfulness practices positively impacted math, science, and social studies grades by 29%, 24%, and 30% respectively. There was no significant effect for the other three subjects, reading, writing, and spelling.

In School B, with 97% White students, using a grading scale of 1 to 4, there was a significant difference in the change of math grades for intervention ($N = 103$, $M =. 053$, $SD = .184$) and control ($N = 103$, $M = -.060$, $SD = .250$) groups; $t(204) = 3.70$, $p < .001$ (two-tailed), 99% CI [.053, .174], $d = .52$. Interestingly, while not significant, verbal communication and science grades appear to be directionally improved by the intervention, whereas social studies grades appear to be directionally reduced. There were also no significant effects in the remaining two subjects – reading and writing. These results suggest that in School B, a daily mindfulness program can improve elementary students' grades in math by 18%.

MBSEL program impact on classroom operations

Program impact on teaching operations were combined from both schools and analyzed together. There was little to no impact of the mindfulness-based intervention on day-to-day teaching operations for participating classrooms in both schools. School A had 45 available days and School B had 44 available days to run the program, excluding holidays, field trips, and teacher institute days. Out of an average of 42.2 school days that the intervention was run (the range was 40 to 45 days), participating teachers implemented the program 95.5% of available days, after one hour of training, which included 30 minutes to review the research protocol. On days the program was implemented, both teachers and students had the opportunity to learn together, with students participating 100% of the time and teachers participating 97.4% of the time. These results show the program can be run every day and that teachers consistently make the choice to participate in the mindfulness practices along with their students. Teachers also indicated every day on the daily tracker that they had been able to accomplish their planned curriculum 99% of the time (the range was 98% to 100%). These results suggest that the intervention had almost no adverse impact on day-to-day classroom activities.

Discussion

Academic achievement

The current study demonstrated positive academic outcomes in both schools for elementary students in first through fifth grade. Students in the intervention condition experienced an improvement in their quarterly GPAs compared to students in the control condition. Students in the intervention condition also experienced by-subject grade improvements in math, science, and social studies in School A, and in math in School B, compared to students in the control condition.

These results are important because this rigorously designed RCT extends nascent findings by previous scholars suggesting a link between mindfulness training in schools and academic achievement (Schonert-Reichl et al., 2015; Bennett & Dorjee, 2015; Bakosh et al., 2015). The present results demonstrate that in spite of differences in geographic location and grading practices, mindfulness practices may prime the brain in a way that fosters an increased capacity to learn.

Embedding MBSEL programs in classrooms with fidelity

The academic improvements reported in this study are comparable to longer-term interventions of school-based academic and SEL programs (Durlak et al., 2011). The MBSEL program researched in this study may help to overcome the recently reported problems of embedding mindfulness training in schools related to program delivery (Johnson et al., 2016). Short, technology driven interventions such as the present MBSEL program are supported by an increasing base of research showing positive outcomes associated with brief (Moore et al., 2012) or technology-facilitated interventions (Krusche et al., 2012; Querstret et al., 2017). These results suggest that it may be plausible for schools to run mindfulness-based programs each day from classroom to classroom and across student sub-populations through the use of technology, without requiring any change to the existing curriculum nor extensive training, scheduling, or cost.

While the current study was conducted for only ten weeks, the program has the potential to be delivered throughout an entire school year or longer. A longitudinal study could be conducted to determine the impact on performance, behavior, and student and teacher well-being over time, measuring the cumulative effect of a daily mindfulness practice on cognitive outcomes, shifts in brain structure and function that support learning (Davidson et al., 2003).

Online materials and resources for further information relating to the program

Belly Breathing (three minutes)

1. Find a place to sit comfortably and quietly without distraction.
2. Close your eyes and taking a few slow breaths as you settle into this moment.
3. Check in with yourself with great kindness as you bring your awareness to how you feel right now (happy, sad, tired, energetic, bored, frustrated, etc.).

4. Place your hand on your belly and taking ten more breaths, at a comfortable pace for you, feeling your belly expanding as you breathe in and contracting as you breathe out.
5. Open your eyes and noticing again how you feel right now.

Start with the Heart (two to three minutes)

1. Find a place to sit comfortably and quietly without distraction.
2. Close your eyes and taking a few slow breaths as you settle into this moment.
3. Place your hand over your heart and bringing to mind a person (or pet) who you love very much.
4. As you continue breathing in and out for five to ten more full breath cycles, sense into your heart, feeling the love as deeply as you can for your person or pet.
5. Open your eyes, aware of what if anything has shifted in your feelings and senses from the beginning of the practice to the end.

Sharkfin (two minutes)

1. Find a place to sit, it can be anywhere, in school, on a bus, at home.
2. Check in with yourself and simply notice how you feel right now as you breathe, just noticing without judging if it's "good" or "bad."
3. Place your thumb on your forehead with your other fingers pointing to the sky (sharkfin hand). Move your hand slowly down from the forehead to your chest, remembering the five S's.

    - Sit Straight
    - Still
    - Silently
    - Softly breathing
    - Shut eyes

4. Place your hand over your heart as you breath in and out three to five more times.
5. Opening your eyes.

Here is a short video that explains this practice to an audience of children:

https://drive.google.com/a/bbrsd.org/file/d/0Bwtflt1_m4zZaDBoOGg2WEQ2cHc/view?usp=sharing

Tools to help individuals stick with daily practice

Download the Inner Explorer, Inc. app for free to access several mindfulness practices to do at home.

Apple https://itunes.apple.com/in/app/inner-explorer-daily-mindfulness practice/id1204849186
Android https://play.google.com/store/apps/details?id=org.innerExplorer.mobileapp&hl=en
If you'd like to bring Inner Explorer to you family or school, visit www.InnerExplorer.org/compass/signup.

Be sure to use the promo code HNDBK2019 and save 10% on your purchase.

References

Bakosh, L. S., Snow, R. M., Tobias, J. M., Houlihan, J. L., & Barbosa-Leiker, C. (2015). Maximizing mindful learning: An innovative mindful awareness intervention improves elementary school students' quarterly grades. *Mindfulness*, 7(1), 59–67.

Bennett, K., & Dorjee, D. (2015). The impact of a mindfulness-based stress reduction course (MBSR) on well-being and academic attainment of sixth-form students. *Mindfulness*, 7(1), 105–114.

Biegel, G. (2009). Mindfulness-based stress reduction for the treatment of adolescent psychiatric outpatients: A randomized clinical trial. *Journal of Consulting and Clinical Psychology*, 77(5), 855–866.

Bogels, S., Hoogstad, B., van Dun, L., de Schutter, S., & Restifo, K. (2008). Mindfulness training for adolescents with externalizing disorders and their parents. *Behavioural and Cognitive Psychotherapy*, 36(2), 193–209.

Broderick, P., & Metz, S. (2009). Learning to breathe: A pilot trial of a mindfulness curriculum for adolescents. *Advances in School Mental Health Promotion*, 2(1), 35–46.

Cohen, J. (1988). *Statistical power analysis for the behavioral sciences* (2nd ed.). Mahwah, NJ: Lawrence Erlbaum Associates.

Collaborative for Academic, Social and Emotional Learning. (2005). *Safe and sound: An educational leader's guide to evidence-based social and emotional learning programs-Illinois edition*. Chicago, IL: Author.

Crane, R. S., Kuyken, W., Williams, M. G., Hastings, R. P., Cooper, L., & Fennell, M. J. (2011). Competence in teaching mindfulness-based courses: Concepts, development, and assessment. *Mindfulness*, 3(1), 76–84.

Davidson, R., Kabat-Zinn, J., Schumacher, J., Rosenkranz, M., Muller, D., Santorelli, S., . . . Sheridan, J. F. (2003). Alterations in brain and immune function produced by mindfulness meditation. *Psychosomatic Medicine*, 65, 564–570.

Durlak, J. A., Weissberg, R. P., Dymnicki, A. B., Taylor, R. D., & Schellinger, K. B. (2011). The impact of enhancing students' social and emotional learning: A meta-analysis of school-based universal interventions. *Child Development*, 82(1), 405–432.

Huppert, F. A., & Johnson, D. M. (2010). A controlled trial of mindfulness training in schools: The importance of practice for an impact on well-being. *The Journal of Positive Psychology*, 5(4), 264–274.

Johnson, C., Burke, C., Brinkman, S., & Wade, T. (2016). Effectiveness of a school-based mindfulness program for transdiagnostic prevention in young adolescents. *Behaviour Research and Therapy*, 81, 1–11.

Kabat-Zinn, J. (2003). Mindfulness-based interventions in context: Past, present, and future. *Clinical Psychology: Science and Practice*, 10(2), 144–156.

Kaiser-Greenland, S. (2010). *Mindful child: How to help your kid manage stress and become happier, kinder, and more compassionate*. New York, NY: Free Press.

Krusche, A., Cyhlarova, E., King, S., & Williams, J. M. G. (2012). Mindfulness online: A preliminary evaluation of the feasibility of a web-based mindfulness course and the impact on stress. *BMJ Open*, 2(3), 1–5.

Kuyken, W., Weare, K., Ukoumunne, O. C., Vicary, R., Motton, N., et al. (2013). Effectiveness of the mindfulness in schools programme: Non-randomised controlled feasibility study. *The British Journal of Psychiatry*, 203(2), 126–131.

Mendelson, T., Greenberg, M. T., Dariotis, J. K., Gould, L. F., Rhoades, B. L., & Leaf, P. J. (2010). Feasibility and preliminary outcomes of a school-based mindfulness intervention for urban youth. *Journal of Abnormal Child Psychology*, 38, 985–994.

Moore, A., Gruber, T., Derose, J., & Malinowski, P. (2012). Regular, brief mindfulness meditation practice improves electrophysiological markers of attentional control. *Frontiers in Human Neuroscience*, 6(18).

Querstret, D., Cropley, M., & Fife-Schaw, C. (2017). Internet-based instructor-led mindfulness for work-related rumination, fatigue and sleep: Assessing facets of mindfulness as mechanisms of change: A randomised waitlist control trial. *Journal of Occupational Health Psychology*, 22(2), 153–169.

Schonert-Reichl, K. A., & Lawlor, M. S. (2010). The effects of a mindfulness-based educational program on pre- and early adolescents' well-being and social and emotional competence. *Mindfulness*, 1(3), 137–151.

Zoogman, S., Goldberg, S. B., Hoyt, W. T., & Miller, L. (2014). *Mindfulness interventions with youth: A meta-analysis, mindfulness*.

Zylowska, L., Ackerman, D. L., Yang, M. H., Futrell, J. L., Horton, N. I., Hale, S., . . . Smalley, S. L. (2008). Mindfulness meditation training in adults and adolescents with ADHD: A feasibility study. *Journal of Attention Disorders*, 11(6), 737–746.

Section V

Mindfulness programs in children and adolescents

Chapter 22

Still Quiet Place
Sharing mindfulness with children and adolescents

Amy Saltzman

How Still Quiet Place came to be

I had been teaching mindfulness to adults for some time when my son, Jason, who was almost three, asked if he could meditate (practice mindfulness) with me. At the time, my daughter, Nicole, was six months old, and we were all adjusting to life with a new baby. My sense is that Jason knew he would have my full and calm attention when we practiced together. His sweet request prompted me to begin sharing mindfulness with him. Some of the practices I shared with him were based on basic, well-known mindfulness practices. Others, like the Feelings practice below, arose spontaneously when we were together, sitting side by side in the upstairs hallway or lying in bed at night.

Creating a mindfulness of feelings practice in the moment

One afternoon Jason wanted something, and I said no. He was very sad and upset. Not knowing exactly what I was offering, I asked if he wanted to do "sads meditation." He said yes. So, intuiting my way as I went, I asked him the following sequence of questions, slowly, allowing him time to gently explore his sadness.

> *Where do the sads live in your body?*
> *What do they feel like?*
> *Are they small or big? . . . Hard or soft? . . . Heavy or light? . . . Warm or cool?*
> *Do they have a color or colors?*
> *Do they have a sound?*
> *What do they want from you?*

To be honest, I only remember the answer to the last question. He said "love," and then promptly asked, "Can we play?" That was that. He had befriended his feeling and was ready to move on.

Creating the program

After sharing practices with my children and reading repeatedly about childhood stress in both the professional and lay literature, I began to wonder:

- Will children and teens benefit if they learn the life skills of mindfulness, and remain familiar with the Still Quiet Place within as they grow older?

- If young people learn to observe their thoughts, feelings, and bodily sensations, will they be less vulnerable to the unhealthy effects of stress?
- If children and teens are able to access their natural sense of peace and trust their own inner wisdom, will they be less susceptible to harmful peer influences and less likely to look for relief in potentially risky behaviors?
- When young people practice mindfulness, does it enhance their natural emotional intelligence? Can it increase their capacity for respectful communication and compassionate action? Will it support them in developing healthy relationships, and in contributing their gifts to the world?

Initially, I explored these questions in an informal way by sharing mindfulness practices with children in elementary school and community settings. Children ages four and older enjoyed and seemed to benefit from the practices. In general, teachers commented that their students were calmer and more focused when they began their day by visiting the Still Quiet Place. Teachers of adolescents reported that their students were more aware of, and thus better able to deal with, the increasingly complex thoughts and emotions of teenage life. This informal exploration led to formal scientific research in the Clinically Applied Affective Neuroscience lab in the Department of Psychology at Stanford University.

Adapting adult MBSR

While the underpinnings of this curriculum come in large part from adult MBSR, it is the adaptations that make it accessible and meaningful to children and teens. The first adaptation is in the definition of mindfulness. When working with young people I define mindfulness as paying attention here and now, with kindness and curiosity, so that we can choose our behavior. "Paying attention here and now," means doing our best not to obsess about the past, or worry or fantasize about the future; it is simply paying attention to what's actually happening here and now in *this* moment. And we pay attention "with kindness and curiosity." Otherwise we can be incredibly hard on ourselves. We tend to see only where we've "made a mistake" or "messed up." With mindfulness, we practice bringing an attitude of kindness and curiosity to ourselves and our experience. Finally, "so that we can choose our behavior": when we bring our kind and curious attention to our thoughts and feelings, to the sensations in our bodies, and to the people and circumstances in our lives, then we have all the information we need to respond in the moment, to difficulties at school, with friends, at home, and in life in general. With ongoing support this definition makes sense to kids and teens, and more importantly helps them apply mindfulness in their daily lives.

Additional modifications to the MBSR curriculum include:

- Making the practices shorter – a useful rule of thumb is that a child or teen can practice as many minutes as they are old; five year olds can practice for about five minutes. This is a general guideline, some five year olds may, over time be able to practice for longer, whereas some teens may need a great deal of ongoing support to be able to practice for 15 minutes.
- Making observing thoughts, and befriending feelings are distinct practices. In adult MBSR these practices are woven into basic sitting practice. However, children and teens benefit from having these practices offered separately.

- Moving the body scan from class one to class six. Even an abbreviated body scan can be 10–12 minutes. For many young people this is an extremely long practice. So it helps to begin with shorter practices to give them a sense of success. Then once they have developed some skills for watching their thoughts, such as "this is boring," and befriending feelings such as agitation, then they can experiment with the longer body scan practice.
- Incorporating a variety of movement practices. Young people (and if we are honest adults) need to move their bodies. Thus, it is helpful to have a variety of simple and more involved movement practices for bringing attention into the body, and raising or lowering energy, in your pocket. For example, if young children come in from recess and are a bit hyper you can invite them to be mindful seaweed anchoring their feet on the floor, making sure they have enough space that won't clonk their neighbor or desk, and then pretending they are seaweed moving in a fast current. Then gradually have the current slow down until they come to stillness. Conversely, if you have a group of low-energy, post-lunch teens, you can invite them to mindfully listen to a rhythm and drum on the tables, do a few energizing stretches, or even just rub the rims of their ears with the thumb and index finger of each hand, noticing the sensations and how their energy shifts.
- Playfully adapting practices for younger children. For example, while the metacognitive ability to observe thoughts may be too advanced for most young children, this skill can be introduced by having them blow and observe bubbles, and loving-kindness can be simplified to the common childhood act of blowing kisses.
- Incorporating the pencil and paper exercises into the class sessions. When I first offered this curriculum to child-parent pairs and entire families within the context of a research study at Stanford University, the kids had the ongoing support of their parents, who were so motivated to provide these skills to their children that they signed up and completed reams of intake questionnaires. When I began offering the curriculum in low-income, high-risk public elementary schools, the parents and care-givers were focused on providing for their kids, and often did not have the time and energy to support them in doing the pencil and paper home practice. So, I chose to do each exercise at least once within a class session. This also allowed for the next modification.
- Making listening to the recorded audio practice the primary home practice. Since participants were doing the pencil and paper exercises in class, the primary home practice they were invited, encouraged and supported to do was to listen to the guided audio recordings.

Course outline

For students in third grade and up, the course is most commonly delivered over eight weeks, offering one session per week during a typical 50–60-minute class period. Alternatively, the course can be divided into five- to fifteen-minute segments for young children, or in settings where an instructor prefers to offers shorter exercises, over a longer period of time. Again, some of the discussions are beyond children ages three to seven years old, and so it is often helpful to replace these discussions by reading a storybook with a relevant theme, or offering a simple related activity, like writing haikus, or drawing their feelings. A detailed course outline is offered on the following pages. The primary practices for each session are marked in

Table 22.1 Program sessions

Session	Elements	Intentions	Home Practice
Introductory Evening	Parents only **Mindful eating** Review data Rationale for the course Commitment Questions	Provide an experience of mindfulness Review data to date for children and teens, and selected data for adults Review the rationale for offering mindfulness to children Discuss the course structure and time commitment Answer questions	
Class 1	Mindful listening (tone bar) Mindful eating Class guidelines Individual introductions **Breath-based practice: Jewel/ Treasure/Rest** Introduce Still Quiet Place Define mindfulness—*paying attention, here and now, with kindness and curiosity, and then choosing our behavior* Mindful listening (tone bar)	Create a safe, welcoming environment Introduce participants to each other and to the Still Quiet Place/ mindfulness Provide an experience and working definition of Still Quiet Place/ mindfulness Give examples of mindfulness in daily life (informal practice)	Jewel/Treasure Rest
Class 2	Review Class 1 and experience with home practice Discuss barriers to practice, generate solutions **Jewel / Treasure / Rest** Pleasant Events Cartoon Investigate how often our attention is in the past or the future Answer questions Encourage home practice	Explore experience of CD and daily life practice Support the children in establishing a daily practice with the CD	Jewel/ Treasure Rest

Session	Elements	Intentions	Home Practice
Class 3	Review Class 2 and experience with home practice **Bubbles / Thought Watching** Nine dots Introduce concept of Unkind Mind (critical internal dialogue)	Discuss experience with CD and daily life practice Cultivate the capacity to observe thoughts Nine dots Perception—how we view ourselves, others Thoughts during a difficult task Introduce the concept of Unkind Mind (critical internal dialogue)	Bubbles/Thought Watching Notice Unkind Mind
Class 4	Review Class 3 and experience with home practice Unpleasant experiences cartoon Suffering = pain x resistance **Feelings** Discuss that this is the halfway point in the course, and a new moment to recommit to the practices	Examine the thoughts and feelings associated with unpleasant experiences Resistance Wanting things to be different Examine how resistance/wanting circumstances, ourselves, others to be different creates upset/suffering Develop emotional fluency	Feelings Haiku/poetry/art depicting a feeling Play with S = P x R Watch how we create suffering
Class 5	Review Class 4 and experience with home practice **Responding vs. Reacting** (Autobiography in five short chapters) Yoga	Explore common "holes" and "different streets" Use holes and streets to discuss *reacting vs. responding* Yoga Self-talk/Self-compassion Balance as dynamic Explore how often Unkind Mind is inaccurate/negative/looking for trouble	Mountain/Stretch and Balance Notice "holes" and "different streets" Continue to notice Unkind Mind
Week 5 Vacation	School schedules often contain vacations. Although it is not always possible, it is best to schedule the course so that vacations fall after week 4, when the students have some momentum.	Maintain practice without support of weekly class	Alternate Feelings and one of the other practices each day Notice "holes" (difficult situations) practice choosing "different streets" (*responding*)

(Continued)

Table 22.1 (Continued)

Session	Elements	Intentions	Home Practice
Class 6	Discuss falling in and staying out of holes **Body Scan** Communication dyads (one person describes one difficult communication, the other listens and then reflects, then the roles are reversed) Introduce possibility of Kind Heart as an antidote to Unkind Mind Walking	Continue developing the capacity to respond rather than react Bring attention into the body Enhance capacity to observe thoughts and feelings Practice using mindfulness during difficult communications Introduce kind heart *Moving* our practice into the world	Alternate Body Scan/Being in the Body, and Walking Thoreau/nature walk Practice *responding* (with Kind Heart) to both Unkind Mind and in difficult situations
Class 7	Share examples of responding, and role-play new responses to situations when the students reacted Aikido **Loving-kindness** Discuss that next week is the last class Request that students bring something for the last class that symbolizes their experience with the course	Continue to develop the capacity to respond (with Kind Heart) rather than react Introduce loving-kindness as a specific practice for developing Kind Heart	Loving-kindness Continue *responding* (with Kind Heart) to both Unkind Mind and in difficult situations Bring something symbolic to share for the last session
Class 8	Discuss experience with loving-kindness **Flashlight or** Group choice Letter to a friend Completion/beginning Making the practice their own	Discuss the natural capacity to send and receive love Share what the course has meant to them Discuss variety of ways they can make the practice their own Discuss the completion of the course Remind them they can always call or e-mail	Your choice Sit/Flashlight Make a commitment (or not) as to how you will continue the CD and daily life practice

bold. However, it is important to note that simply sharing the practices is just the beginning. In the long run, the value of the program is the participants' ability to apply the principles in their lives, and this depends on you offering skillful supported inquiry and dialogue. In turn your ability to offer skillful supported dialogue depends on you developing a committed daily practice, a topic we will return to.

Basic practices

You have already been introduced to a basic feelings practice. In the next few pages I will share an introductory practice for teens and a more advanced practice for young children, tweens, and teens. All of the practices can be scaled up or down for different age groups.

Rest (introductory practice for teens)

Give it a rest. For the next few minutes give it a rest, all of it – homework, parents, the hallway gossip, your inner gossip, the next new thing. . . . Let everything be exactly the way it is. . . . And rest.

Let your body rest. If you feel comfortable, allow your eyes to close. If not, focus on a neutral spot in front of you. Feel your body supported by the chair, the couch, or the floor. Allow the muscles in your body and your face to rest. Maybe even let out a long, slow sigh.

And let your attention rest on the breath . . . the rhythm of the breath in the belly. Feel the belly expand with each in-breath and release with each out-breath. Narrowing your attention to the rhythm of the breath, and allowing everything else to fade into the background. . . . Breathing, resting. . . . Nowhere to go, nothing to do, no one to be, nothing to prove.

Feel the in-breath, from the first sip all the way through to where the breath is still, and the out-breath, from the first whisper all the way through to where the breath is still. Now see if you can let your attention rest in the still quiet place between the in-breath and the out-breath. . . . And rest again in the still space between the out-breath and the in-breath. . . .

Breathing, resting, being. . . . It is more than enough. . . . Just hanging out with the breath and the stillness.

Feel the stillness and quietness that is always inside of you.

And when your attention wanders, which it will, gently return it to the experience of breathing – feeling the rhythm of the breath in the belly.

Choose to rest, to focus your attention on the breath. Allow things to be just as they are. . . . Allowing yourself to be exactly as you are. . . . Nothing to change, or fix, or improve. . . .

Breathing and resting. Resting and breathing.

As this session comes to a close, you may want to remember that in our fast-paced, media-driven world, resting is a radical act. With practice, you can learn to breathe and rest anytime, anywhere: When you're putting on your shoes, when you're struggling in class, when you're hanging out with friends, even when you're arguing with someone. This kind of resting and breathing is especially helpful when you're nervous, depressed, bored, or angry. So give yourself permission and rest.

Once children and teens learn to rest in stillness and quietness and observe their thoughts feelings, physical sensations, circumstances, wants, and consider the thoughts, feelings, physical sensations, circumstances, and wants of those around them, then they have everything they need to choose their behavior.

The entire course has been designed to support young people in applying this approach in their daily lives. Below are three practice mnemonics to support our young friends in doing this: ABCs, for children ages five to seven; STAR for children ages eight to twelve; and PEACE for tweens and teens.

ABCs (ages five to seven)

For young children, it's best to keep it very simple. Most children in this age group are familiar with the alphabet, or at least the first few letters. So you can simply say:

In life it helps to remember our ABCs. This is especially true when things are difficult. So when things are difficult, keep these ABCs in mind:

> A is for attention. Sometimes it is helpful just to stop and pay attention to our
> > B is for breath. Usually when we pay attention to our breath it is easier to
> > C is for choose. When we stop and pay attention to our breath, then sometimes we can make a kind choice, a choice that is kind to us and kind to others.

STAR (ages eight to eleven)

Every spring, all California public school students take assessments called the STAR (Standardized Testing and Reporting) tests. These assessments are often stressful for the students (and teachers), so at the request of some teachers I work with, I created the following practice. In addition to being helpful for stress reduction prior to or while taking the test, this mnemonic is useful in many other challenging situations:

You may find this simple STAR practice helpful when you are taking a test, doing homework, or dealing with any other difficulty. The practice goes like this:

S is for stop. When you are faced with a difficulty, like a question on the test that you don't know the answer to, or any difficulty in life, stop.

T is for take a breath. Usually, taking a few slow, deep breaths relaxes the mind and allows us to. . .

A is for accept. Accept that you're having difficulty, that you don't know the answer, and that you're a bit stressed. (One third grader remembered the A as "All's well.")

R is for restart or resume. When you're ready, after you've taken some slow, deep breaths and accepted things, you can restart, trying to solve the problem again or moving on to another problem.

Remember, this practice can be used with a difficult problem on a test or homework, and with other difficulties in your life.

PEACE (ages twelve to eighteen)

PEACE practice is the most involved of the series of responsive practices. A spoken version of this practice can be found on the *Still Quiet Place: Mindfulness for Teens* CD. While this practice is detailed, with repetition, teens naturally tune into the aspects of the practice that are most relevant to a particular situation, and eventually retain the basic elements of the practice.

If we remember to use it, mindfulness can help us deal with difficult situations, from ordinary everyday difficulties, like losing your cell phone, to more extreme difficulties like failing a class, breaking up with a girlfriend or boyfriend, having a friend go to jail, or maybe even going to jail yourself, getting pregnant, or grieving a death in your family or community.

Mindfulness is much more than just watching the breath. For me, the power and beauty of mindfulness is that using it helps me when things are most difficult.

PEACE is an acronym for a practice that can be used in any difficult situation. Perhaps you can begin by practicing with small daily irritations. If you are dealing with more extreme circumstances, you may need to repeat the practice many times a day, and you may also want to get additional help from a friend, a parent, a counselor, or a doctor.

The practice goes like this:

P is for pause. When you realize that things are difficult, pause.

E is for exhale. When you exhale, you may want to let out a sigh or a groan, or even weep. And after you exhale you want to? . . . Inhale. Just keep breathing.

A is for acknowledge, accept, and allow. As you continue to breathe, acknowledge the situation as it is. Your backpack with all your stuff is gone, your parents are getting divorced, your best friend is now dating the person who just became your ex. Acknowledging a situation doesn't mean you're happy about it. It just means that you recognize the situation as it is, whether you like it or not.

A is also for accept: accepting the situation and your reaction to it, whether you're furious, devastated, heartbroken, jealous, or all of the above.

Finally, A is also for allowing your experience. Do your best to rest in the Still Quiet Place and watch the thoughts, feelings, and body sensations. Notice when you're tempted to suppress your experience by pretending that you're fine, or when you want to create additional drama by rehashing things in your head or with friends. And allow this, too (smile). See if you can discover a middle way – a way of having your thoughts and feelings without your thoughts and feelings having you and making you act in ways you may regret.

C is for choose. When you are ready – and this may take a few moments, days, weeks, or even months, depending on the situation – choose how you will respond. At its best, responding involves some additional Cs: clarity, courage, compassion, and comedy.

Clarity is being clear about what you want, what your limits are, and what you're responsible for.

Courage means having the courage to speak your truth and hear the truth of others.

Compassion means being kind toward yourself and others, and understanding how incredibly difficult it sometimes is to be a human being.

As for comedy, I actually prefer the word "humor," but it doesn't start with C (smile). It's amazing how helpful it can be to have a sense of humor and not take ourselves too seriously.

Finally, E is for engage. After you have paused, exhaled, allowed, and chosen your response, you are ready to engage with people, with the situation, with life.

Remember, if possible, practice with small upsets first, and for extreme circumstances you may have to repeat this process over and over, and receive additional support. The more you practice, the more PEACE you will have.

Research

Below is a simple summary of some of the research regarding the benefits of mindfulness for children and adolescents to date. If you would like more detail I encourage you to review the individual studies, and to keep up to date as more robust studies are published.

Young children

In a study of a 12-week mindfulness-based cognitive therapy intervention, 25 clinic-referred nine- to twelve-year-olds experienced significant reductions in attention problems; those with elevated anxiety at pretest had decreased anxiety. Parents noted reductions in behavioral and anger management problems (Semple, Lee, Rosa, & Miller, 2008).

A pilot study compared a control group of 24 sixth graders to 28 fifth graders in public schools in Madison, Wisconsin. The fifth graders received the mindfulness-based Learning to BREATHE (L2B) program. Students in one of the fifth grade L2B classes were primarily Spanish-speaking. The L2B students' performance on a computerized task of spatial working memory showed statistically significant improvements in strategy use and reductions in error rate. The L2B students also demonstrated fewer symptoms of depression and anxiety and a greater internal locus of control after program completion.

Qualitative reports from teachers indicated that the L2B students were more focused and better able to deal with stressful situations. The reports indicated improvements in social competence, noting that the students learned to pause, if only briefly, and "acknowledge their thoughts and feelings, something that set L2B apart from most social skills programs." Students became more aware of helpful and unhelpful thoughts and actions. The classroom environment was more relaxed and less stressful. Overall, the mindfulness lessons had a strong impact on the classroom climate and individual students stress levels (Broderick, 2013).

A wait-list controlled study of fourth- through sixth-graders and their parents, which I conducted in collaboration with the Department of Psychology at Stanford, showed that the 31 children who participated in 75 minutes of mindfulness training for eight consecutive weeks had decreased anxiety. Further, their written narratives indicated they experienced decreased emotional reactivity, increased focus, and ability to deal with challenges (Goldin, Saltzman, & Jha, 2008).

In a wait-list controlled study, students in six elementary classrooms received a mindfulness education training consisting of four teacher-delivered components: quieting the mind, mindful attention (mindfulness of sensation, thoughts, and feelings), managing negative emotions and thinking, and acknowledgment of self and others. Students in the ME classrooms reported increased optimism, but not improvements in self-concept or affect. Teachers reported improvements in teacher-rated behavior and social competence (Schonert-Reichl & Lawlor, 2010).

In a randomized controlled trial with 32 second and third graders who engaged in Mindfulness Awareness Practices for thirty minutes twice a week for eight weeks, Lisa Flook, PhD, and her colleagues at the Mindfulness Awareness Research Center at UCLA documented that children who began the study with poor executive function had gains in behavioral regulation, metacognition, and overall global executive control. Analyses also showed significant effects for specific executive function capacities, such as attention shifting, monitoring, and initiating. These results demonstrate that Mindfulness Awareness Practice training benefits children with poor executive function (Flook, 2010).

In a randomized controlled trial conducted by Maria Napoli, PhD, 194 first, second, and third graders who participated in a biweekly, 12-session mindfulness and relaxation program showed significant increases in attention and social skills and decreases in test anxiety and ADHD behaviors (Napoli, 2005). (Note: decreased ADHD behaviors basically translate into increased executive function.)

A randomized controlled trial of the Mindful Schools curriculum to 915 elementary school children in the high-crime areas of Oakland found that after four hours of mindfulness training the students demonstrated an increase in their abilities to pay attention and self-calm, and show care for others, as well as an increase in social compliance (Mindful Schools, n.d.).

Adolescents

In a feasibility study, which offered mindful awareness practices and psychoeducation to a mixed group of adults and adolescents with ADHD, combined population findings included improvements in self-reported ADHD symptoms, anxiety, depressive symptoms, and working memory (Zylowska et al., 2008).

In a study of 32 adolescents with learning disabilities (LD) at a private residential school, participants were led in mindfulness meditation for five to ten minutes at the beginning of each class period, five days per week, for five consecutive weeks, by two classroom teachers. Students' self-reports revealed decreased state (short-term) and trait (long-term) anxiety. Teacher ratings showed improvements of students' social skills and academics, and decreases in problem behaviors (Beauchemin, Hutchins, & Patterson, 2008).

A study using mindfulness-based cognitive therapy (MBCT) with a clinical population of fourteen adolescents, 11 to 18 years of age, found improvements in sustained attention, self-reported behavior, personal goals, subjective happiness, and mindful awareness (Bögels, Hoogstad, van Dun, De Shutter, & Restifo, 2008).

In a study of a nine-week MBSR program for 33 urban youth, age 13 to 21, 79 percent of the youth attended the majority of the MBSR sessions and were considered "program completers." Among program completers, 11 were HIV-infected, 77 percent were female, and all were African American. Quantitative data show that, following the MBSR program, participants had a significant reduction in hostility, general discomfort, and emotional discomfort. Qualitative data showed perceived improvements in interpersonal relationships (including less conflict), school achievement, physical health, and reduced stress. Interview data from an HIV-infected sub-group revealed improved attitude, behavior, and self-care (including medication adherence), and decreased reactivity (Sibinga et al., 2011), with transformative experiences of variable levels described by all participants (Kerrigan et al., 2011).

A six-session intervention, which included MBSR, insomnia treatment, and cognitive therapy for 55 substance abusers, 13 to 19 years of age, with current sleep disturbances found improvements in sleep and reduced worry and mental distress (Bootzin & Stevens, 2005).

When compared to 30 control students, 120 senior high school girls who participated in the mindfulness curriculum L2B experienced reductions in negative affect, tiredness, aches, and pains and increases in emotion regulation, feelings of calmness, relaxation, and self-acceptance. The students who participated in L2B were more able to recognize their emotions and more able to label them. They reported that the greatest overall advantage for them was the ability to let go of distressing thoughts and feelings (Broderick & Metz, 2009).

In a randomized controlled trial, 102 adolescents participated in a mindfulness course for two hours a week for eight weeks. The teens reported reductions in perceived stress; symptoms of anxiety, depression, and somatic (physical) distress and interpersonal problems; and increased self-esteem and sleep quality. Independent clinicians documented a higher percentage of diagnostic improvement and significant increases in global assessment of functioning scores in the mindfulness group (versus the control group). In layperson's terms, this means that adolescents who were initially diagnosed as clinically depressed and anxious no longer met clinical criteria for depression or anxiety (Biegel, 2009). Further analysis found that statistically significant increases in mindfulness were present and were significantly related to positive changes in mental health (Brown, 2011).

Before a randomized controlled trial with 400 students in five middle schools in Flanders, Belgium, both the mindfulness group (21%) and the control group (24%) had a similar percentage of students reporting evidence of depression. After the eight weekly 100-minute mindfulness sessions, the number of students with symptoms of depression was significantly lower in the mindfulness group: 15% versus 27% in the control group. This difference persisted six months after the training, when 16% of the intervention group versus 31% of the control group reported evidence of depression. The results suggest that mindfulness can lead to a decrease in symptoms associated with depression and, moreover, that it protects against the later development of depression-like symptoms (Raes, Griffith, Van der Gucht, & Williams, 2013).

Research demonstrates that children who practice mindfulness experience the following benefits:

Increased attention
Increased executive function (working memory, planning, organization, and impulse control)
Decreased ADHD behaviors – specifically hyperactivity and impulsivity
Fewer conduct and anger management problems
Increased emotional regulation
Increased self-calming
Increased social skills and social compliance
Increased care for others
Decreased negative affect, or emotions
Decreased anxiety in general and text anxiety in particular
Decreased depression
Increased sense of calmness, relaxation, and self-acceptance
Increased self-esteem
Increased quality of sleep

Notes and cautions

I hope this chapter has given you a feel for the Still Quiet Place curriculum. If you are interested in exploring this offering in more depth I encourage you to read *A Still Quiet Place: A Mindfulness Program for Teaching Children and Teens to Ease Stress and Difficult Emotions* and or enroll in my online training: www.stillquietplace.com/sqp-10-week-online-training/.

In the meantime if you choose to offer mindfulness to youth it is *essential* that you establish your own devoted daily mindfulness practice, make your offerings universal and accessible, and be aware that in any given classroom or community setting at least one if not more than one child will have experienced trauma.

Establishing a personal practice

The first and most crucial step in preparing to offer mindfulness to youth is to establish your own devoted *daily* practice. The simplest way to begin is to commit to sitting for 15 to 30 minutes each day, resting your attention on the breath, noticing when your mind wanders, and gently returning your attention to the breath. By repeating this process you will discover the tendencies, preferences, and habits of your mind and heart – or more accurately, the human mind and heart. The easiest way to begin is to download a free app, Insight Timer. All of my adult practices, plus Feelings, Rest, and one additional practice from my children's CD and teen CD can be found by searching my name. The app also offers thousands of other guided practices to choose from.

While the rare individual may be able to develop a personal mindfulness (or heartfulness) practice on their own, most of us need much more support. Some support can come from books such as *Full Catastrophe Living*; *Wherever You Go, There You Are*; and *Mindfulness for Beginners*, by Jon Kabat-Zinn, and the *Mindfulness-Based Stress Reduction Workbook*, by Bob Stahl and Elisha Goldstein. However, given that your intention is not just to practice yourself, but rather to share these practices with young people, wholehearted participation in an eight-week Mindfulness Based Stress Reduction (MBSR), Mindfulness Based Cognitive Therapy (MBCT), Mindful Self-Compassion (MSC) course or eleven-week Mindfulness-Based Emotional Balance (MBEB) course is strongly encouraged.

Participating in a course has multiple benefits. You will be supported by a skillful facilitator in establishing your own practice. You will learn from your own experience and the experiences of your classmates. You will be able to observe how the facilitator shares the practices with different individuals and the group as a whole. For those of you who have a longtime practice in another lineage, participation in a secular course will support you in developing a jargon-free perspective and vocabulary.

To find a course near you, search the internet for MBSR, MBCT, MSC and your town, zip code, or area code.

If there is no program in your local area, you can participate in a high-quality online course through the following websites:

www.umassmed.edu/cfm/mindfulness-based-programs/mbsr-courses/mbsr-online/Mindful Living Programs:
www.mindfullivingprograms.com/mbsr_online.php

Lastly, for those who are committed to doing this work with authenticity and excellence, I strongly recommend that you participate in at least one silent mindfulness retreat of seven days or longer. This idea may seem daunting. It's certainly challenging to find seven full days, away from all of life's demands, to devote to anything. And a silent retreat might not be your natural first choice. However, as you deepen your personal practice and take one "next sane step" after another toward sharing mindfulness with children, you will come to see the value of a focused and dedicated retreat. Truly, it is the best gift you can give yourself – and your students.

Universal and accessible

When bringing mindfulness into school, clinical, and community settings – particularly public schools – it is important to emphasize the universal nature of mindfulness. Occasionally I am asked, "Is mindfulness Buddhist?" I usually respond along these lines: "Mindfulness and compassion are innate human qualities that can be cultivated over time. One does not need to be Buddhist to practice them any more than one needs to be Italian to enjoy pizza." If the person asking the question is willing, I guide him through a simple eating or breath awareness practice to allow him to have a personal experience of mindfulness and to realize that he is capable of practicing mindfulness just as he is, with his current beliefs, and without relying on any particular philosophy or religion.

Trauma awareness

In any given classroom or therapy practice, there will be children who have lived through one or more of the following: neglect; divorce; illness; death of a family member; violence in their homes or communities; being uprooted from their homes; war; and emotional, physical, or sexual abuse. Unfortunately, in some settings these experiences are the norm. These circumstances require that we stretch our capacity to respond to suffering with clarity and compassion. Even with the best of intentions, we can do harm if we expose wounds that we don't have the skill to attend to.

You may or may not be a therapist. Regardless of your training, before sharing this curriculum with groups or individuals it is important that you identify local resources for issues that are beyond your expertise. If you are a classroom teacher or someone bringing mindfulness into school (or community) settings, it is important that you understand the institutional policies and the availability and limitations of any allied mental health services, and that you establish effective relationships with counselors and community mental health resources. If you are a therapist, hopefully you are already connected with one or more skilled child and adolescent psychiatrists whom you trust. If not, please establish these relationships *before* you begin teaching. When stuff comes up, it will be crucial that you accompany the child you are referring throughout the process of getting additional support. By "accompany," I mean provide mental, emotional, and in some cases action-oriented support such as taking the initiative, walking the student to the counselor's office, speaking to caregivers, or making an appointment with a therapist.

In conclusion

I applaud your desire to bring these essential life skills to young people. As you move forward, please remember that in the vast majority of research showing that mindfulness benefits children and teens, the programs have been offered by people with a devoted personal practice. Be wary of curricula that are formulaic, and programs that don't explicitly require an ongoing devoted personal practice. We would not want a math teacher who was not well trained in math to instruct our children in math, or a swim coach who had only read about swimming to teach our children to swim. Because skillful mindfulness invites, encourages, and requires essential inner exploration and self-awareness, it is crucial that if you are going to offer these powerful life skills to youth that you do your own work first. Start where you are. Go slow. Take your time. Ask yourself the hard questions about your practice, and your intentions, and then when your heart tells you that you are ready, go out and share what you have learned, and more importantly your embodied, loving presence, with the young people in your life.

References

Beauchemin, J., Hutchins, T. L., & Patterson, F. (2008). Mindfulness meditation may lessen anxiety, promote social skills, and improve academic performance among adolescents with learning disabilities. *Complementary Health Practice Review*, 13, 34–45.
Biegel, G. (2009). Mindfulness-based stress reduction for the treatment of adolescent psychiatric outpatients: A randomized clinical trial. *Journal of Consulting and Clinical Psychology*, 77(5), 855–866.

Bögels, S., Hoogstad, B., Van Dun, L., De Schutter, S., & Restifo, K. (2008). Mindfulness training for adolescents with externalising disorders and their parents. *Behavioural and Cognitive Psychotherapy*, 36(2), 193–209. doi:10.1017/S1352465808004190

Bootzin, R. R., & Stevens, S. J. (2005). Adolescents, substance abuse, and the treatment of insomnia and daytime sleepiness. *Clinical Psychology Review*, 25(5), 629–644.

Broderick, P. C. (2013). *Learning to breathe: A mindfulness curriculum for adolescents to cultivate emotion regulation, attention, and performance*. Oakland, CA: New Harbinger.

Broderick, P. C., & Metz, S. (2009). Learning to BREATHE: A pilot trial of a mindfulness curriculum for adolescents. *Advances in School Mental Health Promotion*, 2, 35–46.

Brown, K. W., West, A. M., Loverich, T. M., Biegel, G. M. (2011). Assessing adolescent mindfulness: Validation of an adapted mindful attention awareness scale in adolescent normative and psychiatric populations. *Psychological Assessment*, December, 23(4), 1023–1033. doi:10.1037/a0021338. Epub 2011, February 14.

Flook, L., Smalley, S. L., Kitil, M. J., Galla, B. M., Greenland, S. K., Locke, J., Ishijima, E., & Kasari, C. (2010). Effects of mindful awareness practices on executive functions in elementary school children. *Journal of Applied School Psychology*, 26, 70–95.

Goldin, P., Saltzman, A., & Jha, A. (2008). *Mindfulness meditation training in families*. ABCT conference abstract. New York, NY: Association for Behavioral and Cognitive Therapies.

Kerrigan, D., Johnson, K., Stewart, M., Magyari, T., Hutton, N., Ellen, J. M., & Sibinga, E. M. (2011). Perceptions, experiences, and shifts in perspective occurring among urban youth participating in a mindfulness-based stress reduction program. *Complementary Therapies in Clinical Practice*, 17(2), 96–101.

Meiklejohn, J., Phillips, C., Freedman, M. L., Griffin, M. L., Biegel, G., Roach, A. et al. (2010). Integrating mindfulness training into K – 12 education: Fostering resilience of teachers and students. *Mindfulness*, 1(1).

Napoli, M., Krech, P. R., & Holley, L. C. (2005). Mindfulness training for elementary school students: The attention academy. *Journal of Applied School Psychology*, 21(1), 99–125.

Raes, F., Griffith, J. W., Van der Gucht, K., & Williams, J. M. G. (2013). School-based prevention and reduction of depression in adolescents: A cluster-randomized controlled trial of a mindfulness group program. *Mindfulness*. doi:10.1007/s12671-013-0202-1

Schonert-Reichl, K. A., & Lawlor, M. S. (2010). The effects of a mindfulness-based education program on pre- and early adolescents' well-being and social and emotional competence. *Mindfulness*. doi:10.1007/s12671-010-0011-8

Semple, R. J., Lee, J., Rosa, D., & Miller, L. F. (2008). Mindfulness-based cognitive therapy for children: Results of a pilot study. *Journal of Cognitive Psychotherapy*, 22(1), 15–28.

Sibinga, E., Kerrigan, D., Stewart, M., Johnson, K., Magyari, T., & Ellen, J. (2011). Mindfulness-based stress reduction for urban youth. *Journal of Alternative and Complementary Medicine*, 17(3), 213–218.

Zylowska, L., Ackerman, D. L., Yang, M. H., Futrell, J. L., Horton, N. L., Hale, T. S., Pataki, C., & Smalley, S. L. (2008). Mindfulness meditation training with adults and adolescents with ADHD. *Journal of Attention Disorders*, 11(6), 737–746. doi:10.1177/1087054707308502

Chapter 23

Mindfulness-Based Cognitive Therapy for Children

Jennifer Lee and Randye J. Semple

Mindfulness-Based Cognitive Therapy for Children (MBCT-C) was developed during an intensely uncertain time in history – shortly after the 9/11 attacks in 2001. As clinicians working at the epicenter in New York City, we conducted our pilot studies with children (ages 9 to 12) who had lived through this national trauma. Initially, anxieties took the form of worrying about an upcoming assignment or test, yet as group members became comfortable with one another, worries became increasingly personal and centered on their own physical safety and the safety of their families. Based on these early clinical experiences, the program evolved into a manualized evidence-based psychotherapy focused on the treatment of childhood anxiety, one which we hoped would offer anxious children a different way of being in the world.

This chapter outlines the development of MBCT-C over the past 15 years and offers a detailed overview of the 12-week group psychotherapy program for children. At the outset, mindfulness-based interventions including Mindfulness-Based Stress Reduction (MBSR; Kabat-Zinn, 1990), Dialectical Behavior Therapy (DBT; Linehan, 1993), Acceptance and Commitment Therapy (ACT; Hayes, Strosahl, & Wilson, 1999), and Mindfulness-Based Cognitive Therapy (MBCT; Segal, Williams, & Teasdale, 2002) were filling a critical void in the compendium of more traditional cognitive-behavioral treatments. After going through the rigor of clinical research trials, these adult interventions earned the distinction of being evidence-based. Building on this foundation, MBCT-C found a receptive audience with researchers and clinicians working with younger populations in need of alternative therapies.

Theoretical background and research

Traditional cognitive therapy facilitates "metacognitive knowledge" of thoughts (Wells, 2002) in which thoughts are recognized as not necessarily accurate (Teasdale, 1999), and therefore can be examined, challenged, and altered. Mindfulness-based therapies, in contrast, is believed to facilitate "metacognitive awareness" or "decentering," which describes the ability to perceive thoughts as transitory events in the mind (Teasdale, 1999; Teasdale et al., 2002). As such, mindfulness training does not directly challenge the veracity of thoughts, but rather aims to change the individual's *relationship* to them (Segal, Williams, & Teasdale, 2002, 2013). Essentially, cognitive therapy focuses on the *content* of thoughts and strives to change maladaptive thinking patterns, whereas mindfulness focuses on the *process* of thinking and promotes purposeful attention to mental states from a nonjudgmental perspective.

By decentering from one's own mental activity, a shift occurs in how an individual relates to his or her own thoughts, feelings, and body sensations (Segal et al., 2002, 2013). These internal events are viewed as shifting, transient phenomena to observe rather than to judge, and as events to be identified rather than changed. With increased awareness, the conditioned, habituated pathway between distressing thoughts and emotional states is interrupted. As a result, mindless reactivity and mindful responsivity are opposite and incompatible states of mind.

If decentering is one of the core mechanisms of change in mindful awareness training, the question arises whether children are capable of metacognitive awareness, and if so, at what age does this capacity develop? Satlof-Bedrick and Johnson (2015) conducted a study to examine children's awareness of the flow of breathing, awareness of the natural stream of consciousness or thoughts in one's mind, and the ability to monitor these experiences that are intrinsic to mindfulness practices. In a group of children ($N = 68$) ages 4, 6, and 8 years old, the authors found significant age-related differences and a steady developmental improvement among the age-stratified sample. By the age of 6, children demonstrate a notable understanding of the breathing process, and by the age of 8, they develop the capacity to successfully monitor their own breathing. There were, however, no changes in thought awareness with performance being consistently poor across all age groups. Given these findings, the lower age limit for children to successfully monitor their own breathing process may be 8 years old, and the capacity for thought awareness may not develop until after the age of 8. This study showcases the need for future research to understand how children develop metacognitive awareness and how specific mindfulness practices, such as breath meditation, can be best utilized to enhance children's emerging metacognitive awareness.

Research on MBCT-C

In systematic reviews, mindfulness interventions with youth have proven to be a promising treatment modality (Black, 2015; Burke, 2010; Harnett & Dawe, 2012; Zoogman, Goldberg, Hoyt, & Miller, 2015). Many of these studies have focused on non-clinical samples and participants recruited from school settings (Zoogman et al., 2015). While there is an interest in integrating mindfulness into school curricula (Semple, Droutman, & Reid, 2017), there is a need for more research focusing on youth in clinical settings.

In one of our first pilot studies (Semple, Reid, & Miller, 2005), we examined the feasibility and acceptability of a mindfulness-training program for children ($N = 5$) ages 7 and 8 years old. The six-week program included age-appropriate activities focused on meditative and sensory practices to enhance attention. Improvements were found for all participants in at least one area, including internalizing or externalizing problems and academic functioning. While clinical observations supported the acceptability, feasibility and helpfulness of mindfulness for clinical populations, there were questions whether children were able to grasp the core theoretical concepts of mindful awareness and decentering given their limited capacities with attention and metacognitive awareness. We concluded that the program offered promise as an intervention for the treatment of anxiety in children, and continued this line of research with a slightly older cohort using the expanded 12-week program that became MBCT-C.

With an augmented curriculum, we conducted a randomized trial of MBCT-C with children ($N = 25$) between the ages of 9 and 12, enrolled in a university clinic-based remedial reading program (Semple, Lee, Rosa, & Miller, 2010). All of the children had significant reading difficulties and most reported stress or anxiety. Significant decreases in anxiety symptoms, attention problems, and behavioral problems were found following the 12-week intervention. Treatment feasibility and acceptability was supported by the high attendance rate, high retention rate, and positive ratings on program evaluations by children and their parents (Lee, Semple, Rosa, & Miller, 2008).

The effectiveness of MBCT-C was further evaluated with children (ages 10 to 13) from divorced families (Esmailian, Tahmassian, Dehghani, & Mootabi, 2013). Participants ($N = 30$) were randomly assigned to either a wait list control group ($N = 16$) or an experimental group ($N = 14$). Questionnaires were administered at baseline, post-intervention, and at six-months following the intervention. Participants in the experimental group reported significant decreases in depression symptoms, negative self-esteem, and interpersonal problems, as well as a significant increase in acceptance and mindfulness. The authors concluded that MBCT-C can be an effective intervention for the treatment of depressive symptoms in children of divorced families.

In one of the most compelling studies done on MBCT-C to date, researchers (Cotton et al., 2015; Strawn et al., 2016) evaluated the neurophysiological correlates of MBCT-C in youth with anxiety disorders who have a biological vulnerability to bipolar disorder. In this open trial, youth between the ages of 9 and 16 and diagnosed with generalized, social, and/or separation anxiety disorder were evaluated with functional magnetic resonance imaging (fMRI) at baseline and after completing the MBCT-C program. The investigators reported increased activity in the cingulate and bilateral insula, parts of the brain responsible for processing cognitive and emotional information and for monitoring the physiological state of the body. Significant decreases were also found in anxiety measures, in both clinician-rated and self-rated trait anxiety. This study, the first of its kind using fMRI, paves an important pathway for future research.

Developmental adaptations and goals

MBCT-C retains the basic structure of the adult program while addressing three key developmental differences: children's limited attentional capacity, their need for multisensory learning, and the importance of family involvement. First, children typically have less developed memory and attention compared to adults, suggesting that they may benefit from shorter, more repetitious interventions. MBCT-C is a 12-week program consisting of weekly, 90-minute sessions, compared to the eight-week adult program of weekly two-hour sessions. Since children may find it more challenging to stay engaged in a single activity for an extended period of time, longer mindfulness activities are replaced with shorter, more frequent ones. Secondly, since children have less verbal fluency, abstract reasoning, and conceptual abilities, it is easier to engage them when games, activities, and stories are integrated into the therapy. The experiential activities of MBCT-C are designed to be participatory and interactive, offering a wide variety of multisensory experiences. Lastly, we consider the child's sociocultural context, and in particular, the influence of the family and the home environment on the child's development. MBCT-C adopts a systemic approach to treatment as parents support and share in their child's home practices, and encourage mindful speech, intentions, and behaviors at home.

Three main themes are interwoven throughout the program. The first involves the *understanding that thoughts, feelings, and body sensations are separate but related entities*. Children learn to recognize that these internal experiences interact to influence their perceptions of day-to-day experiences. The second theme focuses on *differentiating between judging and describing*. Children develop a language to describe internal experiences and external events in the moment, without falling into the habituated tendency to evaluate and judge. The third theme involves *increasing awareness of the present moment* by noticing past, present and future thinking. Children who suffer from anxious thinking learn to decenter from thoughts and redirect their attention away from past or future-oriented thinking and towards an awareness of the present moment.

Overview of the program

MBCT-C is conducted in three phases. Sessions 1 to 3 establish the foundations of mindfulness and introduce basic concepts and practices. Sessions 4 to 10 focus on cultivating mindfulness across the senses including sight, sound, touch, taste, smell, and movement. Sessions 11 and 12 focus on integration and generalization of mindfulness as a new way of being in the world. The following section includes the main activities of each session. For more detailed descriptions and expanded clinical vignettes, we refer the reader to the MBCT-C therapist manual (Semple & Lee, 2011).

Session 1: being on automatic pilot

For many children, the initial session may be fraught with worries, self-consciousness, and self-doubt. The main aims of Session 1 are to establish a safe, therapeutic space, build group cohesion, and introduce the concept of mindfulness. We establish guidelines and expectations to provide children with structure and to convey the importance of active participation in the group. In the icebreaker activity, *Getting to Know You,* children pair up and learn about their partner. After a brief exchange, each child then introduces his or her partner to the group. This is the first mindful listening activity.

Next, children are introduced to the concept of living on automatic pilot. They easily relate to the experience of being "lost in thought" and momentarily forgetting where they are or what they are doing. Children typically are eager to share stories about the day they walked past their school because they weren't paying attention, or how they consumed an entire tub of popcorn at the movies without any recollection. We then invite them to consider, "What if there is a different way of being in the world?"

An activity we call *Discovering Awareness in a Cup* allows children to experience the gradual increase of attention and concentration necessary to meet new demands. Children and therapists sit in a circle and pass around a half filled cup of water, a fairly easy task done with minimal thought or attention. Next, the water cup is filled to the brim and passed around, a moderately challenging task that requires an increase in mindful attention. Finally, the filled cup of water is passed around with the lights turned off or with eyes closed, requiring even greater precision and awareness in coordinating movements between one another.

We also practice *Taking Three Mindful Breaths* together. Children are invited to bring their attention to the sensation of air flowing in through their nostrils or mouth and filling their lungs, and then to the sensation of exhaling. This slowing down and focusing attention on the breath helps children step out of automatic pilot mode and engage with the present-moment sensory experience.

Following each mindfulness activity, children are guided through the inquiry process to help them integrate their personal experiences with the aim of each session. The inquiry consists of three open-ended questions: (1) What did you notice? What was the experience like for you? (2) How was the experience different from our usual way of being? (3) How might you use this practice in your everyday life? (Segal et al., 2013). Through this shared group dialogue, children connect the experiential practice with the application of mindfulness to their daily lives.

We close this and each subsequent session by reviewing the session handouts, reading a short poem or story, reviewing the home practice activities for the coming week, and ending with another brief breathing meditation to help children transition back to their normal activities.

Session 2: being mindful is simple, but it is not easy!

Children arrive to the second session having completed a week's worth of home practice. They start to become familiar with the rhythm of the session, taking off their shoes, taking a seat on a cushion, practicing *Taking Three Mindful Breaths*, and then reviewing the home practice. We prioritize the home practice at the beginning of each session to convey its importance as an essential component of the program. We gently encourage children to share their personal experiences of the home practice, draw points of connection between members, and work through the barriers that might get in the way.

There are two main mindfulness practices in Session 2. *Raisin Mindfulness* is simply the practice of mindfully eating a raisin, and *Mindfully Moooving Slooowly* is the practice of mindful walking. Both practices, commonly used in the MBSR and MBCT programs, need minimal adaptations for use with children. Returning to the concept of automatic pilot, we can shift from mindless eating to a fuller awareness of our food as it passes from our lips to our stomachs. This deliberate practice of exploring a single raisin with all of our senses and savoring each taste in each moment helps disengage us from our automatic ways of being. Similarly, *Mindfully Moooving Slooowly* allows children to tune into the minute sensations of walking, step by step. As we bring a deliberate awareness to each step as we walk slowly around the room, we become aware of our balance, our proprioception, the weight of our body in our feet, and the way our bodies feel in space.

Session 3: who am I?

The activity called *Hey, I Have Thoughts, Feelings, and Body Sensations!* illustrates how these separate phenomena may interact and influence the interpretation of an imagined experience. Children listen to the following passage, adapted from the adult MBCT program (Segal et al., 2013):

> *You are walking down the street, and on the other side of the street you see somebody you know. This person is a good friend of yours. You smile and wave. The person just doesn't seem to notice and walks by.*
>
> (Semple & Lee, 2011, p. 140, emphasis in original)

Children are invited to imagine this scene as vividly as they can, and carefully observe their thoughts, feelings, and body sensations. One child shared the thought, "He didn't want to say hi to me" and reported feeling embarrassed and experiencing the body sensation of warmth in her face. Another child offered, "He was mad at me and tried to ignore me" with an accompanying feeling of anger, tightness in the chest, and a faster heartbeat. During the inquiry process, children share their experiences and explore why each of them had such different responses to the same exact imagined event. We understand how our idiosyncratic "filters," our past and future-oriented thoughts, our present emotional states and associated body sensations impact our interpretation and experience of external events.

The body scan is another practice to enhance awareness of the present moment. While lying down on mats with their eyes closed, children are invited to observe the minute sensations in each part of their body, note the moment-to-moment changes and any urge or wish for a sensation to be different than it actually is. As with the breath meditations, children are reminded to notice when their mind wanders and gently return their attention to their bodies.

Session 4: a taste of mindfulness

In previous sessions, children experience the practice of *Taking Three Mindful Breaths*. Session 4 is the first time children are introduced to the *Three-Minute Breathing Space*, a core breath meditation practice of the adult MBCT program (Segal et al., 2002, 2013). Participants are invited to consider the three steps – Awareness, Gathering and Expanding – as an hourglass, first having a spacious awareness, then gathering attention at the breath, and then expanding awareness. Another analogue is looking through a camera viewfinder – using a wide-angle lens, then zooming into a single precept, which is the breath, and zooming back out to the wide angle perspective again. We have found the original practice to be appropriate for children, and the three steps are easy to remember especially when using the acronym AGE.

Building on Thich Nhat Hanh's (1991) tangerine meditation, the *Opening to One Orange* activity focuses on mindfully exploring a clementine orange with the multitude of our senses. Through guided meditation, children are encouraged to notice the texture of the fruit while slowly peeling its skin, becoming aware of the mist and the scent, and savoring the taste of each segment. During the three-step inquiry process, we highlight our capacity to disengage from automatic pilot mode and approach experiences with a beginner's mind.

Session 5: music to our ears

The practice of mindful listening aims to differentiate thoughts, feelings, and body sensations as separated but interrelated phenomena. In this activity, *Do You Hear What I Hear?*, children lie down on yoga mats and listen to 30-second sound clips from a variety of musical genres while observing emergent thoughts or images, feelings, and body sensations. One child noted that she felt joyful (feeling) when one particular song brought back memories of a family wedding (thought or image), and she noticed that her feet were tapping to the musical rhythms (body sensation). Another child shared that he felt sad as the same song conjured thoughts of a funeral, and noticed that his body felt heavier while lying on the mat. During the inquiry, children understand how their personal filters have a powerful impact on their interpretation and experience of the world around them.

Session 6: sound expressions

While the mindful hearing practice in the previous session focused on receptive listening, this companion session focuses on expressing hearing. In *Sounding Out Emotions – Mindfully*, children have an opportunity to be the conductor of their own symphony. One child may volunteer to be the conductor, while other group members choose among a variety of musical instruments made available to them. The instruments may include a bell, drum, flute, tambourine, or simply anything that makes a sound such as a plastic bottle half filled with water or a plastic container filled with uncooked rice or beans. Children may choose to use their own bodies as instruments – with two hands clapping, whistling, clicking their tongue, or stomping their feet. The conductor is invited to notice how she feels, and compose a song that best expresses her feelings in the moment. With a baton in hand and the other children standing in a semi-circle before her, she will silently instruct each musician to play his or her instrument. If a child is feeling content, she might choose to compose a song where each instrument is clearly heard and played one by one. If a child is feeling irritated, she might instruct the musicians to play their instruments loudly and all at the same time. Children who suffer from anxiety may find this practice challenging because of the need to take center stage, so therapists may volunteer first to model the activity. After the first or second child takes the conductor's stand, the others are usually eager for their turn. Similar to the receptive sounds activity, the purpose of this practice is to understand how our emotions and thoughts can influence our body expressions, and how we can tune into these experiences with greater awareness.

Session 7: practice looking

Visualizing with Clarity is a visualization practice in which children are invited to explore mindful awareness with their sense of sight. We initially start by noticing and "seeing" things that are inside our heads. By doing so, we may learn to see experiences around us with a greater sense of clarity. We offer a verbal prompt to create a pleasant scene such as: *You are walking on a beach. It's a bright, sunny day. You see other children playing in the sand. You hear families playing in the water*. Then we invite children to use their "mind's eye" to experience every detail in the scene as vividly as possible with all of their senses – noticing the feeling of the sand sifting through their feet, the scent of suntan lotion, and the taste of salt water in the air. We may also use a prompt to describe a walk in the park, a picnic, or a playground. After about five minutes, children are invited to write down a brief description of their scene, along with their thoughts, feelings and body sensations.

In *Seeing What Is in the Mind's Eye* activity, children are asked to remember a familiar object that they may use everyday (e.g., phone, television, computer, refrigerator) and draw it from memory, filling in as much detail as possible. If children become self-critical about their drawings, they are encouraged to note the judging thoughts and gently shift their attention back to the activity of drawing. For the home practice, children are invited to take the drawings home, compare them to the actual object, and notice what they might have missed. They are usually surprised they didn't remember some critical detail, despite using the object every day. This practice illuminates how automatic pilot mode makes us less sensitized and less aware of the details around us.

Session 8: strengthening the muscle of attention

In this companion session on mindful seeing, children are shown different optical illusions during the *Seeing Through Illusions* activity and asked to label what they see. Do they see a rabbit or a duck? Do they see the young lady or the elderly woman? If they see one image, are they able to adjust their focus to see the other image? Are they able to see both images at the same time? This practice helps children shift their attention from one image to the other, much in the same way that children shift their attention during the Three-Minute Breathing

Space. Children are often amazed that there is another way of looking at the picture to reveal an image that they initially overlooked. During the inquiry, we draw connections to daily life experiences and how, with intention, we can deliberately shift our focus. Once we become stuck on a worried thought, we can notice and purposefully shift our attention to our breath or our bodies. By becoming more aware of choice points, we can choose to become aware of the thought stream that contributes to distressing emotions and disengage with conscious awareness.

Session 9: touching the world with mindfulness

In the *Being in Touch* activity, children's ability to distinguish between judging and describing is further reinforced. One child is blindfolded at a time, and each is invited to mindfully explore an object with his or her sense of touch – describing the object without labels or judgments. If the child reacts with aversion and expresses, "It feels gross" or "I don't like the feel of it," the rest of the group gently offers feedback that the statement is a judgment rather than a descriptive observation, and the blindfolded child is encouraged to continue with the practice. The observers may ask clarifying questions such as, "Is it hard or soft? Smooth or rough? Cold or hot? Light or heavy?" These interactive exchanges allow children to be in a process of co-discovery with one another, while encouraging the shift from judging to describing experiences.

Session 10: what the nose knows

Mindful smelling closes out the experiential practices of the various senses. In *Judging Stinks!* children are asked to describe what they smell without trying to label or judge what they experience. Small plastic containers are filled with various spices (e.g., cinnamon, cajun spice, oregano) or cotton balls soaked with different liquids (e.g., alcohol, vanilla extract, coconut oil). As the containers are passed around, children try to describe the smell using various adjectives such as sharp, sour, pungent, floral, sweet, fresh, clean, and earthy. This activity can be challenging because words may not fully capture a complex smell. It also tends to elicit strong automatic reactions – repulsion away from putrid scents and attraction towards more pleasing scents. This practice highlights our automatic tendency to judge an experience as *good* or *bad*. If judgment arises, children are gently guided to return to the scent and simply describe what they smell and in the process, learn to be more present with what they are experiencing. Similarly, when feelings of anxiety, fear, anger, or sadness arise, children can simply observe what is happening, without instantly labeling these experiences as bad or negative and without automatically avoiding or pushing them away. By developing a different relationship to their internal experiences, children may become more aware of choice points that allow one to respond rather than react to events with conscious awareness.

Session 11: life is not a rehearsal

The *Feelings Are Not Facts* practice offers another opportunity for children to draw connections between thoughts, emotions, and body sensations. Children are asked to imagine two scenarios as vividly as possible. The *Anger Imagined* scenario reads: You are at school and you're feeling really upset because you just had a fight with a good friend. Then, you see another friend who runs away and says, "I'm too busy to stop and talk." The *Happiness*

Imagined scenario reads: You are at school and you're feeling really happy because you've been included in an activity by a group of children who normally exclude you. Then, you see another friend who runs away and says, "I'm too busy to stop and talk" (Semple & Lee, 2011, pp. 217–218). After both scenarios, children are asked, "What do you think and how do you feel? What is happening in your body?"

Children can easily make the connection that their negative emotions often distort their interpretation of the event. If they are angry, they might project anger onto their friend or fear that everyone is conspiring against them. In the second scenario, the reactions tend to be less emotionally charged. Children might express more understanding and concern, wondering if their friend is overwhelmed with schoolwork or needing to meet urgently with a teacher. How many times does this happen to us in real life? How often do we become upset or anxious without understanding the full context of the event? Our emotions can constrict our perception of reality, and just like our thoughts, they can often mislead. We may automatically jump to conclusions, but with a willingness to look beyond assumptions, we can gather more information and possibly discover something new.

At the end of Session 11, we remind the children that our time together is coming to a close. The home practice for this week is to write a *Letter to My Self*. Children are asked to reflect on their experiences over the past 11 weeks and how they plan to continue their mindfulness practice when the program ends. We also take time to plan the graduation party with activities and food.

Session 12: living with presence, compassion, and awareness

Children typically arrive to the last session with an air of excitement. They arrive with their letters and party supplies in hand. In the beginning of the session, we invite children to share their letters with the group for the *Exploring Everyday Mindfulness* activity. To emphasize choice, we encourage children to share what they feel comfortable sharing. This group experience is a meaningful way for children to reflect on what they learned and what they will take with them, and is also a way for them to express gratitude to the group. Children will leave their letters with the therapists, who will mail them back in three months. This follow-up is intended to encourage children to continue cultivating their mindfulness practices at home.

During the graduation ceremony, children are given certificates of completion and a small gift in the form of a polished stone. Thich Nhat Hanh (2012) teaches the pebble practice, in which a tangible object becomes a symbolic reminder to help children reconnect with their breath and the world around them. We hand out the polished stones and invite children to explore the object with their senses. The stone is also emblematic of the children's shared journey with the group. We can honor the deep learning and meaningful relationships that have been cultivated along the way.

In closing

Through our work with children, we have learned some important lessons. Children have a natural way of being in the present moment and noticing things that adults often overlook. They are creative at expressing themselves with words and through artwork. They might surprise you with their ability to express themselves through movement and their capacity to invent new yoga poses in the moment. Their spirit of discovery allows them to explore their experiences with energy and curiosity. Anyone who has the privilege of working with children can understand how children are often our greatest teachers. The children with whom we've worked in our clinical practices have taught us patience and compassion, and the boundless capacity to discover something new in each moment, if we only pay attention.

Materials and resources

Information about MBCT-C can be found at:

- The California Evidence-Based Clearinghouse for Child Welfare website: www.cebc4cw.org/program/mindfulness-based-cognitive-therapy-for-children-mbct-c/detailed
- Jennifer Lee, Ph.D.: http://jleephd.com
- Randye J. Semple, Ph.D.: http://sites.google.com/site/randyesemplephd
- The MBCT-C treatment manual has been translated into German and French:
- Semple, R. J., & Lee, J. (2013). *Achtsamkeitsbasierte Therapie für Kinder mit Angststörungen*. Paderborn, Germany: Junfermann Verlag. (www.junfermann.de/titel-1-1/achtsamkeitsbasierte_therapie_fuer_kinder_mit_angststoerungen-10038/)
- Semple, R. J., & Lee, J. (2016). *La pleine conscience pour les enfants anxieux: Aller mieux en s'amusant grâce au programme MBCT-C*. Paris, France: De Boeck Supérieur. (www.deboecksuperieur.com/recherche/MBCT-C)
- Clinical training and supervision are available for those interested in integrating MBCT-C into their therapy practices, by the authors and these clinicians:
- Richard W. Sears, Psy.D., Ph.D., is Director of the Center for Clinical Mindfulness & Meditation and clinical/research faculty at the University of Cincinnati Center for Integrative Health and Wellness. Website: http://psych-insights.com/
- Christina M. Luberto, Ph.D., is a Postdoctoral Research Fellow in Integrative Medicine at Harvard Medical School and Clinical Psychology Fellow in Behavioral Medicine at Massachusetts General Hospital. Email: cluberto@mgh.harvard.edu

For researchers, the Mindfulness-Based Cognitive Therapy for Children Adherence Scale (MBCT-C-AS; Semple & Sears, 2014) was developed to ensure fidelity during the program's implementation. The MBCT-C-AS is a 20-item measure of essential components that can be directly observed by a trained rater, including facilitating group cohesion, providing psychoeducation, describing strategies aligned with the overall goals of the program, and reviewing home practices. The scale was adapted from the MBCT Adherence Scale for adults (MBCT-AS; Segal, Teasdale, Williams, & Gemar, 2002), which is a validated measure. The MBCT-C-AS and two program-specific research evaluation questionnaires, one for children and one for parents, are available by request at MBCTforChildren@gmail.com.

References

Black, D. S. (2015). Mindfulness training for children and adolescents: A state-of-the-science review. In K. W. Brown, J. D. Creswell, & R. M. Ryan (Eds.), *Handbook of mindfulness: Theory, research, and practice* (pp. 283–310). New York, NY: Guilford Press.

Burke, C. A. (2010). Mindfulness-based approaches with children and adolescents: A preliminary review of current research in an emergent field. *Journal of Child and Family Studies*, *19*(2), 133–144. doi:10.1007/s10826-009-9282-x

Cotton, S., Luberto, C. M., Sears, R. W., Strawn, J. R., Stahl, L., Wasson, R. S., Blom, T. J., & Delbello, M. P. (2015). Mindfulness-based cognitive therapy for youth with anxiety disorders at risk for bipolar disorder: A pilot trial. *Early Intervention in Psychiatry, 10*, 426–434. doi:10.1111/eip.12216

Esmailian, N., Tahmassian, K., Dehghani, M., & Mootabi, F. (2013). Effectiveness of Mindfulness-Based Cognitive Therapy on depression symptoms in children with divorced parents. *Journal of Clinical Psychology, 3*, 47–57. Available from http://jcp.semnan.ac.ir

Harnett, P. H., & Dawe, S. (2012). Review: The contribution of mindfulness-based therapies for children and families and proposed conceptual integration. *Child and Adolescent Mental Health, 17*(4), 195–208. doi:10.1111/j.1475–3588.2011.00643.x

Hayes, S. C., Strosahl, K., & Wilson, K. G. (1999). *Acceptance and commitment therapy: An experiential approach to behavior change.* New York, NY: Guilford Press.

Kabat-Zinn, J. (1990). *Full catastrophe living: Using the wisdom of your body and mind to face stress, pain, and illness.* New York, NY: Bantam Doubleday Dell.

Lee, J., Semple, R. J., Rosa, D., & Miller, L. (2008). Mindfulness-based cognitive therapy for children: Results of a pilot study. *Journal of Cognitive Psychotherapy, 22*(1), 15–28. doi:10.1891/0889.8391.22.1.15

Linehan, M. M. (1993). *Cognitive-behavioral treatment of borderline personality disorder.* New York, NY: Guilford Press.

Nhat Hanh, T. (1991). *Peace is every step: The path of mindfulness in everyday life.* New York, NY: Bantam Books.

Nhat Hanh, T. (2012). *A handful of quiet: Happiness in four pebbles.* Berkeley, CA: Plum Blossom Books.

Satlof-Bedrick, E., & Johnson, C. N. (2015). Children's metacognition and mindful awareness of breathing and thinking. *Cognitive Development, 36*, 83–92. doi:10.1016/j.cogdev.2015.09.011

Segal, Z. V., Teasdale, J. D., Williams, J. M., & Gemar, M. C. (2002). The mindfulness-based cognitive therapy adherence scale: Inter-rater reliability, adherence to protocol and treatment distinctiveness. *Clinical Psychology & Psychotherapy, 9*(2), 131–138. doi:10.1002/cpp.320

Segal, Z. V., Williams, J. M. G., & Teasdale, J. D. (2002). *Mindfulness-based cognitive therapy for depression: A new approach to preventing relapse.* New York, NY: Guilford Press.

Segal, Z. V., Williams, J. M. G., & Teasdale, J. D. (2013). *Mindfulness-based cognitive therapy for depression* (2nd ed.). New York, NY: Guilford Press.

Semple, R. J., Droutman, V., & Reid, B. A. (2017). Mindfulness goes to school: Things learned (so far) from research and real-world experiences. *Psychology in the Schools, 54*(1), 29–52. doi:10.1002/pits.21981

Semple, R. J., & Lee, J. (2011). *Mindfulness-based cognitive therapy for anxious children: A manual for treating childhood anxiety.* Oakland, CA: New Harbinger Publications.

Semple, R. J., Lee, J., Rosa, D., & Miller, L. F. (2010). A randomized trial of mindfulness-based cognitive therapy for children: Promoting mindful attention to enhance social-emotional resiliency in children. *Journal of Child and Family Studies, 19*, 218–229. doi:10.1007/s10826–009–9301-y

Semple, R. J., Reid, E. F. G., & Miller, L. (2005). Treating anxiety with mindfulness: An open trial of mindfulness training for anxious children. *Journal of Cognitive Psychotherapy, 19*(4), 379–392. doi:10.1891/jcop.2005.19.4.379

Semple, R. J., & Sears, R. (2014). *Mindfulness-based cognitive therapy for children (MBCT-C) adherence scale.* Unpublished assessment scale. University of Southern California, Los Angeles, CA.

Strawn, J. R., Cotton, S., Luberto, C. M., Patino, L. R., Stahl, L. A., Weber, W. A., . . . DelBello, M. P. (2016). Neural function before and after mindfulness-based cognitive therapy in anxious adolescents at risk for developing bipolar disorder. *Journal of Child and Adolescent Psychopharmacology, 26*(4), 372–379. doi:10.1089/cap.2015.0054

Teasdale, J. D. (1999). Metacognition, mindfulness and the modification of mood disorders. *Clinical Psychology and Psychotherapy, 6*(2), 146–155. doi:10.1002/(SICI)1099–0879(199905)6:2<146::AID-CPP195>3.0.CO;2-E

Teasdale, J. D., Moore, R. G., Hayhurst, H., Pope, M., Williams, S., & Segal, Z. V. (2002). Metacognitive awareness and prevention of relapse in depression: Empirical evidence. *Journal of Consulting and Clinical Psychology, 70*(2), 275–287. doi:10.1037/0022–006X.70.2.275

Wells, A. (2002). *Emotional disorders and metacognition: Innovative cognitive therapy*. West Sussex, UK: John Wiley & Sons.

Zoogman, S., Goldberg, S. B., Hoyt, W. T., & Miller, L. (2015). Mindfulness interventions with youth: A meta-analysis. *Mindfulness, 6*, 290–302. doi:10.1007/s12671-013-0260-4

Section VI

Mindfulness programs at work

Chapter 24

Mindful leadership

Jutta Tobias Mortlock and Jennifer Robinson

Development and overview of the program

The Mindful Leadership programme was conceived as a key outcome of the "Mindfulness at Work" conference organised at Cranfield University in 2014. The topic of mindful leadership emerged as a topic of interest in numerous sessions, with individuals debating what exactly mindful leadership is and how it may benefit organisations.

Participants discussed how to bridge the gap between emerging theory on mindful leadership with "the practices" of leading organisations mindfully. Cranfield University's mission is to help organisations translate knowledge into action. Because of this strong focus and close ties to industry, as well as the enthusiasm for mindful leadership generated at the "Mindfulness at Work 2014" conference, it was felt that Cranfield was in a unique position to offer such a programme to its executive clients. Accordingly, the Mindful Leadership programme is structured to emphasise the translation of theory and practise of mindfulness to in situ work contexts.

Since then, Cranfield University has been running Executive Education Programmes on Mindful Leadership. Executives who choose Cranfield programmes are drawn from a wide range of industries and functional backgrounds. Those who participate may or may not hold an official role as a leader, but may in future emerge as leaders (Hosking, 1988; Uhl-Bien & Marion, 2009).

Executives interested in Mindful Leadership self-select to attend the programme at Cranfield. Many who enrol are new to mindfulness. The span of positional power is as wide as CEO to supervisor, but all are considered leaders for the purpose of this programme and the introduction of mindfulness to them is assumed to change both the individual and their relationships as well as the system within which they operate.

Mindfulness can be defined as an "orthogonal rotation in consciousness" (Kabat-Zinn, 1990, p. 426) integrating a fuller understanding of the world derived from increased awareness of thoughts, emotions, sensations, and contextual flux (Fiol & O'Connor, 2003; O'Malley et al., 2009; Brendel & Bennett, 2016). When defining mindfulness it is important to emphasise that this state-change moves beyond the cognitive to an embodied intelligence and as such it is not about "more" or "better" thinking, but a different and new way of knowing (Glomb et al., 2011; Sinclair, 2016).

At Cranfield, through a careful study of the current scholarship in Mindful Leadership, we have come to understand that Leadership in the Mindfulness literature suffers from three conflation. The first is that leaders and leadership are used inter-changeably, yet they are not the same. Often individuals are connoted as leaders simply because they hold positional power, this may or may not make them leaders (Barker, 2001; Pye, 2005). Further, and this is the second conflation, those in positional power may or may not enact leadership practise (Raelin, 2016). The most confusing conflation in the literature is the use of imprecise terms, for instance, leadership is used when what is meant is the leader as a single entity; alternatively, leadership is used when what is meant is the relating that happens between a leader an another. Gronn (2002) provides the key to untangle this muddle by suggesting a unit-of-analysis approach. In this analysis it is possible to parse the literature into three different units. Unit one is within an individual; unit two is between individuals; unit three is across whole systems. When this is applied to the Mindful Leadership literature, it is possible to dis-aggregate three different phenomena. The Cranfield programme is structured across three days to address all three phenomena.

On Day One, the programme considers phenomenon one: mindfulness that is situated within the leader. This draws on the mindful literature that considers the "intra" relational aspects of mindfulness (see for example: Fiol & O'Connor, 2003; Glomb et al., 2011; Kearney, Kelsey & Herrington, 2013; Good et al., 2016; Fraher, Branicki & Grint, 2017). As mindfulness is a self-induced state, much of the teaching on day one is through experiences such as eating or observing or moving. Individuals learn to muster their attention to a single point and to be fully present with whatever is happening in this moment (Kabat-Zinn, 1990; Shapiro et al., 2006). By the end of day one, the intention is to have offered enough variety in the training of mindfulness that individuals can choose their own practises that will activate mindfulness within (Sutcliffe, Vogus & Dane, 2016).

Following the different units of analysis described above, on Day Two, the programme considers phenomenon two: mindfulness that is situated in the relationships between the leader and others. The assumption is that the relationship is changed by the addition of mindfulness (for example, see: Fyke & Buzzanell, 2013; Glomb et al., 2011; Good et al., 2016; Kawakami, White & Langer, 2000; Kearney, Kelsey & Herrington, 2013; Reb, Narayanan & Chaturvedi, 2014; Sauer & Kohls, 2011; Yeo, Gold & Marquardt, 2015). Participants are encouraged to activate a mindful state and consider how this might impact their relationships at work, in meetings, during informal interactions and when dealing with difficult conversations.

Throughout Day Three, the programme considers phenomenon three: mindfulness that is situated in the ongoing social practises of an organisation (Crevani, Lindgren & Packendorff, 2010). The assumption is that the social system is changed by the addition of mindfulness. This system-level of analysis is found in the mindfulness literature of Fiol and O'Connor (2003), Naot, Lipshitz and Popper (2004), Langer (2010), Dunoon and Langer (2011), Fyke and Buzzanell (2013), Yeo, Gold and Marquardt (2015), and Fraher, Branicki and Grint (2017). Participants are invited to make sense of this theory across their own organisation through a series of techniques including a dialogue approach (Ashford & DeRue, 2012; Bohm, 2013).

The programme allows time throughout for personal reflection and personal sense-making and concludes with a review of key points and outstanding issues raised by the participants. This pedagogic approach "place[s] learners directly in their practice worlds" (Raelin, 2007, p. 511) with an accent on action learning and experimentation in real-life enactments.

Through the three-day structure and by utilising three units of analysis – within, between, and across – the Programme on Mindful Leadership avoids the three conflations discussed earlier.

Programme structure

The Mindful Leadership programme unfolds in four phases: (1) onboarding activities before arrival at Cranfield University, (2) a three-day residential workshop, (3) a follow-up webinar approximately four to six weeks following the completion of the workshop, and (4) online support material available through a learning portal. In this way, the programme participants are guided into their personal exploration of what mindful leadership means to them, assisted through this experience at Cranfield University, and supported afterwards, in order to embed and sustain their learning.

Onboarding

Several weeks before the Mindful Leadership programme participants arrive at Cranfield University, they are invited to reflect on a particular leadership challenge they face, which they are prepared to discuss and work through during the programme. They are also invited to complete several self-report surveys including measures of resilience, emotional intelligence, and other surveys related to the practise of leadership.

Residential workshop structure

Having provided the theoretical underpinnings for the Cranfield programme in the foregoing section, in this section, we lay out the general syllabus that is provided each day. We describe this as a general syllabus, in acknowledgement that it would be mindless of us to expect it to be identical each time (Langer, 1997). To begin, therefore we provide a brief introduction on the intentions, attitudes and attentions (Shapiro et al., 2006) we hold in guiding these three days.

Our intention is to hold the group in a safe space to allow for exploration and learning, in large part, experientially (McCowan, Reibel & Micozzi, 2011). In keeping with the precepts of mindfulness, as faculty, we consider ourselves to be Sherpas, simply walking alongside the track of learning; able to describe the journey but "allowing each participant to have their own experience" (McCowan, Reibel & Micozzi, 2011, p. 123). Further, we stand ready to acknowledge that our participants are adults, many of whom hold important roles in organizations, some with high status and power. Stepping into a learning experience with them is to approach the programme as peers and mutual learners. We therefore accompany our participants with an attitude of service and equality, where it is more than possible for us to learn as much as they do.

Our attention is deliberately placed in two ways, both inward and outward. In the first instance to ourselves so that we do not lose connection (Schoeberlein & Sheth, 2009); but also to each other and the group, in the manner often described by Chris Cullen as a state of 50:50 (Williams, Penman & Cullen, 2015). This moving of attention between the intra and the inter mirrors also two of the phenomenon found in the literature.

Holding attention in this way, with intention, and a particular attitude, begins to mark out this syllabus from other leadership development programmes, despite the common thread that is shared by all leadership development training: the course must meet the specific objectives of each participant and provide value for money. Many from the corporate world are curious about meditation, but also cautious. It does not always readily translate into a corporate environment. Hence, the Mindful Leadership programme at Cranfield does not overly rely on meditation as a method of teaching mindfulness. There is meditation, and help for participants to learn to focus, calm and stabilise their mind, but the emphasis in this programme has been moved to mindfulness in situ, with many practises that mimic everyday activities that lend themselves to increased attention and awareness. This approach is aligned to the part of the MBSR curriculum known as informal practise (Blacker et al., 2009). Whereas in mindfulness training targeted as a health intervention, cleaning teeth might be an informal practise; we would offer instead other more office-relevant practises of mindfulness.

Here follows the syllabus in detail:

Day one

As previously set out, the focus of day one is on the individual participant and building their understanding and experience of a personal practise, in whatever way makes best sense to them. Table One below provides an example of the agenda for the day:

Table 24.1 Table one day one

Learning Outcomes	Learning Process	Format
Personal introductions and a mindful learning contract	Using visuals to elicit deeper reflection, get everyone's voice in the room, and encourage them to bring their real self. Understand the challenges they face and their desired learning. Agreeing a learning contract that is psychologically safe and productive for everyone.	Co-creation
Attention and awareness and how they are generated through mindfulness	Defining mindfulness and what it means for the participants. Discussing the business case for mindful leadership. Starting to practise mindfulness individually.	Short presentation Discussion Practise
The road to resilience: How to make personal performance sustainable	Explaining the link between mindfulness practise and neuroplasticity. Exploring ways to increase personal resilience during stress and challenge.	Short presentation Reflection Discussion
Your leadership journey and how mindfulness can increase clarity about it	Inviting participants to consider what leadership is inspirational to them, and where they are on their leadership journey. Practising mindful attention to the challenges they face as leaders.	Reflection Discussion Practise
Increasing choice concerning your own leadership style	Using an established model of leadership (e.g. Boyatzis et al. (2012) six leadership styles), eliciting new insight about their own leadership preference. Exploring how to extend their leadership behavioural repertoire.	Reflection Discussion

Learning Outcomes	Learning Process	Format
Values-based leadership	Using visuals to elicit insight about the difference between goals and the underlying values that drive them. Clarifying which personal values drive their leadership choices and behaviours.	Small group exercise Discussion
Mindful reflections	Reflecting on what was learned and what still needs to be discussed or explored more	Reflection Discussion

Day two

Table 24.2 Table two day two

Learning Outcomes	Learning Process	Format
Returning fully to the workshop	Using mindfulness practise, bringing everyone's attention and voice back into the room, ready for the second day of learning.	Co-creation
Understanding decision-making at a deeper level: why it is so hard to make "the right" decision, and what to do about it	Demonstrating that feelings trump facts and that cognitive schemas are more firmly in place than we often assume. Practising possible ways to become aware of different factors impacting our decisions.	Demonstration Discussion Pair work Practise
Practising making decisions mindfully	Using small group decision exercises (e.g. decision vignettes such as those outlined by Langer (2014)) exploring ways in which we can make decisions more mindfully than habitually.	Small group exercise Discussion Practise
Extending personal mindfulness practise	Reminder that a personal mindfulness practise is the basis for applying mindfulness to work situations. Exploring different ways in which to practise mindfulness at work.	Reflection Discussion Practise
Handling problems mindfully	Returning to the leadership challenges the participants face in their work, exploring all aspects of what such challenges can mean for different individuals, and what new insights can be learned here, individually and through mindful listening to others' perspectives. Using different perspectives and "not knowing" to consider difficult challenges.	Small group exercise Discussion Practise
Setting up a mindful decision making contract	Encouraging participants to continue co-coaching each other and to create an ongoing contract of caring and supporting each other mindfully.	Reflection Discussion

(*Continued*)

Table 24.2 (Continued)

Learning Outcomes	Learning Process	Format
Mindful meetings	Explaining the research underpinning mindful meetings e.g. Pavlov (2010). Discussing mindful ways to apply this knowledge in the participants' workplaces. Reflecting and applying this learning.	Short presentation Discussion Reflection
Mindful reflections	Reflecting on what was learned and what still needs to be discussed or explored more	Reflection Discussion

Day three

Table 24.3 Table three day three

Learning Outcomes	Learning Process	Format
Returning fully to the workshop	Using mindfulness practise, bringing everyone's attention and voice back into the room, ready for the third day of learning.	Co-creation
Personal mindfulness practise	Reminder that a personal mindfulness practise is the basis for applying mindfulness at work. Encouraging participants to practise mindfulness individually, without external support.	Reflection Practise
The meaning of "collective mindfulness" for your organisation	Explaining "collective mindfulness" (Weick & Roberts, 1993) for mindful leaders. Discussing how the elements of this framework apply to the participants' own work contexts.	Short presentation Discussion
Understanding why and how organisational culture matters for mindful leadership	Short presentation about the importance of understanding culture for leadership and strategy formulation. Applying these insights by creating a personal map of the organisation's culture, including where individuals and teams operate mindfully vs on autopilot. Reflection and discussion in plenary.	Short presentation Reflection Discussion
Impacting your own culture mindfully	Returning to the leadership challenges the participants face, or to a newly emerging challenge, exploring in groups what additional factors may be at stake/need to be considered to address the challenge. Co-creating new insight through mindful listening and feedback giving.	Small group exercise Reflection

Learning Outcomes	Learning Process	Format
Your mindful leadership takeaways	Co-creating meaningful takeaway messages, action points, and co-coaching commitments with the participants. Reflecting on what was learned and what remains as open questions. Celebrating the participants' achievements before closing.	Plenary work

Sample curriculum content

In the following section, we provide sample content drawn from the above described curriculum, so that readers can experiment with these ideas in their own relevant training programmes.

Exercise: mindful connections

Intention of the exercise: To allow participants to explore how mindfulness that is held within an individual (i.e. themselves) can effect mindfulness that is between individuals.
  Person A speaks for five minutes. Person B listens.
  Person B speaks for five minutes. Person A listens.
  Dialogue mindfully together about what you learn.
  Pause. Pause some more (!)
  Reflect together on what you notice about this conversation
  Your topics are:
  Describe your perfect day.
  What does leadership mean to you?
  What about leadership challenges you?
  Notes for the teacher who de-briefs this exercise:
  During the de-brief of the exercise, we hold the following intention: help participants to stay with the experience and notice when they are moving to a judgement of the experience
  What happened?
  What did you notice, what did you discover?
  What was unexpected about this conversation?

Exercise: mindful decision making

Intention of the exercise: To allow participants to translate mindfulness to an everyday set of circumstances: decision making is a common executive function and one that can be automatic and mindless. This exercise helps to make manifest hidden ways of thinking and automatic ways of working. Participants are presented with the following vignette and suggestions for reflection:

> You are the general manager of an oil refinery plant. You have budget and decision making responsibility. The plant employs around 300 people and they are rostered around the clock to run the plant 24/7, 365 days. As with any process manufacturing if the plant "stops" getting it back up to speed is time consuming. Each stoppage requires that the plant is stripped and "cleaned" and then re-commissioned in a specific sequence – each step of the sequence needs to be achieved precisely before the next step of the sequence can be initiated.
>
> The plant has a problem, it is not refining oil to the required quality which means that the heavy-oils i.e. a coke residue, remain even after a full cycle. The engineering team have spent months sourcing a cost-effective solution. It is a flexi-coker and it means that the system will be capable of refining a wider range of crude oil types and it will minimize the coke residue.
>
> Installing the flexi-coker requires a shut down.
>
> Shut down will cause a loss of revenue and comes with some risks associated with re-starting the plant. But for $1bn of investment the ROI is expected to be 20%. You authorise a full project plan and final business case to be prepared. When these are presented to you, the costs have nearly doubled.
>
> Read through the above case study. Initially reflect by yourself and consider these questions:
>
> What are your automatic reactions? When you sit in mindfulness, what now emerges? Outline a few mindful actions you might take. Notice how these might differ from your first automatic reactions?

Join others in your group to share themes. Think particularly about how this is relevant to your work situation? What sorts of situations do you regularly face?

Notes for the teacher who de-briefs this exercise:

During the de-brief of the exercise, we hold the following intention: generalise from the exercise to other contexts that they might encounter in the workplace. What did you notice about your conceptualisations of the decision?

What did you notice about the reality of the decision?

What do you discover when you make these distinctions?

What do you take away from this discussion?

Exercise: activating collective mindfulness

Intention of the exercise: To allow participants to experience and experiment with mindfulness that is collective. This is a form of heedful inter-relating where each individual becomes aware of themselves in relation to others and to the system in which they are operating. They begin to understand interconnectivity and how their thoughts and actions interconnect with those of the group. Participants are presented with the following instructions.

Work as a group. Nominate one person to be the scribe: they observe and take notes of what happens, but do not take part in the discussion.

The group task is to make sense of an ambiguous picture.

Notes for the teacher who de-briefs this exercise:

During the de-brief of the exercise, we hold the following intention: Help participants to see their interconnections and heedful inter-relating as well as notice when and where assumptions and conclusions are drawn.

Step one: hear feedback from recorders

Step two: ask others what happened for them

Step three: what aspects of mindfulness/mindlessness arose in the group? What was automatic?

Step four: meta-awareness: so, what's happening now, in this debrief?

Exercise: exploring the unexplored

Intention of the exercise – being mindful in dialogue with ourselves is helpful but often we're in conversation with others and they've not been trained to be mindful! So, how do we use mindfulness in dialogue when others are hitting our hot buttons?

Participants are presented with the following instructions.

Consider the following: Whenever we're in conversation we have another conversation going simultaneously: a narration on whatever is actually happening.

Mindfulness helps us make that visible to ourselves and [sometimes terrifyingly] to the other party. Only when we acknowledge it can we discern what's really happening and make different choices.

Work in pairs. Coach each other on a current work situation where you have difficulty with another person – explain the situation that you face and how you think and feel about it. Particularly make sure that you reveal your hidden thoughts about the situation; about the person. The person who is listening is invited to use open questions to explore the unexplored (a few examples are provided below, but please make up your own).

Questions you might like to ask each other:

- What would you think or feel if this was your [best friend/spouse/child]?
- What might change for you about this situation, if you consider it from the very far future?
- If I wave a magic wand for you, what happens? What do you notice?
- If you assumed completely good intentions in the other person, what shifts inside you?

Notes for the teacher who de-briefs this exercise:

During the de-brief of the exercise, we hold the following intention: generalise more broadly

What difference did this make?

> Where can you use this in your work life?
> What prompts can you create to help yourself step out of automatic? What prompts can you ask others to provide?

Follow-up webinar

Approximately four to six weeks after the three-day programme at Cranfield, there is a follow-up webinar for all participants. During this webinar, the participants are encouraged to share their experiences of returning to work as newly forged "mindful leaders" and their insights since the group spent time together at Cranfield. The webinar is designed to allow space for the emergence of new questions and time for them to be discussed. Typically, there is an exchange ideas of ideas about sustaining their personal mindfulness practise and how to overcome common challenges related to bringing mindfulness into their work and leadership. During the webinar, the facilitators explore where the participants' ongoing leadership are, and the group is encouraged to co-create new answers to the questions the leaders face at this time.

The webinar is also an opportunity for the group to embed important learning from the three-day workshop, to discuss ongoing support, and agree ways to communicate with each other going forward. Some participants choose to establish semi-formal peer-pairs to continue their mindful mentoring of each other. Readers of this chapter might consider doing likewise. Below is an extract from the briefing we provide on how to work as peer coaches:

Peer-to-peer coaching is a way of embedding theoretical learning and a proven way to translate theory into daily practise.

In the past, pairs who have got the most from this sort of arrangement have told us that they do the following:

- Reviewed the guidelines below and talked them through to develop common understanding
- Continued to diary/journal about their mindfulness practise and reflections
- Set up pre-agreed dates for skype calls, approximately every three weeks according to workload and other factors
- Shared, appropriately, extracts from their journal
- Reviewed the slides from the programme, reviewed the learning summary and discovered each other's perspective on key points
- Chosen a behaviour or practise that they would like to embed and experimented over the three weeks with their chosen focus
- Reviewed at the skype call "what's happened" and either recommitted to continuing or trying something else
- Shared resources or helpful new understandings during the skype call
- One person might choose to lead a short/simple mindfulness practise to begin the call; and other to end the call (remember the five senses as a simple way to come into the moment)

> **Guidelines for peer-to-peer coaching**
>
> 1 Hold a positive intention. If you can't think of a constructive for giving feedback, don't give any
> 2 Focus on being objective and encouraging rather than judgemental, and maintain dignity and respect in your comments
> 3 Be aware of feedback overload. Providing feedback can be counter-productive
> 4 Model an attitude of kindness
> 5 Share deeply, you don't need to tell the story, you can start with your inner sense of what is, (e.g. I'm struggling with . . . or, I'm happy about . . .
> 6 Practise open questions to each other so that this is a genuine exploration
> 7 Come with an open mind; accept the possibility that someone else can see things you can't

Online support material

Participants have access to an online learning portal so that they can continue to explore the theory and practise of mindful leadership. There are links to spoken word meditations and videos on the underpinning theory. Some of this material is also in the public domain and relevant links are provided at the end of this chapter.

Empirical research supporting the program

To date, no universally accepted definition of the meaning of "Mindful Leadership" exists; hence we conducted a qualitative research study on what it means to be a mindful leader in relation to the Cranfield programme. The two-fold goal of this longitudinal study was to further understand the experiences and perceptions of programme participants, and to contribute to theory-building on the concept of mindful leadership. The interview data gathered by the researchers provided fertile ground for generating new evidence-based insights on the link between mindfulness and leadership.

The research was exploratory in nature, examining themes related to a recent leadership theory whose tenets conceptually overlap with mindfulness: Drath et al's. (2008) leadership as practise model. In this model, leadership is conceptualised as a multi-level ontology of being, and it emerges predominately as a shared practise and shared perceptions of culture. This practise is centred around the three-pronged sequence of generating Direction – Alignment – Commitment (DAC). Mindfulness too is conceptualised as a multi-level construct (Sutcliffe, Vogus & Dane, 2016), and often referred to as a practise (e.g. Dimidjian & Linehan, 2003).

Sampling and procedure

The research drew on 21 in-depth interviews conducted over the course of six months with eight individuals who had participated in the programme. Five female and three male participants constituted the sample of Mindful Leadership programme "alumni."

They were between 35–56 years old, leading teams of three to 1200 individuals from both private and public sector organisations across the UK, continental Europe, and the Middle East.

Approximately 25 hours of interview data was collected. Interviews were semi-structured, and template analysis (King, 2004) was used to evaluate the data captured.

Data analysis

Building on the ontology proposed by Drath et al. (2008), the mindful leaders surveyed appeared to express their way of being as leaders and their commitment to mindfulness in at least five original, adaptive, and innovative ways.

The five themes that emerged from the data analysis are listed below and explained further in the section that follows:

Formal meditation vs. "in situ" mindfulness
Mindfulness as a practise: culture-changing
Alignment before direction
Commitment before alignment
Direction after commitment

Discussion of emerging research themes

Formal meditation vs. "in situ" mindfulness

First, the more mindful leaders embedded their personal mindfulness practise into their organisational context, the less formal their mindfulness practise became, and the more mindfulness permeated their way of leading at work.

Meditation, on the one hand, seemed to be considered a "holiday" or "escape":

> "I just wanted to get back to sleep when I did that."

There also seemed to be a certain reluctance to practise mindfulness meditation formally whilst back in their work setting.

> "Don't want someone walking into my office meditating."

However, practises discussed during the programme such as "holding the space" were seen as very effective:

> "Practising paying attention to others when they're speaking made me more attentive – noticing works!"

Mindfulness as a practise: culture-changing

Building on the first theme, several participants stressed that "in situ" practise was highly beneficial to them in their work lives. Adopting a mindfulness-based approach to leading and engaging others seemed to impact the collective space and emotional climate of their workplaces.

"My questions are different and the way I listen to the answers has changed. I now really want to hear what people say."

Alignment before direction

Drath et al.'s (2008) Direction-Alignment-Commitment (DAC) model suggests that the practise of leadership starts with providing Direction. However, the evidence put forward by the sampled Mindful Leadership programme alumni indicates that seeking to build Alignment may represent a higher priority for mindful leaders than setting Direction. The focus among the sampled participants seemed to be on nurturing the relational space, especially in situations marked by challenge and conflict.

"A 'no' now means to me 'let's discuss this further'. In the past, I would have heard this as a 'No'. Period."

Commitment before alignment

Drath et al.'s (2008) DAC model also proposes that generating Alignment amongst team members and followers is a higher priority action for leaders than building Commitment. In contrast to this, the Mindful Leadership alumni seemed to have inverted this sequence in that they emphasised demonstrating Commitment, by showing a willingness to accept the situation they have found themselves in and stayed put in the face of difficulty and disagreement.

"I breathe and think about how to move forward constructively rather than brooding on what I should have done."

Direction after commitment

Finally, over time the mindful leaders in the sample tended to use mindfulness techniques in order to change the context in which important decisions were to be shaped. In particular, mindful leaders seemed to proactively promote emergent, bottom-up decision-making, in order to maximise the likelihood of a successful outcome:

"There's more spaciousness in our conversations"

Direction seemed to arise in a less hierarchical, more democratic way. This is in line with one of the tenets of collective mindfulness coined by Weick and Putnam (2006): the idea that in mindful decision-making, the final say should always be deferred to "real-time" experts, in other words those members of the decision-making team who hold the highest degree of expertise in that particular situation and moment in time.

"Now I make sure the real experts have a voice on decisions."

Conclusion

The evidence collected from the sample of Mindful Leadership programme participants suggests that a mindfulness-based leadership practise has the potential to generate a beneficial shift in the leadership context as well as in the relational space in which mindful leaders navigate. This leadership ontology shift may be predominately based on "in situ" mindfulness practise, rather than formal mindfulness meditation.

In extension to Drath et al.'s (2008) DAC leadership as practise model, mindful leaders seem to demonstrate that the order in which the DAC model is constituted may be reversed in mindful leadership. In particular, a focus on Commitment seems to be top priority for mindful leaders, in the sense of remaining committed to making space for experiencing emotional and relational difficulty, rather than rushing to fix or attack it. Second, building Alignment appears to trump Direction giving as a priority of leadership, by remaining open to paying attention to the relational space between mindful leader and those they engage with. Finally, Direction giving may well be the last priority for mindful leaders as a sense of distributed leadership generated from the bottom up seems to be a hallmark of leading mindfully. This evidence suggests that DAC in mindful leadership emerges as CAD: Commitment first, then building Alignment, and finally providing Direction as an emergent quality.

More research is needed to expand this research base, however these early insights, provide fertile ground for more theory-building in mindful leadership.

Online materials and resources for further information on the programme

For more information about Cranfield University's Mindful Leadership Open Programme and several tasters of the mindfulness-based practises taught in the programme, please go to the YouTube channel "Mindful Leadership – Introduction and Practice," available here:

www.youtube.com/playlist?list=PLs0OanxN4Ygg95RREoYtBw_FCM6WxOqWf

References

Ashford, S. J., & DeRue, D. S. (2012). 'Developing as a leader: The power of mindful engagement', *Organizational Dynamics*, 41(2), pp. 146–154. Available at: http://10.0.3.248/j.orgdyn.2012.01.008.

Barker, R. A. (2001). 'The nature of leadership', *Human Relations*, 54(4), pp. 469–494. doi: 10.1177/0018726701544004.

Blacker, M., Meleo-Meyer, F., Kabat-Zinn, J., & Santorelli, S. F. (2009). *Stress reduction clinic Mindfulness-Based Stress Reduction (MBSR) curriculum guide*. Worcester, MA: Center for Mindfulness in Medicine, Health Care, and Society, Division of Preventive and Behavioral Medicine, Department of Medicine, University of Massachusetts Medical School.

Bohm, D. (2013). *On Dialogue*. Netherlands: Schouten & Nelissen. Available at: https://books.google.co.uk/books?hl=en&lr=&id=Bv-gTKx5fTsC&oi=fnd&pg=PP1&dq=david+bohm+dialogue&ots=2iPQaYuCkL&sig=yu0r2d1ECmVhz6dPPQ9Zryc7wuU (Accessed: 30 December 2015).

Boyatzis, R. E., Passarelli, A. M., Koenig, K., Lowe, M., Mathew, B., Stoller, J. K., & Phillips, M. (2012). 'Examination of the neural substrates activated in memories of experiences with resonant and dissonant leaders', *Leadership Quarterly*, Elsevier Inc., 23(2), pp. 259–272. doi: 10.1016/j.leaqua.2011.08.003.

Brendel, W., & Bennett, C. (2016). 'Learning to embody leadership through mindfulness and somatics practice', *Advances in Developing Human Resources*, Sage Publications, 18(3), pp. 409–425. doi: 10.1177/1523422316646068. Brendel, William, College of Education Leadership and Counseling, University of St. Thomas, Minneapolis Opus Hall, Room 427, 1000 LaSalle Avenue, Minneapolis, MN, US, 55403.

Crevani, L., Lindgren, M., & Packendorff, J. (2010). 'Leadership, not leaders: On the study of leadership as practices and interactions', *Scandinavian Journal of Management*, 26(1), pp. 77–86. doi: 10.1016/j.scaman.2009.12.003.

Dimidjian, S., & Linehan, M. M. (2003). 'Defining an agenda for future research on the clinical application of mindfulness practice', *Clinical Psychology Science and Practice*, 10(2), 166–171.

Drath, W. H., McCauley, C. D., Palus, C. J., Van Velsor, E., O'Connor, P. M. G., & McGuire, J. B. (2008). 'Direction, alignment, commitment: Toward a more integrative ontology of leadership', *Leadership Quarterly*, 19(6), pp. 635–653. doi: 10.1016/j.leaqua.2008.09.003.

Dunoon, D., & Langer, E. (2011). 'Mindfulness and leadership opening up to possibilities integral leadership review', *Integral Leadership Review*. Available at: http://integralleadershipreview.com/3729-mindfulness-and-leadership-opening-up-to-possibilities (Accessed: 1 March 2016).

Fiol, C. M., & O'Connor, E. J. (2003). 'Waking up! Mindfulness in the face of bandwagons', *Academy of Management Review*, 28(1), pp. 54–70. doi: 10.5465/AMR.2003.8925227.

Fraher, A. L., Branicki, L. J., & Grint, K. (2017). 'Mindfulness in action : Discovering how US. Navy SEALs develop and sustain mindfulness in High-Reliability Organizations (HROs)', *Academy of Management Discoveries*, Proofcopy, pp. 1–47.

Fyke, J. P., & Buzzanell, P. M. (2013). 'The ethics of conscious capitalism: Wicked problems in leading change and changing leaders', *Human Relations*, 66(12), pp. 1619–1643. Available at: http://10.0.4.153/0018726713485306.

Glomb, T. M., Duffy, M. K., Bono, J. E., & Yang, T. (2011). 'Mindfulness at work', *Research in Personnel and Human Resources Management*, Emerald Group Publishing Ltd. doi: 10.1108/S0742-7301(2011)0000030005.

Good, D. J., Lyddy, C., Glomb, T. M., Bono, J. E., Brown, K. W., Duffy, M. K., Baer, R., Brewer, J., & Lazar, S. W. (2016). 'Contemplating mindfulness at work: An intergrative review', *Journal of Management*, 42(1), pp. 114–142. doi: 10.1002/elan.

Gronn, P. (2002). 'Distributed leadership as a unit of analysis', *The Leadership Quarterly*, 13(May), pp. 423–451. doi: 10.1016/S1048–9843(02)00120–0.

Hosking, D. M. (1988). 'Organizing, leadership and skilful process', *Journal of Management Studies*, 25(2), pp. 147–166. doi: 10.1111/j.1467–6486.1988.tb00029.x.

Kabat-Zinn, J. (1990). 'Full catastrophe living: Using the wisdom of your body and mind to face stress', *Pain, and Illness*, 2005. doi: 10.1037/032287.

Kawakami, C., White, J. B., & Langer, E. J. (2000). 'Mindful and masculine: Freeing women leaders from the constraints of gender roles', *Journal of Social Issues*, United Kingdom: Blackwell Publishing, 56(1), pp. 49–63. doi: 10.1111/0022–4537.00151.

Kearney, W. S., Kelsey, C., & Herrington, D. (2013). 'Mindful leaders in highly effective schools: A mixed-method application of Hoy's M-scale', *Educational Management Administration & Leadership*, 41(3), pp. 316–335. doi: 10.1177/1741143212474802.

King, N. (2004). 'Using templates in the thematic analysis of texts'. In C. Cassell & G. Symon (Eds.), *Essential Guide to Qualitative Methods in Organizational Research* (pp. 256–270). London: Sage Publications.

Langer, E. J. (1997). *The Power of Mindful Learning*. Cambridge, MA: Persus Publishing.

Langer, E. J. (2010). *A call for mindful leadership*, Blog on HBR. Available at: https://hbr.org/2010/04/leaders-time-to-wake-up (Accessed: 1 March 2016).

Langer, E. J. (2014). 'Leadership and organizational behavior'. In A. Ie, C. T. Ngnoumen, & E. J. Langer (Eds.), *The Wiley Blackwell Handbook of Mindfulness*. Chicester, UK: John Wiley & Sons, Ltd.

McCowan, D., Reibel, D., & Micozzi, M. S. (2011). *Teaching Mindfulness*. Berlin: Springer.

Naot, Y. B-H., Lipshitz, R., & Popper, M. (2004). 'Discerning the quality of organizational learning', *Management Learning*, 35(4), pp. 451–472. doi: 10.1177/1350507604048273.

O'Malley, A. L., Ritchie, S. A., Lord, R. G., Gregory, J. B., & Young, C. M. (2009). 'Incorporating embodied cognition into sensemaking theory: A theoretical examination of embodied processes in a leadership context', *Current Topics in Management: Center for Advanced Studies in Management*, pp. 151–181. Available at: https://search.ebscohost.com/login.aspx?direct=true&db=bth&AN=60846780&site=ehost-live.

Pavlov, A. (2010). Reviewing Performance or Changing Routines? An Analysis of the Experience of Participants in Performance Management Review Meeting (unpublished doctoral dissertation). Cranfield, UK, Cranfield University.

Pye, A. (2005). 'Leadership and organizing: Sensemaking in action', *Leadership*, 1(1), pp. 31–50. doi: 10.1177/1742715005049349.

Raelin, J. A. (ed.) (2016). *Leadership-as-Practice Theory and Application*. New York, NY: Routledge.

Raelin, J. A. (2007). 'Toward an epistemology of practice', *Academy of Management Learning and Education*, 6(4), pp. 495–519.

Reb, J., Narayanan, J., & Chaturvedi, S. (2014). 'Leading mindfully: Two studies on the influence of supervisor trait mindfulness on employee well-being and performance', *Mindfulness*, 5(1), pp. 36–45. doi: 10.1007/s12671–012–0144-z. Jochen Reb, Lee Kong Chian School of Business, Singapore Management University, 50 Stamford Road, Singapore, Singapore, 178899: Springer.

Sauer, S., & Kohls, N. (2011). 'Mindfulness in leadership: Does being mindful enhance leaders' business success?' In S. Han & E. Pöppel (Eds.), *Culture and Neural Frames of Cognition and Communication (On Thinking)* (pp. 287–307). Berlin, Heidelberg: Springer. doi: 10.1007/978-3-642-15423-2_17.

Schoeberlein, D., & Sheth, S. (2009). *Mindful Teaching and Teaching Mindfulness*. Boston, MA: Wisdom Publications.

Shapiro, S. L., Carlson, L., Astin, J. A., & Freedman, B. (2006). 'Mechanisms of mindfulness', *Journal of Clinical Psychology*, 62(3), pp. 373–386. doi: 10.1002/jclp.

Sinclair, A. (2016). *Leading Mindfully: How to Focus on What Matters, Influence for Good, and Enjoy Leadership More*. Sydney: Allen & Unwin.

Sutcliffe, K. M., Vogus, T. J., & Dane, E. (2016). 'Mindfulness in organizations: A cross-level review', *Annual Review of Organizational Psychology and Organizational Behavior*, 3(1), pp. 1–57. doi: 10.1146/annurev-orgpsych-041015-062531.

Uhl-Bien, M., & Marion, R. (2009). 'Complexity leadership in bureaucratic forms of organizing: A meso model', *Leadership Quarterly*, Elsevier Inc., 20(4), pp. 631–650. doi: 10.1016/j.leaqua.2009.04.007.

Weick, K. E., & Putnam, T. (2006). 'Organizing for mindfulness: Eastern wisdom and western knowledge', *Journal of Management Inquiry*, 15(3), pp. 275–287. doi: 10.1177/1056492606291202.

Weick, K. E., & Roberts, K. (1993). 'Collective mind in organizations: Heedful interrelating on flight decks', *Administrative Science Quarterly*, 38(3), pp. 357–381. doi: 10.2307/2393372.

Williams, M., Penman, D., & Cullen, C. (2015). *Mindfulness for a Frantic World*. MYRIAD Project study 'Evaluating Mindfulness training routes for school teachers'. Oxford, UK: Oxford Mindfulness Centre.

Yeo, R. K., Gold, J., & Marquardt, M. J. (2015). 'Becoming "leaderful": Leading forward in turbulent times', *Industrial and Commercial Training*, 47(6), pp. 285–292. doi: 10.1108/ICT-04–2015–0032.

Chapter 25

Mindfulness practice and the law

Jurisight and the skillful means to greet the legal profession

Scott Rogers and Sarah Stuart

Introduction

Lawyers around the world are opening to the potential for modern applications of an ancient contemplative practice called "mindfulness" to transform their lives and careers. Set in a context where the legal field is often derided for being too commercial, bottom-line focused, and aggressive, and where the practice of law is often experienced by lawyers as hostile and uncomfortable, some might depict mindfulness in law as an *oxymoron*. Yet the law and legal practice are *uniquely suited* to the interweaving and integration of mindfulness practices and living a mindful life (Rogers, 2014). Considering the central role of the law in society, and of lawyers as shepherds of our legal system, it is heartening to see the robust applications of mindfulness and mindful practices into the law.

This chapter explores the potential for mindfulness to enrich and stabilize the lives of members of the legal profession, our legal system, and society. The first section of this chapter considers the current status of mindfulness permeating legal culture. One of the earliest mindfulness programs to be introduced to members of the legal profession is a program called Jurisight, which will be reviewed in the second section both to convey the methodology and value underlying its structure, utility, and embrace, and to spark ideas for further integrations in the law and other professional fields. The third section summarizes a few of the research studies that shed light on the potential for mindfulness to impact the legal profession and of the ways the Jurisight methodology has been infused in related research. We close by reflecting on the future of mindfulness – in law and life – and further develop our central premise that mindfulness is of fundamental importance to enabling our legal system to continue serving as a stabilizing force in society.

Mindfulness and law

Mindfulness is *attending to present moment experience in a manner that is engaged and unassuming*. (Rogers, 2016c) We are always paying attention to something, but we rarely focus our attention in a purposeful way or are able to sustain our attention for long on a chosen object (Kabat-Zinn, 1994, 2013; Salzberg & Goldstein, 2001). Research has shown that our minds wander upwards to half of the time and that when we are distracted our mood tends to drop due to our tendency to immerse in the woes of our lives, lost in worries about the future or regrets about the past. (Killingsworth & Gilbert, 2010). Mindfulness practice invites us to direct our attention to what is occurring in the present moment, and skillfully remain observant to what is actually unfolding, moment by moment. This is an apt invitation in the context of the law, as mindfulness practice encourages engaging directly with whatever arises, even when it is chaotic and confusing.

A resonate connection exists between the heart of mindfulness practice and the evolution of law. The legal system and laws were created, and have been refined over millennia, to bring order out of chaos. Life was often "nasty, brutish and short" (Hobbes, 1962; Rogers, 2014), involved considerable pain and suffering. The rule of law evolved as a "social contract" under which individuals living in a "state of nature" voluntarily relinquished some of their autonomy in exchange for a system of rules and law enforcement designed to stabilize the disorder and allow for peaceful co-existence and growth (Jean-Jacques Rousseau, 1973; Rogers, 2014). This turning to a "sovereign," for a top-down regulation of erratic, selfish, and unhelpful impulses and actions, relates poignantly to the cultivation of greater awareness in observing the steady stream of often erratic, selfish, and unhelpful thoughts and impulses – so as to bring about a wiser and more compassionate state of mind, body, as well as the governance of our conduct and daily affairs (Rogers, 2014, 2015). Perhaps, this deeply tethered connection is cause to consider both the importance of mindfulness offerings to members of the legal profession, and the lessons and insights that can be learned from the ways mindfulness is taking root in the law.

Interest in mindfulness and mindfulness practice within the law has been growing for about 30 years, with the pace of change increasing significantly in the past decade (Riskin, 2002; Magee, 2010; Halpern, 2012). Mindfulness is spreading rapidly across the legal profession, from law schools, to law firms, to legal organizations and the judiciary. Among the earliest inroads are found in brief mentions in academic legal writings and professional journals directed to law firms' human resource departments (Rogers, 2014, 2015). One of the first law firm mindfulness trainings took place in 1998 when Jon Kabat-Zinn and Ferris Urbanowski introduced an eight-week Mindfulness Based Stress Reduction (MBSR) program at the Boston firm Hale and Dorr (Rogers, 2014). Owing to the time commitment and a variety of additional factors, other law firms were slow to follow suit. In the intervening two decades, as a growing number of mindfulness training programs have been developed for the workplace environment, law firm interest and engagement has proliferated. Currently, law firms such as Mintz Levin and Seyfarth Shaw are offering multi-week MBSR-based courses to their lawyers and staff. Since 2012, Berger Singerman has been offering its attorneys and staff, across all of its offices, multi-session mindfulness trainings and, in 2016, established an in-house Mindfulness and Performance Enhancement Program (Yahoo Finance, 2014; Martinez, 2017). Many other firms around the country are including mindfulness as part of their wellness or training and development initiatives, often in the form of sixty to ninety minute workshops designed to introduce participants to the practice of mindfulness with the potential that they might be inspired to continue on their own, even opening up office space for this purpose. Communities are starting to form at firms and in cities so that mindful lawyers can meet and practice together and/or share their challenges and suggestions for how to incorporate mindfulness into their lives, personally and professionally.

Importantly, judges have become increasingly interested in mindfulness. Federal district court judge Jeremy Fogel who serves as director the Federal Judicial Center, a government education and research center for the courts, wrote a report for judges on the importance of mindfulness. In it he states that his meditation practice became a refuge for him and shares with judges that simple mindfulness practices can help them handle their decision-making responsibilities and prevent mistakes while at the same time easing the stress of their role (Fogel, 2016). Judges Alan Gold, Chris McAliley, and Laurel Isicoff, along with others on both the state and federal bench, have presented on and written about mindfulness and its important connection to the lives of lawyers and judges (Gold, 2016; McAliley, 2016).

The first mindfulness training program created specifically for legal professionals was Jurisight®, a program developed by Scott Rogers that is notable for its use of the language, imagery and culture of the law to introduce fundamental mindfulness insights and exercises. It is one of the first mindfulness programs to impart neuroscience research on mindfulness and teach short form mindfulness trainings. In the past ten years, Jurisight has been introduced to more than 10,000 law students, lawyers, judges and law faculty at local, state, national, and international bar conferences, law firms, legal organization presentations and workshops, and law school programs. It has also been the subject of state bar online practice segments, and has been written about in national and international periodicals and newspapers (Rogers, 2014).

Jurisight: a case study for mindfulness in law

Jurisight was developed at a time when there was little mention of mindfulness in the popular culture and most opportunities to learn and practice mindfulness were found primarily in Buddhist sanghas and centers, and through eight-week MBSR trainings. The Buddhist avenue was rife with confusion over its connection to religion and MBSR called for a significant commitment of time, both of which limited their respective accessibility to members of the legal profession. Born from a recognition of the immense suffering within the legal profession, as exceptionally high levels of stress, anxiety, depression, suicide ideation, and substance abuse were being reported within legal education circles (Benjamin, Kasziniak, Sales, & Shanfield, 1986; Sheldon & Krieger, 2004; Olsen, 2016), Jurisight introduces legal professionals to fundamental mindfulness insights and exercises in a manner that is accessible, enjoyable, and memorable (Rogers, 2009a, 2009b).

The Jurisight method endeavors to meet lawyers where they are by engaging practical discussions of the ways that resistance to moments of challenge can contribute to feelings of overwhelm and compromise performance, and how mindfulness serves to both relieve stress and facilitate a more focused and resilient engagement in daily challenges. These discussions and various demonstrations are communicated through the use of legal imagery, language, and culture – an approach to teaching mindfulness termed "contextually contoured" (Rogers, 2009a, 2009d) and this involves short formal and informal practices that can be integrated into the everyday practice of law (Rogers, 2009b, 2009c). A key aspect of Jurisight is that the insights and exercises resonate with lawyers and law students because they are rooted in the language and culture of legal practice. These *insights* connect to *mindfulness practices* designed to help integrate the teachings in everyday life – conversely, and equally, the *practices* can lead to *insights* that in turn serve to help weave the practice of mindfulness seamlessly into the lives of practitioners. Importantly, Jurisight was developed at a time when neuroscience research began to report on meaningful changes to the structure and function of the brain associated with mindfulness practice, and, from its inception, Jurisight has integrated the science of mindfulness into its teachings.

The Jurisight approach was first introduced to lawyers in 1999 as part of a standard Continuing Legal Education (CLE) Program under the rubric of professionalism (Rogers, 1999). Over the next seven years, as Jurisight was being refined, it was introduced to law school students at the University of Miami School of Law. In 2007 the Florida Bar approved for CLE the two-day workshop "Mindfulness, Balance & the Lawyer's Brain" which integrated mindfulness, law, and neuroscience. Workshop participants were among the first lawyers to be introduced to mindfulness through a program, developed specifically for members of the legal profession. The next year the program's segments were adapted for an eight-week class for law students, and as the popularity of the program grew over the next three years, in 2011 the University of Miami School of Law formed the nation's first Mindfulness in Law Program, offering a series of mindfulness classes as part of the core curriculum. Today, classes include Mindful Ethics, Mindful Leadership, Mindfulness in Law, and Mindfulness and Motivating Business Compliance with the Law, all of which incorporate Jurisight elements, along with the original Jurisight class (Rogers, 2012). Below we set forth the heart of the Jurisight method.

The method

The Jurisight method consists of a series of legal terms, phrases, concepts, and historical figures that are articulated in ways that can be directly connected to fundamental mindfulness insights and practices. In this way, Jurisight reaches with one hand to embrace the attorney (e.g., "Justice") and with the other to join together with a traditional mindfulness practice (observe the moment as it "Just Is"). With one's attention engaged through use of familiar language, imagery, and clever wordplay, the mindfulness insight imparted becomes a discussion point that can be connected to the life and career of a lawyer. As a result, the teachings, which can be playful, surprising, and amusing, offer insights, demonstrations, and practices that are accessible and memorable.

Insights

Justice

One playful yet poignant example of a Jurisight insight is the use of the legal term "Justice," which is split into the two-word phrase, "Just Is." The lesson begins by discussing the legal meaning of the word Justice, a "noble pursuit that calls on wisdom, compassion, courage and commitment" (Rogers, 2009c). It then elaborates that the pursuit of justice is a form of mindfulness in action, which draws on the circumstances of the present moment, without conceptual elaboration and emotional entanglement. The lesson concludes by explaining that, to help bring about justice, whether in one's role as litigator, judge or any other player in the legal process, one can cultivate a mind that acknowledges the arising of an event as it "Just is." Were Jurisight to leave it at this, the opportunity to engage and deepen mindfulness practice would be limited.

The method continues by introducing two mindfulness practices that build upon this creative construction. The first exercise, "Just is Awareness," is a bare attention/open monitoring practice that invites participants to pay attention to whatever "Just Is" arising in the field of awareness. A second exercise, "Just is Changing," builds on the first and invites participants to attend to what "Just Is" arising in the field of awareness for a period of time and then to expand awareness further and notice what "just is" changing. This related practice, which offers a glimpse into the deeper reality that everything is constantly changing in spite of our beliefs to the contrary, opens one to a profound realization about how counterproductive it can be fighting against injustice rather than accepting what is and working for a better tomorrow. It is, of course, an exercise that is applicable at both work and home.

Stare decisis

An insight related to the "Just Is" changing practice is "Stare Decisis," and both are further illuminated by the "Motion to Embrace Life's Uncertain-Tees" exercise. "Stare Decisis" means to "stand by the thing decided," a reminder that the law proceeds with caution and that judicial decisions are made with reference to precedent, leading to a sense that the evolution of case law is predictable and rational. The *Stare Decisis* insight notes that many people are uncomfortable with uncertainty and often want things to remain as they are. Indeed, a fundamental tenet of the law is that it affords predictability to parties. At the same time people can reflect on imperfections from their past with regret, wishing that they could change undesirable and unwanted events and circumstances. So too, the law's growth depends on moving past archaic and inequitable vestiges of a less evolved time and place and embracing more enlightened world views and ways of treating people. This results in a paradox in which one wants to change the past yet maintain the status quo into the future. One of the lessons of *Stare Decisis* is that, by opening to and embracing the fact that everything is uncertain and constantly changing, we reduce the suffering caused by our attachment to the way things are, and free ourselves to see more clearly the road ahead.

Uncertainty

The "Motion to Embrace Life's Uncertain-Tees" exercise is a helpful and entertaining way to illustrate this lesson. The mind's tendency to move into the future and imagine worst-case scenarios, which can lead to a heightened sense of anxiety and negative mood spirals, is a double-edged sword for lawyers, as anticipating and protecting against undesirable outcomes is the lawyer's job. The Jurisight *Uncertain-Tee* demonstration uses elements of surprise to remind us that suffering over a worrisome event may be due more to a resistance to its inherent uncertainty, than to the event itself.

The demonstration begins by handing participants a box of raisins. When part of a multi-session training, the demonstration follows a few weeks after participants experience the mindful eating "raisin" exercise popularized by MBSR. The students are surprised to find that the box does not contain raisins and appears to be empty. Upon further examination, the students discover within the raisin box a snugly fitted golf tee with "One of Life's Uncertain-Tees" embossed on it. After the inevitable laughter and nods of delight, a serious discussion ensues about the series of erroneous assumptions they likely made (the box contains raisins) and the various fleeting feelings they likely experienced (excitement, disappointment, or relief), allowing for fruitful insights across a variety of mindfulness areas. The golf tee can serve as an ongoing reminder that, in spite of the judicial doctrine of stare decisis and implicit preference for certainty and predictability, the practice of law, like life, is constantly changing and forever uncertain. The tee is a mindfulness cue that participants take with them along with a colorful card that on one side comically depicts the "tee" enduring a series of stressful uncertainties, and on the other depicts a legal "Motion to Embrace Life's Uncertain-Tees" that elaborates on the insights discussed and invites participants to embrace the motion – and, physically embrace the tee – as a metaphor for embracing life's uncertainties.

Pain and suffering

A Jurisight insight with profound implications for the practice of law is "Permission to Approach (the Pain)." The lesson begins with the concept of "Pain and Suffering" as a basis for damages in legal actions seeking redress for unpleasant events. It then notes the common belief that the more pain a person feels, the greater will be his or her damages for suffering. In contrast, the Jurisight practice of Permission to Approach the Pain teaches the mindfulness lesson that, by moving *into* rather than *away from* pain, by opening awareness to thoughts, feelings and bodily sensations accompanying "pain," many report a decrease in discomfort (Kabat-Zinn, 1982; Zeidan et al., 2016). This may seem counterintuitive upon first consideration, however, as basic mindfulness treatments have long realized, by engendering a curiosity and open attitude toward the unpleasant event, the accompanying cascade of *resistant thoughts and feelings* often diminishes, leading to a relief from suffering.

This powerful lesson can in turn be extended to unpleasant situations that arise in the midst of daily legal practice, such as negotiating a deal with opposing counsel who is refusing to compromise or working at night on an urgent matter that prevents you from attending a child's performance in a school play. Rather than "fighting against" or using mindful meditation as a way *out of* what may seem like "unfair" circumstances, "Pain and Suffering" suggests instead turning *toward* such experiences; noticing the feelings and bodily sensations that arise in the moment and considering these as unique and invaluable vehicles for the application of mindful practice. This interweaving of mindfulness with the inevitable ups and downs experienced in the legal field, termed "reciprocal practice," encourages looking to our stressful and challenging work situations as pivotal, and perhaps even cherished, opportunities for mindfulness practice, and professional and personal growth (Rogers, 2016c).

Attachment

Another mindfulness insight that flows readily from a basic legal term is the suffering that accompanies "attachments." In the law, a writ of attachment is issued to *satisfy a judgment*. Our minds are continually judging things, based on our preferences. The mind attaches to what it wants *in an effort to satisfy our judgments*. Given the uncertainty inherent in outcomes and the inevitability of change, attachments, as explicitly discussed through wisdom traditions are a reliable source of unhappiness and suffering.

Hearsay

A final Jurisight insight that we will highlight here is called "Hearsay." The legal term hearsay is an "out of court" statement offered as evidence of the truth of the matter asserted. In Jurisight, hearsay is an "out-of-the-mind" thought or statement believed to be true (Rogers, 2009b). In fact, many of the myriad thoughts that we have each day are untrue, yet we not only believe them, we often are guided by them when making crucial decisions. The *Hearsay* insight encourages a recognition that many thoughts are inherently unreliable and warrant further investigation before acting on them. The playful practice involves exclaiming "Objection, Hearsay" just as a lawyer would when opposing counsel attempts to introduce hearsay into evidence. Doing so, we increase our awareness that thoughts are not facts and we decrease our automatic reaction to exaggerations and other stories created in the mind.

Split in the circuits

One of the primary reasons that Jurisight was more fully developed and shared with attorneys in 2007 was the belief that emerging neuroscience findings would prompt attorneys to take mindfulness seriously. In the 2009 treatment, *Mindfulness for Law Students*, a chapter was devoted to neuroscience findings titled, "The Neural Circuit Court" with sections that explored neuroplasticity and the science of mindfulness. One Jurisight insight that dealt with the impact of stress on attention, focus, and decision-making was termed a "Split in the Circuits." In the law, a "split in the circuits" refers to appellate courts reaching different decisions upon similar facts. In Jurisight, it refers to the disconnect between neural circuitry that can lead to the "emotional hijacking" that leads to becoming frazzled.

Demonstrations

A second aspect of the Jurisight method consists of demonstrations which involve an interactive engagement with illustrations, legal motions and orders, and other written materials, crafted to generate insight. One illustration and three motions are briefly discussed here, as they have been addressed in greater detail elsewhere. All of the motions and orders are styled as a legal action of the participant vs. reality.

Attractive nuisance

The legal doctrine of the "Attractive Nuisance," arose from a series of 19th-century cases in which someone dies in an environment that, despite appearances, proved deadly. In the classic "poison pool" cases, young boys, playing in an open field on a hot day, come across an inviting pool of cool water and take a swim. Sadly, the water was toxic and the boys succumbed shortly after jumping in. The legal issue explores the question of liability – the owner of the land who did not have adequate warnings in place or the young trespassers. After recollecting the facts of this legal case, a mindfulness discussion explores the sometimes toxic places our attention wanders. The "Landscape of the Mind" illustration sets in motion a lively, entertaining, and serious conversation and has been found useful in a variety of contexts extending beyond the law (Rogers, 2009b, 2014).

Motion to Recuse

The "Motion to Recuse" addresses the fact that our minds are constantly judging ourselves, others and our experiences. It is grounded in the legal motion to recuse a judge from a case due to a conflict of interest or inherent bias. The motion plays on this by suggesting that "you" must be recused as judge of your own situation since you are constantly judgmental, doubtful, and critical of yourself, others, and situations. The Motion to Recuse plays on legal language and mindfulness concepts in multiple ways. It is a motion where the Petitioner, or person bringing the motion is "You, aka Me" and the Respondent is "Reality." The Motion sites several reasons for recusal, including the fact that you were not elected or appointed to be judge, you had no prior experience, you have multiple conflicts of interest including a personal bias against reality when it does not go your way, you are engaging in "ex parte communications" with yourself, you are using an interpreter of past events, and you prejudge facts. The motion alludes to the insight of non-self, in which we gain considerable freedom by letting go of our fixed concepts of ourselves and open up to the changing nature of everything (Goldstein, 1993).

Motion for Extension of Thyme

The "Motion for Extension of Thyme" practice recognizes that we are often rushing and feeling we do not have enough time to get things done. This leads to increased stress, undermining our ability to perform optimally and adversely affecting our relationships. The mindfulness demonstration involves having participants fill in the blanks in a *Motion for Extension of Time*, identifying areas in which they find themselves short on time and their accompanying thoughts, feelings and body sensations. The motion is granted as an "Order Granting Extension of *Thyme*" where participants are handed an actual sprig (or "extension") of thyme and guided in a mindfulness exercise that incorporates aroma and a "coming to our senses." Participants are reminded that they can keep some thyme handy and practice the simple exercise when they find themselves feeling a sense of urgency.

Practices

Jurisight also offers a series of short mindfulness exercises that can be practiced during the day. These too draw their names from the legal context, including the names of judges and legal doctrine, which may render them more memorable and likely to be looked to during challenging moments.

But for Pause

The *But for Pause* is an informal practice that involves taking a series of mindful breaths when one is feeling agitated and may be on the verge of taking untoward action. In the law, a "But for Cause," invites the inquiry "But for" X, Y would not have happened, to fix responsibility. This short mindful breathing pause, by its very name invites consideration that, *but for the pause*, one may have acted in a way that was not productive or helpful. The insight stemming from this informal practice is relatively simple, yet the ability to see this can lead to profound change over time as one becomes inclined to practice and becomes better able to handle challenging situations and exchanges.

Judge Learned Hand

The *Judge Learned Hand* is taught as a relaxation exercise to help curb anxiety and panic and helps bridge an understanding of the differences and similarities between relaxation and mindfulness practices. Building off the breathing exercise popularized by Dr. Andrew Weil, known as "4-7-8 Breath," this exercise integrates breath and body by bringing the hands into the breath practice (Weil, 2016). Judge Learned Hand is one of the most famous judges in American jurisprudence and the exercise is a play on his name. Because his intellect, the clarity of his writing, and his concentrative faculties are undeniable, the name of the exercise serves to remind people that the exercise can help bring about greater concentration, clarity, and wisdom. Instructions entail exhaling fully while bringing hands into a lightly clenched fist, inhaling and stretching the fingers open to the count of four, holding the breath and fingers outstretched to the count of seven, and exhaling and closing the fingers to the count of eight. Several video demonstrations can be found online (Rogers, 2009d, 2008).

Just Is Holmes

The *Just Is Holmes* is an informal practice that flows from the Jurisight term "Justice," and from the formal "Just Is" awareness exercises. Here, the play on words is the term "Just Is" and the honorific "Justice" bestowed on judges. Supreme Court Justice Oliver Wendell

Holmes, Jr., coined the famous phrase "stop, look, and listen" in a decision prescribing appropriate conduct when approaching train tracks. In the Jurisight exercise known as the "Just Is Holmes," participants are instructed to "Stop, Look and Listen" when approaching a stop sign, when sitting at a traffic light, or anytime for that matter (Rogers, 2011, 2016b). The practice begins by bringing one's attention to the sensations of breathing after which one expands the field of awareness to notice whatever arises within the visual field, and then expand further to notice the arising and passing away of sounds.

Just Is Story

The *Just Is Story* is a formal practice named after Supreme Court Justice Joseph Story. At the heart of many mindfulness practices rests the instruction to pay attention to the arising of thoughts, and the stories that the mind fabricates, so that one can learn to discern the difference between what is actually arising moment by moment and the stories we tell ourselves about what is arising. Jurisight invites participants to listen to the "story" they are telling themselves, cultivating the ability to notice the thought as an event that "just is" (Rogers, 2009a; Tolle, 1999).

Jurisight is an adaptable method allowing for much flexibility. Different aspects of Jurisight are brought to bear in different law school classes based on their subject matter. Presentations and workshops conducted in law firms and legal organizations will draw on Jurisight based on the organization's interests and the length of the program. Moreover, in the various law schools that assign *Mindfulness for Law Students* (Rogers, 2009c) as required reading, teachers draw from the insights, demonstrations, and exercises in ways that are likely in accord with their own personal connection to mindfulness and their particular style of teaching. Jurisight invites and encourages teachers and facilitators, both inside and outside of the law to engage with the core content with openness and a sense of curiosity, pairing insights and exercises in new and playful ways to help elucidate mindfulness teachings and integrate mindfulness practices into participants' daily lives.

Research

Research on the efficacy of mindfulness practices has traipsed into the area of the law. Owing largely to the challenge of conducting research among students in the midst of their stressful law school careers and of pinning down lawyers in the middle of their busy, intense, and unpredictable schedules, with a few notable exceptions (Simon-Thomas, Halpern, Carlin, Shon, & Klein, 2012; Reuben & Sheldon, 2015), there is not much research to report in this area. Preliminary research has looked at whether mindfulness helps lower stress, improve overall wellbeing, and enhance academic performance. However, the contextually contoured approach that underlies Jurisight has been adapted to other domains and has been the subject of scientific research.

Most of these studies have been conducted in collaboration with cognitive neuroscientist Amishi Jha. That approach has led to the development of Mindfulness Based Attention Training (MBAT) and a series of training programs developed for soldiers, firefighters, accountants, undergraduates, teachers, and elite athletes (Rooks, Morrison, Goolsarran, Rogers, & Jha, 2017; Morrison, Goolsarran, Rogers, & Jha, 2014; Sanko, McKay, & Rogers, 2016). A primary research question is the efficacy of short form mindfulness trainings and reported findings indicate that short form trainings can be effective, especially when supported with ongoing daily practice.

Closing

Jurisight emerged at a time when few mindfulness trainings were contextualized for specific audiences. Today that has changed and the rise in contextually tailored programs appears to coincide with a growing interest in the deeper explorations offered by wisdom traditions. Whereas Buddhist centers and MBSR trainings were once looked at askance or deemed impractical, today they are regarded as among the most authentic and useful avenues to deepen one's mindfulness practice. At the same time, these traditional venues, notwithstanding their growing relevance across a broader swath of society and culture, are being threatened by competitive and well-funded contemporary offerings, both through mindfulness studios and other in-person venues as well as through an explosion of digital offerings. These changes present a host of opportunities and challenges. They give rise to complaints of dilution and lack of competence and integrity among newly minted teachers and training programs, while applauding the reach and accessibility of a diverse range of mindfulness offerings. Where all this will lead is uncertain. What is reliable and what is hearsay? Where is the growing pain and suffering cause for concern or an opportunity for positive change? To what extent do we need a little more time before arriving at a judgment and becoming too attached to desired outcomes? After all, isn't the landscape of mindfulness, much as is the terrain of law, something that "just is" and "just is changing?"

Justice and the rule of law evolved to bring order out of chaos, permitting human beings to thrive intellectually, physically, emotionally, economically, and socially. Today, many consider that the practice of law has re-entered a state of nature where rules are undermined, civility is fading, and the bottom line too often trumps other concerns. So too, the foundations of societal, political, economic, and global structures are increasingly vulnerable to attack. As such, mindfulness, like the rule of law, is needed more than ever to help stabilize and steady an increasingly distracted and agitated world, and mindful lawyers and judges may prove to be the skillful means to bring about this noble end.

References

Benjamin, G. A., Kaszniak, A., Sales, B., & Shanfield, S. B. (1986). The Role of Legal Education in Producing Psychological Distress Among Law Students and Lawyers. *American Bar Foundation Research Journal, 11*(2), 225. doi:10.1086/492145

Fogel, J. (2016). *Mindfulness and Judging*. Washington DC: Federal Judicial Center.

Gold, A. (2016). The Art of Being Mindful in the Legal World: A Challenge for Our Times. *The Florida Bar Journal, 90*(4), 16–23.

Goldstein, J. (1993). *Insight Meditation, the Practice of Freedom*. Boston, MA: Shambhala Classics.

Halpern, C. (2012). The Mindful Lawyer: Why Contemporary Lawyers Are Practicing Meditation. 61 *Journal of Legal Education*, 641.

Hobbes, T. (1962). *Leviathan*. New York, NY: Dutton.

Kabat-Zinn, J. (1982). An Outpatient Program in Behavioral Medicine for Chronic Pain Patients Based on the Practice of Mindfulness Meditation: Theoretical Considerations and Preliminary Results. *General Hospital Psychiatry, 4*(1), 33–47. doi:10.1016/0163–8343(82)90026–3

Kabat-Zinn, J. (1994). *Wherever You Go There You Are*. New York, NY: Hyperion.

Kabat-Zinn, J. (2013). *Full Catastrophe Living*. New York, NY: Bantam Books.

Killingsworth, M. A., & Gilbert, D. T. (2010). A Wandering Mind Is an Unhappy Mind. *Science, 330*(6006), 932–932. doi:10.1126/science.1192439

Magee, R. (2010). Educating Lawyers to Meditate? From Exercises to Epistemology to Ethics: The Contemplative Practice and Law Movement as Legal Education Reform. 79 *UMKC Law Review*, 535.

Martinez, N. (2017, January 10). Staying Centered: Miami Law Firms Embrace Mindfulness. *Crain's*. Retrieved from www.crains.com/article/news/staying-centered-miami-law-firms-embrace-mindfulness

McAliley, C. (2016). Mindfulness on the Bench. *The Florida Bar Journal*, 90(4), 24–25.

Mindfulness Training Boosts Business. (2014, February 3). Retrieved May 15, 2017, from https://au.finance.yahoo.com/news/mindfulness-training-boosts-business-040102435.html

Morrison, A. B., Goolsarran, M., Rogers, S. L., & Jha, A. P. (2014). Taming a Wandering Attention: Short-form Mindfulness Training in Student Cohorts. *Frontiers in Human Neuroscience*, 7(897), 1–12. doi:10.3389/fnhum.2013.00897.

Olsen, E. (2016, February 4). High Rate of Problem Drinking Reported Among Lawyers. *The New York Times*.

Reuben, R., & Sheldon, K. (2015). *The Role of Mindfulness on Law Student Stress, Wellbeing and Performance: A Preliminary Study*. Unpublished manuscript, University of Missouri School of Law.

Rogers, S. L. (2009a). *A Context-Contoured Approach to Mindfulness Training: Enhancing Accessibility by 'Speaking Their Language'*. Presentation at Center for Mindfulness 7th Annual International Scientific Conference for Clinicians, Researchers, and Educators [Audio-recording on file].

Rogers, S. L. (2009b). *The Six-Minute Solution: A Mindfulness Primer for Lawyers*. Miami Beach, FL: Mindful Living Press.

Rogers, S. L. (2009c). *Mindfulness for Law Students: Using the Power of Mindful Awareness to Achieve Balance and Success in Law School*. Miami Beach, FL: Mindful Living Press.

Rogers, S. L. (2009d, July 26). *Mindfulness and Stress Reduction '4–7–8 Hands Exercise' Demonstration*. Retrieved May 15, 2017, from www.youtube.com/watch?v=xjMevXTDDX4

Rogers, S. (1999). *Professionalism and the Practice of Law*. Lecture presented at Lorman Educational Services Seminar.

Rogers, S. (2011). Stop, Look & Listen – Regain Your Focus Through Mindfulness. *ABA: The Young Lawyer*, 15(4).

Rogers, S. (2012). The Mindful Law School: An Integrative Approach to Transforming Legal Education. *Touro Law Review*, 28(4), 1189–1205.

Rogers, S. (2014). Mindfulness in Law. In *The Wiley-Blackwell Handbook of Mindfulness* (pp. 487–525). Chicester, UK: Wiley-Blackwell.

Rogers, S. (2015). What Do We Want: Mindfulness in Law! *Louisiana Bar Journal*, 62(4), 268–271.

Rogers, S. (2016a). Mindfulness in Law and the Importance of Practice. *The Florida Bar Journal*, 90(4), 10–14.

Rogers, S. (2016b). Making a Case for Mindfulness and Law Student Wellness. *ABA: Law Student Division*. doi:http://abaforlawstudents.com/2016/04/13/making-a-case-for-mindfulness-and-law-student-wellness/

Rogers, S. (2016c). Mindfulness, Law and Reciprocal Practice. *Richmond Journal of Law and the Public Interest*, 19(4), 331–338.

Rooks, J. D., Morrison, A. B., Goolsarran, M., Rogers, S. L., & Jha, A. P. (2017). 'We Are Talking About Practice': The Influence of Mindfulness vs. Relaxation Training on Athletes' Attention and Well-Being over High-Demand Intervals. *Journal of Cognitive Enhancement*. doi:10.1007/s41465-017-0016-5

Rousseau, J. J. (1973). *The Social Contract and Discourses*. (Cole, G. D. H., trans.). London: J. M. Dent & Sons.

Salzberg, S., & Goldstein, J. (2001). *Insight Meditation Workbook*. Boulder, CO: Sounds True.

Sanko, J., Mckay, M., & Rogers, S. (2016). Exploring the Impact of Mindfulness Meditation Training in Pre-licensure and Post Graduate Nurses. *Nurse Education Today*, 45, 142–147. doi:10.1016/j.nedt.2016.07.006

Sheldon, K. M., & Krieger, L. S. (2004). Does Legal Education Have Undermining Effects on Law Students? Evaluating Changes in Motivation, Values, and Well-Being. *Behavioral Sciences & the Law*, *22*(2), 261–286. doi:10.1002/bsl.582

Simon-Thomas, E., Halpern, C., Carlin, D., Shon, G., & Klein, L. (2012). *Is Mindfulness Good for Lawyers*. Report on preliminary results from assessment from law school mindfulness class.

Tolle, E. (1999). *The Power of Now*. Novato, CA: New World Library.

University of Miami School of Law's *Mindfulness in Law Program*. (n.d.). Retrieved May 15, 2017, from mindfulness.law.miami.edu

Weil, A. (2016). *Three Breathing Exercises*. Retrieved May 15, 2017, from www.drweil.com/health-wellness/body-mind-spirit/stress-anxiety/breathing-three-exercises/

Zeidan, F., Adler-Neal, A. L., Wells, R. E., Stagnaro, E., May, L. M., Eisenach, J. C., McHaffie, J. G., & Coghill, R. C. (2016). Mindfulness-Meditation-Based Pain Relief Is Not Mediated by Endogenous Opioids. *Journal of Neuroscience*, *36*(11), 3391–3397.

Section VII

Mindfulness programs in addiction

Chapter 26

Mindfulness-Oriented Recovery Enhancement

A review of its theoretical underpinnings, clinical application, and biobehavioral mechanisms

Eric L. Garland, Anne K. Baker, Michael R. Riquino, and Sarah E. Priddy

Overview of the program

History of the MORE program

In 2006, Eric Garland began to contemplate developing a mindfulness-based intervention (MBI) for the treatment of addiction. At the time, there were no empirically supported mindfulness-based treatments for addiction, and few studies of mindfulness for addictive behavior had been published in the literature. As one key exception, a quasi-experimental study of traditional Vipassana meditation (Buddhist insight meditation) for incarcerated substance abusers had been published that year (Bowen et al., 2006). Inspired by this study, Garland was motivated to develop a secular mindfulness program to treat addiction that was founded on mechanistic insights from basic biobehavioral research and neuroscience. To inform the treatment development process, Garland reviewed the literature on the cognitive, affective, and psychophysiological mechanisms underpinning addiction. This review identified two key addictive mechanisms that might be effectively targeted by mindfulness: (1) *automaticity* and (2) *allostasis*. With regard to the first mechanism, empirical data suggested that addiction was largely governed by unconscious cognitive and behavioral habits (Tiffany, 1990) – a conclusion echoed in first-person accounts of individuals with substance use disorders that describe feeling automatically compelled to use substances even in the absence of the conscious desire or will to do so. As a result of such addictive automaticity, persons with substance use disorders exhibited an *attentional bias*, or hyperfixation of attention, towards exteroceptive and interoceptive cues (i.e., external and internal stimuli, respectively) associated with past drug use episodes, which "trigger" cue-elicited craving for substances (Field & Cox, 2008). With regard to the second mechanism, neurobiological research indicated that addiction, emotion dysregulation, and chronic pain involve a downward spiral of allostasis (i.e., the process by which the body responds to stress in order to maintain internal equilibrium), in which prolonged exposure to drugs and chronic stress results in heightened sensitivity to threat and decreased sensitivity to natural reward. These neurobiological changes then lead to relatively stable emotional deficits (e.g., anhedonia, or inability to feel pleasure), which in turn precipitate increased dependence on drug use as a means of countering those deficits (Koob & Le Moal, 1997). The resulting allostatic shift in valuation of drug-related reward over valuation of natural rewards (e.g., the pleasure one experiences from beautiful landscapes, healthy food, social affiliation, meaningful accomplishments) was thought to drive addictive use of drugs as a means of preserving a dwindling sense of hedonic well-being (Koob & Le Moal, 2001). Because mindfulness meditation had been classically construed as a means of deautomatization (Deikman, 1966) via attentional training, and mindfulness meditation appeared to be a viable means of reducing stress and increasing well-being (Kabat-Zinn, 1982), Garland surmised that mindfulness might be especially efficacious in treating addiction.

Subsequently, Garland and colleagues developed a conceptual framework of stress-precipitated addictive behavior (Garland, Boettiger, & Howard, 2011) that integrated several prominent theoretical models, including the Cognitive Processing Model of Addiction (Tiffany, 1990), the Allostatic Model of Addiction (Koob & Le Moal, 2001), the Negative Reinforcement Model of Addiction (Baker, Piper, McCarthy, Majeskie, & Fiore, 2004), and the Transactional Model of Stress and Coping (Lazarus & Folkman, 1984). Guided by this conceptual framework, in 2007 Garland wrote the first draft of the Mindfulness-Oriented Recovery Enhancement (MORE) treatment manual for treating alcohol and drug dependence, which was later published by the National Association of Social Workers Press (Garland, 2013).

In 2008, Garland received a Francisco J. Varela Award from the Mind and Life Institute to test MORE as an intervention for alcohol dependent individuals in inpatient treatment at a long-term therapeutic community. Results from this pilot RCT suggested that MORE might produce therapeutic effects on addictive behavior by modifying attentional bias and heart rate variability (HRV) recovery from stress and alcohol-related cues (Garland, Gaylord, Boettiger, & Howard, 2010). This study provided the first scientific evidence that a mindfulness-based intervention could modify attentional biases and autonomic responses to a cue-reactivity paradigm. In light of its potential promise, MORE was then tested in a five-year RCT at the same therapeutic community. In this study funded by the Substance Abuse and Mental Health Services Administration, MORE was found to outperform cognitive-behavioral therapy (CBT) and treatment-as-usual (TAU) on a range of psychiatric and addiction-related outcomes (Garland, Roberts-Lewis, Tronnier, Graves, & Kelley, 2016). In 2010 Garland obtained a R03 grant from the National Institute on Drug Abuse (NIDA) to test a modified version of MORE as a treatment for prescription opioid misuse among chronic pain patients receiving long-term opioid analgesic pharmacotherapy. In this RCT, MORE was found to result in clinically significant reductions in chronic pain symptoms, opioid misuse, and craving (Garland et al., 2014), as well as modulate range of psychophysiological mechanisms (Garland & Howard, 2013; Garland, Froeliger, & Howard, 2014; Garland, Froeliger, & Howard, 2015; Garland, Baker, & Howard, in press). Among the many mechanistic discoveries from this trial, Garland and colleagues found that the effects of MORE on reducing opioid craving and opioid misuse were associated with restructuring reward processing from valuation of drug-related reward to valuation of natural rewards, as indicated by electroencephalography (EEG; Garland, Froeliger, & Howard, 2015) and cardiovascular measures (Garland, Howard, Zubieta, & Froeliger, 2017). In 2015, a pilot study of MORE as a treatment for smoking cessation found similar evidence of restructuring reward processing via fMRI measures of brain reward system function (Froeliger et al., 2017). This evidence that MORE might alter the relative salience of drug and natural rewards was a signal discovery in the history of research on MORE, which launched several new NIH-funded studies in 2016 to explore the effects of MORE on hedonic regulatory mechanisms as indexed by psychophysiology, fMRI, and molecular neuroimaging via PET. In 2017, two additional pilot

RCTs of MORE were completed that suggest that the effects of MORE may be extended into treatment for behavioral addictions. In the first pilot study, MORE was shown to significantly reduce symptoms of internet gaming disorder (Li et al., 2017). In the second pilot, MORE was shown to reduce food attentional bias among obese cancer survivors, which was associated with increased physiological responsiveness to natural reward cues (Thomas et al., under review). These studies will be reviewed in the section on theory and research.

At present, NIH and DOD-funded full-scale clinical trials are underway to determine the efficacy and mechanisms of MORE for civilians and military personnel with chronic pain and other psychiatric comorbidities who are at risk for prescription opioid misuse.

Intended population

MORE is intended to provide a transdiagnostic therapeutic approach for individuals suffering from comorbid addictive behaviors, affective dysregulation, and chronic pain. Unlike Mindfulness-Based Relapse Prevention (MBRP), which is a relapse prevention intervention for individuals who are already abstinent from substance use, MORE is designed to assist individuals in the contemplation, preparation, action, and maintenance stages of change.[1] In that regard, MORE has been tested for individuals in early abstinence (Garland et al., 2016) and long-term abstinence (Garland et al., 2010), as well as for individuals in the contemplation stage of change who are actively engaging in addictive behaviors (Froeliger et al., 2017; Garland et al., 2014; Li et al., 2017; Thomas et al., under review). MORE has not yet been tested among substance users in the precontemplation stage of change; in that regard, MORE provides implicit motivational enhancement by strengthening self-awareness, but does not include any explicit motivational interviewing techniques. One future horizon of research on MORE might examine treatment sequencing by introducing motivational interviewing (MI) prior to, during, or even following participation in MORE, to determine if a MI component might enhance uptake of the intervention in precontemplative individuals.

Goals of the program

The overarching goal of MORE is to reverse the allostatic process of addiction by fostering greater control over automatic, maladaptive behavior and by promoting a recovery-oriented approach rooted in meaning-making and human flourishing, known as eudaimonic well-being (Ryan & Deci, 2001). As described earlier, hedonic valuation systems in the brain are hijacked by addictive drugs during an allostatic process in which drug-related rewards come to be valued over all else, resulting in a void of meaning that the individual attempts to fill with compulsive drug seeking. MORE seeks to remediate this hedonic deficit through a range of strategies, as articulated below.

1. MORE aims to clarify cognitive appraisal processes, enabling the individual to achieve a more adaptive evaluation of the stressor and his or her coping ability.
2. MORE aims to decrease attentional bias towards threat and distressing (e.g., painful) somatic sensations, reducing stressful input that might fuel the allostatic process of addiction.
3. MORE aims to increase regulation of negative emotions by training in reappraisal.
4. MORE aims to directly enhance natural reward processing through savoring practices.

5   MORE aims to disrupt hyperfixated, repetitive cognition through mindful decentering from negative automatic thoughts.
6   MORE aims to strengthen top-down cognitive control over bottom-up drug use action schemas via mindfulness techniques designed to increase awareness of automaticity.
7   MORE aims to decrease addiction attentional bias by strengthening attentional re-orienting capacity through focused attention and open monitoring forms of mindfulness meditation.
8   MORE aims to provide a means of regulating craving by deconstructing the craving experience into its constituent sensations, thoughts, emotions and memories, and then countering them through metacognitive contemplation of the reasons to remain abstinent.
9   MORE aims to provide an effective alternative to suppression of craving through mindful exposure and acceptance.

And finally, MORE aims to downregulate the physiological stress reaction itself. This is accomplished by fostering flexible engagement of the parasympathetic nervous system (which allows us to rest and relax through automatic physiological adjustments such as decreased heart rate and slower respiration) to balance acute and chronic sympathetic activation (which enables our "fight or flight" response through automatic physiological adjustments such as increased heart rate and quickened respiration).

Theory and research

Theoretical background

MORE is an integrative, dual-process intervention that unites complementary aspects of mindfulness training, third-wave cognitive behavioral therapy (CBT), and principles of positive psychology. MORE strengthens top-down proactive cognitive control functions to restructure bottom-up reward learning from valuation of drug rewards to valuation of natural rewards. To restructure valuation processes underpinning addiction, MORE uses mindfulness skills to synergize reappraisal and savoring techniques designed for reevaluating the meaning of conditioned stimuli and responses that have become automatized over repeated cycles of positive and negative reinforcement via addictive behavior. Mindfulness is used to suspend the initial habitual appraisal, broaden awareness to allow for novel information processing, and thereby increase responsivity to the negative consequences of addiction and to the potential rewards of recovery.

MORE is rooted in the Mindfulness-to-Meaning Theory (Garland, Farb, Goldin, & Fredrickson, 2015), a novel conceptual framework that posits that mindfulness meditation facilitates disengagement from automatic schema by producing a metacognitive state of awareness in which attention expands to encompass previously unattended data from which new cognitive appraisals can be constructed. Insofar as mindfulness allows access to an expanded set of information from which established associations may be restructured, it can be used to enhance interoceptive awareness of the hedonic value of various courses of action and experiences. This restructuring of hedonic valuation flexibly re-tunes attention onto novel targets, affording an enriched experience of their reward value in relation to their larger context as hedonic experience becomes infused with eudaimonic meaning. In this way, the Mindfulness-to-Meaning Theory proposes that mindfulness provides a means of restructuring reward learning. Ultimately, MORE is grounded in the notion that through mindfulness, reappraisal, and savoring, one can self-generate a durable, meaningful form of well-being, and thereby free oneself from the need to engage in addictive behavior as a means of obtaining equilibrium.

Empirical evidence in support of MORE

A growing body of studies demonstrates the therapeutic potential of MORE for a range of conditions, including alcohol dependence, co-occurring substance use and psychiatric disorders, opioid misuse among chronic pain patients, smoking, and behavioral addictions. These findings are reviewed below.

Alcohol dependence

A pilot RCT (N=53) comparing the original ten-session version of MORE with a support group (SG) revealed therapeutic outcomes among a sample of alcohol-dependent adults in long-term inpatient treatment (Garland et al., 2010). In this study, participation in MORE was associated with significant reductions in stress and thought suppression, and significantly modified attentional bias to alcohol-related cues during a dot probe task.[2] Moreover, this study revealed that MORE was associated with significantly greater heart rate variability (HRV) recovery and stress relief than the SG following exposure to stress and alcohol-related stimuli, providing evidence that MORE enhances parasympathetic regulation of reactions to stress and alcohol cues. Though the number of relapses in this sample was too small to statistically measure a direct effect on drinking outcomes, MORE's effects on these attentional and autonomic mechanisms suggest its promise as a treatment for alcohol dependence, insofar as alcohol attentional bias and HRV responses to stress and alcohol cues have been shown to predict relapse following treatment for alcohol dependence (Garland, Franken, & Howard, 2012).

Co-occurring substance use disorders and psychiatric disorders

In a large cluster RCT (N=180), a ten-session version of MORE outperformed CBT and treatment-as-usual (TAU) for a sample of previously homeless individuals in long-term treatment for comorbid trauma, substance use, and psychiatric disorders (Garland et al., 2016). Findings revealed participants in MORE evinced significantly greater reductions in substance craving and post-traumatic stress than participants in CBT and TAU, as well as significantly greater improvements in dispositional mindfulness (also known as trait mindfulness, understood as the extent to which one naturally adopts a mindful orientation as a function of personality) and positive and negative emotions. Furthermore, the study revealed that dispositional mindfulness mediated the relationships between the MORE intervention and improved craving and post-traumatic stress outcomes. This finding suggests that MORE may produce therapeutic effects by enhancing mindful awareness. Overall, this RCT lends support for MORE as an integrative therapeutic approach for complex co-morbidities that can match, if not exceed, the efficacy of CBT – a gold standard, empirically supported therapy.

Chronic pain and opioid misuse

A substantial and rapidly growing body of literature is dedicated to the examination of MORE as an effective treatment modality for chronic pain and opioid misuse. Although opioid analgesia can be an effective means by which to attenuate chronic pain, and a majority of chronic pain patients take opioids as prescribed, approximately 25% of this population engage in opioid misuse (Vowles et al., 2015). The integrative, multidimensional nature of MORE makes it especially well-suited to address the network of cognitive, affective and behavioral dysregulation characteristic of opioid misusing chronic pain patients. Results of a RCT (N=115) of an eight-session version of MORE for opioid-treated chronic pain patients revealed that, relative to a SG, participants who received the MORE intervention experienced significant reductions in chronic pain symptoms, stress arousal, opioid craving, and opioid misuse (Garland et al., 2014). Furthermore, reductions in pain severity and interference with function in daily life were mediated by non-reactivity and reinterpretation of pain sensations as innocuous sensory signals.

Several mechanistic sub-studies were conducted to identify the psychophysiological mediators of the MORE intervention in this sample. Results from responses during a dot probe test indicated that MORE significantly reduced opioid attentional bias (Garland, Baker, & Howard, in press) and pain attentional bias (Garland & Howard, 2013), while enhancing cardiac-autonomic responsiveness to natural rewards that mediated the effect of MORE on craving (Garland, Froeliger, & Howard, 2014). Similarly, MORE was found to be associated with enhanced electrocortical indices (captured via EEG) of natural reward processing that were correlated with decreases in opioid craving (Garland et al., 2015). Further, MORE was associated with a shift in the relative salience of drug and natural rewards as indicated by cardiac responses during an affective picture viewing task; this shift was associated with reductions in opioid misuse by three-month follow-up (Garland et al., 2017). Consistent with these psychophysiological effects, an ecological momentary assessment (EMA)[3] study found that participation in MORE was associated with 2.75 greater odds of maintaining or increasing positive affect from moment to moment than the SG, an effect that predicted decreases in opioid misuse (Garland et al., 2017). Taken together, the outcomes and mechanistic data from this trial suggest that MORE may be an efficacious treatment for prescription opioid misuse among chronic pain patients.

Nicotine addiction

More recently, a small neuroimaging study (N=13) employed functional magnetic resonance imaging (fMRI) to measure the effects of a ten-session version of MORE on positive emotion regulation and cue-reactivity among nicotine dependent smokers (Froeliger et al., 2017). Relative to a time-matched comparison group, MORE was associated with significantly greater reductions in smoking (66% reduction in the number of cigarettes smoked over the course of treatment) and significantly greater increases in positive affect. These behavioral effects were complemented by significant changes in brain reward system function in response to cigarette and natural reward-related stimuli. Specifically, MORE was associated with significant decreases in activity in the rostral anterior cingulate cortex (rACC) and ventral striatum (VS) during a cigarette cue-reactivity task, as well as significant increases in these same brain regions during a positive emotion regulation task that involved savoring of natural reward-related images. Increases in reward circuitry activation during savoring were significantly and robustly correlated with decreased smoking, providing additional evidence for the hypothesis that MORE targets addictive behavior by restructuring valuation of drug reward to valuation of natural reward. Furthermore, MORE occasioned significant increases in resting state functional connectivity between the rACC and the orbitofrontal cortex that were associated with decreased smoking behavior. These findings, while preliminary, suggest that MORE may facilitate the restructuring of reward processes by strengthening frontostriatal pathways integral to self-regulation of addictive behavior.

Behavioral addictions

Recently, research has begun to characterize MORE as an intervention for behavioral addictions. A pilot RCT (N=30) examined the effect of an eight-session version of MORE on internet gaming disorder (Li et al., 2017). Relative to a SG control, individuals who participated in MORE evidenced significantly greater improvements in symptoms of internet gaming disorder, craving for video games, and maladaptive gaming-related cognitions. Another pilot RCT (N=51) examined the effects of ten sessions of MORE on overweight cancer survivors who were attempting to lose weight through changes in diet and exercise (Thomas et al., under review). In this study, participants were randomized to receive exercise and nutrition training with or without an additional MORE group. Though participants in both groups lost an average of ten pounds over three months, participants in MORE reported significantly greater increases in interoceptive awareness and savoring ability coupled with significantly greater improvements in food attentional bias and natural reward responsiveness as indicated by facial electromyography (EMG) – an objective marker of positive emotional response. The effect of MORE on reducing food attentional bias was associated with enhanced facial EMG responses to natural reward, again suggesting that MORE may reduce addictive tendencies by restructuring hedonic regulation. Taken together, these findings suggest that MORE may be a promising intervention for behavioral addictions, but additional, larger scale studies are needed to establish MORE's efficacy in these domains.

Program structure of MORE

At its inception, MORE was designed as a ten-session group therapy intervention and later adapted as an eight-week group treatment for opioid-misusing chronic pain patients. Both protocols have been studied in the RCTs described earlier and emphasize the foundational MORE skills of mindfulness, reappraisal, and savoring throughout the sessions. A session-by-session overview of the ten-session protocol is provided below. Once mindfulness, reappraisal, and savoring techniques have been introduced, each session thereafter is devoted to processing, reinforcing, and optimizing the use of these skills for coping in everyday life.

Session 1: mindfulness and the automatic habit of addiction

This session combines psychoeducation and experiential exercises to introduce clients to the concepts of mindfulness, craving, and automaticity. Specifically, clients learn about how mindfulness can help them recognize when they are acting on "automatic pilot" and help them to disrupt addictive habits. This session provides training in mindful breathing and body scan meditations, as well as the "chocolate exercise" – an experiential mindfulness practice designed to increase awareness of automaticity and craving (described later in this chapter). During the debrief of the exercise, a comparison is made between the urge to swallow the chocolate and craving substances. By breaking down the experience of craving into its constituent sensory, affective, and cognitive components, clients learn to consciously and adaptively respond to the urge to use substances rather than automatically reacting to drug cues in maladaptive ways.

Session 2: mindful reappraisal

This session focuses on mindful reappraisal as a means of coping with negative emotions and bringing attention to how the mind reacts to everyday experiences. In addition to reinforcing the concepts of mindfulness taught through mindful breathing practice during the first session, clients learn and practice a three-stage mindful reappraisal procedure during this session: (1) mindful decentering from cognitions and emotions, (2) letting go of automatic thoughts, and (3) generating new and adaptive appraisals. This exercise draws upon principles taught in CBT and integrates them with techniques from mindfulness to teach clients that thoughts are not facts, and how reappraisal improves one's capacity to be emotionally responsive to stressful experiences.

Session 3: shifting the mind to refocus on savoring

After introducing the foundational concepts of mindfulness and reappraisal during the first two sessions, this session introduces the concept of savoring as a means of increasing responsiveness to natural rewards. To learn savoring, patients are first instructed to focus mindful attention on a bouquet of flowers, attending to and appreciating their pleasant colors, textures, and scents, as well as the touch of the petals against their skin. During this process, participants are instructed to adopt a metacognitive awareness of their experience, and to attend to and absorb any positive emotions arising from their encounter with the flowers, as well as any cognitive or affective dimensions of meaning emerging from the experience. This kind of savoring involves not only attending to the most perceptually salient features of an object or event, but also becoming conscious of its more subtle features and affective impressions, broadening and deepening the array of sensations and experiences to be derived from the savored experience. Patients are instructed to practice mindful savoring with naturally rewarding objects and events in their everyday lives.

Session 4: seeing through the nature of craving

This session focuses on applying the foundational MORE skills of mindfulness and reappraisal to the experience of craving, especially as it relates to the ephemeral and subjective experience of craving. Psychoeducation during the session emphasizes reasons why clients want to abstain from using substances, and normalizes craving as a natural impulse. Clients learn to identify symptoms associated with craving and gain awareness of how craving is elicited by substance-related cues. Clients learn and practice a multicomponent mindfulness meditation on craving through a second chocolate exercise in which clients are asked to: (1) imagine holding their drug of addiction rather than a piece of chocolate; (2) use mindful breathing to reduce craving-related distress; (3) deconstruct the craving into its sensory, affective, and cognitive components; and (4) use mindfulness to facilitate contemplation of the consequences of indulging in and abstaining from substance use.

Session 5: overcoming craving by coping with stress

Mindfulness practice can help dismantle the relationship between stress and craving, and ultimately reduce the allostatic load that contributes to lapses and relapses into addictive behavior. This session reviews of the use of mindfulness, reappraisal, and savoring for managing stressful events and the eventual craving that is often triggered by stress. Clients learn to consciously respond to stress and craving rather than automatically react with substance use as a means of coping. During the psychoeducation portion of the session, clients learn to identify the cognitive, affective, and physiological signs of the stress response through an imagery-based stress exposure exercise. During the experiential portion of the session, clients learn imagery and body scan techniques to reduce stress reactivity by engaging the parasympathetically mediated relaxation response.

Session 6: walking the middle way between attachment and aversion

This psychoeducation portion of this session provides clients with an understanding of how thought suppression can exhaust mental and emotional resources, and ultimately lead to increased thoughts and urges to use substances. During the experiential portion of the session, clients are encouraged to find the middle way between the previous attachment they felt towards substances and present feelings of aversion they may be experiencing. By being mindful of thoughts and urges, clients learn to acknowledge, accept, and then let go of drug cravings.

Session 7: mindfulness of the impermanent body

By expounding on the Buddhist notion of impermanence, one of the traditional insights from mindfulness practice, this session focuses on the damaging effects of substances on the body. Rather than simply providing psychoeducation on the negative consequences of substance use on physical health, this session focuses on the experiential cultivation of self-awareness as a means of gaining insight into these consequences. Two mindfulness exercises are conducted as a means of increasing interoceptive awareness: (1) a body scan meditation focused on awareness of how the body has been harmed by substance use, and (2) mindful walking, which introduces kinesthetic sensation as the object of mindfulness practice. Such increased body awareness is intended to promote motivation to change substance use.

Session 8: defusing relationship triggers for relapse

This session focuses on relationship conflict as a cue for relapse given that interpersonal conflict is a powerful source of stress and may promote substance using clients' reasons to remain abstinent. The technique of loving-kindness meditation is introduced to induce positive emotions and help clients adopt a more compassionate, empathetic stance in their interpersonal relationships. By transcending their own egocentric needs, clients learn to acknowledge and attend to the needs of others. However, when emotional distress inhibits clients' ability to feel concern for others, they are encouraged to use the core skill of mindful breathing to address negative feelings and induce self-compassion before attempting to gain insight into their relationship patterns.

Session 9: Interdependence and meaning in recovery

Addiction can lead to feelings of isolation, disconnection, and meaninglessness. In contrast, through mindfulness, clients can regain contact with the meaningfulness of their lives by achieving insight into the interdependence of all events and experiences (i.e., Thich Nhat

Hanh's "interbeing," Hanhn, 1988). Through this insight, one may come to realize that even experiences of adversity can become a source of spiritual growth. During this session, clients engage in a meditation on interdependence, which orients them to a sense of being connected to a larger whole. If the sense of attachment to the individual self is at the root of addictive behavior, then transcending that sense of individuality may ameliorate the processes that lead to substance use.

Session 10: looking mindfully toward the future

The final session is dedicated to reviewing the core concepts covered through the group treatment, discussing how to maintain mindfulness practice, and developing a mindful recovery plan that incorporates the skills learned in group to prevent future relapse. Clients learn and practice success imagery focused on mindful relapse prevention as a means of increasing competence and confidence in their capacity to continue successfully utilizing the skills they have learned during group. By engaging in this final meditation, clients will have a reference experience to draw upon in future situations when they actually encounter challenges similar to the ones they imagined during the rehearsal exercise.

Adaptations for chronic pain

The ten-session MORE treatment was adapted as an eight-session intervention for prescription opioid misuse among chronic pain patients. In this adaptation, an additional session is inserted at the beginning of the treatment series that is focused on helping participants discriminate between nociception (the process by which nerve cells, called nociceptors, signal the brain that the body has endured or might endure damage), pain, and emotional suffering. Sessions 7 and 8 of the original MORE intervention are removed, and material from Session 6 and 9 are integrated into a single session. Each session provides mindfulness training as a means of coping with pain by breaking down the pain experience into its constituent sensory, affective, and cognitive components, parallel to the mindfulness of craving technique described above. This mindfulness practice is intended to help participants reinterpret pain as innocuous sensory information rather than perceive pain as an affectively laden, emotionally anguishing threat. In addition to practicing daily mindful breathing, body scan, reappraisal, and/or savoring exercises, this adaptation of MORE also instructs participants to engage in three minutes of mindful breathing prior to taking their opioid prescription as a means of clarifying whether opioid use was driven by appetitive motivations (i.e., craving) versus a legitimate need for pain relief.

Sample mindfulness exercise

The following script provides an outline of the "chocolate exercise" delivered in Session 1. An elaborated version of this exercise is delivered in Session 4. During this exercise, clients bring their attention to the experience of urge by noticing the sensations associated with eating a piece of chocolate. Clients are first invited to experience their senses in relation to the chocolate (i.e., vision, touch, olfaction) and then asked to become aware of the arising urge to eat the chocolate, without actually eating it. Clients are instructed to adopt a metacognitive awareness of the thoughts, feelings, and sensations associated with the urge, and to notice that urges can be decoupled from action.

Mindfulness-Oriented Recovery Enhancement 337

Sitting comfortably but regally, as if you were a king or queen, with spine straight and belly relaxed, take a few mindful breaths . . . noticing the sensation of the breath moving into the nostrils . . . and then shift the attention to the piece of chocolate in your hand.

Examine the chocolate as if you were seeing chocolate for the very first time, as if you were from a foreign country and have never seen it before. Observe its color and texture. Notice its weight or lightness in your hand. Slowly turn the chocolate so you can see it from different angles. How does it look different from different angles? Is it uniform, or is it irregular and uneven? Look very closely, as if you were looking at the chocolate through a microscope.

Next, smell the chocolate. Notice its scent. You can become aware of the exact moment when you feel the urge to eat it, but don't eat it yet. Bring your attention to your mouth and stomach. Does the smell of the chocolate make your mouth fill with saliva? Notice any feelings of hunger, craving, or urge to eat the chocolate. And we have this word "urge" but what is it really? Sensations of warmth or coolness? Heaviness or lightness? Tingling? Tightness? Emptiness? Where in the body do you notice these sensations? Do the sensations have a center? Do they have edges? Are there spaces inside the sensation where the sensation is not? As you smell the chocolate, bring your attention to your own thoughts and feelings. Notice any thoughts, emotions, imaginations, or memories, but try not to get lost in them. Just make note of them, and then allow your attention to return to your body. Observe what it is like to have the urge to eat chocolate but to not eat it. Notice the state of mind and body while you are having this urge. With each passing moment, those feelings may become weaker, or perhaps they may change in some way. Just take a few moments to notice what happens.

Now, you can let chocolate rest in your hand, and begin to move your attention back to your breath. Just noticing the breath . . . not changing the breath. . . . Just observing the movement of the breath. . . . Perhaps becoming aware of the sensations of air at the tip of the nose or at the lips. . . . Noticing the place where the breath enters the body, and any sensations of warmth or coolness there. . . . And whenever the mind wanders to urges, needs, desires, thoughts, emotions, or sensations, that's okay, because that is what minds do – they wander. . . . Just noticing where the mind has wandered off to, and then letting those urges, thoughts, and feelings go. Just gently bringing the attention back to the breath, noticing what it is like to do that. . . . And with each, passing breath, becoming more aware. . . . And whenever the mind wanders back to the urges, thoughts, or feelings, just noticing where the mind has wandered, letting those urges, thoughts, and feelings go, and then gently returning the attention to the breathing. . . . And the thoughts, feelings, images, and sensations associated with the word urge are like clouds passing in the clear space of awareness. . . . Like clouds drifting, gradually changing shape, and then fading into the distance. . . . The mind like that sky is spotless, stainless, open and vast, just watching, just observing . . . peacefully . . .

Return your attention to the chocolate, and then, when your mind is fully focused on the chocolate, place it in your mouth, but don't chew it yet. Try to pay attention to the exact moment when the urge to chew arises. Where does the urge come from? What does that urge feel like? How do you know that you think you want to chew? Don't chew it yet. Instead, notice how the mouth fills with saliva. Notice the taste of the chocolate on the tongue. Take a few moments to feel those sensations in the body. Notice whatever thoughts and feelings arise in the mind. You might like to play with the feeling of the urge, and notice how the feeling changes the longer you keep from taking a bite. Eventually, when you are ready, chew the chocolate. Really notice and appreciate its flavor, its texture in the mouth. Don't swallow it just yet, but instead, savor the bite in your mouth. See how long you can really enjoy the flavor before it melts away completely. Notice any urge to swallow, but do not obey the urge. Instead, observe the feelings that arise in the body as you allow this chocolate to melt into your mouth with each passing moment. Finally, swallow when ready, and notice the feeling of the swallowing, the feeling of the chocolate going down into your stomach.

Program resources

The published MORE treatment manual contains therapist scripts and patient resources (Garland, 2013), and additional information on MORE can be found at www.drericgarland.com/more. Health care professionals (e.g., social workers, psychologists, nurses, and physicians) can receive training in MORE through a two-day workshop that combines didactic and experiential instruction, including provision of real-time feedback and coaching in the delivery of therapeutic techniques.

MORE therapists engage in weekly supervision that involves review of session audio recordings to fine tune intervention delivery. To ensure treatment fidelity, a MORE fidelity measure has been developed and validated (Garland et al., under review). This measure provides quantitative indices of therapist adherence and competence, and is intended as a tool both for structuring MORE supervision sessions and for implementation science.

Notes

1 The Transtheoretical Model of Behavior Change (Prochaska & DiClemente, 1983) posits there are 5 stages of behavior change: pre-contemplation, contemplation, preparation, action, and maintenance. In pre-contemplation, the individual has yet to recognize a need for change. Such recognition occurs in the contemplation stage, though acknowledgement of necessity is not accompanied by a willingness to change until the preparation stage. In the action stage, the individual actively pursues behavioral change, which is then repeatedly engaged in the maintenance stage.
2 The dot probe task is a cognitive task designed to measure attention. Two photos, matched for size, color/temperature and figure-ground relationships, appear side-by-side on a computer monitor and then quickly disappear. Following a very brief inter-stimulus interval (a plain, black screen), a white dot replaces either the left- or right-side photo. Participants are asked to press corresponding left and right keys on a response box to indicate whether the dot is on the right or the left.
3 Ecological momentary assessment (EMA) is a means by which to repeatedly measure participant behaviors and experiences in real time and in participants' natural environments. Participants are asked to answer study-relevant questionnaires multiple times daily via an electronic device (e.g., smart phone or palm pilot) or by written diary. This methodology is thought to reduce recall bias and increase ecological validity (Shiffman, Stone, & Hufford, 2008).

References

Baker, T. B., Piper, M. E., McCarthy, D. E., Majeskie, M. R., & Fiore, M. C. (2004). Addiction motivation reformulated: An affective processing model of negative reinforcement. *Psychological Review*, *111*(1), 33–51. https://doi.org/10.1037/0033-295X.111.1.33

Bowen, S., Witkiewitz, K., Dillworth, T. M., Chawla, N., Simpson, T. L., Ostafin, B. D., & Marlatt, G. A. (2006). Mindfulness meditation and substance use in an incarcerated population. *Psychology of Addictive Behaviors: Journal of the Society of Psychologists in Addictive Behaviors*, *20*(3), 343–347. https://doi.org/10.1037/0893-164X.20.3.343

Deikman, A. J. (1966). Deautomatization and the mystic experience. *Psychiatry, 29*, 324–388.

Field, M., & Cox, W. M. (2008). Attentional bias in addictive behaviors: A review of its development, causes, and consequences. *Drug and Alcohol Dependence, 97*, 1–20.

Froeliger, B., Mathew, A. R., McConnell, P. A., Eichberg, C., Saladin, M. E., Carpenter, M. J., & Garland, E. L. (2017). Restructuring reward mechanisms in nicotine addiction: A pilot fMRI study of Mindfulness-Oriented Recovery Enhancement for cigarette smokers. *Evidence-Based Complementary and Alternative Medicine, 2017*, e7018014. https://doi.org/10.1155/2017/7018014

Garland, E. L. (2013). *Mindfulness-Oriented Recovery Enhancement for Addiction, Stress, and Pain*. Washington, DC: NASW Press.

Garland, E. L., Baker, A. K., & Howard, M. O. (in press). Mindfulness-Oriented Recovery Enhancement reduces opioid attentional bias among opioid-treated chronic pain patients. *Journal of the Society for Social Work and Research*.

Garland, E. L., Baker, A. K., Priddy, S. E., Riquino, M. R., Thomas, E. A., Kelly, A., Howard, M. O. (under review). The MORE Fidelity Measure: An instrument to assess therapist adherence and competence.

Garland, E. L., Boettiger, C. A., & Howard, M. O. (2011). Targeting cognitive-affective risk mechanisms in stress-precipitated alcohol dependence: An integrated, biopsychosocial model of automaticity, allostasis, and addiction. *Medical Hypotheses, 76*(5), 745–754.

Garland, E. L., Bryan, C. J., Finan, P. H., Thomas, E. A., Priddy, S. E., Riquino, M. R., & Howard, M. O. (2017). Pain, hedonic regulation, and opioid misuse: Modulation of momentary experience by Mindfulness-Oriented Recovery Enhancement in opioid-treated chronic pain patients. *Drug and Alcohol Dependence, 173*(Supplement 1), S65–S72. https://doi.org/10.1016/j.drugalcdep.2016.07.033

Garland, E. L., Farb, N. A., Goldin, P. R., & Fredrickson, B. L. (2015). Mindfulness broadens awareness and builds eudaimonic meaning: A process model of mindful positive emotion regulation. *Psychological Inquiry, 26*(4), 293–314. https://doi.org/10.1080/1047840X.2015.1064294

Garland, E. L., Franken, I. H. A., & Howard, M. O. (2012). Cue-elicited heart rate variability and attentional bias predict alcohol relapse following treatment. *Psychopharmacology, 222*(1), 17–26. https://doi.org/10.1007/s00213-011-2618-4

Garland, E. L., Froeliger, B., & Howard, M. O. (2014). Effects of Mindfulness-Oriented Recovery Enhancement on reward responsiveness and opioid cue-reactivity. *Psychopharmacology, 231*(16), 3229–3238.

Garland, E. L., Froeliger, B., & Howard, M. O. (2015). Neurophysiological evidence for remediation of reward processing deficits in chronic pain and opioid misuse following treatment with Mindfulness-Oriented Recovery Enhancement: Exploratory ERP findings from a pilot RCT. *Journal of Behavioral Medicine, 38*(2), 327–336.

Garland, E. L., Gaylord, S. A., Boettiger, C. A., & Howard, M. O. (2010). Mindfulness training modifies cognitive, affective, and physiological mechanisms implicated in alcohol dependence: Results of a randomized controlled pilot trial. *Journal of Psychoactive Drugs, 42*(2), 177–192.

Garland, E. L., & Howard, M. O. (2013). Mindfulness-Oriented Recovery Enhancement reduces pain attentional bias in chronic pain patients. *Psychotherapy and Psychosomatics, 82*, 311–318. https://doi.org/10.1159/000348868

Garland, E. L., Howard, M. O., Zubieta, J-K., & Froeliger, B. (2017). Restructuring hedonic dysregulation in chronic pain and prescription opioid misuse: Effects of Mindfulness-Oriented Recovery Enhancement on responsiveness to drug cues and natural rewards. *Psychotherapy and Psychosomatics, 86*(2), 111–112. https://doi.org/10.1159/000453400

Garland, E. L., Manusov, E. G., Froeliger, B., Kelly, A., Williams, J. M., & Howard, M. O. (2014). Mindfulness-Oriented Recovery Enhancement for chronic pain and prescription opioid misuse: Results from an early-stage randomized controlled trial. *Journal of Consulting and Clinical Psychology, 82*(3), 448–459.

Garland, E. L., Roberts-Lewis, A., Tronnier, C., Graves, R., & Kelley, K. (2016). Mindfulness-Oriented Recovery Enhancement versus CBT for co-occurring substance dependence, traumatic stress, and psychiatric disorders: Proximal outcomes from a pragmatic randomized trial. *Behaviour Research and Therapy, 77*. https://doi.org/10.1016/j.brat.2015.11.012

Hanh, T. N. (1988). *The Sun My Heart*. Berkeley, CA: Parallax Press.

Kabat-Zinn, J. (1982). An outpatient program in behavioral medicine for chronic pain patients based on the practice of mindfulness meditation: Theoretical considerations and preliminary results. *General Hospital Psychiatry*, *4*(1), 33–47. https://doi.org/10.1016/0163-8343(82)90026-3

Koob, G. F., & Le Moal, M. (1997). Drug abuse: Hedonic homeostatic dysregulation. *Science (New York, N.Y.)*, *278*(5335), 52–58.

Koob, G. F., & Le Moal, M. (2001). Drug addiction, dysregulation of reward, and allostasis. *Neuropsychopharmacology: Official Publication of the American College of Neuropsychopharmacology*, *24*(2), 97–129. https://doi.org/10.1016/S0893-133X(00)00195-0

Lazarus, R., & Folkman, S. (1984). *Stress, Appraisal, and Coping*. New York, NY: Springer.

Li, W., Garland, E. L., McGovern, P., O'Brien, J. E., Tronnier, C., & Howard, M. O. (2017). Mindfulness-Oriented Recovery Enhancement for internet gaming disorder in U.S. adults: A stage I randomized controlled trial. *Psychology of Addictive Behaviors*. https://doi.org/10.1037/adb0000269

Prochaska, J. O., & DiClemente, C. (1983). Stages and processes of self-change of smoking: Toward and integrative model of change. *Journal of Consulting and Clinical Psychology*, *51*, 390–395. doi: 10.1037//0022-006X.51.3.390

Ryan, R. M., & Deci, E. L. (2001). On happiness and human potentials: A review of research on hedonic and eudiamonic well-being. *Annual Review of Psychology*, *52*, 141–166. doi: 10.1146/annurev.psych.52.1.141

Shiffman, S., Stone, A. A., & Hufford, M. R. (2008). Ecological momentary assessment. *Annual Review of Clinical Psychology*, *4*, 1–32.

Thomas, E. A., Mijangos, J., White, S., Walker, D., Reimers, C., Beck, A., Hansen, P., & Garland, E. L. (under review). Mindfulness-Oriented Recovery Enhancement restructures reward processing and interoceptive awareness in overweight cancer survivors: Results from a Stage I RCT.

Tiffany, S. T. (1990). A cognitive model of drug urges and drug-use behavior: Role of automatic and nonamutomatic processes. *Pscyhological Review*, *97*(2), 147.

Vowles, K. E., McEntee, M. L., Julnes, P. S., Frohe, T., Ney, J. P., & van der Goes, D. N. (2015). Rates of opioid misuse, abuse, and addiction in chronic pain: A systematic review and data synthesis. *Pain*, *156*(4), 569–576.

Chapter 27

Mindfulness-Based Relapse Prevention for addictive behaviors

Vanessa Somohano, Taylor Shank, and Sarah Bowen

Background and overview

Substance abuse and dependence is an international epidemic with detrimental health, community, and economic costs. A recent United States survey reported 23% of adults and 5% of adolescents (age 12–17) had a substance use disorder (SUD), a one percent increase from 2013 (NIDA, 2015), with the most prevalent SUD being alcohol use disorder (Center for Behavioral Health Statistics and Quality, 2015). People with SUDs are at higher risk for contracting infectious and chronic diseases, obtaining accidental injuries (e.g., driving under the influence), facing legal problems (NIDA, 2011), and experiencing difficulty obtaining and/ or maintaining employment and stable housing (Henkel, 2011). In 2010, SUDs accounted for nearly 15% of life years lost due to disability, ill-health, and death worldwide (Whiteford et al., 2010). Collectively, these consequences result in approximately $700 billion in U.S. annual costs related to healthcare, crime, and work productivity due to alcohol, tobacco, and illicit drug abuse (NIDA, 2011).

Evidence suggests, however, that greater implementation of evidence-based substance use interventions may attenuate some of these medical and legal costs. Research has shown, for example, a reduction in recidivism rates and an increase in work productivity among individuals whom receive treatment (Ettner, Huang, Evans, Ash, Hardy, Jourabchi, & Hser, 2006). A recent review (SAMHSA, 2009) found that SUD interventions have a monetary benefit-to-cost ratio of 7:1, meaning that for every $1 spent on treatment, the surrounding community saves $7 in medical- and crime-related costs. Additionally, inclusion of SUD treatment coverage by insurance policies has significantly reduced costs for medical and nursing facilities. Individual families have saved between 26–39% of medical costs over time when a family member has received treatment.

SUD treatment has undergone many developments over the past several decades. The most widely used treatments often reinforce abstinence through contingencies (e.g., positively reinforcing abstinence through the use of a reward system), and by teaching individuals to avoid external substance-related cues (e.g. people and places associate with substance use) (NIDA, 2016). While often initially effective, upon treatment end, the external environment can be unpredictable, making contingencies and avoidance of triggers difficult to manage and less likely to have long-term effects (Benishek, Dugosh, Kirby, Matejkowski, Clements, Seymour, & Festinger, 2014). If an individual is faced with an unexpected external trigger, for example, treatments focusing on avoidance may not adequately prepare individuals to navigate through the intense associated internal distress. Furthermore, positive reinforcers for maintaining abstinence in treatment (e.g., tokens) are no longer predictable outside of treatment, thus potentially extinguishing abstinence behaviors reinforced by expected rewards.

Recently, addiction treatments have begun incorporating mindfulness-based approaches to address internal distress (e.g., craving) directly, teaching the individual to manage internal reactions to external cues, thereby decreasing the need to avoid triggering situations (Garland, 2013; Amaro, Spear, Vallejo, Conron, & Black, 2014; Himelstein, Saul, & Garcia-Romeu, 2015). Through mindfulness meditation training, individuals learn to shift and sustain their attention to their internal experience when faced with triggering stimuli. *Observing* the internal events that precede the habitual act of using, rather than *reacting* to them, may allow individuals to access alternative responses to the triggering stimuli. When a person learns to recognize internal reactions while in a triggering situation, she or he is able to access the skills learned in treatment more readily. Thus, mindfulness practices can help increase the generalization of these skills as the individual learns to respond to the experience of elicited craving, rather than each external cue. Individuals may also begin to notice that while substances often provide initial relief, it is short-lived; the discomfort of withdrawal or triggers will return, perpetuating the need to use substances again, and subsequently strengthening the cycle of addiction.

There are several approaches to SUD treatment that involve mindfulness training. One program that has undergone rigorous clinical trial research is Mindfulness-Based Relapse Prevention (MBRP) (Bowen, Chawla, & Marlatt, 2010). MBRP is an eight-week, group-based aftercare program supporting individuals in early abstinence. The program combines mindfulness practices with techniques used in cognitive-behavioral relapse prevention approaches (Marlatt & Gordon, 1985) to enhance awareness of internal processes that can increase relapse risk, and to develop skillful responses to these experiences. While many addiction treatments emphasize willpower and avoidance-based methods to manage situational triggers, practices in MBRP are designed to expose clients to internal reactions that may lead to substance use, and to enhance their relapse prevention skills to better manage triggers and craving.

Some mindfulness practices in MBRP aim to increase awareness and understanding of craving by exploring the constituent sensations, emotions, and thoughts, while other practices aim to support distress tolerance, self-care and lifestyle balance. Through curious exploration of craving, individuals begin to understand substance use as a "false refuge" to escape the discomfort of craving. Although using substances may bring temporary relief, it often strengthens harmful avoidance patterns and increases overall suffering. Individuals learn that cravings, like all experiences, eventually pass. When they witness this for themselves, they begin to trust that cravings will inevitably subside without reaching for a substance to alleviate their discomfort. When discomfort can be accepted as an arising and passing human experience, people can learn to turn toward it with non-judgment, compassion, and curiosity. This allows an opportunity to tune into their own wisdom and develop a clearer understanding of what they *actually* need (e.g., connection or comfort) in these moments, rather than reaching for a "false refuge." Individuals can then begin to implement more wholesome and skillful behaviors when experiencing distress and in daily life as a self-care routine

Theoretical foundations of MBRP

Not long ago, addiction was viewed as a moral weakness. Individuals with substance-related addictive behaviors were viewed as lacking the moral fortitude or will-power to abstain from excessive substance use, and were often punished for their "immoral" behavior (Leshner, 1997). More recently, however, SUD has been conceptualized as a mental illness, shifting treatment from punitive to rehabilitative. Researchers began to understand substance use not as an issue of willpower, but a heavily engrained behavioral pattern that needed to be understood and replaced with more beneficial behaviors (NIDA, 2016).

Driving many advances in SUD treatment is an understanding of the basic patterns of operant and classical conditioning that underlie addictive behaviors. The psychoactive effects of a substance (feeling "high") can be initially positively reinforcing, thus increasing the probability of the behavior being repeated (operant conditioning). Over time, the positive effects become less salient, and use becomes "negatively reinforcing" as the individual uses to eliminate withdrawal symptoms, or to feel "normal." As the frequency of use increases, tolerance increases and the individual often needs a greater amount of the substance to acquire the same "high." Simultaneously, places and people once "neutral," such as a specific location or one's friends, eventually become associated with use. The people or places subsequently serve as "conditioned stimuli," or triggers (classical conditioning). These stimuli may generalize over time, essentially creating an infinite number of triggers and making abstinence difficult to attain.

Methods to extinguish conditioned associations and behaviors are well established in behavioral science. Traditionally, SUD treatment programs focus on changing factors related to reinforcement and conditioning in the external environment (e.g., changing friends and activities) (NIDA, 2012). Such treatment options include contingency management, and 12-step programs, such as Alcoholics Anonymous and Narcotics Anonymous (Herron & Brennan, 2015). While these interventions have shown success for some people, they often fail for others due to the all-or-nothing approach to abstinence. An alternative for these individuals may be treatment incorporating a "middle-way" approach, where recovery is centered around risk reduction rather than abstinence only. Recognizing the need for a more tolerant approach, addictions researchers began developing Relapse Prevention (RP) (Marlatt & Gordon, 1985), an aftercare program to help individuals transition from inpatient or intensive outpatient treatment settings back to everyday life. The aims of RP are to identify intra- and interpersonal factors contributing to a person's drug use, and to develop cognitive-behavioral strategies to reduce the likelihood of a person using. Clients are taught to recognize triggers and high-risk situations that could increase their likelihood of using. Through psychoeducation and skills training, individuals minimize risk of relapse by choosing healthier behaviors when substance-related cues are present, and refusing substances assertively if and when they are offered.

A recent systematic review suggests support for the use of RP in inpatient and outpatient treatment settings (Hendershot, Witkiewitz, George, & Marlatt, 2011). However, much of RP is focused on cognitive and behavioral techniques to avoid external triggers and restructure the perception of internal triggers. While it is often skillful in early abstinence to avoid triggers and engage in alternative behaviors when cravings arise, it is critical to acknowledge the role of internal experiences, such as negative affective states, in the relapse process. Negative affect is often a primary precipitant of relapse (Shiffman & Waters, 2004; Stewart, 2000; Wheeler et al., 2008). Attempting to avoid or change an emotional state, however, cannot only be ineffective, but often causes more discomfort, as the attempted avoidance may actually exacerbate the negative affect (Baker, Piper, McCarthy, Majeskie, & Fiore, 2004).

Interventions with a primary focus on internal triggers can enhance an individual's ability to tolerate distress while experiencing an external trigger by encouraging them to gain insight into the cause of distress rather than attempt to remove or change it. For example, Mindfulness-Based Stress Reduction (MBSR) (Kabat-Zinn, 2003) was first created to assist with the management of chronic pain through cultivating a non-judgmental, curious awareness of the sensations of discomfort, and detaching from thinking patterns that exacerbate the perception of pain. Afterward, Mindfulness-Based Cognitive Therapy (MBCT) (Segal, Williams, & Teasdale, 2012) was developed for managing relapse into depressive symptoms. Like MBSR, MBCT uses mindfulness and meditation-based practices to help clients in remission from major depression manage negative affect and thoughts that lead to depressive relapse. Practices from MBCT were adapted for SUD populations to manage negative affect and craving associated with substance relapse, and combined with skills used in RP, leading to the development of MBRP.

Through MBRP, an individual uses attentional processes to bring awareness to internal stimuli (e.g., body sensations, emotions, or thoughts) that occur between a conditioned stimulus (e.g. contact with a certain triggering environment) and response (e.g. drug use). By shifting the focus from removing or changing the stimulus to observing it, one can begin to perceive craving in its raw form, rather than an insurmountable force or indicator of inevitable relapse. Individuals can learn to shift their relationship to craving, allowing it to exist as merely a series of transient mental, physical and affective experiences. Through this process, they can eventually extinguish conditioned reactions to substance use. Acknowledging the internal response to external events with gentle attention can also relieve some of the distress associated with avoiding aversive, or clinging to appetitive, stimuli. Over time, the experience of distress is shorter lived as the individual is able to observe and accept whatever experiences arise with an open, present-focused attitude. Less perceived distress by resisting negative affective states and greater equanimity toward difficult experiences can become positively reinforcing, and may strengthen the behavior of mindfully and carefully attending to one's suffering.

Structure of the program

Overview

MBRP was originally designed as an eight-week outpatient aftercare program. Each weekly session, lasting about two hours, has a central theme. Typically, sessions begin with a formal mindfulness practice followed by "inquiry" (described below), review of home practice, discussion and practices around the week's theme, "informal" mindfulness practices relating to that theme, review of home practice assignments for the upcoming week, and a brief closing practice. Home practice assignments, to be implemented in the days between sessions, include worksheets, formal mindfulness practice supported by audio recordings, and informal practices that apply the training to everyday life.

Beginning practices

Sessions 1–3 highlight "automatic pilot," or conditioned behaviors described above, by bringing awareness to the habitual and seemingly automatic tendencies of the mind. The facilitator exposes the client to increasingly challenging situations, similar to traditional exposure-response prevention interventions (Eftekhari, Ruzek, Crowley, Rosen, Greenbaum, & Karlin, 2013), starting with recognizing automatic thoughts and sensations during neutral activities, and moving toward maintaining attention to body sensations while imagining distressing circumstances.

In the first session, clients are asked to use all of their senses to explore a raisin, to which they have likely given very little attention in the past. They explore visual, tactile, gustatory, olfactory and even auditory properties of a raisin, as well as thoughts, reactions, judgments, or urges that occur as they engage in this exercise.

The facilitator then leads a discussion on automatic pilot and the common human tendency to "go through the motions," while missing qualities of the present moment. Through inquiry, the facilitator helps the clients understand the connection between this tendency and relapse. Clients then engage in the "body scan" practice, wherein they bring this same curious attention to their present physical experience in a systematic exploration of the often ignored sensations of each body area.

Practices in the second session are designed to cultivate greater awareness of triggers and craving, and habitual responses to them. Based on a practice in MBCT (Segal et al., 2012), clients are asked to imagine a situation in which they wave at someone who does not acknowledge their greeting, and are then encouraged to notice their subsequent thoughts, sensations, emotions and urges to react. This practice helps highlight the mind's automatic tendency to create stories and assumptions, often accepted as facts, and often leading to urges or overt reactive behaviors.

Following this exercise is the Urge Surfing practice, a core exposure response-prevention exercise in MBRP, in which clients are asked to imagine a situation in which they have a tendency to behave reactively. They are asked to imagine what happens right up until the point they would typically react, then pause in that moment to observe their inner experience, turning attention to body sensations, thoughts, and emotions. They are asked to "surf" the fluctuating intensity, bringing curiosity and spaciousness to their experience, and to inquire of themselves what they are truly wanting or needing. Many clients are surprised to notice that the intensity of the craving changes, even within a short amount of time, and are often surprised at their response to the self-inquiry about what they really need.

Urge Surfing is followed by the Mountain Meditation (Kabat-Zinn & Santorelli, 1999), intended to bring clients in contact with their inner "mountain-like" qualities of strength, dignity, and stillness. Clients imagine a mountain, then bring the image of the mountain inside their body so the peak is aligned with the top of the head, the slopes are aligned with the sides of the arms, and the base is aligned with their base on the chair or cushion. The metaphor highlights qualities of the mountain such as dignity, wisdom, equanimity, and stillness, which are maintained regardless of the weather or opinion of others. Clients are invited to access these mountain-like qualities in their own life; to be unmoving and resilient during their own changing external circumstances or internal "emotional storms."

In session 3, SOBER space, another brief exposure response-prevention practice, is introduced. It is intended for use when clients are experiencing reactivity following a trigger. SOBER is an acronym describing the process by which clients can shift from an urge to react to a more intentional and skillful response. Clients are instructed to *Stop* when they notice reactivity, *Observe* body sensations, emotions, and thoughts, then further direct attention inward to notice sensations of the *Breath*. Clients then *Expand* their awareness outward again to include their body sensations, emotions, and thoughts, seeing if they can hold this experience in a more grounded and expansive awareness. They can then choose to *Respond*, versus react, to whatever situation triggered them.

Clients are encouraged to continue to practice SOBER space in a number of challenging situations, including interpersonal interactions and events that arise between sessions. For example, one client reported missing an important court appointment, and instead of turning to substance use, a typical pattern of behavior in past stressful situations, she recalled SOBER space. She noticed her reactivity, thoughts of wanting to use, and feelings of disappointment and anger. However, instead of lapsing, she was able to pause and simply observe her experience rather than habitually react to it. Following this pause, she called her primary counselor to help talk her through cravings and associated thoughts of substance use. She was able to reduce her internal feelings of reactivity and maintain sobriety through a triggering event.

Mid-course practices

Within sessions 4–6, clients are introduced to walking meditation, mindful movement, and awareness of thoughts, as they continue focusing on reframing their relationship with their reactive impulses. By learning to identify high-risk situations, clients are taught to observe the experience of feeling an impulse, rather than habitually acting on the impulse. The focus of these middle sessions shifts from enhancing awareness of autopilot and triggers to applying mindfulness practices in daily life, especially during challenging or triggering situations. Practicing mindfulness outside of the weekly sessions helps equip individuals with easily accessible skills they can use in their daily life to effectively manage triggers and cravings. This integration of practice into daily life is considered to be a foundational mechanism of this approach, and is supported by data suggesting that between-session mindfulness practice mediates positive substance use outcomes (Grow, Collins, Harrop, & Marlatt, 2015). Clients are also taught to expand their attention beyond physical sensations. They are taught various practices to hone attention on sensations such as sight, sound, and emotions. They continue engaging in simple mindfulness practices they can do to help instill mindful awareness while engaging in daily activities, not only while being still. Increasing awareness of all sensations offers clients more stimuli to observe when feeling triggered in challenging situations.

Clients also practice bringing awareness to thoughts and the nature of thinking. They learn to see thoughts as passing mental events, versus reliable reflections of the truth; similar to cravings, thoughts will arise and pass without needing to act on or identify with them. Although subtle, habitual negative thoughts can lead to lapses in abstinence if an individual over-identifies with them (e.g., "I am a failure") (Haller et al., 2016). When clients realize that thoughts are not necessarily accurate descriptions of reality, they may gain more clarity around the ways they contribute to their own suffering. Metaphors are used to foster the process of noticing thoughts and acknowledging them as passing mental events. For example, when a movie plot is engaging, everything else fades from attention as one becomes captivated and emotionally invested in the movie. An individual can feel as though they are experiencing what the characters experience. Although a person can feel the intense emotions of a movie, they can acknowledge it is not reality; they can become an audience to the thoughts rather than subject to their content. As clients strengthen this ability to recognize and pull themselves out of ruminative thought cycles, they have a greater opportunity to experience what is truly happening in the present through awareness of direct sensory stimuli rather than getting embroiled in habit or reactivity.

Final practices

Practices in the final MBRP sessions encourage clients to not only respond skillfully in challenging situations, but to also take time to engage in nourishing and wholesome self-care activities. Sessions 7 and 8 are designed to help clients achieve a balanced lifestyle through self-care, social support, and continued mindfulness practice after course completion. As clients learn to take responsibility for instilling positive contingencies throughout their day by engaging in self-care practices, wholesome behaviors can be strengthened outside of treatment. Clients can also begin embodying a "middle-way" attitude toward life's ups and downs as they continue to practice approaching intense internal stimuli with equanimity. With continued practice, clients can feel empowered to approach life with willingness rather than aversion and feel capable of living a balanced lifestyle.

In the final sessions, clients engage in several additional practices, including an exercise in which they identify and better understand the nourishing and depleting aspects in their daily lives, a formal "loving-kindness" (LK) meditation practice, and a closing meditation practice. LK, based on traditional meditation practices, is intended to train the attention to rest on positive qualities, through sending self and others wishes for well-being. For many clients, offering LK to themselves can be bring up internalized guilt and shame for many years and may experience self-judgment for not being able to offer themselves well wishes. The practice is *not* intended to make clients feel any particular way toward themselves or others; it is important to help clients recognize their judgments as more material to observe, rather than a hindrance.

During the LK practice, the facilitator asks clients to imagine a being toward whom they have an easy, loving relationship, and silently offer this being well-wishes (e.g., "May you be safe, happy, healthy"). Clients may choose other phrases that seem more appropriate to them. Clients then send wishes of LK to themselves, using similar phrases (e.g., "May *I* be safe, happy, healthy"), or other phrases if they choose. Lastly, clients are instructed to expand their wishes of LK to all living beings, which also include themselves (e.g., "May *we* be safe, happy, healthy").

After the LK practice and discussion, clients engage in an exercise based on MBCT in which they are asked to write a detailed list of activities in a typical day from beginning to end. They are then instructed to note "N" for each nourishing activity, and "D" for depleting activities. They are asked to tally and compare the number of Ns and Ds. Some clients are not surprised by the amount of Ns or Ds on their page because it reflects their lived experience accurately. Other clients may be surprised because it is incongruent with their experience. For example, it may be that a client has more nourishing activities listed, but feels depleted most of the time.

There are multiple intentions behind this exercise. Facilitators ask clients how they might adjust their typical day to include more time for nourishing activities and reduce depleting activities. Clients may also identify warning signs of relapse and discuss how consistent self-care practices can reduce exposure to events leading to negative affect and triggers. However, the primary focus is to recognize and explore how the mind can add meaning and value to seemingly neutral events, making them feel either more nourishing or depleting. For example, a person may ascribe their walk to work every day as a mundane or perhaps depleting. However, if a person can notice present moment sensations while walking (e.g., sights, smells) they may re-perceive this activity as nourishing.

To prepare for the end of the course, clients then fill out wallet-sized reminder cards so they can access nourishing activities in the moment when going about their regular day. The importance of support networks in recovery and how to ask for help from others when life seems difficult is also emphasized. Resources such as family, friends, and 12-step programs are reviewed. The facilitator can also offer other mindfulness resources including websites, books, guided meditations on audio files, and information about local meditation groups, courses, and retreats. A closing practice is then facilitated to end the program. The closing practice begins with each client being given a small stone to keep as a reminder of their experience within MBRP. The clients are encouraged to explore their stone, and to allow it to become a tangible representation of their own uniqueness and inner strength. A stone's rough edges, cracks, and crevices are not perceived as flaws or imperfections, but as signs of a real and strenuous journey. Similarly, every person is shaped by their journey and has their own rough edges, cracks, and crevices; these are not imperfections, but signs of living.

Guiding practice

To skillfully guide clients through what is often new experiential territory, and help them navigate the inevitable challenges that arise during mindfulness practice, it is imperative that the clinicians have an established personal mindfulness practice of their own. Although templates for meditation practices are offered in the MBRP clinician's guidebook, as in many other MBI protocols, facilitators are encouraged to guide meditation practices from their own present experience, modeling non-judgmental attention in each passing moment. As clients move through practices, the facilitator offers suggestions on ways to observe experience. Clients are repeatedly reminded that wandering attention is natural, and are instructed to gently guide their attention back to the chosen attentional object. Disabusing ideas that mindfulness practice means having a peaceful and empty mind can instill greater self-efficacy in a novice meditation practitioner, increasing the likelihood of continued engagement with practice.

"Inquiry," an integral part of MBRP and other MBIs, is a dyadic verbal process of exploration between the facilitator and the client. Parallel to processes in formal mindfulness practice, the skilled facilitator redirects clients' tendencies to share stories *about* themselves or their experiences to discussion of their direct, present experience. For example, a client may comment, "I am a bad meditator; I've always known that about myself." Rather than engage in or challenge the content of, or try to refute, this thought, a facilitator might recognize this as a judgment, and comment, "It sounds as though there was some judgment that arose for you. Tell me what else you noticed while you were practicing." Or, "So something happened during the practice, and you decided it meant you were a bad meditator. Do you remember what happened before that thought arose?" This investigation of experience may differ from other process groups in that the primary focus (as in formal practice) is the client's direct experience rather than ideas about or interpretations of what occurred. Where many process groups might encourage discussion of external events or circumstances associated with discomfort, an MBRP clinician is interested in the direct experience of discomfort itself.

Inquiry thus models a different way of relating to experience by redirecting attention from appraisal of ruminative and habitual thought patterns to direct experience of whatever is arising in the perceptual field. The continued practice of gentle redirection of attention can retrain the seemingly uncontrollable tendency of the mind to get caught up in stories and judgments, often the true cause of suffering.

Additional considerations and adaptations

Aside from clinician facilitation of practices and inquiry, there are several other key factors that affect the process of the course. Attendance at each MBRP session is critical, as each week's theme builds on the previous weeks. Often, clients who miss several groups are less engaged and feel lost as they move through later sessions. Closed groups may thus be preferred when feasible. With more exposure to mindfulness practices, individuals gain more mastery of attending to the subtleties of present moment experience and are able to build upon this foundation as the weeks progress. However, several practitioners have worked with open "rolling" groups, modifying practices and structure to accommodate a flow of new clients throughout the course.

While several studies suggest MBIs for SUD clients may be well suited to a variety of populations including incarcerated adults (Bowen et al., 2006), court mandated clients (Witkiewitz, Warner, Sully, Barricks, Stauffer, Thompson, & Luoma, 2014), adolescents (Barnert, Himelstein, Herbert, Garcia-Romeu, & Chamberlain, 2014; Himelstein et al., 2015), individuals with trauma symptoms (King et al., 2013) and ethnic minority women (Witkiewitz et al., 2013; Amaro et al., 2014), it can be helpful to consider population-specific adaptations before implementing these treatments. For example, individuals with trauma histories may benefit from adaptations to some of the meditation practices, such as shortened body-based practices that encompass a broader sweep of the body, rather than a thorough, focused attention to particular areas of the body, which can be triggering for those with histories of physical or sexual abuse. Similarly, practice postures can be adjusted to be less triggering or painful (e.g., sitting in chairs vs. laying down).

As recommended by Himelstein and Saul (2016), adaptations and considerations can also be made to render the practices more accessible to adolescents. For example, it can sometimes be difficult for adults to speak to adolescents as equals. Forming a genuine, non-patronizing human connection is crucial with this age range, as is modeling relational mindfulness (i.e., awareness of how one interacts with and relates to others). Modeling relational mindfulness is especially important in the face of resistance, which will likely be frequent. It is essential to include didactic and process-based activities, along with experiential activities, to alleviate boredom. Young people will also likely need a greater amount of psychoeducation on drug use and relapse-prevention strategies than adults (Himelstein & Saul, 2016).

Research supporting MBRP

Research has demonstrated MBIs are an effective method for reducing cravings and misuse of various substances (Chiesa & Serretti, 2014). Specific to MBRP, the first study evaluating feasibility and initial efficacy using randomized controlled trials was a study comparing MBRP and treatment as usual (TAU), which was a rolling admissions, outpatient-care emphasizing the 12-step model and psychoeducation. Across a four-month follow-up, the MBRP group showed significantly greater decreases in craving severity and drug use, compared to TAU. Craving was found to mediate, or partially explain, the relationship between intervention assignment and drug use following the intervention (Bowen et al., 2009).

A secondary analysis of the previous study was conducted to further understand the mediating effects of cravings. Researchers found the relationship between post-intervention depressive symptoms and days of use measured at 4-month follow-up was significantly mediated by cravings at two-month follow-up. A moderation effect was also found for intervention assignment. Specifically, the MBRP group did not experience a strong, positive relationship between post-intervention depressive symptoms and cravings measured at two-month follow-up, whereas the TAU group did. This suggests individuals in the MBRP group were able to decouple the relationship between depressive symptoms and craving, leading to less drug use days overall. Mindfulness training may help individuals experience cravings as more tolerable, minimizing the causal relationship between depressive symptoms and the desire to alleviate emotional discomfort through substance use (Witkiewitz & Bowen, 2010).

An additional analysis of the initial MBRP trial (Bowen et al., 2009) assessed the effects of MBRP on craving after the intervention (Witkiewitz, Bowen, Douglas, & Hsu, 2013). While the MBRP group experienced an expected decrease in cravings over time, the TAU group showed an increase in craving severity during treatment. This analysis also measured individuals' levels of mindfulness, which encompassed acceptance, awareness, and non-judgment as determined through participant scores on several self-report measures. Level of mindfulness was found to mediate the relationship between treatment and severity of craving at the end of treatment, supporting the efficacy of MBRP for reducing cravings and substance use.

The original Bowen et al. (2009) study sample included a diversity of race, employment status, and drug of choice, implying MBRP may be beneficial for a wide range of people. This finding was further supported by a study of ethnically diverse female criminal offenders in a residential addiction treatment center comparing effects of MBRP and standard relapse prevention (RP) on total drug use days and drug use consequences during a 15-week follow-up (Witkiewitz et al., 2014). The MBRP group reported fewer drug use days and fewer medical and legal problems. Further analyses found that racial and ethnic minority women in MBRP reported significantly lower addiction severity, compared to non-Hispanic and racial and ethnic minority women in RP. Additionally, 0% of the racial and ethnic minority women in MBRP reported drug use at follow-up, while 14.3% of the racial and ethnic minority women in RP did endorse drug use. (Witkiewitz, Greenfield, & Bowen, 2013). These findings are of critical importance, as ethnic minority women often have worse treatment outcomes as compared to non-ethnic minority women (CDC, 2011).

A more recent study assessed the longer-term effects of MBRP. Bowen et al. (2014) found that participants in an MBRP treatment group reported significantly fewer drug use and heavy drinking days at 12-month follow-up than participants in RP and TAU (Bowen et al., 2014). This finding suggests MBRP may be one answer to the consistent issue of treatment outcomes failing to be retained at long-term follow-up points (McLellan, Lewis, O'Brien, & Kleber, 2000). One possible explanation is the emphasis MBRP places on identifying internal triggers, which are often underestimated contributors to relapse.

MBRP has also been specifically targeted to stimulant-use rehabilitation. A recent study found individuals with comorbid diagnoses of SUD and either Major Depressive Disorder or Generalized Anxiety Disorder, who were randomly assigned to MBRP, experienced considerably larger decreases in symptom severity and stimulant use, as compared to individuals assigned to receive health education (Glasner-Edwards et al., 2015). Studies have also been conducted on the beneficial mechanisms of MBRP, such as the quality of the relationship between the therapist and client, and between-session practice. These are thought to be foundational elements for increasing mindful awareness in MBRP participants (Bowen & Kurz, 2012). Continued home-practice following the MBRP is another staple of the course, and an important mediator for preventing relapse (Grow, Collins, Harrop, & Marlatt, 2015).

Online materials for further resources and information relating to the program

Further information and resources can be found on www.mindfulrp.com. Facilitators and clients may use this webpage to access audio recordings of meditations, review current research on MBRP and similar approaches, find professional facilitator trainings and national and international clinicians who facilitate MBRP, and learn about the creation of the program. Facilitators may also refer clients to local meditation groups, where they can sustain their practice after the eight-week MBRP group. Recovery-based meditation groups may include Refuge Recovery and Heart of Recovery, located throughout the United States. General mindfulness-based group meditations and retreat centers may be found online at www.dhamma.org. Furthermore, audio recordings of guided meditations and discussion of meditation practices by teachers and practitioners can be accessed at dharmaseed.org.

References

Amaro, H., Spear, S., Vallejo, Z., Conron, K., & Black, D. S. (2014). Feasibility, acceptability, and preliminary outcomes of a mindfulness-based relapse prevention intervention for culturally-diverse, low-income women in substance use disorder treatment. *Substance Use & Misuse, 49*(5), 547–559.

Baker, T. B., Piper, M. E., McCarthy, D. E., Majeskie, M. R., & Fiore, M. C. (2004). Addiction motivation reformulated: An affective processing model of negative reinforcement. *Psychological Review, 111*(1), 33–51. https://doi.org/10.1037/0033-295X.111.1.33

Barnert, E. S., Himelstein, S., Herbert, S., Garcia-Romeu, A., & Chamberlain, L. J. (2014). Exploring an intensive meditation intervention for incarcerated youth. *Child and Adolescent Mental Health, 19*(1), 69–73.

Benishek, L. A., Dugosh, K. L., Kirby, K. C., Matejkowski, J., Clements, N. T., Seymour, B. L., & Festinger, D. S. (2014). Prize-based contingency management for the treatment of substance abusers: A meta-analysis. *Addiction, 109*(9), 1426–1436.

Bowen, S., Chawla, N., Collins, S. E., Witkiewitz, K., Hsu, S., Grow, J., . . . Marlatt, A. (2009). Mindfulness-based relapse prevention for substance use disorders: A pilot efficacy trial. *Substance Abuse, 30*(4), 295–305.

Bowen, S., Chawla, N., & Marlatt, A. (2010). *Mindfulness-based relapse prevention for addictive behaviors: A clinician's guide*. New York, NY: Guilford Press.

Bowen, S., & Kurz, A. S. (2012). Between-session practice and therapeutic alliance as predictors of mindfulness after mindfulness-based relapse prevention. *Journal of Clinical Psychology, 68*(3), 236–245. https://doi.org/10.1080/08897070903250084.Mindfulness-Based

Bowen, S., Witkiewitz, K., Clifasefi, S. L., Grow, J., Chawla, N., Hsu, S. H., . . . Larimer, M. E. (2014). Relative efficacy of mindfulness-based relapse prevention, standard relapse prevention, and treatment as usual for substance use disorders: A randomized clinical trial. *JAMA Psychiatry, 71*(5), 547–556. https://doi.org/10.1001/jamapsychiatry.2013.4546

Bowen, S., Witkiewitz, K., Dillworth, T. M., Chawla, N., Simpson, T. L., Ostafin, B. D., . . . Marlatt, G. A. (2006). Mindfulness meditation and substance use in an incarcerated population. *Psychology of Addictive Behaviors, 20*(3), 343.

CDC. (2011). CDC health disparities and inequalities report: United States. *Morbidity and Mortality Weekly Report, 60*, 1–116.

Center for Behavioral Health Statistics and Quality. (2015). *Behavioral Health Trends in the United States: Results from the 2014 National Survey on Drug Use and Health*. (HHS Publication No. SMA 15-4927, NSDUH Series H-50. Retrieved from www.samhsa.gov/data/sites/default/files/NSDUH-FRR1-2014/NSDUH-FRR1-2014.pdf\nwww.samhsa.gov/data/

Chiesa, A., & Serretti, A. (2014). Are mindfulness-based interventions effective for substance use disorders? A systematic review of the evidence. *Substance Use & Misuse*, *49*(5), 492–512. https://doi.org/10.3109/10826084.2013.770027

Eftekhari, A., Ruzek, J. I., Crowley, J. J., Rosen, C. S., Greenbaum, M. A., & Karlin, B. E. (2013). Effectiveness of national implementation of prolonged exposure therapy in Veterans Affairs care. *JAMA Psychiatry*, *70*(9), 949–955.

Ettner, S. L., Huang, D., Evans, E., Ash, D. R., Hardy, M., Jourabchi, M., & Hser, Y-I. (2006). Benefit-cost in the California treatment outcome project: Does substance abuse treatment 'pay for itself'? *Health Services Research*, *41*(1), 192–213.

Garland, E. L. (2013). *Mindfulness-oriented recovery enhancement for addiction, stress, and pain.* Washington, DC: NASW Press.

Glasner-Edwards, S., Mooney, L. M., Ang, A., Chokron Garneau, H., Hartwell, E. E., Brecht, M., & Rawson, R. (2015). Mindfulness based relapse prevention improves stimulant use among adults with major depression and generalized anxiety disorder. *Drug and Alcohol Dependence*, *156*, 80. doi: http://dx.doi.org/10.1016/j.drugalcdep.2015.07.1135

Grow, J. C., Collins, S. E., Harrop, E. N., & Marlatt, G. A. (2015). Enactment of home practice following mindfulness-based relapse prevention and its association with substance-use outcomes. *Addictive Behaviors*, *40*, 16–20. https://doi.org/10.1016/j.addbeh.2014.07.030

Haller, M., Norman, S. B., Cummins, K., Trim, R. S., Xu, X., Cui, R., . . . Tate, S. R. (2016). Integrated cognitive behavioral therapy versus cognitive processing therapy for adults with depression, substance use disorder, and trauma. *Journal of Substance Abuse Treatment*, *62*, 38–48.

Hendershot, C. S., Witkiewitz, K., George, W. H., & Marlatt, G. A. (2011). Relapse prevention for addictive behaviors. *Substance Abuse Treatment, Prevention, and Policy*, 2–17.

Henkel, D. (2011). Unemployment and substance use: A review of the literature (1990-2010). *Current Drug Abuse Reviews*, *4*(1), 4–27.

Herron, A. J., & Brennan, T. (2015). *The ASAM essentials of addiction medicine* (2nd ed.). Philadelphia, PA: Wolters Kluwer.

Himelstein, S., & Saul, S. (2016). *Mindfulness-based substance abuse treatment for adolescents: A 12-session curriculum.* New York, NY: Routledge.

Himelstein, S., Saul, S., & Garcia-Romeu, A. (2015). Does mindfulness meditation increase effectiveness of substance abuse treatment with incarcerated youth? A pilot randomized controlled trial. *Mindfulness*, *6*(6), 1472–1480.

Kabat-Zinn, J. (2003). Mindfulness-based stress reduction (MBSR). *Constructive Human Science*, *8*, 73–107.

Kabat-Zinn, J., & Santorelli, S. (1999). *Mindfulness-based stress reduction professional training resource manual.* Worcester, MA: Center for Mindfulness in Medicine, Health Care and Society.

King, A. P., Erickson, T. M., Giardino, N. D., Favorite, T., Rauch, S. A., Robinson, E., . . . Liberzon, I. (2013). A pilot study of group mindfulness-based cognitive therapy (MBCT) for combat veterans with posttraumatic stress disorder (PTSD). *Depression and Anxiety*, *30*(7), 638–645.

Leshner, A. I. (1997). Addiction is a brain disease, and it matters. *Science*, *278*(5335), 45–47. https://doi.org/10.1126/science.278.5335.45

Marlatt, G. A., & Gordon, J. R. (1985). *Relapse prevention: Maintenance strategies in the treatment of addictive behaviors.* New York, NY: Guilford Press.

McLellan, A. T., Lewis, D. C., O'Brien, C. P., & Kleber, H. D. (2000). Drug dependence, a chronic medical illness: Implications for treatment, insurance, and outcomes evaluation. *Journal of American Medical Association*, *284*(13), 1689–1695.

NIDA. (2011). *Trends & Statistics.* Retrieved November 28, 2016, from www.drugabuse.gov/related-topics/trends-statistics

NIDA. (2012). *Principles of Drug Addiction Treatment: A Research-Based Guide* (3rd ed.). Retrieved April 3, 2017, from www.drugabuse.gov/publications/principles-drug-addiction-treatment-research-based-guide-third-edition

NIDA. (2015). *Nationwide Trends*. Retrieved November 28, 2016, from www.drugabuse.gov/publications/drugfacts/nationwide-trends

NIDA. (2016). *Treatment Approaches for Drug Addiction*. Retrieved April 23, 2017, from www.drugabuse.gov/publications/drugfacts/treatment-approaches-drug-addiction

SAMHSA. (2009). *Cost Offset of Treatment Services*. Retrieved April 1, 2017, from www.samhsa-gpra.samhsa.gov/CSAT/view/docs/SAIS_GPRA_CostOffsetSubstanceAbuse.pdf

Segal, Z. V., Williams, J. M. G., & Teasdale, J. D. (2012). *Mindfulness-based cognitive therapy for depression*. New York, NY: Guilford Press.

Shiffman, S., & Waters, A. J. (2004). Negative affect and smoking lapses: A prospective analysis. *Journal of Consulting and Clinical Psychology, 72*, 192–201.

Stewart, J. (2000). Pathways to relapse: The neurobiology of drug- and stress-induced relapse to drug-taking. *Journal of Psychiatry & Neuroscience, 25*, 125–136.

Wheeler, R. A., Twining, R. C., Jones, J. L., Slater, J. M., Grigson, P. S., & Carelli, R. M. (2008). Behavioral and electrophysiological indices of negative affect predict cocaine self-administration. *Neuron, 57*(5), 774–785.

Whiteford, H. A., Degenhardt, L., Jurgen, R., Baxter, A. J., Ferrari, A. J., Erskine, H. E., . . . Vos, T. (2010). Global burden of disease attributable to mental and substance use disorders: Findings from the Global Burden of Disease Study. *The Lancet, 382*(9904), 1575–1586.

Witkiewitz, K., & Bowen, S. (2010). Depression, craving and substance use following a randomized trial of mindfulness-based relapse prevention. *Journal of Consulting and Clinical Psychology, 78*(3), 362–374. https://doi.org/10.1037/a0019172.Depression

Witkiewitz, K., Bowen, S., Douglas, H., & Hsu, S. H. (2013). Mindfulness-based relapse prevention for substance craving. *Addictive Behaviors, 38*(2), 1563–1571. https://doi.org/10.1016/j.addbeh.2012.04.001

Witkiewitz, K., Greenfield, B. L., & Bowen, S. (2013). Mindfulness-based relapse prevention with racial and ethnic minority women. *Addictive Behaviors, 38*(12), 2821–2824. https://doi.org/10.1016/j.addbeh.2013.08.018

Witkiewitz, K., Warner, K., Sully, B., Barricks, A., Stauffer, C., Thompson, B. L., & Luoma, J. B. (2014). Randomized trial comparing mindfulness-based relapse prevention with relapse prevention for women offenders at a residential addiction treatment center. *Substance Use & Misuse, 49*(5), 536–546.

Section VIII

Mindfulness programs in compassion

Chapter 28

Mindful Self-Compassion (MSC)

Christopher Germer and Kristin Neff

Over the past three decades, mindfulness has become part of mainstream Western culture (Williams & Kabat-Zinn, 2011). Compassion has always been an implicit aspect of mindfulness training insofar as we can only be truly mindful when our awareness is warm and kind. More recently, training programs have been developed within the secular, scientific paradigm that *explicitly* teach compassion (Gilbert, 2009; Jazaieri et al., 2013; Pace et al., 2009; van den Brink & Koster, 2015). Mindful Self-Compassion (MSC) is one of those programs.

MSC is a combination of mindfulness and compassion training – a *mindfulness-based self-compassion training program*. MSC relies on mindfulness because we need to know when we're suffering in order to bring kindness to our experience and to ourselves. Self-compassion training also tends to activate difficult emotions, at least in the initial phases of practice, so we need mindfulness to help anchor and stabilize our awareness. Finally, mindfulness training helps to cultivate spacious awareness and equanimity as a basis for compassionate action.

MSC is also a mix of personal development training and psychotherapy. It is primarily a *resource-building* program designed for the general public to enhance our capacity for self-compassion. MSC does not focus on healing old wounds as in psychotherapy. However, when we give ourselves kindness and understanding, we inevitably uncover events in our lives when we were not treated with kindness and understanding. MSC becomes therapeutic to the extent that we meet those old wounds in a new way – with mindfulness and self-compassion.

MSC was developed by two psychologists, Chris Germer and Kristin Neff. Chris is a clinical psychologist who has been working for decades to integrate mindfulness into psychotherapy (Germer, Siegel & Fulton, 2016). Kristin is a pioneering researcher in self-compassion (Neff, 2003a). When they met in 2008, Kristin and Chris wondered if self-compassion could be explicitly taught using a structured curriculum like Mindfulness-Based Stress Reduction and Mindfulness-Based Cognitive Therapy. The first MSC program took place in 2010 and a randomized controlled trial of the program was completed two years later (Neff & Germer, 2013). MSC is now being taught by hundreds of trained teachers worldwide.

Both Chris and Kristin have been practicing mindfulness meditation for most of their adult lives. The necessity of self-compassion became clear to them as they brought mindfulness to bear on their own difficulties. For Kristin, it was the stress of parenting a child with autism, and for Chris, it was the challenge of public speaking anxiety. Self-compassion adds a special element to mindfulness training. Whereas mindfulness is mostly the practice of loving awareness of moment-to-moment *experience*, self-compassion is loving awareness of the *experiencer*. This shift in focus is crucial when we are caught in the grip of intense and disturbing emotions. Sometimes we first need to hold *ourselves* before we can hold our experience in tender awareness.

Theory and research on self-compassion

The construct of self-compassion is drawn from Buddhist psychology, and was first operationally defined and introduced into the psychological literature over a decade ago. Neff (2003b, 2016) proposes that self-compassion is a type of self-to-self relating that represents a compassionate rather than uncompassionate stance toward the self when faced with personal suffering: self-kindness versus self-judgment, a sense of common humanity versus isolation, and mindfulness versus over-identification. These components combine and mutually interact to create a self-compassionate frame of mind. Self-kindness entails being gentle, supportive, and understanding toward oneself. Rather than harshly judging oneself for personal shortcomings, the self is offered warmth and unconditional acceptance. Common humanity involves recognizing the shared human experience, understanding that all humans fail and make mistakes, that all people lead imperfect lives. Rather than feeling isolated by one's imperfection – egocentrically feeling as if "I" am the only one who has failed or am suffering – one takes a broader and more connected perspective with regard to personal shortcomings and individual difficulties. Mindfulness involves being aware of one's present moment experience of suffering with clarity and balance, without running away with a dramatic storyline about negative aspects of oneself or one's life experience – a process that is termed "over-identification." The various elements of self-compassion are conceptually distinct and tap into different ways that individuals emotionally respond to pain and failure (with kindness or judgment), cognitively understand their predicament (as part of the human experience or as isolating), and pay attention to suffering (in a mindful or over-identified manner). Self-compassion can be directed towards the self when suffering occurs through no fault of one's own – when the external circumstances of life are simply painful or difficult to bear. Self-compassion is equally relevant, however, when suffering stems from one's own imprudent actions or personal failures.

Self-compassion has received considerable research attention over the past decade. The vast majority of research has been conducted with the Self-Compassion Scale (SCS; Neff, 2003a), which can be used to assess the three positive and three negative components of self-compassion separately, or else as an overall construct (Neff, Whittaker, & Karl, 2017). Increasingly, however, studies of interventions or else lab-based experimental manipulations of self-compassion are being used to study its impact on wellbeing. Research typically shows that self-compassion is positively associated with psychological health (Barnard & Curry, 2011; Zessin, Dickhäuser & Garbadee, 2015). In fact, one meta-analysis (MacBeth & Gumley, 2012) found a large effect size when examining the inverse relationship between self-compassion and depression, anxiety, and stress in 20 studies. Moreover, self-compassion is directly associated with psychological strengths such as happiness, optimism, and life satisfaction (Hollis-Walker & Colosimo, 2011; Neff, Rude, & Kirkpatrick, 2007), as well as being linked to increased motivation, health behaviors, positive body image, and resilient coping (e.g., Albertson, Neff, & Dill-Shackleford, 2014; Allen, Goldwasser, & Leary, 2012; Breines & Chen, 2012; Sbarra, Smith, & Mehl, 2012). While self-compassion involves recognizing one's own needs and caring for oneself in times of suffering, this is not done in a self-centered or individualistic manner. For instance, self-compassionate individuals are more likely to forgive others, take their perspective and be altruistic than those who lack self-compassion (Neff & Pommier, 2013). Neff and Beretvas (2013) found that people high in self-compassion are described by romantic partners as more emotionally connected and supportive and less detached and controlling than those low in self-compassion.

Paradoxical learning

A subtle challenge emerges when we add self-compassion to mindfulness training. The element of intentionally warming up awareness in self-compassion training, rather than simply opening to whatever is present while practicing mindfulness, can seduce practitioners into striving to feel better. Practiced correctly, however, self-compassion and mindfulness both help us to let go of unnecessary struggle. Self-compassion training may be more *intentional* than mindfulness training but it is not more *effortful*. The heart learns to "melt" in the heat of suffering (i.e., resistance to moment-to-moment experience is abandoned with a warm, loving attitude), much like the heart of a parent toward a child with the 48-hour flu. The parent doesn't give the child compassion in order to drive the flu out. It's going to take 48 hours to pass regardless. Rather, the parent cares for the child because they are sick, and wishes to comfort the child. The central paradox of self-compassion training is "When we suffer, we practice not to feel better but *because* we feel bad." Self-compassion is an inclination of heart – an attitude of warmth, curiosity, connection, and care. Learning to become more self-compassionate is a process of moving from striving to change our experience and ourselves toward embracing who we are already.

Another paradox of self-compassion training is that "when we give ourselves unconditional love, we discover the conditions under which we were unloved." Although self-compassion generates positive emotions in the long run, unpleasant emotions such as grief or shame are likely to emerge during self-compassion training. Why does this happen? One explanation is that we require contrast to know anything – we can only become aware of light because we know dark or hot because we know cold. Similarly, if I say to myself, "May I love myself just as I am," I may remember old messages telling me the opposite: "Don't be so full of yourself!" or "There you go again, you're always getting it wrong."

A metaphor for this phenomenon is *backdraft*. Backdraft occurs when a firefighter opens a door with a fire behind it. When oxygen is introduced to the fire, the fire intensifies. A similar effect can occur when we practice self-compassion. When our hearts are hot with suffering – self-criticism, self-doubt – kind words can open the door of our hearts causing old wounds to resurface. The saying is "Love reveals everything unlike itself." Those feelings are not *created* by self-compassion; we're simply re-experiencing them in the relative safety of our current lives.

Backdraft is part of the healing process. We have an opportunity to heal relational wounds when we treat them with kindness and understanding. Backdraft is not inherently difficult; it's our innate *resistance* to backdraft that makes it a problem. Mindfulness and self-compassion help us to meet backdraft with less resistance and, hence, less suffering.

The effectiveness of the MSC program depends, in part, on participants learning how to work with backdraft and also learning to practice self-compassion as a spontaneous response to suffering rather than as a strategy to directly change who we are or manipulate how we feel.

Structure of MSC

A typical MSC group consists of 10–25 participants in a classroom setting for eight sessions, each two and three quarters of an hour long, plus a four-hour silent retreat. There are one to two teachers depending on the size of the group and, as a safety precaution, the group is either co-led or assisted by a mental health professional.

MSC participants learn mindfulness and self-compassion through a variety of modalities including talks, exercises, meditations, informal practices, discussion, poetry and videos. Participants are taught three core meditations, four other meditations, and 18 informal practices for daily life – 25 practices in all. All the practices blend mindfulness with loving-kindness or self-compassion. At least 30 minutes per day of home practice is encouraged during the eight-week program, either formally (in meditation) or informally throughout the day. Participants are also taught the *principles* of self-compassion training so they can guide their own practice after the program has ended.

Self-compassion is also taught relationally in MSC – by how teachers embody self-compassion and interact with their students. There is an "inquiry" period after each class exercise and practice in which students engage with teachers, one at a time, and share what they directly experienced in the preceding practice. Emotional resonance is the foundation of inquiry, or the participant's sense of "feeling felt" (Siegel & Hartzell, 2013, p. 70) by the teacher. Teachers also create a "culture of kindness" in the classroom that enables students to feel safe and willing to bring compassion to themselves. Some students first need to feel compassion from *others* – teachers and other participants – before they can include themselves in a compassionate embrace.

Overview of the curriculum

The MSC program is carefully scaffolded so that the themes and practices of each session build upon the previous sessions. The sessions are:

- *Session 1 – Discovering mindful self-compassion* – is a welcome session, introducing the participants to the course and to one another. Session 1 also provides a conceptual introduction to self-compassion with informal practices that can be practiced during the week.
- *Session 2 – Practicing mindfulness* – anchors the program in mindfulness. Formal and informal mindfulness practices are taught to participants as well as the rationale for mindfulness in MSC. Participants learn about "resistance" and "backdraft" and how to manage backdraft with mindfulness practices. Sessions 1 and 2 include more didactic material than subsequent sessions in order to establish a conceptual foundation for the entire course.
- *Session 3 – Practicing loving-kindness* – introduces loving-kindness and the intentional practice of warming up awareness. Loving-kindness is cultivated before compassion because it is less challenging. Participants get a chance to discover their own loving-kindness and compassion phrases for use in meditation. An interpersonal exercise helps develop safety and trust in the group.
- *Session 4 – Discovering your compassionate voice* – broadens loving-kindness meditation into a compassionate conversation with ourselves, especially how to motivate ourselves with kindness rather than self-criticism. By Session 4, many participants discover that self-compassion is more challenging than expected so we explore what "progress" means and encourage participants to practice compassion for themselves when they stumble or feel like they are failing to learn self-compassion.

- *Session 5 – Living deeply* – focuses on core values and the skill of compassionate listening. These topics and practices are less emotionally challenging than others in the course, and are introduced in the middle of the program to give participants an emotional break while still deepening the practice of self-compassion.
- *Retreat* – A chance for students to immerse themselves in the practices already learned and apply them to whatever arises in the mind during four hours of silence. Some new practices are introduced, including ones that provide an opportunity for physical activity such as mindfully enjoying nature and compassionate walking,
- *Session 6 – Meeting difficult emotions* – gives students an opportunity to test and refine their skills by applying them to difficult emotions. Students learn three strategies for addressing difficult emotions: labeling and finding emotion in the body, two traditional mindfulness practices, plus a compassion practice called soften-soothe-allow in which we are kind and tender to ourselves because we are experiencing difficult emotions. The emotion of shame is described and demystified in this session because shame is so often associated with self-criticism and is entangled with sticky emotions such as guilt and anger.
- *Session 7– Exploring challenging relationships* – Relationships are the source of much of our emotional pain. This is the most emotionally activating session in the course but most students are ready for it after practicing mindful self-compassion for six to seven weeks. Themes of Session 7 are anger in relationships, caregiver fatigue, and forgiveness. Rather than trying to repair old relationships, students learn to meet and hold their emotional needs, and *themselves*, with more compassion.
- *Session 8 – Embracing your life* – brings the course to a close with positive psychology and the practices of savoring, gratitude, and self-appreciation: three ways to embrace the good in our lives. To sustain self-compassion practice, we need to recognize and enjoy positive experiences as well. At the end of the course, students are invited to review what they have learned, what they would like to remember, and what they would like to practice after the course has ended.

Session outline

MSC is an experiential learning program. The general sequence of activities in each session is:

- *Opening Meditation:* We begin with meditation to refresh the practices for the students and to establish a receptive frame of mind for learning during the session. The core meditations – Affectionate Breathing, Loving-kindness for Ourselves, and Giving and Receiving Compassion (see below) – are repeated two to three times during the course. Opening meditations are usually 20 minutes long, followed by inquiry.
- *Home Practice Discussion:* Participants are encouraged to share their insights and challenges from the previous week, and learn how to motivate themselves to practice regularly with kindness and compassion rather than as an obligation or a chore.
- *Topic:* MSC contains 26 didactic topics that are delivered as succinctly and interactively as possible, usually in less than 15 minutes each. Didactic topics open the door to practice. Examples of topics are the relationship of mindfulness to self-compassion, letting go of resistance, finding personal loving-kindness phrases, stages of progress, core values, compassionate listening, shame, caregiver fatigue, and self-appreciation.

- *Practice or Exercise:* Practices include formal meditations and informal practices for daily life. An example of an informal practice is the Self-Compassion Break (see below). Class exercises are used to illustrate topics. Students are not encouraged to practice class exercises when they are home because the exercises can be emotionally activating.
- *Break:* A 15-minute break is essential for students to refresh themselves.
- *Topic:* A second topic is often presented after the break.
- *Practice or Exercise:* Another practice is usually offered after the break, or an exercise is introduced to illustrate the new topic.
- *Review and Closing:* Students are reminded about what they just learned in the session, what practices are encouraged to try at home, and the session closes with a poem, a silent reflection, or by ringing a bell.

Sample practices

Self-compassion break

This informal practice is taught in Session 1 after students are introduced to the three components of self-compassion. It gives a direct experience of the three components and also shows how self-compassion can be evoked through language. The Self-Compassion Break is taught as a reflective exercise in the program. The individual components of the Self-Compassion Break can be applied either singly or in combination in daily life in response to stress.

- When you notice that you're feeling stress or emotional discomfort, see if you can find the discomfort in your body. Where do you feel it the most? Make contact with the discomfort that you feel in your body.

Then say to yourself, slowly and kindly: "This is a moment of suffering"

That's mindfulness. Other options include:

- *This hurts.*
- *Ouch!*
- *This is stressful.*

Say to yourself: "*Suffering is a part of life*"

That's common humanity. Other options include:

- *I'm not alone. Others are just like me.*
- *We all struggle in our lives*
- *This is how it feels when a person struggles in this way*

Say to yourself: "*May I be kind to myself*"

That's self-kindness. Other options might be:

- *May I give myself what I need.*
- *May I accept myself as I am*
- *May I learn to accept myself as I am*
- *May I forgive myself*

- *May I be strong*
- *May I be patient*
- *May I live in love*

If you're having difficulty finding the right words, imagine that a dear friend or loved one is having the same problem as you. What would you say to this person, heart-to-heart? If your friend were to hold just a few of your words in their mind, what would you like them to be? What message would you like to deliver? (Pause.) Now, can you offer the same message to yourself?

Giving and receiving meditation

Giving and Receiving is a core meditation in the MSC program. It is taught in Session 5 as a support to compassionate listening, and again in Session 7 as a practice that caregivers can apply on the job to prevent caregiver fatigue.

Savoring the breath

- Please sit comfortably, closing your eyes, and if you like, putting a hand over your heart or another soothing place as a reminder to bring not just awareness, but *loving* awareness, to your experience and to yourself.
- Take a few deep, relaxing breaths, noticing how your breath nourishes your body as you inhale and soothes your body as you exhale.
- Now let your breathing find its own natural rhythm. Continue feeling the sensation of breathing in and breathing out. If you like, allow yourself to be gently rocked and caressed by the rhythm of your breathing.

Warming up awareness

- Now, focus your attention on your *in-breath*, letting yourself savor the sensation of breathing in, noticing how your in-breath nourishes your body, breath after breath. . . . and then releasing your breath.
- As you breathe, breathe in kindness and compassion for yourself . . . whatever you need. Just feel the quality of kindness and compassion as you breathe in – letting your breath be warm and kind – or, if you prefer, letting a word or image ride on your breathing.
- Now, shifting your focus now to your *out-breath*, feel your body breathe out, feeling the ease of exhalation.
- Please call to mind *someone whom you love* or *someone who is struggling and needs compassion*. Visualize that person clearly in your mind.
- Begin directing your out-breath to this person, offering the ease of breathing out.
- If you wish, send kindness and compassion to this person with each outbreath, one breath after another.

In for me, out for you

- Now focus again on the sensation of breathing *both* in and out, savoring the sensation of breathing in and out.

- Begin to breath in for yourself and out for the other person. "In for me and out for you." "One for me and one for you."
- And as you breathe, feel free to change the degree to which you focus on yourself ("Two for me and one for you") or the other person ("One for me and three for you"), or just let it be an equal flow – whatever feels right in the moment.
- Let go of any unnecessary effort, allowing this meditation to be as easy as breathing.
- Allow your breath to flow in and out, like the gentle movement of the sea – a limitless, boundless flow – flowing in and flowing out. Let yourself be a *part* of this limitless, boundless flow. An ocean of compassion.
- Gently open your eyes.

Research on MSC

There is increasing evidence to suggest that MSC is effective at increasing self-compassion and other aspects of psychological wellbeing. Neff and Germer (2013) conducted a randomized controlled study of the MSC program that compared outcomes for individuals randomized either to the MSC program or a waitlist control group (N = 52). Participants from both groups were asked to complete a series of self-report scales two weeks before and after the MSC program, while MSC participants were also assessed after six months and again one year later. MSC participants demonstrated significantly greater increases in self-compassion, mindfulness, compassion for others, and life satisfaction, as well as greater decreases in depression, anxiety, stress, and emotional avoidance compared to controls. Moreover, all gains in self-compassion were maintained six months and one year later. The degree to which MSC participants practiced formal meditation or informal self-compassion techniques in daily life were equally predictive of gains in self-compassion. This suggests that self-compassion is teachable skill that is "dose dependent." The more you practice it the more you learn, but it doesn't matter if this is on the cushion or in the supermarket.

A second randomized controlled trial of MSC was conducted by Friis, Johnson, Cutfield and Consedine (2016), which examined people suffering from type 1 and type 2 diabetes (N = 63) and compared outcomes for those randomized to MSC to a waitlist control condition. It was found that MSC participants demonstrated a significantly greater increase in self-compassion and decrease in depression and diabetes distress compared to controls. Also, MSC participants averaged a clinically and statistically meaningful decrease in HbA_{1c} (reflecting change in blood glucose levels) between baseline and three-month follow-up, whereas the control group did not. These findings suggest that MSC may have both emotional and metabolic benefits among patients with diabetes.

An adaptation of MSC for adolescents has been created by Lorraine Hobbs and Karen Bluth called *Making Friends with Yourself* (MFY; Bluth, Gaylord, Campo, Mullarkey, & Hobbs, 2016). This eight-week course roughly parallels the themes and structure of the adult program. It differs mainly in that classes are shorter and more activity based, and guided meditations are shorter, meaning that they are more developmentally appropriate. Bluth and colleagues conducted a mixed-methods study of MFY with adolescents who were randomized to MFY or a wait-list control condition (N = 34). Participants in MFY reported significantly greater gains in self-compassion and life satisfaction and decreases in depression compared to controls, with trends toward significance in terms of increased mindfulness and social connection and decreased anxiety. Given the small sample size, these trends likely would have been significant with more participants. Teens also generally gave positive feedback about the program. These findings are encouraging and suggest that it is possible to teach skills of Mindful Self-Compassion at an early age.

Finally, research has been conducted on brief self-compassion training based on the MSC protocol, in which informal practices from the MSC program were taught, but not formal meditation. Smeets, Neff, Alberts and Peters (2014) randomized female undergraduates (N = 49) to a self-compassion intervention or active time management control group. Both groups met for three consecutive weeks, with two sessions lasting 90 minutes and a closing session lasting 45 minutes. It was found that the brief MSC intervention led to significantly greater increases in self-compassion, mindfulness, optimism and self-efficacy, as well as significantly greater decreases in rumination compared to the control group.

The success of this training suggests that self-compassion may be taught in briefer formats, as well as formats that do not require formal meditation practice. For this reason, the authors of this manual are currently pilot testing brief versions of MSC for populations such as teachers or health care workers at risk of burnout, and people suffering from chronic pain. It remains to be seen how much practice is needed to learn the new habit of self-compassion in a way that makes an impact on wellbeing.

Resources

Online

www.centerformsc.org

- Information about MSC programs around the world, a live online MSC course, and other activities related to self-compassion.
- Audio and video recordings by senior MSC teachers.
- Information on how to become a MSC teacher.

www.self-compassion.org

- Up-to-date bibliography of research on self-compassion.
- Audio and video recordings by Kristin Neff.

www.chrisgermer.com

- Additional materials for self-compassion practice by Chris Germer.

Articles

Friis, A. M., Johnson, M. H., Cutfield, R. G., & Consedine, N. S. (2016). Kindness matters: A randomized controlled trial of a mindful self-compassion intervention improves depression, distress, and HbA1c among patients with diabetes. *Diabetes Care*, dc160416.

Germer, C. K., & Neff, K. D. (2013). Self-compassion in clinical practice. *Journal of Clinical Psychology*, 69(8), 856–867.

Neff, K. D., & Germer, C. K. (2013). A pilot study and randomized controlled trial of the mindful self-compassion program. *Journal of Clinical Psychology*, 69(1), 28–44.

Books

Germer, C. (2009). *The mindful path to self-compassion*. New York, NY: Guilford Press.

Germer, C., & Neff, K. (2019). *Mindful self-compassion: Professional training manual*. New York, NY: Guilford Press.

Neff, K. (2011). *Self-compassion: The proven power of being kind to yourself*. New York, NY: William Morrow.

Neff, K., & Germer, K. (2019). *The mindful self-compassion workbook: A proven way to accept yourself, build inner strength, and thrive*. New York, NY: Guilford Press.

References

Albertson, E. R., Neff, K. D., & Dill-Shackleford, K. E. (2014). Self-compassion and body dissatisfaction in women: A randomized controlled trial of a brief meditation intervention. *Mindfulness*, 1–11.

Allen, A. B., Goldwasser, E. R., & Leary, M. R. (2012). Self-compassion and wellbeing among older adults. *Self and Identity*. DOI: 10.1080/15298868.2011.595082.

Barnard, L. K., & Curry, J. F. (2011). Self-compassion: Conceptualizations, correlates, & interventions. *Review of General Psychology*, 15(4), 289–303.

Bluth, K., Gaylord, S. A., Campo, R. A., Mullarkey, M. C., & Hobbs, L. (2016). Making friends with yourself: A mixed methods pilot study of a Mindful Self-Compassion program for adolescents. *Mindfulness*, 7(2), 479–492.

Breines, J. G., & Chen, S. (2012). Self-compassion increases self-improvement motivation. *Personality and Social Psychology Bulletin*, 38(9), 1133–1143.

Friis, A. M., Johnson, M. H., Cutfield, R. G., & Consedine, N. S. (2016). Kindness matters: A randomized controlled trial of a mindful self-compassion intervention improves depression, distress, and HbA1c among patients with diabetes. *Diabetes Care*, dc160416.

Germer, C. K., Siegel, R. D., & Fulton, P. R. (2016). *Mindfulness and psychotherapy*. New York, NY: Guilford Publications.

Gilbert, P. (2009). *The compassionate mind*. London: Constable & Robinson.

Hollis-Walker, L., & Colosimo, K. (2011). Mindfulness, self-compassion, and happiness in non-meditators: A theoretical and empirical examination. *Personality and Individual Differences*, 50, 222–227.

Jazaieri, H., Jinpa, G. T., McGonigal, K., Rosenberg, E. L., Finkelstein, J., Simon-Thomas, E., . . . Goldin, P. R. (2013). Enhancing compassion: A randomized controlled trial of a compassion cultivation training program. *Journal of Happiness Studies*, 14(4), 1113–1126.

MacBeth, A., & Gumley, A. (2012). Exploring compassion: A meta-analysis of the association between self-compassion and psychopathology. *Clinical Psychology Review*, 32, 545–552.

Neff, K. D. (2003a). Development and validation of a scale to measure self-compassion. *Self and Identity*, 2, 223–250.

Neff, K. D. (2003b). Self-compassion: An alternative conceptualization of a healthy attitude toward oneself. *Self and Identity*, 2, 85–102.

Neff, K. D. (2016). The Self-Compassion Scale is a valid and theoretically coherent measure of self-compassion. *Mindfulness*, 7(1), 264–274.

Neff, K. D., & Beretvas, S. N. (2013). The role of self-compassion in romantic relationships. *Self and Identity*, 12(1), 78–98.

Neff, K. D., & Germer, C. K. (2013). A pilot study and randomized controlled trial of the mindful self-compassion program. *Journal of Clinical Psychology*, 69(1), 28–44.

Neff, K. D., & Pommier, E. (2013). The relationship between self-compassion and other-focused concern among college undergraduates, community adults, and practicing meditators. *Self and Identity*, 12(2), 160–176.

Neff, K. D., Rude, S. S., & Kirkpatrick, K. (2007). An examination of self-compassion in relation to positive psychological functioning and personality traits. *Journal of Research in Personality*, 41, 908–916.

Neff, K. D., Whittaker, T., & Karl, A. (2017). Evaluating the factor structure of the Self-Compassion Scale in four distinct populations: Is the use of a total self-compassion score justified? *Journal of Personality Assessment*, *99*(6), 596–607.

Pace, T. W., Negi, L. T., Adame, D. D., Cole, S. P., Sivilli, T. I., Brown, T. D., . . . Raison, C. L. (2009). Effect of compassion meditation on neuroendocrine, innate immune and behavioral responses to psychosocial stress. *Psychoneuroendocrinology*, *34*(1), 87–98.

Sbarra, D. A., Smith, H. L., & Mehl, M. R. (2012). When leaving your ex, love yourself: Observational ratings of self-compassion predict the course of emotional recovery following marital separation. *Psychological Science*, *23*(3), 261–269.

Siegel, D., & Hartzell, M. (2013). *Parenting from the inside out*. New York, NY: Tarcher/Perigree.

Smeets, E., Neff, K., Alberts, H., & Peters, M. (2014). Meeting suffering with kindness: Effects of a brief self-compassion intervention for female college students. *Journal of Clinical Psychology*, *70*(9), 794–807.

van den Brink, E., & Koster, F. (2015). *Mindfulness-based compassionate living: A new training programme to deepen mindfulness with heartfulness*. London: Routledge.

Williams, J. M. G., & Kabat-Zinn, J. (2011). Mindfulness: Diverse perspectives on its meaning, origins, and multiple applications at the intersection of science and dharma. *Contemporary Buddhism*, *12*(1), 1–18.

Zessin, U., Dickhäuser, O., & Garbade, S. (2015). The relationship between self-compassion and well-being: A meta-analysis. *Applied Psychology: Health and Well-Being*, *7*(3), 340–364.

Chapter 29

Mindfulness-Based Compassionate Living (MBCL)
A deepening programme for those with basic mindfulness skills

Erik van den Brink and Frits Koster

MBCL's rationale, development and application

With the rise in mindfulness courses in preventive and clinical health care, it is no surprise that the interest in follow-up and deepening programmes is also growing. Mindfulness-Based Compassionate Living (MBCL) is a programme offering participants further training in deepening their mindfulness skills with practice in compassion toward themselves and others. It is designed as a group training for those who have preferably followed Mindfulness-Based Stress Reduction (MBSR; Kabat-Zinn, 1991), Mindfulness-Based Cognitive Therapy (MBCT; Segal, Williams, & Teasdale, 2013) or an equivalent training.

The attitude of kindness and compassion is implicitly present in MBSR and MBCT and many participants seem to develop self-compassion along the way (Shapiro et al., 2005, 2007; Kuyken et al., 2010). The founders of MBCT have expressed their reservation about offering explicit compassion exercises to patients vulnerable to depression, as it may increase feelings of inadequacy or unworthiness (Segal et al., 2013). In their view, it is sufficient for trainers to embody the compassionate attitude and indirectly convey it to participants. On the other hand, there are arguments that not only mindfulness, but also self-compassion is vital for mental health (MacBeth & Gumley, 2012) and several compassion training courses were developed for participants without previous mindfulness experience (e.g. Fredrickson et al., 2008; Jazaieri et al., 2013; Neff & Germer, 2012; Pace et al., 2009). Empirical evidence is so far lacking as to whether compassion training should be offered *with* or *without* previous mindfulness training. Based on clinical experience, people find it helpful to have already acquired basic mindfulness-skills before exploring more challenging compassion exercises. It requires sufficient stability and a safe inner holding in mindful awareness to meet our pain, see it clearly and open our hearts for what is needed.

We initially developed the MBCL programme for out-patients attending the mental health services. EvdB is a psychiatrist and psychotherapist, who trained in Western science and psychology, and FK is Vipassana meditation teacher, psychiatric nurse and former Buddhist monk, who studied Buddhist psychology. As experienced meditators and pioneering mindfulness teachers and trainers in the Netherlands, we had trained many patients and professionals in MBSR/MBCT. Frequently, participants expressed a need to deepen their practice and do more inner work on developing kindness and compassion, particularly towards themselves. We found that offering practices based on Loving Kindness Meditation (LKM) too early, could elicit strong adverse reactions, as they can stir up old pain and grief. Germer (2009) coined the term 'backdraft' for this, and Gilbert (2010) – the founder of Compassion Focused Therapy (CFT) – emphasised that dealing with the fear of compassion is key to successful therapy. Backdraft is often an issue for participants with backgrounds of insecure attachment, trauma and neglect, who often suffer from harsh self-criticism, shame and unworthiness. However, less intense adverse reactions are also common in non-clinical settings, among clients and professionals, including ourselves, when we began practising LKM. We therefore decided to develop a programme that gently introduces the more explicit practice in compassion towards ourselves and others in an advanced mindfulness-based course, building on the work of self-inquiry that started with MBSR/MBCT.

We have closely collaborated since 2007, teaching client groups, professional groups and teacher-training seminars. We trained in compassion focused approaches with founding teachers and integrated elements of their work in MBCL. Extensive qualitative evaluations and session to session feedback from participants on content, guidance and course material, were used to shape the curriculum into its current format. MBCL can be offered as a preventive programme and to those with current health problems, complementing conventional treatments. It is trans-diagnostic in scope, as it provides a way of dealing with suffering, not as a substitute for methods aimed at *cure*, but to complement these by cultivating an attitude of *care*. MBCL is suitable for clinical and non-clinical settings, for people who seek care and give care, for health workers, counsellors, therapists, teachers and pastoral workers. In fact, it can be offered to all those who benefitted from mindfulness training, wishing to deepen their practice with 'heartfulness', as the explicit cultivation of kindness and compassion is increasingly referred to by mindfulness teachers.

Defining compassion

In the search for a pragmatic definition suitable for the health care setting, we follow Gilbert and Choden (2013), who define compassion as the capacity to be sensitive to the suffering of ourselves and others and the commitment to relieve and prevent it. So, compassion involves both being receptive to suffering, as well as taking responsibility for dealing with it (Gilbert, 2014). Compassion has several key attributes necessary to engage with suffering:

- the fundamental motivation to care for the well-being of oneself and others;
- sensitivity to our own and others' needs;
- sympathy, the ability to resonate with the inner state of others;
- distress tolerance, the courage to face the difficult and endure it;
- empathy, the ability to 'feel into' and understand what goes on in our inner worlds; and
- a mindful and non-judgmental attitude.

Compassion is incomplete if one of these attributes is lacking. Together they enable us to develop the skilful means to deal wisely with the suffering we encounter.

Although compassion is concerned with suffering, it is associated with positive emotions, health and happiness, rather than fatigue and burn-out, as pointed out by Ricard (2015). He argued that the term 'compassion fatigue' is better replaced by 'empathy fatigue' (Ricard, 2015). Compassion needs empathy, but empathy is not necessarily compassionate. Empathy can even harm others or ourselves if other key attributes of compassion are lacking. For instance, salesmen can use empathy for their own gain, trying to convince us to buy their products. When we care for others, empathy can exhaust us if we forget to care for ourselves.

Compassion has a transpersonal quality, as it involves commitment to alleviate and prevent suffering, *regardless of who the (potential) sufferer is*. In the MBCL programme we therefore make it clear from the start that, whenever we speak of 'compassion', we include 'self-compassion'.

Aims of the MBCL programme

Participants applying for the course often state that they wish to develop a kinder and warmer relationship with themselves, a healthier balance between caring for others and caring for themselves, and finding ease with life's inevitable pain and 'dis-ease'. The overall aim of the MBCL programme is to alleviate suffering and enhance physical, psychological and social well-being by offering a science-based training in (self-) compassion, building on already established mindfulness skills. More specific goals are:

- Acknowledging pain and suffering as part of human life.
- Understanding how our brain has evolved to help us survive, and that its imperfect design is not our fault.
- Gaining insight into three basic emotion regulation and motivation systems: the threat system, the drive system and the soothing system.
- Understanding how influences from outside and from inside, such as an 'inner critic' and persisting maladaptive patterns, can easily cause imbalances.
- Learning practices in (self-)compassion, such as soothing breathing, kindness meditation, compassionate imagery, compassionately dealing with inner difficulties and cultivating an 'inner helper', 'taking in the good' (what nourishes us and contributes to happiness).
- Cultivating a sense of common humanity and learning how to connect with the Four Friends for Life (loving kindness, compassion, sympathetic joy and equanimity).
- Integrating and exploring ways of applying what has been learned in daily life.

We will first discuss some relevant theoretical issues and scientific insights on which the programme is based before we describe its content and practices in more detail.

Theoretical background

MBCL combines ancient wisdom from contemplative traditions with modern insights from neuroscience, evolutionary psychology, attachment theory, positive psychology, and third generation behaviour therapies, such as mindfulness-based approaches, Compassion Focused Therapy (CFT; Gilbert, 2010) and Acceptance and Commitment Therapy (ACT; Hayes, Strohsal, & Wilson, 2012). From an evolutionary perspective, compassion is not a luxury but a necessity for survival (Gilbert, 2017). The more vulnerable and fewer the offspring of a species, the more important it is that individuals care for each other. The human brain evolved to become highly sensitive to seeking, receiving and giving care but retains many features of older evolutionary stages.

The multi-layered brain

MacLean (1990) described three layers in the brain corresponding with phases in evolution, enabling us to adapt to our environment in various ways. There are the very old automatic reflexes of *the reptilian brain* (brain stem) and the emotional reactions of *the old mammalian brain* (limbic system), which are together referred to as 'old brain'. *The new mammalian brain* (neocortex) or simply 'new brain' is much younger and evolved when our predecessors became 'smart'. The most substantial parts of the new brain support a vast repertoire of social behaviour, enabling us to survive in ever more complex communities. This allows language and imagination, memories of past events, fantasies about future events, concepts of self and others, and open unlimited possibilities for learning new behaviour. Thanks to our new brain, we can intentionally overrule automatic old-brain reactions. On the other hand, our new-brain-processes can easily be hijacked by old-brain-instincts, sometimes with devastating results. For instance, despotic leaders who, driven by old-brain lust for power, use destructive war machinery against innocent people. Our new brains can be both a curse and a blessing. We can be boundlessly cruel and boundlessly compassionate. Gilbert (2014) therefore speaks of 'a tricky brain', as the interaction between old and new layers is far from harmonious and can easily exacerbate our suffering.

At some stage in our lives we encounter trauma, loss, illness, aging and eventually death. This primary suffering is inevitable. Buddhist and Western psychologies agree that the more we try to avoid what is unavoidable and try to hold on to what is impermanent, the more we suffer (Hanson, 2009; Hayes, Strohsal, & Wilson, 2012). However, a lot of secondary suffering is generated by counterproductive reactions to primary suffering. Fortunately, secondary suffering can be alleviated by our capacity to observe the processes in our mind and transform unconscious automatic reactions into conscious responses. We can refer to a very young part of our brain as *the mindful brain* (corresponding with parts of the medial forebrain), which can become stronger with practice (Siegel, 2007).

The imperfect design of our brain is not our fault. We have neither chosen the many imperfections wired into our brains and bodies, nor the family and culture of our up-bringing. However, although it is not our fault, it is our responsibility to deal with it; and this is where compassion comes in. It is a helpful response to the realisation that we find ourselves in an imperfect, impermanent and vulnerable existence, prone to suffering. Whereas mindfulness as a meta-cognitive capacity is relatively young, compassion has deep roots in the motivational and emotion regulation systems of the old brain.

Three emotion regulation systems

From the perspective of evolution, all emotions, whether pleasant or unpleasant, are useful messengers, designed to inform us whether we are on the right track for survival. Three basic emotion regulation and motivation systems are deeply rooted in the old brain (Gilbert, 2009). Figure 29.1 is an adaptation of Gilbert's model that we use in MBCL.

The multi-layered brain and emotion regulation systems can deepen our understanding of why humans are so prone to stress. It is an extension of the basic stress theory offered in MBSR/MBCT, which can easily be linked to the 'doing mode' (driven by threat and drive systems) and the 'being mode' (grounded in the soothing system). The *threat system* is focussed on protecting ourselves from danger. Unpleasant emotions (anxiety, anger, disgust) alert us to imminent dangers and elicit behaviour such as fight, flight or freeze. In mammals, a fourth stress reaction became known as 'tend and befriend' (Taylor, 2006), characterised by protecting the young and vulnerable and gathering group members in case of threat. The threat system is crucial for physical survival and escape from external threats. In humans, imagined threats activate the old brain's alarm system just as easily, causing a similar cascade of neurophysiological reactions (LeDoux, 1998). The threat system is the oldest and

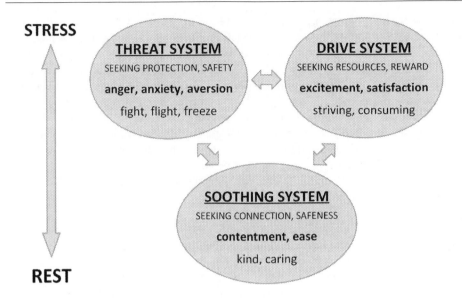

Figure 29.1 The three emotion regulation systems.

Source: Reproduced with kind permission from A practical guide to Mindfulness-Based Compassionate Living by Van den Brink and Koster, Routledge, 2018.

most fundamental. Its urgency immediately takes us over and dictates our behaviour. This works along the lines of 'better to be safe than sorry' and is the evolutionary advantage of the so-called 'negativity bias', which is the tendency to perceive and remember negative rather than positive events (Baumeister et al., 2001).

The *drive system* is focussed on reward and access to resources such as food, sex, and material or immaterial gains. Here also, real or imagined needs can be the triggers. The emotions involved are often pleasant. Chasing after a reward gives transient excitement and vitality and getting what we want gives intense but short-lived satisfaction.

Both the threat and drive systems were already part of reptilian life. Reptiles also show a restorative 'rest and digest' state, which evolved into a *soothing system* in mammalian species, when social bonding and attachment became important. Here, attention is not narrowed by the threat or reward focus but open to kind and peaceful affiliation, characterised by soothing behaviour, wonder, play and creativity. Gilbert (2009) uses the word 'safeness' here, to be distinguished from 'safety' as escape from danger, which the threat system seeks. The emotions of the soothing system are pleasant but they differ from the drive system in that they are characterised by longer-lasting calmness, warmth and contentment (Depue & Morrone-Strupinsky, 2005). The threat and drive systems increase levels of stress and consume energy. They are designed for short term survival. The soothing system is necessary for recovery and nourishment and it is supported by activity of the vagus nerve, which is associated with calmer breathing, lower blood pressure, slower heartbeat, increased heart rate variability, relaxed muscles, and increased activity of the digestive and immune systems (Porges, 2007).

We humans cannot access our soothing system as easily as many other mammals and we often get caught up in our threat and drive systems for much longer than they are designed for (Gilbert, 2009). With our new-brain abilities we can *imagine* all kinds of possible threats and unfulfilled needs. Thus, we can become chronically stressed. Overactive threat and drive systems give rise to prolonged sympathetic activity, which is physically and emotionally exhausting and undermines our health. We need the counterbalance of the calming parasympathetic system to recover and be nourished. All three emotion regulation systems are important for survival, but they need to be in balance for well-being. Hence, many exercises in the MBCL programme begin with mindful practice of the soothing breathing rhythm which supports a healthier balance by activating parasympathetic activity.

The evolving mind

It makes sense to view minds and brains as evolving interdependently (Siegel, 2007). When our minds change in response to experiences, our brains change alongside. When our brains change, it is more likely certain experiences will repeat and shape our minds in certain ways. Habitual mindsets are referred to as patterns, modes or mentalities – durable constructs offering some stability in the flux of life. Such patterns developed during human evolution to help us survive the complexity of living in groups: distinguishing friend from foe, competing for rank and status, cooperating and sharing, seeking, receiving and giving care. Gilbert (2014) refers to these archetypal patterns as *social mentalities*. They can proliferate around old-brain emotion regulation systems, and involve not only basic motivations, emotions and instincts, but also mental pictures, stories and role-scripts enabled by new-brain imagery, thinking and reasoning. A *threat mode* dominates when our mind is preoccupied with avoiding social threats (shame, blame, abuse, neglect or rejection). A *competition mode* prevails when our mind is set on gaining social rewards (approval, power, success). We can be driven by desire for superiority or fear of inferiority. Social comparison and self-evaluation are common strategies for judging and securing our position in rank and status, which can fuel our threat and drive systems. If we perceive a gap between our actual self (how we are) and our ideal self (how we think we should be), we can easily develop a habit of criticising ourselves. Because of the negativity bias it comes more naturally to say we are no good or should do better, than to accept and befriend ourselves. Many people suffer from an inner critic or even an inner bully, while they need an inner helper. On top of these common patterns, more specific patterns develop in individual lives. For example, schema therapists distinguish various maladaptive patterns that stem from early childhood and persist into adulthood, hindering psychological health (Young, Klosko, & Weishaar, 2003).

So, there appears to be a spectrum of wholesome and unwholesome attitudes towards ourselves. This is reflected in Neff's Self-Compassion Scale (2003a, 2003b), consisting of three subscales – *self-kindness*, *common humanity* and *mindfulness*. It is interesting that their opposites *self-criticism*, *self-isolation* and *over-identification* (as opposed to mindful non-identification) can be identified as the psychological expressions of *fight, flight* and *freeze* (Germer, 2009), which may also have survival value. Self-criticism or fighting (parts of) ourselves may protect us from being criticised by others. Self-isolation or hiding (parts of) ourselves from others may prevent us from being ignored or rejected by others. And over-identifying with our views and opinions, a psychological way of freezing, may feel safer than opening ourselves to unpleasant emotions and unfamiliar perspectives. We could add self-sacrifice and excessive anxiety for others' well-being as the psychological distortions of the instinctual *tend and befriend* reaction. These tendencies are often confused with compassion towards others, but may increase rather than alleviate levels of suffering, for example by causing burn-out symptoms.

Most intra- and interpersonal patterns did not evolve to make us happy, but to help us survive in the complexities of social life. Patterns that we rigidly repeat leave deep traces in neural networks, which make them more likely to persist. But the brain is a very plastic organ which changes with experience, referred to as 'neuro-plasticity' (Davidson, 2012). Although deeply ingrained habits are difficult to unlearn, we can still learn new and healthier behaviour (Brewin, 2006). Initially this may feel like diverting from the motorway and struggling on a barely visible path, but this is how our minds (and brains) evolve. The more we travel it, the more visible the path becomes. When we practice mindful compassion, a new, healthier repertoire is wired into our brains. Instead of feeding an inner critic, we feed an inner helper. Although maladaptive patterns may be very persistent, they are less likely to operate on autopilot when we recognise them mindfully and learn to relate to them compassionately, flexibly and playfully. This is an important part of the inner work done in the MBCL course.

The founders of ACT point out that experiential avoidance and 'fusion' (over-identification) with the constructs of our mind play a key role in psychopathology (Hayes et al., 2012). Psychological health begins with experiential acceptance (including inevitable pain) and 'defusion' (dis-identification) from unhealthy views, opening the way to committing ourselves to what we really value. Practices in MBCL help us to 'meet our pain', with gentleness and courage, and to respond compassionately. They also invite us to 'take in the good' (Hanson, 2013) and here we apply insights from positive psychology (Fredrickson et al., 2008; Kok et al., 2013; Seligman, 2002). By broadening our awareness for nourishing, engaging and meaningful experiences we build resources and create positive spirals that work as an antidote against negativity-bias and narrow mind-sets.

In MBCL participants cultivate an inner helper or *compassion mode* as a gateway to increased connectedness, well-being and happiness. The 'common humanity' perspective, the awareness that we are not alone in our suffering, is empowered by exercises in kindness and compassion that expand from oneself to others. Thus, participants begin to understand the transpersonal dimension of suffering by extending the practice of compassion to loved, neutral and difficult persons. This way, one realises that this practice is not limited to family, group, species, race or nation. It can expand boundlessly, to all beings, even the ones we dislike.

Compassion and health

There is a strong correlation between self-compassion and mental health (reviewed by MacBeth & Gumley, 2012). Also compassion to others is associated with individual and social well-being (Crocker & Canevello, 2008). Most of the ingredients of MBCL, such as kindness and compassion meditations, compassionate imagery and compassionate letter writing, were empirically evaluated in intervention studies with positive outcome. Several controlled studies have evaluated stand-alone compassion training programmes, showing considerable overlap with MBCL in structure, themes and practices but not requiring previous mindfulness training. Compared to controls, results showed increases on measures for mindfulness and self-compassion, decreases on measures for depression, anxiety, worry, emotional suppression, physical complaints and perceived stress, and increases on measures for wellbeing, happiness and empathic accuracy (Fredrickson et al., 2008; Jazaieri et al., 2013, 2014; Mascaro et al., 2013; Neff & Germer, 2012; Pace et al., 2009; Wallmark et al., 2013).

Goleman (2006) argued there seems to be a 'low road' (through the old brain) and a 'high road' (through the new brain) towards compassion. Both roads can be trained by practice. For instance, practicing soothing breathing rhythm trains the low road and practicing with compassionate imagery stimulates the high road. It is likely that low and high roads reinforce each other and Barbara Fredrickson's research team provided empirical evidence for this (Kok et al., 2013). Hence, we have woven practices to stimulate both low and high roads into the MBCL programme. For a more extensive review of research underpinning MBCL, we refer to the research chapter in Van den Brink and Koster (2015).

Empirical evaluation of MBCL

The first research on the MBCL programme itself is beginning to emerge. A Dutch feasibility study (Bartels-Velthuis et al., 2016) into MBCL following MBSR or MBCT with a heterogeneous psychiatric out-patient sample (n=33) showed a significant decrease in depressive symptoms and a non-significant decrease in anxiety symptoms, as well as significant increases in levels of mindfulness and self-compassion. The research team led by Anne Speckens at Radboud University, Nimwegen, in the Netherlands did a feasibility study (Schuling et al., 2017) with patients suffering from recurrent depression, which was positively evaluated and followed by larger study with a randomised controlled trial design (Schuling et al., 2016). Included in this study were patients diagnosed with recurrent depression (three episodes or more), who had previously participated in MBCT. Results of this last study were presented by Schuling et al. (2018). The intervention group (N=60) showed a significant decrease of depressive symptoms and a significant increase of self-compassion and mindfulness skills, compared to the control group (N=62) who received treatment as usual.

A Swiss pilot study of an MBCL-based online programme among self-referring individuals with high levels of self-criticism, showed a significant increase in mindfulness, self-compassion, ability to reassure themselves and satisfaction with life; and a significant decrease in feelings of inadequacy, self-hatred, perceived stress and fear of compassion (Krieger, Martig, Van den Brink, & Berger, 2016). Results correlated with the time spent in the programme and were maintained at six-week follow-up.

The structure and content of the MBCL programme

The MBCL programme has a similar structure to MBSR/MBCT, with eight thematic sessions of two and a half hours and a silent session (half-day or day) between session 6 and 7. The sessions offer guided exercises, sharing and inquiry into insights and difficulties, teachings about relevant themes and discussion of home practice. In between sessions, participants are requested to spend three-quarters of an hour to an hour daily on formal practice and undertake informal exercises. They are given audio material and a workbook to support home practice. An important difference with MBSR/MBCT is that the MBCL provides a range of suggestions for home practice following each session, rather than specific homework. This supports participants with tuning into their deeper needs and compassionately choosing the exercises that help them learn best. Participants can always continue practising what was offered in earlier sessions or return to basic mindfulness exercises. We designed the manual as a guideline to be followed flexibly rather than a protocol to be obeyed rigidly.

Several elements are adaptations from traditional practices:

- *Metta* (renamed 'Kindness Meditation'), where one mindfully sends kind wishes to oneself or others;
- *Tonglen* (renamed 'Compassionate Breathing'), where one imagines inhaling what is painful in oneself or other persons and exhaling a wholesome energy which relieves the pain; and
- *Brahmaviharas* or The Four Immeasurables (renamed 'The Four Friends for Life'), where one practises four self-transcending heart qualities that complement each other (kindness, compassion, sympathetic joy and equanimity).

Other practices are adapted from contemporary sources. For instance, the practice of Soothing Breathing Rhythm and compassionate imagery (Safe Place, Compassionate Companion, Embodying Compassion) and letter writing were adapted from CFT (Gilbert, 2009, 2010). Compassionately dealing with resistance, desire and forgiveness exercises were inspired by the work of Brach (2004). Important short informal practices are the Breathing Space with Kindness (to be practised any moment) and the Breathing Space with Compassion (to be practised in difficult moments), which are developed from the Three-Minute Breathing Space in MBCT (Segal et al., 2013). The Self-Compassion Mantra was derived from Neff (2011). Calendar exercises provide a focus week by week to mindfully explore an everyday experience.

Below, we give an overview of the entire curriculum, followed by two examples of key exercises.

Session overview of the MBCL curriculum

Session 1	How we evolved – The threat, drive and soothing systems
Themes	Defining compassion. Evolutionary brain model: the design is not our fault.
	How the three emotion regulation systems can get out of balance.
Practices	Soothing Breathing Rhythm. Nourishing the soothing system through the senses, e.g. Pleasure Walk. Safe Place. Kindness Meditation (KM): Self.
Informal	Breathing Space with Kindness. Calendar: Soothing System.
Session 2	Threat and self-compassion
Themes	Instinctual stress reactions (fight, flight, freeze, tend and befriend) and their psychological equivalents. The three components of self-compassion: self-kindness, common humanity and mindfulness. How imagery can work for and against us. Dealing with difficulties such as 'backdraft'.
Practices	Compassionately relating to Resistance (exploring a stressful situation, embodying 'No' or 'Yes'). Compassionate Companion. KM: Benefactor.

Informal	Breathing Space with Kindness. For difficult moments: Breathing Space with Compassion; or Self-Compassion Mantra (SCM): 1. *This is suffering*; 2. *Suffering is part of life*; 3. *May I be kind to myself.* Calendar: Threat System.
Session 3	*Untangling desires and patterns*
Themes	Understanding desires and inner patterns. Threat mode, competitive mode, caring mode. The Inner Critic and self-conscious emotions (shame, shyness, guilt).
Practices	Compassionately relating to Desire (exploring an area of desire/attachment, surfing on the urge). Compassionately relating to Inner Patterns (exploring a familiar pattern). KM: Good Friend.
Informal	Breathing spaces, SCM. Calendar: Drive System.
Session 4	*Embodying Compassion*
Themes	Attributes of Compassion: care for well-being, sensitivity to needs, sympathy, empathy, courage and tolerance of distress, wisdom. Skilful Means of Compassion: attentional, sensory, imagery, reasoning, emotional, behavioural. How to cultivate an Inner Helper.
Practices	Embodying Compassion. Kindness to the Body. Walking and Moving with Kindness. KM: Neutral Person.
Informal	Breathing spaces, SCM. Calendar: Inner Critic.
Session 5	*Self and others – Widening the circle*
Themes	Understanding images of self and others as impermanent. How over-identification can be restricting and non-identification can be liberating. How practising kindness to others can disclose areas in need of self-compassion (e.g. worry, jealousy, old pain).
Practices	Writing a Compassionate Letter (from a compassionate self to a suffering self). Compassionate Breathing (imagining inhaling what hurts and exhaling what heals). KM: Difficult Person.
Informal	Breathing spaces (third phase can be extended with compassionate breathing), SCM. Calendar: Inner Helper.
Session 6	*Growing happiness*
Themes	The wish to be happy and free from suffering connects all human beings. The Four Friends for Life (kindness, compassion, joy, equanimity). Discovering what contributes to happiness: the joyful life, the engaged life, the meaningful life.
Practices	Forgiveness (forgiving oneself, asking and offering forgiveness). Savouring and revisiting the good. Silver lining. Gratitude. Core values. KM: groups, all beings.
Informal	Breathing spaces, SCM. Calendar: Receiving Compassion.
Silent Session	Guided programme of silent practice; depending on logistics, from 2.5 hours to full day. An integration of imagery exercises, appreciative body scan, sitting, walking and moving with kindness. Whole sequence of KM. Metaphor like The Horse Whisperer.

Session 7	Weaving wisdom and compassion into daily life
Themes	Recognising the motivation from threat, drive and caring modes. Draining or sustaining activities. From formal to informal practice. Practical ethics. Caring for the future.
Practices	Equanimity Meditation (. Sympathetic Joy Meditation. A Day in Your Life (Exploring care for self and others in daily life). A Compassionate Prevention Plan.
Informal	Breathing spaces (also for wise and compassionate action), SCM. Calendar: Giving Compassion.
Session 8	Living with heart
Themes	How to continue the healing work of compassion? Evaluation of the course.
Practices	Compassionate Body Scan. River of Life: a metaphor for intimate connectedness and boundless openness. Choose formal and informal practices to continue after the course.

Breathing Space with Kindness

1 Open, kind awareness

Allow a comfortable position, whether you are sitting, lying or standing. . . . Noticing what presents itself right now . . ., whether it be thoughts, feelings, physical sensations, or sounds. . . . Kindly acknowledging whatever arises, the pleasant and the unpleasant. . . . Welcoming all experiences, just as they present themselves.

2 Focus on the breath and allow a soothing breathing rhythm

Then let your attention rest on the breath, following every in- and out-breath with relaxed attention. Allowing a calming, soothing breathing rhythm by gently slowing down and deepening the movements of the breath. Letting the out-breath flow out all the way, until the direction of flow changes by itself. Letting the body fill on the in-breath, until the next out-breath naturally follows. A soothing breathing rhythm may be supported by consciously allowing a gentle smile on your face . . . softness in your belly and muscles . . . spaciousness in your chest . . . opening your heart as a flower towards the light. If you like you can place a hand on your heart, your belly or another place where touch has a soothing effect. When the breath has found its soothing rhythm, you can just let it follow its own course. Any moment you realise your mind has drifted off, mindfulness has returned. Acknowledging what is there right now, and gently guiding your attention back to the breath, and if you lost the soothing rhythm, allowing it to return.

3 Expand awareness to the whole body and offer a kind wish

Then expanding your awareness holding the body as a whole in relaxed attention, the breathing body as it sits, lies or stands here. Attuning to yourself, what comes up when you ask yourself: 'What could be a kind, supportive wish to myself right now? Is there something I really value? For instance, 'May I feel safe' . . . or 'May I feel healthy . . . happy . . . at ease'. Choose the words that come from your heart and that can be taken to heart. . . . If you like you can allow this wish to flow through you on the rhythm of the breath. For instance, 'May I . . . ' on the in-breath and ' . . . feel safe' on the out-breath. Repeating the whole phrase or just one or two keywords and mindfully acknowledging what arises while letting this kind wish flow through you. Every experience, pleasant or unpleasant, can be welcomed as part of the practice. You may end this Breathing Space with Kindness when you are ready to do so and return to it again whenever you find a good moment for it.

A Compassionate Companion

You can start with step one and two of the Breathing Space with Kindness, mindfully holding in your awareness what presents itself in this moment . . . allowing a soothing breathing rhythm. . . . And any time you can return to these two steps. . .

As in any exercise in this course, you do not have to force anything, allow a playful atmosphere. Let yourself be surprised by the free gift of your imagination. You can start with imagining a safe place, in whatever way it presents itself . . . allowing all senses to be involved . . . a place welcoming you, however you feel in the present moment . . . Then allowing another image to emerge from this safe place or independent from it, opening yourself for the presence of a compassionate being. . . . It can arise from memory or fantasy or both. It can be a human being, or an animal, a natural being, or a celestial being. . . . In any case, a being committed to your well-being, embodying compassion in all its qualities . . . it is kind and patient, sensitive, playful and caring, wise and understanding; it has courage and resilience in the face of life's difficulties and stays firmly on your side when you suffer. It accepts you just as you are, with all your imperfections and possibilities, wishing you the very best from its heart, willing to relieve your suffering wherever it can.

What does your compassionate companion look like? What colour, what shape . . . big or small . . . old or young . . . male or female . . . where do you image him or her . . . in front of you, beside or behind you . . . at what distance? And if this kind being would look at you, how do you imagine the facial expression would be . . . how the glance in the eyes? A visual image may vary in clarity, various images may come and go. Other senses may be clearer. Perhaps feeling a kind of presence or atmosphere, perhaps a fragrance? . . . How would this being relate to you? If it would speak to you, how would the voice sound?

How does it affect to you imagining yourself being near this compassionate being? What bodily effects do you notice . . . in your face, your chest, your belly, your arms and legs? . . . How does it affect your thoughts and feelings, your mind, your mood state? . . . Now imagining this being really appreciates your presence and values being with you. No matter how you are, imagine it welcomes you from the heart. How does that make you feel?

And remember, it is a practice. It may be difficult to connect to it, or various fleeting images may pass by. Notice your reactivity to what arises, your likes and dislikes.

> *All experiences belong to the practice. Mindfully acknowledge and welcome whatever shows itself, pleasant or unpleasant, joyful or sad, tendencies to hold on or hold off. . . . Allowing for a mindful pause. . . . Allowing for the breath to sooth you. . . . And return to the imagery practice when you feel the space to do so . . . imagining a compassionate being turning to you with this very experience you have right now. . . . How would it relate to you? What would it wish for you?*
>
> *Continuing with this practice until you are ready to end it, perhaps with a goodbye and expression of gratitude or appreciation, in your own way, and letting the image dissolve. No need for a definitive goodbye. You can return any moment to this practice of imagining a compassionate being, wherever you are, however you feel and however it will show itself.*

Additional resources

More information on MBCL can be found in the textbook *Mindfulness-Based Compassionate Living – A new training programme to deepen mindfulness with heartfulness* by Erik van den Brink and Frits Koster (2015) which was published by Routledge and written for (semi-) professionals. *A practical guide to Mindfulness-Based Compassionate Living – Living with heart*, by the same authors, is intended for a wider audience and scheduled to be published by Routledge early 2018. This can be used as a self-help guide and by participants of group trainings. Most exercises are available on audio recordings and can be downloaded together with worksheets from www.routledge.com. Those interested in introductory foundation courses and teacher training seminars can find information on www.compassionateliving.info and www.mbcl.org.

Summary

In this chapter we described how we developed the Mindfulness-Based Compassionate Living course, an eight-session deepening programme for those who already acquired basic mindfulness skills through MBSR, MBCT or equivalent training. We outlined the relevant theoretical background, particularly the expansion of the stress theory with insights from evolutionary psychology, as well as the science base, content and structure of the programme. A session-overview and two examples of key practices were given.

References

Bartels-Velthuis, A. A., Van der Ploeg, K., Koster, F., Fleer, J., Schroevers, M. J., & Van den Brink, E. (2016). A Mindfulness-Based Compassionate Living training in a heterogeneous sample of psychiatric outpatients: A feasibility study. *Mindfulness*, 7, 809–818.
Baumeister, R. F., Bratslavsky, E., Finkenauer, C., & Vohs, K. D. (2001). Bad is stronger than good. *Review of General Psychology*, 5, 323–370.
Brach, T. (2004). *Radical acceptance*. New York, NY: Bantam.
Brewin, C. R. (2006). Understanding cognitive behaviour therapy: A retrieval competition account. *Behaviour Research and Therapy*, 44, 765–784.

Crocker, J., & Canevello, A. (2008). Creating and undermining social support in communal relationships: The role of compassionate and self-image goals. *Journal of Personality and Social Psychology, 95*, 555–575.

Davidson, R. J. (2012). The neurobiology of compassion. In C. K. Germer & R. D. Siegel (Eds.), *Compassion and wisdom in psychotherapy* (pp. 111–118). New York, NY: Guilford Press.

Depue, R. A., & Morrone-Strupinsky, J. V. (2005). A neurobehavioral model of affiliative bonding. *Behavioral and Brain Sciences, 28*, 313–395.

Fredrickson, B. L., Cohn, M. A., Coffey, K. A., Pek, J., & Finkel, S. (2008). Open hearts build lives: Positive emotions, induced through loving-kindness meditation, build consequential personal resources. *Journal of Personality and Social Psychology, 95*, 1045–1062.

Germer, C. K. (2009). *The mindful path to self-compassion*. New York, NY: Guilford Press.

Gilbert, P. (2009). *The compassionate mind*. London: Constable & Robinson.

Gilbert, P. (2010). *Compassion focused therapy*. London: Routledge.

Gilbert, P. (2014). The origins and nature of compassion focused therapy. *British Journal of Clinical Psychology, 53*, 6–41.

Gilbert, P. (2017). Compassion as a social mentality: An evolutionary approach. In P. Gilbert (Ed.), *Compassion: Concepts, research and applications* (pp. 31–68). London: Routledge.

Gilbert, P., & Choden, K. (2013). *Mindful compassion*. London: Constable & Robinson.

Goleman, D. (2006). *Social intelligence: The new science of human relationships*. New York, NY: Bantam.

Hanson, R., with Mendius, R. (2009). *Buddha's Brain: The practical neuroscience of happiness, love & wisdom*. Oakland, CA: New Harbinger Publications.

Hanson, R. (2013). *Hardwiring happiness – The new brain science of contentment, calm, and confidence*. New York, NY: Harmony.

Hayes, S., Strohsal, K., & Wilson, K. (2012). *Acceptance and Commitment Therapy: The process and practice of mindful change*. New York, NY: Guilford Press.

Jazaieri, H., Jinpa, J. T., McGonigal, K., et al. . . . Goldin, P. R. (2013). Enhancing compassion: A randomized controlled trial of a compassion cultivation training program. *Journal of Happiness Studies, 14*, 1113–1126.

Jazaieri, H., McGonigal, K., Jinpa, T., Doty, J. R., Gross, J. J., & Goldin, P. R. (2014). A randomized controlled trial of compassion cultivation training: Effects on mindfulness, affect, and emotion regulation. *Motivation and Emotion, 38*, 23–35.

Kabat-Zinn, J. (1991). *Full catastrophe living: How to cope with stress, pain and illness using mindfulness meditation*. New York, NY: Dell.

Kok, B. E., Coffey, K. A., Cohn, M. A., et al. . . . Fredrickson, B. L. (2013). How positive emotions build physical health: Perceived positive social connections account for the upward spiral between positive emotions and vagal tone. *Psychological Science, 24*, 1123–1132.

Krieger, T., Martig, D. S., van den Brink, E., & Berger, T. (2016). Working on self-compassion online: A proof of concept and feasibility study. *Internet Interventions, 6*, 64–70.

Kuyken, W., Watkins, E., Holden, E., et al. . . . Dalgleish, T. (2010). How does mindfulness-based cognitive therapy work? *Behavior Research and Therapy, 48*, 1105–1112.

LeDoux, J. (1998). *The emotional brain*. London: Weidenfeld & Nicolson.

MacBeth, A., & Gumley, A. (2012). Exploring compassion: A meta-analysis of the association between self-compassion and psychopathology. *Clinical Psychology Review, 32*(6), 545–552.

MacLean, P. D. (1990). *The triune brain in evolution: Role in paleocerebral functions*. New York, NY: Springer.

Mascaro, J. S., Rilling, J. K., Tenzin Negi, L., & Raison, C. L. (2013). Compassion meditation enhances empathic accuracy and related neural activity. *Social Cognitive and Affective Neuroscience, 8*, 48–55.

Neff, K. (2011). *Self-compassion: Stop beating yourself up and leave insecurity behind*. New York, NY: Harper Collins.

Neff, K. D. (2003a). Self-compassion: An alternative conceptualization of a healthy attitude toward oneself. *Self and Identity, 2*, 85–102.

Neff, K. D. (2003b). Development and validation of a scale to measure self-compassion. *Self and Identity, 2*, 223–250.

Neff, K. D., & Germer, C. K. (2012). A pilot study and randomized controlled trial of the mindful self-compassion program. *Journal of Clinical Psychology, 69*, 28–44.

Pace, T. W. W., Negi, L. T., Adame, D. D., et al. . . . Raison, C. L. (2009). Effect of compassion meditation on neuroendocrine, innate immune and behavioral responses to psychosocial stress. *Psychoneuroendocrinology, 34*, 87–98.

Porges, S. W. (2007). The polyvagal perspective. *Biological Psychology, 74*, 116–143.

Ricard, M. (2015). *Altruism – The power of compassion to change yourself and the world*. London: Atlantic Books.

Schuling, R., Huijbers, M. J., Van Ravesteijn, H., Donders, R., Kuyken, W., & Speckens, A. E. M. (2016). A parallel-group, randomized controlled trial into the effectiveness of Mindfulness-Based Compassionate Living (MBCL) compared to treatment-as-usual in recurrent depression: Trial design and protocol. *Contemporary Clinical Trials*. doi: 10.1016/j.cct.2016.07.014.

Schuling, R., Huijbers, M. J., Van Ravesteijn, H., Donders, R., Kuyken, W., & Speckens, A. E. M. (submitted February 2018). Effectiveness of Mindfulness-Based Compassionate Living compared with treatment-as-usual in recurrent depression: An RCT. *Journal of Clinical and Consulting Psychology*.

Schuling, R., Huijbers, M. J., Jansen, H. C. . . . Speckens, A. (2017). The co-creation and feasibility of a compassion training as a follow-up to Mindfulness Based Cognitive Therapy in patients with recurrent depression. *Mindfulness* (accepted for publication June 2017).

Segal, S. V., Williams, J. M. G., & Teasdale, J. D. (2013). *Mindfulness-Based Cognitive Therapy for depression: A new approach to preventing relapse*. New York, NY: Guilford Press.

Seligman, M. (2002). *Authentic happiness: Using the new positive psychology to realize your potential for lasting fulfillment*. New York, NY: Free Press.

Shapiro, S. L., Astin, J. A., Bishop, S. R., & Cordova, M. (2005). Mindfulness-based stress reduction for health care professionals: Results from a randomized trial. *International Journal of Stress Management, 12*, 164–176.

Shapiro, S. L., Brown, K. W., & Biegel, G. M. (2007). Teaching self-care to care-givers: Effects of mindfulness-based stress reduction on the mental health of therapists in training. *Training and Education in Professional Psychology, 1*, 105–115.

Siegel, D. J. (2007). *The mindful brain: Reflection and attunement in the cultivation of well-being*. New York, NY: W.W. Norton.

Taylor, S. (2006). Tend and befriend: Biobehavioral bases of affiliation under stress. *Current Directions in Psychological Science, 15*, 273–277.

Van den Brink, E., & Koster, F. (2015). *Mindfulness-Based Compassionate Living – A new training programme to deepen mindfulness with heartfulness*. London: Routledge.

Van den Brink, E., & Koster, F. (2018). *A practical guide to Mindfulness-Based Compassionate Living: Living with heart*. London: Routledge.

Wallmark, E., Safarzadeh, K., Daukantaitė, D., & Maddux, R. E. (2013). Promoting altruism through meditation: An 8-week randomized controlled pilot study. *Mindfulness, 4*, 223–234.

Young, J. E., Klosko, J. S., & Weishaar, M. E. (2003). *Schema therapy – A practitioner's guide*. New York, NY: Guilford Press.

Section IX

Mindfulness programs in psychological flourishing

Chapter 30

Mindfulness-Based Strengths Practice (MBSP)

Roger Bretherton and Ryan M. Niemiec

A pause for you

Mindfulness is strangely paradoxical. On the one hand, it is the easiest thing in the world to learn – many people pick it up effortlessly, and quickly discover the benefits of its practice. On the other hand, there are depths of mindfulness, infinite subtleties to learn and obstacles to overcome that can make it one of the most difficult things to maintain as a part of everyday life, let alone apply to vexing medical or psychological problems. Mindfulness-Based Strengths Practice (MBSP), like many of the other programs profiled in this volume, uses a combination of theoretical teachings and experiential practices to help people to establish regular mindful practice. It emphasises the powerful integration of mindfulness and character strengths for creating sustainable mindful practice and for enhancing positive qualities of character.

With this pragmatic attitude in mind, we would like to start with an exercise. We begin the chapter with a short activity that captures the integration of the concepts we will explore below. It is called "the mindful pause," and it involves two simple steps:

- First, we invite you to pause. Mindfully attend to your breathing. Allow your awareness to rest effortlessly on the rising and falling of your body as you breathe for about 20 seconds.
- Second, having created a bit more clarity in your mind, pose the following question to yourself: what character strength might I bring forth right now? Attend to your mind and body – notice what strength rises to the forefront through thoughts/ideas, images, emotions, and body sensations. This is an invitation to action – to take action in some way in your thoughts, feelings, or behaviours by bringing forth your best qualities in this moment.

Participants in MBSP programs around the world have reported this exercise to be exceptionally useful when applied to their routine activities, to stressful situations, and to positive experiences of daily life at home, school, work, and community. This activity is one simple example of the integrated approach to mindfulness and character strengths that defines MBSP.

Concepts/definitions

Mindfulness-Based Strengths Practice (MBSP) was first comprehensively described in the volume *Mindfulness and Character Strengths: A Practical Guide to Flourishing* (Niemiec,

2014), the early parts of which are dedicated to clarifying the principle constructs involved. The integration of mindfulness and character strengths is no meagre feat. Both are vast areas of psychological research. It is estimated that well over five hundred peer-reviewed articles on mindfulness are published every year. Meanwhile, scientific work on character strengths has continued to rise steadily over the last decade or so (Niemiec, 2013) and is viewed as the backbone of the science of well-being/positive psychology. Both fields, largely as a result of this thriving, contain multiple definitions and conceptualisations offered by scientists, thought leaders, and practitioners. It is therefore necessary, to start by delineating our understanding of the principle concepts.

In terms of mindfulness, we primarily reference the operational and scientific definition offered by Bishop and colleagues (2004). This distinguished group of mindfulness luminaries aimed to operationalize the construct of mindfulness so as to avoid its becoming confused or diluted. Upon review of the literature on mindfulness over the decades, this working-group of scientists concluded that mindfulness, at its core, consists of two elements: a) the self-regulation of attention and b) an attitude of curiosity, openness, and acceptance. This definition has the twin advantages of not only achieving a widespread scholarly consensus in the field, but also, conveniently for our purposes, utilises at least two character strengths (self-regulation and curiosity) formally recognized in the literature (Peterson & Seligman, 2004).

When it comes to defining character strengths, there are many ways of approaching the construct. It should be acknowledged that there are different categories of strengths exhibited by human beings, such as hard-wired talents, acquired skills, external resources that support us, and interests or passions in life (Niemiec, 2014, 2017). Character strengths, however, can be differentiated from these other forms of strength, they are trait-like capacities for thinking, feeling, and behaving (Park, Peterson, & Seligman, 2004), the expression of which determines the full life – a life of pleasure, engagement, and meaning (Peterson, Ruch, Beerman, Park, & Seligman, 2007). They are often thought of as pathways to the great virtues (Peterson & Seligman, 2004), and in this respect character strengths could be construed as the basic building blocks and routes to well-being or flourishing (Seligman, 2011). Character strengths, in contradistinction to other categories of strength, are central to human identity and thereby crucial in allowing us to actualize our talents/abilities, skills, passions, and external support.

This is the notion of character strength on which MBSP focusses. It draws upon the classification of 24 universal character strengths and six virtues developed by Peterson and Seligman (2004), in collaboration with 55 scientists, as the result of a worldwide project of the VIA Institute for Character (2016). The 24 character strengths of this VIA Classification are summarised as follows:

- Wisdom (cognitive strengths that help us acquire and use knowledge): curiosity, creativity, love of learning, perspective, and judgment/critical thinking.
- Courage (emotional strengths that help us face adversity): bravery, zest, perseverance, and honesty.
- Humanity (interpersonal strengths that help us tend and befriend others): kindness, love, and social intelligence.
- Justice (civic strengths that help us build healthy communities): fairness, leadership, and teamwork.

- Temperance (self-control strengths that help us manage and control our vices): forgiveness, humility, prudence, and self-regulation.
- Transcendence (strengths that help us connect outside of ourselves): appreciation of beauty and excellence, gratitude, hope, humour, and spirituality.

The VIA classification represents a consensual nomenclature or common language, established by scientists for talking about what is good in people, a language every bit as sophisticated and comprehensive as the language of pathology found in psychiatric diagnostic systems. For this reason, Peterson and Seligman (2004) referred to the classification as a "manual of the sanities." Niemiec (2017) summarises this approach by suggesting that ultimately character strengths perform three crucial functions. They are a set of positive traits which a) reflect our personal identity by indicating who we are; b) produce positive outcomes for ourselves and others, such as well-being, positive relationships, and achievement; and c) contribute to the collective good.

How and why MBSP was created

When explaining the integration of mindfulness and character strengths to our MBSP participants, we often use a short parable, the parable of the two trees. It goes like this:

> Picture this: Two, tall trees growing side by side as they branch out towards the limitless sky. With solid trunks that twist around each other, each tree has an extensive root system spreading several yards long and wide. Some of their roots intertwine and begin to depend on one another becoming one and the same; other roots go their separate ways, extending deeper and deeper. The trees are of similar height and are so close to one another that their branches interconnect. As time goes on, the branches from each tree weave in and around one another. This occurs so seamlessly that when the passer-by gazes up at the tress their tops have become one.
>
> (Niemiec, 2014, p. 154)

The story of the two trees points towards the integration of mindfulness and character strengths found in MBSP. These two are often viewed as unique entities with separate expressions in the world, yet they can be brought together in a harmonious way that benefits oneself and others.

In the West, mindfulness has often been presented from a deficit-reduction perspective, as a technical solution to problems such as stress, pain, hypertension and so on. However, it has been asserted that there is an alternative view that practices mindfulness with an intention more closely aligned to that of positive psychology (e.g., Ivtzan, Niemiec, & Briscoe, 2016). Rather than alleviating mental illness, mindfulness can be practiced with the intention of improving mental health. It is this flourishing perspective, as opposed to a deficit perspective, that legitimises the inclusion of mindfulness within the field of positive psychology. MBSP was arguably the first formal mindfulness program to adopt this perspective (Niemiec et al., 2012). By targeting character strengths, it took a different starting point than the other mindfulness-based programs up to that point. Rather than addressing a specific problem area or disorder, it emphasised what is best in the human being. Rather than correcting what is wrong in a person, it sought to capitalize on what is right. It integrates the science, practices, and resources of mindfulness and character strengths to help people reach greater levels of flourishing, such as greater well-being, better relationships, more engagement and meaning/purpose in life. In addition, it does not omit or turn from problems. To the contrary, MBSP assists with the development of resilience, building skills such as buffering, managing, and/or transcending problems, stressors, and conflicts. It begins with a character strengths-based focus and then uses this mindset and approach to address obstacles and life challenges.

With this purpose in view, MBSP was developed as the result of extensive research in both mindfulness and character strengths. These vast fields of scholarly activity were aggregated and integrated into program form, with well-defined criteria for experts to test it cross-culturally. Qualified professionals and mindfulness practitioners were given access to the program, and tracked through the struggles and successes they encountered in delivering it. This feedback was then used to make appropriate changes to the program, which was then published in manualized form by Niemiec (2014). As a result, MBSP is being deployed in various countries and settings with a variety of cultural and demographic samples. Early publications, as well as pilot studies and ongoing trials are outlined below.

Research and theory underpinning MBSP

There are several theoretical innovations which could be considered distinctive to MBSP. In 2015, Ruth Baer, one of the world's leading mindfulness experts, described it as the only mindfulness-based program to theoretically integrate mindfulness with strengths and positive human functioning. In recent years, other programs have emerged that also link mindfulness to the psychology of human flourishing (see the review by Ivtzan & Lomas, 2016). MBSP also has an implicitly existential inflection, particularly in the way that MBSP participants are invited to consider notions of meaning and purposeful engagement with life (Littman-Ovadia & Niemiec, 2017).

The distinctiveness of MBSP is readily viewed in how it weaves together mindfulness and character strengths. It teaches two main ways of doing this:

1 Strong Mindfulness (Niemiec, Rashid, & Spinella, 2012) means to use character strengths to benefit mindfulness, meditation, and mindful living. Participants in the MBSP program are encouraged at various points to use their character strengths to assist their practice of mindfulness. Several exercises in the program invite participants to reflect upon which of their strengths could help them when seeking to establish a sustainable mindfulness practice. It is therefore not unusual to hear MBSP participants talking about how gratitude, or perseverance, or the playful joy of humour, could be brought to bear on their mindfulness practice and ways of mindful living (e.g., mindful driving, eating, and working). MBSP invites participants to strengthen mindfulness by bringing what is best in them to the practice.

2 Mindful Strengths Use (Niemiec, 2012) means to use mindfulness practices to discover and actualize character strengths. The precision of mindful awareness offers a lens to bring balance to character strengths use (managing strengths overuse and underuse), a newfound savvy for responding with strengths in interactions, and allows people to contextualize their strengths use to the situation they are in. In addition, MBSP takes popular mindfulness-based program activities such as "bring mindfulness to a routine activity" (e.g., bringing mindfulness to brushing teeth, showering, feeding a pet, climbing stairs) to a new level. Participants use the energy of mindfulness to tune into the

character strengths they are using in the moment, such as: self-regulation when brushing their teeth, humility when speaking with their boss, zest when they rise out of bed, or gratitude when they speak to the clerk at the grocery store. At the same time, they use mindfulness to consider adjustments to these routines, or how they might weave different character strengths into that routine in the future.

In operationalizing these two approaches to integration, MBSP is congruent with a growing literature on the power of combining mindfulness and character strengths (see Baer & Lykins, 2011). Research consistently endorses a strong link between mindfulness and character strengths. Mindfulness allows people to overcome blind spots in self-knowledge, by increasing the quality and quantity of information they have about themselves, and thereby allowing them to process personally salient information that may otherwise have been overlooked (Carlson, 2013). In addition, mindfulness and the strength of curiosity close the self-discrepancy gap, in that each helps to align one's actual self and beliefs about who one thinks one is and one's ideal self and the image of who one would like to be (Ivtzan, Gardner, & Smailova, 2011). In these ways, mindfulness is intimately associated with the sense of identity which comes through knowledge of one's core self, or character strengths.

Over the last decade and a half, there has been substantial research connecting the 24 individual character strengths with mindfulness, too extensive to detail here (for summaries, see Baer & Lykins, 2011; Niemiec, 2014). In short, character strengths have been used to delineate:

1 the *essence* of mindfulness, such as curiosity and self-regulation (Bishop et al., 2004);
2 the *process* of mindfulness, such as humility or quieting the ego (Heppner & Kernis, 2007); and
3 the *outcomes* of mindfulness practice, such as greater gratitude (Bryant & Veroff, 2007), and increased prudence in leaders (Boyatzis & McKee, 2005; Giluk, 2009).

In addition, character strengths are frequently a central component in mindfulness practices such as perspective/wisdom (Kristeller, Wolever, & Sheets, 2013) and kindness/compassion (Neff, 2011). It is also worth noting that the explicit benefits of most mindfulness programs (e.g., MBCT and MBSR) involve the cultivation of character strengths. For example, Segal and colleagues (2013) describe benefits such as observing negative thoughts with curiosity and kindness, learning to accept oneself and stop wishing things to be different, letting go of old habits, and noticing small beauties and pleasures in the world. It is easy to associate the character strengths of curiosity, kindness, judgment/critical thinking, self-regulation, forgiveness, perspective, bravery, perseverance, and appreciation of beauty and excellence with these intended outcomes.

In addition to each of the 24 character strengths being linked with mindfulness in some way, there is compelling new research enhancing our understanding of the synergistic relationship between character strengths and mindfulness.

Experimental data suggests that the use of character strengths improves well-being even for those already well-practiced in mindfulness and psychologically well (Lykins, 2014). A study emerging from a large database of well-being instruments noted a significant positive correlation between mindfulness and the amount of time spent using strengths (Jarden et al., 2012). A small correlational study in Holland with 43 subjects found that mindfulness was related to higher levels of strength use (Alberts, 2015). In addition, not only were both character strengths and mindfulness positively correlated and independently linked with life satisfaction, but mindfulness accounted for 24% of the variance in strength use (Alberts, 2015).

Duan and Ho (2017) also concluded that mindfulness and character strengths work together to facilitate mental well-being. They found that practicing the character strengths related to temperance and interpersonal relationships highly contributed to the association between mindful observing and flourishing. Their longitudinal analysis found that the observing facet of mindfulness predicted temperance strengths which then predicted flourishing. The observing facet of mindfulness was positively related to interpersonal-, intellectual-, and temperance-related character strengths.

In the Chinese context, a study by Duan (2016) found that character strengths explain the relationship between dispositional mindfulness, a measure of a person's natural tendency to enter a mindful state, and psychological well-being, thus making the argument that mindfulness training can be offered to help participants increase awareness and use of character strengths.

In addition, there are a number of other studies that, without measuring mindfulness per se, have revealed important benefits to well-being or flourishing for those who are aware of their strengths and even more benefits to those who use their strengths (Hone et al., 2015; Littman-Ovadia & Steger, 2010).

Taken together, these findings lay important groundwork for the concept of mindful strengths use, painting a picture that the practice of mindful attention may be an important prerequisite to using one's character strengths, and that engagement with character strengths may be an important way of sustaining, enhancing, and even flourishing with mindfulness practice. While promising, further studies are needed to bring additional evidence to these hypotheses.

Research on the MBSP program

Despite the fact that the MBSP program was published in 2014, a number of pilot studies have been completed, as well as several ongoing trials. The first pilot study was reported in Niemiec (2014), as part of the research and development phase of the MBSP program. Eight individuals completed MBSP, with seven assigned to a control group. All completed the Five Factor Mindfulness Questionnaire (Baer, Smith, Hopkins, Krietemeyer, & Toney, 2006), the Satisfaction with Life Scale (Diener, Emmons, Larsen, & Griffin, 1985), the Flourishing Scale- which additionally measures meaning (Diener et al., 2009), and the Orientations to Happiness Scale which addresses engagement in life (Rashid, 2008). Additional items targeting signature strengths use (those strengths most energizing, effortless to use, and essential to the individual) and depression were included. In pre- and post-test comparisons, the experimental group exhibited five meaningful differences over the control group: they scored higher in flourishing, engagement and use of signature strengths in work, community and relationships. Qualitative data concerning participants' experience of the program was also gathered, and was consistent with the data above.

Another pilot study examined the effects of MBSP upon elements of flourishing among a group of 8 Mexican leaders. All elements of well-being improved following the program, with the largest change occurring for meaning, followed by positivity, achievement, positive relationships, engagement, and health, as well as large decreases in loneliness and negativity (Morales Cueto, 2017). A further study demonstrated that using MBSP with a work crew at a technical college enhanced well-being and significantly decreased both self-reported levels of anxiety and depression (Wingert, 2017).

Ivtzan, Niemiec and Briscoe (2016) conducted an empirical study of MBSP with a non-randomized control methodology. Nineteen participants completed MBSP, and twenty were assigned to a non-intervention control group. Participants completed measures of life satisfaction, flourishing, engagement and signature strengths use, pre- and post-intervention. Wilcoxon signed-rank tests found that MBSP participants scored significantly higher in all four measures post-MBSP, whereas participants in the control group did not, with the exception of a slight increase in satisfaction with life scores.

A controlled study, currently in progress, compared the effectiveness of MBSP and MBSR with a waitlist control group across a number of variables, such as perceived stress, well-being, job satisfaction, and supervisor-rated task performance. At the three-month post-intervention mark, both MBSP and MBSR were equivocally superior to the control group in decreasing stress, increasing well-being, and increasing job satisfaction. In terms of increasing performance, MBSP was significantly higher than placebo after the intervention and one-month post-intervention, whereas MBSR showed no difference from placebo at any time point (Pang & Ruch, 2017). A similar study found MBSP and MBSR to be superior to a control group in fostering the strength of humour, with MBSP being stronger than MBSP, and for effects lasting six months (Hofmann et al., 2019).

Alongside these empirical projects, there are a number of published application reports across contexts. The combination of mindfulness and character strengths makes MBSP an adaptable program which can be delivered in various modalities (e.g., groups, couples, or one-to-one sessions) and contexts (e.g., education, business, health). Utilisation in the following contexts has been described: organizations (Niemiec & Lissing, 2016), teachers and parents in early childhood education (Lottman, Zawaly, & Niemiec, 2017), gifted children (Sharp, Niemiec, & Lawrence, 2016), older adolescents (Stephenson & Bretherton, 2017), the classroom setting during school hours (Cummins, 2016), psychotherapists (Niemiec, 2015), physicians (Niemiec, 2014), and those with disabilities (Shogren et al., 2017). These reports testify to the wide-range of applicability of MBSP, and add to the future promise of its extending evidence-base.

MBSP has been successfully delivered in various countries across a wide range of settings and populations. This lends evidence to not only the feasibility of MBSP across contexts but also the widespread relevance and applicability with a myriad of populations. The following are only a handful of examples that have garnered positive feedback from MBSP leaders *and* received self-reported benefits from the client populations: healthy adults, college students, graduate students in supervision, employees of non-profit and for-profit companies, parents of school-aged children, dementia caregivers, clients with eating disorders at a psychiatric facility, impoverished single mothers, religious/spiritual persons, war veterans, young entrepreneurs, youth with ADHD, psychotherapist peer-support groups, staff/clients at children's centres, and coaching clients.

A close review of participants' perceptions of the MBSP program (across contexts/populations) – examining the structure, homework, mindfulness and character strengths activities, and perceived benefits – has revealed additional findings. One of the authors (RN), is tracking the feedback of those who participate in MBSP around the globe. Some clear themes have emerged such as the most reported obstacles to meditation (i.e., being too busy, forgetting to practice, and becoming distracted). The program engagement is high with a majority of participants completing 50% or more of the numerous weekly homework tasks. The most favoured activities to practice are mindfulness meditation, reflection on past strengths use, observing and appreciating the strengths of others, and tracking and using strengths. Commonly reported areas of personal development include being more aware of one's highest signature strengths, deepening mindful practice, using strengths to address challenges, and spotting and appreciating strengths in others. To date, not a single negative effect of MBSP has been reported by any participant. On the contrary, overwhelmingly, participants report MBSP directly improves their sense of well-being, purpose, meaning, engagement, accomplishment, and stress management. Finally, there are two additional benefits of completing MBSP that consistently emerge in participant feedback and are particularly intriguing: Participants report: a) improved relationships with others, and are able to cite a specific relationship in their life that has benefited from MBSP; and b) an enhanced ability to manage problems with resilience.

Further controlled trials of MBSP are warranted to add specificity to our understanding of the benefits of MBSP and the psychological mechanisms that underlie them. While it would be premature at this point to draw final conclusions, there are important themes emerging in relation to the well-being benefits of MBSP in regard to the boosting of positive relationships, happiness, productivity and meaning (flourishing elements) and the management of problems (resilience elements). In addition to deepening the evidence with those outcomes, research is needed to explore the benefit of taking a strengths-based as opposed to a deficit-focussed approach. There is emerging evidence, from clinical practice and workplace interventions, that focusing on strengths is superior in some ways to remediating deficits (Cheavens et al., 2012; Meyers et al., 2015), but how might the difference play out in the mindfulness context, comparing MBSP, which starts with the operating focus of what's best in people, with the majority of mindfulness-based programs, with their (at least partial) focal point of "disorders"? Research into alternative program structures is necessary to ascertain essential structural elements, for instance, whether the MBSP program can be reduced in terms of number of weeks and maintain benefits.

MBSP program outline

Mindfulness-Based Strengths Practice is usually delivered in eight sessions at weekly intervals. The most common delivery methods have been delivered live to groups and online (live) to participants across the globe, through the web-based platform dedicated to mindfulness training, eMindful. According to the current evidence, both formats appear to be equally effective. The eight sessions are designed to introduce both mindfulness and character strengths and then integrate them over the course of the program, with tasks such as dealing with obstacles, improving relationships, being authentic and enhancing engagement. The MBSP program also includes an optional half-day MBSP retreat which further applies the practices to activities of everyday life such as conversation, eating, walking, sitting, food preparation, and so on. The eight sessions may also be followed by "booster" sessions a month or so later, intended to remind participants to practice and to pick up any obstacles or difficulties that may have emerged since the end of the formal program. A brief outline of the sessions can be seen in Table 30.1.

The optimal delivery of MBSP requires at least 90 to 120 minutes per session, each of which follows a particular internal structure: starting with an opening mediation, followed by small or large group discussion and feedback, didactic offering, practising a core skill, a virtue circle involving mindful speaking and listening, homework review, and a concluding meditation. These seven ingredients are outlined in Table 30.2 and, while they represent the

Table 30.1 Core topic areas of MBSP

Session	Core Topic	Description
1	Mindfulness and Autopilot	The autopilot mind is pervasive; insights and change opportunities start with mindful attention.
2	Your Signature Strengths	Identify those strengths that are most essential to who you are; this can unlock potential to engage more in work and relationships and reach higher personal potential.
3	Obstacles are Opportunities	The practice of mindfulness and of strengths exploration leads immediately to two things – obstacles/barriers to the practice and a wider appreciation for the little things in life.
4	Strengthening Mindfulness in Everyday Life (Strong Mindfulness)	Mindfulness helps us attend to and nourish the best, innermost qualities in ourselves and others, while reducing negative judgments of self and others; conscious use of strengths can help us deepen and maintain a mindfulness practice.
5	Valuing Your Relationships	Mindful attending can nourish two types of relationships: relationships with others and our relationship with ourselves. Our relationships with ourselves contributes to self-growth and can have an immediate impact on our connection with others.
6	Mindfulness of the Golden Mean (Mindful Strengths Use)	Mindfulness helps to focus on problems directly and character strengths help to reframe and offer different perspectives not immediately apparent.
Optional Retreat	MBSP Half-Day Retreat	Mindful living and character strengths apply not only to good meditation practice but also to daily conversation, eating, walking, sitting, reflecting, and the nuances therein (e.g., opening the refrigerator door, turning a doorknob, creating a smile). This day is therefore, a *practice* day.
7	Authenticity and Goodness	It takes character (e.g., courage) to be a more authentic "you" and it takes character (e.g., hope) to create a strong future that benefits both oneself and others. Set mindfulness and character strengths goals with authenticity and goodness in the forefront of the mind.
8	Your Engagement with Life	Stick with those practices that have been working well and watch for the mind's tendency to revert back to automatic habits that are deficit-based, unproductive, or that prioritize what's wrong in you and others. Engage in an approach that fosters awareness and celebration of what is strongest in you and others.

Source: Adapted with permission from Niemiec, 2014

Table 30.2 Standard structure of MBSP sessions

Part	Focus Area	Description
I	Opening meditation	Start group with "practice," allows for letting go of preceding tension and ushers in a different focus.
II	Discussion: whole group or multiple small groups	Review participants' practice from last week with the following catalyst: what went well?
III	Lecture/input	Offering new material aligned with core themes.
IV	Experiential	Core practice in which mindfulness and character strengths are experienced.
V	Virtue circle	Structured, respectful approach for mindful listening/speaking practice and strengths-spotting/appreciating practice.
VI	Suggested homework	Review of focus areas in between sessions.
VII	Closing meditation	Letting go of session to come fully into the present moment; mindful transitioning to the next part of the day.

Source: Adapted with permission from Niemiec, 2014

ideal structure of each MBSP session, elements of it may require adaptation in some contexts. For example, one of us (RB), in delivering MBSP to adolescents in an education context was required to reduce the length of the session and emphasise the key learning points more strongly. He therefore omitted the virtue circle and, using opening and closing meditations to bookmark the beginning and end of sessions, delivered the other four elements under catchy titles. They were re-named: catch-up (how did you do this week?), idea (one thing you need to know), experiment (let's give it a try), and challenge (what to do this week?). This allowed the main principles and practices of MBSP to be covered in a slightly shorter time and to be held vividly in mind by the young people participating in the group.

MBSP places a substantial emphasis on the importance of practising exercises related to both mindfulness and character strengths. Each session aims to introduce a new practice to participants, which build from session to session to further establish strong mindfulness and mindful strengths use. These practices have been selected on the basis of previous research or as the result of positive feedback from participants who have completed them. One example of a novel practice used in each session is provided in Table 30.3.

It is worth noting how these practices contribute to the development of strong mindfulness and mindful strengths use. For example, the statue meditation in Session 3 allows participants to bring their strengths to bear on the challenges and obstacles of being mindful. The exercise requires participants to stand still, to bring awareness to their breath and then hold their arms out in front of them, bent at the elbow, in a posture that looks as if they are giving a hug to an invisible person. As they hold this position for a few minutes, they naturally begin to feel discomfort. They are invited to consider their mindful breathing and any of the 24 strengths they might draw upon to maintain mindfulness and manage the challenge. It is not a comfortable exercise, and some participants are vocal in their dislike of having to stand still in such a difficult position. Nevertheless, the exercise illustrates how individuals have more inner resources than they know and that they can deliberately turn to their character strengths in any situation. Participants report the need to draw on strengths such as perseverance to remain in the stance, on hope to remind themselves that it will eventually come to an end, on teamwork to realize they are "all in this together" as a group, on humour to make the

Table 30.3 Core practices across the eight MBSP sessions

Session	Core Practice	Explanation	Rationale
1	Raisin exercise/mindful eating and/or mindful drinking of water	Eating one raisin as if "for the first time"; eating with all five senses. And/or applied to drinking water.	Poignant practice in beginner's mind; offers a microcosm by which mindfulness can be applied into daily life.
2	Strengths-spotting	In pairs, participants share recent positive experiences and practice steps involving the spotting of strengths.	Offers a shift in how we perceive stories and how we typically approach conversations; combats strength blindness.
3	Statue meditation	Participants engage in a challenge involving holding up their arms and facing the mental & physical obstacles and discomforts that ensue.	Facing meditation obstacles and reframing difficulties and stressors that arise as "obstacles" that can be targeted with *any* of the 24 character strengths and mindful breathing.
4	Mindful walking/ movement	Practising standing and walking meditation, and spotting strengths that arise and that are used during walking.	Strengthening mindfulness in daily life; bringing strengths to a task often taken for granted; deepening the experience of mindfulness through strengths.
5	Use of both a targeted strengths meditation and an open-ended meditation on strengths	Practice of traditional meditation focused on cultivating warmth and compassion; followed by an open meditation on a strength of the participants' choosing.	Experiencing the potential to target any of the 24 strengths, in both a guided format and an open-ended format; distinction of two different types of meditation.
6	Character strengths 360	Review of feedback of a two- to five-minute survey in which participants receive feedback from several people on his or her character strengths.	Offers numerous mindfulness opportunities involving strengths awareness, blindness, potential opportunities, appreciation, and handling feedback; implications for positive relationships.
7	Best possible self and defining moments exercise	Structured exercises involving a choice of envisioning a future best self or reflecting on one of life's defining moments.	Mindful reflection or mindful envisioning with strengths; linking goals, identity, and strengths.

(Continued)

Table 30.3 (Continued)

Session	Core Practice	Explanation	Rationale
8	Golden nuggets	Sharing key insights and long-term practices.	Linking current experiences with next steps; use of positive cueing.

Source: Adapted with permission from Niemiec & Lissing, 2016

exercise bearable by recognising the silliness of the situation, and self-regulation to remain focused and undistracted in holding their position. These are just a few examples of how the statue meditation teaches strong mindfulness.

Mindful strengths practice is also incorporated into many of the practices. For example, the Character Strengths 360 exercise asks participants to distribute a short strengths survey to a handful of people who know them, such as friends, family, neighbours, or colleagues, and asks these people to indicate from a list the strengths they see in the participant, and one example for each strength denoted. The participants are then invited to collate this feedback into a single table and reflect upon it. Some of the findings are aligned with the participant's signature strengths results on the VIA Survey; others represent strengths the participant had been blind to. The most common reactions of participants across the globe, after assembling the 360 results, are that it is validating, uplifting, and powerful, especially in providing a new dimension of knowledge to how the participants view themselves. They attain a mindful awareness of how others perceive their strengths.

The Character Strengths 360 exercise almost always involves a few surprises. Sometimes participants find that their peers unanimously spot a strength in them that they didn't realize they had. One young woman, for example, found that when she collated her 360 feedback, each of the surveys noted her strength of kindness, yet she had largely taken her kind actions towards others for granted. As a result of the exercise she became aware of this blind spot, a strength she expressed strongly but failed to recognize, and could turn mindful awareness to the times her kindness was in evidence. By the same token, participants may also find that strengths they believe they are highest in, go unrecognized by those around them. One MBSP participant, when completing the VIA Survey, had found love to be his highest ranking strength, yet none of the feedback in the Character Strengths 360 recognized this in him. Initially he found this disheartening, thinking he was failing to adequately demonstrate his love to those around him, but he was invited to view this result as a potential opportunity. He brought mindful awareness to the times he felt love rise most strongly and then considered how he could best apply or express this strength in ways that felt authentic but also allowed others to see his care for them.

MBSP involves various activities that enable its participants to explore the integration of mindfulness with character strengths. Several examples of exercises are summarised in Table 30.4.

Over the last few years we have been delighted to see how the MBSP program has brought energy, meaning, and engagement to its participants. We offer two illustrative examples: one delivered online and one program delivered in a school.

The first case involves a man who was participating in an online MBSP programme that involved several participants living in different time-zones scattered across the globe. During group conversation, he had shared the problems he experienced regulating his alcohol consumption. It was not a diagnosable clinical problem, but he was concerned that he was

Table 30.4 A sampling of ten integration activities in MBSP

Name of Practice	Description	Type of Integration	Research Base or Source
Signature strengths use	Bring attention to and use one of your highest, most authentic strengths in a new way each day.	Mindful strengths use	Gander et al. (2013); Seligman et al. (2005).
Strengths-spotting	Spot strengths in another person's sharing; spot strengths in your daily routines; spot strengths in the media (e.g., movies, books).	Mindful strengths use	Linley (2008); Niemiec (2013); Niemiec and Wedding (2014).
Strengths appreciation (also called the "Speak Up!" exercise)	Share the value and impact that someone else's strengths expression had upon you.	Mindful strengths use	Adler and Fagley (2005); Algoe, Gable, and Maisel (2010); Bao and Lyubomirsky (2013); Kashdan et al. (2017).
Facing meditation obstacles	Name one barrier to your meditation practice (e.g., mind wandering; noises; scheduling, discomfort), and describe how each of your top strengths could help you face or overcome it.	Strong mindfulness	Brahm (2006); Kornfield (1993) Lomas et al. (2014); Niemiec (2014); Niemiec, Rashid, and Spinella (2012).
Bring strengths to mindful living	Identify one area of routine that you could bring mindfulness to (e.g., driving, eating, listening, walking). Notice the strengths that are already present in the experience. How might the experience be invigorated with additional strengths?	Strong mindfulness	Nhat Hanh (1979); Nhat Hanh (1993); Niemiec (2013).
Body mindfulness meditation	Pure present moment mindfulness while using strengths to explore, maintain attention, and be gentle to oneself.	Strong mindfulness	Call, Miron, and Orcutt (2013); Kabat-Zinn (1990); Kabat-Zinn (2005); Mirams et al. (2012); Ussher et al. (2012).
Find balance by attending to strengths overuse and underuse	Examine life situations for strengths overuse and underuse and consider how other strengths can bring balance.	Mindful strengths use	Biswas-Diener, Kashdan, and Minhas (2011); Grant & Schwartz (2011); Niemiec (2014); Freidlin et al. (2017).
Targeting specific strengths	Use meditation to explore and boost any of the 24 strengths.	Mindful strengths use	Amaro (2010); Brach (2003); Fredrickson et al. (2008); Salzberg (1995).
Positive reappraisal with strengths	Skilful use of mindful listening and speaking to reframe challenges with character strengths language.	Both	Garland, Gaylord, and Fredrickson (2011); Garland, Gaylord, and Park (2009).
Character strengths breathing space	Mindfulness practice involving the use of curiosity, self-regulation, and perspective.	Both	Bishop et al. (2004); Niemiec (2014); Segal, Williams, and Teasdale (2013).

Source: Adapted with permission from Niemiec, 2014

becoming dependent on nightly alcohol to reduce stress and allow sleep. When he shared this with the group they encouraged him not to judge his behaviour but to bring non-judgemental awareness and his signature strengths to bear on the concern. By the close of the programme he reported a significant reduction in a problem that had preoccupied him for several years. He reported not only improved self-regulation but also more meaningful relationships with his family. To the latter point, he chose to conduct one of the MBSP homework activities, the character strengths interview exercise, on his eldest son, who was nine years old at the time. To his surprise, it became one of the most meaningful moments of contact he had ever experienced with his son, and as a consequence he felt that his appreciation and understanding of someone he thought he knew well achieved new depths. Moments of insight and change like these are not uncommonly reported by MBSP participants.

The second case example involves delivery of an MBSP programme to sixteen and seventeen year olds in a school in the UK. The school had been considering running a mindfulness programme for some time and had an ethos of character education for which the character strengths element of MBSP was a good fit. A twenty-minute presentation on mindfulness and character strengths was delivered to all six hundred students in that age category, following which they were invited to submit applications and provide parental consent to attend the group as an after-school club delivered over eight weeks. Fifteen students committed to the programme, and completed both quantitative and qualitative assessments of progress before and after participation. Over the course of the eight weeks, a series of beneficial changes were found in the participants. One young man described how he had attended the group looking for help with debilitating Chronic Fatigue Syndrome. In the final session, he reported that thanks to the group he no longer dreaded getting out of bed in the morning. He would practice mindfulness as soon as he woke up, and then call upon whatever character strength he needed that morning to raise his head from the pillow – sometimes it was curiosity about what would happen in the day ahead, other times it was gratitude, hope, bravery, or zest. Another young woman, an academic high-flyer, noted that mindful walking had allowed her to rediscover her strength of appreciation of beauty in the natural world. This gave her some peace amidst her usual worries of failure and concern about academic accomplishment.

These are short anecdotal examples but they nevertheless enrich our understanding of how the synthesis of mindfulness and character strengths in MBSP can benefit people in different ways. While MBSP is a relative new-comer to the scene of mindfulness programmes, the research around it is gathering pace, and is promising. As a programme, it has established its application to a diverse range of contexts, nations, and demographics, and the evidence base attesting to its beneficial effect on well-being, engagement, meaning, and productivity is taking shape. The MBSP integrated approach to mindfulness and character strengths is proving to be a powerful and productive amalgam for producing psychological change.

Resources

The latest developments in Mindfulness and Character Strengths can be followed via the resources outlined below.

www.viacharacter.org

> The global hub on all-things-character. Take the VIA Survey, learn about each of the 24 character strengths, get in-depth reports, take on-demand courses, watch videos, read articles. Under the courses tab, individuals can sign up for the MBSP program

(live, remotely), as well as the MBSP-2 course which trains practitioners who want to lead MBSP with their unique population.

www.viacharacter.org/mindfulness

A developing component of the above site. Offers resources for practitioners wanting to learn more about MBSP, including tools for marketing, application ideas, audio meditations, and more. An individualized report and workbook that integrates mindfulness and the user's VIA Survey results is expected in 2018.

www.psychologytoday.com/blog/what-matters-most

Dr. Ryan Niemiec's blog on Psychology Today (titled "What Matters Most?"), which offers user-friendly articles and research summaries on mindfulness, character strengths, positive psychology, and related topics.

References

Adler, M. G., & Fagley, N. S. (2005). Appreciation: Individual differences in finding value and meaning as a unique predictor of subjective well-being. *Journal of Personality, 73*(1), 79–114.
Alberts, H. (2015). Personal communication. February 17, 2015.
Algoe, S. B., Gable, S. L., & Maisel, N. C. (2010). It's the little things: Everyday gratitude as a booster shot for romantic relationships. *Personal Relationships, 17*, 217–233.
Amaro, A. (2010). Thinking: II: Investigation, the use of reflective thought. *Mindfulness, 1*(4), 265–268.
Baer, R. (2015). Ethics, values, virtues, and character strengths in mindfulness-based interventions: A psychological science perspective. *Mindfulness, 6*, 956–969.
Baer, R. A., & Lykins, E. L. M. (2011). Mindfulness and positive psychological functioning. In K. M. Sheldon, T. B. Kashdan, & M. F. Steger (Eds.), *Designing positive psychology: Taking stock and moving forward* (pp. 335–348). New York, NY: Oxford University Press.
Baer, R. A., Smith, G. T., Hopkins, J., Krietemeyer, J., & Toney, L. (2006). Using self-report assessment methods to explore facets of mindfulness. *Assessment, 13*(1), 27–45.
Bao, K. J., & Lyubomirsky, S. (2013). Making it last: Combating hedonic adaptation in romantic relationships. *Journal of Positive Psychology, 8*(3), 196–206.
Bishop, S. R., Lau, M., Shapiro, S. L., Carlson, L., Anderson, N. D., Carmody, J., et al. (2004). Mindfulness: A proposed operational definition. *Clinical Psychology: Science and Practice, 11*, 230–241.
Biswas-Diener, R., Kashdan, T. B., & Minhas, G. (2011). A dynamic approach to psychological strength development and intervention. *Journal of Positive Psychology, 6*(2), 106–118.
Boyatzis, R., & McKee, A. (2005). *Resonant leadership: Renewing yourself and connecting with others through mindfulness, hope, and compassion*. Boston, MA: Harvard Business School Publishing.
Brach, T. (2003). *Radical acceptance: Embracing your life with the heart of a Buddha*. New York, NY: Bantam.
Brahm, A. (2006). *Mindfulness, bliss, and beyond: A meditator's handbook*. Boston, MA: Wisdom Publications.
Bryant, F. B., & Veroff, J. (2007). *Savouring: A new model of positive experience*. Mahwah, NJ: Lawrence Erlbaum Associates.
Call, D., Miron, L., & Orcutt, H. (2013). Effectiveness of brief mindfulness techniques in reducing symptoms of anxiety and stress. *Mindfulness, 5*(6), 658–668.
Carlson, E. N. (2013). Overcoming the barriers to self-knowledge: Mindfulness as a path to seeing yourself as you really are. *Perspectives on Psychological Science, 8*(2), 173–186.

Cheavens, J. S., Strunk, D. R., Lazarus, S. A., & Goldstein, L. A. (2012). The compensation and capitalization models: A test of two approaches to individualizing the treatment of depression. *Behaviour Research and Therapy, 50*, 699–706. http://doi.org/10.1016/j.brat.2012.08.002

Cummins, T. (2016). Mindfulness and character strengths in schools: Teaching students the key pathways to flourishing. *Psychology Today*. Retrieved from www.psychologytoday.com/blog/what-matters-most/201604/mindfulness-and-character-strengths-in-schools

Diener, E., Emmons, R. A., Larsen, R. J., & Griffin, S. (1985). The satisfaction with life scale. *Journal of Personality Assessment, 49*(1), 71–75.

Diener, E., Wirtz, D., Biswas-Diener, R., Tov, W., Kim-Prieto, C., Choi, D., & Oishi, S. (2009). New measures of well-being. In E. Diener (Ed.), *Assessing well-being: The collected works of Ed Diener* (pp. 247–266). New York, NY: Springer.

Duan, W. (2016). Mediation role of individual strengths in dispositional mindfulness and mental health. *Personality and Individual Differences, 99*, 7–10.

Duan, W., & Ho, S. M. Y. (2017). Does being mindful of your character strengths enhance psychological wellbeing? A longitudinal mediation analysis. *Journal of Happiness Studies*. doi: 10.1007/s10902-017-9864-z

Fredrickson, B. L., Cohn, M. A., Coffey, K. A., Pek, J., & Finkel, S. M. (2008). Open hearts build lives: Positive emotions, induced through loving-kindness meditation, build consequential personal resources. *Journal of Personality and Social Psychology, 95*(5), 1045–1062.

Freidlin, P., Littman-Ovadia, H., & Niemiec, R. M. (2017). Positive psychopathology: Social anxiety via character strengths underuse and overuse. *Personality and Individual Differences, 108*, 50–54.

Gander, F., Proyer, R. T., Ruch, W., & Wyss, T. (2013). Strength-based positive interventions: Further evidence for their potential in enhancing well-being and alleviating depression. *Journal of Happiness Studies, 14*, 1241–1259. http://doi.org/10.1007/s10902-012-9380-0

Garland, E. L., Gaylord, S. A., & Fredrickson, B. L. (2011). Positive reappraisal mediates the stress-reductive effects of mindfulness: An upward spiral process. *Mindfulness, 2*(1), 59–67.

Garland, E. L., Gaylord, S. A., & Park, J. (2009). The role of mindfulness in positive reappraisal. *Explore: The Journal of Science and Healing, 5*(1), 37–44.

Giluk, T. L. (2009). Mindfulness, big five personality, and affect: A meta-analysis. *Personality & Individual Differences, 47*(8), 805–811.

Grant, A. M., & Schwartz, B. (2011). Too much of a good thing: The challenge and opportunity of the inverted u. *Perspectives on Psychological Science, 6*(1), 61–76.

Heppner, W. L., & Kernis, M. H. (2007). Quiet ego functioning: The complementary roles of mindfulness, authenticity, and secure high self-esteem. *Psychological Inquiry, 18*, 248–251.

Hofmann, J., Heintz, S., Pang, D., & Ruch, W. (2019). Differential relationships of light and darker forms of humor with mindfulness. *Applied Research in Quality of Life*. https://doi.org/10.1007/s11482-018-9698-9

Hone, L. C., Jarden, A., Duncan, S., & Schofield, G. M. (2015). Flourishing in New Zealand workers: Associations with lifestyle behaviors, physical health, psychosocial, and work-related indicators. *Journal of Occupational and Environmental Medicine, 57*(9), 973–983. http://doi.org/10.1097/JOM.0000000000000508

Ivtzan, I., Gardner, H. E., & Smailova, Z. (2011). Mindfulness meditation and curiosity: The contributing factors to wellbeing and the process of closing the self-discrepancy gap. *International Journal of Wellbeing, 1*(3), 316–326.

Ivtzan, I., & Lomas, T. (Eds.). (2016). *Mindfulness in positive psychology: The science of meditation and wellbeing*. Abingdon: Routledge.

Ivtzan, I., Niemiec, R. M., & Briscoe, C. (2016). A study investigating the effects of Mindfulness-Based Strengths Practice (MBSP) on wellbeing. *International Journal of Wellbeing, 6*(2), 1–13. doi: 10.5502/ijw.v6i2.1

Jarden, A., Jose, P., Kashdan, T., Simpson, O., McLachlan, K., & Mackenzie, A. (2012). *International Well-being Study*. Unpublished raw data.

Kabat-Zinn, J. (1990). *Full catastrophe living: Using the wisdom of your body and mind to face stress, pain, and illness*. New York, NY: Dell.

Kabat-Zinn, J. (2005). *Coming to our senses*. New York, NY: Hyperion.

Kashdan, T. B., Blalock, D. V., Young, K. C., Machell, K. A., Monfort, S. S., McKnight, P. E., & Ferssizidis, P. (2017). Personality strengths in romantic relationships: Measuring perceptions of benefits and costs and their impact on personal and relational well-being. *Psychological Assessment, online*, 1–18. doi: 10.1037/pas0000464

Kornfield, J. (1993). *A path with heart*. New York, NY: Bantam Books.

Kristeller, J. L., Wolever, R. Q., & Sheets, V. (2013). Mindfulness-based eating awareness training (MB-EAT) for binge eating: A randomized clinical trial. *Mindfulness*. doi: 10.1007/s12671-012-0179-1

Linley, A. (2008). *Average to A+: Realising strengths in yourself and others*. Coventry, UK: CAPP Press.

Littman-Ovadia, H., & Niemiec, R. M. (2017). Meaning, mindfulness, and character strengths. In P. Russo-Netzer, S. E. Schulenberg, & A. Batthyany (Eds.), *To thrive, to cope, to understand: Meaning in positive and existential psychology*. New York, NY: Springer.

Littman-Ovadia, H., & Steger, M. (2010). Character strengths and well-being among volunteers and employees: Toward an integrative model. *Journal of Positive Psychology*, 5(6), 419–430. doi: 10.1080/17439760.2010.516765

Lomas, T., Cartwright, T., Edginton, T., & Ridge, D. (2014). A qualitative analysis of experiential challenges associated with meditation practice. *Mindfulness*. doi: 10.1007/s12671-014-0329-8

Lottman, T., Zawaly, S., & Niemiec, R. M. (2017). Well-being and well-doing: Bringing mindfulness and character strengths to the early childhood classroom and home. In C. Proctor (Ed.), *Positive psychology interventions in practice*. New York, NY: Springer.

Lykins, E. (2014). *Mindfulness, character strengths, and well-being*. Presentation at the Society for Personality and Social Psychology, Austin, Texas. doi: 10.1037/e578192014-915

Meyers, M. C., van Woerkom, M., de Reuver, R., Bakk, Z., & Oberski, D. L. (2015). Enhancing psychological capital and personal growth initiative: Working on strengths or deficiencies? *Journal of Counseling Psychology*, 62(1), 50–62. http://doi.org/10.1037/cou0000050

Mirams, L., Poliakoff, E., Brown, R. J., & Lloyd, D. M. (2012). Brief body-scan meditation practice improves somatosensory perceptual decision making. *Consciousness and Cognition*, 22(1), 348–359.

Morales Cueto, C. (2017). Personal communication. January 10, 2017.

Neff, K. D. (2011). *Self-compassion: Stop beating yourself up and leave insecurity behind*. New York, NY: William Morrow.

Nhat Hanh, T. (1979). *The miracle of mindfulness: An introduction to the practice of meditation*. Boston, MA: Beacon.

Nhat Hanh, T. (1993). *For a future to be possible: Commentaries on the five mindfulness trainings*. Berkeley, CA: Parallax Press.

Niemiec, R. M. (2012). Mindful living: Character strengths interventions as pathways for the five mindfulness trainings. *International Journal of Wellbeing*, 2(1), 22–33. doi: 10.5502/ijw.v2i1.2

Niemiec, R. M. (2013). VIA character strengths: Research and practice (The first 10 years). In H. H. Knoop & A. Delle Fave (Eds.), *Well-being and cultures: Perspectives on positive psychology* (pp. 11–30). New York, NY: Springer.

Niemiec, R. M. (2014). *Mindfulness and character strengths: A practical guide to flourishing*. Cambridge, MA: Hogrefe.

Niemiec, R. M. (2014). Mindfulness-based strengths practice (MBSP) for physicians: Integrating core areas to promote positive health. In M. W. Snyder (Ed.), *Positive health: Flourishing lives, well-being in doctors* (pp. 247–263). Bloomington, IN: Balboa Press.

Niemiec, R. M. (2015). Mindfulness and character strengths: Advancing psychology to the next level. *New Jersey Psychologist*, 65(3), 22–24.

Niemiec, R. M. (2017). *Character strength interventions: A field-guide for practitioners*. Boston, MA: Hogrefe.

Niemiec, R. M., & Lissing, J. (2016). Mindfulness-based strengths practice (MBSP) for enhancing well-being, life purpose, and positive relationships. In I. Ivtzan & T. Lomas (Eds.), *Mindfulness in positive psychology: The science of meditation and wellbeing* (pp. 15–36). New York, NY: Routledge.

Niemiec, R. M., Rashid, T., & Spinella, M. (2012). Strong mindfulness: Integrating mindfulness and character strengths. *Journal of Mental Health Counseling, 34*(3), 240–253.

Niemiec, R. M., & Wedding, D. (2014). *Positive psychology at the movies: Using films to build character strengths and well-being*. Cambridge, MA: Hogrefe.

Pang, D., & Ruch, W. (2017). Personal communication. March 31, 2017.

Park, N., Peterson, C., & Seligman, M. E. P. (2004). Strengths of character and well-being. *Journal of Social and Clinical Psychology, 23*(5), 603–619.

Peterson, C., Ruch, W., Beerman, U., Park, N., & Seligman, M. E. P. (2007). Strengths of character, orientations to happiness, and life satisfaction. *The Journal of Positive Psychology, 2*(3), 149–156. doi: 10.1080/17439760701228938

Peterson, C., & Seligman, M. E. P. (2004). *Character strengths and virtues: A handbook and classification*. Oxford: Oxford University Press.

Salzberg, S. (1995). *Lovingkindness: The revolutionary art of happiness*. Boston, MA: Shambhala.

Segal, Z. V., Williams, J. M. G., & Teasdale, J. D. (2013). *Mindfulness-based cognitive therapy for depression: A new approach to preventing relapse* (2nd Ed.). New York, NY: Guilford.

Seligman, M. E. P. (2011). *Flourish*. London: Nicholas Brealey Publishing.

Seligman, M. E. P., Steen, T. A., Park, N., & Peterson, C. (2005). Positive psychology progress: Empirical validation of interventions. *American Psychologist, 60*, 410–421.

Sharp, J. E., Niemiec, R. M., & Lawrence, C. (2016). Using mindfulness-based strengths practices with gifted populations. *Gifted Education International*. doi: 10.1177/0261429416641009

Shogren, K. A., Singh, N., Niemiec, R. M., & Wehmeyer, M. (in press). Character strengths and mindfulness. In M. Wehmeyer (Ed.), *The Oxford handbook of positive psychology and disability*.

Stephenson, J. M., & Bretherton, R. (2017). *Mindfulness-Based Strengths Practice with 16–18 Year Olds in a UK School*. Unpublished Data.

Ussher, M., Spatz, A., Copland, C., Nicolaou, A., Cargill, A., Amini-Tabrizi, N., & McCracken, L. M. (2012). Immediate effects of a brief mindfulness-based body scan on patients with chronic pain. *Journal of Behavioral Medicine, 37*(1), 127–134.

VIA Institute for Character. (2016). *VIA Strengths Inventory*. Retrieved from www.viacharacter.org/www/

Wingert, H. (2017). Personal communication. April 26, 2017.

Chapter 31

Mindfulness Based Flourishing Program (positive mindfulness program)

Tarli Young and Itai Ivtzan

Overview of the Mindfulness Based Flourishing Program

Reducing negative cognitive and emotional responses is a worthy goal but it does not necessarily increase positive variables, which are an integral part of complete mental health (Keyes, 2002). As such, a complete theory of mindfulness must also include positive mental states (Garland, Farb, Goldin & Fredrickson, 2015). Positive psychology is a relatively new field which focuses on positive variables such as wellbeing (Lomas, Hefferon, & Ivtzan, 2014) and Positive Psychology Interventions (PPIs) which have been successfully used to strengthen those variables (Parks & Biswas-Diener, 2013). In this way, positive psychology can offer new perspectives on mindfulness (Shapiro, Schwartz, & Santerre, 2002).

Interestingly, many Western mindfulness programs which focus on reducing negative variables can also produce incidental improvements in positive variables such as positive affect, (Geschwind, Peeters, Drukker, Van Os, & Wichers, 2011) and interpersonal relationships (Goleman, 2006). It could therefore be suggested that, if existing deficit-focused programs increase positive variables, then it is unnecessary to have a mindfulness program specifically focused on positive outcomes. But this approach would miss the potential benefits of combining positive psychology and mindfulness to affect the *intention* participants bring to their mindfulness practice.

Shapiro, Carlson, Astin and Freedman (2006) proposed the Intention, Attention, and Attitude (IAA) model of mindfulness. They define intention as a practitioner's purpose in undertaking mindfulness practice and suggest that intentions are a vital component of mindfulness which affect the outcome of practice (Shapiro et al., 2006). The importance of intention is underscored in Shapiro's (1992) study showing the majority of meditators attained positive effects in line with their intentions. For example, if they aimed for self-exploration they were more likely to achieve self-exploration. These findings indicate that the intentions of a mindfulness program will affect its outcomes.

When prominent mindfulness programs such as the MBSR and the Mindfulness Based Cognitive Therapy program (MBCT) were developed, the primary intention was to decrease negative variables such as stress and depression (Kabat-Zinn, 1982; Teasdale et al., 2000). Conversely, the MBFP combines PPIs and mindfulness with the specific intention of increasing wellbeing and a range of positive variables. The MBFP thus provides a unique theoretical foundation for a relationship between PPIs and mindfulness, which is captured in the 'positive mindfulness cycle'.

Positive mindfulness cycle

We developed the *'positive mindfulness cycle'* to illustrate the mutual support PPIs and mindfulness provide each other, forming a cycle which leads to increased wellbeing (Ivtzan et al., 2016). This process allows mindfulness and PPIs to mutually enhance each other until they contribute more than the individual practices. The positive mindfulness cycle suggests the PPIs of each session shape the intention for the mindfulness practice of that session. For example, Session 3 on self-compassion includes a PPI that aims to increase self-compassion and also invites the participant to further explore the experience of self-compassion in the mindfulness practice that follows. Thus the PPIs in the MBFP set positive intentions for the mindfulness component of the program.

Mindfulness in turn supports the use of PPIs through the process of savouring. Savouring relates to generating and prolonging enjoyment and appreciation (Bryant & Veroff, 2007). It has been identified as a potential pathway between mindfulness and positive outcomes (Garland et al., 2015). Mindfulness enables us to monitor ongoing sensory and perceptual events, thereby helping us notice and appreciate and *savour* (Lindsay & Creswell, 2015). Savouring in turn increases practitioners' awareness of the positive outcomes triggered by PPIs. This is important because while PPIs often lead to the experience of positive events or emotions; without savouring, the practitioner may not be able to appreciate or prolong these positive outcomes. Mindfulness promotes savouring, which is required to fully utilise the benefits of PPIs. For example, when the PPI in Session 3 has increased self-compassion, mindfulness allows the practitioner to notice, appreciate, and prolong the benefits of self-compassion. Thus, through the positive mindfulness cycle, the PPIs and mindfulness in the MBFP continuously enhance each other, leading to greater increases in wellbeing than the individual practices. (To see a more detailed account of this cycle please see the original paper by Ivtzan and colleagues [2016].)

Structure of the MBFP

The MBFP is delivered online with eight sessions and a ninth concluding video. The sessions are completed over four weeks and combine mindfulness, PPIs, and recorded talks on positive psychology theory. Each of the eight sessions targets a different positive variable: (1) self-awareness, (2) positive emotions, (3) self-compassion, (4) self-efficacy (strengths), (5) autonomy, (6) meaning, (7) positive relations with others and (8) engagement.

By targeting these specific variables, the sessions are also designed to increase overall wellbeing. For example, we included the sessions on gratitude and engagement to enhance hedonic wellbeing, which emphasises the attainment of pleasure and pain avoidance (Deci & Ryan, 2008). The remaining positive variables were included to promote eudaimonic wellbeing; the wellbeing which comes from living in a meaningful and deeply satisfying manner (Ryan & Deci, 2001). Eudaimonic wellbeing is represented in the psychological wellbeing (PWB) model which includes six factors (Ryff & Keyes, 1995). Five of these are targeted in the MBFP sessions: self-acceptance (self-compassion), autonomy, environmental mastery (self-efficacy), purpose in life (meaning) and positive relations with others. The sixth PWB factor of personal growth is targeted throughout the entire program and discussed in the concluding video. Mindfulness promotes both hedonic (Brown & Cordon, 2009) and eudaimonic wellbeing (Brown, Ryan, & Creswell, 2007) in its own right and we sought to enhance this effect by specifically targeting these two types of wellbeing.

The eight sessions each include an eight- to ten-minute video and an audio file. The audio files include two aspects: a ten-minute meditation and a two-minute 'daily practice'. Table 31.1 provides full details on the session topics, videos, meditations and daily practices.

The videos feature an experienced trainer summarising the theoretical basis of the session's topic. To allow the reader of this chapter to experience a session, we have provided

Table 31.1 Outline of MBFP eight topics and activities

Session	Variable	Theory video	Meditation	Daily practice
1	Self-awareness	Introduction to mindfulness, self-awareness, positive psychology and meditation	Introductory meditation focusing on awareness of breath and body	Keeping aware of thoughts and reactions throughout the day
2	Positive emotions	Discussion of the benefits of positive emotions and gratitude	Gratitude meditation focusing on who or what one appreciates	Expressing gratitude for positive situations
3	Self-compassion	Explanation of the self-compassion concept, research and methods to increase self-compassion	Adapted version of Loving Kindness meditation focusing on self-compassion (Neff & Germer, 2013)	Replacing internal criticism with statements of kindness
4	Self-efficacy	Introduction to character strengths and self-efficacy including enhancement methods	Meditation focusing on a time when participant was at his/her best anstscharacter strengths	Completing the Values in Action character strengths survey (Peterson & Seligman, 2004) and using strengths
5	Autonomy	Introduction to autonomy and its connection with wellbeing	Meditation on authentic self and action	Taking action in line with one's values and noticing external pressure on choices
6	Meaning	Discussion of meaning and well-being. Completion of writing exercise, 'Best Possible Legacy' adapted from the Obituary Exercise (Seligman et al., 2006)	Meditation on future vision of self, living one's best possible legacy	Acting according to best possible legacy. Choosing meaningful activities
7	Positive relations	Discussion of benefits of positive relationships with others and methods for relationship enhancement	Loving Kindness Meditation	Bringing feelings of loving kindness into interactions

(Continued)

Table 31.1 (Continued)

Session	Variable	Theory video	Meditation	Daily practice
8	Engagement	Introduction to engagement and savouring and their connection with positive emotions	Savouring meditation focusing on food	Engagement

details on Session 2 below. This session is on positive emotions and the trainer in the video does the following:

- Defines emotions and describes the benefits of positive emotions
- Explains relevant theories such as the 'Broaden and Build' theory (Fredrickson, 2004) and negativity bias (Rozin & Royzman, 2001)
- Introduces the PPI of gratitude to be used to increase positive emotions
- Discusses different types of gratitude and outlines the benefits of gratitude
- Troubleshoots common problems with the gratitude intervention
- Invites the participant to proceed to the relevant audio file

Each video allows participants to understand the relevant theory while highlighting the benefits of the relevant variable to motivate practice. After the video, participants then continue to the audio file which includes a meditation and a 'daily practice'.

The meditations are central to the MBFP and provide mindfulness practices focused on the specific topic for that session, further developing ideas from the video talk. All meditations start with simple instructions on mindfulness of breath and then focus on that session's topic. Continuing with the example of Session 2 on positive emotions and gratitude; participants were first guided into a mindful state and then given the following instructions (punctuated by many pauses):

From this state of relaxation . . . allow yourself to ponder the question:

Who or what do I appreciate in my life right now?
Breathe in . . . and out . . . and ask yourself again. . .
Who or what do I appreciate in my life right now?
Notice the first thing that comes to mind and bring your attention here. . .
Continue to breathe, allowing yourself to focus on that first thing that came into your mind. . .
There are many things in life that we can be grateful for, but for this meditation try to focus on one aspect of your life that you appreciate in this moment. . .
Continue to breathe and focus on that one thing that came to your mind first. The thing you are grateful for in this moment . . . visualise it clearly and notice the feelings that arise in your body . . . breathe in . . . and out . . . and focus on gratitude. . .
Try not to focus on any thoughts . . . if thoughts arise, just let them pass . . . and come back to focusing on how you feel as you visualise something you are grateful for.
Breathing in . . . and breathing out . . . continue to picture this one thing that you appreciate in your life right now and notice how you are feeling. . .

Notice the sensations in your body as you focus on gratitude . . . breathe in . . . and out . . . observe these sensations and appreciate them. . .
Breathe in . . . and out . . . feeling gratitude for that one thing in your life that you are grateful for right now. . .
Watching with kindness and acceptance as you experience gratitude. . .

The meditation then ended with instructions about gently returning to the present moment; an ending used in all eight meditations. The meditations were all designed to blend mindfulness with a PPI, in this case, gratitude. They were at the core of the program and yet, a third element was required: daily practice.

The daily practice was included at the end of the audio file to invite participants to apply the insights gained from that session's video talk and meditation to their everyday lives. Meditation can have a greater influence once it becomes an integrated aspect of life rather than an island within our daily activities (e.g. Krishnamurti, 1975). The daily practice provided a bridge between the meditations and the participants' daily lives, allowing them to apply their meditative insights. While participants watched each video just once, they were invited to download the audio file and listen to it every day until the next session. Thus they regularly completed the meditations and daily practices.

Research on the MBFP

We have tested the MBFP extensively and it has led to consistently strong results. Here we will outline seven studies in various stages of publication. In our original study (Ivtzan et al., 2016) we used a randomised wait-list controlled trial and 168 participants (128 females, mean age = 40.82) took part. Participants were recruited to represent three groups: educators, office workers and meditators. Those with severe depression on Beck's Depression Inventory (Beck, Steer, Ball, & Ranieri, 1996) were screened from the study; a process that was completed in all subsequent studies due to research indicating that meditation can have adverse effects on severely depressed individuals (Shapiro, 1992).

The experimental participants who completed the MBFP showed a significant improvement in all 11 dependent variables: wellbeing, mindfulness, gratitude, self-compassion, autonomy, self-efficacy, presence of meaning, compassion for others, engagement, depression and perceived stress. At the one-month follow up, they had maintained their significant improvements in ten out of the 11 measurements (self-efficacy gains were not maintained) and interestingly their overall wellbeing had continued to increase. These results were very encouraging and indicated that the MBFP may be effective in enhancing participant wellbeing and other positive variables, and that participants may continue to benefit after the program ends.

One of the largest results in the study was the decreased levels of depression in the experimental group compared to the control group. In addition, participants with higher levels of depression gained more from the program. These results do not relate to participants with severe depression as they were screened out, but they are encouraging regarding the use of the MBFP for participants with mild depression. This supports the notion that Positive Psychology may also be suitable for individuals with psychological difficulties (Fava et al., 2005), by shifting people from 'languishing' towards 'flourishing' on the mental health continuum (Keyes, 2002).

This study demonstrated the efficacy of the new MBFP with a population that was mixed in age, income and location. This meant the results can be somewhat generalised to a wide population. But while participants came from twenty countries, the majority were from English-speaking Western cultures. Hence a key suggestion was for future research on the cross-cultural effects of the MBFP. We addressed this suggestion with a subsequent cross-cultural study.

Cross-cultural study

The cross-cultural study (Ivtzan, Young, Lee, Lomas, Daukantaitė, & Kjell, 2017) tested the MBFP with Hong Kong Chinese and British groups. This study took on the dual aim of trying to replicate the results of the previous study (Ivtzan et al., 2016), while also testing the MBFP with different cultures. We used a randomised wait-list controlled design with 115 participants (92 females, mean age = 31.50).

Both the British and the Hong Kong Chinese experimental groups showed significant improvements, with large effect sizes, in mindfulness, gratitude, self-compassion, meaning, and negative affect, but no significant changes in positive affect. The same five variables were also significantly higher for the two experimental groups at post-intervention when compared to their control counterparts.

We also compared the results of the British and Hong Kong Chinese experimental groups and results for both groups showed large effect sizes for mindfulness, self-compassion, meaning, and negative affect. These results suggest that the MBFP had a similar effect in both countries and supports the idea that the MBFP can be used across different cultures. Having established the MBFP with broad populations, we decided to test the program with a very specific population: business leaders.

Authentic leadership study

There is a growing level of interest in the development of mindfulness within an organisational context and there are many leadership theories that position mindfulness practice as a central component of authentic leadership (see Boyatzis & McKee, 2005). Our study used a randomised waitlist control trial with 80 Australian business leaders. Variables tested included: mindfulness, self-esteem, dispositional authenticity, and work-based meaning. The experimental participants showed significant improvements in all dependent variables with the exception of self-esteem. They also showed significant improvements in the same three variables when compared to the control group. These promising results indicate that participation in the MBFP can have beneficial effects for leaders. This is important because boosting the wellbeing of leaders can have flow-on effects for the employees and organisations they lead (Nielsen & Daniels, 2012).

Unpublished studies

In addition to the above studies, there have been four studies which we are preparing for publication. While these have not yet been peer-reviewed, they provide us with new information about the MBFP. For example, Ivtzan, Young and Logeswaran (2017) tested the MBFP with prehypertensive adults. Prehypertension is a precursor to hypertension and refers to 'borderline' or 'high-normal' blood pressure readings which increase the risk of cardiovascular disease (Chobanian et al., 2003). The study included self-report measures of perceived stress, self-compassion, self-efficacy and physical symptoms. It also measured participant's blood pressure, making it the first study of the MBFP to use an objective measure related to physical health. A total of 42 participants were involved in this randomised wait-list control trial. Experimental participants exhibited a significant reduction in systolic blood pressure (rate during heart contraction) and perceived stress as a result of the programme. Reductions in systolic blood pressure were comparable with other interventions (e.g. Hughes et al., 2013). However, there were no significant changes in diastolic blood pressure (rate during heart relaxation) and the other self-report measures.

While diastolic blood pressure did not change, systolic blood pressure can be used as the primary indication of prehypertension (Kannel, Gordon, & Schwartz, 1971) and it is often viewed as more important as there is a stronger association between systolic blood pressure and chronic heart disease and the importance of systolic blood pressure increases over the lifespan (Kannel et al., 1971). This suggests that by helping to control systolic blood pressure, the MBFP may provide a new way of improving blood pressure.

These results are promising given that high blood pressure is a major risk factor for medical conditions, accounting for up to 62% of stroke cases and 49% of coronary heart disease cases (World Health Organisation, 2002). Poor blood pressure control results in 9.4 million deaths worldwide per year (Lim et al., 2012). The effect of the MBFP supports previous research which found positive variables such as positive emotions and self-compassion can reduce blood pressure (e.g. Cosley et al., 2010; Ostir et al., 2006). The reductions in perceived stress in the study participants was suggested as a pathway of change between the MBFP and blood pressure as reduced stress through mindfulness programs has been associated with BP reduction (e.g. Carlson et al., 2007; Hughes et al., 2013).

The second unpublished study also examined stress but focused on office workers and workplace stress (Ivtzan, Young, & Verkest, 2017). For this study we used a randomised waitlist control trial. The primary dependent variable was perceived stress and secondary dependent variables included: mindfulness, work engagement, and meaningfulness of work. These variables were tested with self-report scales pre- and post-intervention. 37 participants completed the study and the experimental group showed significant improvements in the primary dependent variable of perceived stress, and the secondary dependent variable of mindfulness. The experimental group also showed non-significant increases in levels of perceived work meaning and work engagement.

These results suggest the MBFP could be an effective programme to reduce workplace stress which would be beneficial for both workers and organisations given the high rates of stress-related illness and the workplace costs of stress (EU-OSHA, 2014). The result is particularly promising given the MBFP requires only 1.6 hours per session and is delivered online; making it a low cost and flexible option for organisations where costs and time are often central concerns.

As the MBFP had been tested multiple times in organisational setting, the final two unpublished studies aimed to test the program with a very different population: athletes. The first of these focused on elite athletes and examined the effect of the MBFP on 25 Muay Thai fighters (Ivtzan, Young, & Bakhshov, 2017) with a randomised control trial. When compared to the control group at post-intervention, the experimental group had significantly higher levels of mindfulness, flow, psychological skills, and self-efficacy. There was also a significant decrease in amotivation but no significant increase in levels of intrinsic motivation.

The second athlete study examined whether the MBFP could increase the quality of physical training among non-professional athletes who exercise on the regular basis (Ivtzan, Young, & Matvejeva, 2017). Specifically, we measured sports motivation, training satisfaction and exercise self-efficacy in a randomised wait-list control trial. 38 participants completed the study and showed significant improvements in motivation and training satisfaction compared to the control group, but no significant difference in exercise self-efficacy.

Taken together, these two studies suggest the MBFP may be a useful intervention for improving athletes' levels of mindfulness, flow, psychological skills, self-efficacy, motivation and training satisfaction. These results support existing research which shows that mindfulness interventions can have positive outcomes for those involved in sport (Gardner & Moore, 2004; Thompson, Kaufman, De Petrillo, Glass, & Arnkoff, 2011). By including both professional and non-professional athletes in these studies, we can suggest that the MBFP can be used with a wide range of individuals undertaking physical exercise.

Limitations and future studies

While we have seen many promising results while studying the application of MBFP, there are areas which warrant further exploration. A key limitation is that the program has only been compared to wait-list control groups. This does not control for nonspecific effects of the MBFP such as online learning, demand characteristics and expectancy effects (Grossman et al., 2004). To explore these effects future trials should also include an active control, such as an online educational course. To help address this issue, we are currently undertaking a comparison study, to compare the MBFP to an existing face-to-face positive psychology program. This will help us ascertain whether the MBFP can be as effective as well-established positive psychology interventions. Given the MBFP was created to complement existing mindfulness programs, it would also be useful to compare the MBFP with a mindfulness program such as the MBSR. This is another aim for future studies. In considering comparisons with existing mindfulness programs, one possible advantage of the MBFP is its ability to offer support without a focus on pathology. Given the unfortunate stigma around mental health issues, the MBFP focus on wellbeing may make it more appealing to the general population. As such it would be interesting to explore the factors and barriers (such as stigma) that individuals consider when choosing between different mindfulness programs.

Another area for future research is the addition of objective measures to reduce reliance on self-report scales. One existing study of the MBFP measured blood pressure and showed successful effects (Ivtzan, Young, & Logeswaran, 2017). This result indicates the self-report scales are reflecting a real change in MBFP participants and it would be useful to have more research which includes objective measures of physical health or behaviour change. Partly in response to this issue we are currently testing the MBFP in a large health organisation and measuring the program's effect on workplace outcomes such as sick leave levels. This will provide us with an objective measure while also tracking outcomes for an institution in addition to individual participants. This is important as positive psychology has been criticised for focusing heavily on individual-level outcomes (Wong, 2011) and we hope this study will help address these concerns.

Another problem that has recurred throughout our research is high levels of attrition. This is common in online interventions (e.g. Ouweneel et al., 2013) and may be addressed with in-person delivery. Future research could test the program in a face-to-face format. On the other hand, the online delivery is also a key strength of the MBFP as it means the program is inexpensive to deliver, does not require a trained facilitator, and can be delivered to people in the familiar settings of their own homes (Krusche et al., 2012). This means the program can be delivered to large populations worldwide.

Delivering the MBFP to large and varied populations is particularly important since participants experienced significant changes in levels of depression. Mental health systems are under heavy pressure to deliver more for less (Kuyken, 2011) and people can go untreated due to the high cost of other interventions (Layous, Chancellor, Lyubomirsky, Wang, & Doraiswamy, 2011). Given this situation and rising levels of depression, online programs such as the MBFP may assist over-burdened healthcare systems (Krusche et al., 2012). As such, a key future area for research is to test the efficacy of the MBFP with depressed individuals.

Addressing concerns

Mindfulness interventions focused on positive variables (such as the MBFP) commonly attract concern that the intervention may generate an attachment to pleasant or positive experiences, leading to potential suffering when the positive experience inevitably fades (Garland et al., 2015). However, effective and established mindfulness interventions such as the Mindfulness Based Stress Reduction program (MBSR) were developed to reduce negative states such as stress (e.g. Kabat-Zinn, 1982) but do not teach an aversion to such states, instead encouraging a non-judgemental and open relationship with these experiences. The intention set by the program does not change the key mindfulness components which are taught. Similarly, the MBFP sets the intention of increasing wellbeing and at the same time teaches participants to have a non-attached, open relationship with their experiences; thereby strengthening the practitioner's capacity to let go of any potential attachment.

A related common concern is that mindfulness programs emphasising positive variables do not align with the original Buddhist context of mindfulness. Addressing this concern, Wallace and Shapiro (2006) state that, 'A common misperception is that Buddhism uniformly denies the value of stimulus-driven pleasures, as if it morally wrong to enjoy the simple pleasures of life' (p. 692). Positive outcomes are a natural part of mindfulness practice and Carlson (2015) indicates they are not a concern, as long as the intentions and savouring of positive outcomes are accompanied and balanced by equanimity and non-attachment. She further suggests that awareness of impermanence allows beauty and non-attached joy because the practitioner knows the positive experiences will fade away and change. This non-attached attitude is an important component taught within the MBFP and allows participants to experience positive states while simultaneously reducing attachment.

Conclusion

Creating and testing the MBFP has been an encouraging process for us. We aimed to develop a mindfulness intervention with the specific purpose of increasing wellbeing, and the results to date have been promising. Our studies suggest that the MBFP could complement existing mindfulness programs and be used to increase positive outcomes such as wellbeing, while also decreasing variables such as depression. This is particularly promising since the intervention is delivered online and could be made available to a large and varied population. We hope that future studies will help us continue to strengthen the program and allow broader testing so the MBFP may be beneficial for a wide range of participants.

References

Bach, P., & Hayes, S. C. (2002). The use of acceptance and commitment therapy to prevent the rehospitalization of psychotic patients: A randomized controlled trial. *Journal of Consulting and Clinical Psychology, 70*(5), 1129.

Beck, A. T., Steer, R. A., Ball, R., & Ranieri, W. F. (1996). Comparison of beck depression inventories-IA and -II in psychiatric outpatients. *Journal of Personality Assessment, 67*(3), 588–597.

Boyatzis, R. E., & McKee, A. (2005). *Resonant leadership: Renewing yourself and connecting with others through mindfulness, hope, and compassion*. Boston, MA: Harvard Business Press.

Brown, K. W., & Cordon, S. (2009). Toward a phenomenology of mindfulness: Subjective experience and emotional correlates. In *Clinical handbook of mindfulness* (pp. 59–81). New York, NY: Springer.

Brown, K. W., & Ryan, R. M. (2003). The benefits of being present: Mindfulness and its role in psychological well-being. *Journal of Personality and Social Psychology, 84*(4), 822–848.

Brown, K. W., Ryan, R. M., & Creswell, J. D. (2007). Mindfulness: Theoretical foundations and evidence for its salutary effects. *Psychological Inquiry, 18*(4), 211–237.

Bryant, F. B., & Veroff, J. (2007). *Savoring: A new model of positive experience*. Mahwah, NJ: Lawrence Erlbaum Associates, Inc.

Carlson, L. E. (2015). The mindfulness-to-meaning theory: Putting a name to clinical observations. *Psychological Inquiry, 26*(4), 322–325.

Carlson, L. E., Speca, M., Faris, P., & Patel, K. D. (2007). One year pre – post intervention follow-up of psychological, immune, endocrine and blood pressure outcomes of mindfulness-based stress reduction (MBSR) in breast and prostate cancer outpatients. *Brain, Behavior and Immunity, 21*(8), 1038–1049.

Cosley, B. J., McCoy, S. K., Saslow, L. R., & Epel, E. S. (2010). Is compassion for others stress buffering? Consequences of compassion and social support for physiological reactivity to stress. *Journal of Experimental Social Psychology, 46*(5), 816–823.

Deci, E. L., & Ryan, R. M. (2008). Hedonia, eudaimonia, and well-being: An introduction. *Journal of Happiness Studies, 9*(1), 1–11.

EU-OSHA. (2014). *Report-calculating the cost of work-related stress and psychosocial risks*. Retrieved from https://osha.europa.eu/en/tools-and-publications/publications/literature_reviews/calculating-the-cost-of-work-related-stress-and-psychosocial-risks.

Fava, G. A., Ruini, C., Rafanelli, C., Finos, L., Salmaso, L., Mangelli, L., & Sirigatti, S. (2005). Well-being therapy of generalized anxiety disorder. *Psychotherapy and Psychosomatics, 74*, 26–30.

Forette, F., Seux, M., & Staessen, J. (1998). Prevention of dementia in randomised double-blind placebo controlled systolic hypertension in Europe (Syst-Eur) trial. *The Lancet, 352*, 1346–1351.

Fredrickson, B. L. (2004). The broaden-and-build theory of positive emotions. *Philosophical Transactions of the Royal Society B: Biological Sciences, 359*(1449), 1367.

Gardner, F. L., & Moore, Z. E. (2004). A Mindfulness-Acceptance-Commitment (MAC) based approach to performance enhancement: Theoretical considerations. *Behavior Therapy, 35*, 707–723.

Garland, E. L., Farb, N. A., Goldin, P., & Fredrickson, B. L. (2015). Mindfulness broadens awareness and builds eudaimonic meaning at the attention- appraisal-emotion interface: A process model of mindful positive emotion regulation. *Psychological Inquiry, 26*(4), 293–314.

Geschwind, N., Peeters, F., Drukker, M., Van Os, J., & Wichers, M. (2011). Mindfulness training increases momentary positive emotions and reward experience in adults vulnerable to depression: A randomized controlled trial. *Journal of Consulting and Clinical Psychology, 79*, 618–628.

Goleman, D. (2006). *Social intelligence: The new science of human relationships*. New York, NY: Bantam.

Grossman, P., Niemann, L., Schmidt, S., & Walach, H. (2004). Mindfulness-based stress reduction and health benefits: A meta-analysis. *Journal of Psychosomatic Research, 57*(1), 35–43.

Hanh, T. N. (1991). *Peace is every step: The path of mindfulness in everyday life*. New York, NY: Bantam.

Harmell, A. L., Mausbach, B. T., Roepke, S. K., Moore, R. C., von Känel, R., Patterson, T. L., . . . Grant, I. (2011). The relationship between self-efficacy and resting blood pressure in spousal Alzheimer's caregivers. *British Journal of Health Psychology, 16*(2), 317–328.

Hughes, J. W., Fresco, D. M., Myerscough, R., van Dulmen, M. H., Carlson, L. E., & Josephson, R. (2013). Randomized controlled trial of mindfulness-based stress reduction for prehypertension. *Psychosomatic Medicine, 75*(8), 721–728.

Ivtzan, I., & Lomas, T. (2016). *Mindfulness in positive psychology: The science of meditation and wellbeing*. London: Routledge.

Ivtzan, I., Young, T., & Bakhshov, I. (2017). *The effect of a Positive Mindfulness Programme (PMP) on athletes' flow, motivation, self-efficacy and psychological skills: An 8-week randomised controlled trial*. Unpublished manuscript.

Ivtzan, I., Young, T., Lee, H. C., Lomas, T., Daukantaitė, D., & Kjell, O. (in press). Mindfulness based flourishing program: A cross-cultural study of Hong Kong Chinese and British participants. *Journal of Happiness Studies*.

Ivtzan, I., Young, T., & Logeswaran, S. (2017). *Outcomes of the mindfulness based flourishing program for prehypertensive adults*. Unpublished manuscript.

Ivtzan, I., Young, T., Martman, J., Jeffrey, A., Lomas, T., Hart, R., & Eiroa-Orosa, F. J. (2016). Integrating mindfulness into positive psychology: A randomised controlled trial of an online positive mindfulness program. *Mindfulness, 7*(6), 1396–1407.

Ivtzan, I., Young, T., & Matvejeva, J. (2017). *Effects of mindfulness based flourishing program on the of quality physical training*. Unpublished manuscript.

Ivtzan, I., Young, T., & Verkest, E. (2017). *The effect of the mindfulness based flourishing program on stress levels at work*. Unpublished manuscript.

Kabat-Zinn, J. (1982). An outpatient program in behavioral medicine for chronic pain patients based on the practice of mindfulness meditation: Theoretical considerations and preliminary results. *General Hospital Psychiatry, 4*(1), 33–47.

Kannel, W. B., Gordon, T., & Schwartz, M. J. (1971). Systolic versus diastolic blood pressure and risk of coronary heart disease: The Framingham study. *The American Journal of Cardiology, 27*(4), 335–346.

Keyes, C. L. (2002). The mental health continuum: From languishing to flourishing in life. *Journal of Health and Social Behavior*, 207–222.

Krishnamurti, J. (1975). *Freedom from the known*. London: HarperOne.

Krusche, A., Cyhlarova, E., King, S., & Williams, J. M. G. (2012). Mindfulness online: A preliminary evaluation of the feasibility of a web-based mindfulness course and the impact on stress. *BMJ Open, 2*(3).

Kuyken, W. (2011). *Mindfulness training in the UK*. Reykjavik, Iceland: 41st Annual European Association for Behavioural and Cognitive Therapies (EABCT) Conference.

Layous, K., Chancellor, J., Lyubomirsky, S., Wang, L., & Doraiswamy, P. (2011). Delivering happiness: Translating positive psychology inter-vention research for treating major and minor depressive disorders. *The Journal of Alternative and Complementary Medicine, 17*(8), 675–683.

Lim, S. S., Vos, T., Flaxman, A. D., Danaei, G., Shibuya, K., Adair-Rohani, H., . . . Wilkinson, J. D. (2012). A comparative risk assessment of burden of disease and injury attributable to 67 risk factors and risk factor clusters in 21 regions, 1990–2010: A systematic analysis for the Global Burden of Disease Study 2010. *The Lancet, 380*(9859), 2224–2260.

Lindsay, E. K., & Creswell, J. D. (2015). Back to the basics: How attention monitoring and acceptance stimulate positive growth. *Psychological Inquiry, 26*(4), 343–348.

Lomas, T., Hefferon, K., & Ivtzan, I. (2014). *Applied positive psychology: Integrated positive practice*. London: Sage Publications.

Neff, K. D., & Germer, C. K. (2013). A pilot study and randomized controlled trial of the mindful self-compassion program. *Journal of Clinical Psychology, 69*(1), 28–44.

Nielsen, K., & Daniels, K. (2012). Does shared and differentiated transformational leadership predict followers' working conditions and well-being? *The Leadership Quarterly, 23*(3), 383–397.

Parks, A. C., & Biswas-Diener, R. (2013). Positive interventions: Past, present and future. In T. Kashdan & J. Ciarrochi (Eds.), *Mindfulness, acceptance and positive psychology: The seven foundations of well-being* (pp. 140–165). Oakland, CA: Context Press.

Peterson, C., & Seligman, M. E. P. (2004). *Character strengths and virtues: A handbook and classification.* New York, NY: Oxford University Press; and Washington, DC: American Psychological Association.

Ostir, G. V., Berges, I. M., Markides, K. S., & Ottenbacher, K. J. (2006). Hypertension in older adults and the role of positive emotions. *Psychosomatic Medicine, 68*(5), 727–733.

Ouweneel, E., Le Blanc, P. M., & Schaufeli, W. B. (2013). Do-it-yourself: An online positive psychology intervention to promote positive emotions, self-efficacy, and engagement at work. *Career Development International, 18*(2), 173–195.

Seligman, M. E., & Csikszentmihalyi, M. (2014). Positive psychology: An introduction. In *Flow and the foundations of positive psychology* (pp. 279–298). Netherlands: Springer.

Seligman, M. E. P., Rashid, T., & Parks, A. C. (2006). Positive psychotherapy. *American Psychologist, 61*, 774–788.

Shapiro, D. H. (1992). A preliminary study of long term meditators: Goals, effects, religious orientation, cognitions. *Journal of Transpersonal Psychology, 24*(1), 23–39.

Shapiro, S. L., Carlson, L. E., Astin, J. A., & Freedman, B. (2006). Mechanisms of mindfulness. *Journal of Clinical Psychology, 62*(3), 373–386.

Shapiro, S. L., Schwartz, G. E., & Santerre, C. (2002). Meditation and positive psychology. *Handbook of Positive Psychology, 2*, 632–645.

Rozin, P., & Royzman, E. B. (2001). Negativity bias, negativity dominance, and contagion. *Personality and Social Psychology Review, 5*(4), 296–320.

Ryan, R. M., & Deci, E. L. (2001). On happiness and human potentials: A review of research on hedonic and eudaimonic well-being. *Annual Review of Psychology, 52*(1), 141–166.

Ryff, C. D., & Keyes, C. L. M. (1995). The structure of psychological well-being revisited. *Journal of Personality and Social Psychology, 69*(4), 719.

Teasdale, J. D., Segal, Z. V., Williams, J. M. G., Ridgeway, V. A., Soulsby, J. M., & Lau, M. A. (2000). Prevention of relapse/recurrence in major depression by mindfulness-based cognitive therapy. *Journal of Consulting and Clinical Psychology, 68*(4), 615.

Thompson, R. W., Kaufman, K. A., De Petrillo, L. A., Glass, C. R., & Arnkoff, D. B. (2011). One year follow-up of mindful sport performance enhancement (MSPE) with archers, golfers, and runners. *Journal of Clinical Sport Psychology, 5*(2), 99–116.

Wallace, B. A., & Shapiro, S. L. (2006). Mental balance and well-being: Building bridges between Buddhism and Western Psychology. *American Psychologist, 61*(7), 690–701.

Wong, P. T. P. (2011). Positive psychology 2.0. *Canadian Psychology, 52*(2), 69–81.

World Health Organisation. (2002). *World Health Report 2002 – Reducing Risks, promoting healthy life*. Geneva: Switzerland. Retrieved from www.who.int/whr/2002.

Index

Note: Page numbers bold indicate a table and page numbers in italic indicate a figure on the corresponding page.

500 Calorie Challenge 199

acceptance 8, 9, 12–13, 33–34, 174, 206–207
Acceptance and Commitment Therapy (ACT) 7; acceptance 8, 9, 12–13; cognitive defusion 13–14; committed action 15–16; creative hopelessness 12; dropping emotional control and preparing for acceptance 11–12; effective action 7; empirical support 10; functional contextualism 7; "Leaves on a stream" exercise 14; metaphors used in 13; mindfulness 8; online resources 16; in practice 10–11; present moment awareness 14; psychological flexibility 9–10; self as context 14; sessions 11–12; values 15; willingness 12
accessibility: of Mindfulness-Based Cancer Recovery 165; of Still Quiet Place program 279
active listening 224–225
activities: in the Mindful Self-Compassion (MSC) program 361–362; in the Mindfulness-Based Cognitive Therapy for Children (MBCT-C) program 285–290; in the Mindfulness-Based Strengths Practice (MBSP) programme **397**; in the Mindfulness-Based Therapy for Insomnia (MBTI) program **207–208**
adaptations: for dialectical behavior therapy (DBT) 19–20; of the Mindful Self-Compassion (MSC) program 364–365; of the Mindfulness-Based Relapse Prevention (MBRP) program 349
addiction 327; mindfulness training as treatment for 342; negative reinforcement 343; positive reinforcement 343; Relapse Prevention (RP) 343; theoretical models 328; treatments 342; triggers 327
addiction programmes 2; *see also* Mindfulness-Based Relapse Prevention (MBRP); Mindfulness-Oriented Recovery Enhancement (MORE)
addictive automaticity 327
adho mukha svanasana 117
adolescents: effectiveness of Still Quiet Place 277–278; Learning to BREATHE (L2B) 241; Mindfulness-Based Strengths Practice (MBSP) 394, 397; *see also* Learning to BREATHE (L2B); Still Quiet Place
adverse childhood experiences (ACEs) 54–55
aging 123; and MBIs 126
Akiva, T. 73
alcohol dependence, effectiveness of Mindfulness-Oriented Recovery Enhancement (MORE) on 331
all-day retreat session (MBRE) 109
allostatic load 53, 56, 327, 329; *see also* stress
Alzheimer's Disease (AD) 125; mindfulness programs for 133–134
amygdala 35
anterior cingulate cortex (ACC) 56–57, 59
anxiety 284; allostatic load 53; *see also* allostatic load; stress
applied behavior analysis 43
archers, mindful sport performance enhancement (MSPE) for 183
artwork exercise 151
assisted living: practicing mindfulness at ISRAA 129–130; working with elders in 130, **131**
Association for Contextual Behavioral Science (ACBS) 16
Astin, J. 403
athletics *see* sports
attachment insight 318
attention 29, 162; and concentration 176; hyperfixation of 327; Learning to BREATHE (L2B) program 247; strengthening the muscle of 180–181
attentional control 56; Contact Point Exercise 58

attitude 29
"Attractive Nuisance" 319
attunement 146
authentic leadership study, Mindfulness Based Flourishing Program (MBFP) 408
automatic pilot parenting 97
automaticity, addictive 327
autonomic nervous system 167–168
awareness 12, 290, 314, 344, 363, 394; body 223–224; and MBCP pain practices 84–85; One-Mindfulness 21; presentness 145; *sati* 46; triangle of *147*; *see also* mindfulness

backdraft 359, 369
baddha konasana 116
Baer, R. 244, 388
Bakosh, L. 251, 252
balasana 117
Bardacke, N. 113
Barrack, N. 79
Beall, B. 174
"beginner's mind" 32, 33, 36; parenting 97
Behavior Rating Inventory on Executive Functions (BRIEF) 236–237
behavioral addictions, effectiveness of Mindfulness-Oriented Recovery Enhancement (MORE) on 333
Behavioral Assessment Interview Questions 44, **44**, **45**
behavioral interventions 42, 43
Behavioral Regulation Index 237
Belly Breathing exercise 260–261
Benn, R. 73
binge eating disorder (BED) 195; and eating regulation theory 194–195
Birrer, D. 174
Bishop, S. R. 386
Bluth, K. 364
body awareness 223–224
body satiety 195
body scans 81, 161, 166, 180, 209, 224, 245, 254, 269
body-based trauma therapy 56
Bogels, S. 97
Bohy, N. 109
borderline personality disorder 18, 19; dialectical behavior therapy (DBT) 19
bound angle pose (*baddha konasana*) 116
brahmaviharas 376
BREATHE (Body, Reflections, Emotions, Attention, Tenderness/Take it As It Is, Habits for a Healthy Mind, leading to Empowerment) 241; and the Learning to BREATHE (L2B) program 245–248
breathing 167–168; diaphragmatic 180, 181; Learning to BREATHE (L2B) program 245;

limits imagination exercise 101; MBCP pain practices 84–85; Mindful Self-Compassion (MSC) exercises 363–364; Mindfulness-Based Compassionate Living (MBCL) programme 378–379; seated meditation on 116
Briscoe, C. 391
Broderick, P. 241, 242, 243
Buber, M. 145
Buddhism 64, 66, 129, 133, 136, 160, 176–177, 192, 220, 322, 368, 371, 411; and MBIs 123; *metta* 224; self-compassion 358; traditions 67; *see also* mindfulness
building mindfulness fundamentals 179–180
burnout 226; in teachers 219–220
But for Pause practice 320

CALM intervention 115
cancer patients 161
caregivers 123; in behavioral interventions 42, 43; formal 124; inclusion 145; informal 124; MBEC for 128–129; MBIs for 125–126; and Mindful Medical Practice (MMP) 156; Mindful Medical Practice (MMP) participants 151–153; Mindfulness-Based Living Course (MBLC) 131, 132–133; Mindfulness-Based Positive Behavior Support (MBPBS) training program 48; stepped care 43–44; stress in 126; well-being of 42–43
Carlson, L. E. 160, 403, 411
Carson, R. L. 105
cat/cow pose 117
centering 224
CenteringPregnancy (CP) 89
CenteringPregnancy with Mindfulness Skills (CPMS); *see also* expectant families; pregnancy
chaining 199
chair yoga 200
character strengths 386, 387, 388; cultivating 389; integrating with mindfulness 388–389
Character Strengths 360 exercise 396
Chaskalson, M. 131
check-in, M-Yoga 115
childbirth 79, 81; effectiveness of Still Quiet Place 275–276; pain practices (MBCP) 82, 83–87; *see also* Mindfulness-Based Childbirth and Parenting (MBCP); pain practices (MBCP)
children 2, 267; ACEs 54–55; and trauma 280; *see also* adolescents; Mindfulness-Based Cognitive Therapy for Children (MBCT-C); Still Quiet Place
chronic insomnia 204
chronic pain: Dolomite project 134–135; effectiveness of Mindfulness-Oriented Recovery Enhancement (MORE) on 331–332,

336; studies of Mindfulness-Based Stress Reduction (MBSR) on 34; *see also* pain practices (MBCP)
Chukwu, O. C. 231, 238
classes: mindful-based social emotional learning (MBSEL) impact on 259; Mindfulness-Based Childbirth and Parenting (MBCP) 81–82; in the Mindfulness-Based Emotional Balance (MBEB) program 67, **68–69**; Still Quiet Place **270–272**; *see also* sessions
classroom effects of Mindfulness-Based Emotional Balance (MBEB) 72
Coccia, M. A. 225
Cognitive and Affective Mindfulness Scale 130
Cognitive Behavioral Therapy (CBT) 18, 19, 126, 199, 328
cognitive defusion 13–14
cognitive loss, in elders 125
Cognitive Stimulation Lab 131
Cognitive-Behavior Therapy for Insomnia (CBT-I) 204–205; *see also* Mindfulness-Based Therapy for Insomnia (MBTI)
Cohn, M. A. 146
Collaborative for Academic, Social and Emotional Learning (CASEL) 221, 241
college athletes, mindful sport performance enhancement (MSPE) for 184–186
Collins, D. 177
committed action 10, 15–16
common humanity 146
community and assisted living dwelling elders, Mindfulness-Based Elder Care (MBEC) for 127
compassion 3, 34, 65, 99, 290, 370; defining 369–370; and health 374–375; self- 93; *see also* Mindful Self-Compassion (MSC); Mindfulness-Based Compassionate Living (MBCL)
Compassion Focused Therapy (CFT) 368
compulsive overeating, eating regulation theory 193–195
concentration 176
conditioned behaviors 344
connecting 149
consciousness 160; normal state of 1
Contact Point Exercise 58
contemplative practices 66–67; *see also* meditation; mindfulness
contextual psychotherapies 7
Continuing Legal Education (CLE) Program 315–316
contractions, MBCP pain practices 82, 83–87
control 86
coping mechanisms 54, 168; emotion-focused 161
core mindfulness themes and practices, Mindful Parenting program 97–98

core performance facilitators 176–178, 180–181; concentration 176; establishing a sense of harmony and rhythm 177; forming key associations 177–178; letting go 176–177; relaxation 177
couples: Mindfulness-Based Relationship Enhancement (MBRE) 106–107; *see also* Mindfulness-Based Relationship Enhancement (MBRE); relationships
course outline, Still Quiet Place 269, 272
Cranfield Leadership programme 297–298; *see also* Mindful Leadership
craving 334
creative hopelessness 12
cross-cultural study, Mindfulness Based Flourishing Program (MBFP) 408
Csikszentmihalyi, M. 175
Cullen, C. 64, 65, 71
cultivating: character strengths 389; mindfulness 29; observation 33
Cultivating Awareness and Resilience in Education (CARE) for Teachers 219, 221; caring and listening practices 224–225; emotion skills instruction 222–223; intention setting 222; mindful awareness practices (MAPs) 223–224; mindful listening 224–225; program structure 221–222; Prosocial Classroom Model 221; research support for 225–227; scripts 223, 225; self-care 222; social validity assessments 227; theoretical background 221
Cultivating Emotional Balance (CEB) program 64, 64–65, 220, 221
curriculum: Mindful Tool Kit (MTK) **233–234**; *see also* sessions

D2 Test of Attention 130
daily practice, Still Quiet Place 278–279
daytime fatigue 211
decentering 282–283, 330
decision-making, mindful 309
deep well analogy of Wise Mind 23
defusion 9, 374
depression 244, 368; and eating regulation theory 195–196; in the elderly 125; in expectant women 113, 114; and the Mindfulness Based Flourishing Program (MBFP) 407–408; postpartum 80, 112; *see also* M-Yoga
describing without judgment 23–24
designing PBS plans 45, **45**
Desmond, C. 231, 233, 235, 238
dharma 67
diabetes prevention, and the Learning to BREATHE (L2B) program 244
dialectical behavior therapy (DBT) 18, 199, 282; adaptations 19–20; brining attention to

the present moment 22–23; central dialectic in 19; Describe skill 22–23; describing without judgment 23–24; distress tolerance skills 22; Emotion Regulation skills 22; Emotional Mind 18; exercises 22–25; "How" skills 21; interpersonal effectiveness skills 22; Mindfulness 5-5-5 exercise 22–23; Observe skill 24–25; One-Mindfulness 21; online resources 25; outpatient program 20; Reasonable Mind 18; "What" skills 21; Wise Mind 18, 19, 20, 21–22, 22, 22–23, 23, 25
diaphragmatic breathing 180, 181
dieting 199–200; Mindfulness-Based Eating Awareness Training (MB-EAT) 192–193, 195–196
Direction-Alignment-Commitment (DAC) model 309–310
distractions 24
distress tolerance skills 242–243
Dobkin, P. L. 145
Dolomite project 134–135
downward facing dog (*adho mukha svanasana*) 117
drive system 372, 373
duality, of activity and attention 1–2
Duan, W. 390
Duncan, L. 79

eating, and mindfulness 191
eating regulation theory 193–195
education programmes 2; *see also* Cultivating Awareness and Resilience in Education (CARE) for Teachers; Learning to BREATHE (L2B); mindful-based social emotional learning (MBSEL); Mindfulness-Based Emotional Balance (MBEB); Wellness Works in Schools (WWiS)
effective action 7
eight-week MBPS program 49
Ekman, P. 64, 65, 66
elders: in assisted living 131; bringing MBIs to 123–124; caregiving 124; cognitive loss 125; and depression 125; Dolomite project 134–135; MBIs for 124–125, 125–126; mindfulness programs for AD sufferers 133–134; Mindfulness-Based Elder Care (MBEC) 125, 126–127; practicing mindfulness at ISRAA 129–130
embedded mindful-based social emotional learning (MBSEL) programs 260
embodiment 33, 182; of mindfulness 242
emergence of the Mindfulness-Based Emotional Balance (MBEB) program 65
emotion regulation systems 371, 372
Emotional Mind 18

emotions 246; attunement 146; and eating regulation theory 193–195; Four Rs, the 223; integrating with mindfulness 66–67; joy 69–70; negative 93; skills instruction, CARE program 222–223; universal 65
empathy 106, 369–370; inclusion 145
empirical support: for Acceptance and Commitment Therapy (ACT) 10; for Mindful Medical Practice (MMP) 153–154, 155, 156; for mindful sport performance enhancement (MSPE) 183–186; for the mindful-based social emotional learning (MBSEL) program 255; for Mindfulness-Based Cancer Recovery 162–164; for M-Yoga 114–115
Empowering Educators through Mindfulness Training 71
envy 69–70
Epstein, R. 156
establishing a sense of harmony and rhythm 177
eudaimonic well-being 329, 404
Eva, A. L. 244
evolution: and the brain 370–371; and the human brain 373–374
executive functioning 57, 237–238; Behavior Rating Inventory on Executive Functions (BRIEF) 236–237
exercises: artwork 151; Belly Breathing 260–261; breathing 180; dialectical behavior therapy (DBT) 22–25; Jurisight 315–316, 317–318; lemon 167; limits imagination 101; Mindful Leadership programme 303–306; Mindful Medical Practice (MMP) 148, 149–151; "mindful pause, the" 385; Mindful Self-Compassion (MSC) 363–364; mindful sport performance enhancement (MSPE) 174; mindful-based social emotional learning (MBSEL) 253; Mindfulness-Based Compassionate Living (MBCL) 378–380; Mindfulness-Based Eating Awareness Training (MB-EAT) **197–198**; Mindfulness-Based Emotional Balance (MBEB) 69–70; Mindfulness-Based Mind Fitness Training (MMFT) 58; Mindfulness-Based Strengths Practice (MBSP) 396; Mindfulness-Oriented Recovery Enhancement (MORE) 336–338; "minis" 167–168; morning stress 94; Partner Eye-Gazing 108–109; Partner-Focused Loving-Kindness Meditation 108; pencil and paper 269; rupture and repair imagination 100
expectant families 79; Prenatal Education About Labor Stress (PEARLS) 88; *see also* Mindfulness-Based Childbirth and Parenting (MBCP)
experiences: ACEs 54–55; impact of mindfulness on 1–2; psychological inflexibility 8
experiential avoidance 9, 12

extended triangle pose 118
eye-gazing exercise 108–109

family programmes 2; *see also* Mindful Parenting program; Mindfulness Based Elder Care (MBEC); Mindfulness-Based Childbirth and Parenting (MBCP); Mindfulness-Based Relationship Enhancement (MBRE); M-Yoga
final resting pose 118–119
Fitzgerald, M. 177
flexibility, of Acceptance and Commitment Therapy (ACT) 11
flow 173, 175–176
Fogel, J. 314
forgiveness 65, 69, 200
formal caregivers 124; MBEC for 128–129; Mindfulness-Based Living Course (MBLC) 131, 132–133
forming key associations 177–178
four foundations 66
"Four Immeasurables, The" 64, 65
Four Rs, the 223
Fredrickson, B. 375
Freedman, B. 403
functional contextualism 7
Fung, J. 244

Garland, E. 327, 328
Germer, C. 357, 364–365
Gestalt psychotherapy 129
Gioia, G. A. 236
Giving and Receiving meditation 363
goals: of mindful-based social emotional learning (MBSEL) 253–254; of Mindfulness-Based Childbirth and Parenting (MBCP) 79–80; of Mindfulness-Based Cognitive Therapy for Children (MBCT-C) 284–285; of the Mindfulness-Based Compassionate Living (MBCL) programme 370; of Mindfulness-Based Eating Awareness Training (MB-EAT) 191–192; of Mindfulness-Based Mind Fitness Training (MMFT) 55–56; of the Mindfulness-Oriented Recovery Enhancement (MORE) program 329–330
Gold, A. 314
Goldstein, Joseph 66
Goleman 375
golfers, mindful sport performance enhancement (MSPE) for 183
Gordhamer, S. 174
Gottman, J. 109
grade performance, mindful-based social emotional learning (MBSEL) impact on 257, 258–259
Greenberg, M. T. 225
guided meditation 67, 165, 208, 287

guided reflections, "Stone in the Well" 81
guiding practice, Mindfulness-Based Relapse Prevention (MBRP) 348
Guo, S. 244
Guy, S. C. 236

Hanh, T. N. 287
Hanich, L. B. 231
Hartzell, M. 93
Hatha yoga 161
head to knee pose (*janu sirsasana*) 116–117
Healing Relationship Model 146, 146–147
healing relationship processes: connecting 149; nonjudgmental stance 148–149; presence 149–151
health-care programmes 2; *see also* Mindful Medical Practice (MMP); mindful sport performance enhancement (MSPE); Mindfulness-Based Cancer Recovery (MBCR); Mindfulness-Based Eating Awareness Training (MB-EAT); Mindfulness-Based Stress Reduction (MBSR); Mindfulness-Based Therapy for Insomnia (MBTI)
"Hearsay" insight 318
Hedberg, B. 65
Hicks, L. M. 113
high blood pressure, impact of Mindfulness Based Flourishing Program (MBFP) on 408–409
high intensity care 44
Himelstein, S. 349
Ho, S. M. Y. 390
Hobbs, L. 364
home practices: Mindful Parenting program 100, 101; mindful sport performance enhancement (MSPE) 182; Mindfulness-Based Childbirth and Parenting (MBCP) 82, 85, 86; Mindfulness-Based Cognitive Therapy for Children (MBCT-C) 286; Mindfulness-Based Relapse Prevention (MBRP) 344; Mindfulness-Based Therapy for Insomnia (MBTI) program 207; Still Quiet Place 269
Houlihan, J. 251, 252
"How" skills 21
human brain, the 370–371; drive system 372; emotion regulation systems 371, 372; and evolution 373–374; neuro-plasticity 374; reactions to stress 371; soothing system 372–373; tend and befriend reaction 374; threat system 371, 372
hunger, and eating regulation theory 193–195
Hutchinson, T. 145
hyperfixation of attention 327

hypertension, impact of Mindfulness Based Flourishing Program (MBFP) on 408–409
hypothalamic-pituitary-adrenal (HPA) axis 55

"ice contractions" 84
I-It relationships 145, 147
Impact Foundation 65
implementations of the Mindful Parenting program 103
impulse control 57
inclusion 145
infant mental health (IMH) movement 103
informal caregivers 124; MBEC for 128–129
Inner Explorer (IE) 251, 252–254, 254–255
inner wisdom 191, 195, 196, 198
innovativeness of the mindful-based social emotional learning (MBSEL) program 255
inquiry 348, 360, 369
insecure attachment, and backdraft 369
Insight Dialogue 150
insights: attachment 318; "Hearsay" 318; Jurisight 315; justice 316; "Permission to Approach (the Pain)" 317–318; "Split in the Circuits" 318–319; *Stare Decisis* 317; Uncertain-Tee demonstration 317
insomnia: behavioral strategies for 209–210; daytime fatigue 211; metacognitive model of **206**; mindfulness-based approach for 205; mindfulness-based interventions 212–213; relapse prevention plan 211; taking a mindful stance with 210–211; territory of 210–211; *see also* Mindfulness-Based Therapy for Insomnia (MBTI)
insula cortex 56–57, 59
integrated regulation 193
intended population and targets: of Mindfulness-Based Childbirth and Parenting (MBCP) 79; of Mindfulness-Based Mind Fitness Training (MMFT) 53–55; of Mindfulness-Oriented Recovery Enhancement (MORE) 329
intention 29, 162, 222, 299, 403
Intention, Attention, and Attitude (IAA) model of mindfulness 403
interoception 56–57, 58, 191–192, 198
introduction and check-in, M-Yoga 115
invisibile gorilla video 97
Irving, J. A. 153
Isicoff, L. 314
Isquith, P. K. 236
Istituto per Servizi di Ricovero e Assistenza agli Anziani (ISRAA) 131; Alzheimer's Cafe 133–134; *Casa Albergo* 130; Dolomite project 134–135; integrated care model 135–136; practicing mindfulness at 129–130
I-Thou relationships 145, 147
Ivtzan, I. 391

janu sirsasana 116–117
Jennings, K. W. 225, 226
Jha, Amishi 70, 71
Jin, J. 244
Johnson, C. 283
joy 69–70
Judge Learned Hand practice 320
judgment 23–24
Jurisight 313, 315; attachment insight 318; "Attractive Nuisance" 319; *But for Pause* practice 320; development of 315–316; exercises 315–316; "Hearsay" insight 318; insights 315; *Judge Learned Hand* practice 320; *Just Is Holmes* practice 320–321; *Just is Story* practice 321; justice insight 316; method 316; "Motion for Extension of Thyme" 319–320; "Motion to Recuse" 319; "Permission to Approach (the Pain)" 317–318; practices 320–321; research support for 321; "Split in the Circuits" insight 318–319; *Stare Decisis* insight 317; Uncertain-Tee demonstration 317
Just Is Holmes practice 320–321
Just is Story practice 321
justice insight 316

Kabat-Zinn, J. 29, 34, 64, 65, 79, 112, 125, 143, 173, 174, 177, 192, 253, 279, 314; *Wherever You Go, There You Are* 129
Kenworthy, L. 236
Kinder, W. 231, 235
Kinhin meditation 47, 50
Kitwood, T. 129
kneeling postures 117
Kornfield, J. 66
Koster, F., *Mindfulness-Based Compassionate Living – A new training programme to deepen mindfulness with heartfulness* 380
Kramer, G. 150

Lancaster Osteopathic Health Foundation 233
language: M-Yoga 119; Relational Frame Theory (RFT) 7–8
Lau, A. 244
law firms, mindfulness training in 314
leadership 297–298; authentic leadership study, Mindfulness Based Flourishing Program (MBFP) 408; *see also* Mindful Leadership
Learning to BREATHE (L2B) 241, 242; attention 247; BREATHE acronyms 245–248; for diabetes prevention 244; distress tolerance skills 242–243; lessons 244–245; mindfulness 242; movement practices 247–248; online resources 249; pilot studies 244; program structure 244–248; research support for

243–244; Surfing the Waves 246; theoretical background 242–243
"Leaves on a stream" exercise 14
legal profession, and mindfulness 313–315
lemon exercise 167
letting go 176–177, 206–207
limits imagination exercise 101
Linehan, M. 18, 20, 23
listening 269; mindful 224–225, 287
long-distance runners, mindful sport performance enhancement (MSPE) for 183
longevity 124
Loving Kindness Meditation 148, 168, 347, 368, 369; *metta* 224
loving-kindness practice 200; Mindfulness-Based Childbirth and Parenting (MBCP) 86–87
low intensity care 44

MacPherson, A. C. 177
macro-level self-regulation 56
malasana 118
Mashburn, A. J. 73
McAliley, C. 314
McBee, L., *Mindfulness Based Elder Care* 127
McMindfulness 156
meditation 96–97, 174, 181, 182, 192, 193, 198, 328, 342, 391, 392, 403, 406–407; and concentration 176; Giving and Receiving 363; Kinhin 47, 50; Loving Kindness 148, 168, 347, 368, 369; *metta* 168, 224, 376; in the Mindful Leadership programme 299; in the Mindful Parenting program 98; Mindfulness-Based Cancer Recovery program 166–167; Mindfulness-Based Childbirth and Parenting (MBCP) 85; Mindfulness-Based Stress Reduction (MBSR) sessions 30–32; "mountain" 31, 345; seven-day MBPS program 47–48; sitting 180; versus *in situ* mindfulness 308; "Stone in the Well" guided reflection 81; Tamatha 64; trainspotting 208–209; Vipassana 327; walking 168
mental training paradox 178–179
mentalities 373
Metacognition Index 237
metacognitions 205, **206**, 210, 282–283
metaphors: in Acceptance and Commitment Therapy (ACT) 13, 14; backdraft 359; in Mindfulness-Based Relapse Prevention (MBRP) 346; "mountain" meditation 31
metta 224, 376
Metz, S. 243
micro-level self-regulation 56
"Milk, Milk, Milk" 13
Mind and Life dialogue on Destructive Emotions 64

mind-body connection 167
mindful awareness practices (MAPs) 220, 223–224, 232, 236
Mindful Birthing and Parenting Foundation (MBPF) 79
mindful brain 371
mindful eating 36
Mindful Leadership 297; activating collective mindfulness exercise 304–305; conflation regarding leadership in mindfulness literature 297–298; Cranfield programme 297–298; day one **300–301**; day three **302–303**; day two **301–302**; development of 297–298; Direction-Alignment-Commitment (DAC) model 309–310; discussion of emerging research themes 308–309; exploring the unexplored exercise 305–306; follow-up webinar 306; guidelines for peer-to-peer coaching 307; meditation 299–300; mindful connections exercise 303; mindful decision making exercise 303–304; onboarding 299; online support material 307; research support for 307–308; residential workshop 299–300
mindful listening 224–225
Mindful Mamas 113
Mindful Medical Practice (MMP) 143, 146; artwork exercise 151; common humanity 146; connecting 149; developing competencies 147, 148; exercises 148, 149–151; Healing Relationship Model 146–147; mindfulness 156; and Mindfulness-Based Stress Reduction (MBSR) 153–154, 155, 156; nonjudgmental stance 148–149; outline of the program **144–145**; participants 151–153; presence 149–151; theoretical background 145, 146; yoga 148
Mindful Parenting program 91, 92; automatic pilot parenting 97; beginner's mind parenting 97; compassion 99; content 96–97; core mindfulness themes and practices 97–98; home practices 100, 101; limit setting 100; limits imagination exercise 101; meditation practices 98; mindfulness 98, 99; morning stress exercise 94; ongoing implementation and future directions 103; and parenting stress 92–93; program overview **95–96**; reconnecting with the body 97–98; research support for 101, 102–103; responding versus reacting 98; rupture and repair imagination exercise 100; self-compassion 98–99; self-kindness 98; structure 94, 96; unique themes and practices 99, 100
"mindful pause, the" 385
mindful seeing 97
Mindful Self-Compassion (MSC) 357; activities 361–362; breathing exercises 363–364;

Index

Cultivating Awareness and Resilience in Education (CARE) for Teachers 357; Giving and Receiving meditation 363; online resources 365; program structure 359–360; research support for 364–365; Self-Compassion Break 362–363; sessions 360–362

mindful sport performance enhancement (MSPE) 173, 174; adapting for college teams 185–186; for archers and golfers 183; body scans 180; breathing exercises 180; building mindfulness fundamentals 179–180; committing to mental training 179–180; core performance facilitators 174, 176–178, 180–181; embodying the mindful performer 182; embracing "what is" in stride 181–182; exercises 174; final session 182–183; flow 175–176; formal mindfulness practice 179–180; formal practice 182; future research 186–187; for high-school teams 186; home practices 182; for long-distance runners 183; mental training paradox 178–179; mindfulness 175–176; one-year follow-up 183–184; online resources 187; overview of the program 173–174; pathways to peak performance 178–179; program structure 179; research support for 183–186; sessions 179–183; strengthening the muscle of attention 180–181; stretching the body's limits mindfully 181; studies with collegiate athletes 184–186; theoretical background 174; True Athlete Project 186

Mindful Tool Kit (MTK) 233, **233–234**, 239

mindful walking 37, 38

mindful-based social emotional learning (MBSEL) 251; and academic achievement 260; age stages 253; audio-guided practices 253; benefits to school classrooms 252; body scans 254; classroom kit 254; development of 251–252; embedded programs 260; exercises 253; goals of 253–254; impact on classroom operations 259; impact on grade performance 257, 258–259; implementation in schools 254–255; innovativeness of 255; mindfulness practices 260–261; online materials and resources 260–261; practices 254; program purpose and content 252–254; Randomized Controlled Trial (RCT) 256–257; theoretical background 255–256

mindfulness 56, 65, 67, 80, 81, 98, 127, 135, 143, 145, 155, 156, 160, 166, 168, 173, 174, 178, 179, 181, 182, 185, 196, 198, 208, 209, 223, 231, 232, 241, 242, 251, 252, 253, 260–261, 268, 269, 297, 299, 327, 330, 331, 342, 348, 357, 358, 360, 368, 385, 386, 388, 392, 394, 404, 410; in Acceptance and Commitment Therapy (ACT) 8; at *Casa Albergo* 130, 131; centering 224; CenteringPregnancy with Mindfulness Skills (CPMS). *See also* expectant families; cognitive defusion 13–14; and core performance facilitators 176–178; cultivating 29; and decentering 282–283; distractions 24; and eating regulation theory 194–195; and flow 175–176; fundamentals 179–180; impact on experiences 1–2; Inner Explorer (IE) 251; integrating with character strengths 388–389; integrating with emotions 66–67; interpersonal 150; and the law 313–315; listening 287; versus meditation 308; mental training paradox 178–179; Mindful Parenting program 99; in the mindful sport performance enhancement (MSPE) program 175; Mindfulness-Based Cognitive Therapy for Children (MBCT-C) activities 285–290; and Mindfulness-Based Eating Awareness Training (MB-EAT) 193; in Mindfulness-Based Positive Behavior Support (MBPBS) 46; in Mindfulness-Based Stress Reduction (MBSR) 29; Observe skill 24–25; One-Mindfulness 21; operationalizing 10; as part of patient-centered care 146; as a practice 308–309; practicing at ISRAA 129–130; programmes 2; programs for AD sufferers 133–134; and relationships 105–106; and self-compassion 359; and sports 174; of thoughts 245–246; training for children 283; training in 129–130; for treating addiction 328; Western 160, 387, 403; while eating 191; and Wise Mind 20, 21–22; and yoga 112–113; *see also* Buddhism

Mindfulness 5-5-5 exercise 22–23

Mindfulness and Performance Enhancement Program 314

Mindfulness Based Attention Training (MBAT) 321

Mindfulness Based Elder Care (MBEC) 127

Mindfulness Based Flourishing Program (MBFP) 403; authentic leadership study 408; cross-cultural study 408; impact on hypertension 408–409; limitations and future studies 410–411; meditations 406–407; 'positive mindfulness cycle' 404; Positive Psychology Interventions (PPIs) 403–404; program structure 404–405, **405–406**, 406–407; research support for 407–408; savouring 404; unpublished studies 408–409

Mindfulness Self-Compassion (MSC) 279

Mindfulness-Based Attention Training (MBAT)-Spouse 71

Mindfulness-Based Cancer Recovery 160; accessibility to 165; breathing techniques 167–168; drop-in sessions 162–163; improvements in psychological and biological

Index 423

outcomes 163–164; lemon exercise 167; mindfulness interventions 161; "noble silence" 169; program structure 165; recent studies on 164–165; research support for 162–164; theoretical background 160–162; week 2: mindfulness and breath awareness 166; week 3: mindfulness attitudes 166–167; week 4: mind-body wisdom and healing 167; week 5: balance in the autonomic nervous system 167–168; week 6: mindful coping 168; week 7: cultivating beneficial states of heart and mind 168; week 8: deepening and expanding 169; week 9+: moving into the world 169; weekend retreat 169

Mindfulness-Based Cancer Recovery (MBCR) 161

Mindfulness-Based Childbirth and Parenting (MBCP) 79; Body Scan 81; classes 81–82; home practices 82, 85, 86; *Mind in Labor (MIL): Working with Pain in Childbirth* 88; intended population and targets 79; intentions informing 79–80; loving-kindness practice 86–87; meditation 85; pain practice 82; phone interview 80; research support for 88–89; Reunion gathering 87–88; silent practice 86; teaching on breastfeeding 87; teaching on Causes and Conditions 85–86; yoga sequence 82

Mindfulness-Based Cognitive Therapy for Children (MBCT-C) 282; activities 285–290; developmental adaptations and goals 284–285; home practices 286; mindful listening 287; online resources 291; research support for 283–284; theoretical background 282–283; visualization practice 288

Mindfulness-Based Cognitive Therapy (MBCT) 13, 115, 148, 173, 282, 344, 368, 403

Mindfulness-Based Compassionate Living (MBCL) 368, 371, 374, 375; defining compassion 369–370; exercises 378–380; goals of 370; program structure 375–376; research support for 375; sessions **376–378**; theoretical background 370–371, 372–375

Mindfulness-Based Eating Awareness Training (MB-EAT) 187, 191; development of 192; dieting 199–200; eating regulation theory 193–195; exercises **197–198**; goals of 191–192; and mindfulness 193; online resources 201; program structure 196, 198–200; Quality over Quantity (QOQ) challenge 199–200; research support for 195–196; sensory-specific satiety (SSS) 194–195; theoretical background 192–193; wisdom 193

Mindfulness-Based Elder Care (MBEC) 125, 126–127; for caregivers 128–129; for community and assisted living dwelling elders 127; for nursing home elders 127; working with professional caregivers 131, 132–133

Mindfulness-Based Emotional Balance (MBEB) 64, 279; in education, research on 70–72, 73–74; emergence of 65; exercises 69–70; fidelity of implementation 72; and forgiveness 65; integrating mindfulness and emotion 66–67; other names of 64; pilot program 70–71; research studies in military settings 74; teacher training programs 65; theory of change *72*

Mindfulness-Based Interventions (MBIs) 52, 55, 65, 136, 327; bringing to the elderly 123–124; and Buddhism 123; for elders 124–125, 125–126; inquiry 348; for insomnia 212–213; *see also* Mindfulness-Oriented Recovery Enhancement (MORE)

Mindfulness-Based Living Course (MBLC) 129; working with professional caregivers 131, 132–133

Mindfulness-Based Mind Fitness Training (MMFT) 53; Contact Point Exercise 58; goals of 55, 55–56; intended population and targets of 53–55; interoception 56–57; program structure 57–58; research support 59; self-regulation 59; theoretical background 56–57

Mindfulness-Based Positive Behavior Support (MBPBS) 43; caregiver training program 48; eight-week program 49; mindfulness 46; Positive Behavior Support (PBS) 43–44, 45; research support for 46–47; seven-day intensive program 47–48, **48–49**; three-day program 50

Mindfulness-Based Relapse Prevention (MBRP) 329, 341, 342; adaptations 349; beginning practices 344–346; final practices 347–348; guiding practice 348; inquiry 348; metaphors 346; mid-course practices 346; online resources 351; program structure 344–348; research support for 349–350; SOBER space 345–346; theoretical background 342–344

Mindfulness-Based Relationship Enhancement (MBRE) 105, 106; all-day retreat session 109; clinical trial 109; mindfulness 106; Partner Eye-Gazing exercise 108–109; Partner-Focused Loving-Kindness Meditation exercise 108; qualitative research on 109–110; sessions 107–108

Mindfulness-Based Strengths Practice (MBSP) 385, 403; for adolescents 397; character strengths 386, 387, 388; mindful strengths practice 396; online resources 398–399; parable of the two trees 387; pilot studies 390–391; program structure 392, **393–394**, 394, **395–396**, 396, **397**, 398; research support

for 390–392; theoretical background 388–390; virtues 386
Mindfulness-Based Stress Reduction (MBSR) 29, 55, 64, 79, 92, 106, 125, 143, 148, 160, 161, 173, 192, 241, 251–252, 279, 282, 344, 357, 368, 411; adapting for the Still Quiet Place program 268–269; "beginner's mind" 32, 33; for chronic pain 34; cultivating observation 33; discovering embodiment 33; effects on healthy individuals 35; growing compassion 34; implementation in law firms 314; mindful eating 36; and Mindful Medical Practice (MMP) 153–154, 155, 156; mindful walking 37, 38; moving towards acceptance 33–34; neuroscience findings 35; participant learnings 32, 33–34; preliminary exploration of 35–36; research 34–35; resources 38–39; sessions 29–32; week 1: introduction and orientation 165–166
Mindfulness-Based Therapy for Insomnia (MBTI) 204, 204–205, 205; future directions 213; home practice 207; insomnia relapse prevention plan 211; meditation retreat 211; program structure 207, 208; published resources on **213–214**; quiet meditations 209; research support for 212–213; sessions 207, 208–211; sleep reconditioning 210; sleep restriction 210; synchronizing sleep behaviors 209–210; taking a mindful stance with insomnia 210–211; themes and activities **207–208**; theoretical background 205, 206–207; trainspotting meditation 208–209
Mindfulness-Oriented Recovery Enhancement (MORE) 328; adaptations for chronic pain 336; alcohol dependence, effectiveness on 331; for behavioral addictions 329; behavioral addictions, effectiveness on 333; chronic pain, effectiveness on 331–332; defusing relationship triggers for relapse 335; goals of 329–330; intended population and targets 329; interdependence and meaning in recovery 335–336; looking mindfully toward the future 336; mindful reappraisal 334; mindfulness and the automatic habit of addiction 333–334; mindfulness and the impermanent body 335; mindfulness exercise 336–338; nicotine addiction, effectiveness on 332–333; for opioid addiction 328; opioid addiction, effectiveness on 331–332; overcoming craving by coping with stress 334–335; program resources 338; program structure 333–336; psychiatric disorders, effectiveness on 331; seeing through the nature of craving 334; shifting the mind to refocus on savoring 334; substance abuse, effectiveness on 331; theoretical background 330–331; walking the middle way between attachment and aversion 335

Mindfulness-to-Meaning Theory 330
Mindfulness-Based Cognitive Therapy (MBCT) 239
mini-meditations 167–168, 195
mood disorders during pregnancy 114
Morgan, L. 174
morning stress exercise 94
"Motion for Extension of Thyme" 319–320
"Motion to Recuse" 319
"mountain" meditation 31, 345
mountain pose (*tadasana*) 117–118
movement practices, Learning to BREATHE (L2B) 247–248
Multidimensional Assessment of Interoceptive Awareness (MAIA) 88
mutual eye-gazing 108–109
M-Yoga 112; empirical support 114–115; introduction and check-in 115; language 119; overview of 112–113; research on 113–114; resources 120; seated meditation on the breath 116; seated postures 116–117; theoretical background 113–114

Nairn, R. 129, 131
National Institutes of Health (NIH) 195–196, 196
Neff, K. 357, 364–365, 376; Self-Compassion Scale 373
negative reinforcement 343
neuro-plasticity 374
new mammalian brain 371
nicotine addiction, effectiveness of Mindfulness-Oriented Recovery Enhancement (MORE) on 332–333
Niemiec, R. 387, 388, 391, 399; *Mindfulness and Character Strengths: A Practical Guide to Flourishing* 385–386
"noble silence" 169
nonjudgmental stance 148–149
non-striving 181–182
non-suicidal self-injury (NSSI) 19; Cognitive Behavioral Therapy (CBT) 18, 19
nursing home elders: *Casa Albergo* 130, 131; Mindfulness-Based Elder Care (MBEC) for 127

Obhi, S. S. 177
observation, cultivating 33
Observe skill 24–25
'old brain' 371
onboarding, Mindful Leadership programme 299
One Mindful Step 135–136
One-Mindfulness 21

online resources: Acceptance and Commitment Therapy (ACT) 16; dialectical behavior therapy (DBT) 25; Learning to BREATHE (L2B) 249; Mindful Self-Compassion (MSC) 365; mindful sport performance enhancement (MSPE) 187; mindful-based social emotional learning (MBSEL) 260–261; Mindfulness-Based Cognitive Therapy for Children (MBCT-C) 291; Mindfulness-Based Relapse Prevention (MBRP) 351; Mindfulness-Based Strengths Practice (MBSP) 398–399; Mindfulness-Based Stress Reduction (MBSR) 39
operationalizing mindfulness processes 10
opioid addiction, and Mindfulness-Oriented Recovery Enhancement (MORE) 328, 331–332
outer wisdom 191, 192, 196, 199
outpatient treatment, dialectical behavior therapy (DBT) 20
over-identification 358, 373–374

pain practices (MBCP) 82, 83–87; *see also* chronic pain
parable of the two trees 387
paradox of self-compassion training 359
parasympathetic nervous system 167–168
parenting 79, 92; infant mental health (IMH) movement 103; stress 92–93; *see also* Mindfulness-Based Childbirth and Parenting (MBCP)
participant learnings, Mindfulness-Based Stress Reduction (MBSR) 32, 33–34
Partner Eye-Gazing exercise 108–109
Partner-Focused Loving-Kindness Meditation exercise 108
pathways to peak performance 178–179
patient-centered care 146
PEACE practice 274–275
peak performance, pathways to 178–179
peer-to-peer coaching, Mindful Leadership programme 307
pencil and paper exercises, Still Quiet Place 269
"Permission to Approach (the Pain)" 317–318
Person-Centered Care 129
Peterson, L. G. 387
phone interview, Mindfulness-Based Childbirth and Parenting (MBCP) program 80
pilot studies, Mindfulness-Based Strengths Practice (MBSP) 390–391
Pineau, T. P. 184, 185
Positive Behavior Support (PBS) 43–44, 45; plans, designing 45, **45**
'positive mindfulness cycle' 403–404
positive psychology 403, 407

Positive Psychology Interventions (PPIs) 403, 404
positive reinforcement 343
postpartum depression (PPD) 80, 112
post-traumatic stress disorder (PTSD) 55
practices: Jurisight 320–321; Mindfulness-Based Compassionate Living (MBCL) 376; Mindfulness-Based Relapse Prevention (MBRP) 344–348; Mindfulness-Based Strengths Practice (MBSP) 394, **395–396**, 396; Still Quiet Place 273–275
pregnancy 119; CenteringPregnancy (CP) 89; mental illness during 112; mindfulness group interventions 115; mood disorders during 114; and toxic stress 114; *see also* childbirth; expectant families; M-Yoga; parenting
Prenatal Education About Labor Stress (PEARLS) 88
prenatal yoga *see* M-Yoga
presence 149–151
present moment awareness 9, 14, 290
presentness 145
primary arousal 205, **206**
primary care 44
problem-focused coping 161
professional caregivers: and Mindfulness-Based Living Course (MBLC) 132–133; Mindfulness-Based Living Course (MBLC) 131
Prosocial Classroom Model 221
psychiatric disorders, effectiveness of Mindfulness-Oriented Recovery Enhancement (MORE) on 331
psychological flexibility 8, 11; acceptance 8, 9; committed action 10, 15–16; defusion 9; present moment awareness 9; self as context 9–10, 14; values 10, 15
psychological flourishing programmes 3; *see also* Mindfulness Based Flourishing Program (MBFP); Mindfulness-Based Strengths Practice (MBSP)
psychological wellbeing (PWB) model 404
psychotherapeutic mindfulness programs 160, 161, 357; *see also* Mindfulness-Based Stress Reduction (MBSR)
published resources on Mindfulness-Based Therapy for Insomnia (MBTI) **213–214**

qualitative research, on Mindfulness-Based Relationship Enhancement (MBRE) 109–110
Quality over Quantity (QOQ) challenge 199
Questions About Behavior Function (QABF) rating scale 44
quiet meditations 209

raisin exercise 208
Randomized Controlled Trial (RCT) 256–257
Reasonable Mind 18
receptive listening 287
reconnecting with the body 97–98
Relapse Prevention (RP) 343
Relational Frame Theory (RFT) 7–8
relationships 105; healing 148; *I-It* 145, 147; *I-Thou* 145, 147; maintaining 105; and Mindfulness-Based Strengths Practice (MBSP) 392; *see also* Mindfulness-Based Relationship Enhancement (MBRE)
relaxation 177
reptilian brain 370–371
research support: for Cultivating Awareness and Resilience in Education (CARE) for Teachers 225–227; for Jurisight 321; for Learning to BREATHE (L2B) 243–244; for MBIs for elders 125–126; for the Mindful Leadership programme 307–308; for Mindful Parenting program 101, 102–103; for Mindful Self-Compassion (MSC) 364–365; for mindful sport performance enhancement (MSPE) 183–186; for Mindfulness Based Flourishing Program (MBFP) 407–408; for Mindfulness-Based Cancer Recovery 162–164; for Mindfulness-Based Childbirth and Parenting (MBCP) 88–89; for Mindfulness-Based Cognitive Therapy for Children (MBCT-C) 283–284; for the Mindfulness-Based Compassionate Living (MBCL) programme 375; for Mindfulness-Based Eating Awareness Training (MB-EAT) 195–196; for Mindfulness-Based Emotional Balance (MBEB) in education 70–72, 73–74; for Mindfulness-Based Mind Fitness Training (MMFT) 59; for Mindfulness-Based Positive Behavior Support (MBPBS) 46–47; for Mindfulness-Based Relapse Prevention (MBRP) 349–350; for Mindfulness-Based Stress Reduction (MBSR) 34–35; for Mindfulness-Based Therapy for Insomnia (MBTI) 212–213; for Still Quiet Place 275–278; for Wellness Works in Schools (WWiS) 235–238
residential workshop, Mindful Leadership programme 299–300
restorative positions 118–119
Reunion gathering, Mindfulness-Based Childbirth and Parenting (MBCP) 87–88
Rising, S. 89
Roeser, R. 70, 71, 73
Rogers, S. 315
Röthlin, P. 174
rule of law 314, 322
rupture and repair imagination exercise 100

Samatha meditation 47
sati 46
Satipatthana Sutta 66
Satlof-Bedrick, E. 283
Saul, S. 349
savasana 118–119
savouring 334, 363, 404
Schellekens, M. P. 164
Schonert-Reichl, Kimberley 70
schools: Learning to BREATHE (L2B) program 242; mindful-based social emotional learning (MBSEL) 252; mindful-based social emotional learning (MBSEL) implementation in 254–255; *see also* mindful-based social emotional learning (MBSEL)
Schussler, D. L. 226
Scott, J. G. 146
scripts 223, 225
seated meditation on the breath 116
secondary arousal 205, **206**
self as context 9–10, 14
self-acceptance 192, 200, 404
self-care, in the Cultivating Awareness and Resilience in Education (CARE) for Teachers program 222
self-compassion 93, 98–99, 99, 148, 357–358, 359, 369–370, 404, 407; and mindfulness training 359; *see also* Mindful Self-Compassion (MSC); Mindfulness-Based Compassionate Living (MBCL)
self-criticism 373
Self-Determination Theory 193
self-invalidation 24
self-isolation 373
self-kindness 98, 358
self-regulation 55–56, 57–58, 59, 163, 175, 176, 193, 195, 196, 243, 386; eating regulation theory 193–195; executive functioning 57; in teachers 219–220
Seligman, M. 387
sensory-specific satiety (SSS) 194–195
sessions 198–200; Acceptance and Commitment Therapy (ACT) 11–12; Cultivating Awareness and Resilience in Education (CARE) for Teachers 221–222; Learning to BREATHE (L2B) 245; Mindful Leadership programme **300–303**; Mindful Parenting program 94, 96; Mindful Self-Compassion (MSC) 360–362; mindful sport performance enhancement (MSPE) 179–183; Mindfulness Based Flourishing Program (MBFP) 404–405, **405–406**, 406–407; Mindfulness-Based Cancer Recovery 165–169; Mindfulness-Based Cognitive Therapy for Children (MBCT-C) 284–285, 285–290; Mindfulness-Based Compassionate Living (MBCL)

375–376, **376–378**; Mindfulness-Based Eating Awareness Training (MB-EAT) **197–198**, 198–200; Mindfulness-Based Emotional Balance (MBEB) 67, **68–69**; Mindfulness-Based Mind Fitness Training (MMFT) 57–58; Mindfulness-Based Relapse Prevention (MBRP) 344–348; Mindfulness-Based Relationship Enhancement (MBRE) 107–108; Mindfulness-Based Strengths Practice (MBSP) 392, **393–394**, 394, **395–396**; Mindfulness-Based Stress Reduction (MBSR) 29–32; Mindfulness-Based Therapy for Insomnia (MBTI) program 207, 208–211; Mindfulness-Oriented Recovery Enhancement (MORE) 333–336; Still Quiet Place **270–272**; Wellness Works in Schools (WWiS) 232
seven-day MBPS program 47–48, **48–49**
Shapiro, S. L. 403, 411
Sharp, J. E. 226
Siegal, D. J. 93
silent practice: Mindfulness-Based Childbirth and Parenting (MBCP) 86; "noble silence" 169
simple cross-legged pose (*sukhasana*) 116
Singh, N. 46–47
Skinner, E. 73
sleep medications 204
sleep quality: metacognitions 205, **206**; MMFT effect on 59; primary arousal 205; secondary arousal 205; and stimulus control 209–210; *see also* Mindfulness-Based Therapy for Insomnia (MBTI)
sleep reconditioning 210
sleep restriction 210
Snowberg, K. E. 225
SOBER space 345–346
social and emotional competencies (SEC) 221
social mentalities 373
Social-Emotional Learning (SEL) 241, 251
Somatic Experiencing 56
soothing system 372–373
Speca, M. 160
"Split in the Circuits" insight 318–319
sports: core performance facilitators 176–178; and flow 175–176; and mindfulness 174; and mindfulness based flourishing program (MBFP) 409–410; and self-regulation 175–176; True Athlete Project 186
squat pose 118
standing postures 117–118
STAR practice 274
Stare Decisis insight 317
Statistical Package for Social Science (SPSS). 132
stepped care 43–44

Still Quiet Place 267, 278; accessibility of 279; body scans 269; course outline 269, 272; development of 267–268; establishing a personal practice 278–279; home practices 269; introductory practice for teens 273; listening 269; movement practices 269; notes and cautions 278; pencil and paper exercises 269; practices 273–275; research support for 275–278; sessions **270–272**; trauma awareness 280
stimulus control 209–210
"Stone in the Well" guided reflection 81
Story, Joseph 321
strengthening the muscle of attention 180–181
stress 231, 411; allostatic load 53, 56; in caregivers 126, 129; chronic 114; and eating regulation theory 193–195; executive functioning 57; impact of Mindfulness Based Flourishing Program (MBFP) on 408–409; interoception 58; parenting 92–93; reactions of the brain to 371; self-regulation 55–56, 57–58; in teachers 219; tolerance for challenging experience 56; toxic 114; *see also* allostatic load; Mindfulness-Based Mind Fitness Training (MMFT); Mindfulness-Based Stress Reduction (MBSR)
stress inoculation training (SIT) 54
stress-contagion 220
Stress-Management and Relaxation Training (SMART)-in-Education Program 64, 65
stretching the body's limits mindfully 181
structure: of the Cultivating Awareness and Resilience in Education (CARE) for Teachers program 221–222; of the Learning to BREATHE (L2B) program 244–248; of the Mindful Parenting program 94, 96; of the Mindful Self-Compassion (MSC) program 359–360; of Mindfulness Based Flourishing Program (MBFP) 404–405, **405–406**, 406–407; of the Mindfulness-Based Cancer Recovery program 165; of the Mindfulness-Based Cognitive Therapy for Children (MBCT-C) program 284–285; of the Mindfulness-Based Compassionate Living (MBCL) programme 375–376; of the Mindfulness-Based Eating Awareness Training (MB-EAT) program 196, 198–200; of the Mindfulness-Based Emotional Balance (MBEB) program 67, **68–69**; of the Mindfulness-Based Mind Fitness Training (MMFT) program 57–58; of the Mindfulness-Based Relapse Prevention (MBRP) program 344–348; of the Mindfulness-Based Strengths Practice (MBSP) programme 392, **393–394**, 394, **395–396**, 396, **397**, 398; of the Mindfulness-Based Therapy for

Insomnia (MBTI) program 207, 208; of the Mindfulness-Oriented Recovery Enhancement (MORE) program 333–336; *see also* sessions
student effects of Mindfulness-Based Emotional Balance (MBEB) 72
substance abuse: and addiction 327–328; effectiveness of Mindfulness-Oriented Recovery Enhancement (MORE) on 331; evidence-based interventions 341
substance abuse disorder (SUD) 341; Relapse Prevention (RP) 343; theoretical background for Mindfulness-Based Relapse Prevention (MBRP) 342–344; treatments 341–342, 343
suffering 371; and self-compassion 359
Sukhasana 116
"sun salutation" 169
supported wide leg child's pose (*balasana*) 117
Surfing the Waves 246
survival response 93, 94
syllabus, Mindful Leadership programme **300–303**
sympathetic nervous system 167–168, 330
synchronizing sleep behaviors 209–210

tadasana 117–118
Tamatha meditation 64
teachers: effects of Mindfulness-Based Emotional Balance (MBEB) on 72, 73; self-regulation 219–220; and stress-contagion 220; *see also* Cultivating Awareness and Resilience in Education (CARE) for Teachers
tend and befriend reaction 374
territory of insomnia 210–211
Thayer, N. M. 244
themes: in the Mindful Leadership programme 308–309; in the Mindful Parenting program 96–97, 97–98; in the Mindfulness-Based Cognitive Therapy for Children (MBCT-C) program 284–285; in the Mindfulness-Based Compassionate Living (MBCL) programme **376–378**; in the Mindfulness-Based Therapy for Insomnia (MBTI) program **207–208**
theoretical background: of Cultivating Awareness and Resilience in Education (CARE) for Teachers 221; of Learning to BREATHE (L2B) 242–243; of Mindful Medical Practice (MMP) 145, 146; of mindful sport performance enhancement (MSPE) 174; of mindful-based social emotional learning (MBSEL) program 255–256; of Mindfulness-Based Cancer Recovery 160–162; of Mindfulness-Based Cognitive Therapy for Children (MBCT-C) 282–283; of Mindfulness-Based Compassionate Living (MBCL) 370–371, 372–375; of Mindfulness-Based Eating Awareness Training (MB-EAT) 192–193; of Mindfulness-Based Mind Fitness Training (MMFT) 56–57; of Mindfulness-Based Relapse Prevention (MBRP) 342–344; of Mindfulness-Based Strengths Practice (MBSP) 388–390; of Mindfulness-Based Therapy for Insomnia (MBTI) 205, 206–207; of Mindfulness-Oriented Recovery Enhancement (MORE) 330–331; of M-Yoga 113–114
therapy programmes 2; *see also* Acceptance and Commitment Therapy (ACT); dialectical behavior therapy (DBT); Mindfulness-Based Emotional Balance (MBEB); Mindfulness-Based Mind Fitness Training (MMFT); Mindfulness-Based Positive Behavior Support (MBPBS); Mindfulness-Based Stress Reduction (MBSR)
thoughts, mindfulness of 245–246
threat system 371, 373
three-day MBPS program 50
tolerance for challenging experience 56
tonglen 376
toxic stress 114
tracks, mindful-based social emotional learning (MBSEL) 253–254
traditions, of Buddhism 67
training: *Istituto per Servizi di Ricovero e Assistenza agli Anziani* (ISRAA) 136; in mindfulness 129–130; mindfulness in the legal field 314; Mindfulness-Based Emotional Balance (MBEB) 65; *see also* mindful sport performance enhancement (MSPE)
trainspotting meditation 208–209
Transcendental Meditation 192
trauma 280; Mindfulness-Based Mind Fitness Training (MMFT) 52; *see also* Mindfulness-Based Mind Fitness Training (MMFT)
Trauma Resilience Model 56
treatment-as-usual (TAU) 328
triangle of awareness *147*
True Athlete Project 186

Uncertain-Tee demonstration 317
unique themes and practices, in the Mindful Parenting program 99, 100
universal emotions 65
university cross-country team, mindful sport performance enhancement (MSPE) for 184
unpublished studies, Mindfulness Based Flourishing Program (MBFP) 408–409
upavistha konasana 116
Urbanowski, F. 314
Urge Surfing practice 345
utthita trikonasana 118

values 10, 15
van den Brink, E., *Mindfulness-Based Compassionate Living – A new training programme to deepen mindfulness with heartfulness* 380
vedana 66
VIA classification of character strengths 386–387
videos, Mindfulness Based Flourishing Program (MBFP) **405–406**, 406
Vipassana 66
Vipassana meditation 327
virabhadrasana 118
virtues 386
Visser, U. 65
visualization practice, Mindfulness-Based Cognitive Therapy for Children (MBCT-C) 288
Vygotsky, L. S., social-cognitive theory 235

walking meditation 31, 168
Wallace, A. 64, 65, 411
Wallace, L. 65
Wansink, B. 193
warrior pose (*virabhadrasana*) 118
well-being: of caregivers 42–43; eudaimonic 329, 404
Wellness Works in Schools (WWiS) 231, 231–233, 239; mindful awareness practices (MAPs) 236; Mindful Tool Kit (MTK) 233, **233–234**, 239; research support for 235–238; sessions 232
"What" skills 21
Whitebird, R. R. 126
wide angle seated pose (*upavistha konasana*) 116
willingness 12
wisdom 193, 389; inner 191, 195, 198; outer 191, 192, 196, 199
Wise Mind 18, 19, 20, 21–22, 22, 22–23, 23, 25
work-oriented programmes 2; *see also* Jurisight; Mindful Leadership
workplace stress, impact of Mindfulness Based Flourishing Program (MBFP) on 409

yoga 31, 106, 119, 181; chair 200; experiencing pain during 113; Hatha 161; at ISRAA 130; kneeling postures 117; in Mindful Medical Practice (MMP) 148; and mindfulness 112–113; in Mindfulness-Based Cancer Recovery program 166; in Mindfulness-Based Childbirth and Parenting (MBCP) 82; restorative positions 118–119; seated postures 116–117; standing postures 117–118; "sun salutation" 169; *see also* M-Yoga

Zen Buddhism 133; *see also* Buddhism; mindfulness

Printed in the United States
by Baker & Taylor Publisher Services